BIHLMEYER - TÜCHLE

# CHURCH HISTORY

# CHURCH HISTORY

by
### Dr. Karl Bihlmeyer
late Professor at the University of Tübingen
revised by
### Dr. Hermann Tüchle
Professor at the University of Munich

translated from the thirteenth German edition
by
### Victor E. Mills, O. F. M., M. A., Litt. D.,
Province of the Most Holy Name

Volume One

## Christian Antiquity

### THE NEWMAN PRESS

Westminster, Maryland

The original and further German editions of CHURCH HISTORY were
published under the title KIRCHENGESCHICHTE by
Ferdinand Schöningh at Paderborn Germany

Imprimi potest:

Celsus R. Wheeler, O.F.M.
Minister Provincialis

New York
September 12, 1956.

Nihil obstat:

Damian Blaher, O.F.M., J.C.D.
Censor deputatus.

Imprimatur:

+ Patrick A. O'Boyle
Archbishop of Washington.

May 6, 1957.

The *nihil obstat* and *imprimatur* are official declarations that a book or pamphlet is free
of doctrinal or moral error. No implication is contained therein that those who have
granted the *nihil obstat* and the *imprimatur* agree with the content, opinions or statements expressed.

# From the Preface to the Tenth Edition (1936)

The author of a textbook who desires his work to reflect the results of the latest research in the field can never consider his work complete. A textbook calls for almost constant revision and amplification. Until now, the first part of the present work was based largely on the work of Dr. F. X. Funk — and his presentation of the history of Christian Antiquity was generally considered the best part of his Church history. However, I have devoted so much time and effort to revising and supplementing Funk that I feel justified in considering even this first part as essentially my own work. With exception of a few minor changes, the original division and arrangement of matter have been retained. Suggestions, which I fully appreciated, were made that I introduce a freer and less schematic disposition of the matter. But such a radical change would have delayed the publication of the work which was then long overdue. Hence I was obliged to abandon any such plan; and consoled myself with the thought that in the acquisition of knowledge, it is the teacher rather than the textbook that matters; and that every professor of Church History will naturally treat the subject according to his own good judgment and in the best interests of his students.

A work like the present one, in spite of the more recent interesting facts which have been added, must remain a textbook; and hence will never be an easy book to read. It demands the most earnest application of those who use it. I refer to what I said in the preface to the Third Part (1933) where I endeavored briefly to outline the point of view. It seemed to me that the most important thing was an exact, authentic an impartial statement of facts as the necessary foundation for the formation of sound judgment. Lengthy observations and reflections in an attempt to synthesize ideas, facts and trends, as valuable as they may be, are, in my opinion, the task of the teacher rather than of the textbook, which is limited to a concise presentation of facts. The textbook can give only the starting point for synthesis and reflection.

**Karl Bihlmeyer.**

V

## Foreword to the Twelfth Edition

Before the revered editor of six editions of this Church History died in the spring of 1942, he expressed the wish that I undertake a revision of the work. Hence this present edition is an attempt to carry out the request of my former professor. A number of interested persons suggested that I recast the entire work; but this I could not bring myself to do. I felt that I would be wanting in reverence if I endeavored to make of the first revision after Dr. Bihlmeyer's death a work which would no longer be "Bihlmeyer."

However, this edition contains the results of the latest research and the bibliography has been brought up to date. The task was not always an easy one. After the appearance of the second volume it did, indeed, become easier to correspond with scholars of other lands; but economic difficulties in Germany still rendered it impossible to keep abreast of the research being carried on in various countries. In fact it was often quite impossible to acquire articles appearing in periodical publications of distant places. Hence I shall be most grateful to colleagues who can furnish me with copies of articles which they think should receive attention in a work of this kind.

The manuscript was completed about the middle of 1950. While the work was in press only relatively few alterations or additions could be made. In the event of another revision, I have in mind to limit the bibliography to works which have appeared since 1930. On this point, too, I shall be grateful for any suggestions.

Paderborn, July 2, 1951.

**Hermann Tüchle.**

# TABLE OF CONTENTS

### Introduction

## PART I

## THE ANCIENT CHURCH

### First Period

## FROM THE FOUNDATION TO THE EDICT OF MILAN (313)

### Chapter I

### Foundation, Spread and Persecution of the Church

### Chapter II

### The Constitution of the Church

## Chapter III

### Worship, Discipline and Morals

## Chapter IV

### Development of Doctrine. Heresies and Schisms

## Chapter V

### Ecclesiastical Literature and Learning

### Second Period

## FROM THE EDICT OF MILAN TO THE COUNCIL IN TRULLO
### (313—692)

## Chapter I

### Spread of Christianity and Obstacles Encountered

VIII

## Table of Contents.

### Chapter V
### Ecclesiastical Literature and Learning

# ABBREVIATIONS

AB = Analecta Bollandiana

Abh. = Abhandlungen der Akademie bzw. Gesellschaft der Wissenschaften, philos.-histor. Klasse, in Berlin, Göttingen, Heidelberg, Leipzig, München, Wien.

AkKR = Archiv für katholisches Kirchenrecht.

AnnHVNiedRh = Annalen des historischen Vereins für den Niederrhein.

AntChrist = Antike und Christentum. Kultur- u. Religionsgeschichtliche Studien by F. J. Dölger (1929 ff.).

ArchFH = Archivum Franciscanum Historicum.

ArchHistMA = Archives d'histoire doctrinale et littéraire du moyen âge.

ArchLKGMA = Archiv für Literatur- und Kirchengeschichte des Mittelalters.

ArchRelW = Archiv für Religionswissenschaft.

ArchSRom = Archivio della R. Società Romana di storia patria.

ASS = Acta Sanctorum of the Bollandists (§ 2, 8).

BeitrGdSL = Beiträge zur Gesch. der deutschen Sprache und Literatur.

BenMS = Benediktinische Monatsschrift.

BKV = Bibliothek der Kirchenväter, new adaptation (§ 2, 9).

BlwürttKG = Blätter für württembergische Kirchengeschichte.

BullLA = Bulletin d'ancienne littérature et d'archéologie chrétiennes·

BullLE = Bulletin de litterature ecclésiastique.

CIC = Codex iuris canonici.

CivCatt = Civiltà Cattolica.

CSCO = Corpus Scriptorum Christian. Orientalium.

CSEL = Corpus Scriptorum Ecclesiasticorum Latinorum (§ 2, 9d).

DAGM = Deutsches Archiv für Geschichte des MA (continuation of NA 1937 ff.).

DictAC = Dictionnaire d'archéologie chrétienne et de liturgie (§ 2, 1).

DictApol = Dictionnaire apologétique (§ 2, 11).

DictHE = Dictionnaire d'histoire et de géographie ecclésiastiques (§ 2, 11).

DictSpir = Dictionnaire de spiritualité ascétique et mystique (§ 2, 11).

DictThC = Dictionnaire de théologie catholique (§ 2, 11).

DLZ = Deutsche Literaturzeitung.

DVSLGG = Deutsche Vierteljahrsschrift für Literaturwissenschaft und Geistesgeschichte.

EphThLov = Ephemerides Theologicae Lovanienses.

FranzSt = Franziskanische Studien.

FreiDA = Freiburger Diözesan-Archiv.

FunkAU = Funk, Kirchengeschichtliche Abhandlungen und Untersuchungen, 3 vols. 1897—1907.

GeschAL = Geschichte der altkirchlichen (Bardenhewer) or altchristlichen (Harnack) Literatur.

Harduinus = Acta conciliorum ed. J. Harduinus (§ 2, 2).

HarvThR = Harvard Theological Review.

Hauck = A. Hauck, Kirchengeschichte Deutschlands.

Hefele, Hefele-Leclerq = Konziliengeschichte by C. J. von Hefele, 2nd ed., or the French revision of the same (§ 2, 2).

HJG = Historisches Jahrbuch der Görresgesellschaft.

HistVS = Historische Vierteljahrsschrift.

HpBl = Historisch-politische Blätter.

HZ = Historische Zeitschrift.

IntkZ = Internationale kirchliche Zeitschrift.

Janssen = J. Janssen, Geschichte des deutschen Volkes seit dem Ausgang des Mittelalters.

JbLW = Jahrbuch für Liturgiewissenschaft (§ 2, 5).

JThSt = Journal of Theological Studies.

Kath. = Der Katholik (Mainz).

KL = Kirchenlexikon 2. A. (§ 2, 11).

MélAH = Mélanges d'archéologie et d'histoire.

MG = Monumenta Germaniae historica (§ 2, 10); SS = Scriptores.

MIÖG = Mitteilungen des Instituts für österreichische Geschichtsforschung.

MissWRelW = Missionswissenschaft und Religionswissenschaft (continuation of the ZMW 1938 ff.).

MSR = Mélanges de science religieuse.

NA = Neues Archiv der Gesellschaft für ältere deutsche Geschichtskunde.

Nachr. = Nachrichten (s. Abh.).

NedAKG = Nederlandsch Archief voor Kerkgeschiedenis.

NJklA = Neue Jahrbücher für das klassische Altertum, Geschichte und deutsche Literatur.

NkZ = Neue kirchliche Zeitschrift.

OrChrAn = Orientalia Christ. Analecta.

OrChrPer = Orientalia Christ. Periodica.

Pastor = L. v. Pastor, Geschichte der Päpste seit dem Ausgang des Mittelalters.

PG, PL = Migne, Patrologiae cursus, series graeca, series latina (§ 2, 9c).

QFItalAB = Quellen und Forschungen aus italienischen Archiven und Bibliotheken.

RE = Realenzyklopädie für protest. Theologie 3rd ed. (§ 2, 11).

REKraus = Realenzykl. der christl. Altertümer, ed. F. X. Kraus (§ 2, 1).

RE Pauly-Wissowa = Paulys Realenzyklopädie des klassischen Altertums, revised by G. Wissowa et al. (§ 3, 5).

RClFr = Revue du clergé français.

RechSR = Recherches de science religieuse.

RechThAM = Recherches de Théologie ancienne et médiévale.

RevAM = Revue d'ascétique et de mystique.

RevBén = Revue Bénédictine.

RevHEFrance = Revue d'histoire de l'Église de France.

RevHPhR = Revue d'histoire et de philosophie religieuses.

RevHR = Revue de l'histoire des religions.

RevOC = Revue de l'Orient chrétien.

RevSPhTh = Revue des sciences philosophiques et théologiques.

RevSR = Revue des sciences religieuses.

RHE = Revue d'histoire ecclésiastique.

RHLR = Revue d'histoire et de littérature religieuses.

RLAntChr = Reallexikon für Antike und Christentum.

RivArchCrist = Rivista di archeologia cristiana.

RottMS = Rottenburger Monatsschrift für praktische Theologie.

RQ = Römische Quartalschrift für christliche Altertumskunde und Kirchengeschichte.

RQH = Revue des questions historiques.

Sb = Proceedings of the Academies mentioned under Abh.

Sp = Speculum.

StMBenO = Studien und Mitteilungen aus dem Benediktiner- und Zisterzienserorden, bzw. zur Geschichte des Benediktiner-Ordens und seiner Zweige.

StML, StZ = Stimmen aus Maria-Laach, Stimmen der Zeit.

ThGl = Theologie und Glaube (Paderborn).

ThLZ = Theologische Literaturzeitung.

ThQ = Theologische Quartalschrift.

ThRev = Theologische Revue.

ThStKr = Theologische Studien und Kritiken.

TU = Texte und Untersuchungen zur Geschichte der altchristlichen Literatur (§ 2, 9).

VC = Vigiliae Christianae.

Wolf, QKdRG = G. Wolf, Quellenkunde der deutschen Reformationsgeschichte, 2 vols. in 3 parts 1915—1923.

WürttVLG = Württembergische Vierteljahrshefte für Landesgeschichte.

ZAszMyst = Zeitschrift für Aszese und Mystik.

ZfdA = Zeitschrift für deutsches Altertum und deutsche Literatur.

ZfdGeistG = Zeitschrift für deutsche Geistesgeschichte.

ZGORh = Zeitschrift für die Geschichte des Oberrheines.

ZKG = Zeitschrift für Kirchengeschichte.

ZkTh = Zeitschrift für katholische Theologie (Innsbruck).

ZMW = Zeitschrift für Missionswissenschaft (und für Religionswissenschaft).

ZntW = Zeitschrift für (die) neutestamentliche Wissenschaft (und die Kunde der älteren Kirche).

ZRGkan = Zeitschrift der Savigny-stiftung f. Rechtsgeschichte, kanonistische Abteilung.

ZThS = Zeitschrift für Theologie und Seelsorge (Bonn).

ZwürttLG = Zeitschrift für württembergische Landesgeschichte (continuation of the WürttVLG 1937 ff.

ZwTh = Zeitschrift f. wissenschaftliche Theologie.

N.B. — The three volumes of this work are arranged in sections numbered consecutively throughout and indicated by §. All references and cross references are to the sections. Thus (§ 39, 5) within or at the end of a sentence means that the same or related matter will be found in the fifth *numbered* paragraph of section 39.

# INTRODUCTION

## § 1.

## Task, Method and Division of Church History.[1]

1. The task of Church History[2], as a theological discipline, is to give a clear, intelligent and scientific account of the external and internal development of the *institution* founded by Christ

---

[1] C. KREIG, Enzyklopädie der theol. Wissenschaften, [2]1910, 181/221. P. WERNLE, Einführung in d. theol. Studium, [3]1921, 203/92. L. HALPHEN, Introduction à l'histoire, Paris 1946. P. GUILDAY, An Introduction to Church History, St. Louis, 1925. A. EHRHARD, Die hist. Theologie und ihre Methode, Festschrift S. Merkle, 1922, 117/36. W. KÖHLER, Idee u. Persönlichkeit in der KG., 1910. A. HARNACK, Das Verhältnis der KG. zur Universalgesch., in: Aus Wissensch. u. Leben II, 1911, 43/62. E. SEEBERG, Über Bewegungsgesetze der Welt- und KG., 1924. Ideen zur Theologie der Gesch. des Christentums, 1929; ZKG 1941, 309/31 (History and the historical attitude of the ancient Church). W. KOEHLER, Histoire u. Metahistorie in der KG., 1930 (Lecture). E. BERNHEIM, Lehrb. der hist. Methode, [5/6]1908. A. FEDER, Lehrb. der geschichtlichen Methode, [3]1924. J. G. DROYSEN, Historik, publ. by R. Hübner, [3]1948. G. WOLF, Einführung in das Studium der neueren Gesch., 1910. WILH. BAUER, Einführung in das Studium der Gesch., [8]1928. L. FONCK, Wissenschaftliches Arbeiten, [3]1926. KR. ERSLEV, Hist. Technik, from the Danish by E. Brandt, 1928. FR. SAWICKI, Geschichtsphilosophie, 1920. A. DEMPF, Weltgesch. als Tat u. Gemeinschaft, 1924. E. SPRANGER, Der Sinn der Voraussetzungslosigkeit in den Geisteswissenschaften, Sb. Berlin 1929. I. E. KEYSER, Die Geschichtswissenschaft, Aufbau u. Aufgaben, 1931. F. KAUFMANN, Geschichtsphilosophie der Gegenwart, 1931 (Philosoph. Forschungsberichte 10). K. HEUSSI, Die Krisis des Historismus, 1932. P. SIMON, Die Geschichte als Weg des Geistes, ThQ 1933, I/39; Das Menschliche in der Kirche Christi, [3]1948. E. BOENI, Der Kampf um die Kirche. Studien zum Kirchenbegriff des christl. Altertums, Vevey 1934 (liberal). E. LASLOWSKI, ZfdGeistG 1935, 125/32 (the Church as an historical phenomenon). O. BAUHOFER, Das Geheimnis der Zeiten, christl. Sinndeutung d. Geschichte, 1935. TH. HAECKER, Der Christ u. die G., [2]1949. TH. MICHELS, Das Heilswerk der Kirche, 1935. A. SCHÜTZ, Gott in der Geschichte, 1936. H. GÖRGEN, ZfdGeistG 1936, 55/64 (theology of history). F. MEINECKE, Die Entstehung des Historismus, 2 vols. [2]1946; Vom geschichtl. Sinn u. vom Sinn der G., [2]1951; also W. HOFER, G.-Schreibung u. Weltanschauung, 1950. H. J. BADEN, Der Sinn der G., 1948. K. JASPERS, Vom Ursprung u. Ziel der G., 1948. O. WAGNER, Geschichtswissensch., 1951. W. ECKERMANN, Neue G.-Wissenschaft, 1950. G. EBELING, KG. als G. der Auslegung der Heiligen Schrift, 1947. H. U. V. BALTHASAR, Theologie der G., 1950. J. ZEILLER, RHE 1933, 571 ff. 827 ff. (the concept of the Church in the first four centuries). E. GÖLLER Die Periodisierung der KG. und die epochale Stellung des MA.s, 1919. K. HEUSSI, Altertum, MA. u. Neuzeit in d. KG., 1921. G. V. BELOW, Über hist. Periodisierungen, 1925 (disagrees with Heussi).

[2] The first "Church History" (Ἐκκλησιαστικὴ ἱστορία) was compiled by Eusebius of Caesarea (§ 4, 1) who also most probably invented the term. Walafried Strabo (Liber de exordiis, etc. 7) in the ninth century correctly

1

*for the salvation of mankind.* In endeavoring to fulfill this task, Church History must consider the spread of Christianity over the earth from the beginning to the present day *(History of the Missions)*; the relations of the Church with the converted *peoples*, with *States* and with *rulers (History of Ecclesiastical Polity)*; the *persecutions* to which she has been subjected by adverse powers as well as the *obstacles* placed in the way of her development by non-Christian or heterodox Christian groups. Of still greater importance is the history of the Church's *internal* development — of the religious-social life that is peculiarly her own. Vincent of Lérins (Commonitorium c. 29. 30), in the fifth century, used the example of the organic growth of plants and human beings to explain this development and to show that it takes place in virtue of powers and principles which God implanted in her. Her *constitution* and organization, her *worship* and *liturgy*, her *discipline, customs* and *culture*, her *art* and *literature*, her *doctrine* and *science* (theology) have developed in accordance with these laws. Her dogma, of its very nature, is immutable, but this fact by no means excludes a formal development. Partly of her own accord and partly because of the attacks of heresy, the Church, under the guidance of the Holy Ghost who never forsakes her (John 14. 16) continues to clarify, explain, and give a more lucid concept of the revealed truths which have been committed to her. Naturally, Church History can indicate only the bare outline of the development of doctrine; for a more detailed treatment a special discipline, the *History of Dogma*, must be consulted.

2. The *method* used in Church History is determined, on the one hand, by the generally recognized principles of historical research and presentation; on the other hand by the special demands of a theological discipline. The church historian must be acquainted with and make use of the latest verified findings and approved scientific methods. There are three principles in particular which

---

recognized the word "Church" as coming from the Greek. It is from κυριακόν, in popular speech κυριχόν, the word οἰκεῖον being understood (Eus. H. E. IX, 5, 2; 10, 10. 12). But it is disputed whether the term was taken directly from the Greek by the Visigoths on the Balkan peninsula and transmitted by them to the other Germans and the Slavs (Kluge, et al.) or whether it had first found its way into Vulgar Latin (cyricon?) and was adopted by German tribes in the fourth century (Stutz, Braune). The Romanic peoples adopted the biblical word ἐκκλησία ecclesia into their languages. Cfr. P. Kretschmer, Zeitschr. f. vergleich. Sprachforsch. 39, 1906, 539 ff.; U. STUTZ, Internationale Wochenschr. 1909, 1640 ff.; F. KLUGE, BeitrGdSL 35, 1909, 124 ff.; W. BRAUNE, ib. 43, 1918, 424 ff.

must govern the writing of Church History: 1) It must be *authentic* and *critical*, that is, the matter must be carefully sifted from the best available sources according to the rules of external and internal criticism; 2) It must be *objective*, that is, unbiased, revealing lights and shadows with strict adherence to truth and without any intent to influence opinion contrary to fact. Absolute objectivity, on which the Liberal School prides itself, is, of course, impossible, since one's judgment in historical matters is always influenced more or less by one's philosophy of life. And 3) It must be *pragmatic-genetic*, that is, didactically evolutionary (explanatory): the historian must seek to find the causative relationship in the development of events; he must examine the motives and aims of the persons involved as well as the deeper roots of mass movements, the formative ideas and the driving forces in back of the processes of development. The observance of these principles will make Church History like general World History in very truth the magistra vitae.

However, since the Church is not merely a human, but primarily a divine institution, or more exactly, a synthesis of the divine and human, it follows that Church History 4) must of necessity take a *religious* orientation. Nor does this in any way exclude the full and proper use of scientific methods; for theology and history if truly scientific, can never be at variance, since both are devoted to the acquisition of truth, which is *one*. Church historians use the yardstick of historical interpretation, always conscious of Christian religious values. The idea that the Kingdom of God became a reality among men according to the divine plan and under the guidance of the Holy Ghost, must be their lode star. Church History together with the Scriptural sciences forms *historical theology* whose task is "to lay the real historical foundation for the entire structure of scientific theology." (Pfeilschifter).

*History of Religion* and *Psychology of Religion,* both receiving so much attention today, can make use of Church History to great advantage. It can help them to investigate more thoroughly the relationship between Christianity and Judaism and the culture developed under the pagan religions; and it can help to a better understanding of the personal piety of prominent men and leaders and of the religiosity of the masses. It must, however, beware of the generalizations so frequent in these disciplines and of the unwarranted conclusion that Christianity merely built on a pagan foundation. And it must reject resolutely the assertion so often made that Church History is not distinct from the History of the Christian Religion. For the formal object of Church History is not the evolution of the Christian religion and Christian piety as such; it is rather the development in all the fullness of its life-processes of the institution founded by Christ for man's salvation. — *H. Schrörs*, Kirchengesch. und nicht Religionsgesch., 1905 (a lecture). — *B. Bartmann*, Dogma und Religionsgesch., 1922. — *H. Pinard de la Boullaye, SJ.*, Histoire comparée des religions t. I—II, Paris 1922/5. — *B. Heigl*, Religionsgeschichtl. Methode und Theologie, 1926 (Bibl. Zeitfr. XII, 1/2). — *G. Mensching*, Allgem. Religionsgesch., ²1949. — *M. Gorce et R. Mortier*, Histoire générale des religions, Paris 1948 ff.

3. The tremendous amount of matter which must be treated in Church History may be arranged *topically* or *chronologically*. A combination of the two methods allows a treatment of matter which is not purely schematic but in which the time element governs the disposal of the matter. Topical treatment must give attention to the various facets of ecclesiastical life mentioned above; The Mission and Spread of Christianity; Relationship of Church and State; Suppression and Persecution; Organization and Discipline; Worship and Liturgy; Customs and Culture; Art and Literature; Doctrine and Learning. A strictly chronological division is rarely followed in modern texts. The division of history into three great periods: *Antiquity, Middle Ages* and *Modern Times,* was introduced by the Humanists of the fifteenth and sixteenth centuries and was first used in textbooks of world history in the seventeenth century (Christopher *Cellarius*, Historiae antiquae, mediae, novae nucleus, Jenae 1675/76). It has been used in the writing of Church History since the days of the Romanticists (Möhler, Hase). Today these terms are somewhat vague because no one can fix a line of demarcation between Antiquity and the Middle Ages on which every one will agree. Yet the division still serves a purpose. However, its didactic-typological value is greater than its chronological importance. Any division of time can be of relative value only, in marking the constant flow of history.

The following division is generally followed by most Church Histories: *Antiquity*, during which the Church was active chiefly within the framework of Greco-Roman culture. It extends from the birth of Christ to the end of the seventh century (692, the Trullan Synod of Constantinople). The year 313, when Constantine the Great granted State recognition to the persecuted Church, divides this age into two periods. The *Middle Ages* marks the time when the Catholic faith and the Church played the leading role in all departments of public and cultural life among the Germanic-

Romanic peoples. This age comprises more than eight centuries (692—1517). The dates of accession of Gregory VII (1073) and of Boniface VIII (1294) divide the age into three periods, often called the Early, the High, and the Late Middle Ages. Finally, *Modern Times* begins with Luther's consequential revolt against the Church (1517) and extends to the present day. The nineteenth and twentieth centuries are sometimes distinguished as the *"Latest Period"* of Modern Times. The boundary lines of this period are marked by the Peace of Westphalia (1648), the French Revolution (1789 ff.) and World War I (1914/18).

# § 2.
## Sources of Church History.

The sources of Church History are those written records and monuments which supply us with information regarding the Christian past. They may be *original*, or *reproductions* of the original; they may be *public* (official) or *private*. Original and official sources are naturally the most important. In recent times the most important sources have been made available in large *collections*, an acquaintance with which is necessary for a study of Church History.

**1. Inscriptions and Monuments:** *F. Piper*, Einleitung in die monumentale Theologie, 1867. — *H. Leclercq*, DictAC VII, 850/1089 (Collections of inscriptions). — *J. B. de Rossi*, Inscriptiones christianae urbis Romae VII saec. antiquiores I—II, I, Romae 1861/88; Suppl. ed. *J. Gatti* fasc. I, Romae 1915; Nova series ed. *A. Silvagni*, 2 vol. Romae 1922/35. — *E. Le Blant*, Inscriptions chrét. de la Gaule, 3 vol. Paris 1856/92, reprinted 1923. — *Aem. Hübner*, Inscriptiones Hispaniae christ., 1871, Suppl. 1892/1900; Inscriptiones Hispaniae christ., 1871, Suppl. 1892/1900; Inscriptiones Britanniae christ., 1876. — *J. Vives*, Inscriptiones cristianas de la España romana y visigoda, Barcelona 1941 ff. — *F. X. Kraus*, Die christl. Inschriften d. Rheinlande, 2 vols. 1890/4. — Corpus inscriptionum latinarum vol. XIII p. 6; Inscriptiones trium Galliarum et Germaniarum latinae, 1933. — *E. Egli*, Die christl. Inschriften der Schweiz vom 4.—9. Jh., 1895. — *St. Gsell*, Inscriptions latinas d'Algérie I, Paris 1922. — *H. Grégoire*, Recueil des inscriptions grecques chrét. d'Asie Mineure, Paris 1922 ff. — *L. Jalabert* et *R. Mouterde*, Inscriptions grecques et latines de la Syrie I, Paris 1929. — *E. Diehl*, Inscriptiones latinae christianae veteres, 3 vol. 1924/31; Inscriptiones latinae, 1912 (50 tables). — *C. Wessel*, Inscriptiones graecae christianae veteres occidentis, Dissertation 1936. — *J. B. Fey*, Corpus inscriptionum iudaicarum I, Rome 1936. — *J. B. de Rossi*, La Roma sotteranea cristiana, 3 vol. Rome 1864/77; Supplement by *J. Wilpert*, 1909, *O. Marucchi*, Roma 1909. — Roma sotteranea cristiana per cura del Pontif. Istituto di archeologia cristiana, Rome 1936 ff. — *R. Krautheimer*, Corpus Basilicarum Christianarum Romae, Rome 1937 ff. —- *J. Wilpert*, Die Malereien

der Katakomben Roms, 2 vols. 1903; Die röm. Mosaiken u. Malereien der altkirchl. Bauten vom 4.—13. Jh., 4 vols. [2]1917; I sarcofagi cristiani antichi,
3 vol. Rome 1929/36; *F. Gerke*, Die christlichen Sarkophage der vorkonstantinischen Zeit, 1940. — *C. Cecchelli*, Monumenti christiano-eretici di Roma,
Rome 1944; Iconografia dei Papi, Rome 1938 ff. (I: S. Pietro). — *G. B. Ladner*,
Papstbildnisse des Altertums und Mittelalters I, Rome 1941. — Realenzyklop.
der christl. Altertümer, edited by *F. X. Kraus*, 2 vols. 1882/86. — Dictionnaire
d'archéologie chrét. et de liturgie, publ. p. *F. Cabrol et H. Leclercq*, Paris,
1907 ff. (Now complete). — Reallexikon für Antike und Christentum, ed. by
*Th. Klauser* et al., 1950 ff. — Bibliographie der christl. Archäologie by
*J. P. Kirsch* in RQ 1900 ff. and in Rivista di archeologia cristiana, Rome
1929 ff. — *A. Egger*, Kirchliche Kunst- u. Denkmalspflege, Brixen [2]1933. —
Reallexikon zur deutschen Kunstgeschichte, ed. by *O. Schmitt*, 1937 ff. —
*W. Otto*, Handbuch der Archäologie I, 1939. — Die deutschen Inschriften,
publ. by the Deutsche Akademien der Wissenschaften Berlin, Göttingen,
Heidelberg, Leipzig, München, Wien, 1942 ff. — Cfr. also § 3,3 and § 71.

**2. Councils:** *Concilia* generalia ecclesiae catholicae, 4 tomi Romae 1608/12.
— *Ph. Labbe* et *G. Cossart*, Sacrosancta concilia, 17 fol. Paris 1674; ed. *Coleti*,
23 fol. Venet. 1728/34; Suppl. 6 fol. (to 1720) ed. *Mansi*, Lucae 1748/52. —
*J. Harduinus*, Acta conciliorum et epistolae decretales ac constitutiones
summorum pontificum, 12 fol. (to 1714) Paris 1715. — *J. D. Mansi*, Sacrorum
conciliorum nova et amplissima collectio, 31 fol. (to 1439) Flor. et Venet.
1759/98; photostatic reprint with additions by *J. B. Martin* and *L. Petit* to
1902 in 53 vols., Paris 1901/27; cfr. *H. Quentin*, Mansi et les grandes collections conciliaires, Paris 1900. — *Ed. Schwartz*, Acta conciliorum oecumenicorum
(431—879), 1914 ff. (§ 54, 55, 58). — *Bruns, Lauchert, Turner* and others,
§ 65. — *Collectio Lacensis*, Acta et decreta s. conciliorum recentiorum, 7 vol.
(1682—1870) 1870/90. — *J. Sirmond-La Lande*, Concilia antiqua Galliae, 4 fol.
Paris 1629/66. — *A. W. Haddan-W. Stubbs*, Councils and ecclesiastical Documents rel. to Great-Britain and Ireland, 4 vol. Oxford 1689/78. — *J. Hartz-
heim*, Concilia Germaniae, II fol. Col. 1749/90. — MG Concilia, see no. 10
below. — *C. J. v. Hefele*, Conziliengeschichte, 7 vols. 1855/74; I—VI 2. A.
(V—VI revised by A. Knöpfler) 1873/90; VIII—IX (to 1541) by J. Hergenröther 1887/90; French translation (Histoire des Conciles) with revisions by
*H. Leclercq*, vol. I—VIII Paris 1907/21; supplement vol. IX; Concile de
Trente par P. Richard, Paris 1930/31; vol. X, 1 par A. Michel, Paris 1938.

**3. Acts and Documents of Popes and Collections of Bulls:** *Bullarium
Romanum*, various editions, but none complete or reliable; the best is Bullarium Romanum (from the 6th vol. on) by *C. Cocquelines*, 14 fol. Romae 1739/44
(ed. Taurinensis cura A. Tomassetti, 24 tom. in 4⁰ 1857/72), to 1740; a Continuatio from Benedict XIV to Pius VIII (1830) appeared in 10 Fol. vols.
at Prato 1853/67, a second, from Clement XIII to Gregory XVI (1846) ed.
by *A. Barberi, A. Spetia* and *R. Segreti*, 19 vols. Rome 1835/57. — *Pontificum
Romanorum* a S. Clemente I usque ad S. Leonem *M. Epistolae* genuinae ed.
*P. Coustant* I (to 440, Paris 1271 (ed. Schoenemann, Gottingae 1796); a
S. Hilaro (461) usque ad S. Hormisdam (523) ed. *A. Thiel* 1863. — *Regesta*
Pontif. Romanorum ab condita ecclesia ad a. 1198 ed. *Ph. Jaffé* 1851; ed. II
cur. F. Kaltenbrunner, P. Ewald, S. Loewenfeld, 2 vol. 1885/8; ab a. 1198 ad

## § 2. Sources of Church History.

a. 1304 ed. *A. Potthast*, 2 vol. 1874/75. — Supplement to Jaffé: *J. v. Pflugk-Harttung*, Acta pontificum Romanorum (to 1198), 3 vols. 1881/88. — *P. Fr. Kehr*, Regesta pontificum Romanorum: Italia Pontificia I—VIII cong. P. Fr. Kehr 1907/35; Germania Pontificia I—III, cong. *A. Brackmann* 1910/35 (id., Studien und Vorarbeiten zur Germania Pontificia I 1912; *J. Haller*, Internat. Wochenschrift 1910, 1627 ff. 1659 ff.); *P. Fr. Kehr*, Papsturkunden in Spanien 1/2, Abh. Göttingen 1926/28; Sb. Berlin 1934, 71/92 (on the collection and editions of the older papal documents to Innocent III). — *W. Wiederhold*, Papsturkunden in Frankreich, Nachr. Gött. 1906/7, 1910/13. — *H. Meinert*, Papsturkunden in Frankreich NF., 2 Teile, Abh. Gött. 1932/33. — *J. Ramackers*, Papsturkunden in den Niederlanden, 2 Teile, Abh. Gött. 1933/34; id., Papsturkunden in Frankreich NF. 2—4, Abh. Gött. 1937/42. — *W. Holtzmann*, Papsturkunden in England, 2 Teile, Abh. Gött. 1930/36. — *H. Leclercq*, Lettres des Papes (Collections), DictAC VIII, 2942/82. — *Corpus iuris canonici* ed. Aem. *L. Richter*, 1839; ed. *E. Friedberg*, 2 tom. 1879/82. — *Codex iuris canonici* Pii X iussu digestus, Benedicti XV auctoritate promulgatus, Romae 1917; ed. Herder-Pustet, 1918. — Codicis iur. can. *fontes* cura *Petri Card. Gasparri* et *Iustiniani Card. Serédi* editi I—IX, Romae 1923/39. — Codicis iur. can. interpretationes authenticae (1917/50), 2 vol. Romae 1935/50. — *N. Hilling*, Codicis iur. can. supplementum, 1924; Continuatio I (1924/30), 1931. — *C. Sartori*, Enchiridion canonicum, Rome 1947. — *Acta Apostolicae Sedis*, Commentarium officiale, Romae 1909 ff. – *K. Mirbt*, Quellen zur Gesch. des Papsttums u. des Röm. Katholizismus, [4]1924 (somewhat biased). — *A. Galante*, Fontes iuris canonici selecti, 1906. — *H. J. Schroeder*, Disciplinary Decrees of the General Councils (325—1215), text, translat. and commentary, St. Louis 1937. — The papal *registers* for the second half of the Middle Ages have been published by various authors; those from Gregory IX to Benedict XI by French scholars of the Bibliothèques des Écoles françaises d'Athènes et de Rome, Paris 1884 ff. — The following Regesta have been published or are being published: Honorius III—IV, Gregory IX—X, John XXI, Innocent IV, Alexander IV, Urban IV, Clement IV—V, Nicholas III—IV, Martin IV, Boniface VIII, Benedict XI to XII, Leo X. — Cfr. G. Brom, Guide aux archives du Vatican Rome [2]1911; Sussidi per la consultazione dell'Archivio Vaticano I, Rome 1926 (Studi e testi 45); *K. A. Fink*, Das vatik. Archiv, [2]1951. — *Liber Pontificalis* and collections of lives of the popes, § 78, 3; 85; 138 (Duchesne, Watterich, Baluzius). — For the *Greek-Oriental* Church: Sacra Congregazione Orientale, Codificazione canonica orientale — Fonti, Rome 1930 ff.

4. **Concordats and Civil Laws Relating to the Church:** Codex Theodosianus cum perpet. commentariis *Jac. Gothofredi* ed. *J. D. Ritter*, 6 fol. Lips. 1739/43; ed. *Th. Mommsen* et *P. Meyer*, 2 vol. 1904/5; recogn. *P. Krueger*, 1923/26. — *O. Gradenwitz*, Heidelberger Index zum Theodosianus, 1925; Supplement, 1929. — Corpus iuris civilis ed. *Dion. Gothofredus*, 6 fol. Lugd. 1589; ed. *Mommsen—Krüger—Schöll—Kroll*, 3 vol. 1872/95. — *H. Leclercq*, Lois Romains (empire chrétien), DictAC IX, 2229/73. — Monumenta Germaniae histor. ed. *Pertz*, Leges I—V fol. 1835 ff.; see below 10 c. — *E. v. Münch*, Vollst. Sammlung aller älteren und neueren Konkordate, 2 vols. 1830/31. — *F. Walter*, Fontes iuris eccl. antiqui et hodierni, 1862. — *V. Nussi*, Conven-

tiones de rebus ecclesiasticis (1122—1862), 1870. — *Ph. Schneider*, Fontes iuris eccles. novissimi, 1895. — (*A. Mercati*), Raccolta di Concordati (1098—1914), Roma 1919. — *J. M. Restrepo.* Concordata regnante SS. D. Pio PP XI inita latine et gallice reddita, Romae 1934. — *A. Perugini*, Concordata vigentia, Romae 1934. — *E. Eichmann*, Quellensammlung zur kirchl. Rechtsgesch. u. zum KR., 1912 ff. — *Z. Giacometti*, Quellen zur Gesch. der Trennung von Staat und Kirche, 1926.

**5. Liturgies:** *J. Goar*, Euchologion s. Rituale Graecorum, Paris 1647, Venet. 1730. — *E. Renaudot*, Liturgiarum orientalium collectio, 2 vol. Par. 1716. — *L. A. Muratori*, Liturgia Romana vetus, 2 vol. Venet. 1748. — *J. A. Assemani*, Codex liturgicus ecclesiae univ., 13 vol. Rome 1749/66; ed. nova Par. 1902; ed iterata, Par. 1922 ff. — *H. A. Daniel*, Codex liturgicus eccl. univ., 4 vol. Lips. 1847/53. — *H. Denzinger*, Ritus orientalium, 2 vol. 1863/64. — *C. A. Swainson*, The Greek Liturgies, London 1884. — *F. E. Brightman*, Liturgies Eastern and Western I, Oxford 1896. — *N. Nilles*, Kalendarium manuale utriusque ecclesiae orient. et occident., 2 vol. [2]1896/7. — *A. v. Maltzew*, Die Liturgien der russisch-orthod. K., 10 vols. 1894/1904. — *K. Kirchhof*, Die Ostkirche betet, 4 vols. 1934/38. — *F. Cabrol* et *H. Leclercq*, Monumenta ecclesiae liturgica I, Paris 1902/13; V 1904. — Dictionnaire d'archéologie chrét. et de liturgie, cfr. no. 1. — Liturgiegeschichtl. Quellen, ed. *K. Mohlberg* and *A. Rücker*, 1918 ff.; Liturgiegesch. Forschungen publ. by Mohlberg, Rücker and *F. J. Dölger*, 1919 ff. — Jahrb. f. Liturgiewissenschaft, ed. by *O. Casel*, 15 vol. 1921/41; Index to vols. I—X, 1933. — Archiv f. Lit.-wissensch., ed. *H. Emonds*, 1950 ff.; Liturg. Jahrb., ed. *J. Pascher*, 1951 ff. — *Jos. Braun*, Liturg. Handlexikon, [2]1924. — *G. M. Dreves* et *Cl. Blume*, Analecta hymnica medii aevi, Lipsiae 1886 ff. 55 vols.). -— *U. Chevalier*, Repertorium hymnologicum, 6 vol. Brux, 1892/1920. — *J. Julian*, Dictionary of Hymnology, London [2]1907. — *F. G. Holweck*, Calendarium liturgicum festorum Dei et Dei Matris Mariae, Philadelphiae 1925. — *R. Aigrain*, Liturgia. Encyclopédie populaire des connaissances liturgiques, Paris 1930. — *H. Leclercq*, Liturgistes, DictAC IX, 1729/49. — *Ph. Oppenheim*, Introductio in literaturam liturgicam, Torino 1937. — Opuscula et textus, Series liturgica, see no. 9 below. — Cfr. literature in § 23 and § 67.

**6. Creeds and Books of Symbols:** *H. Denzinger*, Enchiridion symbolorum, definitionum etc., 1854: ed. 26. par. *J. B. Umberg*, 1947 (cfr. J. Koch, ThQ 1932, 138/57). — *F. Cavallera*, Thesaurus doctrinae cathol. ex documentis magisterii ecclesiastici ordine methodico dispositus, Paris [2]1937. — *A. Hahn*, Bibl. d. Symbole und Glaubensregeln der alten Kirche, 1942; 3. ed. (by *L. Hahn*), 1897. — *Ph. Schaff*, Bibl. symbolica eccl. universalis, 3 vol. New York [4]1884. — *A. E. Burn*, Facsimiles of the Creeds, London 1909. — *H. Lietzmann*, Ausgewählte Symbole der alten Kirche, [3]1931. —- *J. Neuner*, and *H. Ross*, Der Glaube der Kirche in den Urkunden der Lehrverkündigung, [3]1951. — *J. T. Müller*, Die symbol. Bücher der evangl.-luth. Kirche, [12]1928. — *J. Michalcescu*, Die Bekenntnisse und wichtigsten Glaubenszeugnisse der griech.-orient. Kirche, 1904. — Corpus Confessionum. Die Bekenntnisse der Christenheit, ed. *C. Fabricius*, 1923 ff. — Die Bekenntnisschriften der evangelisch-luth. Kirche, publ. by the Deutsche evang. Kirchenausschuß, 2 vols. 1930. — Cfr. also § 22, 2.

**7. Rules of Religious Orders:** *Luc. Holstenius,* Codex regularum monastica-rum et canonicarum, 3 fol. Rome 1661; auctus a *Mar. Brockie,* 6 fol. Aug. Vind. 1759. — *H. U.v. Bathasar,* Die großen Ordensregeln, 1935. — Enchiridion de statibus perfectionis I, Rome 1949.

**8. Acts of Martyrs and Lives of Saints:** *B. Mombritius,* Sanctuarium seu Vitae Sanctorum (1477), ed. nova 2 vol. Paris 1910 (cfr. G. Eis, Die Quellen des Sanctuarium des Mombritius, 1933). — *L. Surius,* De probatis sanctorum vitis, 6 fol. Colon. 1570/75 and thereafter. — *Th. Ruinart,* Acta primorum martyrum sincera, Par. 1689; ed Galura, 3 vol. Aug. Vind. 1802; Ratisbonae 1859. — *J. Bollandus S.J.* et socii, Acta Sanctorum, Antverpiae 1643 ff., reprinted Paris 1854 ff. (follows the order of the Roman calendar); the latest volumes, 65th, for November 4th (9.—10.), appeared at Brussels 1925. Table of contents for the ASS in Potthast (see no. 11 below) and in the Bibliotheca hagiographica. Analecta Bollandiana, supplements the work of the ASS, 1882 ff. cfr. *H. Delehaye,* L'oeuvre des Bollandistes 1615—1915, Brux, 1920; also in Anal. Boll. 1937, V/XLV; *F. Pelster,* StZ 99, 1920, 517/31; *F. Baix,* RHE 1938, 270/96. — *A. Mercati* in Misc. Historiae Pontificiae n. 4, Rome 1940 (Bollandiana in the Vatican Archives). — *St. E. Assemani,* Acta SS. Martyrum oriental. et occident., 2 vol. Rome 1748. — *J. Mabillon,* Acta Sanctorum O. S. Bened., 9 fol. (500—1100) Paris 1668/1701; reprint (with vol. X and appendices), Mâcon 1935 ff. — *Martyrologium Hieronymianum,* edd. de Rossi et Duchesne (ASS Nov. II), Paris 1894; New edition by H. Quen-tin and commentary by H. Delehaye in ASS Nov. II, 2, Bruxellis 1931. — *Martyrologium Romanum,* ed. typica Vaticana, Rom. 1914, ed. tertia post. typ., Rome 1949. — *H. Delehaye* et al., Propylaeum ad Acta Sanctorum Decembris. Martyrologium Rom. ad formam ed. typicae scholiis historicis instructum, Bruxellis 1940. Das römische Martyrologium German transl., 1935. — *H. Quentin,* Le Martyrologes hist. du moyen âge, Paris 1908, reprinted 1923. — *H. Delehaye,* Étude sur la Légendier romain. Les saints de novembre et décembre, Brux. 1936. — *Bibliotheca hagiographica* latina, edd. socii Bollan-diani, 2 vol. Brux. 1898/1901, reprinted 1949, Suppl. ²1911; Bibliotheca hagiograph. graeca, ²1909 (additions by *F. Halkin* in Anal. Boll. 1935, 366/81); Bibliotheca hagiograph. orientalis, 1910. — *F. E. Stadler,* Vollständ. Heiligen-lexikon, 5 vols. 1858/62 (not critical). — *R. Buchwald,* Calendarium Ger-maniae. Die Sonderfeste der deutschen Diözesen, 1920. — *F. G. Holweck,* Biographical Dictionary of the Saints, St. Louis 1924. — *J. Baudot,* Dictionnaire d'hagiographie, Paris 1925 (popular); Le Martyrologe romain, Paris 1925. — *Fr. Doyé,* Heilige und Selige der römisch-katholischen Kirche, 2 vols 1925/30. — *A. Schütte,* Handb. der deutschen Heiligen, 1941. — *W. Schamoni,* Das wahre Gesicht der Heiligen, ³1950. — *J. Braun,* Tracht u. Attribute der Heiligen in der deutschen Kunst, 1943.

**9. Works of the Fathers and Ecclesiastical Writers:**

a) *Maxima Bibliotheca* veterum patrum etc., 27 fol. Lugd. 1677/1707 (up to the sixteenth century. The Greek authors appear only in Latin translation).

b) Bibliotheca veterum patrum etc. ed. *A. Gallandi,* 14 fol. (to 1200) Venet. 1765/81.

c) Patrologiae cursus completus accurante *J. P. Migne:* 1. Patrologia latina, 221 tomi (218—21 Indices) usque ad Innocentium III, Par. 1844/64;

(A revision of this work is planned by the Benedictines of the Abbey of Steenbrugge); 2. Patrologia graeca, 161 tomi usque ad s. XV, 1857/66; indices digessit F. Cavallera, Paris 1912; Index locupletissimus a Th. Hopfner, Paris 1928/45. Migne is the most complete and frequently used collection of patristica (the work is cited henceforth as PG or PL); cfr. also *P. de Labriolle*, BullLa 1913, 203/9; *H. Leclercq*, DistAC XI, 941/57; Chr. Baur, ThQ 1919, 251/69 (Duplicate in PG). The Latin series is continued by *Horoy* under the title Medii aevi Bibliotheca patristica 1879/83 in 5 vols. To distinguish the Latin Fathers in Migne from other collections *M. Vatasso* wrote, Initia patrum aliorumque scriptorum ecclesiasticorum latin., 2 vol. Romae 1906/8. This work was continued by *A. G. Little*, Initia operum s. XIII—XV, Manchester 1904. Cfr. also *A. Noyon*, Inventaire des écrits théol. du XIIᵉ siècle non insérés dans la Patrologie lat. de Migne, fasc. 1—2 Paris 1912/13 (Revue des Bibliothèques). — *L. Thorndike* and *P. Kibre*, A Catalogus of Incipits of Mediaeval Scientific Writings in Latin, Cambridge, Mass. 1937. — *F. Lot*, Bulletin Du Cange 1939, 113/230 (Index scriptorum operumque latino-gallicorum medii aevi [500—1000]). Very important for later Greek literature is the work of *A. Ehrhard*, Überlieferung und Bestand der hagiographischen und homiletischen Literatur der griech. Kirche von den Anfängen bis zum Ende des 16. Jh.s, Abt. I: Die Überlieferung, 1936 ff. (TU 50 ff.); Vols. I—III, 1, were published 1937/43.

d) Corpus scriptorum ecclesiasticorum latinorum Academiae Litterarum Caesareae, Vindob. 1866 ff. The Fathers whose works appear in this edition are indicated (§ 36 ff. § 74 ff.) by **, or by *, if the works are not yet complete.

e) ,,Die Griechischen Christlichen Schriftsteller der ersten drei Jahrhunderte", under the direction of *A. Harnack* published by the Kirchenväter-Kommission der Berliner Akademie der Wissenschaften, 1897 ff., 54 vols. proposed (cfr. ThLZ 1950, 116). The works in this collection are indicated by a double or single asterisk, as above.

f) SS. Patrum opuscula selecta ed. *H. Hurter*, ser. I in 48 small eds., 1868/85 (several editions of some volumes); ser. II in 6 vols., 1884/92. — *Texte* und *Untersuchungen* zur Gesch. der altchristl. Literatur, ed. by *O. Gebhardt*, *A. Harnack, C. Schmidt, E. Klostermann*, 1882 ff. 1st series vols. 1—15, 1882/97; 2nd series vols. 16—30, 1897/1906; 3rd series vol. 31 ff., 1907 ff. — Sammlung ausgewählter kirchen- und dogmengeschichtl. Quellenschriften, ed. *G. Krüger*, 1st series in 12 parts, 1891/96; 2nd series, 1901 ff. — Cambridge Patristic Texts ed. *J. A. Mason*, Cambridge 1899 ff. — *Florilegium Patristicum* digessit vertit adnotavit G. Rauschen, fasc. 1—12, 1904/19; Nova series ed. *P. Br. Albers*, 1920 ff., ed. *B. Geyer* et *J. Zellinger*, 1926 ff. (includes some works of the Middle Ages). — Textes et documents pour l'étude historique du christianisme, publ. p. *H. Hemmer* et *P. Lejay*, Paris 1904 ff. — *Opuscula* et *textus* historiam ecclesiae eiusque vitam atque doctrinam illustrantia. Series scholastica, edd. *M. Grabmann* et *Fr. Pelster*, 1926 ff.; Series liturgica, edd. *R. Stapper et A. Rücker*, 1933 ff. — Testi Cristiani con versione italiana, dir. da *O. Manacorda*, Firenze 1930 ff. — Pontificia Universitas Gregoriana, *Textus* et *documenta* in usum exercitationum et praelectionum academicarum. Series philosophica, Series theologica, Rome 1932 ff. — *M. J. Rouët de Journel*, Enchiridion Patristicum (for History of Dogma), ed. XIV, 1947. — *M. J.*

§ *2. Sources of Church History.*

*Rouét de Journel* et *J. Dutilleul*, Enchiridion Asceticum, [4]1947. — *J. de Guibert*, Documenta ecclesiastica christianae perfectionis studium spectantia, Rome 1932. — *Bibliothek der Kirchenväter*, Auswahl patristischer Werke in deutscher Übersetzung, ed. by *F. X. Reithmayr* and *V. Thalhofer*, 80 small volumes, (with general index) 1869/88. Revised ed., by *O. Bardenhewer*, *Th. Schermann* *(J. Zellinger)*, *K. Weyman*, 61 vols. 1911/28; Index (vols. 62—63) by J. E. Stöckerl, 1931. *Bibliothek der Kirchenväter*, 2nd series (in 18 vols), by *O. Bardenhewer*, *J. Zellinger* and *J. Martin*, 1932/37.

g) *Oriental Christian Literature: J. S. Assemani*, Bibliotheca Orientalis Clementino-Vaticana, 4 vol. Rome 1719/28. — Patrologia Syriaca accur. *R. Graffin* t. I—III, Paris 1894/1926. — Patrologia Orientalis, publ. p. *R. Graffin* et *F. Nau*, Paris 1903 ff. — Corpus Scriptorum Christianorum Orientalium cur. *J. B. Chabot*, *J. Guidi*, *H. Hyvernat*, *B. Carra de Vaux*, Paris 1903 ff. (Syrian, Coptic, Arabic and Ethiopic works arranged in separate groups). — Cfr. also § 75, 8, 9.

**10. Collections of National Histories:** a) Rerum *Italicarum* scriptores ed. *L. A. Muratori*, 25 fol. Mediol. 1273/51. Reprinted by Carducci and Fiorini, Città di Castello 1900 ff.

b) Rerum *Gallicarum* et *Francicarum* scriptores, also known under the title: Recueil des historiens des Gaules et de la France, edd. *M. Bouquet* etc., 23 fol. Paris 1738/1904; nouv. ed. p. *L. Delisle*, 19 fol. 1869/80. Nouvelle série 7 vol. 1899/1906. — Chartes et diplômes relatifs à l'hist. de France publ. p. les soins de l'Académie des Inscriptions et belles Lettres. Paris 1908 ff.

c) Monumenta *Germaniae* historica edd. *G. H. Pertz* etc., (the following parts are to be noted) Scriptores, 30 fol. 1826 ff., Continuation in Quart I—II 1902 ff.; Auctores antiquissimi I—XV, 1877 ff.; Scriptores rerum Merovingicarum I—VII (II—VII Passiones vitaeque Sanctorum), 1884/1920; Leges, vide supra no. 4; Legum sectio II: Capitularia regum Francorum I—II, 1883 ff.; sectio III: Concilia I—II, 1893 ff.; sectio IV: Constitutiones et Acta publica imperatorum et regum I—VI, VIII, 1883 ff.; Diplomata Regum Germaniae ex stirpe Karolinorum I—III, 1932/40; Diplomata regum et imperatorum I—VI, VIII, 1879 ff.; Epistolae I—X, 1885 ff.; Antiquitates: Poetae lat. aevi Carolini I—V, 1, Libri confraternitatum, Necrologia I—V, 1880 ff. Indices to the MG by *O. Holder-Egger* and *K. Zeumer*, 1890. — Cfr. *H. Bresslau*, Gesch. der Monumenta Germ. hist., 1921. — *W. Th. Miller Gamble*, The Monumenta Germaniae Hist., its Inheritance in Source-valuation and Criticism, Dissertation, Washington Cath. Univ. 1927. — Supplements to the MG in NA and DAGM (see list of abbreviations). — Cfr. P. Kehr. Sb. Berlin 1935 (new organization of the MG).

d) Fontes rerum *Austriacarum*: Scriptores, 8 vol. 1855/75; Diplomataria et Acta I—VII, 1849/1904. — Scriptores rer. *Hungaricarum*, 2 vol. Budapest 1937/8.

e) Rerum *Britannicarum* medii aevi scriptores, 98 works in 244 vols. London 1858/96.

f) Corpus scriptorum hist. *Byzantinea* edd. *Niebuhr* etc., 50 vol. 1829/97.

**11. Historical Source-Material, Bibliographies, Reports of Learned Societies, Encyclopedias and Reference Works:** *P. Herre*, *A. Hofmeister*, *R. Stübe*, Quellenkunde zur WG., 1910. — *W. Trillmich*, Kl. Bücherkunde zur Geschichtswissenschaft, 1950. — *A. Potthast*, Bibliotheca historica medii aevi, 2 vol. ²1896. — *U. Chevalier*, Répertoire des sources hist. du moyen âge. — Bio-Bibliographie, 2 vol. Paris ²1905/7; Topo-Bibliogr., 2 vol. Montbéliard 1894/1903. — *Dahlmann-Waitz*, Quellenkunde der Deutschen Gesch., 9th. Ed. by *H. Haering*, 1931, Reg. 1932 (cfr. H. Haering, HZ 136, 1927, 266/89). — *V. Loewe*, Bücherkunde der deutschen Gesch., ⁵1919. — *W. Wattenbach*, Deutschlands Geschichtsquellen im MA. bis z. Mitte d. 13. Jh.s, 2 vols ⁶1894, I ⁷1904; Revised ed. by *R. Holtzmann*, 1938/43. — *O. Lorenz*, Deutschlands Geschichtsquellen im MA. von d. Mitte d. 13. Jh.s bis z. Ende d. 14. Jh.s, 2 vols. ³1886/87. — *H. Vildhaut*, Quellenkunde zur allg. Gesch. bis z. Auftreten des Humanismus, 4 vols. ²1906/8. — *K. Jakob*, Quellenkunde der deutschen Gesch. im MA. I ³1922, II (to 1250) ²1926 (Samml. Göschen). — Grundriß der Geschichtswissenschaft, ed. *Al. Meister*, 2 vols. in 16 parts (some of this work in new editions) 1906 ff.; especially (I, 7): *M. Jansen-L. Schmitz-Kallenberg*, Quellen u. Historiographie der deutschen Gesch. bis 1500, ²1913. — *G. Wolf*, Einführung in das Studium der neueren Gesch., 1910; Quellenkunde der deutschen Reformationsgesch., 2 vols. with index 1915/23.— *E. Fueter*, Gesch. der neueren Historiographie, ³1926. — *Wilh. Bauer*, Einführung in das Studium der Gesch., ³1928. — *K. u. M. Uhlirz*, Handb. der Gesch. Österreichs u. seiner Nachbarländer Böhmen u. Ungarn, 4 vols. 1927/44. — *Histoire littéraire de la France*, 36 vol. Paris 1733/1927. — *A. Molinier*, Les sources de l'hist. de France (to 1494), 6 vol. Paris 1901/6. — *G. Monod*, Bibliographieque de l'hist. de France, Paris 1888. — *Répertoire Bibliographique de l'histoire* par P. Caron et H. Stein I—V (1920/29), Paris 1923/34. — *H. Pirenne*, Bibliographie de l'hist. de Belgique, Brux. ²1931. — *Ch. Gross*, The Sources and Literature of English History (to 1485), London ²1915. — *E. Calvi*, Bibliografia generale di Roma I (476—1499), Roma 1906; Suppl. 1908. — *R. Ballester*, Bibliografia de la Historia de España, Gerona 1921.

*H. Stein*, Manuel de bibliographie generale, Paris 1898. — *Ch. V. Langlois*, Manuel de bibliogr. hist., 2 vol. Paris ²1901/4. — *R. Dimpfel*, Biographische Nachschlagewerke, 1922. — *G. Schneider*, Handbuch d. Bibliographie, ⁴1930; Einführung in die Bibliographie, 1936. — Internationaler Jahresbericht der Bibliographie, ed. *J. Vorstius*, 1930 ff. — *K. Löffler*, Einführung in die Katalogkunde, 1935. — *Deutscher Gesamtkatalog* der öffentl. Bibliotheken in Deutschland u. Österreich, 1935 ff. — Lexikon des gesamten Buchwesens, ed. *K. Löffler* and *J. Kirchner* I, 1935. — *E. M. Coulter* and *M. Gerstenfeld*, Historical Bibliographies, Berkeley 1935. — *M. Arnim*, Internationale Personalbibliographie 1850—1935, 1936. — Répertoire de bibliographie française 1501—1930, Paris 1935 ff. — *E. H. Lehmann*, Einführung in die Zeitschriftenkunde, 1936. — World-List of Historical Reviews, in Bulletin of Historical Sciences Nr. 31, Paris 1936. — *H. Bohatta* et al., Internationale Bibliographie, 1939 ff.

Theol. Jahresbericht, Abt. KG. 1—32, 1880/1913. — Bibliographisches Beiblatt der Theologischen Literaturzeitung, 1921 ff. — Bibliographie der *Revue d'histoire ecclésiastique*, Louvain 1900 ff. Tables générales a 1—36 (1900/40), ib. 1928/46. — *A. Esdaile*, A Student's Manual of Bibliography, London 1931. — *G. M. Dutcher*, *H. R. Shipman* et al., A Guide to Historical Literature, New York 1931. — *S. J. Case*, J. T. McNeill et al., A Biographical

## § 2. Sources of Church History.

Guide to the History of Christianity, Chicago 1931. — *L. J. Paetow*, A Guide to the Study of Mediaeval History, New York ²1931. — *International Bibliography of Historical Sciences*, Internationale Bibliographie der Geschichtswissenschaften, Washington-Paris-Berlin 1931 ff. — *Jahresberichte der Geschichtswissenschaft*, by F. Abraham, J. Jastrow et al. vols. I—XXXVI (1878/1913), 1880/1916. — *Jahresberichte der deutschen Gesch.*, ed V. Lowew, M. Stimming and O. Lerche vols. I—VII (1918/24), 1920/26. — *Jahresberichte für deutsche Gesch.*, ed. A. Brackmann and F. Hartung. 1927 ff. — *Bio-Bibliographien der Wissenschaften*, ed. V. Lowew, l. H.: Deutsche Gesch., 1931.

*Kirchenlexikon* oder Encyklopädie der kath. Theol., 2nd ed. by *J. Hergenröther* and *Fr. Kaulen*, 12 vols. with index 1882/1903. — *Kirchliches Handlexikon*, hg. von M. Buchberger, 2 Bde 1907/12; reprinted 1921. — *Lexikon für Theologie u. Kirche*, 2nd revised ed. of the Kirchl. Handlexikon, ed. M. Buchberger, 10 vols 1930/38. — *Realencyklopädie für protestantische Theologie und Kirche*, 3rd ed. by *A. Hauck*, 21 vols. with index 1896/1909 and two supplementary vols. 1913. — *Kraus* RE and *Cabrol*, Dict. d'archéol. chrét. et de liturgie. cfr. no. 1 above. — *W. Smith* and *H. Wace*, Dictionary of Christian Biography, Literature, Sects and Doctrines (to 700), 4 vols. London 1877/87; the same condensed in one vol. by H. Wace and W. C. Piercy, London 1911. — *J. Hastings*, Dictionary of the Apostolic Church, 2 vols. Edinburgh-London 1915/18. — *H. Hurter*, Nomenclator literarius theologiae cath., 5 tom. (II², III²—V, 1³) 1903/13. — *The Catholic Encyclopedia*, 15 vol. with index, New York 1907/14 and Suppl. I (= vol. XVII), 1922. — Dictionnaire d'histoire et de géographie ecclésiastique, publ. p. *A. Baudrillart* et autres, Paris 1909 ff. Dictionnaire de théologie cath., publ. p. *A. Vacant—E. Mangenot—E. Amann*, Paris 1903 ff. — Dictionnaire apologétique de la foi cath., publ. p. *A. d'Alès*, 4 vol. Paris 1911/29; Index and Suppl. 1931. — Dictionnaire de droit canonique, publ. p. A. Villien et autres, Paris 1935 ff. — Dictionnaire pratique des connaissances religieuses, publ. p. *J. Bricout*, 6 vol. and 2 Suppl., Paris 1925/30. — Dictionnaire de sociologie, dir. p. *Th. Mainage*, Paris 1931 ff. — Dictionnaire de spiritualité ascétique et mystique, publ. p. *M. Viller S. J.*, Paris 1932 ff. — *R. Streit* and *J. Dindinger*, Bibliotheca Nissionum vol. I—XI, 1916/39; R. Streit, J. Dindinger and G. *Rommerskirchen*, Bibliographia Missionaria, 1934 ff. — A Dictionary of the Popes, ed. by *D. Attwater*, London 1939. — Reallexikon f. Antike u. Christentum, ed. by *Th. Klauser*, 1950 ff. — *A. Anwander*, Wörterbuch der Religion, 1948. — *Die Religion in Geschichte u. Gegenwart*, Handwörterbuch, ed. by Fr. M. Schiele and L. Zscharnack, 5 vols 1909/13; 2nd revised ed. by H. Gunkel and L. Zscharnack, 5 vols 1927/31, Index 1932. — *J. Hastings*, Encyclopedia of Religion and Ethics, 12 vol. Edinburgh 1908/22; Index 1926. — *C. Clemen*, Religionsgeschichtl. Bibliographie 1—10 (1914/23), 1917/25. — *Theologisches Wörterbuch* zum Neuen Test., ed. *G. Kittel*, 1932 ff. — *R. Eisler*, Wörterbuch der philosoph. Begriffe, 3 vols ⁴1927/30. — *Allgemeine Deutsche Biographie*, 56 vols 1875/1912. — *H. Korff*, Biographia Catholica 1870—1926, 1927. — *S. J. Brown*, International Index of Catholic Biographies, London ²1935. — *Verfasserlexikon des deutschen Mittelalters*, ed. *W. Stammler*, 1931 ff. — *W. Kosch*, Das katholische Deutschland*, biographisch-bibliographisches Lexikon, 1935 ff. — *W. Kosch*, Deutsches Literatur-Lexikon. Biographisches u. bibliographisches Handbuch,

[2]1949 ff. — *H. W. Eppelsheimer*, Handbuch der Weltliteratur, 1937. — Dictionnaire de biographie française, Paris 1929 ff. — *Staatslexikon* der Görresgesellschaft, the revised edition by H. Sacher, 5 vols. 1926/32. — *E. Haberkern* u. *J. Fr. Wallach*, Hilfswörterbuch für Historiker (Middle Ages and Modern Times), 1935. — *H. Schulthess* et al., Europäischer Geschichtskalender Jahrg. 1—25, 1860/84; NF. 1—79, 1884/1939.

## § 3.
## Auxiliary Sciences.

1. **Paleography and Papyrology, Literature and Library Science:** *Th. Birt*, Das antike Buchwesen, 1882. —*W. Wattenbach*, Das Schriftwesen im MA., [2]1896. — *L. Traube*, Zur Paläographie u. Handschriftenkunde, 1909. — *A. Bauckner*, Einführung in das mittelalterl. Schrifttum, 1923. —*F.H.Ehmcke*, Die hist. Entwicklung der abendländ. Schriftformen, 1927. — *K. Löffler*, Einführung in die Handschriftenkunde, 1929. — *H. Degering*, Die Schrift, Atlas der Schriftformen des Abendlandes, 1929. — *G. Mehring*, Schrift und Schrifttum, 1931. — *H. Leclercq*, Art. Paléographie, DictAC XII, 610/736.

*B. Montfaucon*, Palaeographia graeca, Paris 1708. — *W. Wattenbach*, Anleitung zur griech. Paläographie, [3]1895. — *V. Gardthausen*, Griech. Paläogr., 2 vols. [2]1911/13. — *E. M. Thompson*, An Introduction to Greek and Latin Palaeography, Oxford [2]1912. — *V. A. v. Groningen*, Short Manual of Greek Palaeography, Leiden 1940. — *G. Battelli*, Lezioni di Paleografia, Roma [3]1949. — *W. Schubart*, Einführung in die Papyruskunde, 1918; Griech. Paläographie, 1925; Griech. Papyri vom 4. Jh. vor bis z. 8. Jh. nach Chr., Text u. Kommentar 1927. — *Archiv f. Papyrusforschung*, ed. U. Wiloken 1900 ff. — *H. Leclercq*, Art. Papyrus, DictAC XIII, 1370/1520. — *K. Preisendanz*, Papyrusfunde und Papyrusforschung, 1933. — Papyri u. Altertumswissenschaft, Vorträge des 3. internationalen Papyrologentages in München (1933), ed. *W. Otto* u. *L. Wenger*, 1934.— J. Jeremias, ThLZ 1950, 55/8 (status of early Christian papyrology).

*F. Steffens*, Latein, Paläographie, [2]1929. —*M. Ihm*, Palaeographia latina I, [2]1931. — *M. Prou*, Manuel de paléographie latine et française, Paris [4]1924.— *B. Bretholz*, Latein. Paläogr., [3]1926 (in Al. Meisters Grundriß der GW. I, 1). — *P. Lehmann*, Latein. Paläogr., 1925 (in Einleitung in die Altertumswiss., ed. Geroke and Norden I, 10). — *A. C. Millares*, Paleografia española, 2 vol. Barcelona 1929. — *A. Capelli*, Lexicon abbreviaturarum, [2]1928.

*Tabulae in usum scholarum* ed. J. Lietzmann: 1. Specimina cod. graec. Vaticanorum coll. *P. Franchi de 'Cavalieri* et *J. Lietzmann*, [2]1929; 2. Papyri graecae Berolinenses coll. *W. Schubart*, 1911; 3. Specimina cod. lat. Vaticanorum coll. *Fr. Ehrle* et *P. Liebaert*, [2]1927; 4. Inscriptiones latinae coll. *E. Diehl*, 1912; 5. Handschriften der Reformationszeit, ausgewählt von *G. Mentz*, 1912. — *K.* and *S. Lake*, Dated Greek Minuscule Manuscripts to 1200, Boston, Mass. 1934 ff. — *Fr. Dölger*, Facsimiles byzantin. Kaiserurkunden, 1931. — *A. Arndt* u. *M. Tangl*, Schrifttafeln zur Erlernung der lat. Paläographie, 3 vols. 1904/7. — *A. Chroust*, Monumenta palaeographica, Denkmäler der Schreibkunst des Mittelalters, 1899 ff. — *Br. Katterbach*, Specimina Supplicationum ex Registris Vaticanis, Rome 1927. — *Br. Katterbach, A. Pelzer* et *C. Silva-Tarouca*, Exempla scripturarum . . . Bibliotheca et Tabularii Vaticani,

## § 3. Auxiliary Sciences.

Fasc. 1—2, Rome 1929/30. — E. Carusi, C. Silva-Tarouca et C. Erdmann, Pontificum Romanorum diplomata papyracea phototypice expressa, Rome 1929. — E. A. Lowe, Codices latini antiquiores I—II, Oxford 1934/35. — A. Bruckner, Scriptoria medii aevi Helvetica I—V, Genf 1935/43. — Fr. Wilhelm, Corpus der altdeutschen Originalurkunden bis 1300, I (1200—1282), 1932. — B. Bischoff, Die südostdeutschen Schreibschulen . . . I, 1940. Handbuch der Bibliothekswissenschaft, ed. Fr. Milkau, 2 vols. 1931/3, ²1951 ff. — R. Hoecker u. a., Internationale Bibliographie des Buch- und Bibliothekwesens, NF. 1926 ff. — E. C. Richardson, A Union World Catalogue of Manuscripts, Fasc. 1—5, New York 1933/35 (cfr. A. Pelzer RHE 1936, 621/30). — Verzeichnis der Handschriften im Deutschen Reich, 1938 ff. — Buch u. Papier, Festschr. H. H. Bockwitz, 1949. — K. Haebler, Handbuch der Inkunabelkunde, 1925. — E. v. Rath, Der Buchdruck des 15. Jh.s, eine bibliograph. Übersicht, 1929/36. — Gesamtkatalog der Wiegendrucke, 1925 ff.

**2. Diplomatics and Archives:** J. Mabillon, De re diplomatica, Paris ²1709. — H. Bresslau, Handbuch der Urkundenlehre für Deutschland und Italien, 2 vols. ²1912/31. — R. Thommen, L. Schmitz-Kallenberg, H. Steinacker, R. Heuberger, Diplomatik, 1913/21 (in A. Meisters Grundriß der GW. I, 2). — W. Erben, L. Schmitz-Kallenberg, O. Redlich, Urkundenlehre I, 1907; III, 1911. — M. Modica, Diplomatica, Milano 1942. — Fr. Philippi, Einführung in d. Urkundenlehre d. deutschen Mittelalters, 1920. — H. Steinacker, Die antiken Grundlagen der früh. mittelalterl. Privaturkunde, 1927 (in Grundriß der GW., Suppl. I). — A. de Boüard, Manuel de diplomatique française et pontificale I, Paris 1929. — Urkunden u. Siegel in Nachbildungen, ed. G. Seeliger, Heft 2—4, 1914. — H. Leclercq, Art. Chartes, DictAC III, 876/977. — R. Rosenmund, Der Fortschritt der Diplomatik seit Mabillon, 1897. — Archiv für Urkundenforschung, ed. K. Brandi et al. 1907 ff. — H. Zatschek, MIÖG 44, 1930, 457 ff.; 48, 1935, 463 ff.; 50, 1937, 394 ff. (Report on the Literature of Diplomatics). — L. Santifaller, Urkundenforschung, Methode, Ziel, Ergebnisse, 1937; Abkürzungen in den ältesten Papsturkunden (788—1002), 1939. — F. Dölger, Athos-Klöster, 1949 (Byzantine Diplomatics). — Guide international des Archives Europe, Leipzig 1935. — H. Nabholz u. P. Kläui, Internationaler Archivführer, Zürich 1936. — H. O. Meissner, Urkunden u. Aktenlehre der Neuzeit, 1950.

**3. Epigraphy:** J. B. de Rossi, Inscriptiones (2, 1), Introd. — E. Hübner, Röm. Epigraphik, ²1892. — E. Le Blant, L'epigraphie chrétienne en Gaule et dans l'Afrique Romaine, Paris 1890. — W. Larfeld, Hdb. d. griech. Epigraphik, 1898/1907; Griech. Epigraphik, ³1914. — R. Cagnat, Cours d'épigraphie lat., Paris ⁴1914. — S. Ricci, Epigrafia latina, Milano 1898. — L. Jalabert, Épigraphie, DictApol I, 1910, 1404/57. — O. Marucchi, Epigrafia cristiana, Milano 1910. — C. M. Kaufmann, Hdb. der altchristl. Epigraphik, 1947 (cfr. E. Diehl, ThLZ 1918, 200/5). — J. E. Sandys, Latin Epigraphy, Cambridge 1919. — A. Grossi Gondi, Trattato di Epigrafia crist., Rome 1920. — H. Dessau, Latein. Epigraphik, 1925 (in Einl. in die Altertumswiss. I, 10). — L. Jalabert et R. Mouterde, Inscriptions grecques chrétiennes, DictAC VII, 623/94; H. Leclercq, Inscriptions latines chrét., id. VII, 694/850 (also E. Peterson, ThLZ 1927, 397 f.). — J. P. Kirsch, Die christl. Epigraphik u. ihre Bedeutung für die kirchengesch. Forschung, 1898 (Archive). — Cfr. § 2, 1.

**4. Numismatics, Sphragistics, Heraldry and Genealogy:** *J. H. Eckhel*, Doctrina nummorum veterum, 8 vol. Vindob. 1792/8, IX, 1826. — *H. Dannenberg*, Grundzüge der Münzkunde, ³1912. — *A. Luschin von Ebengreuth*, Allg. Münzkunde u. Geldgesch. des MA.s u. der neueren Zeit, ²1926; Grundriß d. Münzkunde I 1918. — *F. Friedensburg*, Die Münze in der Kulturgesch., ²1926; Die Symbolik der mittelalt. Münzen, 3 Parts 1914/22; Münzkunde u. Geldgesch. der Einzelstaaten des Ma.s u. der neueren Zeit, 1926. — *F. v. Schrötter*, Wörterbuch der Münzkunde, 1930. — *W. Jesse* u. *R. Gaettens*, Handb. der Münzkunde v. Mittel- u. Nordeuropa, 1939 ff. — *H. Leclercq*, Monnaie etc., DictAC XI, 2260/2350. — *B. Müller*, Medaillen u. Münzen im Dienste der Religion, 1915. — *V. Schultze*, Münze u. KG., Geschichtl. Studien A. Hauck dargebracht, 1916, 326/30. — *A. Suhle*, Die deutschen Münzen des MA.s, 1936.

*Th. Ilgen, E. Gritzner, F. Friedensburg*, Sphragistik, Heraldik und deutsche Münzgesch., ²1912 (in A. Meisters Grundriß der GW. I, 4). — Siegel in Nachbildungen, vide supra no. 2. — *P. Sella*, I sigilli dell'Archivio Vaticano, 1937 ff. — *W. Ewald* und *F. Hauptmann*, Siegel- und Wappenkunde, 1914. — *L. D. Galbreath*, Handbüchlein der Heraldik, 1930. — *E. Beck*, Grundfragen der Wappenlehre u. des Wappenrechts, 1931. — *J. Siebmacher*, Großes u. allgem. Wappenbuch, new edition by *O. T. v. Hefner*, 1854 ff. — *J. B. Rietstap*, Armorial général, Lyon 1950 ff. — *J. Meurgey* Armorial de l'église de France, Mâcon 1938. — *H. W. Singer*, Allg. Bildniskatalog, 14 vols. 1930/36. — *S. H.* und *Chr. Steinberg*, Die Bildnisse geistlicher u. weltl. Fürsten u. Herren I (950—1200), 1931. — *S. H. Steinberg*, Bibliographie z. Gesch. d. deutschen Porträts, 1934.

*E. Wentscher*, Einführung in die praktische Genealogie, 1933. — *O. Lorenz*, Genealog. Handb. der eürop. Staatengesch., ³1908. — *H. Koch*, Regententafeln, 1910. — *W. K. Prinz von Isenburg*, Stammtafeln zur Gesch. der europ. Staaten I—II, 1935/37; Ahnentafeln der Regenten Europas u. ihrer Gemahlinnen, 1938; Histor. Genealogie, 1940. — *O. Forst de Battaglia*, Wissenschaft. Geneal., 1948.

**5. Philology and Archaeology:** *Ch. Du Fresne Dom Du Cange*, Glossarium ad scriptores mediae et infimae latinitatis, 3 fol. Par. 1678; several times republished and enlarged, e. g., by *G. Henschel*, 7 vols. Paris 1840/50, by *L. Favre*, 10 vols. Niort 1882/87. — *E. Forcellini*, Lexicon totius latinitatis, 4 fol. Patav. 1771; revised by *V. de Vit*, 6 vols. Prato 1858/79, by *F. Corradini* and *J. Perin*, 6 vols. Padua 1940; Onomasticon totius latinitatis ed. *J. Perin*, 2 vol. Patavii 1913/20. — *Thesaurus* linguae latinae, Lipsiae 1900 ff. — *E. Brinckmeier*, Glossarium diplomaticum 2 vols. 1850/63. — *L. Diefenbach*, Novum Glossarium latino-germanicum mediae et infimae aetatis, 1857. — *K. E. Georges*, Ausführl. lat.-dtsch. Handwörterb., 2 vols. ⁸1912/19. — *Ch. Du Fresne D. Du Cange*, Gloss. ad scriptores mediae et infimae graecitatis, 2 fol. Lugd. 1688. — *J. C. Suicer*, Thesaurus ecclesiasticus e patribus graecis, 2 fol. Amsterdam 1682, Traiecti ³1746; Suppl. ed. Nothnagel, 1821. — *H. Stephanus*, Thesaurus graecae linguae edd. C. B. Hase etc., 8 tom. Paris 1831/55. — *E. A. Sophocles*, Greek Lexicon of the Roman and Byzantine Periods (146—1100), New York ³1888. — *Fr. Passows*, Wörterbuch der griech. Sprache, revised by V. Rost et al., 2 vols. 1841/57. — *H. G. Liddell* and *R. Scott*, Greek-

## § 3. Auxiliary Sciences.

English Lexicon, new ed. by H. S. Jones et al., Oxford 1925 ff. — *E. Preuschen-W. Bauer*, Griech.-Deutsches Wörterbuch zu den Schriften des N. Test. u. der übrigen urchristl. Lit., [4]1950 f. — *Fr. Preisigke* u. E. *Kiessling*, Wörterbuch der griech. Papyrusurkunden, 3 vols. 1925/31. — *A. Sleumer*, Kirchenlatein. Wörterbuch, [2]1926; Deutschkirchenlat. Wörterbuch, 1937. — *J. Schmid*, Kurzes Handwörterbuch des Kirchenlateins, 1934. — *R. Köstler*, Wörterbuch zum Cod. iur. can., 1928/30. — *A. Souter*, A Glossary of Later Latin to 600 A.D., Oxford 1949. — *E. Habel*, Mittellatein. Glossar, 1931. — *J. H. Baxter* and *Ch. Johnson*, Medieval Latin Word-list from British and Irish Sources, Oxford 1934. — *V. Gay*, Glossaire archéologique du moyen âge et de la Renaissance, 2 vol. Paris 1882/1928. — *H. Leclercq*, Lexique archéologique, DictAC VIII, 2996/3048; Lexique liturgique grec et latin, id. IX, 1/30. — *A. Jolivet* et *F. Mossé*, Manuel de l'allemand du moyen âge, Paris 1942. — *Deutsches Rechtswörterbuch*, published by the Preuss. Akad. der Wiss., 1914 ff. — *E. Haberkern* u. *J. Fr. Wallach*, § 2, 11.

*Paulys* Realenzyklopädie des klass. Altertums, revised by *G. Wissowa, W. Kroll*, et al., 1893 ff. — *F. Lübkers* Reallexicon des klass. Altertums, 8th ed. by *J. Geffcken* and *E. Ziebarth*, 1914. — Einleitung in die klass. Altertumswissenschaft, ed. *A. Gercke* and *E. Norden*, 3 vols. [2]1912/23, [3]1921 ff. — *J. Lavalleye*, Introduction aux études d'archéologie et d'histoire de l'art, Tournai-Paris 1942.

*H. Usener*, Vorträge und Aufsätze, 1907, 3/35 (Philology and History). — *E. Preuschen*, Die philol. Arbeit an den älteren Kirchenvätern, 1907. — *L. Traube*, Einl. in die lat. Philologie des MA.s, 1910. — *P. Lehmann*, Vom MA. und von der lat. Philologie des MA.s, 1914. — *O. Stählin*, Editionstechnik, [2]1914. — *H. Kantorowicz*, Einführung in die Textkritik, 1921. — *H. P. V. Nun*, Introduction to Ecclesiastical Latin, Cambridge 1922. — *Chr. Mohrmann*, Misc. G. Mercati, 1946, I, 437/66; VC 1948/9. (Christian Latinity). — *Bulletin du Cange*, Archivum latinitatis medii aevi, Paris 1925 ff. — *K. Strecker*, Einführung in das Mittellatein, [3]1939. — *W. Bulst*, Über die mittlere Latinität des Abendlandes, 1946. — *F. Ermini*, Medio evo latino, Modena 1938. — *W. Stach*, Mittelalterl. Philologie u. GW., HistVS 1931, 1/12. — *H. Leclercq*, Latin, DictAC VIII, 1422/1528. — *R. Meister*, Bedeutung u. Umfang des latein. Schrifttums im MA. u. in der Neuzeit, 1933. — *S. Hellmann*, HistVS 1935, 625/80 (medieval philology). — *K. Langosch*, Wilhelm Meyer aus Speyer u. Paul v. Winterfeld, Begründer der mittellat. Wissenschaft, 1936; Mittellatein als Deutschkunde, 1937.

**6. Geography and Statistics:** *S. J. Neher*, Kirchl. Geogr. u. Statistik, 3 vols. 1864/68. — *G. Droysen*, Allg. hist. Handatlas, 1886. — *Meyers* hist. Handatlas, 1911. — *J. Calmette, R. Grousset* et *J. J. Gruber*, Atlas historique II—III, Paris 1936/37. — The Cambridge Medieval History, Vol. of Maps, Cambridge 1936. — The Cambridge Modern History Atlas, ed. by *Ward* et al., Cambridge 1912. — *H. Österley*, Hist.-geogr. Wörterbuch des deutschen MA.s, 1883. — *L. de Mas-Latrie*, Trésor de chronologie, d'hist. et de géographie pour l'étude et l'emploi des documents du moyen-âge, Paris 1889. — *Chevalier*, Répertoire: Topo-Bibliogr., *The Catholic Encyclop.* and DictHE, § 2, 11. — *J. G. Th. Graesse*, Orbis latinus oder Verzeichnis der wichtigsten latein. Orts- und Ländernamen, [2]1909. — *K. Kretschmer*, Hist. Geogr. v. Mitteleuropa, 1904. —

*E. Gordon,* An Historical Geography of Europe, London 1935. — *R. Kötzschke,* Quellen u. Grundbegriffe der hist. Geogr. Deutschlands u. seiner Nachbarländer, [2]1913. — *L. Mirot,* Manuel de géographie hist. de la France, Paris 1930. — *H. Leclercq,* DictAC IX, 741/984 (Gallic place names). — *R. de Riess-L. Heidet,* Atlas Scripturae Sacrae, [3]1924. — *L. Tellier* et *H. Holstein,* Atlas historique de N.T., Paris [2]1945. — *K. Heussi* u. *H. Mulert,* Atlas zur KG., [3]1937. — *K. Pieper,* Atlas orbis christiani antiqui, 1931. — *O. Werner,* Kath. Missionsatlas, [2]1885; Kath. Kirchenatlas, 1888; Orbis terrarum catholicus . . . geographicus et statisticus, 1890. — *K. Streit,* Kath. Missionsatlas, 1906; Atlas hierarchicus, descriptio geographica et statistica S. Romanae Ecclesiae, [2]1929. — *L. Grammatica,* Testo e atlante di geografia ecclesiastica e missionaria, Bergamo 1928. — *J. Thauren,* Atlas der kath. Missionsgesch., [2]1933. — *H. P. Beach* and *Ch. H. Fahs,* World Missionary Atlas, London 1925 (Protestant).

*P. M. Baumgarten,* Kirchl. Statistik, 1905. — *Z. V. Lobkowitz,* Statistik d. Päpste, 1905. — *G. B. Ladner,* Die Papstbildnisse des Altertums u. MA.s I, Rome 1941. — *P. B. Gams,* Series episcoporum eccl. cathol., 1873, Suppl. 1879, 1886; reprinted 1931. — *C. Eubel,* Hierarchia cath. medii et recentioris aevi I (1198—1431) [2]1913; II (1431—1503) [2]1914; III (1503—1600) [2]1923; vol. IV (1592—1667) ed. *P. Gauchat,* 1935. — *H. Leclercq,* Listes épiscopales, DictAC IX, 1207/1536. — *M. Le Quien,* Oriens Christianus, 3 vol. Paris 1740. — *L. Lemmens,* Hierarchia latina Orientis 1622—1922, 2 vol. Rome 1923/24 (= Orientalia Christiana 5. 10). — *J. Silbernagl,* Verfass. u. gegenwärt. Bestand sämtl. Kirchen des Orients, 2nd. ed. by J. Schnitzer, 1904. — *K. Lübeck,* Die christl. Kirchen des Orients, 1911; cfr. A. Baumstark, ThRev 1912, 89/94. — *F. Ughelli,* Italia sacra, 10 tom. Venet. [2]1717/22. — *F. Lanzoni,* Le diocesi d'Italia (fino 604). Rome [2]1927. — *P. Fr. Kehr,* Italia Pontificia, § 2, 3). — *D. de Sainte-Marthe* et *B. Hauréau,* Gallia christ. (nova), 16 tom. Par. 1715 to 1865; *J. H. Albanès* et *U. Chevalier,* Gallia christiana novissima I—VII, Montbéliard-Paris-Valence 1899/1920. — *L. Duchesne,* Fastes épiscopaux de l'ancienne Gaule I[2]—II[2], Paris 1907/10, III 1915. — *Les Églises de France,* Répertoire historique et archéologique par département, éd. p. M. Aubert, J. Verrier et R. Planchenault, Paris 1932 ff. — *V. Carière* et autres, Introduction aux études d'hist. ecclésiastique locale (3 vol.) II, Paris 1934; III, Paris 1936. — *A. Vincent,* Toponymie de la France, Brux. 1937. — *L. H. Cottineau,* Répertoire topo-bibliographique des abbayes et prieurés, 2 vol. Mâcon 1935/9. — *M. Duportet,* Topo-bibliographie de la France, Montluçon 1947 ff. — *C. J. Böttcher,* Germania sacra, 2 vols 1874. — *Germania sacra,* Historischstatist. Darstellung der deutschen Bistümer, Domkapitel, Kollegiat- u. Pfarrkirchen, Klöster usw., published by Kaiser-Wilhelm-Institut f. deutsche Gesch., 1929 ff. — *Klosterverzeichnis* der deutschen Benediktiner u. Zisterzienser, 1917 (StMBenO 1911, 1914/16). — *N. Backmund,* Monastaicon Praemonstratense, 1949 ff. — *A. Brackmann,* Germania Pontificia, § 2, 3. — Kirchl. Handb. für das kath. Deutschland, ed. *H. A. Krose* (et *J. Sauren*), 1908 ff.; id., Konfessionsstatistik Deutschlands, 1904. — *P. Pieper,* Kirchl. Statistik Deutschlands, [2]1900 (Protestant). — Kirchl. Jahrb. f. die evang. Landeskirchen Deutschlands, ed. *J. Schneider,* 1873 ff. — *Die kath. Kirche unserer Zeit,* publ. by der österreich. Leogesellschaft, 3 vol 1899/1902; 2nd

## § 3. Auxiliary Sciences.

ed. in 2 vols. 1904/7. — *Annuario Pontificio*, Roma 1912 ff. — *Annuare Pontifical Catholique*, Paris 1898 ff. — *G. Monti*, Handb. der kath. Organisationen, 1924. — *H. A. Krose*, Kath. Missionsstatistik, 1908; Statistik der Religionsgemeinschaften im Deutschen Reich, 1937. — *G. Michl*, Religions- und kirchl. Statistik in Deutschland, 1921. — *Missionse catholicae* cura S. Congregationis de Propaganda Fide descriptae, Rome 122.

7. **Chronology**: *D. Petavius*, Opus de doctrina temporum, 2 tom. Par. 1627. — *H. Grotefend*, Zeitrechnung des deutschen MA.s und der Neuzeit, 2 vols. 1891/98; Taschenbuch der Zeitrechn. des deutschen MA.s u. der Neuzeit, [6]1928; Abriß der Chronol. des MA.s u. der Neuzeit, [2]1912. — *Mas-Latrie*, vide no. 6. — *F. Blatt*, Misc. G. Mercati, 1946, II, 581/92 (formulas used in medieval texts). — *B. M. Lersch*, Einl. in die Chronol., [2]1899. — *K. F. Ginzel*, Handb. der mathem. und techn. Chronol., 3 vols. 1906/14. — *R. Schram*, Kalendariograph. u. chronol. Tafeln, 1908. — *J. Bach*, Die Zeit- u. Festrechnung der Juden, mit immerwährendem Kalender, 1908. — *J. Dowden*, The Church Year and Calendar, Cambridge 1910. — *P. V. Neugebauer*, Tafeln zur astron. Chronol., 3 vols. 1912/22; Astron. Chronologie 2 vols. 1929; Hilfstafeln zur techn. Chronol., 1937. — *W. Foerster*, Kalenderwesen u. Kalenderreform, 1914. — *E. Cavaignac*, Chronologie de l'histoire mondiale, Paris [3]1946. — *W. Kubitschek*, Grundriß der antiken Zeitrechnung, 1928. — *A. Cappelli*, Cronologia, Cronografia e Calendario perpetuo, Milano [2]1930. — *E. Bickermann*, Chronologie, 1933. — *H. Lietzmann*, Zeitrechnung für die Jahre 1—2000 nach Christus, [2]1945. — *H. Brinkmann*, Alte u. neue Zeitrechnung, 1939. — *H. Leclercq*, Kalendaria, DictAC VIII, 624/67. — *B. Krusch*, Studien zur christlich-mittelalterl. Chronologie, Abh. Berlin, 1937, 8.

The following **methods for computing time** are most frequently encountered in history:

a) The reckoning from the year of the building of *Rome,* Anno Urbis Conditae, A.U.C. (753 B.C.), or by the Roman *consulate* and *post-consulate years.* — *W. Liebenam*, Fasti consulares imperii Romani, 1909 (Kleinere Texte 41/43).

b) *The Cyclus Indictionum* (Roman Indiction), a cycle of 15 years, used from the reign of Diocletian (297) to the sixteenth century.

c) The *World Era*, from the creation of the world. It is found in several forms: 1. The Byzantine calendar began with the year 5509 B.C., and was used by the Russians until Peter the Great (1700) and by the Greeks, Serbs and Roumanians until into the nineteenth century; 2. The Alexandrian calendar began with the year 5492 B.C.; and, 3. The Jews began with the year 3761 B.C.

d) *The Christian Era*, beginning with the year of the birth of Christ was popularized at Rome in 525 or 526 by the Monk *Dionysius Exiguus* (§ 65, 4; § 78, 2) and is often, therefore, called the *Dionysian Era*. This method gradually supplanted all other methods in the West. Dionysius took the year 753 A.U.C. as the year of Christ's birth, so that 754 A.U.C. became the first year of the Christian Era. As a matter of fact, Christ was born 5 to 7 years earlier, that is, between 746 and 748 A.U.C.

The **day on which the year was considered as beginning** was not the same everywhere. January 1; March 1 (in Russia); September 1 (in Constantinople);

Christmas; the feast of the Annunciation (March 25) and Easter were dates on which the year commenced in various places. In places where the feast of the Annunciation marked the beginning of the year, some took the feast before January 1 (Calculus Pisanus), and some after January 1 (Calculus Florentinus). It was not until the sixteenth century that January 1 was generally adopted as the beginning of the year.

In 46 B.C. *Julius Caesar* computed the **length of the year** and his computation was accepted until the sixteenth century. But the Julian year exceeded the solar year by eleven hours and fourteen minutes. To correct this discrepancy, Pope Gregory XIII in 1582 suggested that ten days be dropped from that year (October 5—14) and to prevent a recurrence of the same error, that three intercalary days (in leap years) be dropped every 400 years. The *Gregorian* calendar or calendar of the *New Style* (N.S.) was not adopted in Protestant countries until the eighteenth century. The Greeks, Russians and other peoples adhering to the Orthodox religion retained the Julian calendar or calendar of the *Old Style* (O.S.) until recent years with the result that they were 13 to 14 days behind in their reckoning. But since the beginning of the twentieth century *commercial* life in Russia and the Balkan States demanded conformity with the rest of the world and the Synod of the Orthodox Eastern Churches approved the change in 1923. — A movement has long been on foot to establish a fixed date for the *celebration of Easter*. The matter was discussed by the now defunct League of Nations; but opposition of the churches, especially of the Roman Catholic Church, prevented any action from being taken.

## § 4.
### The Writing of Church History[1].

1. **Eusebius[2]**, Bishop of Caesarea in Palestine, († 339 cfr. § 75, 1) is rightly called the "Father of Church History." He not only

---

[1] A. KNÖPFLER, KL VII, 536/77. F. CHR. BAUR, Die Epochen der kirchl. Geschichtsschreibung, 1852. G. LOESCHKE, Zwei kirchengesch. Entwürfe, 1913. M. JANSEN, Die Geschichtsauffassung im Wandel der Zeit, HJG 1906, 1/33. M. RITTER, Die Entwicklungder GW. an den führenden Werken betrachtet, 1919. K. BRANDI, Gesch. der Geschichtswissenschaft, 1947. W. NIGG, Die Kirchengeschichtsschreibung, 1934 (biased). F. J. FOAKES-JACKSON, A History of Church History, Cambridge 1939. H. LECLERCQ, Historiens du Christianisme, DictAC VI, 2533/2735. Cfr. also § 2, 11.

[2] Eusebius Chronik, ed. A. Schöne, 2 vols. 1866/75; from the Armenian by J. Karst, 1911; Eusebius-Hieronymus Chronik, ed. R. Helm, 2 vols. 1913/26, by J. K. Fotheringham, London 1923. Cfr. R. HELM, Sb. Berlin 1929, 371/408; Philologus Suppl. 21, 2, 1929; E. CASPAR, Gött. Gel. Anz. 1927, 161/84. Eusebius' Church History, the best ed. is that of ED. SCHWARTZ, 3 vols. 1903/9 (with Rufin's Latin revision, by Th. Mommsen); a small ed. ³1922; French translation by E. Grapin, 3 vols. Paris 1905/13; English translation with commentary by Lawlor and Oulton, 2 vols. London 1927/8; German translation by Ph. Häuser, BKV 2. R. I, 1932, sep. 1938. R. LAQUEUR, Eus. als Historiker s. Zeit, 1929. Socrates and Sozomenus H. E., ed. R. Hussey, Oxford 1853, 1860; PG 67. THEODORET H. E., ed. L. Parmentier, 1911. EVAGRIUS H. E. edd. J. Bidez et L. Parmentier, London 1898. Philostorgius' Fragmente, ed. J. Bidez, 1913. Gesamtausgabe der Kirchenhisto-

compiled a *chronicle* preserved in an Armenian translation, with Book II (chronological tables) continued in Latin to 378 by Jerome; but he also wrote a *Church History* proper ('Εκκλησιαστικὴ ἱστορία) in ten books. The first copy stopped with 311, but was later brought by the author himself to 324. This truly epoch-making work, although conceived as a collection of available material rather than as a pragmatic historical narrative, is invaluable for the numerous documents it quotes and for fragments from works of the first Christian centuries now lost. During the fifth century the History was continued by three others: — two lawyers and a bishop. *Socrates* and *Sozomen*, both of Constantinople continued the work to 439 and 425 respectively and Bishop *Theodoret* of Cyrus in Syria brought the work up to the year 438. While all these efforts are not without merit, the continuation by Socrates is by far the best. Another lawyer, *Evagrius* (Euagrius) of Antioch, extended the work to 594. We possess only fragments of the continuation by Theodore of Constantinople (up to 527) as well as of the work of the Arian, *Philostorgius* (in 12 books 300—425).

2. Besides *Jerome*, the *Latin Church* of Antiquity produced several historians, none of them quite the equal of the Orientals.

*Rufinus* (§ 6, 7) translated Eusebius' History somewhat faultily and much abbreviated and added two books extending the original by another 70 years. *Sulpicius Severus* (§ 76, 7) in classical style and not without a certain critical sense, compiled two books of a Chronicle from the beginning of the world to the end of the fourth century. *Orosius* (§ 76, 7) in his Historiarum libri VII attempted a sort of Christian universal history which developed into an apology against paganism. He was encouraged in this by *St. Augustine* who himself powerfully influenced the interpretation of history throughout the Middle Ages by his magnificent work De civitate Dei (§ 76, 3). Finally the Historia (ecclesiastica) tripartita of *Cassiodorus* (§ 78, 2) which is merely a summary of the first three continuations of Eusebius, was a favorite text-book of Church History during the Middle Ages. — *J. E. L. Oulton*, JThSt 1929, 150/74 (Rufinus CH). — *M. Villain*, RechSR 1946, 164/210 (Rufinus and CH). — *A. Glas*, Die KG des Gelasios von Kaisareia, 1914 (refutes the opinion that Books X and XI of Rufinus are only a Latin revision of the lost work of Gelasius of Caesarea [† 395], cfr. P. van den Veen, Muséon 1915, 92/115; 1946, 281/94; — P. Peeters, AB 1932, 30/32; — F. Diekamp, Analecta Patristica, Rome 1938, 16/49; — *P. Heseler*, Beiträge zur KG des Gelasius v. Cäs., Dissertation 1934). — *W. v. Loewenich*, Augustin u. das christl. Geschichtsdenken, 1947. — *A.* Jäger, Hochl. 1949/50, 467/74 (Orosius).

riker von Eus. bis Evagrius by Henri de Valois (Valesius), 3 fol. Paris 1659/73, revised by W. Reading, 3 fol., Cambridge 1720. G. GENTZ u. K. ALAND, ZntW 1949, 101/41 (establishes the text).

3. The *Middle Ages*[1] produced very few works embracing the entire field of Church History. They were for the most part, unoriginal and often uncritical *compilations*, and for the period of antiquity, were limited to summaries of earlier works (Jerome, Rufinus, Cassiodorus).

During this same period, the Greek Church had but a single noteworthy church historian in the person of *Nicephorus Kallisti* († c. 1341), whose history extends to 610. It is, however, nothing more than an adaptation of an older work of the tenth century. In the West Bishop *Haymo* (or Haimo) of Halberstadt († 853) compiled a Breviarium historiae eccl. (as far as 400) which is derived chiefly from Rufinus. Histories relating events in the church down to their own times were written by: The Roman librarian *Anastasius* († 879; cfr. § 87, 2. 3 and § 89, 4); *Ordericus Vitalis*, monk of St. Evroul in Normandy († c. 1143; cfr. *J. Spörl*, no. 1 supra); the Dominican, *Vincent* of Beauvais († 1264, Speculum historiale; cfr. § 135, 3b), *Bartholomew* (Tolomeo) of Lucca († 1327) and *St. Antonine*, Archbishop of Florence († 1459; Summa historialis, the most comprehensive work of its kind; cfr. § 145, b4; Monog. on St. Antonine by R. Morcay, Paris 1914; A. Masseron, Paris 1926; E. Sanesi, Florence 1940; J. B. Walker, The "Chronicles" of St. Antonine, Dissertation, Washington 1933). — As a rule, far better work was done in the numerous *national and local histories, annals* and *chronicles* of the period. In keeping with the character of the times, no distinction was made between Church History stricto sensu and profane history.

4. Since the fifteenth century, the age of *Humanism* and the *Renaissance,* a very noticeable change gradually took place in the field of Church History[2]. There was a rebirth of historical criticism which had all but disappeared during the Middle Ages; the old sources, now made more easily available by printing, were sought out and used, and a growing sense of realism caused historians to recognize as untenable many legends (e. g. of the Popess Joan, cfr. § 87, 2) and to question the genuinity of documents (Donatio Constantini, cfr. § 85, 3; the Pseudo-Isidorean Decretals cfr. §87,4) and works (Pseudo-Dionysius Areopagita cfr. § 77, 1) theretofore accepted as authentic. One consequence of the *religious schism* of the sixteenth century was that Church History began to be written

---

[1] J. SPÖRL, Grundformen hochmittelalterlicher Geschichtsanschauung, 1935; HJG 1933, 281/303 (medieval historical thought).

[2] E. FUETER, G. WOLF, § 2, 11. E. MENKE-GLÜCKERT, Die Geschichtsschreibung d. Reformation u. Gegenref., 1912. M. RITTER, HZ 109, 1912, 1914, 29 ff. (Humanism to the Enlightenment). K. HEUSSI, Centuriae, Harnack-Ehrung, 1921, 328/34. E. CL. SCHERER, Gesch. u. KG. an den deutschen Universitäten (16.—18. Jh.), 1927. P. POLMAN, RHE 1931, 27/73 (Flacius Illyricus); L'élément historique dans la controverse religieuse du XVIe siècle, Thèse Louvain 1932. H. BARON, HZ 147, 1932, 5/20 (Revival of historical interest in the fifteenth century). A. WALZ, Angelicum 1940, 88/110 (Baronius).

primarily to serve the special interests of religious groups. This actually precluded an impartial historical view. Nonetheless, the religious quarrel powerfully stimulated the study of Church History and, as time went on, the polemico-apologetic tendency, although never entirely abandoned, received less emphasis and permitted a more sincere search for historic truth.

The pace was set by the Ecclesiastica historia . . . congesta per aliquot studiosos et pios viros in urbe Magdeburgica (13 fol. Basileae 1559/74). The work was divided into centuries (I—XIII) and was compiled by a group of Protestant scholars, headed by Matthias *Flacius* (Vlacich) of Istria. Because the work was undertaken at Magdeburg and the first five volumes written there, it became popularly known as the *"Magdeburg Centuries"* and the *compilers*, as *"Centuriators of Magdeburg"*. Owing to the extensive use of sources, the work is not without merit; but throughout, it evidences a bitter hatred toward the old Church and the papacy. It immediately called forth a number of rejoinders, the best and most important being the *Annales ecclesiastici* of the Oratorian cardinal, Caesar *Baronius* († 1607). The chief value of this work (12 fol. Rome 1588/1607) which closes with the year 1198, is the large number of documents not merely quoted but printed in full for the first time.

The work was reprinted several times and during the sixteenth and seventeenth centuries was revised and augmented by other Catholic scholars. *Spondanus* (Henri de Sponde) Bischop of Pamiers, added the years up to 1622 (2 fol. Paris 1639) and the Dominican, *Bzovius*, covered the years 1198 to 1571 (9 fol. Cologne 1621/1630). The most notable of the continuators were the three Oratorians: *Raynaldus*, who carried the history to 1565 (9 fol. Rome 1646/77); Laderchi, who took up where Raynaldus left off, and added the years to 1571 (3 fol. Rome 1728/1731); and August Theiner who continued to the year 1583 (3 fol. Rome 1856). A critique which both amends and supplements Baronius, was published by the French Franciscans Anthony and Francis *Pagi* (4 vols. Antwerp 1689/1705).

5. This intense activity in writing Church History was followed by a standstill. For some time scholars were satisfied to acquaint their co-religionists with the contents of these two great works by means of extracts and summaries. Moreover, the increased stress placed on scholastic training, especially as established by the Ratio Studiorum of the Society of Jesus (1599) caused the Catholic universities to favor the faculties of philosophy and speculative theology over the faculty of history. New and important works

first began to appear in *France* where, during the reign of Louis XIV, there was a deeping of intellectual life. Many scholars, especially of the Benedictine Order *(Congregation of St. Maur* cfr. § 188, 2) devoted themselves to the study and application of the auxiliary sciences (cfr. § 3; 178, 1e) and published editions of the Fathers and scholarly monographs still admired and consulted. The Jesuits laid the foundation for the gigantic work, Acta Sanctorum (Antwerp 1643 ff.). Noël or Natalis *Alexander,* a Dominican imbued with Gallican ideas, published a comprehensive history of the Church to 1563 under the title Selecta historiae eccles. capita in 26 volumes (Paris 1676/86). The work was corrected by the author himself in 1699 (Paris 8 volumes) and the revised edition was called *Historia ecclesiastica Vet. Novique Test.* Still more important are the excellent Mémoires pour servir à l'histoire ecclésiastique of the secular priest Le Nain de *Tillemont* († 1698). The work is a critical Church History to 513 published in monographs, the more important passages of which are fitted together as in a mosaic and annotated (16 vols. Paris 1693/1712). Another work of the same author, Histoire des Empereurs (16 vols. Paris 1690/1738) although written first, carries the history to 518. Only the first four volumes of both works were published during the author's lifetime.

Mention must also be made of works intended for more general reading, written by Claude *Fleury* (Histoire ecclésiastique, 20 vols. Paris 1691/1720 up to 1414, continued by Claude Fabre, 16 vols. Paris 1722/37 up to 1595 and in Latin translation continued to 1768; a good monograph on Fleury by Fr. Gaquère, Paris 1925) and by A. H. Bérault-*Bercastel* (Histoire de l'Église, 24 volumes Paris 1778/90 up to 1721, German translation 24 volumes 1787/91 and continued by various French and German scholars) as well as the essay on the philosophy of history, Discours sur l'histoire universelle (Paris 1681 up to Charlemagne) by the brilliant Bishop of Meaux, *Bossuet.* — Among Church historians in *Italy,* the Dominican Cardinal *Orsi* occupies a prominent place by reason of his Storia ecclesiastica (21 volumes, Rome 1746/62 up to 600) which was continued up to 1587 (28 volumes, Rome 1770/97) by his fellow religious *Becchetti.*

6. The study of Church History was zealously pursued in the *Protestant universities of Germany*[1]. As a result of the general in-

---

[1] E.CL.SCHERER, vide supra. E.SEEBERG, G.ARNOLD, 1923. K. HEUSSI, J. L. MOSHEIM, 1906. K. VÖLKER, Die Kirchengeschichtsschreibung der Aufklärung, 1921. FR. MEINECKE, Die Entstehung des Historismus, 2 vols. [2]1946. K. TH. SCHNEIDER, A. NEANDER, 1894. H. JURSCH, Schleiermacher als Kirchenhistoriker I, 1933. K. BAUR, BlwürttKG 1921, 1/70; 1922, 1/60 (F. CHR. BAUR as a church historian). FR. SMEND, A. V. HARNACK, Verzeichnis seiner Schriften, 1927. J. DE GHELLINCK, RHE 1930, 962/91 (Harnack's development). A. V. ZAHN-HARNACK, ADOLF V. HARNACK [3]1951. H. BÖH-

tellectual development in the seventeenth century, universal history was divided into Profane History and Church History and the latter became an independent discipline in the faculty of theology. Godfrey *Arnold*, a Pietist, wrote "Unparteiische Kirchen- und Ketzerhistorie[1]" (Frankfurt 1699) in which he severely criticized the intolerant orthodox Lutherans of his day. The Institutiones historiae ecclesiasticae (1755) of J. L. *Mosheim* easily holds first place by reason of the skillful use of sources and presentation. The very detailed "Christliche Kirchengeschichte" of his pupil, J. M. *Schröckh* (45 vol. 1768/1812) is not quite of the same high order. The *Enlightenment*, averse to all dogma, exerted a strong even devastating effect, on the writing of Church History. It was only in the nineteenth century when the old Rationalism had been overcome and the historical method had developed that Church History began to make real progress. But the various tendencies of conservative and liberal Protestant theology are clearly reflected in it. (Cfr. Part. III § 210 and 222, 7).

The following works are deserving of mention: Allgemeine Geschichte der christlichen Religion und Kirche, of the learned theologian *August Neander*[2] strongly tinged with the ideas of Schleiermacher (5 volumes [4]1863/65 to 1431); the manual of *J. K. L. Gieseler* is concise in presentation, but contains many citations from the sources (5 vols. 1824/54; a fourth revised edition was published 1844/48; this two-volume edition was translated into English by S. Davidson and revised and edited by H. B. Smith 2 vol. New York 1857); *Ferdinand Chr. Baur*, head of the Tübingen School, published a Church History which, while proving most stimulating, also proved very disturbing in the field of criticism (5 vols. 1863/63); *Fr. Böhringers*, Die Kirche Christi und ihre Zeugen oder KG. in Biographien (24 vols. [2]1860/79, up to the Reformation) is based on authentic sources; an extensive work by *K. R. Hagenbach* (7 vols. 1869/72, I—III 5. ed by Fr. Nippold 1885/87); Abriß der gesamten KG. by *J. J. Herzog* (3 vols. 1876/82, 2nd ed. A. v. Koffmane, 2 vols. 1890/92); KG auf der Grundlage akademischer Vorlesungen of the brilliant aesthetic *Karl Hase* (3 vols. 1885/92; Lehrbuch der KG by *W. Möller* (I—II 1889/91, II[2] 1893, III (Reformation and Counter Reformation) ed. G. Kawerau [3]1907; vol. I revised by *H. v. Schubert*, 1902 and continued under the title: Geschichte der Christlichen Kirche im Früh-MA., 1917/21); the very excellent Kirchengeschichte by *Karl Müller* († 1940; 2 vols. up to 1689, 1892/1919,

---

MER, Beiträge zur sächs. KG. 33, 1919, 1/78 (A. HAUCK). H. RÜCKERT, BlwürttKG 1940, 49/68 (K. MÜLLER).

[1] "An Unbiased History of Churches and Heresy" — actually the work was very biased.

[2] Called in German "pectoral theology" because of his favorite saying, "Pectus est quod facit theologum". He represented a trend in Protestant theology to attempt to judge the merits of a man and his work by the piety evinced.

partly reprinted, Vol I revised 1924/29, II ³1941); Handbuch der KG published by *G. Krüger* († 1940) in collaboration with G. Ficker, H. Hermelink, E. Preuschen, H. Stephan (4 parts 1909/12, Index 1913, revised edition by the above together with W. Maurer and H. Leube, 1923/31. The School of *Albrecht Ritschls* († 1889) had a very beneficent and stimulating influence in the field of Church History. Its undisputed master was *Adolf von Harnack* († 1930), by all means the outstanding Protestant church historian of modern times. Other eminent writers, now deceased, were *Albert Hauck* († 1918), *K. Holl* († 1926), *Friedr. Loofs* († 1928), and *Hans v. Schubert* († 1931). The most complete Protestant church history in English is the History of the Christian Church by *Philip Schaff* (7 vols. New York ⁵1889/92).

Shorter manuals of Protestant Church History have been compiled by *K. Hase* (1834 ²1900 condensed); *J. H. Kurtz* (1849 14th ed. in 2 vols. revised by Bonwetsch and Tschackert 1906); *O. Zöckler* (³1889); K. Heussi (Kompendium der KG., ¹⁰1949 the most popular of the manuals; chronological tables to supplement the work were published in 1917; Abriß (der KG ³1925); *S. M. Deutsch* (1909); *H. Appel* (³1925); *K. Aner* (4 small vols. 1928/31): *J. v. Walter* (Die Gesch. des Christentums, 2 vols. 1932/8, ²1948 f.). Good surveys have been published by: *R. Sohm* (KG in Grundriß, ¹¹1909): *Fr. Loofs* (Grundlinien ²1910); *H. v. Schubert* (Grundzüge ¹¹1950): *H. Achelis* (KG 1921); *H. Weingarten* (Zeittafeln und Überblicke z. KG ⁶1905): *T. Brandt* (Die Kirche im Wandel der Zeiten 1—2, 1933/34); *W. v. Loewenich* (Die Gesch. der Kirche, 1938); H. Lother (Gesch. des Christentums I, 1939); Jülicher, Harnack, Bonwetsch, K. Müller and Funk collaborated in writing an Inter-Faith „Geschichte der christl. Religion" (Ehrhard took Funk's place on the second edition) and Tröltsch (Kultur der Gegenwart I, 4 ²1909, enlarged ed. 1922). *Hans Lietzmann* of Berlin († 1942) published a Geschichte der alten Kirche which has a satisfactory religious basis (4 vols. 1932/44). The profane historian *Erich Caspar* († 1935) published 2 volumes of a *Gesch. des Papsttums* von den Anfängen bis zur Höhe der Weltherrschaft (1930/33) which ends with the year 750. Das Papsttum Idee und Wirklichkeit (I—III₁ 1934/5; ²1950) by *John Haller* (Tübingen) is fascinating but hyper-critical.

7. Chairs of Church History were established at the *Catholic universities of Germany* as a result of Maria Theresia's reforms. But most of the works produced during the period of *Enlightenment* are superficial and permeated with Febronianism and Josephinism[1]. A decided improvement is noticeable with the beginning of Romanticism in the nineteenth century. The convert Count *Friedrich Leopold zu Stolberg* († 1819) struck a warm religious tone in his "Geschichte der Religion Jesu Christi" (15 vols. 1806/18 up to 430). His work was continued to 1190 by *Fr. von Kerz* (30 vols 1825/48) and to 1245 by *J. N. Brischar* (8 vols. 1850/64). Professor

---

[1] K. ZINKE, Zustände u. Strömungen in der kath. Kirchengeschichtsschreibung des Aufklärungszeitalters im deutschen Sprachgebiet, (Dissertation 1933).

## § 4. The Writing of Church History.

*Theodore Katerkamp* of Münster wrote a Church History (5 vols. 1819/34) which is valuable, but which, unfortunately, was never continued beyond 1153. The theological faculties of the universities strove zealously and successfully to broaden and deepen the study of Church History. Leaders in this movement were *John Adam Möhler* († 1838) and *Karl Joseph Hefele* († 1893) at Tübingen, *Ignaz Döllinger* († 1890) at Munich and *Joseph Hergenröther* († 1890) (cfr. § 208, 1 and § 220, 1.2 and the bibliography found in these sections). During the last decades of the century excellent work was done in research as well as in the publication of monographs and collections. Old and new problems were eagerly investigated. The most noted scholars were *Franz X. Kraus* († 1901), *Fr. X. Funk* († 1907), *Henry S. Denifle*, O.P. († 1905), Cardinal *Francis Ehrle*, S.J. († 1934) and *Albert Ehrhard* († 1940).

A general history of the Church by *J. A. Möhler* appeared after his death (3 vols. 1867/68. Index 1870). It was completed by *B. Gams* from Möhler's lectures. *Hefele's* monumental Konziliengeschichte (cfr. § 2, 2) is the equivalent of a universal history of the Church carried down to the fifteenth century. Besides numerous monographs and researches, *Döllinger* published a manual of Church History (2 vols. [2]1843 up to 1517). Manuals were also written by *J. N. Hortig* (2 vols. [II 2 by Döllinger] 1826/28); *J. J. Ritter* (3 vols. 1826/35, 6th ed. by Ennen 2 vols. 1862); *John Alzog* (1840, 10th ed. by F. X. Kraus, 2 vols. 1882) and especially by *Joseph* (Cardinal) *Hergenröther*, Handbuch der allgem. KG. (3 vols. 1876/80; revised by *J. P. Kirsch* with Supplements, 4 vols. [6]1924/25). Hergenröther's manual is the most complete German work of its kind and maintains a thoroughly ecclesiastical spirit throughout. It has been revised into a *"Kirchengeschichte"* of 4 volumes by *J. P. Kirsch* in collaboration with A. Bigelmair and J. Greven († 1934), J. Hollnsteiner and L. A. Veit († 1939). This work also appeared in 4 volumes as follows: I (Antiquity) by J. P. Kirsch, 1930; II 2 (from 1200 to 1450) by J. Hollnsteiner, 1940; III 2 (from 1555 to 1648) by K. Eder, 1949 and IV (from 1648 to the present) by *L. A. Veit*, 1881/3. The principal Catholic works, whose excellence is attested by translation into various languages and by adaptation as textbooks, were written by *H. Brück* (1874, 9th ed. by *J. Schmidt*, 1906); *J. Marx* (1903, 9th ed. by F. Pangerl, 1929); *F. X. Kraus* ([4]1896); *Al. Knöpfler* (1895, based on the lectures of Hefele, [6]1920, reprinted 1924 and 1930); *F. X. Funk* (1886, [5]1907; other editions since 1911, gradually enlarged to 3 volumes by K. Bihlmeyer [† 1942]); *J. Schmidt* (Grundzüge der KG., 1925); *Joseph Lortz* (Gesch. der Kirche in ideengeschichtl. Betrachtung 1930, [15/16]1950 [4th German ed. translated into English and adapted by Kaiser, C.PP.S, 1938]); *Albert Ehrhard* (Die kath. Kirche im Wandel der Zeiten und der Völker I 1935/7 and II [2]1950, by *W. Neuss*, an excellent, independent and pleasing presentation, which gives more attention than usual to the Eastern Church). Mention should also be made of the Dissertationes selectae in historiam eccl. of *A. Weiss*, (I—II, 1907/10) and two popular-scientific works: "Illustrierte

Geschichte der Kirche", by *J. P. Kirsch* and *V. Luksch* (1905) and "Illustrierte Kirchengeschichte" by *G. Rauschen, J. Marx* and *J. Schmidt* (1912). *F. X. Seppelt*, began the publication of a scientific *Papstgeschichte* in 6 volumes (thus far Vols I, II, IV and V, 1931/41, I² 1939). And *Seppelt* and *K. Löffler* issued a popular, illustrated Papstgeschichte in one volume (1933, ⁵1950). The 16 volume work of the layman, *Ludwig Freiherr von Pastor*, "Geschichte der Päpste seit dem Ausgang des Mittelalters" is very valuable for the study of Church History. This work published 1886—1933 has already appeared in several editions, and is being continued by *Joseph Schmidlin* from 1800 to the present in Papstgeschichte der neuesten Zeit (I—IV, 1933—1939). An English translation of all the volumes of Pastor is published by Herder. *G. Castella* also compiled a History of the Popes in 3 volumes (1944/6).

8. In *Italy, Gaetano Moroni* compiled the very profuse, but uncritical Dizionario di erudizione storico-ecclesiastica (103 vols. and 6 vols. of indices, Venice, 1840/78). Textbooks of Church History in Italian have been published by *L. Todesco* (Corso di storia della Chiesa, 6 vols. Turin 1922/30, I—V ⁴1947 ff.); *G. Lucca* (Storia della Chiesa (3 vols. Rome ²1932/3); *G. Pagnini* (Manuale di storia ecclesiastica, 4 vols. Milan 1928/33), *P. Paschini* (Lezioni di storia ecclesiast. 3 vols. Turin ²1933/35), *F. Callaey*, (Praelectiones historiae ecclesiasticae, Rome 1936/7) and *A. Saba* (Storia della Chiesa, 3 vols. Turin 1938/43). The three volume work of E. Buonaiuti (Storia del cristianesimo, Milan 1942/6; German transl. I 1948) is tinged with Modernism.

In *France, R. F. Rohrbacher* published an extensive Histoire universelle de l'Église catholique (29 vols. Nancy 1942/49, 9th ed. in 20 volumes [XV—XX a continuation to 1889 by Chantrel and Chamard], Paris 1899/1903). A great part of the work was translated into German by Hülskamp, Rump, Knöpfler et al. 1860 ff., and some of it was completely revised. Even more profuse, but uncritical, is the Histoire général de l'Église by *Darras*, Bareille and Févre (44 vol. Paris 1861/1907). During the last decades the study of Church History was pursued with lively interest in France and Belgium and the number of scholarly works in the field multiplied rapidly. Chief credit for this is due to *Louis Duchesne* († 1922; cfr. J. Guiraud, RQH 97, 1922, 130 ff., 350 ff.; 98, 1923, 394 ff.; F. Cabrol, JThSt 1923, 253/81), the most noted Church historian of France in modern times. His Histoire ancienne de l'Église (3 vols. Paris 1906/10) was placed on the Index because of its hypercritical trend. Credit is also due to his disciple Pierre Batiffol († 1929; cfr. G. Bardy, RechSR 1929, 122/41). Perhaps the greatest influence was exerted by the School of Church History founded at the University of *Louvain* by A. Cauchie († 1922) with its scientific periodical Revue d'histoire ecclésiastique (1900 ff.), and the College of the *Neo-Bollandists* at Brussels directed by *H. Delehaye S. J.* († 1941). Textbooks in French, patterned after German manuals, were publishd by *L. Marion* et *V. Lacombe* (3 vols. Paris 1905, 4 vols. ⁹1928); *F. Mourret* et *J. Carreyre* (3 vols. Paris 1924); *C. Poulet* (2 vols. Paris 1926 ¹⁷1947; translated into English and adapted from the 4th French ed. by Raemers, 2 vols. St. Louis, 1934); *A. M. Jacquin* (I—II Paris 1929/36). Larger works were written by *F. Mourret* (Histoire générale de l'Église, 9 vols. Paris 1909/21, nouv. ed. 1924/26; transl. into English by Thompson, 6 vols. St. Louis 1930/46); *A. Dufourcq* (Histoire de l'Église, 8 vols. Paris ³1908/14, 6th ed. 1924 ff.);

## § 4. The Writing of Church History.

*A. Boulenger* (Hist. générale de l'Église, vol. I—V Paris 1931/5); *C. Poulet* (Hist. du Christianisme, 4 vols. Paris 1932 ff.; Initiation à l'histoire ecclésiastique 2 vols. Paris 1944/6); *G. de Plinval* et *R. Pittet* (Hist. illustrée de l'Église 2 vols. Paris 1947/8). *Fliche* and *Martin* are publishing Histoire de l'Église in 24 volumes, of which volumes I—X and XII, XVII and XX (Paris 1935/50) have appeared. This work is also being translated into English. Thus far the translation of the first 3 volumes of the French edition has been issued in 6 volumes (London 1942/52). A popular History of the Church by *Philip Hughes* (3 vols. London 1934/47) has been well received by the English-reading public and has gone into a second edition.

PART I

THE ANCIENT CHURCH

# FIRST PERIOD

## FROM THE FOUNDATION TO THE EDICT OF MILAN[1]

### CHAPTER I

### FOUNDATION, SPREAD AND PERSECUTION OF THE CHURCH

### § 5.

#### Preparation of the Pagan World for the Redemption[2].

1. Christianity did not appear in a world entirely unprepared to receive it. According to the words of St. Paul (Gal. 4:4; Eph. 1:10)

---

[1] Cfr. the sources in § 2 and the Church Histories in § 4, 6—8. C. KIRCH, Enchiridion fontium historiae ecclesiasticae antiquae, ⁶1947. Scriptorum paganorum I—IV. saec. de christianis testimonia ed. W. DEN BOER, Leyden 1948. K. PIEPER, Atlas orbis christiani antiqui, 1931. L. DUCHESNE, Hist. ancienne de l'Église I⁴, Paris 1908 (cfr. § 4, 8). P. BATIFFOL, Le Catholicisme des origines à S. Léon, 4 vol. Paris 1909/24. A. EHRHARD, Das Christentum im röm. Reich bis Konstantin, ²1932 (lecture); Die Kirche der Martyrer, ihre Aufgaben u. ihre Leistungen, 1932. Die kath. Kirche im Wandel der Zeiten u. der Völker I, 1, 1935. J. ZEILLER, L'Empire Romain et l'Église des premiers siècles, Paris 1928. F. HAASE, Altchristl. KG. nach oriental. Quellen (bis 451), 1925. Histoire de l'Église (cfr. § 4, 8) t. I—II (to 313, by J. LEBRETON u. J. ZEILLER), Paris 1935. F. CALLAEY, Praelectiones historiae ecclesiasticae antiquae, Rome 1936. A. DUFOURCQ, Le christianisme antique, Paris 1939. H. DANIEL-ROPS, L'église des apôtres et des martyrs, ib. 1948. PH. HUGHES, A History of the Church I, London ²1948. Protestant Works: Propyläen-Weltgesch. Bd. II: Hellas u. Rom u. d. Entstehung d. Christentums, 1931. E. KORNEMANN, Weltgesch. des Mittelmeerraumes II, 1949. H. M. GWATKIN, Early Church History (to 313), 2 vol. London 1909. H. ACHELIS, Das Christentum in den ersten drei Jhh., 2 vols. 1912, condensed into one vol. 1924. C. F. ARNOLD, Geschichte der alten Kirche bis auf Karl d. Gr., 1919. B. J. KIDD, History of the Church to A. D. 461, 3 vol. Oxford 1922. E. G. SIHLER, From Augustus to Augustine, Cambridge 1923. C. J. CADOUX, The Early Church and the World (to 313), Edinb. 1925 (Excellent extracts from the sources). H. LIETZMANN, Gesch. der alten Kirche I—II, 1932/6; I² 1937. J. MACKINNON, From Christ to Constantine, London 1936. FR. HEILER, Die kath. Kirche des Ostens u. Westens I: Urkirche u. Ostkirche, 1937, II: Die römischkath. Kirche, Teil I, 1941. K. MÜLLER, Kirchengeschichte I, 1, ³1941. H. LOTHER, Gesch. des Christentums I, 1939.

[2] J. DÖLLINGER, Heidentum u. Judentum, Vorhalle z. Gesch. des Christentums, 1857. O. HOLTZMANN, Neutest. Zeitgesch., ²1906. J. FELTEN (Catholic), Neutest. Zeitgesch. oder Judent. u. Heident. z. Zeit Christi u. der Apostel, 2 vols. ³1925. W. STÄRK, Neutest. Zeitgesch., 2 small vols. ³1921. F. J. FOAKES-JACKSON and K. LAKE, The Beginnings of Christianity I—II, London 1920/33. R. KNOPF, Einführung in das N.T., ⁴1934. CH. F. JEAN, Le milieu biblique avant Jésus-Christ, 3 vol. Paris 1922/6. Ἄγγελος, Archiv f. neutest. Zeitgesch. und Kulturkunde, ed. J. LEIPOLDT, 1925 ff. C. SCHNEIDER, Einf. in die neutest. Zeitgesch., 1934. H. PREISKER, Neutest. Zeitgesch., 1937. L. FRIED-

Christ appeared in the "fullness of time," i. e., after divine Providence had prepared mankind to accept Redemption. But because God's judgments are incomprehensible and His ways unsearchable

LÄNDER, Darstellungen aus der Sittengesch. Roms von Augustus bis z. Ausgang der Antonine (192), 4 vols. [10]1921/23. G. GRUPP, Kulturgesch. der röm. Kaiserzeit, 2 vols. 1903/4; I[3], 1921. G. BOISSIER, La religion romaine d'Auguste aux Antonins, 2 vol. Paris [7]1909. J. TOUTAIN, Les cultes païens dans l'empire Romain, 3 vol. Paris 1907/20. J. KAERST Gesch. des Hellenismus I[3], 1927; II[2], 1926. E. ROHDE, Psyche, Seelenkult u. Unsterblichkeitsglaube der Griechen, [10]1925. E. REISINGER u. R. WAGNER, Die antike Kultur in ihren Hauptzügen, [2]1925. P. WENDLAND, Die hellenist.-röm. Kultur in ihren Beziehungen zum Judent. u. Christent., [3]1912. A. DEISSMANN, Licht vom Osten. Das N.T. u. die neuentdeckten Texte d. hellenist.-röm. Welt, [4]1923. H. LIETZMANN, Der Weltheiland, 1909. E. KREBS, Der Logos als Heiland im 1. Jh., 1910; Das religionsgeschichtl. Problem des Urchristentums, 1913 (Bibl. Zeitfr. VI, 4/5). J. ROHR, Griechent. u. Christent., 1912 (Bibl. Zeitfr. V, 8). E. NORDEN, Agnostos Theos, 1913; Die Geburt des Kindes, Gesch. einer relig. Idee, 1924, reprinted 1931. F. CUMONT, Die oriental. Religionen im röm. Heidentum, Germ. tr. by G. GEHRICH, [3]1931. R. REITZENSTEIN, Die hellenist. Mysterienreligionen, [3]1927. J. GEFFCKEN, Der Ausgang des griech.-röm. Heidentums, [2]1929; Relig. Strömungen im 1. Jh. nach Chr., 1922. E. R. BEVAN, Hellenism and Christianity, London 1921. W. WEBER, Der Prophet u. s. Gott. Studie zur 4. Ekloge Vergils, 1925. S. DILL, Roman Society to Marcus Aurelius, London 1925. W. R. HALLIDAY, The Pagan Background of Early Christianity, Liverpool 1926. O. KERN, Die Religion der Griechen (to Julian the Apostate), 3 vols. 1926/38. P. FIEBIG, Die Umwelt des N.T., religionsgesch. Texte übers., 1926. H. HAAS u. J. LEIPOLDT, Die Religionen in der Umwelt des Christentums, 1926/30 (A picture atlas for the history of religion). K. LATTE, Die Religion der Römer u. der Synkretismus der Kaiserzeit, [2]1927. H. KLEINKNECHT, Πάνθειον, Religionsgesch. Texte des Griechentums, 1929. H. GRESSMANN, Die oriental. Religionen im hellenist.-römischen Zeitalter, 1930. R. LAQUEUR, H. KOCH and W. WEBER, Probleme der Spätantike, 1930. W. NESTLE, Griech. Religiösität von Homer bis Proklos, 3 vols. 1930/34; Vom Mythos zum Logos, [2]1942. F. PFISTER, Die Religion der Griechen u. Römer, Darstellung u. Literaturbericht 1918/30, 1930 (Jahresber. über die Fortschritte der klass. Altertumswiss., Suppl. vol. 229). S. WIDE u. M. P. NILSSON, Griech. u. röm. Religion, 1931. M. P. NILSSON, Gesch. d. griech. Religion, 2 vols. 1941/50. F. ALTHEIM, Röm. Religionsgesch. II—III, 1932/33. M. ROSTOVTZEFF, Gesellschaft u. Wirtschaft im röm. Kaiserreich, German by L. WICKERT, 2 vols. 1931. K. PRÜMM, Scholastik 1929, 51 ff. 221 ff. 498 ff.; 1931, 539 ff.; 1932, 239 ff. (4. Ekloge Vergils; cfr. O. KURFESS, ThGl 1936, 454/64); id. in ZkTh 1933, 254 ff.; id., Der christliche Glaube u. die altheidnische Welt, 2 vols. 1935 (also O. CASEL, JbLW XIV, 1938, 197/224, and PRÜMM, ZkTh 1938, 545/68); id., Christentum als Neuheitserlebnis. Studien zur Umformung des relig. Denkens der Antike, 1939; Religionsgesch. Handb. f. den Raum der altchristl. Umwelt, 1943. E. LICHTENSTEIN, Festschrift W. Goetz, 1948, 1/21 (PHILIPPI, an historical-theological study of the introduction of Christianity into the West.). H. LEISEGANG, Logos, RE Pauly-Wissowa XIII, 1033/81. K. BORNHAUSEN, Der Erlöser, s. Bedeutung in Gesch. u. Glaube, 1927. H. HERZOG-HAUSER, Soter, die Vorstellung eines Retters im altgriech. Epos, 1931. W. STAERK, Soter I—II, 1933/8. G. KITTEL, Urchristentum, Spätjudentum, Hellenismus, 1926 (lecture); Die Religionsgesch. u. das Urchristentum, 1932. A. FESTUGIÈRE, L'idéal religieux des Grecs et l'Évangile, Paris 1932; A. FESTUGIÈRE et P. FABRE, Le monde gréco-romain au temps de Notre-Seigneur, 2 vol. ib. 1935. L. GERNET et A. BOULENGER, Le génie grec dans la religion, Paris 1932. B. HEIGL, Antike Mysterienreligionen u. das Christentum, 1932 (Bibl. Zeitfr.

(Rom. 11:33) there is a certain amount of mystery surrounding this preparation. Yet it is not entirely incomprehensible; for as God reveals Himself in creation, so also He makes Himself manifest in history (Acts 14:16 f.).

The preparation of *the heathen world* for the coming of the Kingdom of God is evident in several ways. The Greeks and Romans, the most advanced peoples of antiquity, had reached an astonishing degree of profane culture: the Greeks, as poets, philosophers and artists; the Romans, as organizers, legislators and rulers. But the brilliance of these achievements served only to throw into relief their utter bankruptcy of religion and morals. The old polytheistic religions and cult of State had, for the time that they were kept on a lofty plane, succeeded in promoting reverence for the divine and in stimulating to virtue; but they had degenerated and no longer exerted any influence over the large mass of the people. While it is true that the simple people still retained some faith and a measure of morality, the educated class in the last days of the Roman republic had become rank atheists. The efforts of Emperor Augustus to restore the cult of State and the piety of the ancients met with little success. As a sort of substitute for belief in the gods there was introduced from the Hellenic Orient since the beginning of the Empire, *the cult of the Emperor* with divine honors paid to the deceased (apotheosis, consecratio) and soon (since Cajus Caligula) even to the living emperor or to his genius. But even before this trend became evident, *Oriental religions* and *mystery cults* had found their way into the West

XIII, 11/12).   H. LIETZMANN, Die Umwelt des jungen Christentums, Antike 1932, 254/75.   W. KROLL, Die Kultur der Ciccronianischen Zeit, 2 vols. 1933. ST. LÖSCH, Deitas Jesu u. antike Apotheose, 1933.   C. CLEMEN, Der Einfluß des Christentums auf andere Religionen, 1933.   A. D. NOCK, Conversion, The Old and New in Religion from Alexander the Great to Augustine of Hippo, Oxford 1933.   P. M. SCHUHL, Essai sur la formation de la pensée grecque, Paris 1934. H. KEES, A. GÖTZE u. a., Kulturgesch. des alten Orients, 1933 ff.   The Cambridge Ancient History vol. X: The Augustan Empire (to 70 A. D.), Cambridge 1934.   C. BAILEY Religion in Virgil, Oxford 1935. K. HÖNN, Augustus u. s. Zeit, [3]1943. M. POHLENZ, Der hellen. Mensch, 1947. TH. HAECKER, Vergil, Vater des Abendlandes, [5]1947.   L. BIELER, Θεῖος 'Ανήρ, Das Bild des "göttlichen Menschen" in Spätantike u. Frühchristentum, 2 parts 1935/6.   J. HESSEN, Platonismus u. Prophetismus, 1939.   EDW. EYRE and others, European Civilization, Its Origin and Development (7 vol.), I—II Oxf. 1935.   ED. WECHSSLER, Hellas im Evangelium, [2]1947.   E. PETERSON, Der Monotheismus als polit. Problem im Imperium Romanum, 1936. W. SCHU-BART, Die relig. Haltung des frühen Hellenismus, 1937.   K. KERÉNYI, Apollon. Studien über antike Religion u. Humanität, 1937; Die antike Religion, Amsterd. 1940.   E. PETERICH, Die Theologie der Hellenen, 1938.   R. BULT-MANN, Das Urchristentum im Rahmen der antiken Religionen, 1949.

and appealed strongly to the masses. Especially the cult of the Phrygian Magna Mater Cybele and Attis, the various Syrian Baalim, the Egyptian deities Isis and Osiris-Serapis and the Persian god of light, Mithras, had many devotees in the West. Alongside of these there flourished all sorts of religious superstitions: astrology, magic, incantation and necromancy. Hand in hand with the decline of religion among the upper classes especially in the larger cities, went a frightful brutilization of morals. The Apostle Paul (Rom. 1:24—32) paints the gloomy picture in sharp lines and his opinion is substantiated in all essentials by pagan authors such as Seneca, Tacitus and Juvenal.

2. *Philosophy* which had replaced religion in the case of many educated persons, was itself in a state of decay. The profound speculation of Plato and Aristotle had given way to other more eclectic systems which abandoned metaphysics and stressed the practical. *Epicurus of Samos* († 270) and his school rejected speculation and taught a materialistic Hedonism ("pleasure, the highest good"). *Stoicism,* founded by Zeno of Cittium († c. 260), the most popular philosophy immediately before and after the coming of Christ, was somewhat better. It considered moral perfection the objective of all philosophy. But its theology is pantheistic-monistic and it subjects the evolution of the universe to the blind, immutable forces of fate. Many, especially of the Neo-Platonists, surrendered to *Scepticism* and gave up all hope of ever having knowledge of truth (cfr. Pilate's question, John 18:38). The Cynics, in their unrestricted individualism, subjected all religion to frivolous criticism. All post-Aristotelian philosophy aware of its own inadequacy showed a pessimistic strain. It had also developed a strong cosmopolitan tendency. *Political* and *national life* which had formerly held so much interest and had nurtured so much civic virtue, was no longer a dominant influence. The Grecian republics, Athens and Sparta, with their ardent patriots had passed out of existence; the Roman world-empire, which comprised almost the entire known and civilized world had gradually yielded to tedium and had reached the end of her conquests. And so the human heart was no longer fascinated by the external; open to truth, it seized it all the more eagerly, the more hopeless its pursuit appeared. At no time was the feeling of helplessness and the consciousness of a general decadence stronger and more widespread than at the moment that Christ entered the world.

3. But besides these negative factors there were also in Paganism several *positive* points of contact for Christ's message of salvation and many *favorable external circumstances* which promoted its rapid spread. They are found chiefly in the religious and philosophic trends already noted. While the *Oriental religions* and *mystery cults* sanctioned orgiastic and revolting practices, they also contained some grains of truth. In spite of jejune legalism, some of the forms of the Roman religions, appealed powerfully to the imagination and the emotions; they spoke of sin and guilt, expiation and rebirth, of immortality and a blissful existence beyond the grave. By means of mysterious rites and sacred banquets they strove to attain salvation (σωτηρία) and immediate union with Divinity; their priests even gave courses of instructions and spiritual guidance.

4. In spite of the large number of polytheistic cults, there is noticeable a certain spiritualization of the notion of God and an unconscious *trend toward monotheism.* Following upon the decline of religion, toward the end of the republic, there arose a new and gradually swelling wave of religiosity, which was predominately *syncretistic.* Representations of the gods harmonized with the cults in many ways, especially the Oriental cults. Even the idea of a universally revealed religion offering universal redemption constantly grew stronger and gained more adherents. Pious pagans agonized with ardent yearning for enlightenment and help from above. The expectation that *the world would be transformed and renewed* (a "Golden Age"), indeed, even the expectation of an historical savior and redeemer, a great prophet and leader is found among the Orientals and Greeks at an early date. In the Orient of remote antiquity, the king was looked upon as the son of God and the predestined ruler of the world, endowed with wisdom and priestly dignity; he was the "redeemer" or "savior", and the beginning of each new reign (epiphany) was expected to mark a new and happy era. Even the Roman emperor was given the honorary title κύριος—σωτήρ (Lord-God-Savior). The same idea is expressed in the famous fourth Eclogue of Virgil and in the literature relating to the legendary Hermes Trismegistos (cfr. § 17, 2) as well as in the Stoic idea of a universally ruling *Logos*, the mediator between God and the world, who everywhere scatters the "seeds" of truth. In fact, *Greek philosophy*[1] besides containing many errors, also

---

[1] FR. ÜBERWEG, Grundriß der Geschichte der Philosophie I[12], ed.

contained many elements of truth which for the earnest pagan could form a bridge to Christianity (Justin, Tatian, etc.). *Plato,* the author of philosophical Idealism identifies the idea of the highest good with God; and *Aristotle* in his metaphysics arrived at the knowledge of the first unmoved mover of the world and of an absolute self-conscious Mind. The theological speculation of the Stoic *Posidonius* of Apamea in Syria († c. 50 B.C.), the last independent Greek thinker for a long time, combined in an unusual degree a critical mind with deep mystical piety, which strongly influenced the subsequent philosophy of religion both pagan and Christian. The ethics of the later Stoa, of a *Seneca* ("saepe noster" Tertullian says of him: De anima 20; in the fourth century it was asserted that he had corresponded with St. Paul), of *Epictetus* and *Marcus Aurelius* harmonize in many points with Christian ethics. It recognizes a divine moral law and a guiding Providence; it speaks of the equality and homogeneity of all men; prescribes mortification and struggle against the flesh; and demands charity toward all men, even toward enemies. The avowal of such noble sentiments in paganism led Christian thinkers of the second and third centuries to see Hellinism as the precursor and preparatory school of Christianity. *Clement of Alexandria* calls philosophy "God's gift to the Greeks" (Strom. I, 2, 20) and says (Strom. I, 5, 28) that "as the law prepared the Hebrews (Gal. 3:24) so philosophy prepared the Grecian world for Christ."

---

K. PRAECHTER, 1927. H. MEYER, Gesch. der abendländ. Weltanschauung I, 1947. TH. HOPFNER, Orient u. griech. Philosophie, 1925. E. HOWALD, Ethik des Altertums, 1927. J. STENZEL, Metaphysik des Altertums, 1931. G. KAFKA u. H. EIBL, Das Ausklingen der antiken Philosophie u. das Erwachen einer neuen Zeit, 1928. FR. WAGNER, Der Sittlichkeitsbegriff in der antiken Ethik, 1928. A. BILL, La morale dans la philosophie antique, Paris 1928. H. EIBL, Die Grundlegung der abendländ. Philosophie, 1934. M. POHLENZ, Die Stoa, 2 vols. 1948; Stoa u. Stoiker I, 1950. AD. DYROFF, Die Ethik der alten Stoa, 1897. M. SCHNEIDEWIN, Die antike Humanität, 1897. E. ELORDUY, Die Sozialphilosophie der Stoa, 1936. P. BARTH, Die Stoa, ⁵1941. J. HEINE-MANN, Poseidonios' metaphys. Schriften, 2 vols. 1921/8. K. REINHARDT, Poseidonios, 1921; Neue Untersuchungen über Poseid., 1926. P. SCHUBERT, Die Eschatologie des Posidonius, 1927. W. THEILER, Die Vorbereitung des Neuplatonismus (Posidonius), 1930. M. BAUMGARTEN, Seneca u. das Christentum, 1895. C. W. BARLOW, Epistolae Senecae ad Paulum, Rome 1938. P. BENOÎT, Rev. bibl. 1946, 7/35. K. DEISSNER, Paulus u. Seneca, 1917. TH. SCHREINER, Seneca im Gegensatz zu Paulus, Dissertation 1935. TH. ZAHN, Epiktet u. s. Verhältnis z. Christent., ²1895. A. BONHÖFFER, Die Ethik des Stoikers Epiktet, 1894; E. u. das N.T., 1911. M. J. LAGRANGE, Rev. bibl. 1912, 5 ff. 192 ff. (Epictetus); 1913, 243 ff. 394 ff. 568 ff. (Marcus Aurelius); Rev. THOMISTE 1928, 324 ff. (Seneca). G. LOISEL, Marc-Aurelia, doctrine néostoicienne, Paris 1929.

The most important and most direct preparation of the heathen world for the true religion was effected by contact in the diaspora with Judaism and its monotheistic creed. (cfr. infra § 6, 2).

5. Among the favorable *external* circumstances must be considered the *political* unity of the old civilized world and the *Hellenization* of the East and, to some extent, of the West, which had been going on since the days of Alexander the Great. When the lands bordering the Mediterranean from Syria to Spain and from the Nile to the Danube had become *one* political organism, peoples that had once been mutually hostile, realized that they had common interests. A common legal system and government, the diffusion of the *Greek language* (κοινὴ διάλεκτος) and a common *culture* necessarily created a certain unity in manner of life and thought. A brisk and well-protected *commerce*[1] by land and sea made possible a rapid exchange of goods and ideas. A closely knit *social* and *business life*, a communal and provincial organization provided the Christians with all manner of contacts. The world torn and exhausted by long civil wars rejoiced in the peace and order established by Emperor Augustus. Discerning Christians recognized the historic world-mission of the Roman Empire. *St. Melito of Sardes* pointed out about 175 (Eus. H. E. IV, 26) that Christianity and the imperial rule entered the world about the same time and grew up together, hence were evidently intended by Providence to complement each other. And the brilliant *Origen* writing about 248 (contra Cels. II, 30), said: "God prepared the nations and disposed things so that the Roman Emperor ruled the whole world ... for the existence of many kingdoms would have proved a hindrance to the spread of Christ's doctrine."

## § 6.

### Judaism before Christ and Its Messianic Expectation[2].

1. The significance of the Jewish people for world history consists exclusively in their religion. It became apparent to the

---

[1] TH. ZAHN, Weltverkehr und Kirche; in: Skizzen aus dem Leben der christlichen Kirche, ³1908, 1/41. A. STEINMANN, Die Welt des Paulus im Zeichen des Verkehrs, 1915 (Progr. Braunsberg). FRIEDLÄNDER (vide Supra) I u. II.

[2] Cfr. literature in § 5 (DÖLLINGER, FELTEN, KNOPF etc.). E. SCHÜRER, Gesch. des jüdisch. Volkes im Zeitalter Jesu Christi, 3 vols. ⁴1901/9, Reg. 1911 (important). P. VOLZ, Jüd. Eschatologie von Daniel bis Akiba, 1903; 2nd ed

surrounding pagan nations that the Jews had received a divine revelation and that they were governed by a special divine Providence. *Monotheism* and the promise of a *Messias* were the stars which led Judaism through the darkest night and sustained it in the most grievous afflictions. By means of various trials and visitations the people of Israel were preserved in the belief in one true God or were recalled from idolatry when, as sometimes happened,

---

entitled: Die Eschatologie der jüd. Gemeinde im neutest. Zeitalter, 1934. W. BOUSSET, Die Religion des Judentums im spät-helenist. Zeitalter, [3]1926. A. SCHLATTER, Israels Gesch. v. Alexander d. Gr. bis Hadrian, [3]1926; Die Theologie des Judentums nach d. Bericht des Josefus, 1932. M. J. LAGRANGE, Le Messianisme chez les Juifs, Paris 1909; Le Judaisme avant Jésus-Christ, ib. 1931. A. BERTHOLET, Das Ende des jüd. Staatswesens, 1910; Bibl. Theologie des A.Test., 1911; Kulturgesch. Israels 1919; Die Religion des A. T., [2]1932. J. DÖLLER, Die Messiaserwartung im A. T., 1911 (Bibl. Zeitfr. IV, 6/7). J. JUSTER, Les Juifs dans l'empire Romain, 2 vol. Paris 1914. E. KÖNIG, Gesch. der alttest. Religion, [4]1924. J. GÖTTSBERGER, Die göttl. Weisheit als Persönlichkeit im A. T., 1919 (Bibl. Zeitfr. IX, 1/2). ED. MEYER, Ursprung und Anfänge des Christentums II, [5]1925. R. KITTEL, Die Religion d. Volkes Israel, [2]1929; Gesch. des Volkes Israel I—II, [6/7]1925/32; III, 1927/9; Die hellenist. Mysterienreligion u. das A. T., 1924; Gestalten u. Gedanken in Israel, [2]1932. G. HÖLSCHER, Gesch. der israelit. u. jüd. Religion, 1922. E. SELLIN, Gesch. des israelitisch-jüd. Volkes I—II, 1924/32, I[2] 1935; Alttest. Theologie auf religionsgesch. Grundlage, 2 vols. [2]1936. S. ÖTTLI, Gesch. Israels bis Alex. d. Gr., [2]1925. L. DÜRR, Ursprung u. Ausbau der israelitisch-jüd. Heilandserwartung, 1 25; Wollen u. Wirken der alttest. Propheten, 1926; Die Wertung des göttl. Wortes im A. T. u. im antiken Orient, 1938. G. KITTEL, Die Probleme des palästinens. Spätjudentums u. das Urchristentum, 1926. G. F. MOORE, Judaism in the First Centuries of the Christian Era, 3 vol. Cambridge 1927/30. P. RIESSLER, Altjüdisches Schrifttum außerhalb der Bibel übers. u. erläutert, 1928. R. STORR, Die Frömmigkeit im A. T., 1928. L. DENNEFELD, Le Messianisme (from DictThC X), Paris 1929 [this article was placed on the Index Dec. 16, 1930]; Judaïsme, DictThC VIII, 1581/1668; Histoire d'Israël et de l'ancien Orient, Paris 1935. H. GRESSMANN, Der Messias, 1929. H. LECLERCQ, Judaïsme, DictAC VIII, 1/254. A. CAUSSE, Les dispersés d'Israel, Paris 1929. ST. LÖSCH, Epistula Claudiana, der neuentdeckte Brief des Kaisers Klaudius vom Jahre 41 n. Chr. u. das Urchristentum, 1930. F. FELDMANN, Gesch. der Offenbarung des A. T. bis z. Babyl. Exil, [3]1930. A. JEREMIAS, Das A. T. im Lichte des alten Orients, [4]1930. A. JIRKU, Gesch. des Volkes Israel, 1931. J. MEINHOLD, Einführung in das AT., [3]1931. A. VINCENT, Le Judaïsme, Paris 1932. TH. H. ROBINSON and W. O. E. OESTERLEY, A History of Israel (to A. D. 135), 2 vol. Oxford 1932. M. HOEPERS, Der neue Bund bei den Propheten, 1933. W. EICHRODT, Theologie des A.T., 3 vols. 1933/9, I[2] 1939. J. BONSIRVEN, Les idées juives au temps de Notre-Seigneur, Paris 1934; Le Judaïsme palestinien au temps de Jésus-Christ, 2 vol. Paris 1935; Juifs et chrétiens, ib. 1936. A. LODS, Les prophètes d'Israël et les débuts du Judaïsme, Paris 1935. L. KÖHLER, Theologie des A.T., 1936. K. HOLZHEY, Jahve der Gott Israels u. sein Kampf gegen die fremden Götter von Moses bis Christus, 1936. A. ALLGEIER, Biblische Zeitgeschichte, 1937. E. DHORME, L'évolution relig. d'Israël I, Paris 1937. U. HOLZMEISTER, Historia aetatis Novi Testamenti, Rome 1938. P. VOLZ, Prophetengestalten des Alten Testamentes, 1938. J. HEMPEL, Das Ethos des A.T., 1938. P. HEINISCH, Theologie des A.T., 1940. N. JOHANSSON, Parakletoi. Vorstellungen von Fürsprechern für die Menschen vor Gott in der alttest. Religion, im Spätjuden- u. Urchristent., Lund 1940. O. PROCKSCH, Theologie des A.T., 1950.

they were allured by the example of their pleasure-loving neighbors. This was accomplished chiefly by the *prophets,* who were the divinely commissioned leaders of the people. It was the mission of the prophets to make God's will known to the people, to reprimand them for their infidelity and to remind them of the Savior who would spring from their midst. As a result *the hope in a Messias* grew more ardent especially at the time of the Machabees when the Syrian king Antiochus Epiphanes (175—164 B.C.) endeavored to rob them of their faith and impose on them a pagan religion and pagan morals. The danger was averted by the courage of the people and their leaders, and political independence was regained after bitter strife (142 B.C.). In the hour of trial when the political power of Israel was declining, the Jews clung the more tenaciously to the *Law.* At this time their spiritual leaders were the *Pharisees* who, in unremitting study and scrupulous observance of the prescriptions of the Law, sought by "separation" from all that was not Jewish to promote their own and the people's welfare. The Pharisees were opposed by the aristocratic party of the *Sadducees,* a group with epicurean tendencies, who dallied with Grecian culture. Under the later Machabean princes, the *Hasmoneans,* who waged ruthless civil and fratricidal wars, the theocratic government of the Jews came to an *end.* Pompey took Jerusalem in the year 63 B.C. The tribal principalities were left unchanged (37—4 B.C. the Idumaean Herod the Great held the crown of all Judea); but Judea became a vassal state of Rome and in the year 6 B.C. was merged with the province of Syria and governed by a procurator residing at Caesarea. During the time that the people were oppressed by foreign rulers, *the Messianic idea* remained their greatest consolation. Unfortunately, however, the idea had become distorted and had been given a strongly *political* and national interpretation so that the Expected One was looked to as the liberator of Israel from the Roman yoke and as the restorer of worldly power and greatness (Luke 24:21; Act 1:6). Still there were many pious Jews deeply interested in the speculations of the apocalyptics, and who were convinced that the Messias would be a wise king of the house of David, endowed with extraordinary powers to establish a supernatural kingdom of God and redeem mankind from the wretchedness of sin. In the person of the "Precursor", *John the Baptist,* there appeared the last and greatest of the prophets to prepare the way for the Messias.

**41**

The New Testament makes no mention of the sect of **Essenes**. They cut themselves off from the society and worship of the Jews, since they spurned the Temple and sacrifices, renounced marriage and private property, and lived a strict ascetical life in isolated colonies especially on the west shore of the Dead Sea (Desert of Engaddi). Cfr. § 28, 3. *Schürer* II[4], 651/80; *C. Bugge*, ZntW 1913, 145/74. — *W. Bauer*, RE Pauly-Wissowa Supp. IV 386/430. — *L. Marchal*, Dict. de la Bible, Supp. (Paris 1926 ff.) 1110/32. — *L. Cerfaux*, RechSR 1929, 248/65 (Baptism among the Essenes). Cfr. Literature § 28. — In their attitude toward religion, the **Therapeutae** were closely related to the Essenes. They were Jewish ascetics who lived in Lower Egypt near Alexandria and devoted themselves chiefly to the study of the Scriptures. Philo speaks of them in his De Vita contemplativa (ed. F. C. Conybeare, Oxford 1895; Philonis opp. edd. Cohn-Wendland VI; Lucius and others have erroneously denied the authenticity of the work). Eusebius (H. E. II, 16—17) and later, Lucius (1879) without sufficient reason, thought that the Therapeutae were Christian ascetics and precursors of later monasticism. *Schürer* III[4] 687 ff. — *P. Wendland*, Jahrb. f. klass. Philol. Suppl. 22, 1896, 693 ff. — *H. Strathmann*, Gesch. d. frühchristl. Askese I, 1914, 148 ff. — *I. Heinemann*, RE Pauly-Wissowa 2. R. V, 2321/46.

2. For a long time many Jews had been forced to live outside of Palestine. In 722 B.C. (or probably 708), the Assyrians conquered the land and in 597 B.C. (or 586) it was invaded by the Chaldeans. On both occasions large numbers of the people were taken captive and scattered through the neighboring countries. Upon release many of these exiles as well as some Jews who had remained in Palestine began to seek their fortunes in other countries, so that soon Jews were to be found in almost every city of the known world. The Egyptian Ptolemies (328—198 B.C.) brought thousands of them to Egypt. In the third century B.C., the first Greek translation of the Old Testament, known as the *Septuagint*, was made by Jewish scholars at Alexandria. The Jews living in the *"diaspora" (Hellenists)* gathered together in closely-knit groups and mingled but little with other people. They had their own synagogues, but kept in contact with the central sanctuary at Jerusalem by the payment of the annual temple tax and by more or less regular visits. Yet they could not withdraw themselves entirely from the influence of the foreign world in which they lived. They accommodated themselves to Hellenism not only in language and manner of life, but even began to adopt something of the Greek philosophy of religion. This is seen most clearly in the writings of the learned Jew **Philo**[1] of Alexandria († c. 40 A.D.) who was of

---

[1] Philonis opera edd. L. COHN, P. WENDLAND and S. REITER, with index by H. LEISEGANG, 8 vols. 1896/1930; edd. F. H. COLSON and G. WHITAKER

a prominent priestly family and a contemporary of Christ. By means of an allegorical interpretation of the Old Testament, he endeavored to harmonize the religious concepts of the Jews, to which he, as an orthodox Jew held fast, with the Platonic, Stoic and Neo-Pythagorean philosophies popular at the time. Naturally he did not succeed in creating a unified system. But his *allegorical* exegesis and his doctrine of the *Logos* as the external revelation of the idea of God and as mediator between God and the world, exerted a powerful influence on Christian theology of the first centuries.

In spite of their isolation the very presence of the Jews had a telling effect on the pagan world about them. Their more exalted idea of God, their imposing ritual and their purer morals made a deep impression on thinking minds. The consciousness of their own religious superiority and their necessary controversies with pagans aroused the Jews of the diaspora to a fairly lively literary activity. Because of the contempt, even abhorrence, which Greeks and Romans generally felt toward the Jewish race, very few pagans actually embraced the religion as *proselytes* (προσήλυτοι, Acts 7:11) by the rite of circumcision and purification or took

I—IX, London 1929/41 (with English translation). Philos Werke deutsch übers. von L. COHN u. I. HEINEMANN I—VI, 1909/38. PHILON, Von den Machterweisen Gottes, übers. u. bearb. v. H. LEWY, 1935. H. LEISEGANG, Philon, RE Pauly-Wissowa XIX, 1/50. P. HEINISCH, Der Einfluß Philos auf die älteste christl. Exegese, 1908; id. in Bibl. Zeitfr. I, 12; VI, 6/7; VII, 3; VIII, 1/2; XI, 1/2, 1913/22. P. KRÜGER, Hellenismus u. Judentum im hellenist. Zeitalter, 1908. E. BRÉHIER, Les Idées philos. et relig. de Philon, Paris ²1925. H. WINDISCH, Die Frömmigkeit Ph.s u. ihre Bedeut. f. das Christentum, 1909. M. LOUIS, Philon, Paris 1911. W. BOUSSET, Jüdisch-christl. Schulbetrieb in Alexandria u. Rom, 1915. H. LEISEGANG, Der Heilige Geist. Wesen u. Werden der intuit. Erkenntnis in d. Philosophie u. Religion d. Griechen, 1919. O. STÄHLIN in W. v. Christ, Gesch. d. griech. Lit. II⁶, 1924, 535/662. ED. STEIN, Die allegorische Exegese des Philo aus Alex., 1929. M. ADLER, Studien zu Philon v. Alex., 1929. G. KUHLMANN, Theologia naturalis bei Philon u. bei Paulus, 1930. J. PASCHER, Der Königs-weg zu Wiedergeburt u. Vergottung bei Philo v. Alex., 1931. K. STAEHLE, Die Zahlenmystik bei Philon v. A., 1931. I. HEINEMANN, Philons griech. u. jüd. Bildung, 1932. FR. GEIGER, Philon v. A. als sozialer Denker, 1932. H. LEWY, Sb. Berlin 1932, 4 (quotations from Philo in Ambrose). H. SCHMIDT, Die Anthropologie Philons v. A., Dissertation 1933. S. TRACY, Philo Iudaeus and the Roman Principate, Williamsport (U.S.A.) 1933. W. KNUTH, Der Begriff der Sünde bei Philon v. A., 1934. G. BARDY, Philon, DictThC XII, 1439/56. H. WILLMS, Eikon I: Philon v. A., 1935. W. VÖLKER, Fortschritt u. Vollendung bei Philo v. A., 1938. E. R. GOODENOUGH, The Politics of Philo Iudaeus, New Haven 1938; An introduction to Philo Iudaeus, ib. 1940. A. MEYER, Vorsehungsglaube u. Schicksalsidee in ihrem Verhältnis bei Philo v. A., Dissertation 1939. S. BELKIN, Philo and the Oral Law, Cambridge, Mass. 1940. H. A. WOLFSON, Philo, 2 vol. ib. ²1948. M. POHLENZ, Nachr. Göttingen 1942, 5, 409/87.

upon themselves the observance of the Law in its entirety. But a very great number did accept Monotheism and the observance of certain practices (Sabbath, dietary laws, religious purification) and thus drew close to Judaism. These "religious" *"Godfearing"* people (φοβούμενοι or, σεβόμενοι τὸν θεόν, Acts 10:2; 13:50; 16:14) were fertile soil for the reception of Christianity because it offered them that for which their hearts yearned and at the same time did not impose upon them Jewish rites and customs which they found repugnant.

### § 7.

### Jesus Christ, Savior of the World and Founder of the Church.

1. "When the fullness of time was come, God sent his Son, made of a woman, made under the law; that he might redeem them who were under the law; that we might receive the adoption of sons." (Gal. 4:4,5). In these few words St. Paul describes the birth, mission and work of the Redeemer. The Son of God came to abolish the Old Covenant, and to establish a new one, — a Covenant of grace, not of law. About thirty years after His wondrous birth (concerning the year cfr. § 3,7) of the Virgin *Mary*, He began His public life in Palestine and proved His divine mission by signs and wonders. He was not merely a reformer of the Jewish religion; He introduced something new: God is the Father Who, out of love, gives Himself to men. The Law, the temple and works of the Law were to come to an end. Christ united religion and ethics, the two concepts of salvation of the Jewish and pagan worlds and announced the "Kingdom of God" i. e., a new, supernatural realm for the salvation and sanctification of man, which would embrace all mankind and would last to the end of time. For this purpose, He gathered disciples about Him and from their number selected twelve Apostles whom He endowed with plenipotentiary powers. He gave to them the same commission He Himself had received and commanded them to teach all nations; to baptize and to govern the faithful with God-given authority. He appointed Simon Peter as the foundation of His Church and chief shepherd of the flock, and thus assured the continuance of the work He had come to do.

But only a small portion of the Jewish people acknowledged Jesus as the promised Messias. "He came unto his own and his own received him not" (John 1:11). The zealous *Pharisees* as well as the freethinking *Sadduccees* strenuously opposed Him. He ended His life on the cross after a brief public career of two to three years, a victim of the hatred of the Jewish hierarchy. This occurred on the 14th or 15th Nisan of a year which can not be determined with certainty (between 30 and 33 of our era). Marvelous incidents occurred at His death and bore witness to His divine mission. The veil of the Temple was rent as a sign that the Old Covenant which God had made with the Jews had ceased and a new one had begun. As He had foretold, He arose after three days in the grave and remained on earth for forty days before returning to the Father who had sent Him.

The more recent works by *Catholics* on the life of Jesus are the following: J. Grimm, 7 vols. 1876/99, 3rd ed. by J. Zahn I—VI, 1 1906/20; *C. Fouard*, 2 vol. Paris [11]1901; *E. P. Le Camus*, 3 vol. Paris [6]1901, German tr. by E. Keppler, 2 vols. 1893/95; *J. Sickenberger*, 1915/31 (from Bibl. Zeitfr. Bd. VII—XIV); *L. C. Fillion*, 3 vol. Paris [2]1925, German tr. by H. Mühlen, 1927; *G. Papini*, German tr. by M. Schwarz, 1941; *A. Reatz*, [4]1925; *Fr. Mauriac*, German tr. by R. Scherer, [3]1947, *K. Pieper*, 1947. — *H. Daniel-Rops*, Paris [2]1947. — *G. Bichlmair*, [4]1948. — *J. Ricciotti*, German tr. by H. Harder, 1949. — Cfr. also: *H. Schell*, Christus, 1903. — *I. Rohr* in Bibl. Zeitfr. I, 3—4, [4]1912. — *H. Felder*, Jesus Christus, Apologie seiner Messianität u. Gottheit, 2 vols. [2]1920/1; Jesus von Nazareth, 1936. — *P. X. Kiefl*, Der geschichtl. Christus u. die moderne Philosophie, 1911. — *Fr. Tillmann, G. Esser* u. *St. v. Dunin-Borkowski* über Christus u. die Kirche in „Religion, Christentum u. Kirche", ed. by G. Esser u. J. Mausbach, Vol. II, 1913. — *A. Meyenberg*, Leben-Jesu-Werk, 3 vols. 1922/32. — *L. de Grandmaison*, Jésus dans l'histoire et dans le mystère, Paris 1925; Jésus-Christ, sa personne, son message, ses preuves, 2 vol. Paris 1928. — *O. Graber*, Der Kampf um Christus, 1926. — *A. Dufourcq*, L'Avenir du christianisme, t. II : La révolution religieuse de Jésus, Paris [6]1927. — *H. Pinard de la Boullaye*, Jésus et l'histoire, Paris 1929; Jésus Messie, le thaumaturge et le prophète, 2 vol. Paris 1930/1. — *M. Lepin*, Le Christ Jésus, son existence historique et sa divinité, Paris 1929. — *J. Lebreton*, La vie et l'enseignement de Jésus-Christ, 2 vol. Paris 1931. — *F. Prat*, Jésus-Christ, 2 vol. ibid. 1933. — *K. Adam*, Jesus Chr., [7]1946. — *J. Pickl*, Messiaskönig Jesus und seine Zeitgenossen, [3]1939. — *R. Guardini*, Jesus Chr., sein Bild in den Schriften des N.T., 1940. — *L. Kösters*, Unser Christusglaube, [2]1939 (excellent bibliography). — *J. M. Vosté*, De passione et morte Jesu Christi, Rome 1937. — *J. Bonsirven*, Les Juifs et Jésus, Paris 1937. - *F. M. Braun*, Jésus. Histoire et critique, ib. 1947. — *Th. Quoidbach*, Le Christ cet inconnu, 2 vol. Bruxelles 1947. — *K. Schelkle*, Die Passion Jesu in der Verkündigung des N. T., 1949. — J. Michl, München. ThZ 1950, 5/15 (death of Jesus). — *J. Blinzler*, Der Prozeß Jesu, 1951. — *R. Schmittlein*, Umstände und Ursache von Jesu Tod, 1950. — Recent *Protestant* works: B. *Weiss*, Leben Jesu, 2 vols. [4]1902. — *Ad. Schlatter*, Gesch. des Christus, [2]1923. — *Ed. Meyer*, Ursprung u. Anfänge d. Christentums, 2 vols. 1924/5. — *W. Bousset*, Kyrios

Christos, Gesch. des Christusglaubens bis Irenäus, [4]1935. — *A. C.Headlam,* Jesus der Christus, German tr. J. Leipoldt, 1926. — *R. Bultmann,* Jesus, [2]1951 (radical). — *S. J. Case,* Jesus, Cambridge 1927. — *Th. Zahn,* Grundriß der Gesch. des Lebens Jesu, 1928. — *K. L. Schmidt,* Art. Jesus Chr., in „Die Religion in Gesch. u. Gegenwart" III[2], 1929, 110/51. — *P. Feine,* Jesus, 1930. — *M. Goguel,* La vie de Jésus, Paris 1932, German tr. 1934. — *Ch. Guignebert,* Jésus, ibid. 1933 (radical). — *Alb. Schweitzer,* Gesch. der Leben Jesu-Forschung, [6]1951. — *G. Pfannmüller,* Jesus im Urteil der Jahrhunderte, [2]1938. — *J. Leipoldt,* Vom Jesusbilde der Gegenwart, [2]1925. — *Er. Seeberg,* Wer ist Christus? 1937. — *M. Dibelius,* Jesus, [2]1947. — *W. Grundmann,* Jesus der Galiläer u. das Judentum, 1940. — *J. Leipoldt,* Jesu Verhältnis zu Griechen u. Juden, 1941. — *F. Buchsel,* Jesus, 1947. — *T. R. Glover,* The Jesus of History, London [2]1949. — *J. G. H. Hoffmann,* Les vies de Jésus et le Jésus de l'histoire, Paris 1947. — *J. Maiworm,* Die Gesch. Jesu, 1946; Die Familie Jesu, 1948. — *J. Isaac,* Jésus et Israel, Paris 1948 (Jewish). — *Chronology* of the life of Jesus: *U. Holzmeister,* Chronologia vitae Christi, Rome 1933. — *M. Dibelius* u. *W. Köhler,* Theol. Blätter 13, 1934, 65/71 (the day of Jesus' death). — *R. Hennig,* Das Geburts- u. Todesjahr Christi, 1936 (Born: 7 B.C.; Died: Friday, April, 3, 33 A.D.). — JThSt 1941, 190/3. 1942, 187/8 (date of the Crucifixion). — *G. Hölscher,* Sb. Heidelberg, 1939/40, 3 (The list of the high priests in Josephus and the chronology of the Gospels).

2. The *denial* of the historical *existence* of Jesus by A. Kalthoff, P. Jensen, A. Drews, P. L. Couchond and others, who explain the Redeemer as a purely mythical personage, based on an idea originating in the Near East and on the Jewish notion of a Messias, is a serious aberration of radical criticism. The validity of the testimony of the Evangelists and of the Apostle Paul remains unshaken. A recently discovered papyrus fragment of the Gospel of St. John dating from the beginning of the second century, proves that at the time of Trajan, the statements regarding Jesus were the same as we read today. Besides, we have fully authenticated testimonies from pagan and Jewish pens. *Tacitus* († ca. 120) in his Annales XV, 44 in connection with the persecution of Nero speaks of the execution of Christ by the procurator Pontius Pilate (auctor nominis Ejus [scil. Chrestianorum] Christus Tiberio imperitante per procuratorem Pontium Pilatum supplicio affectus erat; cfr. E. Panneels, Nova et Vetera 1947, 43/55). *Pliny,* the Younger, in a letter to Trajan (Ep. X, 96) about 112 says that the Christians of Bithynia in their services are accustomed to sing a hymn (carmen dicere) to Christ as God (Christo quasi Deo). And the Jewish historian *Flavius Josephus* (Cfr. B. Brünne, 1913; R. Laqueur, 1920; W. Weber, 1921; St. J. Thackeray, New York 1929; G. Bardy, RHE 1948, 179/91) writing about the year 93 speaks of James the Younger as "the brother of Jesus, who is called the Christ," (Antiq. Jud. XX, 9. 1) — Some doubt is cast on the remarkable passage in the Antiq. XVIII 3, 3: "About this time lived Jesus, a man full of wisdom, [if indeed one may call Him a man, for He was] the doer of incredible things. [and the teacher of such as gladly received the truth.] He thus attracted to Himself many Jews and many of the Gentiles. He was the Christ. On the accusation of the leading men of our people, Pilate condemned Him to death upon the cross; nevertheless those who had previously loved Him still remained faithful to Him. [For on

the third day He again appeared to them living, just as, in addition to a thousand other marvelous things, prophets sent by God had foretold.] And to the present day the race of those who call themselves Christians after Him has not ceased." Since the words in brackets break the connection and are not in the style of Josephus, it has been thought that they were revisions or marginal notes added by an unknown Christian hand to a copy of the work seen by Eusebius (H. E. I, 11, 7—8) but not known to Origen. However, even to the present day there are scholars who defend the genuinity of the passages (e. g. A. Harnack, F. C. Burkitt, A. Seitz, C. Willems, and still more recently L. Wohleb, RQ 1927, 151/69 and F. Dornseiff, AntW 1936, 143/55); while others (e. g., E. Schürer, E. Norden, P. Batiffol, P. Corssen etc.) hold that they are an interpolation of a later date by a Christian hand. Five fragments of an *old Russian translation* (eleventh-twelfth century) of *Josephus' Jewish Wars* (German transl. by A. Berendls and K. Grass, Dorpat 1924) contain accounts of Jesus' life and sufferings, which in spite of their defence by R. Eisler (vid. infra) and others, are undoubtedly spurious. (see the literature, especially Bienert). — Cfr. *J. Aufhauser*, Antike Jesuszeugnisse [2]1925; *A. Seitz*, Christus-zeugnisse aus dem klass. Altertum, 1906. — *H. L. Strack*, Jesus, die Häretiker und die Christen nach den ältesten jüd. Angaben 1910. — *F. Meffert*, Die geschichtl. Existenz Jesu [9-13]1921. — *C. Clemen*, Der geschichtl. Jesus, 1911. — *E. Klostermann*, Die neuesten Angriffe auf die Geschichtl. Jesu, 1912. — *K. Linck*, De antiquissimis veterum quae ad Jesum Nazarenum spectant testimoniis, 1913. — *J. Moreau*, Le plus anciens témoignages profanes sur Jésus, Brussels, 1944. — *M. Goguel*, HarvThR. 1926, 115/42 (against the myth theory) *M. J. Lagrange*, Rev. Bibl. 1932 5/30 (against Couchond). — J. R. Geiselmann ThQ 1949, 257/77 (*J. E. Kuhn* vs. *D. Strauß*). — For further literature see no. 1 above. — *R. Eisler*, Ιησοῦς βασιλεὺς οὐ βασιλεύσας, 2 vols. 1929/30. — Bibliotheca sacra 1—2, St. Louis 1930, 1/60. — Also F. Kampers, HJG 1925, 558/65. — H. Dieckmann, ZkTh 1926 463/75. — M. Goguel, Rev. Hist. 1929 II, 217/67. — M. J. Lagrange, Rev. Bibl. 1930, 29/46. — R. Draguet, RHE 1930, 833/79. — H. Vogels, Hochland 1930/31 I, 363/71. — W. Bauer ThLZ 1930, 557/63. — A. Goethala, Anti-Eisler, Brussels 1932. — F. Bickermann, Mél. Fr. Cumont, Brussels 1936. 53/84. — W. Bienert, Der "älteste nichtchristl. Jesusbericht" unter bes. Berücksichtigung des alt-russ. Josephus, 1936.

The correspondence of Prince *Abgar* of Edessa (cfr. § 12. 9) with Jesus, mentioned in Eusebius (H. E. I. 13) is certainly spurious. Cfr. E. V. Dob-schütz, Christusbilder, TU 18, 1899, 102 ff. — ZwTH 1900, 422 ff. — C. Picard, Bull. de correspondance hellénique 44, 1920, 41/69. — H. C. Youtie, HarvThR 1930, 299/302. — Apocryphal, too, are the report of *Pilate* to Emperor Tiberius on the death and resurrection of Jesus and the letter of *Lentulus* (the supposed predecessor of Pilate) to the Senate describing Jesus' physical features. — Cfr. Dobschütz, ZntW 1902, 29 ff. — Christusbilder 308 ff. — A daring forgery of more recent times is the so-called *letter of Benan* with accounts of Jesus and His disciples, which, according to the publisher or inventor, Ernest Edler von der Planitz (1910) is supposed to have been written by the Egyptian physician Benan in the year 83 A. D. — Cfr. C. Schmidt and H. Grapow in TU 44, 1, 1921.

## § 8.

## The Christian Community at Jerusalem
## and the Growth of the Church. The two Jameses[1].

The first community of believers in Jesus as the Messias and Son of God was formed at Jerusalem. During the forty days

[1] Catholic Commentaries and Monographs on the Acts of the Apostles: J. FELTEN, 1892; J. KNABENBAUER, 1899; J. BELSER, 1905; A. STEINMANN, [4]1934; E. JACQUIER, Paris 1926; A. WIKENHAUSER, 1938; see also the author's work, Die AG. u. ihr Geschichtswert, 1921. H. WIRTZ, 1942; A. TRICOT, Paris 1946. J. GEWIESS, Die urapostol. Heilsverkündigung nach der AG., 1939. — J. DUPONT, Les problèmes du Livre des Actes d'apres les praveaux récents, Louvain 1950. Protestant Commentaries: E. PREUSCHEN, 1912; G. HOENNICKE, 1913; TH. ZAHN, 2 vols. [3/4]1922/27; H. W. BEYER, [2]1935; F. J. FOAKES-JACKSON and K. LAKE, London 1933 (The Beginnings of Christianity I, 4—5); O. BAUERNFEIND, 1939; U. SMIT, 1941; W. L. KNOX, Cambridge 1948. K. BORNHÄUSER, Studien zur AG., 1934. Catholic Works on Christian Antiquity: J. DÖLLINGER, Christent. u. Kirche in der Zeit der Grundlegung, [2]1868. E. P. LE CAMUS, Origines du christianisme, 3 vol. Paris 1904/5. P. BATIFFOL, L'Église naissante et le catholicisme, Paris [6]1927; English tr. entitled: Primitive Christianity, by H. L. BRIANCEAU, New York 1911; German tr. by F. X. SEPPELT, 1910. A. DUFOURCQ, Hist. de la fondation de l'Église, 2 vol. Paris [6]1927/29. FR. MEFFERT, Das Urchristentum, apologet. Abhandlungen, 4 parts 1920 (popular). A. EHRHARD, Urchristentum u. Katholizismus, 1926. J. LEBRETON, La vie chrétienne au premier siècle de l'Église, Paris 1927. K. PIEPER, Jesus u. die Kirche, 1932; Die Kirche Palästinas bis zum J. 135, 1938. G. BARDY, L'Église à la fin du premier siècle, Paris 1932. E. PETERSON, Die Kirche aus Juden u. Heiden, 1933. L. KÖSTERS, Die Kirche unseres Glaubens, [3]1938. Theology of the New Testament: O. KUSS, [3]1938; M. MEINERTZ, 2 vols. 1950. N. ADLER, Das erste christl. Pfingstfest (Acts 2:1—13), 1938. Protestant Works: A. NEANDER, Gesch. der Pflanzung u. Leitung der christl. Kirche durch die Apostel, [5]1862. G. V. LECHLER, Das apost. u. nachapost. Zeitalter, [3]1885. E. RENAN, Hist. des origines du christianisme, 8 vols. Paris 1863/83, Vol. 1—4 in German 1866/73. K. WEIZSÄCKER, Das apost. Zeitalter, [3]1902. O. PFLEIDERER, Das Urchristentum, 2 vols. [2]1902; Die Entstehung des Christentums, [2]1907. E. V. DOBSCHÜTZ, Die urchristl. Gemeinden, 1902; Probleme des apost. Zeitalters, 1904; ZntW 1929, 107/18. G. HEINRICI, Das Urchristent. i. d. KG. d. Eusebius, 1902. P. WERNLE, Die Anfänge unserer Religion, 1904. CH. GUIGNEGERT, Manuel de l'hist. ancienne du christianisme, Paris 1906. E. DE FAYE, Étude sur les origines de l'Église de l'âge apostolique, Paris 1909. C. CLEMEN, Religionsgeschichtl. Erklärung des N.T., [3]1924. JOH. WEISS, Das Urchristentum, 2 parts 1913/17. H. WEINEL, Bibl. Theologie des N.T., [4]1928. Theology of the New Testament: P. FEINE, [8]1850; F. BÜCHSEL, [2]1937; E. STAUFFER, [4]1949; R. BULTMANN, 1948 ff. R. KNOPF, Einführung in das N.T., [4]1934. ED. MEYER, Ursprung u. Anfänge des Christentums III, 1923. H. TÖGEL, Die ersten Christen, [3]1928. F. C. BURKITT, Christian Beginnings, London 1924. J. V. BARTLET, The Apostolic Age, London 1926. AD. SCHLATTER, Gesch. der ersten Christenheit, [3/4]1927. F. J. FOAKES-JACKSON, The Rise of Gentile Christianity, London 1927. TH. ZAHN, Grundriß der neutest. Theologie, 1928; Grundriß der Gesch. des apostol. Zeitalters, 1929. W. MICHAELIS, Täufer, Jesus, Urgemeinde, 1928. R. FRICK, Gesch. des Reich-Gottes-Gedankens in der alten Kirche bis Origenes u. Augustin, 1928. F. KATTENBUSCH, Die Vorzugstellung des Petrus u. d. Charakter der Urgemeinde zu Jerusalem, Festgabe K. MÜLLER, 1922, 322/51. K. L. SCHMIDT, Die Kirche des Urchristentums, lexikograph. u. biblisch-theol.

that He remained on earth after His Resurrection, Christ instructed His disciples regarding the organization of the "Kingdom of God" which He had preached. He commanded them to remain in the Holy City until the "other Paraclete" (John 14:16) the Holy Ghost, would come upon them. Then, endowed with that power, they were to be witnesses to Him in Jerusalem, and in all Judea, and Samaria, and even to the uttermost parts of the earth (Acts 1:8). On the Jewish feast of the Harvest, the tenth day after Christ's Ascension, (*Pentecost*, II Mach. 12:32), the "promise of the Father" was fulfilled, after which, at Peter's suggestion, an election was held and *Matthias* was chosen to take the place of the traitor Judas so that the college of the "Twelve" was again complete. The descent of the Holy Ghost on the assembly of 120 persons was accompanied by extraordinary signs: a roaring wind, tongues of fire and speech in strange languages. *Peter*, who appears as head of the apostolic band and director of the primitive community, courageously and publicly preached Jesus crucified, the risen and exalted Lord of all. The result of this sermon was that on the same day 3 000 Jews declared their faith and were baptized (Acts 2). Thus with the first feast of Pentecost, the real *history of the Christian Church* begins: it was solemnly proclaimed to the whole world as the new, universal Messianic Kingdom, independent of the Synagogue, and endowed with the "Spirit of Truth" that would abide with it forever, (John 14:17).

Other conversions soon followed. The number of the faithful increased daily (Acts 2:47). After the cure of the man who had been lame from his mother's womb, the number reached 5 000 persons (Acts 4:4). The life of the young community was ideally beautiful: "The multitude of believers had but *one* heart and *one* soul; neither did any one say that aught of the things which

---

Studie, ²1932. G. KITTEL, Die Religionsgesch. u. das Urchristentum, 1932. E. LOHMEYER, Das Urchristentum I (John. the Baptist), 1932. C. SCHNEIDER, Einführung in die neutest. Zeitgesch., 1934. L. ALBRECHT, Die ersten fünfzehn Jahre der christl. Kirche, ²1935. O. DIBELIUS, Die werdende Kirche, Einführung in die AG., ⁴1941. K. WEISS, Urchristentum u. Geschichte in der neutest. Theologie seit der Jahrhundertwende, 1929. M. S. ENSLIN, Christian Beginnings, New York 1938. W. GRUNDMANN, ZntW 1939, 45/73 (Hellenic Christianity in the Community at Jerusalem); Christentum u. Judentum, 1940. R. ASTING, Die Verkündigung des Wortes im Urchristentum, 1939. W. FÖRSTER, Neutestamentl. Zeitgesch. I, 1940. M. GOGUEL, Jésus et les origines du christianisme II/III, Paris 1946/7. M. VEIT, Die Auffassung von der Person Jesu im Urchristent. 1946. G. JALLAND, The Origins and Evolution of the Christian Church, London 1950. Cfr. literature in § 5 and 6, § 9—12.

he possessed was his own ... and great grace was in them all" (Acts 4:32f.). The needy were generously aided by the brotherhood so that "all things were common unto them" (Acts 2:44; 4:32). Their life was a sort of religio-ethical communism based on pure charity, entirely without compulsion[1]. The distribution of alms and the general direction of the work of charity was at first left to the Twelve. But as the community continued to grow the task of "serving tables" (Acts 6:2) became so burdensome that the Apostles were not able to give themselves to the "ministry of the word." Hence, when the Hellenists, i. e., those born in foreign lands and those Jews who spoke Greek, (§ 6,2) complained that their widows were being neglected in the daily ministration, the Apostles suggested that seven men (deacons, § 18,1) be chosen to oversee the care of the poor. These seven, among whom were Stephen and Philip were brought before the Twelve who inducted them into their office by prayer and the imposition of hands. (Acts 6).

2. At first, the believers lived as Jews; they visited the Temple daily at the prescribed hours of prayer and observed the Mosaic law as they had previously done. But they also held their own religious services in private houses: "They were persevering in the doctrine of the Apostles, and in the communication of the breaking of bread and in prayers." (= the Eucharistic liturgy or the simple agape or both together?) (Acts 2:42). In spite of the "believers'" loyal observance of the Law, the Sanhedrin, the chief administrative and judicial authority of the Jews, could not look on indifferently as the numbers increased. Twice the Apostles were commanded to desist from preaching the name of Jesus; then they were arrested and scourged. But because of fear of popular sentiment and because the celebrated doctor of the law, Gamaliel, counselled prudence, no other action against them was taken for a time. But when *Stephen* spoke of the abrogation of the Law by Christ, he became the first martyr of the Church, being stoned by the Jews in the most brutal manner (in the year 32 or 33). This was the signal for a bitter persecution of the community, especially of the Hellen-

---

[1] F. X. KIEFL, Die Theorie des modernen Sozialismus über den Ursprung des Christentums, 1915. A. STEINMANN, Jesus u. die soziale Not der Gegenwart, [2]1925. E. LOHMEYER, Soziale Fragen im Urchristentum, 1921. A. BIGELMAIR, Festgabe A. EHRHARD, 1922, 73/93. S. J. CASE, The Social Origins of Christianity, Oxford 1924. J. JEREMIAS, Jerusalem zur Zeit Jesu II, 1924/37. R. SCHUMACHER, Die soziale Lage der Christen im apostol. Zeitalter, 1925. I. ROHR, Die soziale Frage im N.T., 1930 (Bibl. Zeitfr. XIII, 5/6).

ists; many fled to the country districts of Judea and Samaria; but the Apostles remained in the city. (Acts 3—8).

The dispersion of the believers contributed to the spread of the faith, for they "went about preaching the word of God." (Acts 8:4). The "Evangelist" *Philip*, one of the seven, preached in *Samaria*. The inhabitants of this district, like the Jews, were monotheists and looked for the coming of the Messias; but they retained nothing else of Jewish religion or practices and were despised by the Jews as a mixed race. When the news of Philip's success reached Jerusalem, Peter and John went to Samaria to impose hands on those who had been baptized and to confer on them the Holy Ghost. The "first-born of the pagan world" (Eusebius H. E. II, 1, 3) was the *Eunuch* of Candace, Queen of the Ethiopians, baptized by Philip. (Acts 8:26 ff.). He was followed by another God-fearing man, the centurion *Cornelius*, who was received into the Church by Peter without being obliged to comply with the Jewish law. The doubts which the Apostles had entertained about such immediate reception of pagans, were resolved by a series of miracles. (Acts 10—11). In **Antioch**[1], the capital of Syria, there arose a community consisting chiefly of Gentile Christians, the direction of which was committed by the Apostles to the Levite *Barnabas*, a native of Cyprus. It was here that the pagans began to call the followers of Christ χριστιανοί, *Christians* (Acts 11:26). The Jews usually referred to them as *Galileans* or Nazarenes (Acts 1:11; 24:5); while they themselves used such terms as brethren, saints, faithful, disciples of the Lord and the like (Acts 1:15; 6:1,2,7; Rom. 1:7; Eph. 1:1 etc.).

3. After a short time Christian blood flowed again in Jerusalem. In order to conciliate the Jews, Herod Agrippa permitted the execution of the Apostle **James the Elder**, a brother of John. *Peter*, for whom the same fate had been planned, escaped the hands of Herod by a miraculous liberation from prison. This happened during the Paschal season (Acts 12:3) of the year 42 or 43; for Herod died soon thereafter and his death occurred in the year 44. About this time, according to ancient tradition, the Apostles set out on their missionary journeys. **James the Younger**[2], son of

---

[1] K. BAUER, Antiochia in der ältesten KG., 1919. H. DIECKMANN, Antiochien, ein Mittelpunkt der urchristl. Missionstätigkeit, 1920. E. PETERSON, Misc. G. Mercati I, Rom 1946, 355/72 (Christianus). cfr. § 12, 9.
[2] M. MEINERTZ, Der Jakobusbrief u. sein Verfasser, 1905. FR. MAIER, Bibl. Z. 1906, 164 ff. 255 ff. FR. HAUCK, Der Brief des Jakobus, 1926.

Alpheus (Mt. 10:3) who, in all probability, is the same as the Apostle James, "brother of the Lord" (Gal. 1:19) remained in Jerusalem as director of the first community and head of the sacerdotal college there. In the second century, the Jewish Christian, Hegesippus (quoted in Eusebius H. E. II, 1. 23) expressly mentions him as *bishop* of Jerusalem. He was highly esteemed by the other Apostles and Paul calls him one of the "pillars" of the church of Jerusalem. (Gal. 2:9). It was James who suggested the method for settling the difficulty at the Council of Jerusalem (cfr. § 9,2). Because of his strict ascetical life and his unswerving adherence to the Law, he was surnamed the *"Just."* The canon of the New Testament contains his splendid encyclical "to the twelve tribes in the diaspora" i. e., to the Jewish Christians scattered throughout the pagan world. But he himself finally fell a victim to Jewish fanaticism; the high priest Annas (Ananus) had him stoned to death in the year 62 or 63 (Flavius Josephus, Antiq. XX 9.1; the account of Hegesippus in Euseb. H. E. II 23 is slightly different.).

## § 9.
### Paul, the Apostle of the Gentiles[1].
### The Dispute at Antioch.

1. The great Apostle of the ancient Church and the most remarkable character of all those who were chosen to spread the Kingdom

H. LECLERCQ, Jacques le Mineur, DictAC VII, 2109/16.  G. KITTEL, ZntW 1931, 145/57; 1942, 71/105.  K. PIEPER, ThGl 1936, 661/78.  E.THURNEYSEN, Der Brief des Jakobus, 1941.  K. ALAND, ThLZ 1944, 97/104.
   [1] Catholic Monographs on St. Paul: C. FOUARD, 2 vol. Paris [12]1925; F. X. PÖLZL, 1905; F. PRAT, Paris [4]1922; A. TRICOT, ibid. 1928; J. HOLZNER, [22]1949.  E. B. ALLO, Paris 1942, German tr. by E. KAMNITZER, 1946. A. PENNA, Alba 1945.  G. RICCIOTTI, Rome 1946.  P. DE AMBROGGI, Rovigo 1949. H. LECLERCQ, S. Paul, DictAC XIII, 2568/2699.  L. VOUZUX, Les actes de Paul et ses lettres apocryphes, Paris 1913. Πράξεις Παύλου, Acta Pauli, ed. C. SCHMIDT, 1936 (see also A. KURFESS, ZntW 1939, 164/70).  F. PRAT, La théologie de S. Paul, 2 vol. Paris [20]1937.  E. MOSKE, Die Bekehrung des hl. Paulus, 1907.  K. BENZ, Die Ethik des Ap. Paulus, 1912.  B. BARTMANN, Paulus, die Grundzüge s. Lehre, 1914; Paulus als Seelsorger, 1921.  K. PIEPER, Die Missionspredigt des hl. Paulus, 1921; Paulus, s. missionarische Persönlichkeit u. Wirksamkeit, [2/3]1929; Paulus u. die Kirche, 1932.  L. MURILLO, Paulus et Pauli scripta I, Romae 1926.  A. STEINMANN, Der Werdegang des Paulus, 1928.  L. TONDELLI, Il pensiero di S. Paolo, Milano 1928.  A. WIKENHAUSER, Die Christusmystik des hl. Paulus, 1928. (Bibl. Zeitfr. XII, 8/10); Die Kirche als der mystische Leib Christi nach dem Ap. Paulus, [2]1940.  W. KÖSTER, Die Idee der Kirche beim hl. P., 1929.  E. PRUCKER, Γνῶσις Θεοῦ bei P., 1937. J. DUPONT, Gnosis. La connaissance religieuse dans les épîtres de St. Paul, Louvain 1949.  F. AMIOT, L'enseignement de S. Paul, 2 vol. Paris [4]1946. Protestant Works on St. Paul: C. CLEMEN, 2 vols. 1904; H. WEINEL, [2]1915; F. FARRAR, 2 vol. London 1904, German tr. by RUPPRECHT u. BRANDNER,

of Christ was *Saul*, a native of Tarsus and a scion of the tribe of Benjamin. After the conversion of the proconsul, Sergius Paulus of Cyprus, all Scriptural references to Saul use the Roman form of the name, *Paul* (Acts 13:9). As a youth he had familiarized himself with Hellenic culture and later had become a doctor of the law in the school of Gamaliel at Jerusalem. His zeal for the law made him a participant in the martyrdom of Stephen and led him to persecute the disciples, — even those dwelling outside the city. He was suddenly converted by an apparition of Christ while on his way to Damascus. This happened about the year 33, seventeen years before the Council of Jerusalem (Gal. 1:18; 2:1). After being baptized by Ananias, Paul was eager to begin preaching the new

---

3 vols. 1905/8; E. VISCHER, 1921; AD. DEISSMANN, ²1925; E. DE FAYE, Paris ²1913; F. J. FOAKES-JACKSON, London 1927, 1933; A. LICHTENHAN, 1928; K. LAKE, London 1934; E. RENAN (Paulus, German tr. and commentary by E. FRANZEN), 1935; A. P. CHRISTLIEB, 1936; A. D. NOCK, London 1938, German tr. by H. H. SCHAEDER, 1940; T. R. GLOVER, ib. 1938; W. V. LOEWENICH, ²1949; E. J. GOODSPEED, Philadelphia ²1947; M. DIBELIUS, ²1951. A. SCHWEITZER, Gesch. der paulin. Forschung, ²1933; Die Mystik des Ap. P., 1930. A. JUNCKER, Die Ethik des Ap. Paulus, 2 vols. 1904/20. W. M. RAMSAY, St. Paul the Traveller and the Roman Citizen, London ⁷1905, (German tr. by H. GROSCHKE: P. in der AG., 1898); The Cities of St. Paul, London 1907. R. KNOPF, Probleme der Paulusforschung, 1913. H. BÖHLIG, Die Geisteskultur in Tarsos, 1913. B. WEISS, P. u. seine Gemeinden, 1914. A. OEPKE, Die Missionspredigt des Ap. Paulus, 1920. L. BRUN u. A. FRIDRICHSEN, P. u. die Urgemeinde, 1921. K. HOLL, Der Kirchenbegriff des Paulus, Sb. Berlin 1921, 920/47, also in Ges. Aufsätze zur KG. II, 1928, 44/67. K. DEISSNER, Paulus u. die Mystik 3. Zeit, ²1921. W. MUNDLE, Das religiöse Leben des Ap. Paulus, 1923; Der Glaubensbegriff des Paulus, 1932. H. LEISEGANG, Der Ap. Paulus als Denker, 1923. W. L. KNOX, St. Paul and the Church of Jerusalem, Cambridge 1925; St. Paul and the Church of the Gentiles, London 1939. J. WAGENMANN, Die Stellung des Paulus neben den Zwölf in den ersten 2 Jhh., 1926. E. V. DOBSCHÜTZ, Der Ap. Paulus (his importance in world history and in art), 2 parts 1926/28. P. FEINE, Der Ap. Paulus, das Ringen um das geschichtl. Verständnis des P., 1927. TH. WILSON, St. Paul and Paganism, Edinburgh 1928. JUL. RICHTER, Die Briefe des Ap. Paulus als missionarische Sendschreiben, 1929. JOH. SCHNEIDER, Die Passionsmystik des Paulus, 1929. E. LOHMEYER, Grundlagen paulinischer Theologie, 1929. O. KIETZIG, Die Bekehrung des Paulus, 1932. H. WINDISCH, Paulus u. Christus, biblisch-religionsgesch. Vergleich, 1934; Paulus u. das Judentum, 1935. W. SCHMAUCH, In Christus. Eine Untersuchung zur Sprache u. Theologie des Paulus, 1935. J. LEIPOLDT, Jesus u. Paulus — Jesus oder Paulus, 1936. G. HARDER, Paulus u. das Gebet, 1936. M. SCHLUNK, Paulus als Missionar, 1937. W. STRAUB, Die Bildersprache des Ap. Paulus, 1937. E. ALEITH, Das Paulusverständnis der alten Kirche, 1937. M. DIBELIUS, Paulus auf dem Areopag, Sb. Heidelberg 1938/39, 2. A. RÖDER, Die Geschichtstheologie des Ap. Paulus, 1938. W. D. DAVIES, Paul and Rabbinic Iudaism, London 1948. J. KLAUSNER, Von Jesus zu Paulus, 1950. F. X. PÖLZL, Die Mitarbeiter des Weltapostels Paulus, 1911. R. SCHUMACHER, Der Alexandriner Apollos, 1916; Aquila u. Priscilla, ThGl 1920, 86/99. A. STEGMANN, Silvanus, 1917. J. CLADDER u. H. DIECKMANN, Korinth, die Kirche des hl. Paulus, 1923. Cfr. literature in § 8.

doctrine; but upon the advice of his newly-found friends, he retired to the Arabian desert where he prepared himself for his apostolic career. Three years later, he returned to Damascus; but, obliged to flee from the Jews, he went to Jerusalem. There he remained for fifteen days with Peter and James the Younger, the only Apostles he found in the city, (Gal. 1:18 f.) and continued on to Tarsus. Finally, accepting the invitation of Barnabas, he went to *Antioch* (42 or 43), where his work in the vineyard of the Lord properly began.

But Paul's activity was not confined to this one city. He had been called by the Lord to "carry his name before the Gentiles, and kings, and the children of Israel" (Acts 9:15). "As a debtor to the Greeks and to the barbarians, to the wise and to the unwise," Paul, encompassed by needs and perils, tirelessly traversed countries from Syria to Spain, "as far as the olive grows." (Deissmann). He perceived that it was his life's work to free the Church of Christ from the narrowness of Judaism and from the confines of Palestine and to make it truly universal. He dedicated all the faculties of his great soul to a systematic mission which led him first to the populous cities around the Mediterranean, the focal point of commerce and Hellenic culture. His ultimate aim was to carry his message to Rome, the capital of the world and even to Spain. (Acts 19:21; Rom. 15:24,28). Such success attended his efforts that he could say he had labored more abundantly than all the other Apostles. (1 Cor. 15:10). Recognizing the "right of the firstborn," he turned first of all to the Jews, his "kinsmen according to the flesh" (Rom 9:3); but when he found them stiff-necked, he went to the *pagans* and was phenomenally successful in gaining them to the Church. His "Gospel" — not the work of man, but the revelation of Jesus Christ (Gal. 1:6—13) consisted chiefly in stressing the doctrine of salvation for all men through faith in Christ, without circumcision or other works of the Law. In writing his numerous Epistles, Paul became the founder of Christian *theology.*

2. Paul's *first mission journey,* occupying the years 45 to 48, led him to *Cyprus,* where he converted the proconsul Sergius Paulus, and passed on to *Asia Minor.* Here he preached at Perge in Pamphylia, at Antioch of Pisidia, at Iconium, Lystra and Derbe of Lycaonia. *Barnabas* had been appointed to assist him and, for a time, he was also accompanied by John *Mark* (Acts 13 and 14).

## § 9. St. Paul and the Dispute at Antioch.

A series of remarkable events soon paved the way for the final separation of the Church from the Synagogue. Brethren from Palestine came into the community at *Antioch* insisting that converts from paganism in order to be saved must submit to circumcision and all the other observances of the Old Law. Such unreasonable demands threatened the liberty of the *pagan converts* and a *spirited controversy* arose[1]. It was decided to send Paul and Barnabas to resolve the question before the congregation at *Jerusalem*. The Apostles met in conference with the "Elders." The **Council of Jerusalem** (in the year 49 or 50) as this meeting is usually called, decided, in the main, against such demands and the "pillars" (James the Younger, Peter and John) approved Paul's mission to the Gentiles no longer fettered by the Old Law. However, in order to facilitate the fusion of pagans and Jews into *one* Church, the so-called *Apostolic Decree* demanded that the pagan converts abstain from certain things particularly obnoxius to Jews, namely, "things sacrificed to idols, and from blood, and from things strangled, and from fornication." (Acts 15:28 f.).

Soon after the Council of Jerusalem[2] even the Jewish converts residing outside of Palestine were also freed from the yoke of the Law. At *Antioch*, the metropolis of the pagan converts, where Jewish observances did not oblige under penalties as in Palestine, the converts from Judaism began very early to abandon Jewish practices. Even *Peter*, disregarding the dietary laws, ate with the brethren from the pagan world; as Paul expressed it, he lived "after the manner of the Gentiles." (ἐθνικῶς) (Gal. 2:14). But his action was motivated rather by a kind consideration of the brethren than by a clear understanding of the situation. For when brethren from Judea were scandalized, he ceased to associate on such friendly terms with the pagan converts and his example was followed by Barnabas and other Jewish Christians. But this attitude, interpreted as a slight to the pagan converts or as a means of morally

---

[1] K. SIX, Das Aposteldekret, 1911. R. STEINMETZ, Bibl. Zeit- u. Streitfragen VII, 5, 1911. H. GROSCH, Der Gal. 2, 11—14 berichtete Vorgang in Antiochia, 1916. W. LÜTGERT, Gesetz u. Geist, 1919. K. BÖCKENHOFF, Das apostol. Speisegesetz in den ersten 5 Jhh., 1903. H. WAITZ, ZKG 1936, 227/63 (The Apostolic decree). M. DIBELIUS, ThLZ 1947, 193/7 (Council of Jerusalem).

[2] Following St. Augustine (Cfr. Jerome, Ep. 116, 11), some modern scholars (T. ZAHN, V. WEBER, J. BELSER) hold that the dissension between Peter and Paul took place at Antioch; and that the Epistle to the Galatians was written before the Council of Jerusalem. However, the evidence does not support such an opinion.

forcing them to live after the manner of the Jews, was a serious obstacle to Paul's work and led to the eventual solution of the problem. *Paul* "withstood Peter to the face" (Gal. 2:11), and the defense of his position before the assembled congregation had the desired result. For, although Paul was often obliged later to combat the efforts of Judaizers, especially in Galatia and Corinth, the idea that the Church was totally independent of the Synagogue was never again seriously questioned. The *destruction of Jerusalem* by Titus in the year 70 completed the separation. "When there was no longer an earthly Jerusalem, the Christian ideal of the future Church was of a Church universal" (Mommsen). Jewish converts constituted a minority and a considerable number of them withdrew to themselves and became heretical (§ 28).

3. After the incident at Antioch, Paul started on his *second great* mission tour among the pagans (in the year 50 (49)—52). He was accompanied by *Silas* (Silvanus), and later by *Timothy* and *Luke*, while Barnabas, influenced by his nephew John Mark, separated from Paul and the two kinsmen sailed to Cyprus. The Apostle first visited the congregations in Lycaonia and Pisidia and then passed through Phrygia, Galatia and Mysia (Moesia). From Troas, he went to *Macedonia* and *Greece*, and worked at Philippi, Thessalonica, Beroea and in Athens, where his sermons before the Areopagus converted the judge Dionysius and a few others. He then preached with great success for a year and a half in the populous and wealthy city of *Corinth*, where he was entertained by *Aquila* and his wife *Priscilla*, Jewish Christians who had been expelled from Rome during the Claudian persecution. Somewhat later the Jewish convert *Apollo* (Apollonius), an eloquent and learned native of Alexandria began to preach at Corinth. *Gallio*, proconsul of Achaia and brother of the philosopher Seneca, refused to press the charges which the Jews made against Paul. A recently discovered Delphic inscription definitely fixes the date of Gallio's term of office at Corinth from 51 to 52 A.D. On his return trip to Antioch, Paul passed through Ephesus and Jerusalem (Acts 15:35—18:22).

A third journey, undertaken soon thereafter, may be assigned, approximately to the years 53 to 58. After visiting the congregation in Galatia and Phrygia, Paul remained at *Ephesus* for two years and a half. The disturbance incited by the silversmith Demetrius because the spread of Christianity interfered with the sale of miniature silver temples in honor of the goddess Diana, forced Paul to leave. He went to Troas, *Macedonia* and *Greece* (Corinth) and probably also to Illyricum (Rom. 15:19). And all the while he was busy promoting the cause of the Gospel by writing a series of Epistles; at this time, the ones to the Corinthians, the Romans and the Galatians (Acts 18:23—21:15).

4. Paul's return to *Jerusalem* in the year 58 to bring the alms he had collected, marked the end of his travel for a long time. The hatred of the Jews was aroused against the "renegade" to such a degree that the tribune, Lysias, was obliged to intervene and, to save Paul's life, sent him to the procurator Felix at *Caesarea*. Felix kept him in custody for two years (58—60 A.D.). When Paul, insisting on his rights as a Roman citizen, appealed to the emperor, Felix's successor, Festus, sent him to *Rome* for further examination (60 A.D.). After a perilous voyage, including shipwreck near Malta, Paul reached Rome in the spring of the year 61. His detention in the capital city did not, however, prevent contact with the outside world; for two years he lived in his own hired lodging where he received all who came to him "without prohibition" and preached to them the Kingdom of God (Acts 21 to 28). The Acts of the Apostles closes with an unfinished description of this house-arrest. It has been and still is supposed by many that the Apostle remained a prisoner until his death by martyrdom in the persecution of Nero in the year 64. But it is more probable that his trial resulted in acquittal and that he then made the trip to *Spain* which he had previously planned[1]. The Muratorian Fragment (§ 38) speaks very definitely of a "profectio Pauli ab urbe ad Spaniam proficiscentis"; and the words of Clement of Rome (§ 37) in his Epistle to the Corinthians 5, 7, (written ca. 96), in which he speaks of the Apostle as the herald of the Gospel "as far as the extremity of the West," (ἐπὶ τὸ τέρμα τῆς δύσεως), are to be understood in this same sense. Moreover, Paul's pastoral Epistles (I and II Tim. and Titus), compared with the Epistles to the Philippians, the Ephesians and the Colossians, imply a second and far more rigorous imprisonment in Rome. This ended with the Apostle's execution by the sword

---

[1] R. STEINMETZ, Die 2. röm. Gefangensch. des Apostels Paulus, 1897. J. FREY, Die letzten Lebensjahre des P., 1910. F. DUBOWY, Klemens von Rom u. die Reise nach Spanien, 1914. E. SAVOI, CivCatt 1914, I, 424 ff. 560 ff. H. LIETZMANN, Petrus u. Paulus in Rom, [2]1927. JOS. SCHMID, Zeit u. Ort der paulin. Gefangenschaftsbriefe, 1921. A. ST. BARNES, The Martyrdom of St. Peter and St. Paul, Oxford, 1933 (also, DELEHAYE, AB 1934, 69/72). O. MARUCCHI, Pietro e Paolo a Roma, Torino, [4]1934. G. CELI CivCatt 1935 II, 247 ff.; III, 167 ff.; IV, 116 ff.; 1936 I, 129 ff.

probably in the year 67 (June 29?). His tomb is in the beautiful basilica of Saint Paul-outside-the-walls on the Via Ostia (testimony of the Roman priest Gaius (§ 10, 2 f.); the place of execution is pointed out on the nearby estate called Tre Fontane, now a Trappist Abbey.

The *chronology* of the main events in St. Paul's life is disputed. The point at which the reckoning usually begins, is Paul's departure for Rome, or the appointment of Festus to succeed Felix as procurator of Palestine (Acts 24:27). Most modern scholars, for good reasons, place that event in the year 60. Others, however, especially A. von Harnack and E. Schwartz prefer the year 56 (55) and the year 54 (53) as the date of Paul's arrest. In this case all the other events of his life would have to be dated four to five years earlier. But the inscription referring to Gallio (mentioned above, No. 3) certainly favors the year 60. Harnack (Berlin, 1912, 673/82) places Paul's conversion in the autumn of 31 or 30. Cfr. *G. Hoennicke*, Chronologie des Lebens des Apostels Paulus, 1903; *F. Stober*, Chronologie des Lebens und der Briefe Pauli, 1904. — F. J. Goodwin, A Harmony of the Life of St. Paul, London ³1950. — *F. X. Kugler*, Von Moses bis Paulus, 1922, 423 ff. — *O. Gerhardt*, NkZ 1922, 89/114. — *A. Deissmann*, Paulus, ²1925, 203 ff. — G. Hölscher, cfr. sup. § 7, 1. For the year of Paul's death, cfr. *O. Procksch*, Luthertum, 1936, 225/38; H. Katzenmayer, IntKZ 1940, 38/48.

## § 10.
### The Apostle Peter and His Martyrdom at Rome[1].

1. Far scantier than in the case of St. Paul is the information we possess regarding the Apostle whom the Lord made the firm foundation of His Church and the keeper of its keys — the fiery, impulsive *Simon Peter* (Matt. 16:18 f.; John 21:15 ff.). The Acts of the Apostles (1 to 11) relate only his activities in Jerusalem and Palestine during the first years after Christ's ascension: the sermon on Pentecost, the cure of the lame man at the gate of the temple,

---

[1] Monographs on St. Petri: by C. FOUARD (Catholic), Paris ¹1905, German tr. 1910; L. C. FILLION (Catholic), Paris ²1906; F. SIEFFERT, RE XV, 156/212; F. X. STEINMETZER, 1917 (Bibl. Zeitfr. VI, 3); W. BRANDT, ¹1939; F. J. FOAKES-JACKSON, London 1927; U. HOLZMEISTER (Vita S. Petri Ap., Paris 1936 = Introduction to Cursus Scripturae Sacrae III, 13, 1, 1937). TRICOT, DictThC XII, 1747/92; F. UNDERHILL, London 1938; W. T. WALSH, ibid. 1949; R. AIGRAIN, Paris 1938; E. FASCHER, RE Pauly-Wissowa XIX, 1335/61. A. T. ROBERTSON, Epochs in the Life of Simon Peter, New York 1933. W. ELERT, Die Religiosität des P., 1911. A. HARNACK u. F. KATTENBUSCH in Festgabe K. Müller, 1922, 1 ff. 322 ff. K. G. GOETZ, Petrus als Gründer u. Oberhaupt der Kirche u. Schauer von Gesichten, 1927. L. VOUZUX, Les Actes de Pierre, Paris 1922; cfr. C. SCHMIDT, ZKG 1924, 321/48; 1926, 481/513. G. STUHLFAUTH, Die apokryphen Petrusgeschichten in der altchristl. Kunst, 1925. L. VAGANAY, L'Évangile de Pierre, Paris 1930. E. DINKLER, Die ersten Petrusdarstellungen, 1937. C. CECCHELLI, Iconografia dei Papi I: S. Pietro, Rome 1938.

two occasions when he was imprisoned and his work in Samaria and Judea. From the beginning, as we saw above (§ 8,1), Peter always appears as the head of the primitive community. The author of the Acts does not say where he went after his miraculous release from the prison into which Herod Agrippa had cast him; but merely adds "he went to another place" (12:17 ἐπορεύϑη εἰς ἕτερον τόπον). Tradition, however, has always considered him the founder of the episcopal see of *Antioch* (Origen, Eusebius); so it is probable that he went to Syria first. There is also a strong probability that during the reign of Emperor Claudius (41—54) or at the beginning of Nero's reign (54—68) he went to *Rome*, where a fairly large Christian community consisting of Jewish and pagan converts had been formed at an early date. He was again in Jerusalem for the Council in the year 50 and appears at Antioch soon thereafter when he and Paul adjusted their differences. The mention of a party of Cephas among the divisions of the Church of *Corinth* (1 Cor. 1:12) suggests the possibility of a brief sojourn in that place: and John 21:18 f. alludes to his martyrdom. According to the testimony of the Roman priest Gaius, Rome was certainly the place of his *death* and *burial*, more exactly, the foot of the Vatican Hill, where under Constantine the Great, a church was erected in his honor and where today stands the great basilica of St. Peter with the resting place (Confessio) of the Prince of the Apostles. According to Origen (in Eusebius III, 1) and the apocryphal Acts of Peter (second or third century), Peter met his death by crucifixion and, at his own request, with his head down. The date of his death falls between the years 64 and 67.

2. A tradition traceable to the fourth century (Catalogue of the Popes, 354, Jerome), holds that Peter *resided in Rome* for 25 years, without implying that the sojourn was uninterrupted. At any rate it is historically certain that Peter exercised his supreme apostolic power in the capital of the Empire and that he met death there during the persecution of Nero[1]. A former hypothesis, aimed at

---

[1] M. LECLER, De Romano S. Petri episcopatu, Dissertation Louvain 1888. J. B. LIGHTFOOT, St. Clement of Rome, London 1890, I, 201/345; II, 481/502. JOH. SCHMID, Petrus in Rom, 1892. W. ESSER, Des hl. Petrus Aufenthalt, Episkopat u. Tod zu Rom, ³1897. C. A. KNELLER, Petrus, Bischof v. Rom, ZkTh 1902, 33 ff. 225 ff. 351 ff. (opposes Erbes). H. LIETZMANN, Petrus u. Paulus in Rom ²1927. J. FLAMION, RHE 1913, 249 ff. 473 ff. (opposes Guignebert). E. BÖMINGHAUS, StZ 95, 1918, 251/67 (opposes A. Bauer). E. VACANDARD, Études de critique et d'hist. relig. IV, Paris 1923. M. BESSON, S. Pierre et les origines de la Primauté Romaine, Genf 1929. H. KATZEN-

disproving these facts was inspired by sectarian bias. It has now been entirely abandoned by all serious historians. The concluding words of the first Epistle of St. Peter (5:13) indicate clearly enough the residence of the writer. Expositors have proved beyond doubt that "Babylon" must refer to Rome, the only city so designated in ancient Christian literature. Furthermore, the *unanimous tradition* of Christian antiquity both East and West furnishes incontrovertible evidence. A series of noted and trustworthy writers of the first two centuries bear ample witness to the facts.

a) *Clement of Rome* (§ 37, 3) writing about the year 96, just a generation after the events, says in his Epistle to the Corinthians (c. 5—6) that Peter and Paul were victims together of jealousy and strife; that they fought to the death and gave testimony before the authorities (μαρτυρεῖν = to confess Christ before a judge who imposes the death penalty), and so departed for the place of glory. Since the writer connects the Apostles so closely with the victims of the persecution under *Nero*, which he proceeds to mention immediately (6, 1), it is clear that he believed both of them had died in Rome.

b) *St. Ignatius the Martyr*, Bishop of Antioch (§ 37, 4), was aware of a special bond of St. Peter with Rome; for he says in his Epistle to the Romans (4, 3), written about 110: "I do not command you as did Peter and Paul," (οὐχ ὡς Πέτρος καὶ Παῦλος διατάσσομαι ὑμῖν). Now tradition knows nothing of any written communication from St. Peter to the Romans; hence Ignatius must refer to oral commands.

c) *Clement of Alexandria* in speaking of the origin of the second Gospel (in Eusebius II, 15; VI, 14) says that *Mark*, who was Peter's interpreter, was requested by the *Romans* to put in writing the instructions Peter gave them. This testimony dating from the early third century agrees so perfectly with the narrative of *Papias* (§ 37, 6), a disciple of St. John[2], it may safely be traced to a tradition of the earliest days of the Church.

d) Bishop *Dionysius of Corinth* writing to the Romans about the year 170, says that Peter and Paul died the death of martyrs at Rome "about the same time" (κατὰ τὸν αὐτὸν καιρόν), (Eusebius II, 25).

e) *Irenaeus of Lyons*, writing between the years 180—190, speaks of the foundation of the Roman Church by the glorious Apostles Peter and Paul

---

MAYER, IntkZ 1938, 129/40; 1939, 85/93 (Peter in Rome and the date of his death). L. HERRMANN, Latomus 1946, 303/10 (first sojourns of Peter in Rome). A. ST. BARNES u. O. MARUCCHI, cfr. § 9, 4. The Petrine tradition challenged by CH. GUIGNEBERT, Rev. Hist. 168, 1931, 225/53; H. DANNENBAUER, HZ 146, 1932, 239/62 (see opposite view of Krüger, ZntW 1932, 301/6) u. HZ 159, 1939, 81/88; J. HALLER, Das Papsttum I, 1934, 11 ff. 443 ff.; K. HEUSSI, War Petrus in Rom? 1936; War Petrus wirklich röm. Martyrer? 1937; Neues zur Petrusfrage, 1939 — adding no new or convincing argument Cfr. opposite opinion of H. LIETZMANN, Petrus röm. Martyrer, Sb. Berlin 1936, 29; B. ALTANER, ThRev 1937, 177/88; 1939, 365/6; HJG 1949, 25/30; E. MOLLAND, ThLZ 1937, 439/44; H. G. OPITZ, ThLZ 1940, 24/6.

[2] The only difference being that the narrative of PAPIAS (found in Eusebius III, 30), does not expressly mention Rome.

(Adv. haer. III, 3, 2, 3) and adds a list of Roman bishops from Peter to his own day, a list which is considered reliable. (Cfr. § 21, 1).

f) The Roman priest *Gaius* (about 200) declares most emphatically that it was still possible to point out the τρόπαια = signs of victory, i. e., the burial places of the two Apostles in Rome: the grave of Peter on the Vatican and that of Paul on the road toward Ostia (Eusebius II, 25). Cfr. A. Zisterer, ThQ 1892, 121/32; K. Erbes, TU 19, 1 (1899) and ZKG 1924, 38/92; H. Lietzmann, (vide supra) 209 ff.

g) *Tertullian*, writing about the same time, speaks of Peter's work and death in Rome (De praescriptione 32. 36; Scorpiace 15).

3. To this evidence found in the literature of antiquity may be added *archeological* proofs. In 1626 when work was in progress on the foundation for the great dome of St. Peter's, old pagan burial places which had been in use as late as the third century, were discovered quite near the spot always believed to be the site of St. Peter's grave. Excavations in the large Grotte Vaticane undertaken in 1840 resulted in the discovery of the circus of Nero nearby and the exact location of the basilica of Constantine. In spite of technological and psychological difficulties, Constantine had built his church on the slope of the Vatican Hill in the center of a graveyard because he wished the grave of Peter to form the center of the apse of the new church. Fragments of pre-Constantinian monuments with inscriptions (invocations of St. Peter) were also found. In later years, when Christians had their own cemeteries in Rome, and when reliable tradition had been forgotten, the Christians no longer looked for the grave of *St. Peter* in the place where Gaius had pointed it out about the year 200. The burial place of St. Paul on the road to Ostia was also forgotten. The Depositio Martyrum in the Chronograph of Philocalus of the year 354 (cfr. the Martyrologium Hieronymianum) speaks of a local commemoration service in honor of Peter and Paul on June 29th in the Church of *San Sebastiano* ad Catacumbas on the Via Appia outside of Rome. In ancient times this church was called the Basilica or Memoria Apostolorum. An inscription of Pope Damasus († 384) in the same church says that both Apostles "dwelt" there (habitare); but whether this means that they resided there for a time or were buried there is not clear. During excavations in San Sebastiano which began in 1915, an assembly room (Triclia) was discovered containing numerous inscriptions (graffiti) invoking both Apostles. The graffiti had been placed there by those who had held a memorial banquet (refrigerium) in the Apostles' honor. Attempts have been made to explain this by assuming that for safety sake the remains of the Apostles were hidden in the catacombs of San Sebastiano during the Valerian persecution (258) and that later on when the Church attained freedom under Constantine the Great (312) they were returned to their original burial places where the great basilicas now stand. But there are other scholars (Delehaye, Kirsch, Kalsbach) who maintain that it would have been scarcely possible to transfer the remains of the dead in Rome in those days. — Cfr. *Lietzmann, Barnes* and *Marrucchi* (§ 9, 4). — *J. P. Kirsch*, RQ 30, 1916/22, 5/28; JbLW 3, 1923, 33/50; 4, 1924, 294/97. — *P. Styger*, ZkTh 1921, 549/72; Die röm. Katakomben, 1933, 331/51. — *L. Duchesne*, Atti della Pontif. Academia Romana di Archeologia, Memorie I, 1, Rome, 1923 1/22. — *A. Kalsbach*, RQ 1927, 247/57. — *H. Delehaye*, AB 1927,

297/310; Mél. P. Thomas, Paris 1930, 201/7. — *A. Prandi*, La Memoria Apostolorum in Catacumbus I, Rome 1936. — *F. Toletti*, RivArchChrist 1947/48, 13/116 (On the Memoria Ap.). — *G. Belvedere*, Le tombe apostoliche nell'età paleo-cristiana, Rome 1948. For the recent excavations in St. Peter's cfr. Acta Ap. Sedis 1942, 162 f. — *N. M.-D. Boulet*, RechSR 1947, 385/406; — *E. Kirschbaum*, Gregorianum 1948, 544/557.

## § 11.
### John[1] and the Other Apostles.

1. John, the son of Zebedee and brother of James the Elder, was the youngest of the Apostles and the favorite disciple of the Lord. On several occasions, we find him occupying a place of importance together with Peter: at the cure of the man born lame, in the presence of the Sanhedrin, and on the mission to Samaria. He was in *Jerusalem* during the Council of the Apostles (ca. 49/50) together with Peter and James the Younger and was looked upon as a "pillar" of the infant Church (Gal. 2:9). Most probably he remained in the Holy City until after the death of Jesus' Mother, who had been committed to his care[2]. A statement ascribed to Papias and

---

[1] Monographs on St. John by: C. FOUARD, 1904; F. C. FILLION, 1907; L. PIROT, 1923 (all publ. at Paris); H. PREUSS, 1939; J. BEAUFAYS, Brux. [2]1944; W. H. G. THOMAS, Grand Rapids 1946. L. VENARD, DictThC VIII, 537/93. R. KNOPF, Das nachapost. Zeitalter (61—138), 1905. G. BARDY, L'Église à la fin du premier siècle, Paris 1933. Introduction to the Commentary on the Gospel of St. John by M. J. LAGRANGE, Paris [3]1927; FR. TILLMANN, [4]1931; A. WIKENHAUSER, 1948; TH. ZAHN, [5/6]1921; R. BULTMANN, [11]1941. Commentary on the Apocalypse E. B. ALLO, Paris [3]1933; J. SICKENBERGER, [2]1942; A. WIKENHAUSER, 1947. TH. ZAHN, 2 vols. 1924/6; J.BEHM, 1935. TH. ZAHN, Forschungen VI, 1900. F. BOLL, Aus der Offenbarung Johannis, 1914. J. FREUNDORFER, Die Apokalypse des Ap. Joh. u. die hellenist. Kosmologie u. Astrologie, 1929. R. SCHÜTZ, Die Offenb. des Joh. u. Kaiser Domitian, 1933. P. TOUILLEUX, L'Apocalypse et les cultes de Domitien et de Cybèle, Paris 1935. W. OEHLER, Zum Missionscharakter des Joh.-evang., 1941. St. John at Ephesus and the Question of the Presbyter John: F. SPITTA, ZntW 1910, 39 ff.; V. WEBER, Kath. 1913 II, 434 ff.; E. RIGGENBACH, NkZ 1921, 692 ff. (all disagree with E. SCHWARTZ, Abh. Göttingen 1904, 1/53 u. ZntW 1910, 89 ff.) J. CHAPMAN, John the Presbyter and the Fourth Gospel, Oxford 1911. K. ERBES, ZKG 1912, 159/239; 1916, 283/318. W. LARFELD, Die beiden Joh. in Ephesus, 1914 (see also J. BELSER, ThQ 1915, 161 ff.); Byzant.-neugriech. Jbb. 3, 1922, 282/85. S. TROMP, Mnemosyne 1926, 279/320. J. DONOVAN, Irish Eccles. Record 31, 1928, 337/50. P. VENUTELLI, De Presbytero Joanne apud Papiam, Rome 1933 (weak). G. M. PERRELLA, Div Thom. (Plac.) 1940, 47/56 (the text of Papias on the Presbyter John).

[2] According to tradition, the place of the "Dormitio" or "Transitus" of Mary, the Mother of God, is in Jerusalem on Mt. Sion near the Coenaculum where the German Benedictines have the church and monastery called Dormitio B. Mariae. Some few scholars (TH. WEGENER, J. NIESSEN et al.) relying on the visions of Anna Catherine Emmerick (d. 1824) have endeavored to prove that the Panagia Kapuli at Ephesus is the spot of the Transitus Mariae. Cfr.

found in the history of Philip of Side (fifth cent.) according to which John "the Theologian" was put to death by the Jews in Jerusalem in the year 44 together with his brother James, is unworthy of credence. Apparently John the Apostle is here confused with John the Baptist. There is, however, a reliable tradition dating from the second century that the Apostle John later (from about the year 60) functioned as "Highpriest" at *Ephesus*, appointed bishops and established congregations in Asia Minor, and having reached an old age, died a natural death early in the reign of Emperor Trajan (c. 100). *Irenaeus* of Lyons (Adv. haer. II, 22, 5; III, 1, 1; 3, 4) a native of Asia Minor and a disciple of Polycarp of Smyrna, who was in turn a disciple of St. John, states these facts as certain. Polycrates of Ephesus, who pointed out the grave of John in Ephesus (Eusebius III, 31, 3) and Clement of Alexandria (Quis dives salvetur 42) make the same assertions.

A fairly widespread modern opinion holds that these statements of ancient writers regarding John in Ephesus refer to a *"presbyter" John*, a disciple of the Lord, who is not the same as the Apostle John. The opinion is based on a rather obscure passage from Papias (Eusebius III, 39) which Eusebius interprets as meaning that two Johns, the Apostle and the "Presbyter", lived in Ephesus at the same time, and that the Apocalypse is to be ascribed to the latter. More recent critics also assign the fourth Gospel and the Joannine Epistles to the "Presbyter." But Eusebius' interpretation is questionable, to say the least. Even if a presbyter John actually existed and is not merely a literary double of the son of Zebedee, the Ephesian tradition regarding the Apostle is too clear and definite to be disregarded. According to the Apocalypse 1:9, John was banished to the island of Patmos, evidently during the reign of Domitian, "for the word of God and for the testimony of Jesus," where he received the wonderful revelations contained in this book. The story that John was previously tortured in boiling oil at Rome (Tert. De praescriptione 36) is legendary.

By his long life, John not only linked the apostolic office with the post-apostolic age from which very few documents have been preserved (§ 37) but he also mirrors quite clearly in his writings the changes which occured in Christianity after the catastrophe of the year 70. The fourth or "pneumatic" Gospel (Clement of Alexan-

J. NIRSCHL, Das Grab d. hl. Jungfrau Maria, 1896; Recent studies: C. MOMMERT, Die Dormitio, 1900. J. NIESSEN, Ephesus, die letzte Wohnstätte der hl. Jungfrau Maria, 1931. A. D'ALÈS, RevOC 1932, 376/89. J. RIVIÈRE, RechThAM 1936, 5/23 (Text of the 'Transitus V. Mariae'); see also B. CAPELLE, ib. 1940, 209/35; AB 1949, 21/48. M. IUGIE, La mort et l'assomption de la sainte Vierge (Studi e Testi 114), Rom 1944. G. M. GAGOV, Misc. francescana 1947, 132/51 (Tradition of the first five centuries regarding the death and burial of the B. V. M). C. BALIĆ, Testimonia de assumptione B. V. Mariae ... I, Rome 1950.

dria) was intended for pagan converts; it was written to strengthen their faith in the Messiasship and Divinity of Jesus and combatted the docetic-gnostic denial of the Redeemer's true human nature and of His identity with the historical Jesus — a denial just then being made by Cerinthus and other heretics (Iren. Adv. haer. III, 11, 1; cfr. § 28, 2). By employing the *logos-concept* then so familiar to the Hellenic and late Israelitic world and by giving it a new and infinitely deeper meaning, this Gospel made it possible for Christianity to become truly a world religion "because it utilized the deepest thought of Greek philosophy and the best element of Hellenic religiosity in the service of Christianity without losing its own religious character" (A. Ehrhard).

2. The fates of the other Apostles, all of whom died probably before 70, are almost entirely unknown. Origen, as reported by Eusebius (H. E. III, 1), says that *Thomas* worked in Parthia (§ 12, 11) and *Andrew* in Scythia. *Bartholomew* went as far as India (Eus. V, 10) by which southern Arabia is most probably meant. *Matthew* preached first to the Jews and afterwards to other nations (Eus. III, 24). But Eusebius is silent regarding the missionary activities of *Philip, Simon Zelotes, Judas Thaddaeus* or Lebbaeus and *Matthias*. The grave of an "Apostle" *Philip* at Hieropolis in Phrygia, of which Bishop Polycrates of Ephesus speaks, was probably, as Eusebius thinks (III, 31), the grave of the "Evangelist" Philip (Acts 21: 8—9) one of the seven deacons. Cfr. *Th. Zahn*, Forsch. VI, 158 ff. — *P. Corssen*, ZntW 1901, 289/99.

The Evangelist *Mark*, the "interpreter for Peter" (Papias in Eus. III, 39, 15), is looked upon as founder of the Church of Alexandria (Eus. II, 16). The Churches of Venice and Aquileia, with less right, also consider him their founder. According to the Acts of the Apostles and the Epistles of St. Paul, *Luke*, the learned pagan convert and physician, was the companion and co-worker of the Apostle of the Gentiles. It is believed that he worked later in Achaia. Cfr. H. A. Kellner, ThQ 1905, 596 ff. (where it is held that Luke died at Thebes in Boetia). — A. Harnack, Lucas d. Arzt, 1906; for further literature see § 9 (Pölzl, etc.).

3. Since the second century pious fantasy endeavored to supply what tradition failed to furnish regarding the later lives of the Apostles. Thus, by fabricating all sorts of stories, a whole series of *apochryphal Acts of the Apostles* came into being. (Acta Petri, Pauli, Pauli et Theclae, Andreae, Joannis, Thomae, Philippi, Mathaei, etc.). They belong to the popular literature of their times and are of an edifying and entertaining character with little or no historic value. They consist chiefly of curious moral tales of miracles after the fashion of Hellenic "aretalogy." Some of them (Acts of John, of Thomas and of Andrew) originated in heretical circles (Gnostic) or at least have been revised and given an heretical trend. Since the fifth century, it has been believed that a certain Lucius was the author of a collection of such legends of the Apostles. — Acta apostolorum apochrypha *edd. R. A. Lipsius* et *M. Bonnet*, 2 vol. 1891/1903. — *E. Hennecke*, Neutest. Apokryphen, [2]1924,

163 ff. — *M. Rhodes James*, The Apocryphal New Testament Newly Translated, Oxford 1924. — *R. A. Lipsius*, Die apokryphen Apostelgeschichten und Legenden, 2 vols. with supplement 1883/90. — *Th. Schermann*, Propheten- und Apostellegenden, TU 31, 3, 1907. — *F. Haase*, Apostel und Evangelisten in den orientalischen Überlieferungen, 1922. — *F. Piontek*, Die katholische Kirche u. die häret. Apostelgeschichten, Kirchengesch. Abh. ed. M. Sdralek VI, 1908, 1/71. — *E. v. der Goltz*, Apostellegenden als Geschichtsquellen, Harnack-Ehrung, 1921, 143/58. — *L. Hertling*, ZkTh 1925, 219/43. — *K. Kerényi*, Die griechisch-oriental. Romanliteratur in religionsgesch. Beleuchtung, 1927. — *R. Söder*, Die apokr. Apostelgeschichten u. die romanhafte Lit. der Antike, 1932. — R. Helm, Der antike Roman, 1948. — *M. Blumenthal*, Formen u. Motive in den apokr. Apostelgesch., 1953. — G. Bornkamm, Mythos und Legende in den apokr. Thomasakten, 1933; and in RE Pauly-Wissowa 2. R. XI, 316/23. — *K. L. Schmidt*, Kanon u. apokr. Evangelien u. Apostelgeschichten, 1944. — Ch. C. Torrey, The Apocryphal Literature, New Haven 1945.

# § 12.
# The Spread of Christianity[1].

The distance covered by St. Paul and the other Apostles on their missionary journeys warrants the belief that the Gospel was planted in most provinces of the Roman Empire even in apostolic times (cfr. Rom. 1:8; Col. 1:6 and 23). Later it reached the other provinces and lands not subject to the Imperium Romanum. At a very early date important congregations were to be found in the larger cities. For a time Christianity remained a city religion and only gradually found its way into rural districts (§ 20, 1). The first points of contact were the widespread Jewish diaspora and the "God-fearing" pagans. The new religion gained its first converts from the *middle* and *lower* classes of society (artisans, merchants, slaves) and among *women*. Yet, as the Acts of the Apostles and

---

[1] K. PIEPER, Atlas orbis christiani antiqui, 1931; RQ 1926, 111/27 (Mission routes of Christian antiquity). A. HARNACK, Die Mission und Ausbreitung des Christent. in den ersten 3 Jhh., 2 vols. [4]1924. H. LECLERCQ, DictAC V, 978/1014. M. MEINERTZ, Jesus u. die Heidenmission, [2]1925. A. DEISSMANN, Das Urchristentum u. die unteren Schichten, [2]1908. A. RUEGG, Die Mission in der alten Kirche, ihre Wege und Erfolge, 1912 (Basler Missionsstud. 40). A. BIGELMAIR, Der Missionsgedanke bei den vorkonstantin. Vätern, ZMW 1914, 264/77. W. M. RAMSAY, The Church in the Roman Empire Before 170, London [10]1913. F. J. FOAKES-JACKSON, The Rise of Gentile Christianity (to 150), 1927. J. ZEILLER, L'Empire Romain et l'Église, Paris 1928; RechSR 1935, 560/82 (the Church about 310); L'année théol. 1944, 193/208 (spread of Christianity in the West). L. HERTLING, ZkTh 1934, 243/53 (number of Christians about the year 300). K. S. LATOURETTE, A History of the Expansion of Christianity I, New York 1937. R. LIECHTENHAN, Die urchristl. Mission, 1946. G. BARDY, La conversion au christianisme durant les premiers siècles, Paris 1949.

the Pauline Epistles prove, there were also some wealthy, distinguished and educated persons to be found in the ranks of Christians from the beginning; and from the end of the second century the number of wealthy and educated persons, patricians, soldiers and officials continued to grow. By about the year 250 Christianity had been so firmly established that the more severe persecutions, then beginning, were unable to check its eventual victory. By the beginning of the fourth century Christians in the Empire numbered at least seven million in a total population of about fifty million. Most of the Christians were in the East in Asia Minor, Macedonia, Syria, Armenia, Egypt and in parts of lower and central Italy, northwest Africa, Spain and southern Gaul. Clement of Alexandria and Origen, and especially the teachers of the fourth and fifth centuries, saw in the astonishingly rapid growth of the Christian religion in spite of all obstacles (§ 14), a convincing proof of its supernatural origin.

1. The growth of the congregation at **Rome** (§ 10, 1) is attested especially by *Tacitus* (Annal. XV, 44) who says that an "ingens multitudo" of Christians died as martyrs under Nero. Pope *Cornelius* (d. 253) speaks of a vast number of Roman Christians directed by 46 priests, 7 deacons and about 100 clerics in lower orders, who had in their midst 1500 widows and orphans in need of support. A proof of the spread of Christianity in the rest of **Italy** are the 60 bishops whom the same Pope Cornelius summoned to a synod at Rome (Eus. VI, 43, 2) in 251 at the outbreak of the Novatian schism (§ 35, 1). The oldest bishopric of Upper Italy is *Ravenna* (between 120 and 170), followed by *Milan* (about 200), *Verona* and *Aquileia* (240/260). *Brescia, Bergamo* and *Bologna* were probably episcopal sees before the reign of Constantine the Great. In central Italy, *Ostia* and *Porta*, and in Lower Italy, *Puteoli* (cfr. Acts 28:14) and *Naples* must be accounted among the oldest churches. It is quite probable that there were Christians in the cities destroyed by the eruption of Vesuvius in the year 79 A.D. In 1936 a copy of the now famous Sator-square was found at *Pompeii* (as previously at Dura-Europos on the Euphrates, § 23, 5) and in 1939 traces of a wooden cross were discovered at *Herculanum*. Naturally the Christian character of this cross is questioned. — *F. Lanzoni*, Le diocesi d'Italia dalle origini all' anno 604, Faenza [2]1927. — *H. Leclercq*, Italie, DictAC VII, 1612/841. — On Rome: *G. La Piana*, HarvThR 1927, 183/403. — *A. Mackinnon*, The Rome of St. Paul, London 1930; The Rome of the Early Church, London 1933. — *P. Styger*, Juden u. Christen im alten Rom, 1934. — *A. St. Barnes*, Christianity at Rome in the Apostolic Age, London 1938. — See also § 15, 1. On *Pompeii* and the Sator Square: F. Grosser, ArchRelW 24, 1926, 165/9. — F. Dornseiff, ZntW 1937, 222/38. — A. Ferrua, CivCatt 1937 III, 127/39; 1940 I, 60/5. — Grumel, OrChristPer 1947, 515/21. — M. della Corte, I Cristiani a Pompei, Napoli 1939. — G. de Jerphanion, OrCristPer 1941, 5/35 (Herculanum).

2. The earliest Christian history of **France** is thickly interwoven with legend (the presence of Lazarus, Martha and Mary Magdalene in Provence; Lazarus, the first bishop of Marseilles, Dionysius the Areopagite, the first bishop of Paris; the foundation of parishes by immediate disciples of the Apostles; the seven missionaries sent to Gaul by Pope Fabian as related by Gregory of Tours, Hist. Franc. I, 28). Improbable, too, is the preaching there of Paul's disciple Crescens (2 Tim. 4:10 where Γαλατία evidently means Galatia, not Gaul). It is only in the second century that we are on safe historic ground. During the reign of Marcus Aurelius, there were flourishing congregations at *Lyons* and *Vienne* composed of Greek immigrants who suffered much in the persecution of that Emperor (§ 15, 4). Irenaeus, Bishop of Lyons, preached to the Celts (Adv. haer. praef.) and speaks (I, 10, 2) of churches among them. Episcopal sees were established in the second and partly in the third century at Marseilles, Arles, Vienne, Orange, Toulouse, Autun, Rouen, Paris, Sens, Bordeaux, Bourges, Reims and probably at other places. Sixteen bishops were present at the Synod of Arles in 314. Cfr. the excellent work of *L. Duchesne*, Fastes épiscopaux de l'ancienne Gaule, 3 vol. Paris 1894/1915, I—II ²1907/10 (here I², 231 ff. on the Provençal legends which originated in the eleventh and twelfth centuries; cfr. also E. Vacandard, RQH 100, 1924, 257/305). — E. Griffe, La Gaule chrétienne à l'époque romaine I, Paris 1947. — *H. Leclercq*, DictAC V, 2116/575 (France); VI, 310/473 (Église gallicane); VIII, 2357/440 (Légendes gallicanes). — C. Jullian, Histoire de la Gaule, 8 vol. Paris 1908/26. — *H. Bruders*, ZThS 1927, 197/218 (Ecclesiastical organization in Gaul and along the Rhine). — *M. Schuler*, Trierer Z. 1931, 80/103. — J. Leflon, Hist. de l'église de Reims du I^er au V^e s., Reims 1942. — J. Rupp, Hist. de l'église de Paris, Paris 1948. — Ch. Martin, RHE 1942, 143/52 (Irenaeus and the deacon Demetrius of Vienne). — *F. Staehelin*, Die Schweiz in römischer Zeit, ³1948.

3. Most probably it was *St. Paul* who first preached Christianity in **Spain.** The legend that the Gospel was brought there by James the Elder is not older than the seventh century. Irenaeus (Adv. haer. I, 10, 2) and Tertullian (Adv. Jud. 7) speak of Churches there, and about the middle of the third century Cyprian (Ep. 67) wrote to the churches of *Leon-Astorga* and *Merida* and mentions the church of *Saragossa* (Caesaraugusta). At the Synod of *Elvira* (Illiberis-Granada) held about 306, there were present 19 bishops and 24 priests. The 81 canonical decrees of this synod deal with penance, matrimony, the celibacy of the clergy, etc., and prohibit the introduction of pagan vices and customs among Christians. — *P. Gams*, KG. von Spanien I, 1862. — *H. Leclercq*, L'Espagne chrétienne (to 711), Paris ²1916; DictAC V, 407/523. — A. Eitel, Festgabe Finke 1925, 1/23. — *Z. Garcia Villada*, Historia ecclesiástica de España I—III, 2 (to 1085), Madrid 1929/36; also in Jahresber. der Görresgesellschaft für 1925/26 (1927) 64 ff. Historia de España, dir. p. *R. Menéndez Pidal*, t. II: España Romana (to 411), Madrid 1935. — *A. Ferrua*, CivCatt 1940 IV, 421/31. — On the synod of Elvira: L. Duchesne, Mél. Renier, Paris 1887, 159/74; Bareille, DictThC IV, 2378/97; H. Koch, ZntW 1916, 61/67; D. Stiefenhofer, ZThS 1924, 232/50.

4. St. Irenaeus (Adv. Haer. I, 10, 2) speaks of Churches "in Germaniis;" — a proof that Christianity had adherents in **Germany** before the end of the

second century. The Roman provinces in Upper and Lower Germany along the left bank of the Rhine were naturally the places to become acquainted with the new religion at an early date. The churches known to Irenaeus were most likely communities governed by bishops, but which later ceased to exist. Bishops Maternus of *Cologne* and Agroetius of *Trier* (Belgian-Gaul) were present at the Synod of Arles in 314. Both of these sees were probably established in the third century. Monuments and inscriptions prove that there were Christians at *Metz* (Belgian-Gaul), *Mainz* and *Strassburg* as early as the fourth century, if not earlier. Excavations begun in the minster of *Bonn* in 1928 resulted in the discovery of a fourth century basilica of the soldier-martyrs Cassius and Florentius (believed to have been members of the Theban Legion § 16, 4) and the still older ruins of a room for memorial services were found in the martyrs' crypt of St. Victor's Church at *Xanten* (= ad Sanctos). — Cfr. *H. Leclercq*, DictAC VI, 1187/222 (Germanie). *H. Friedrich*, Bonner Jbb. 1926, 10/113 (The beginnings of Christianity on the lower and middle Rhine and along the Moselle). — E. de Moreau, Histoire de l'Église en Belgique I, Brux. ²1947. — A. M. Burg, Hist. de l'Église d'Alsace, Colmar 1946. — *H. Tüchle*, KG. Schwabens I, 1950. — Bruders u. Schuler, vide supra no. 2. — *W. Levison*, AnnHVNiedRh 116, 1930, 5/28 (legends of the old episcopal sees in the Rhineland). — *W. Neuss*, Die Anfänge d. Christentums im Rheinlande, ²1933 (also W. Bader, Theol. Blätter 1933, 335 ff.). — *W. Siebert*, StZ 130, 1936, 551/64 (the first Christian communities among the Germans). — *K. Corsten*, AnnHVNiedRh 129, 1936, 1/50 (early Christianity in Cologne and the history of the old cathedral); O. Doppelfeld, Der unterirdische Dom (in Cologne), 1948. — Th. K. Kempf, Trierer Theol. Z. 1947, 2 ff., 33 ff., 118 ff. (The old cathedral of Triers). — J. Mösch, Z. f. schweizer. KG. 1949, 61/3 (historical basis of the legend of the Theban Legion). On the recent discoveries at *Bonn*: H. Lehner, RQ 1930, 133/51; Lehner u. Bader in Bonner Jbb. 1932; Th. Klauser in F. Nussbaum, Bonn u. sein Münster, 1939, 35/9; in *Xanten*: W. Neuss, RQ 1934, 177/80; W. Bader, Bonner Jbb. 1934. — F. Rütten u. A. Steeger, Rheinische Vierteljahrsbl. 1933. 281/320.

The introduction of Christianity into the **territory along the Danube**, i. e., the provinces of Rhaetia, Noricum and Pannonia, is dated by the martyrs who died during the Diocletian persecution; *St. Afra at Augsburg* (MGSS rer. Merov. VII, 192—204; the Conversio and Passio are not historically trustworthy, cfr. A. Bigelmair, Die Afralegende, Archiv des Hochstifts Augsburg I, 1910, 139/221; HpBl 1914 II, 624/31; O. Riedner, Der geschichtl. Wert d. Afralegende, 1913); *Irenaeus of Sirmium*, the bishops Victorinus of Pettau (Poetovio) in Styria (§ 40, 4) and *Quirinus of Sissek* (Siscia) in Croatia in 308 or 309. It is possible that *Lorch* (Lauriacum) was a bishopric (archbishopric?) before the reign of Constantine. (Martyrdom of St. Florian). The Passio quattuor coronatorum (ASS Nov. III, 748/84), Christian sculptors supposed to have been martyred in *Pannonia* under Diocletian, has been the subject of much recent research. It now appears that the sculptors were confused with four Roman soldiers who met death about this time. (J. P. Kirsch, HJG 1917, 72/97; H. Delehaye, Les passions des martyrs, Brussels 1921, 328 ff.). — In 1949 a cemetery chapel from about the year 400 was discovered at Regensburg; and a small Christian chapel dating from the fourth century was found at

Carnutum in Upper Pannonia (between Vienna and Pressburg). — *J. Ziber-mayer*, Noricum, Bayern u. Österreich, 1944. *R. Bauerreiss*, KG. Bayerns I, 1949. — A number of Christian communities existed in *Moesia* and *Dacia* on the lower Danube as early as 300. St. Paul sent his disciple Titus to *Dalmatia* (2 Tim. 4:10). *Salona* (Spalato-Macarsca) became a bishopric in the third century, but recent discoveries prove that Christianity was known there even earlier. Cfr. *J. Zeiler*, Les origines chrét. de la province romaine de Dalmatie, Paris 1906; Les origines chrét. de la province romaine de Dalmatie, Paris 1906; Les origines chrét. dans les provinces Danubiennes de l'empire Romain, Paris 1918. — H. Leclercq, Dalmatie, DictAC IV, 21/111; Illyricum, ib. VII, 80/180.

5. Tertullian (Adv. Jud. 7) mentions **England**: inaccessa Romanis loca, Christo vero subdita. Recent study has established good reason for believing that Christianity was introduced into England directly from Asia Minor by way of the sea. (K. Holl, Abh. Berlin 1923, 5, 33 f.). Bishops from *York* (Eboracum), *London* and *Lincoln* took part in the Synod of Arles in 314. The Liber Pontificalis (§ 78, 3) and Venerable Bede (H. E. I, 4) relate that a British king, *Lucius*, asked Pope Eleutherius (174—189) for missionaries and that the king and some of his people became Christians. A. von Harnack (Sb. Berlin 1904, 909 ff.) shows that this account resulted from confusing the English Lucius with King Lucius Abgar of Edessa, who corresponded with Pope Eleutherius. — F. Cabrol, L'angleterre chrét. avant les Normands, Paris 1909. — H. Williams, Christianity in Early Britain, Oxford 1912. — J. C. Wall, The First Christians of Britain, London 1927. — R. G. Colling-wood, Roman Britain, London 1932. — *J. Chevalier*, DictHE III, 145 ff.

6. Northern **Africa** was probably evangelized from Rome toward the end of the first century. A hundred years later, Tertullian (Ad Scap. 2) says, in his usual rhetorical style, that the population of the cities was almost entirely Christian. Roman Africa had a great many sees, even the smaller towns being the residences of bishops. Cyprian (Ep. 59, 10) tells of a heretic being con-demned about the year 240 by 90 bishops. The Synod of Carthage held by Agrippinus about the year 220 was attended by 70 bishops and Cyprian presided over 87 bishops in the synod he held in 256. — *H. Leclercq*, L'Afrique chrétienne, 2 vol. Paris 1904. — *J. Mesnage*, (same title), Paris 1912; Le christianisme en Afr., 3 vol. Paris 1915. — *St. Gsell*, Hist. ancienne de l'Afr. du Nord, 6 vol. Paris 1927/28. — E. Buonaiuti, Il cristianesimo nell'Africa Romana, Bari 1928 (also H. Koch, ThLZ 1930, 229/34). — J. P. Brisson, Gloire et misère de l'Afr. chrétienne, Paris 1949. — *G. G. Lapeyre*, L'ancienne Église de Carthage, 2 vol. Paris 1932; Lapeyre and *A. Pellegrin*, Carthage latine et chrétienne, Paris 1950. — A. Schwarze, RE 14, 159/65; 24, 271/75. — A. Audollent, DictHE I, 705/861. — *D. D. Sullivan*, The Life of the North Africans as Revealed in the Works of S. Cyprian, Dissertation Washington 1933. — *G. Metzger*, Die afrikan. Kirche [according to the letters of St. Augu-stine, 1934; Kirche u. Mission in den Briefen Augustins, 1936. — *R. Höslinger*, Die alte afrikan. Kirche im Lichte der Kirchenrechtsforschung, 1935.

7. In **Egypt**, the Church of *Alexandria* (founded by St. Mark?) first ap-pears in history in a flourishing condition. By the end of the second century we find the famous catechetical school already organized (§ 39, 1). From

Alexandria Christianity spread among the Greek and Coptic population in the cities and country as far as Thebes and Libya. During the third century the number of bishoprics increased to almost 100 as we see in the Synod of Alexandria of the year 318. — Faivre, DictHE II, 289/369. — H. Leclercq, DictAC IV 2401/271. A. Heckel, Die Kirche v. Ägypten bis z. Nicänum, Dissertation, Strassb. 1918. — *W. Schubart*, Ägypten von Alexander d. Gr. bis auf Mohammed, 1922. — A. Böhlig, RLAntChrist I, 128/38. — G. Bardy, Mémorial Lagrange, Paris 1940. 203/17 (Christianity among the Copts).

8. Christianity made even greater progress in **Asia Minor**. About the year 112 Pliny (Ep. X. 96; § 15, 8) the governor of Bithynia and Pontus spoke of the many Christians of all ages and conditions. The temples of the gods were deserted, and sacrifices to the gods had almost ceased. Several synods were held in Phrygia about 172—180 to deliberate regarding the errors of the Montanists (Eus. V, 16). The pagan satirist Lucian (Pseudomant. 25) about the year 170 represents one of his characters as complaining that the Pontus was full of "atheists" and Christians. The other parts of Asia Minor presented a similar picture, especially the province of Asia with Ephesus as its capital. Cfr. *V. Schultze*, Altchristl. Städte u. Landschaften II: Kleinasien, 2 Teile 1922/26. — The letter which Bishop Dionysius of Alexandria wrote to the bishops of Roman *Armenia* (Eus. VI, 46) regarding the Novatian schism is an indication of how Christianity had spread in that province. The independent *kingdom* of **Armenia** (Armenia Major) became a Christian country in the third century (§ 42, 2).

9. In **Syria**, especially Hellenized *West Syria* (Celesyria), there were scarcely fewer Christians than in Asia Minor. Antioch, the capital, had been the starting-point (§ 8, 2) and, in a sense, remained the metropolis for the pagan converts of all the Near East. Many important synods were held there since the middle of the third century. Cfr. *V. Schultze*, Altchristl. Städte u. Landschaften III: Antiocheia, 1930. C. Karalevskij, Antioche, DictHE III, 563 ff. W. Eltester, ZntW 1937, 251/86 (the churches of Antioch in the fourth century). — *East Syria* (for the recent discoveries at Dura-Europos see § 23, 5) and the territory of *Osrhoëne*, east of the Euphrates, which had become subject to Rome under Trajan, especially its capital city, **Edessa** (now Urfa), had received the new religion by the middle of the second century, if not earlier. Legend (Eus. H. E. I, 13 and Doctrina Addaei of the early fifth century) places the conversion of the country in apostolic times. King Abgar V, who was ill, wrote to Christ begging Him to come and heal him. In His reply Christ promised to send one of His disciples (§ 7, 2). After the Ascension, *Addaeus* or *Thaddaeus*, one of the Seventy, undertook the task and preached the Gospel at Edessa. After the year 170 *Tatian* "the Assyrian" (§ 38 A 3) worked in East Syria and somewhat later the influential Christian philosopher (Gnostic ?) and poet, *Bardesanes* (§ 30 B 3), a boyhood friend of King Agar IX (179—216), also preached there. The veracity of the old story that the king and his household embraced Christianity and made it the state religion is now seriously contested (W. Bauer, J. O. de Urbina). During the Easter controversy about the year 190 (§ 25, 3) the bishops of Osrhoëne addressed a letter to Rome (Eus. V, 23). A Christian church was built at Edessa in 201. The ecclesiastical language was Syrian. On Tatian's Diatessaron see § 38 B 5. —

## § 12. The Spread of Christianity.

H. Leclercq, Édesse, DictHE IV, 2055/110. — *J. Tixeront*, Les origines de l'Église d'Édesse, Paris 1888; *J. P. Martin* (same title), Paris 1889. — *R. Duval*, Hist. politique, relig. et littéraire d'Édesse, Paris 1892. — *F. C. Burkitt - E. Preuschen*, Urchristentum im Orient, 1907. — A. Baumstark, RQ 1908, 17/35. — W. Bauer, Rechtgläubigkeit u. Ketzerei im ältesten Christentum, 1934, 6/48. — J. Ortiz de Urbina, Gregorianum 1934, 82/91. — *H. Lietzmann*, Sb. Berlin 1935, 729 f. (Beginnings of christianity in Syria).

From Osrhoëne Christianity spread northward along the trade route into **Mesopotamia**. Bishop Dionysius of Alexandria about 260 assumed that the Church was well organized there (Eus. VII, 5) and Eusebius (VIII, 12, 1) speaks of martyrs in the Diocletian persecution. According to the Chronicle of Arbela, the authenticity of which is questioned, the "Apostle" Addai and his disciple Pekidha, preached with great success in the territory of **Adiabene** (Assyria) about the year 100. The same Chronicle states that about the year 225 there were 17 episcopal sees in Assyria and Mesopotamia. Christianity reached **Parthia** and **Persia** in the third century at the latest. The Persian king Sapor I (Schapur) (241—272) brought back many Christian prisoners of war from his expedition into Syria. Thus in 256 he took captive Bishop Demetrius of Antioch. — *E. Sachau*, Die Chronik v. Arbela, Abh. Berlin 1915, 6; 1919, 1; Sb. Berlin 1916, 958 ff. Lat. Übersetzung der Chronik v. *Fr. Zorell* in Orientalia Christ. VIII, 4, Rome 1927, 142/204. — Cfr. A. Allgeier, Kath. 1916 I, 393 ff.; 1918 II, 224 ff.; 289 ff.; F. Haase, ThQ 1920, 226 ff.; P. Peeters, AB 1925, 263, 303 f.; J. Ortiz de Urbina, OrChrPer 1936, 5/32; G. Messina, CivCatt 1932 III, 362/76. See also § 42.

10. Because of the hatred of the Jews, Christianity encountered obstacles in **Palestine** and hence was confined chiefly to the Hellenized cities. Until well into the fourth century, Judaism and, to some extent, paganism continued in control. It was only in the third century that the bishop and his congregation (composed chiefly of pagan converts) began to play an important role in Jerusalem (called Aelia Capitolina since the time of Hadrian). The bishop of Caesarea was metropolitan of the Syrio-Palestinian province (§ 20, 2). Many of the Jewish Christians became heretical (§ 28). Cfr. *K. Pieper*, Die Kirche Palästinas bis 135, 1938. Cfr. also § 8. — There were soon Christians also in the parts of **Arabia** bordering on Palestine, as we learn from the Synod of Bostra in 244 (§ 39, 1). According to Eusebius (V, 10) *Pantaenus*, the renowned catechist of Alexandria, preached in "India" about the year 190; but by India is probably meant the southwestern part of Arabia (Yemen where the Apostle Bartholomew is said to have gone (§ 11, 2). — R. Aigrain, Arabie, DictHE III, 1158/339. — H. Charles, Le christianisme des Arabes nomades, Paris 1936. — R. Devreesse, Vivre et penser 1942 110/46 (Christianity in Arabia).

11. According to the apochryphal Acta of Thomas of the third century, and according to Ephraem, Ambrose, Jerome and others, (Origen speaks of *Parthia*, § 11, 2), the Apostle *Thomas* preached the Gospel in **India**. After wandering eastward as far as Kalamina (near Mailapur?) he was put to death with a lance by order of King Misdai (Mazdai). His remains are said to have been brought back to Edessa. The so-called *Thomas Christians* of the Malabar coast in southwest India take their name from him and hold to the tradition

that they received the faith from him. This tradition has recently received some support (J. Dahlmann, Die Thomaslegende, 1912; A. Väth, Der hl. Thomas, der Apostel Indiens, [2]1925) from the discovery that King Gundaphor whose name constantly recurs in the Acts was an historical person. It has further been proved that lively trade relations existed between Syria and India in the first Christian century, and that the sea route from Egypt to India was known as early as the second century. But, at best, this merely proves the possibility of a mission to India in apostolic times; it does not prove that there actually was one. Probably Christianity found its way into India in the third century by way of Syria (Edessa) and into the southern part (Malabar) in the fourth century through travelers from Persia or Armenia. All that is known with certainty is that about 530 Cosmas Indicopleustes, "the Indian Voyager," speaks of the existence of Christian congregations (§ 77, 3). — *O. Wecker*, ThQ 1910, 538 ff. and in art. India, RE Pauly-Wissowa IX, 1322 f. — *R. Garbe*, Indien u. das Christentum, 1914 (also K. Beth, DLZ 1915, 893 ff. 957 ff.). — H. Bruders, ThGl 1926, 521/5. — A. Mingana, Bulletin of J. Rylands Library Manchester 8, 1925, 297/371; J. N. Farquhar, Manchester 80/111; 11, 1927, 20/30. — A. Anwander, ThQ 1927, 317 ff.; 1928, 257 ff. (India and the Catechetical School of Alexandria). — G. Bornkamm, Cfr. § 11, 3.

## § 13.
### Reasons for the Rapid Spread of Christianity[1].

1. The spread of Christianity over the then known world in such a short time constitutes a phenomenon to which history offers no parallel. In attempting to explain the marvel, we naturally recall what has been said (§ 5 and 6) about the negative and positive preparation of the ancient world for the Redemption; the inability of old religious forms to satisfy the human heart; the search for a more adequate substitute; the growing attraction of monotheism; the general adoption of the Greek language and culture throughout the Roman Empire, etc. However, these factors alone would never account for the Church's growth, had not the Gospel con-

---

[1] W. DEN BOER, Scriptorum Paganorum I—IV saec. de Christianis testimonia, Leyden 1948. A. HARNACK, etc. § 12. M. SDRALEK, Über die Ursachen, welche den Sieg d. Christent. im röm. Reiche erklären, 1906 (Lecture). J. LORTZ, Tertullian als Apologet, 2 vols. 1927/8. G. KITTEL in "Zeitwende" 1926, 237/52. J. LEIPOLDT, Festschrift L. Ihmels, 1928, 49/83; Allg. Ev. Luth. K. Ztg. 1938, 1130 ff. 1157 ff. H. SCHUHMACHER, Kraft der Urkirche 1934. H. VOGELS, Hochland 1935/36, I, 289/99 (the laity in Christian Antiquity). A. MICHEL, DictThC XIII, 692/708. O. KARRER, Urchristliche Zeugen, 1937. H. D. WENDLAND, Geschichtsanschauung u. Geschichtsbewußtsein im N.T., 1938. O. BAUERNFEIND, Z. f. syst. Theol. 1938, 347/78 (historical concept of Christian Antiquity). K. PRÜMM, Christentum als Neuheitserlebnis, 1939. W. OEHLER, see p. 60. W. KAMLAH, Christentum u. Selbstbehauptung, 1940. W. W. HYDE, Paganism to Christianity in the Roman Empire, Philadelphia 1946. Cfr. § 26.

tained within itself the compelling *force of truth*. And this force proved all the more effective since the Gospel in content and clarity so far surpassed all worldly wisdom and answered so much more satisfactorily the great questions which had always plagued the human mind: the existence of God, the immortality of the soul, the purpose of life, and so forth. As a matter of fact, Christianity attracted many, like the apologists Justin and Tatian and Dionysius of Alexandria, who had earnestly striven to find truth in the various systems of pagan learning. And in it they found, as Justin says (Dial. 8) "the only trustworthy and useful philosophy." Pagans discerned in Christ's doctrine something entirely new and unparalled. It brought them "the Gospel of a Savior and salvation, the Gospel of love and service, a religion of the spirit and of power (1 Cor. 2:4), of moral values and holiness, a religion of authority and reason, of mystery and transcendental knowledge, the message of a new race, the religion of the Book and the fulfillment of history." (A. v. Harnack). Those who confessed Christ were aware that with their religion something entirely new had entered the world and that old standards had passed away (2 Cor. 5:17). Ignatius of Antioch wrote to the Romans (3, 3): "It is not the power of persuasion that counts when Christianity is hated by the world, but it is the greatness which abides in Christianity itself." Nor must we forget that the *charismata* of the early Church (1 Cor. 12—14) especially healing, exorcism of unclean spirits and other extraordinary gifts and *miracles* also attested to the truth of the new religion (Justin, Apol. II, 6; Dial. 121. — Iren. Adv. haer. II, 32, 4. — Tert. Apolog. 23; De anima 47. — Origen. C. Cels. I, 6, 46; III, 28. — Cypr. Ad Donatum 5. — Eus. H. E. V, 3, 4).

2. In the second place, the *zeal* of the first Christians was not without effect. Men and women, great and lowly, freemen and slaves, learned and ignorant, rich and poor, officials, merchants, and soldiers, all became lay apostles devoted to the spread of the Gospel. It was their firm belief that baptism imposed on every Christian the duty of being a missionary of the faith. Not only Christians, but also pagan authors (Pliny the Younger, Celsus, Galenus, Julian the Apostate) testify that the *lives* of Christians preached a powerful sermon to their pagan neighbors and that their example of virtue brought many into the Church. Their austerity, their chastity, their *fraternal love* and their admirable *works of charity* (§ 26) caused their lives to shine brightly against the dark background of a world

full of vice, of hatred and of greed. The apologists of the second century, especially Aristides (c. 15, 16) and the author of the Epistle to Diognetus stress these virtues when depicting for the pagans the conduct of Christians. (Cfr. also Tert. Apolog. 39; M. Felix, Octav. 9, 31). According to Origen (C. Cels. III, 29) the Christians, when compared with the pagan populace, shone "like the stars of heaven in the world" (Phil. 2:15). Justin (Apol. 5, 16) ascribes numerous conversions to their virtuous example. Tertullian (Apolog. 39) says that the pagans derided Christian charity but at the same time unwillingly expressed their admiration for it when they exclaimed: "See how they love one another and how ready they are to die for one another!" Julian the Apostate (Ep. 49) thought that Christianity owed its growth chiefly to works of charity, solicitude for the dead and to the holy lives of its adherents. However Julian professed to remain unimpressed because Christian sanctity to him was hypocritical.

But the one factor that operated most effectively in favor of Christianity and that attracted a great many converts was the *steadfastness* of Christians during the *persecutions* and the *heroic courage of the martyrs* who gave their lives for Christ. Justin (Apol. II, 12) says that in his own case, this attitude of the Christians sufficed to disprove all the charges made against them and impelled him to become one of them. Tertullian (Apolog. 50) addressed the pagan judges in his usual vehement fashion: Cruciate, torquete, damnate, atterite nos; ... *plures efficimur, quotiens metimur a vobis, semen est sanguis Christianorum.* And many other Fathers and Christian writers of the second and third centuries express the same idea. (Justin Dial. 110; Acta Apollonii 24; Iren. Adv. haer. IV, 33, 9; Ep. ad Diogn. 7; Orig. C. Cels. VII, 26). Lactantius (Instit. V, 19, 9) is perhaps summarizing what others had written when he remarks: Augetur religio Dei, quanto magis premitur.

## § 14.

## Obstacles to the Spread of Christianity and Causes of the Persecutions[1]. The Legal Process.

1. St. Paul says (1 Cor. 1:23) that preaching Christ crucified was "unto the Jews indeed a stumblingblock, and unto the Greeks

---

[1] H. RAHNER, Abendländ. Kirchenfreiheit, 1943.   J. E. WEIS, Christenverfolgungen, Gesch. ihrer Ursachen 1899.   A. BIGLMAIR, Die Beteilig. der

foolishness." Paganism and Christianity contrasted most sharply in the domain of public life. The pagan religion was not merely a private affair, but was also, and chiefly, a concern of the State; the family, society and culture were most intimately linked with polytheism. The Roman State insisted on due honor being paid to the national gods. Conquered peoples were, as a rule, permitted to retain their own form of worship, and their gods were readily admitted into the pantheon of the Roman gods. Naturally this latter concession could not be granted to adherents of a monotheistic religion, since, unlike other subject peoples, they could not honor the gods of Rome alongside their God. Yet Rome was generally tolerant of the *Jews* because the Jewish religion had a strong national character and for a long time there were relatively few proselytes to Judaism. Hence Tertullian (Apolog. 21, 1) calls Judaism a "religio certe licita," in whose shadow Christianity was at first tolerated.

But with the *Christians* the case was different. Their religion was not an ancient, national religion like Judaism. It was something entirely new and made a universal appeal. It drew its adherents from all the nations and peoples; indeed, it aimed at the religious

Christen am öffentl. Leben in vorkonstantin. Zeit, 1902. A. HARNACK, Der Vorwurf d. Atheismus, TU 28, 4, 1905. F. AUGAR, Die Frau im röm. Christenprozeß, ib. (cfr. Linsenmayer, HpBl 1908 I, 886/94). A. PIEPER, Christentum, röm. Kaisert. und heidn. Staat, 1907. H. WEINEL, Die Stellung des Urchristent. zum Staat, 1908. H. LECLERCQ, Accusations contre les chrétiens, DictAC I 265/307; Église et État, op. cit. IV, 2238/79; Meurtre rituel, op. cit. XI, 887/98 (also J. P. WALTZING, Bull. de l'Académie R. de Belgique 1925, 205/30; F. J. DÖLGER, Sacramentum infanticidii, AntChrist 1933, 188/228). A. CAUSSE, RevHR 1918, 98/142; 1919, 195/223 (the conflict between Christianity and Roman civilization). A. JACOBY, ArchRelW 1928, 265/82 (onolatry imputed to Jews and Christians). W. NESTLE, ib. 1941, 51/100 (Principal accusations made against Christians). J. LORTZ, vide supra § 13, 1. H. WINDISCH, Imperium u. Evangelium im N.T., 1931 (Lecture). K. PIEPER, Urkirche u. Staat, 1935. F. HERZOG-HAUSER, RE Pauly-Wissowa Suppl. IV, 806/53 (apotheosis of the Emperor). E. LOHMEYER, Christenkult u. Kaiserkult, 1919. E. BICKERMANN, Die röm. Kaiserapotheose, ArchRelW 1929, 1/34. ST. LÖSCH, Deitas Jesu u. antike Apotheose, 1933. FR. SAUTER, Der röm. Kaiserkult bei Martial u. Statius, 1934. H. KRUSE, Studien z. offiz. Geltung des Kaiserbildes im röm. Reich, 1934. F. TAEGER, ZKG 1942, 1/26 (deification of human beings in Antiquity). H. P. L'ORANGE, Sol Invictus Imperator, in Symbolae Osloenses 14, 1935, 86/114. K. SCOTT, The Imperial Cult under the Flavians, Stuttgart 1936. L. BIEHL, Das Gebot für Kaiser u. Reich, 1937. K. BORNHÄUSER, Jesus imperator mundi (Phil. 3:17—21; 2:5—12), 1938. G. KITTEL, Christus u. Imperator, 1939. O. ECK, Urgemeinde u. Imperium, 1940. D. M. PIPPIDI, Recherches sur le culte impérial, Paris 1940. M. DIBELIUS, Rom u. die Christen im 1. Jh., Sb. Heidelberg 1941/2, 2. P. BREZZI, Christianesimo e impero Romano, Rom ²1944. E. STAUFFER, Christus u. die Caesaren, 1948. F. M. STRATMANN, Die Heiligen u. der Staat I—II, 1950.

conquest of the whole world and sought to supplant all other religions. Because of the close, apparently indissoluble bond between the State and polytheism, many saw in Christianity a serious threat to the very foundation of the State. Such fear appeared the more justified because Christians were prohibited by the first principles of their religion from paying *divine honors to the emperor.* Worship of the living emperor as the very life of the State (and his apotheosis when dead) which had been practised in the East, was introduced into the West under Nero and by the time of Domitian had become the focal point of the Roman State religion. It was the touchstone of loyalty and patroitism, so that any person refusing to pay such honor was charged with high treason. Herein lay a special peril for Christians. Moreover, they refrained from taking part in the dissolute revelries of the pagans, refused to decorate and illumine their houses on the occasion of public festivals and some rigorists, like Tertullian and Origen, maintained that it was contrary to Christian principles to serve in the army. On all other points the Christians were certainly obedient citizens. They observed faithfully the injunctions of their Founder (Matt. 22:21 and parallel passages) and of the Apostles (Rom. 13, 1; 1 Pet. 2: 13—17), conscientiously fulfilled their duties as subjects of the State and in all of their religious services prayed fervently for the Emperor and the Empire (Clem. I Cor. 61; Polyc. Phil. 12, 3; Athenag. Legatio 37. Theoph. Ad Autol. I, 11. Tert. Apolog. 30). Yet membership in the Christian congregation sufficed to bring them under suspicion as enemies of the State (Tert. Apol. 35).

2. Moreover, at a very early date, the most unfavorable and fantastic notions regarding Christians began to be circulated. Tacitus (Annal XV, 44) and Suetonius (Nero 16), Roman historians who wrote in the first part of the second century, record these fabrications. The Jews in the diaspora who hated the Christian religion contributed their share toward this campaign of vilification. For some time Christianity was thought to be a Jewish sect and since there was a strong anti-Semitic sentiment among the majority of pagans, many of them helped to color and spread the stories to give vent to their anti-Semitism. There were three main accusations. The Christian attitude toward the State religion and their own pure form of worship without idols led to the charge of *atheism* (Justin, Apol. 6, 13; Athenag. Leg. 3—12; Mart. Polyc. 3) the worst of all crimes; their Eucharistic banquets and the agape were repre-

sented as *"Thyestean banquets"* (sacramentum infanticidii et pabu-
lum inde, Tert. Apolog. 7, 1) and as occasion for *Oedipean orgies*
(incest) (Just. Apol. I, 26; Dialog. 10; Athenag. Leg. 31—36; Theoph.
Ad Autol. III, 4—15; M. Felix Actav. 9, 30, 31; Tert. Apolog. 7—9).
Other charges such as superstition, magic, sun worship, onolatry,
etc., are mentioned by Suetonius (l. c. superstitio nova et malefica),
Tertullian (Apolog. 16) and Minucius Felix (Octav. 9). Tacitus,
Epictetus and Marcus Aurelius further accused the Christians of
misanthropy (odium humani generis) and of cultivating an unnatural contempt of death. Toward the end of the second century
it was suggested and widely believed that the Christian's disdain
for the national gods was the cause of *public calamities* such as
plagues, floods, famine and attacks of barbarians (Tert. Apolog. 40;
Orig. In Matt. Comm. ser. 39; Cypr. Ad Demetr. 2, 3; Arnob. Adv.
nat. I, 13, 26; Aug. De civ. Dei II, 3). While most of the other
charges were gradually forgotten, this latter indictment proved
to be as dangerous as it was widespread and persistent. It was still
heard in the fourth and fifth centuries. Those pagans who earned
their livelihood from the cult of the gods; priests, artists, writers,
fortune tellers, merchants, were quite naturally bitterly opposed
to a religion which seriously affected their business. Hence Christians
were represented as an *unproductive* class of society (infructuosi
negotiis, Tert. Apolog. 42, 43; cf. Acts 19:24 ff.). The pagan Cacci-
lius (M. Felix, Octav. 8, 4) calls them "a sneaky people who shun
the light" (latebrosa et lucifuga natio), recruited from the lowest
dregs of humanity. The philosopher Celsus (in Orig. C. Cels. III, 55;
VI, 14) had the same opinion of them.

3. As a result of such misrepresentation, there occurred at an
early date, especially during the second century, bloody manifestations of *popular wrath* against the followers of Christ in various
places. At times, the *governors* of provinces proceeded against them,
urged thereto by secret information, by popular demand or on
their own initiative. From the middle of the third century the State
itself began to direct the persecutions systematically. The *emperors*
issued general *edicts* ordering them; the purpose being to extermi-
nate the Christian Church as an enemy of the State. The decisive
battle between the Roman State and the Church was fought from
the reign of Decius to that of Diocletian (294—305).

The *legal basis* of the Christian persecutions is not quite clear, at least
in the period before Decius. Some (e. g. Le Blant and K. J. Neumann), think

that the *penal prescriptions* of the older *common law* were appealed to: the laws against illegal assemblies or hetairae (made more severe by Trajan), against criminal magic, against sacrilege and atheism (crimen laesae Romanae religionis, Tert. Apolog. 24) and especially the Lex Julia majestatis which punished with confiscation of property and death any act hostile to the Roman people or endangering their security. Such laws could easily be invoked against Christians who refused to pay *divine honor to the emperor* (crimen laesae majestatis imperatorum, Tert. Apolog. 28). Sacrilege and lese majesty constituted high treason. Hence even a Roman citizen could be punished for them by penalties considered particularly degrading for a Roman, such as crucifixion, burning at the stake, or by being thrown to wild animals. The rack could be used to extract a confession in the case of these crimes. Apparently some of these provisions of the common law were actually invoked; for Tertullian writes (Apolog. 10, 1): sacrilegii et majestatis rei convenimur, summa haec causa, immo tota est. Some scholars (Allard, Duchesne, Callewaert, Leclercq, Lortz, Haidenthaller et al.), basing themselves on Tertullian (Apolog. 4), think that *special laws* were passed *for the persecution* of Christians as early as the reign of Domitian or even of Nero. Most probably, however, these were not exactly special laws — otherwise the persecutions would have been more general and uniform at an early date and Pliny who wrote to Trajan for instructions as to how to proceed, (§ 15, 3), would have known how to act — but were *legal opinions* which had crystalized since the persecutions of Nero and had become precedents for the court (Pieper, Hüntemann). At any rate, since Nero's day Christians were tried and executed on no other charge than that they were Christians. This is the constant complaint of the apologists of the second century (illud solum expectatur ... confessio nominis, non examinatio criminis ... Ideo torquemur confitentes et punimur perseverantes et absolvimur negantes, quia nominis proelium est, Tert. Apolog. 2, cfr. 44; Ad nat. I, 6; Ad Scap. 4 — Justin Apol. I, 4. — Athenag. Leg. 1, 2).

Th. Mommsen[1] heads a list of historians who maintain that the *trial* of an accused Christian was not the ordinary criminal one, but was an application of the police power of the State whereby the Roman officials (the emperor,

---

[1] Der Religionsfrevel nach röm. Recht, HZ 64, 1890, 389/429, and in Ges. Schriften III, 3, 1907, 389/422. Opposite views: AUGAR 59 ff.; PIEPER 35 ff.; C. CALLEWAERT, RHE 1901, 1902, 1911; RQH 74 (1903), 76 (1904), 82 (1907); C. A. KNELLER, StML 1898 II, 1 ff. et passim. cfr. also H. LECLERCQ, Droit persécuteur, DictAC IV, 1565/648; Édits et Rescrits, op. cit. IV, 2119/211; Jurisdiction, op. cit. VIII, 438/503. A. PRUFOMO, Le fonti ed. i. tempi dello incendio Neroniano, Roma 1905, 197/251. L. CEZARD, Hist. juridique des persécutions contre les chrétiens (to 202), Dissertation Paris 1911. O. SILD, Das altchristl. Martyrium in Berücksichtigung der rechtl. Grundlage der Christenverfolgung, 1920. L. DE REGIBUS, Storia e diritto romano negli Acta martyrum, Torino 1927. J. LORTZ, Tertullian als Apologet II, 206 ff. 232 ff. U. HÜNTEMANN, ThQ 1932, 72/93. M. HAIDENTHALLER, ThGl 1933, 37/70. G. KRÜGER, Die Rechtsstellung der vorkonstantin. Kirchen, 1935. H. V. CAMPENHAUSEN, Die Idee des Martyriums in der alten Kirche, 1936. H. W. SURKAU, Martyrien in jüdischer u. frühchristl. Zeit, 1938. L. DIEU, RHE 1942, 5/19 (Institutum Neron. une loi fantôme); also J. ZEILLER, Misc. G. Mercati V, 1946, 1/6; AB 1949, 49/54. E. WOLF, ThLZ 1947, 223/31. E. GRIFFE, BullLE 1949, 129/45.

praefectus urbi, governor of a province) could use *coercive measures*. In virtue of this authority they could proceed summarily against subjects who had disturbed public peace and order without observing the usual form of trial and, in certain cases could even decree the death penalty. There were undoubtedly many cases in which both methods were used. This could easily happen, especially in the provinces where the governor was at the same time the court magistrate. At any rate the trial of a Christian was something rather unique in the Roman legal system and can not be precisely classified; for as a rule, the "crime" had to be proved before the magistrate by a refusal to sacrifice on the spot, while the Christian who abjured his faith was released.

4. In spite of the length and rigor of the persecutions, the Christian faith which held out to its followers the promise of an eternal reward, could not be exterminated. A few, and at times relatively many, quailed at the thought of torture and death and renounced the faith (lapsi); but for the most part they proved themselves more patient in enduring their sufferings than their executioners were in inflicting them. Men and women, youths and maidens, the aged and children vied with one another in attaining the crown of martyrdom, so that by their deaths as well as by their lives the Christian martyrs proclaimed the divine origin of the new religion.

Since Orosius (Hist. adv. pag. VII, 27) and Augustine (De civ. Dei XVIII, 52; cfr. also Brewer, ZkTh 1912, 852 ff.) it has been customary to enumerate *ten* persecutions. But this number was arrived at in an attempt, for symbolic reasons, to parallel the persecutions with the plagues of Egypt.

Recent studies regarding the origin and application of the **term martyr** have not succeeded in shedding much additional light on the subject. The word μάρτυς or μάρτυρ was first applied to the Apostles, the trustworthy eye and ear witnesses to the life and Resurrection of Christ (Acts 1:8 and 22; 1 Cor. 15:1 ff.). It was later used to designate those who testified to the truth of Christianity by constancy in the faith in spite of hardship or peril, even danger of death; and finally was restricted to those who sealed the faith with their blood during the persecutions (Apoc. 2:13; Mart. Polyc. 2, 2; 14, 2, etc.). One who professed his faith before a court and in consequence was mistreated, tortured, imprisoned or exiled, but was not put to death, was called ὁμολογητής, *confessor* (cfr. Matt. 10:32). But even Cyprian does not use the terms consistantly. — H. *Delehaye*, Martyr et Confesseur, AB 1921, 20/49 (and earlier works) also his "Sanctus", Brux. 1927. — F. *Dornseiff*, ArchRelW 1923/24, 133/53. — O. *Michel*, Prophet und Martyrer, 1932. — H. v. *Campenhausen* (vide supra). — E. *Peterson*, Zeuge der Wahrheit, 1937. — H. *Strathmann*, Art. Μάρτυς etc. im Theol. Wörterb. z. N.T. IV, 1939, 477 ff. — E. *Günther*, Μάρτυς, 1941. — J. *Ernst*, HJG 1913, 328/53. — E. L. *Hummel*, The Concept of Martyrdom According to St. Cyprian of Carthage, Washington 1946.

According to Origen (C. Cels. III, 8) the *number* of martyrs down to the middle of the third century was not large. Yet we must not ignore the "multitudo ingens" during the reign of Nero (§ 15, 1). Later the number increased greatly. Cyprian (De mortal. 26) speaks of a "martyrum innumerabilis populus"; and there were mass executions during the reign of Diocletian (L. Hertling, Gregorianum 1944, 103/29). From the beginning the Church held martyrs and confessors in high regard (cfr. § 24, 1 on their intercession for penitents); and confessors were readily accepted into the ranks of the clergy. The anniversary of a martyr's death was celebrated as his birthday to a higher life (ἡμέρα γενέθλιος, Mart. Polyc. 18: dies natalis) with special services above or near his tomb, with the reading of the acts of his martyrdom (Passio) and a memorial banquet. The names of martyrs were entered in the calendar of feasts, from which later developed the voluminous *martyrologies* (Synaxaria, menologia § 70, 1).

Unfortunately not many original and authentic *acts of martyrs* have been preserved which give the official minutes of the courts with little or no additions (Acta martyrum in the proper sense of the word, such as the acts of Justin and of the martyrs of Scillium) or are at least based on the testimony of eye and ear witnesses (Passiones or Acta Martyrum) such as the accounts of the martyrdom of St. Polycarp, the martyrs of Lyons, Perpetua and Felicitas, St. Pionius, St. Cyprian and others. The historian Eusebius made a collection of the older acta, which has been lost with the exception of his account of the martyrs of Palestine 303—311. The acts, mentioned in § 15 and 16, which have remained substantially unchanged are indicated by a †. Far greater is the number of *legends of martyrs*, most of which originated in the period immediately following the persecutions. They run the gamut from slight revisions of older authentic material to fantastic embellishment and pure fiction. Collections of acts and legends of the martyrs are found in the ASS of the *Bollandists* and in *Ruinart* (§ 2, 8). A. Ehrhard in his excellent work "Überlieferung und Bestand der hagiographischen und homiletischen Literatur der griechischen Kirche," 1937/43 (§ 2, 9) gives a survey of the Greek tradition. — *O. v. Gebhardt*, Acta martyrum selecta, 1902; G. Barra, Turin 1945. — *R. Knopf*, Ausgewählte Martyrerakten, [3]1929. German tr. by *G. Rauschen*, BKV 14, 1913 and *H. Rahner*, Die Martyrerakten des 2. Jh., 1941; French tr. by *H. Leclercq*, Les Martyrs II, Paris 1903, and *P. Hanozin*, La geste des martyrs, Paris 1935, German tr.: Helden der Urkirche, by E. Lense, 1938; English by *E. C. E. Owen*, Some authentic Acts of the early martyrs, Oxford 1927. — Surveys of earlier works: O. Bardenhewer, GeschAL II[2], 664 ff.; A. Harnack, GeschAL I, 807 ff.; II, 2, 463 ff.; H. Leclercq, DictAC I, 373/446; Dufourcq, Nau, Tournebize, DictHE I, 381/415. General: *E. Le Blant*, Les actes des martyrs, Paris 1883; Les persécuteurs et les martyrs, ibid. 1893. — *A. Ehrhard*, Die griech. Martyrien, 1907. — *P. Allard*, Dix leçons sur le martyre, Paris [3]1907; DictApol III, 331/491. — *H. Leclercq*, Martyre, DictAC X, 2359/512. — *J. Geffcken*, Die christl. Martyrien, Hermes 1910, 481/506. — *A. Harnack*, Das ursprüngl. Motiv d. Abfassung von Martyrer- u. Heilungsakten in der Kirche, Sb. Berlin 1910, 106/25. — *W. Hellmanns*, Wertschätzung d. Martyriums als eines Rechtfertigungsmittels in d. altchristl. Kirche, Dissertation 1912. — *K. Holl*, NJklA 33, 1914, 521/56 (also in Ges. Aufsätze

z. KG. II, 1928, 68/102). — *R. Reitzenstein*, Nachr. Gött. 1916, 417/67; Hermes 1917, 442/52. — M. Viller, RevAm 1925, 3 ff. 105 ff.; Viller and K. Rahner, Aszese u. Mystik in der Väterzeit, 1939, 29/40 (Martyrdom and Perfection). — *O. Sild*, cfr. § 14, 3. — *D. W. Riddle*, The Martyrs. A Study in Social Control, Chicago 1931. Principal works: *H. Delehaye S.J.*, Les passions des martyrs et les genres littéraires, Bruxelles 1921; Les origines du culte des martyrs, Brux. ²1933; Cinq leçons sur la méthode hagiographique, Brux. 1934. *H. v. Campenhausen*, Die Idee des Martyriums, § 14, 3. Cfr. literature in § 15, 16 and 70.

# § 15.
## The Christian Persecutions from Nero to the Middle of the Third Century[1].

The Roman emperors of the Early Christian Era did not persecute the adherents of the new religion. *Claudius* (41—51) proceeded

---

[1] P. ALLARD, Histoire des persécutions, 5 vol. Paris ³1903/8; Le christianisme et l'empire Romain de Néron à Théodose, Paris ⁹1925. B. AUBE, Hist. des persécutions (to 284), 3 vol. Paris 1875/86. K. J. NEUMANN, Der röm. Staat u. die allg. Kirche bis Diokletian I, 1890. W. M. RAMSAY, see § 12. E. G. HARDY, Christianity and the Roman Government, London 1894 (2. ed.: Studies in Roman History, 1906). H. HÜLLE, Die Toleranzerlasse röm. Kaiser für das Christentum bis 313, 1895. G. UHLHORN, Der Kampf des Christentums mit dem Heidentum, ⁶1899. A. LINSENMAYER, Die Bekämpfung des Christentums durch den röm. Staat bis Julian, 1905. H. B. WORKMAN, Persecution in the Early Church, London 1906. L. H. CANFIELD, The Early Persecutions of the Christians (to 138), New York 1913. U. FRACASSINI, L'Impero e il Cristianesimo da Nerone a Costantino, Perugia 1913. A. MANARESI, L'Impero Romano e il Cristianesimo, Torino 1914. ED. MEYER, Ursprung u. Anfänge des Christent. III, 1923, 500/65 (to Trajan). E. TR. MERRILL, Essays in Early Christian History, London 1924. G. SCHOENAICH, Der Kampf zw. Römertum u. Christentum in geschichtl. Entwicklung, 1927 (Lecture). W. WEBER, Röm. Kaisersgesch. u. KG., 1929; Rom, Herrschertum n. Reich im 2 Jh., 1937. L'HOMO, Les empereurs Romains et le christianisme, Paris 1931. A. EHRHARD, Die Kirche der Martyrer, 1932 (important). Prosopographia Imperii Romani s. I—III, Pars I—II², edd. E. GROAG et A. STEIN, 1933/6. G. SAMA, Bibliografia generale dell'età romana imperiale, Firenze 1938 ff. TH. MOMMSEN, Röm. Gesch. V (The Roman provinces from Caesar to Diocletian), ¹⁰1927. H. SCHILLER, Gesch. der röm. Kaiserzeit, 5 vols. 1883/7. V. DURUY-G. F. HERTZBERG, (same title) 5 vols. 1884/9. A. V. DOMASZEWSKI, Gesch. der röm. Kaiser, 2 vols. ³1922. R. V. POEHLMANN, Röm. Kaiserzeit u. Untergang der antiken Welt, in Weltgesch., ed. J. V. PFLUGK-HARTTUNG I, 1909. E. KORNEMANN, Die röm. Kaiserzeit, in Einl. in die klass. Altertumswiss. III³, 1933; Röm. Gesch. II: Die Kaiserzeit, 1939. G. FERRERO u. C. BARBAGALLO, Das alte Rom, 1927. B. W. HENDERSON, Five Roman Emperors (Vespasian to Trajan), Cambridge 1927. J. WOLF, Die römische Kaiserzeit, 1932. E. MEYER, Grundzüge der Gesch. der röm. Kaiserzeit, 1935. M. CARY, History of Rome down to the Reign of Constantine, London 1935. H. M. D. PARKER, A History of the Roman World A. D. 138—327, London 1935. The Cambridge Ancient History vol. XI (70—192); XII (193 to 324), Cambridge 1936/9. L. HOMO, Le Haut-Empire, Paris 1937 (= Histoire générale, publ. par G. GLOTZ, III p.: Hist. Romaine, t. 3). M. BESNIER, L'Empire romain de l'avènement des Sévères au Concile de Nicée, Paris 1937 (Hist. générale etc., t. 4). F. ALTHEIM, Die Soldaten-

against the Jews of Rome about the year 50 and expelled them as he had done earlier (41) at Alexandria, because, as Suetonius relates (Claud. 25), they had caused constant disturbances "at the urging of the Chrestus" (impulsore Chresto)[1]. The ordinance naturally affected Jewish Christians who were then thought to be a Jewish sect (Acts 18:2; Aquilla and Priscilla); but this can not be called a Christian persecution. The distinction of having inaugurated Christian persecutions belongs to the infamous Emperor **Nero** (54—68)[2] (Eus. II, 25, 5). According to *Tacitus* (Annal. XV, 44), Christian baiting began with the burning of Rome in July, 64. The populace suspected the emperor of having criminally caused the conflagration. To divert suspicion from himself and to satisfy the popular demand for retributive justice, Nero made use of the Christians as suitable victims. With the help of informers (Jewish?) he caused the arrest of a great number (multitudo ingens) of Christians, who, because they practised "pernicious superstition" (exitiabilis superstitio) and committed "shameful crimes" were hated by the people. They were not accused of having burned the city but were rather convicted of "hatred of the human race" (odio humani generis) and summarily condemned to death. There is much in this account that is not clear. Some recent critics rather unconvincingly question a direct connection between the burning of Rome and the subsequent proceedings, since, they say, Tacitus was biased and endeavored to paint Nero in the blackest colors.

---

kaiser (Sept. Severus—Diocletian), 1939; Die Krise der Alten Welt, 1943 ff. See literature in §5 and 14. For bio-bibliography of the martyrs cfr. R. KNOPF, Ausgew. Martyrerakten, [3]1929, and H. DELEHAYE (§ 14 and especially the Analecta Bollandiana.

[1] It is still disputed whether "Chrestus" refers to Christ, erroneously considered by Suetonius to be still living, or whether the disturbances arose from heated discussions regarding the Messias, or an unknown Jewish agitator in Alexandria at that time. Cfr. W. SESTON, Rev. d'hist. et de philos. relig. 1931, 275/304; H. JANNE, MEL. BIDEZ II, Paris 1934, 531/53; MEL. F. CUMONT, Brussels, 1936, 273/95; G. MAY, Revue hist. de droit français et étranger 1939, 1/46. For a discussion of the Jewish question in Alexandria in the year 41 see ST. LÖSCH, Epistula Claudiana, 1930.

[2] M. CANAVESI, Nerone, Milan 1945. M. A. LEVI, Nerone e i suoi tempi, Milan 1949. C. F. ARNOLD, Die Neron. Christenverfolgung, 1888. A. PROFUMO, see note § 14, 3. TH. KLETTE, Die Christenkatastrophe unter Nero, 1907. G. SEMERIA, Il primo sangue cristiano, Roma [2]1907. G. SCHOENAICH, Die Neron. Christenverf., 1911 (in Festschr. publ. by schles. Philologenverein). H. JANNE, L'Antiquité Classique II, 1933, 331/56 (Persecution of Christians of rank under Nero A.D. 65). STYGER, MACKINNON and BARNES, see § 12, 1. On Tacitus: B. GRUNDL, ThQ 1904, 1/10; J. STIGLMAYR, StML 1910 I, 169/84; C. WEYMAN, Festgabe M. Schanz 1912, 167/72; H. LECLERCQ, DictAC VII, 481/501; XII, 1124/50; A. KURFESS, Mnemosyne 1938, 261/72; H. FUCHS, VC 1950, 65/93.

The executions took place in the imperial gardens as a spectacular form of public entertainment, and presented every refinement of torture (crucifixion, wild beasts, burning as living torches and various forms of death to represent mythological characters: Danaids and Dircae, cfr. I Clem. 6). Apparently the persecution was confined to the capital city, and continued there until the end of Nero's reign. Among the victims were the Apostles *Peter* and *Paul* (§ 9 and 10). The impression made on the Roman world was as vivid as it was lasting; henceforth the name Christian was depised; it stood for all that was abominable and deserving of death (§ 14, 3).

2. During the reign of the first two emperors of the Flavian dynasty, *Vespasian* and *Titus*, the Christians enjoyed relative peace. But in the last years of **Domitian** (81—96)[1], who fostered the cult of the emperor even to the extent of calling himself Dominus et deus, and whose reign was generally odious, their troubles began anew. The cousin of the emperor, Titus *Flavius Clement*, senator and ex-consul, was charged with "atheism" or "of adopting Jewish customs" and executed; while his wife, Flavia *Domitilla*, was exiled. It seems that the consul *Acilius Glabrio*, another victim of Domitian's cruelty, must also be considered a martyr. The martyrs of Asia Minor mentioned in the Apocalypse (2:13 Antipas of Pergamus and 20:4) were put to death at this time; for it appears that they were executed for refusing divine honors to the emperor. The Apostle *John* was banished to Patmos (§ 11, 1). If Hegesippus is to be believed (Eus. III, 19, 20) the suspicious tyrant caused the living relatives of Christ to be brought to Rome, but released them when he became convinced that they had no political ambitions. Compared with the persecution of Nero, this one was relatively mild (Tert. Apolog. 5: Domitianus portio Neronis de crudelitate). Yet the historian Dio Cassius and others speak of many victims.

3. *Nerva* was more kindly disposed. He even forbade accusations of lese majesty to be made and would allow no charges to be pressed against those who lived according to the Jewish (Christian)

---

[1] DIO CASS. Hist. Rom. 67, 14. SUET. Domit. 10. 15. FUNK, AU I, 308/29 (T. Flavius Clement, a Christian, but not Bishop of Rome). J. B. LIGHTFOOT, St. Clement of Rome I, London 1890, 14/103. H. ACHELIS, Acta Nerei et Achillei, TU 11, 2, 1893. D. MCFAYDEN, Americ. Journal of Theol. 1920, 46/66 (Causes of the persecution). H. LECLERCQ, DictAC VI, 1259/74 (A. Glabrio). R. L. P. MILBURN, The Church Quarterly Rev. 1945, 154/64. Cfr. also § 11 and 14.

form of life (Dio Cassius 68, 2). But under **Trajan** (98—117)[1] a capable ruler of strict military discipline, who extended the boundaries of the Empire as far as they were ever to reach, a new persecution broke out. It was accompanied by the enforcement of the statute prohibiting illegal assemblies (hetairae). Simeon, the 120 year old bishop of Jerusalem and kinsman of the Lord, was crucified, and *Ignatius*, Bishop of Antioch, (§ 37, 4), was thrown to wild beasts in the Roman arena. The accounts of the persecution in *Asia Minor* are more detailed. *Pliny* the Younger was proconsul in Bithynia and Pontus at the time. After executing many Christians and causing many others to defect, he became alarmed at the great number of those who stubbornly clung to this "most perverse superstition" (§ 12, 8) and in 112 wrote to the emperor for instructions. Trajan replied: that Christians were not to be hunted down, but if they were denounced and brought to trial, they were to be punished (conquirendi non sunt; si deferantur et arguantur, puniendi sunt). Renegades, of course, were to be released. Moreover, he forbade any attention to be paid to anonymous information; yet the lot of Christians was serious enough. The highest authority had expressly declared their religion to be illegal and had threatened them with death. Trajan's rescript, contradictory as it was (Tert. Apolog. II, 8) imposed no obligation on his successors yet it long remained a sort of precedent for future assaults on the Church.

Trajan's two immediate successors were more indulgent. By imperial edicts they took under their protection the Christians of *Greece* and *Asia Minor* who were frequently the victims of *mob violence*. The laws, however, remained in force. *Hadrian* (117—138), a religious man, and a progressive ruler, in a rescript to the governor of the provinces of Asia, *Minucius Fundanus*[2] about 125, threatened to punish denunciations made against Christians for motives of gain and insisted that trials be conducted strictly in accordance with legal principles. *Antoninus Pius* (138—161) took the same stand. According to a

---

[1] PLIN. Ep. X, 96. 97.   C. F. ARNOLD, Studien z. Gesch. der Plinianischen Christenverfolgung, 1887.   A. J. KLEFFNER, Der Briefwechsel zw. d. jüng. Plinius u. K. Trajan die Christen betreff., 1907.   J. MEYER, Der Briefwechsel des Plinius u. Trajan, Dissertation Straßb. 1909.   CH. BABUT, RHLR 1910, 289/315.   DAVIES, JThSt 1913, 407/14.   W. WEBER, Festgabe K. Müller 1922, 24/45.   A. KURFESS, ZntW 1937, 295/98; Mnemosyne 1939, 237 ff. J. KRAEMER, Classical Philology 1934, 293/300.   S. L. MOHLER, op. cit. 1935, 167/79; R. M. GRANT, HarvThR 1948, 273/4.
[2] IUST. Apol. I, 68.   EUS. IV, 9. Rightly understood, the genuinity of Hadrian's rescript can not be questioned. Cfr. FUNK, AU I, 330/45; J. M. MECKLIN, Hadrians Reskript, 1899; C. CALLEWAERT, RHLR 1903, 152/89; B. CAPELLE, RevBén 1927, 365/68.   H. LECLERCQ, DictAC VI, 1967/81 (Hadrian). W. HÜTTL, Antoninus Pius I, Prag 1936.

rescript cited by Eusebius (IV, 13) but probably not genuine, he is supposed to have forbidden the governors of Asia to allow the charge of "atheism" to be made against Christians. Yet the apologies composed by *Quadratus, Aristides* and *Justin* (§ 38), show how cruelly Christians had to suffer. During the reign of Hadrian, the Christians of *Palestine* were severely oppressed by the Jews (Justin, Apol. I, 31) because they refused to take part in the uprising led by Simon Bar-Cochba (132—135). Irenaeus (Adv. haer. III, 3, 3) reports the martyrdom of Pope *Telesphorus* (136 ?). The martyrdom of *St. Ptolemaeus* and two other Christians occurred in Rome under Antoninus Pius and induced Justin to write his second apology. About the same time, *St. Polycarp,* the eighty-six year old bishop of Smyrna (§ 37, 5) underwent his "glorious martyrdom" (Irenaeus III, 3, 4). According to the best reckoning, he died on February 22, 156, preceded in death by eleven companions.

4. A fourth and greater persecution began under **Marcus Aurelius** (160—180)[1], an otherwise good ruler and philosopher of the Stoic School. His reign was ushered in by a series of calamities; famine and pestilence devastated the Empire and hordes of barbarians threatened the borders. In many places the people rose against the Christians whom they assumed to be the cause of these misfortunes and shamefully maltreated them. The emperor himself could see in Christianity nothing but a spirit of contradiction and rank folly (Medit. XI, 3). The renowned rhetorician *Fronto,* the emperor's teacher, delivered a diatribe against Christians (possibly under Hadrian); and *Celsus* published his "True Word" (§ 17, 1). The severity of the persecution is seen from the apologies of *Athenagoras, Melito, Apollinaris* and *Miltiades* (§ 17, 1) which were addressed to the emperor. No special edict of persecution was issued; but an imperial rescript of 176 could easily be invoked against Christians. It forbade the incitement of the people by introducing new religions and punished the crime by banishment in the case of persons of rank and by death for those of the lower class. When questioned by the proconsul of Gaul regarding the treatment of Christians, the emperor endorsed the principles of Trajan.

A number of renowned martyrs died at this time. The outstanding apologist *Justin* (§ 38), was beheaded at Rome with six companions. In *Lyons,* where the persecution began with a popular uprising against Christians in 177, there were about 50 victims,

---

[1] J. DARTIGUE-PEYRON, Marc-Aurèle dans ses rapports avec le christianisme, Thèse Paris 1897. K. HUBIK, Die Apologien Justins, 1912, 339/72. H. EBERLEIN, K. Mark Aurel u. die Christen, Dissertation Breslau 1914. G. LOISEL, La vie de Marc-Aurèle, Paris 1930. C. P. PHIPPS, Hermathena 22, 1932, 167/81. A. CHAGNY, Les martyrs de Lyon de 177, Lyon 1936. H. DELEHAYE, AB 1940, 142/76 (Acts of the martyrs of Pergamus). Cfr. § 5, 4.

among them the ninety year old bishop *Pothinus*, the deacon *Sanctus* of Vienne, the young slave-girl *Blandina* and the youth *Ponticus* (Eus. H.E. V, 1—2: the letter from Lyons and Vienne to the churches of Asia Minor describing the persecution). In the East, the bishops, *Publius* of Athens and *Sagaris* of Laodicaea were martyred. It was probably at this time that Bishop *Carpus*, the deacon *Papylus* and the newly-converted woman *Agathonice* (Agathonica) perished in the flames at Pergamus. The old legend that Marcus Aurelius forbade further persecution of the new religion after his campaign against the Quadi and Marcomanni, is not deserving of credence. The emperor himself ascribed the rain which saved the army and resulted in victory to Jupiter Pluvius and not to the prayers of the Christians in his army, as the story of the Legio fulminata (fulminea)[1] relates the event.

Peace was restored again under Marcus Aurelius' unworthy son *Commodus* (180—192). This was due chiefly to the influence of the emperor's concubine or morganatic wife, Marcia, who at least favored the Christians if she was not one of them. Her mediation obtained the release of Christians who were languishing in the lead mines of Sardinia. It was even possible to hold synods in several provinces in an attempt to settle the Easter controversy (§ 25, 3). Yet there were several martyrs. Six Christians (three men and three women) from *Scillium* in Numidia were beheaded at Carthage (July 17, 180). The noble and well-educated (senator?) *Apollonius* died at Rome about 185 after delivering an elegant plea before the court. For a time the proconsul Arrius Antoninus of Asia Minor bestirred himself to uproot Christianity in his province.

5. The African **Septimius Severus** (193—211)[2] continued the tolerant policy of his predecessors and even showed himself personally well-disposed toward Christians. But his attitude soon changed, due to Jewish insurrections and probably also to some apprehensions aroused by the increasing number of Christians in high offices. In 201 he forbade under severe penalties the formal initiation into Judaism by circumcision and in 202 under the same penalties, he prohibited his subjects from joining the new religion. Hence this persecution affected especially catechumens and the recently baptized. We have some details of its course in Egypt

---

[1] TERT. Apolog. 5; Ad Scap. 4. EUS. V, 5. DIO CASS. 71, 9. Cfr. A. HARNACK, Sb. Berlin 1894, 835/82; J. GEFFCKEN, N JklA 3, 1899, 253 ff.; J. PETERSEN, Rhein. Mus. f. Philol. 1895, 453/74; K. WEIZSÄCKER, Das Regenwunder unter M. Aurel, 1894 (lecture); W. WEBER, Sb. Heidelberg I, 7, 1910. F. GUEY, MélAH 1948/49 (the miraculous rainfall).
[2] M. PLATNAUER, The Life and Reign of L. Septimius Severus, Oxford 1918. FLUSS, RE Pauly-Wissowa 2. R. II, 1923, 1940/2002. H. U. JUSTINAKY, Klio 1942, 200/19. A. CALDERINI, I Severi, Rome 1949. The Cambridge Ancient History XII, M. BESNIER, F. ALTHEIM, etc., cfr. § 15, 1.

(Eus. VI, 1—5) and Africa. *Leonides* and several catechumens of his son Origen were martyred at Alexandria; and the well-known martyrs *Perpetua* and *Felicitas*[1] with three others died in the arena at Carthage (March 7, 202 or 203). The acts of this latter martyrdom are among the best now extant. They were probably written by Tertullian.

During the last years of Septimius Severus' reign (i. e. from about 208) a semblance of peace was restored and endured for some time. However, the (lost) collection of imperial rescripts against Christians made by the eminent jurist Domitius *Ulpianus* (about 215) (Lactant. Instit. V, 11), proves that higher officials never abandoned their hostile attitude. The leniency of M. Aurelius Antoninus called *Caracalla* (211—217), one of the most depraved of the emperors, was probably due to some favorable impressions made upon him by Christians when he was a child (lacte christiano educatus, Tert. Ad Scap. 4). Since the laws continued in force, it was always possible for local officials to apply them; as happened in Africa under the Proconsul Scapula (211—212) to whom Tertullian addressed one of his most trenchant exhortations.

6. With Caracalla began the reign of the so-called **Syrian emperors** (211—235)[2], a dynasty established through Caracalla's mother, the Aramaean Julia Domna, daughter of the highpriest of the sun at Emesa, and wife of Septimius Severus (§ 17, 2). This period was one of the most disturbed and unfortunate in Roman history and was characterized by domination of the army and the rule of women (Julia Domna, her sister, Julia Maesa and their daughters the four Julias). The East began to assume equal importance with the West in the Empire and in 212 Caracalla granted Roman citizenship to all subjects who were not slaves. The mystery cults

---

[1] The best edition of the Passio SS. Perpetuae et Felicitatis is that of C. J. VAN BEEK I, Noviomagi 1936, and of the same author in Floril. patrist. 43, 1938. W. H. SHEWRING, RevBén 1931, 15/22 (Tertullian the compiler of the Passio). F. J. DÖLGER, AntChrist 1930, 16/40 (the vision of Dinocrates). H. LECLERCQ, DictAC XIV, 393/444. E. RUPPRECHT, Rhein. Mus. f. Philol. 1941, 177/192 (Tertullian *not* the compiler of the Passio).

[2] J. RÉVILLE-G. KRÜGER, Die Religion zu Rom unter den Severern, [2]1906. K. BIHLMEYER, Die „syrischen" Kaiser zu Rom u. das Christentum, 1916. J. GEFFCKEN, Der Ausgang des griech.-röm. Heidentums, [2]1929. For literature on the Oriental Mystery cults (TOUTAIN, CUMONT, REITZENSTEIN, GRESSMANN, PRÜMM etc.) see § 6. J. LEIPOLDT im Handb. d. Rel. Wissenschaft, ed. G. MENSCHING I, 4, 1948; Die Religion des Mithra, 1930. H. LECLERCQ, Mithriacisme, DictZC XI, 1498/1554. A. D. NOCK, Journ. of Rom. Stud. 1937, 108/13 (the Spirit of Mithraism). H. P. L'ORANGE, § 14. A. HOLLARD, Les cultes des mystères, Paris 1938. General works on mystery cults, Syncretism and Christianity: J. BLÖTZER, StML 1906 II; 1907 I; ST. V. DUNIN-BORKOWSKI, ZkTh 1911; StML 1912 I; H. DIECKMANN, StML 1912 II; K. BENZ, HJG 1919, 1/30; M. J. LAGRANGE, Rev. bibl. 1919, 157/217, 419/80; H. RAHNER, Eranos-Jb. 1944, 347 ff.

of the East (§ 5, 1, 3) especially *sun-worship* (Sol invictus Mithras) became very popular in the West. It is probable that Caracalla issued a special edict recognizing alien (Oriental) religions and incorporating them into the Roman state-religion. It was at this time, too, that *Neo-Platonism*, an idealistic, religious philosophy began to flourish at Alexandria (§ 17, 2).

The youthful **Heliogabalus** (218—222) who disgraced the throne by every manner of vice and orgy, supplanted the Roman state-religion for a few years by the worship of Baal of Emesa and called himself Sacerdos amplissimus Dei invicti Solis Elagabali. It is said that he planned to merge all religions, even Judaism and Christianity with his sun worship. His cousin, the noble-minded and dutiful, but weak, **Severus Alexander** (222—235) was more kindly disposed toward the Christians than any other Roman emperor. His biographer, Lampridius (Alex. Sev. 22) says of him: Christianos esse passus est. He not only tolerated many Christians among his attendants but was also on friendly terms with the learned lay theologian Julius Africanus (§ 39, 5). He caused the Golden Rule (Matt. 7:12), expressed negatively, to be inscribed on palaces and public buildings and in a legal dispute with restaurateurs, he promised the Christians of Rome the piece of property under litigation to be used for purposes of worship. However, the statement of his unreliable biographer (c. 43) that Alexander built a temple to Christ and intended to enroll Him among the gods of Rome, is not deserving of credence. And the further assertion that he placed an image of Christ in his lararium alongside of Apollonius of Tyana (§ 17, 2), Abraham, Orpheus and the apotheosized emperors, is doubtful to say the least. His mother, the gifted but ambitious Julia *Mamaea*, took an active interest in Christianity and was acquainted with the foremost theologians. About 232, she summoned *Origen* to Antioch to deliver lectures on religion, and the Roman priest *Hippolytus* dedicated a work on the Resurrection to her; but it was only in the fifth century that Rufinus, Orosius and other historians began to allege that she was a Christian. The Christian Church profited greatly by the favorable circumstances and came nearer to public recognition than at any other time prior to the reign of Constantine the Great.

But even in this period of relative peace there were some victims of the still extant laws. The martyrdom of *St. Cecilia* is usually placed at the time of Severus Alexander, since the acts mention a Bishop Urban (= Pope Urban 222—230?). Still a later date (the persecution of Valerian or Diocletian) is not wholly impossible. These acts, like those of other martyrs of the city of Rome, Sts. *Agnes, Lawrence, Sebastian, Martina*, etc., are largely legendary. But there can be no doubt about these martyrs themselves for the veneration paid to them from the earliest times is sufficient proof that they died for the faith. On *St. Cecilia*: J. P. Kirsch, Die hl. Cäcilia in der röm. Kirche des Altertums, 1910. — H. Quentin, DictAC II, 2712/38. — P. Frenchi de' Cavalieri, Studi e Testi 24, Rom 1912. — H. A. Kellner und P. A. Kirsch in ThQ 1912/16. — L. Saltet, BullLE 1912, 169/79. — Pr. Guéranger, Sainte Cécile, Paris 1874, nouv. éd. 2 vol. Paris 1933 (popular). — On *St. Agnes*: P. Franchi de' Cavalieri,

San Agnese nella tradizione e nella legenda, RQ Suppl. 5, 1899. — F. Jubaru, S. Agnès, Paris 1907. — H. Grisar, ZkTh 1927, 532/47. — A. Monaci, Nuovo bullettino di archeol. crist. 28, 1922, 33/42. —The Bollandist, *H. Delehaye*, has made a critical study of the Roman martyrs whose feasts are celebrated in November and December in his Étude sur Légendier romain, Brussels 1936. (For St. Cecilia, cfr. pp. 194/220.)

7. The murder of Alexander and Mamaea in an encampment on the Rhine effected a sudden and drastic change. The army bestowed the purple on **Maximus Thrax** (235—238), the "first barbarian" to ascend the imperial throne. He maltreated all the partisans of his predecessor, but vented his passion in a special manner on the Christians whom Alexander had favored. His edict was aimed primarily at the overseers of congregations, i. e., the higher clergy. Pope Pontian and the antibishop Hippolytus (§ 32, 4:39, 4) were exiled to Sardinia where the torrid climate soon released them from worse sufferings. Hippolytus was buried in the cemetery which bears his name in the Via Tiburtina and the epitaph of Pontianus was discovered in 1909 in the catacombs of St. Callistus. Yet it seems that this was not a major persecution except in the provinces of Cappadocia and the Pontus, where the populace arose against the Christians whom they blamed for a destructive earthquake. Nor did the hostilities last long. Maximus himself, it appears, took no active part in it. Peace was restored under *Gordian III* (283—44) and under *Philip the Arabian* (244—249), the son of a Beduin sheik of Bostra. Origen corresponded with Philip and his wife Severa. In fact, Philip was so friendly toward Christians that a rumor spread among them (Eus. VI, 34; VII, 10, 3) that he was a Christian and that he had submitted to the penitential discipline of the Church (at Antioch) to atone for his bloody deeds. But on coins commemorative of the thousand-year anniversary of Rome (248) he is represented as the Pontifex Maximus offering sacrifice; and in his public life he always appeared to be a thorough pagan.

## § 16.
### The Great Persecutions from Decius to Diocletian.
### The Victory of the Church.

1. Excepting the brief persecution under Maximus the Church had enjoyed peace for forty years, a period sufficiently long for her to increase notably in members and to organize without much molestation. More than ever before she was a factor to be reckoned

with in the State and in society. But her internal development had not kept pace with her external growth — the long peace had begotten laxity. Many of her members, both lay and clerical had become lukewarm and worldly-minded. St. Cyprian says (De lapsis 5) it was for this reason that God sent a new persecution "to try His family." It was not long, but it was exceedingly violent and devastating. It began under **Decius** (249—251)[1] a poorly educated but energetic soldier-emperor. He was of Pannonian-Illyrian descent and from the beginning of his reign resolved to carry out a policy of restoration on a large scale. The Empire had been brought close to ruin by corruption, especially since the adoption of Oriental religions and ways of life. Decius' first care, therefore, was to strengthen the defenses against internal and external foes so that Rome's ancient glory would not be made a mockery by barbarians. Since, in his opinion, the Christians were the most dangerous enemies of the State, he felt himself obliged to force them to conform to the ancient religion which had unified the Empire. He set about the work so energetically and systematically that his persecution surpassed in importance all previous ones (§ 14, 3). An edict issued toward the end of 249 or the beginning of 250 commanded all subjects, men, women and children, to offer a solemn sacrifice (supplicatio) to the gods. Those who hesitated were goaded to action by all known means of coercion: imprisonment, confiscation of property, banishment, the mines, the rack and when all other means failed, the death penalty. However, as cruel as this persecution was, the death penalty was not inflicted in very many cases. Bishops especially were marked out as victims (tyrannus infestus sacerdotibus, Cypr. Ep. 55, 9). Decius would have tolerated a rival to his throne, sooner than a Christian bishop in Rome (l. c.).

Since the blow fell unexpectedly, the terror of the Christians was the greater and their power of resistance unfortunately was not at its peak. In large cities such as Alexandria, Carthage, Smyrna and Rome there were many defections (Eus. VI, 39—41; Cypr. De lapsis, 7—9): even some bishops renounced the faith. Some of the recreants (lapsi) offered sacrifices or incense to the gods (sacrificati,

---

[1] J. A. F. GREGG, The Decian Persecution, Edinburgh 1897. G. SCHOE-NAICH, Die Christenverf. des Kaisers Decius, 1907. K. BIHLMEYER, ThQ 1910, 19/50. H. LECLERCQ, DictAC IV, 309/39. E. LIESERING, Untersuchungen zur Christenverf. des K. Decius, Dissertation 1933. A. ALFÖLDI, Klio 1938, 323/48 (Persecutions from Decius to Gallienus). The Cambridge Ancient History XII (§ 15), 165 ff. F. ALTHEIM, Die Krise der alten Welt im 3. Jh. I u. III, 1943.

turificati), others, without sacrificing fraudulently obtained certificates (libellus) testifying that they had conformed and were officially registered as being Christians no longer. But there was also "a multitude" (Cypr. De lapsis 2) of steadfast confessors and martyrs of both sexes and of every age. Pope *Fabian* was one of the first victims (his office remained vacant for over a year). The priest *Pionius* of Smyrna was burned. The bishops *Babylas* of Antioch and *Alexander* of Jerusalem died in prison[1] and the aged *Origen* suffered the rack and imprisonment before being liberated. Many others like Cyprian of Carthage, Dionysius of Alexandria and Gregory Thaumaturgus of Neocaesarea saved their lives by flight. In the spring of 251 the persecution began to abate, since Decius was diverted by an attack of the Goths in Moesia. When he fell in battle against them on the lower Danube in May or June 251, Christians again began to enjoy peace. The Church had been violently convulsed, but by no means overthrown. Many of the lapsi contritely sought their way back to the fold; but in Rome and Carthage their readmission gave rise to a heated controversy (§ 35, 1, 2).

More than forty original libelli or fragments of libelli written on papyrus have been discovered in Egypt in relatively recent times; thirty-four of them in the village of Theadelphia in Fajum (Central Egypt). It is doubtful how many of these were issued to Christians; for one of them unquestionably was issued to a pagan priestess. The texts of these libelli are given by *J. R. Knipfing*, HarvThR 1923, 345/90; *Ch. Wessely* in Patrologia Orientalis IV, 2 u. XVIII, 3, Paris 1907, 1924; Michigan Papyri III, ed. *J. G. Winter*, Ann Arbor 1936, 133 ff. Cfr. also *P. M. Meyer*, Abh. Berlin 1910, 5; Griech. Texte aus Ägypten, 1916. — *G. Schoenaich*, Die libelli u. ihre Bedeut. f. die Christenverfolg. des K. Decius, 1910. — *A. Bludau*, Die ägyptischen Libelli u. die Christenverfolg. des K. Decius, 1931. — *H. Leclercq*, DictAC IV, 309 ff.; V, 1067 ff.; IX, 78 ff.; XIII, 1402 ff. — *L. Faulhaber*, ZkTh 1919, 439 ff. 617 ff.

Decius' successor Emperor **Gallus** (251—253) did not at first molest the Christian Church; but her trials were not yet over. When a terrible plague began to ravage the empire, Gallus ordered expiatory sacrifices to Apollo. And although there was no persecution on a large scale, Christians felt the effect of this new edict. However, they were now better prepared and even some who had lapsed in

---

[1] This was probably also the fate of Pope Fabian (Jan. 20, 250) since Cyprian in Ep. 28, 1, of August 25th speaks of martyrdom being "consummated by rack and execution only in Africa and not in Rome. On the other hand, Fabian's "martyrdom" is attested by Eusebius (VI, 39, 1) and the Roman Chronographer of 354. Cfr. H. KOCH, IntkZ 1920, 234 f.; H. LECLERCQ, DictAC V, 1058/64.

the previous persecution made amends for their weakness by their steadfastness in this one. Pope *Cornelius* died in exile and his successor *Lucius* was banished.

2. Peace was again restored when **Valerian** (253—260)[1] ascended the throne. The new emperor even took Christians into his service. But, with the Empire facing ruin, Valerian was easily induced by his minister of finance, Macrianus, to adopt a hostile attitude toward the Church (Eus. VII, 10—12). This persecution was calculated especially to destroy the organization of Christian congregations and to make it impossible for them to exist. A decree of 257 ordered bishops, priests and deacons to sacrifice under pain of banishment; visiting cemeteries (§ 28, 5) or attending assembles for religious worship was punished by death. A second edict in 258 (Cypr. Ep. 80, 1) ordered that clerics who refused to sacrifice were to be executed forthwith; laymen of the higher classes were to receive the same penalty if loss of position and property did not constrain them to obey; women of rank were to be exiled; and officials of the imperial household were to be reduced to slavery. In many of the provinces the persecution was accompanied by much bloodshed, especially in the East where Macrianus, now the emperor's rival, continued it as long as he could. In the West it practically ceased with Valerian's capture (259) in the war with Persia. Several of the martyrs of this period were illustrious churchmen. Pope *Sixtus II* was surprised while conducting services in the catacombs of St. Callistus and, together with four deacons, was beheaded on the spot (August 6, 258). Four days later his deacon *Lawrence* met death (by fire?). In Africa a great number, whose names are unknown (massa candida), were martyred at Utica together with their bishop Quadratus. It was in this persecution that *Cyprian*, the great bishop of Carthage, was beheaded (September 14, 258). In Spain Bishop *Fructuosus* of Tarragona and his deacons, Augurius and Eulogius †, were burned in the amphitheater (259).

Valerian's son and successor *Gallienus* (260—268) not only abrogated the laws against Christians but even restored to them the cemeteries that had

---

[1] P. J. HEALY, The Valerian Persecution, Boston 1905. P. CORSSEN, ZntW 1915, 147/66 (Sixtus II). On St. Lawrence: P. FRANCHI DE' CAVA-LIERI, RQ 1900, 159 ff. u. Studi e Testi 33, Rome 1920, 65/72; H. LECLERCQ, DictAC VI, 1827/31; VIII, 917/61. On the Massa candida: P. FRANCHI DE'CAVALIERI, Studi e Testi 9, 1903; G. MORIN, Rendiconti d. Pontificia Accad. Romana di archeol. 3, 1925, 289/312; H. LECLERCQ, DictAC X, 2649/63. On St. Fructuosus and companions: P. FRANCHI DE'CAVALIERI, Studi e Testi 65, Rome 1935, 129 ff.

been confiscated during the persecution, as well as the places of worship they had been able to acquire (§ 19, 3 and 23, 5) in spite of prohibitory laws enacted toward the end of the second century. It is probable that the emperor's benevolence extended even to individual Christians and that they recovered the property and dignities of which they had been deprived. These measures of Gallienus actually amounted to an edict of toleration. — H. Gregoire, Byzantion 1938, 587/8.

3. Thus about the year 260 there began an era of peace for Christians which lasted for over forty years and was disturbed only by a minor persecution under **Aurelian** (270—275). Aurelian known as Restitutor Orbis, was a votary of the gods, especially *Sol invictus* (of Palmyra). The *cult of the sun,* joined with the cult of the emperor, became, for a long time, the *State religion.* Yet, at first, Aurelian respected the edicts of Gallienus. He settled a dispute among the Christians of Antioch (272) and restored to the rightful bishop, Domnus, the church building claimed by the heretical and deposed bishop, Paul of Samosata (§ 32, 3). Political considerations, however, influenced the decision, since Paul was a partisan of Queen Zenobia of Palmyra, whom Valerian had vanquished. In 275 an edict of persecution was issued; but it had little effect since the emperor was murdered soon thereafter and his successor made no effort to carry it out. — *E. Groag,* Domitius Aurelianus, RE Pauly-Wissowa V, 1347/1419.

4. Emperor **Diocletian** (284—305)[1] did nothing to disquiet the Christians. As a ruler of ability and energy, he was chiefly concerned with a plan for the thoroughgoing reorganization of the Empire. It was to be an absolute military monarchy dependent only on the favor of Jupiter and made externally brilliant by an elaborate Oriental court ceremonial. The emperor's residence was transferred to the East (Nicomedia) and the administration of the whole Empire was divided into four prefectures, twelve dioceses and ninety-six pro-

---

[1] Principal sources: LACTANTIUS, De mortibus persecutorum (316/7); EUSEBIUS H. E. VIII—IX (314/15); De martyribus Palaestinae. E. STEIN, Gesch. des spätröm. Reiches I (284—476), 1928. W. SESTON, Dioclétien et la Tétrarchie I, Paris 1946. J. VOGT, Constantin d. Gr. u. sein Jahrh., 1949. A. J. MASON, The Persecution of Diocletian, Cambridge 1876. P. ALLARD (cfr. § 15) IV—V. J. BELSER, Zur Dioklet. Christenverf., 1891. B. VIOLET, Die paläst. Märtyrer des Eusebius, TU 14, 4, 1896. T. DE BACCI VENUTI, Dalla grande persecuzione alla vittoria del Cristianesimo, Milano 1913. P. BATIFFOL, La paix Constantinienne et le Catholicisme, Paris [4]1929. K. BIHLMEYER, ThQ 1912, 411 ff. 527 ff. (Galerius' edict of toleration). CH. BABUT, Rev. hist. 123, 1916, 225/52 (causes of the persecutions); M. GELZER, in Festschrift Eb. Vischer, Basel 1935, 35/44. H. DELEHAYE, Bull. de l'Acad. R. de Belgique 1921, 150/66 (persecution in the army); AB 1922, 5 ff. 241 ff. (Martyrs in Egypt). K. STADE, Der Politiker Diokletian und die letzte große Christenverf., 1926. H. FLORIN, Untersuchungen zur Dioklet. Christenverf., Dissertation 1928. R. LAQUEUR, Eusebius als Historiker s. Zeit, 1929. H. LECLERCQ, Maximien Hercule, DictAC X, 2778/83; MAXENCE, op. cit. X, 2752/67. The Cambridge Ancient History XII, 324 ff. 661 ff. E. GROAG, Maxentius, RE Pauly-Wissowa XIV, 2417/84; W. ENSSLIN, Maximianus Herculius, l. c. 2486/516; Maximianus Galerius, 2516/28. See also literature in § 41.

vinces with a great complex of officials. As co-emperor in the West, he appointed his companion-in-arms, *Maximianus Herculeus* (286—305) and named his son-in-law *Galerius* and *Constantius Chlorus*, co-regents and successors (293), both with the title of Caesar: Galerius in the East and Constantius in the West.

During the peace which had lasted since 260, the Christian Church had had an opportunity to grow as never before. Imposing buildings had been erected in most of the larger cities; one in a very conspicuous location at Nicomedia, the residence of the emperor. Many Christians held important offices in the army and the court, and the emperor's wife Prisca and daughter Valeria were apparently closely associated with them. In a total population of about fifty million for the Empire, there were perhaps seven to ten million Christians. It seemed but a matter of a short time until the new religion would prevail over the old, especially in the East. However, some of the pagans, led by *Neo-Platonists* incited the warlike and fanatical Caesar, Galerius, to action. He in turn represented to Diocletian that the work of restoration and centralization of the Empire would not not be complete until the enemies of the State religion had been suppressed. Lactantius says (De mort. 16) that the instigator of the persecution (auctor et consiliarius) was *Hierocles*, the governor of Bithynia, who was a Neo-Platonist and had written inflammatory tracts against the Christians (§ 17, 1).

Then began the last great persecution, the most cruel and the longest of all — the decisive battle between Christianity and Paganism. The purification of the army formed the prelude. Soldiers were given the alternative of sacrificing or losing their rank, some were put to death at once (Marcellus, Dasius; on the Theban Legion see below). The storm broke in all its fury in 303. Within less than a year, four edicts appeared containing systematic measures for the complete extinction of Christianity. The first, dated February 23, 303 (Eus. VIII, 2; Lact. De mort. 13) ordered church buildings to be demolished and sacred books to be burned: Clerics who surrendered the Scriptures were called traditores and constituted a new class of lapsi (§ 52, 1, 2). All Christians were deprived of their civil rights, those holding positions of honor were degraded and stripped of titles and dignities and those in the imperial service were reduced to slavery. The first attempts to enforce the decree led to bloodshed in several places, especially in Nicomedia where there were several martyrs. Christians were blamed for fires which broke out in the imperial palace and all Christians in the city who refused to sacrifice were executed, including Bishop *Anthimus*, many of the clergy and court officials. A mutiny in the army in Syria and Cappadocia became the pretext for further reprisals. Two more edicts (Eus. VIII, 6) ordered the incarceration of all clerics until they would consent to sacrifice. Finally a fourth edict (Eus. De mart. Palaest. 3) issued in the spring of 304 was a general command that all Christians be compelled to sacrifice. Those who remained steadfast on the rack were put to death with all the refinements of cruelty the executioners could invent. Christian blood flowed in streams, especially in the East (Aera martyrum). Eighty-four martyrs from the small province of Palestine are known by name. Eusebius (H.E. VIII, 9, 3—4) relates that in Egypt (Thebes) there were mass executions with as many as ten to one hundred martyrs in a single day. There were, of course, some who weakened and apostatized (Eus. VIII, 3)[1]. The prefecture of Gaul, which included France, Spain, and Britain, escaped the general persecution, since *Constantius*, the ruler of this domain restricted himself to the enforcement of the first edict only.

We first hear of the martyrdom of the **Theban Legion** (i. e. recruited from the province of Thebes in Egypt) from Bishop Eucherius of Lyons, about 450 (Passio Agaunensium martyrum, ed. Krusch, MGSS rer Merov. III, 20/41). According to this account, the entire Legion consisting of Christians, refused to have any part in the persecution of their brethren. The legion was then quartered at *Agaunum* (now St. Maurice in Valais, Switzerland) where the co-emperor Maximian was directing the persecution. Twice he ordered the legion to be decimated and finally caused all who survived to be massacred. The names of some of the legion's officers are included in the account: *Maurice*, Candidus, Exsuperius and Victor. Other later versions of the event say that divisions of the Legion were stationed along the Rhine (Bonn, Cologne, Xanten, Trier § 12, 4) and met a like fate. Although some modern scholars (Krusch, Egli et al.) have rejected the historicity of the Theban Legion, the account can not be dismissed as utterly false. Recent excavations at St. Maurice have proved that the story has a basis in fact, although the details have undoubtedly been elaborated, and, so far, it has not been possible to fix the event definitely between the years 284 and 305. Recent works on the Theban Legion: Fr. Stolle, Dissertation Breslau 1891 (also HJG 1892, 783/98); Joh. Schmid, 1893; R. Berg, 1895; M. Besson, Monasterium Agaunense, Fribourg 1913; Étude sur

---

[1] According to the Liber Pontificalis of the sixth century (§ 78, 3), Pope Marcellinus offered incense and soon thereafter atoned for his inconstancy by dying a martyr's death. The Donatist bishop, Petilian, asserts that Marcellinus was a traditor and a turificatus; but St. Augustine (C. lit. Petiliani II, n. 202), disproves the assertion. Cfr. DÖLLINGER, Papstfabeln, ²1890, 48 ff.; E. CASPAR, ZKG 1927, 321/33; H. LECLERCQ, DictAC X 1762/73; E. AMANN, DictThC IX, 1999/2001.

les commencements du christianisme en Suisse romande, ib. 1921; N. Peissard, La découverte du tombeau de St. Maurice, martyr d'Agaune, St. Maurice 1922 (also HJG 1923, 104). — H. Leclercq, DictAC X, 2699/729. — *A. J. Herzberg,* Der hl. Mauritius, 1936, 10 ff. — J. Mösch, cfr. § 17, 4. — L. Blondel, Vallesia 1948, 9/57 (Les anciennes basiliques d'Agaune).

Of far more legendary character is the account of the martyrdom of **St. Ursula** and **eleven thousand companions,** who were said to have been put to death by the Huns about the year 452. The Passio in the form it eventually assumed in the tenth century (cfr. L. Zoepf, Das Heiligenleben im 10. Jh., 1908, 64 ff.) relates that these virgins were returning to Britain after a pilgrimage to Rome, when they underwent the death of martyrs. The story is not without historical foundation. An inscription belonging indisputably to the fifth, and probably to the fourth century, found in the choir of the Church of St. Ursula at Cologne, describes how a man of senatorial rank (vir clarissimus) named *Clematius* made a vow to erect or restore a basilica on his own property in honor of the virgin martyrs. In the ninth century the names Saula, Martha, Pinnosa, Ursula, etc., began to be applied to the martyrs, whose number was variously given as 5, 8, then 11, and finally, about the same time, as 11,000. This latter number is best explained as a false reading of the Latin numeral XI M. V. (undecim martyres virgines, as undecim millia virginum). Since the tenth century the legend of St. Ursula and eleven thousand companions has undergone all sorts of romantic revisions and occurs in the visions of St. Elizabeth of Schönau (1156/57). Cfr. the excellent work of *W. Levison,* Das Werden der Ursula-Legende, 1928; also *M. Coens,* AB 1929, 89/110. — *G. de Tervarent,* La légende de S. Ursule dans la littérature et l'art du moyen âge, 2 vol. Paris 1931. — *W. Neuss* (§ 17, 4) 28 ff., 80 f. — *F. Schubel,* Die südenglische Legende von den 11 000 Jungfrauen, 1938.

5. In 305 Diocletian and his co-emperor abdicated and were succeeded by Constantius and Galerius, while Severus and Galerius' nephew, Maximinus Daja (Daza), became Caesars. But the persecution continued. The usurper *Maxentius* (306—213), the son of Maximianus, who had displaced Severus, soon relaxed the severity of the persecution for the Christians of Italy and Africa. After the death of Constantius, the army proclaimed his son *Constantine,* Augustus (July, 306) and he continued his father's tolerant policy in Gaul. *Licinius,* who had been made Augustus for Pannonia and Noricum (308) was less hostile toward Christians than Galerius. But in the East the bloodshed continued with few interruptions for several years, since Galerius could now give free rein to his hatred of Christianity; and his Caesar, *Maximin,* surpassed him in cruelty. There died at this time, among others, the learned priests *Pamphilus* of Caesarea (§ 39, 6) and *Lucian* of Antioch (§ 37, 3), the bishops *Peter* of Alexandria (§ 35, 3), *Methodius* of Olympus

(§ 39, 6) and *Silvanus* of Gaza (the latter with 39 companions). (See § 12, for *Victorinus, Quirinus, Afra* and the *Quattuor Coronati*). In spite of the ferocity of the long campaign and with all the advantages apparently on the side of the civil power, Rome was finally obliged to admit defeat. A horrible disease from which Galerius had suffered for some time brought him to a better frame of mind. Together with two of his co-regents, Licinius and Constantine, he issued an **edict of toleration** at Sardica in April 311. (Lact. De mort. 34; Eus. VIII, 17). This put an end to the great but ineffectual persecution of Christians, gave legal status to their religion and sanctioned its practice, subject to an easily observed condition (*ut denuo sint Christiani* et conventicula sua componant, ita ut ne quid contra disciplinam agant). The Edict concludes with a request that Christians offer prayers for the emperor and the Empire. Maximin refused to accept the edict for his domains, but his power was soon broken.

6. In the meantime the political situation in the West rendered inevitable a decisive contest between **Constantine**[1] and Maxentius, which began in 312. Up to this time Constantine had practiced a form of syncretic monotheism which consisted in the worship of Apollo-Sol; but as he prepared for his hazardous campaign, he was

---

[1] V. SESAN, Kirche u. Staat im römisch-byzant. Reiche seit Konstantin I 1911. W. SCHNYDER, Die Anerkennung der christl. Kirche unter Konst, d. Gr., Progr. Luzern 1913; also the ,,Acht Studien zur christl. Altertumswiss. u. zur KG.", Luzern 1937, 29/79. M. BESNIER, § 15. H. LECLERCQ, Paix de l'Église, DictAC XIII, 483/99. J. MAURICE, Les origines relig. de Constantin le Gr., BullLA 1914, 37/45. F. J. DÖLGER, Konst. d. Gr. nach neueren. Forschungen, ThRev 1914, 353 ff. 385 ff. H. SCHRÖRS, Die Bekehrung Konst. d. Gr. in der Überlief., ZkTh 1916, 238/57. N. H. BAYNES, Constantine the Great and the Christian Church, London 1931 (British Academy Proceedings XV). J. VOGT, § 15, 4; ZKG 1942, 171/90 (the significance of the year 312 for the religious policy of Constantine). H. V. SCHÖNBECK, Beiträge zur Rel.-Politik des Maxentius u. Const., 1939. H. P. L'ORANGE, Der spätantike Bilderschmuck des Konst.-bogens, 1939. A. ALFÖLDI, The Conversion of Constantine and Pagan Rome, Oxford 1948. H. GRÉGOIRE, Revue de l'Univ. de Bruxelles 36, 1931, 231/72; Byzantion 1938, 561/83 (Constantine's conversion to Christianity an act of political expediency). W. SESTON, RevHPhR 1936, 250/64, u. in Mél. F. Cumont, Brux. 1936, 403/21; F. STÄHELIN, Z. f. schweiz. Gesch. 1937, 385 ff. 1939, 396 ff. H. LIETZMANN, Der Glaube Konstantins d. Gr., Sb. Berlin 1937, 263/75. See literature in § 41. On the Edixt of Milan: J. WITTIG, RQ Suppl. 19, 1913, 40/65; V. SESAN I, 128/237; BATIFFOL, BullLA 1913, 241/64; J. MAURICE et F. MARTROYE, op. cit. 1914, 45/52; K. BIHLMEYER, ThQ 1914, 65 ff. 198 ff. (Did Constantine issue an Edict of toleration in 312?); J. R. KNIPFING, ZKG 1922, 206/18 (without convincing reasons, holds that Constantine did not issue an Edict at Milan); R. LAQUEUR, in Gedenkschrift H. Swoboda, 1927, 132/41; H. LECLERCQ, DictAC IV, 2202/11; E. STEIN, Byz. Z. 1932, 117 ff.; J. R. PALANQUE, Byzantion 1935, 607/17, and also H. GRÉGOIRE, in the same number 616/19 and in 1938, 552 ff.

drawn rather toward Christianity. In consequence of a phenomenal apparition, he placed himself and his army under the protection of the God of the Christians and His "saving sign", and defeated Maxentius in battle at the Milvian bridge near Rome (October 28, 312). The religious problem received Constantine's immediate attention. Toward the end of 312 he addressed a communication to Maximin who was still persecuting Christians in the East, ordering him to desist, exempted the African clergy from the local tax and in a conference with his brother-in-law, Licinius at **Milan** in February, 313, took the magnanimous action for which he has since been noted. The result of their meeting was "a very perfect and comprehensive *law in favour of Christians*" (Eus. IX, 9, 12; 9a, 12), the so-called *Edict of Milan*, more properly, a rescript or circular mandate to the governers of provinces. The general tenor of this important law has been preserved for us by Lactantius (De mort. 48) and Eusebius (X, 5, 2—14) but only in the form of a decree for the East, issued by Licinius after his victory over Maximin. Besides removing the restrictions placed by Galerius in 311, it guaranteed every person in the Empire, especially Christians, freedom of worship. Moreover, it ordered that all buildings and properties confiscated during the persecution be returned or indemnification be made to the corpus Christianorum, i. e. to the congregations as now legally existing corporations. This decree definitely and fundamentally severed the relationship which had heretofore linked pagan worship with the Roman State; it introduced a totally new era in that State's religious policy and it constituted *one of the most important turning points* in the history of the Christian Church. There remained only one obstacle to the universal operation of the new law: Maximin, the relentless enemy of Christianity, renewed his efforts to annihilate it. But **Licinius** met him in battle at Adrianople on April 30, 313. Maximin was put to flight and died at Tarsus, after which the East, which had suffered the full severity of persecution for almost ten years, was quite ready to welcome the proclamation of Milan. The Christian Church had emerged victorious from her struggle with the powers of a pagan State and she could now face the future with abounding joy.

The much-discussed **apparition** in which Constantine is supposed to have seen a cross, is related in Eusebius' highly eulogistic Vita Constantini, I, 28—31, compiled in 337. Eusebius assures us that the account he gives is based on the emperor's own sworn word. When Constantine was preparing for his capaign against Maxentius (he was apparently still in Gaul or upper

Italy), he prayed to the God of his father for help. Late one afternoon, he and his entire army beheld immediately above the sun the sign of the cross formed of light with the words: τουτῷ νίκα = in this sign thou shalt conquer. That night Christ appeared to him with the same sign and ordered him to make a banner, or *labarum* with the monogram of Christ (formed of the Greek

chi X crossed with a P)  ☧  or  ⳩   This account is open to grave suspicion.

For Lactantius in his De mortibus persecutorum (compiled 316/7) c. 44, speaks only of a portentious dream in which Constantine is instructed, ut caeleste signum Dei notaret in scutis atque ita proelium committeret. And Eusebius himself in the part of his Church History dealing with this event (IX, 9) relates only the emperor's prayer to the God of the Christians, the divine aid obtained, and the erection of a statue at Rome representing Constantine with the sign of salvation in his right hand, and with the inscription ordered by the emperor, that by means of that saving sign he had freed Rome from the yoke of the tyrant. It is a bit difficult to admit a miraculous occurrence such as the Vita Constantini relates because the emperor who then practised a religion in which some Christian elements were mingled with much paganism, used the cross as a sort of magic charm against his enemies. Yet the story is not pure invention. It contains a germ of subjective truth, which after the impressions of so many years of successful reign is elaborated and retold in glorified form. Even though the details can no longer be established with certainty, it can scarcely be doubted that Constantine had some sort of religious experience, related to the sun worship he had been practising, but at the same time, definitely inclining him to Christianity. Many possibilities suggest themselves: the parhelion, halo or light rings at first taken to be a manifestation of the sun god, was then, in consequence of a dream, given a Christian interpretation(?) The emblem on the labarum was similar to the gamma cross, much used in the East as a symbol of the sun and of life. When Constantine first caused the labarum to be made and used is not certain; Alföldi holds for 312, Lietzmann for 317. There is no justification, however, for the opinion (H. Grégoire) that a pagan vision in 310 was used as the pattern for the story of 312. — *J. B. Aufhauser,* Quellenzeugnisse zu Konstantins Kreuzesvision, 1912 (Kleine Texte 108). — *Funk,* AU II, 1/23. — *H. Schrörs,* Konstantins d. Gr Kreuzerscheinung, 1913 (also F. J. Dölger, ThRev 1914, 354 ff.); ZkTh 1916, 485/523. — *F. Kampers,* Vom Werdegang der abendländ. Kaisermystik, 1924, 144/73. — *V. Gardthausen,* Das alte Monogramm, 1924, 73/102. — *M. Sulzberger,* Byzantion 1926, 337/448. — *H. Grégoire,* op. cit. 1929, 477/92 (Labarum = laureum, laureatum signum); L'Antiquité classique 1932, 135/43; Byzantion 1939, 341/51 (and *J. Zeiller,* 329/40 as well as in Revue des études anciennes 1940, 498 ff.). — A. Brasseur, Latomus 1946, 35/40 (the two visions). — *A. Alföldi,* in Pisciculi, Festschrift F. J. Dölger, 1939, 1/18. — *H. Leclercq,* Labarum, DictAC VIII, 927/62. — *N. H. Baynes* (vide supra) S. 9, 58 ff. (with good bibliography). — *J. Vogt,* Mél. H. Grégoire I, Brüssel 1949, 593/606 (accounts of the vision in the fourth century). — The following support the credibility of the accounts: M. Desroches, Le Labarum, Paris 1894; A. Knöpfer, HpBl 1908, I, 183/99; J. Wilpert, 3 Vereinsschr. d. Görresges. f. 1913, 5/17; F. Savio, CivCatt, 1913 II/III etc. See also the literature listed in no. 6 above.

# § 17.
## Literary Attacks on Christianity[1].

1. The Pagan State attacked Christianity with all the known weapons that could inflict bodily death; but pagan scholars employed the even more insidious weapon — the pen. A great number of works appeared openly or covertly assailing Christians and impugning their belief and conduct. Of the more direct attacks, three works are deserving of special mention: The "True Word" or "True Discourse" ('Αληθὴς λόγος) of the philosopher **Celsus**, written about 178; the fifteen books of the Neo-Platonist, *Porphyrius*, "Against the Christians," compiled about 270/275; and the Λόγοι φιλαλήθεις of *Hierocles*, the Neo-Platonic governor of Bithynia (§ 16, 4). All of these works have been lost, partly because Theodosius II (§ 41,6) ordered them to be burned in 488, and partly because they held no interest for succeeding generations. They are known to us only from quotations used by Christian theologians in refuting them. The most important of these works seems to have been that of *Celsus*. Origen refuted it about 248 (Contra Celsum) and in doing so, repeated almost the entire text. Celsus bitterly attacks Christianity by comparing it with Judaism and paganism; and to him paganism means Platonism and loyalty to the Empire. He was

---

[1] H. KELLNER, Hellenismus u. Christentum, 1866. B. AUBÉ, Hist. des persécutions II, Paris 1878. G. SCHMITT, Die Apologie der 3 ersten Jhh., 1890. J. ZAHN, Die apologet. Grundgedanken in d. Lit. der 3 ersten Jhh., 1890. J. GEFFCKEN, Das Christentum im Kampf u. Ausgleich mit der griech.-röm. Welt, ³1920; Der Ausgang des griech.-röm. Heidentums, ²1929. P. DE LABRIOLLE, La réaction païenne Paris 1934 (valuable). W. NESTLE, ArchRelW 1941, 51 ff. (principal accusations). Celsus True Word reconstructed by O. GLOECKNER in Kleine Texte 151, 1924. R. BADER, Der 'Αληθὴς Λόγος des Kelsos, 1940 (disagrees with Glöckner). A. WIFSTRAND, Die wahre Lehre des Kelsos, Lund 1942. FUNK, AU II, 152/61 (time of composition). J. F. MUTH, Der Kampf des Philosophen Celsus gegen das Christentum, 1899. A. MIURA-STANGE, Celsus u. Origenes, 1926. H. CHADWICK, HarvThR 1948, 83/102 (resurrection of the body according to Origen and Celsus). W. VÖLKER, Das Bild vom nichtgnostischen Christentum bei Celsus, 1928. O. GLOECKNER, Philologus 1927, 329/52 (Celsus' Weltanschauung). P. DE LABRIOLLE (vide supra), 111/69. On Porphyrius: A. HARNACK, TU 37, 4, 1911; Abh. Berlin 1916, 1; Sb. Berlin 1921, 266/84, 835 f.; Reden u. Aufsätze NF. III, 1916, 45/66. L. VAGANAY, DictThC XII, 2550/90; P. DE LABRIOLLE (vide supra), 223/96; P. BENOÎT, Rev. bibl. 1947, 543/72. A. B. HULEN, Porphyry's Work against the Christians, Scottdale Pa. 1933. A. J. KLEFFER, Porphyrius, der Neuplatoniker u. Christenfeind, 1896. J. BIDEZ, Vie de Porphyre, Gand 1913. W. THEILER, Porphyrius u. Augustin, 1933.

acquainted with the Old Testament, the Gospels and a number of Christian writings. His objections to the doctrines of the Incarnation and Redemption are worthy of note, since all subsequent opponents of Christianity down to the freethinkers of the eighteenth and nineteenth centuries have never been able to invent new ones. But he deliberately falsifies history when he speaks of the life of Jesus.

2. *Porphyrius* was probably himself a Christian catechumen for a short time. He *attacked* Christianity directly in the work "Against Christians" and *indirectly* in his "Philosophy derived from the Oracles." In this latter work he attempts to prove to pagans that they possess a religion founded on divine revelation such as the Christians have in the Scriptures. His objective was to strengthen pagans in their old belief and restrain them from accepting the new religion. This was in fact the main purpose of the **Neoplatonic School**[1], founded in Alexandria by Ammonius Saccas († ca. 242). This school was systematically developed by **Plotinus**, its foremost representative, who taught at Rome (244—270), by his pupil, *Porphyrius* († 306), by *Jamblichus* († 330) and later especially by *Proclus* († 485) at Athens. *Neoplatonism* became of vast importance not only for paganism, but also for Christian theology of latter times (especially for Augustine and the Pseudo-Dionysius and through these for the whole Middle Ages). It was chiefly concerned with religious and ethical problems, indeed it was an idealistic philosophy of religion (the swan-song of Greek philosophy). By means of allegorical interpretation of pagan myths, and by emphasizing ascetics and ecstacy, it endeavored to purify and justify poly-

---

[1] For literature on Neoplatonism see § 5, 4 (especially ÜBERWEG). T. WHITTAKER, The Neo-Platonists, Cambridge ²1928. W. THEILER, Die Vorbereitung des Neuplatonismus, 1930. On Ammonius Saccas: F. HEINEMAN Hermes 1926, 1/27. E. SEEBERG, ZKG 1942, 136/170. E. HOFFMANN, Platonismus u. Mystik im Altertum, Sb. Heidelberg 1934/35, 2. Works of Plotinus: edd. by P. HENRY and H.-R. SCHWYZER, Paris 1951 ff.; German by R. HARDER, 5 vols. 1930/7; cfr. HARDER in Hermes 1936, 1/10. Monographs on Plotinus: M. WUNDT I, 1919; F. HEINEMANN 1921; G. MEHLIS, 1924; H. OPPERMANN, 1929; G. FAGGIN, 1945; L. PELLOUX, 1945. C. SCHMIDT, Plotins Stellung zum Gnosticismus und zum kirchl. Christentum, TU 20, 4, 1901. W. R. INGE, The Philosophy of Plotinus, 2 vols. London ³1929. C. CARBONARA, La filosofia di Plotino, 2 vols. Rome 1938/9. W. THEILER, Museum Helviticum 1944, 209/225 (Plotinus and the philosophy of antiquity). E. BREHIER, La philosophie de Plot., Paris, 1948. P. O. KRISTELLER, Der Begriff der Seele in der Ethik des Plotin, 1929. E. KRAKOWSKI, P. et le paganisme religieux, Paris 1933. J. GUITTON, Le temps et l'éternité chez P. et S. Augustin, Paris 1933. A. DAHL, Augustin und Plotin, Lund 1945. P. HENRY, P. et l'Occident, Louvain 1934, also Études plotiniennes I, Louvain 1938. A. MANSION, Revue Neoscol. Philos. 1939, 229/251 (lists the more recent works on Plotinus).

theism, satisfy the inner craving for religion and thus by a sort of pagan pietism provide a counterpoise to Christianity. But in spite of the fact that Neoplatonism and Christianity held some ideas and ideals in common, they soon found themselves in opposition (cfr. § 16, 4 for the origin of Diocletian's persecution). — With a purpose similar to that of Porphyrius, the *Neo-Pythagorean*, Flavius *Philostratos*, wrote a life of the magician and imputed worker of miracles, *Apollonius of Tyana*[1]. This work which appeared in the early part of the third century, is said to have been composed at the command of the Empress Julia Domna, wife of Septimius Severus (§ 15, 6). Apollonius is represented as a model of piety and virtue ennobled by philosophy and the work was offered to the *syncretism* of the times as the life of Christ was presented to Christians in the Gospels. However it was not intended as a mockery nor as hostilely offensive to Christians. In the second and third centuries similar attempts to satisfy the longing for a more perfect religion were made by studying and popularizing *Orphic* and *Hermetic* (Hermes Trismegistos identified with Thoth) rites and teaching[2] with colorful Hellenic-Egyptian wisdom and doctrine. (Poimandres contributes the most important work among the Hermetica).

3. Finally, mention must be made of the free-thinker and rhetorician, *Lucian of Samosata*, a friend of Celsus, and like him, a foe of Christianity. In his satire, De morte Peregrini (Peregrinus Proteus, a false philosopher and magician) written about 170, he ridicules Christians for their charity and their scorn of death. At least he includes them in his derision, for it is probable that the work was directed primarily against the Cynics. — Lucian's

---

[1] J. GÖTTSCHING, Apollonius v. Tyana, 1889. R. REITZENSTEIN, Hellenist. Wundererzählungen, 1906. J. HEMPEL, Untersuch. z. Überlieferung von Apoll. v. Tyana, 1921. M. WUNDT, ZwTh 1906, 309/66. ED. MEYER, Hermes 1917, 371/424. H. DOERGENS, ThGl 1933 292/304. G. HERZOG-HAUSER, Jb. d. österreich.-Leogesellschaft 1930, 177/200. M. MEUNIER, Apollonius de Tyane, Paris 1936.

[2] Hermetica, ed. W. SCOTT, 4 vol. Oxf. 1924/36 (with English translation and commentary). Corpus Hermeticum, ed. A. D. NOCK et A.-J. FESTUGIÈRE, 2 vol. Paris 1945 (with French translation). R. REITZENSTEIN, Poimandres 1904. J. KROLL, Die Lehren des Hermes Trismegistos, ²1928. C. F. G. HEINRICI, Die Hermesmystik u. das N.T., 1918 (also REITZENSTEIN, Gött. Gel. Anz. 1918, 241/74). F. BRÄUNINGER, Untersuchungen zu d. Schriften des Hermes Trism., Dissertation 1926. V. MACCHORO, ZAGREUS, Studi intorno al Orfismo, Firenze 1930. M. P. NILSSON, HarvThR 1935, 184/230 (early Orphic mysteries). P. RAINGEARD, Hermès psychagogue, Paris 1935. W. GUNDEL, Neue astrologische Texte des Hermes Trism., Abh. München 1936. M. J. LAGRANGE, Critique historique I: Les mystères, l'Orphisme, Paris 1937 (aus Rev. biblique 1924 ff.); also A. D'ALÈS, RechSR 1938, 134/49. A. FESTUGIÈRE, Hermetica, HarvThR 1938, 1/20; La révélation d'Hermès Trismégiste, 2 vol. Paris 1944/9.

works: in Italian by L. Settembrini et A. Savinio, 2 vol. Milan 1944; De morte Peregrini, German tr. by W. Nestle, 1925. — Cfr. J. Bernays, Lucian u. die Cyniker, 1879. — K. Meiser, Sb. München 1906, 281/325. — H. Leclercq, Lucien de S., DictAC IX, 2619/35. — *P. Riessler*, ThQ 1933, 64/72 (Lucian of S. and Holy Scripture). — *M. Caster*, Lucien et la pensée relig. de son temps, Paris 1937.

## CHAPTER II
## THE CONSTITUTION OF THE CHURCH[1]

## § 18.
### The Clergy and the Hierarchical Organization[2].

1. In the beginning the direction of the church was naturally in the hands of the *Apostles*. After His Resurrection Christ had given

---

[1] J. BINGHAM, Origenes ecclesiasticae or the Antiquities of the Christian Church, 10 vol. London 1708/22, Latin by GRISCHOW, 10 vols. Halle 1724/38. G. SEMERIA, Dogma, gerarchia e culto nella chiesa primitiva, Roma 1902. H. DE GENOUILLAC, L'Église Chrét. au temps de St. Ignace d'Antioche, Paris 1907. TH. SCHERMANN, Die allg. Kirchenordnung usw. II, 1915. N. LÄMMLE, Beiträge zum Problem des Kirchenrechts, 1933. E. RÖSSER, Göttliches u. menschl., unveränderl. u. veränderl. Kirchenrecht von der Entstehung der Kirche bis z. Mitte des 9. Jh., 1934. FR. HEILER, Die kath. Kirche des Ostens u. Westens I—II, 1, 1937/41. J. V. BARTLET, Church Life and Church Order during the First Four Centuries, Oxford 1943. G. J. EBERS, Grundriß des Kath. Kirchenrechts. Rechtsgesch. u. System, 1950. H. E. FEINE, Kirchl. Rechtsgesch. I, 1950. See literature § 8.

[2] L. SOBKOWSKI, Episkopat u. Presbyterat in den ersten christl. Jhh., 1893. A. MICHIELS, L'origine de l'épiscopat, Diss. Louvain 1900. ST. V. DUNIN-BORKOWSKI, Die neueren Forsch. über die Anfänge d. Episkopats, 1900; supplementary essays on the foregoing works in ZkTh 1903/5. P. BATIF-FOL, Études d'hist. et de théol. positive, Paris [7]1926, 225/80. H. BRUDERS, Die Verfassung der Kirche bis 175, 1904. E. METZNER, Die Verf. der Kirche in den 2 ersten Jhh., 1920. H. DIECKMANN, Die Verf. der Urkirche, 1923; De ecclesia, tractatus historico-dogmatici, 2 vol. 1925. J. B. WALZ, Die Sichtbarkeit der Kirche, 1924. Article Évêque: A. MICHIELS im DictApol I, 1750/86; F. PRAT in DictThC V, 1656/1701; L. MARCHAL im Dict. de la Bible, Suppl. II, Paris 1934, 1297/1333. H. LECLERCQ, Épiscopat, DictAC V, 202/38. J. COPPENS, L'imposition des mains et les rites connexes dans le Nouveau Test. et dans l'Église ancienne, Wetteren (Belg.) 1925; cfr. P. GALTIER, DictThC VII, 1302/1424; F. CABROL, DictAC VII, 391/413; A. MICHEL, Ordre, Ordination, DictThC XI, 1193/405. K. PIEPER, Jesus u. die Kirche, 1932. R. HANSLIK, Jb. d. österreich. Leogesellschaft 1933, 29/71 (Beiträge z. Gesch. des Urchristentums). L. KÖSTERS, Die Kirche unseres Glaubens, [3]1938. Protestant literature: E. HATCH-A. HARNACK, Die Gesellschaftsverfass. der christl. Kirchen im Altertum, 1883; Die Grundlegung d. Kirchenverfass. Westeuropas im frühen MA., 1888. J. RÉVILLE, Les origines de l'épiscopat, Paris 1894. CH. GORE, The Church and the Ministry, London [2]1919. T. M. LINDSAY, Church and Ministry in the Early Centuries, London [2]1924. K. E. KIRK, The Apostolic Ministry, London 1947. R. SOHM, Kirchenrecht I, 1892; Wesen u. Ursprung des Katholizismus, Abh. Leipz. 1909, separate [2]1912. A. HARNACK, Entstehung u. Entwicklung der Kirchenverf. u. des KR.s in den ersten 2 Jhh., 1910 (= RE 20, 508/46). [Opposing Sohm and Harnack:

them the command to teach, baptize and guide all mankind (Matt. 28:19 and 20). They were assisted by *Prophets* and *Doctors* endowed with charismatic gifts (1 Cor. 12:28 f.; Acts 13:1; Ephes. 4:11; Did. 11, 13, 15), whose duty it was to edify and further instruct the faithful, while the Apostles were engaged in the work of conversion. The charismatics did not exercise any definite local authority, but their influence in the congregations was very great. The title of *Apostle* was given not only to the Twelve, but also to their assistants and companions, like Barnabas, as well as to the first heralds of the Gospel or wandering preachers (Did. 11, 3—6) who were also called *Evangelists.* (Ephes. 4:11; Acts 21:8; Eus. III, 37; V 10). On the other hand, especially in congregations of pagan converts, we find, even in the infant Church, *bishops, priests* and *deacons* (Acts 20:17—28; Phil. 1:1; 1 Tim. 3:2—12; 5:17, 19; Tit. 1:5, 7; Did. 15, 1; 1 Clem. 42, 44) who were admitted to their office by a special rite (imposition of hands and prayer). These offices were retained permanently whereas, after the Church had been firmly established i. e. after apostolic times, the *charismatics* gradually disappear or rather the function they performed like those of prophets and doctors were merged with the *"permanent"* offices. Other officials like the Evangelists also lost their importance as the Church grew. Acts 20:28 says of *bishops* in particular that they had been placed by the Holy Ghost to rule the Church of God. Thus there developed the *hierarchy* of the New Testament to continue the duties which the Apostles had been commissioned to perform for the Church. This is made clear in the Epistle of *Clement* of Rome, a disciple of the Apostles. Writing to the Corinthians about the year 96, he says (42, 4; 44, 2) that the Apostles went from land to land and from city to city, preaching the Gospel,

---

P. A. LEDER, Das Problem der Entstehung des Katholizismus, ZRGkan 1911, 276/308; N. LÄMMLE (vide supra)]. W. LÜTGERT, Amt und Geist im Kampf, 1911. H. LIETZMANN, Zur altchristl. Verfassungsgesch., ZwTh 1914, 97/153. A. C. HEADLAM, The Doctrine of the Church and Christian Reunion, London 1920. K. MÜLLER, Beiträge z. Gesch. der Verf. der alten Kirche, Abh. Berlin 1922, 3; ZntW 1924, 216/22; Aus der akad. Arbeit, 1930, 101/31. B. H. STREETER, The Primitive Church, London 1929. A. J. MACLEAN, The Position of Clergy and Laity in the Early Church, London 1930 (excellent use of sources). FR. GERKE, Die Stellung des 1. Klemensbriefes innerhalb der altchristl. Gemeindeverf. u. des Kirchenrechts, TU 47, 1, 1931. O. LINTON, Das Problem der Urkirche in der neuesten Forschung, Diss. Uppsala 1932. L. SCHMIDT, Art. im Theol. Wörterb. zum N.T. III, 502/39. K. H. HENGSTORF, ἀπόστολος, ib. I, 406/46. H. W. BEYER, ib. II, 604/17. G. SASS, Apostelamt u. Kirche 1939. E. MOLLAND, Festschrift J. Norregaard, Copenhagen 1947. 157/76 (Irenaeus and apostolic succession); also RHE 1948, 783/4.

and from among their earlier converts appointed men whom they had tested in the Spirit to act as bishops and deacons for the future believers. Afterwards they laid down the rule that when these men died, other approved men were to succeed to their sacred ministry. The same Clement insists (42, 1 f.) that these men received their commission from Christ and God through the Apostles and bases his whole argument on the fact that there was a well-established hierarchy. The members of the Church, therefore, fall into two groups, the directors and the simple faithful, *clerics* and *laics*, expressions which can be traced back to the earliest Christian times (Acts 1:17; 1 Clem. 40, 5; Tert. De monog. 12). The body of those believing in Christ and united in charity form the "Catholic", i. e. *universal* Church, ἡ καθολικὴ ἐκκλησία, a term first used by Ignatius (Smyrn. 8, 2).

2. The directors or heads of the Church are always mentioned in the plural in Holy Scripture, sometimes as "Elders" (πρεσβύτεροι). sometimes as "Overseers" (ἐπίσκοποι), terms which are used synonomously. They form, therefore, a *college*, called presbyterium (1 Tim. 4:14). No doubt this arrangement was based on the organization found among the Jews, whose synagogues in the diaspora were governed by a council of "Elders". Naturally the collegium had a presiding officer. Since the government of the congregation in post-apostolic times was left more and more in his hands, his authority increased until finally he alone was given the title ἐπίσκοπος, which term originally had a much wider meaning. The monarchical episcopacy therefore did not develop as a result of individual priests usurping more authority: rather the priesthood was gradually distinguished from the original presbyter-episcopate by restrictions and limitations. The letters of *St. Ignatius* of Antioch (§ 37, 4) written about 110 show clearly this change in Syria and western Asia Minor (Eph. 6, 1; Magn. 6, 1; Trall. 3, 1; Philad. 4) and picture a highly developed ecclesiastical organization along *monarchical* lines. But there is nothing essentially new in it, for the episcopacy as such is derived from the authority of the Apostles (cfr. Clement of Rome in No. 1 above) and is the continuance in the Church of the Apostolic office. However, we must not forget that the organization of the mission churches was necessarily very rudimentary and that the terminology for the various offices did not become fixed for some time. Yet in some of the provinces ecclesiastical organization developed with surpris-

ing rapidity. But if the original system had been a strong democratic government of priests alone, as most non-Catholics assume and as *Jerome* held, it would be difficult to explain how a monarchical episcopacy could have been substituted and spread so universally without precipitating a serious crisis, especially since Rome, the principal congregation of the universal Church was not then powerful enough to impose such a revolutionary change on the scattered congregations.

The sources for the years from about 60 A.D. to 100 A.D. are, unfortunately, extremely meagre; yet they are not without proofs of a monarchical episcopacy. Paul's disciples, *Timothy* at Ephesus and *Titus* on the island of Crete, are clearly monarchical bishops, as are also the "angels" of the seven churches of Asia Minor (Apoc. 1:20; 2—3). Hegesippus speaking of *James* the Younger, the "Brother of the Lord", expressly calls him Bishop of Jerusalem (§ 8, 3) and Scriptural references do the same (Gal. 1:19; 2:9; Acts 15:13). Finally, the *lists of bishops* compiled by Hegesippus and Irenaeus of Lyons in the last quarter of the second century are of great importance. In refuting the Gnostics, these two writers traced the succession of bishops of all the principal churches, especially of *Rome*, from the Apostles down to their own day. If they had not been convinced that the episcopacy was of apostolic origin, they were perpetrating a fraud that could easily have been discovered at the time they wrote.

*Jerome* held (Comment. in Tit. 1:5; Ep. 69 ad Ocean. 3; Ep. 146 ad Evangelium 1) that originally there were only priests and that the episcopacy was called into being in the course of time, when one of the priests set himself above the others to lead the attack on schism. This supposition is based on an erroneous misinterpretation of some passages in ancient documents but is not entirely free from personal bias, since Jerome quarrelled long and bitterly with the bishops of Jerusalem and disliked bishops generally. — Cfr. L. Sanders, Études sur St. Jerôme, Paris 1903, 296/344; F. Prat Rech SR 1912, 463/475.

3. During the second century the episcopal office was more clearly defined and became more influential as the Church was forced to parry the attacks of heresy and schism (§ 29, 5). The **bishop** now appears as the real head of the congregation, its teacher, leader and pastor, the director of worship and the minister of the sacraments. As the center of the congregation's life and unity, he represented it in all important matters. **Presbyters** (priests) formed the bishop's council ("Senate" according to St. Ignatius); they were his helpers in the office of teaching and divine worship,

and took his place in his absence or when the see was vacant. Except in the case of large congregations their duties were not burdensome. Hence the Didascalia of the third century (II, 28) allows the faithful to decide whether any part of the offerings (§ 19, 3) is to be given to the presbyters, whereas it makes clear that the bishop and deacons have a strict right to a share in the oblata. In the next period (§ 62) the presbyters attained to greater importance with the rise of large parishes. This developement took place even earlier in Rome and in some of the other larger cities (§ 10, 1).

4. The **diaconate**[1], a grade of the clergy inferior to the episcopate and priesthood, is first mentioned by name in Phil. 1:1. It appears to have been introduced with the election of the "seven men" to serve the tables in the congregation at Jerusalem (Acts 6:1—6; § 8, 1); for the duty of these men did not consist merely in the actual distribution of alms, but was, as in the case of Stephen and Philip, of greater scope, including even pastoral and mission work. In general, deacons were the bishop's assistant's and their duties were manifold. They assisted him in the care of the poor, in supervising temporal affairs, in divine services, especially in administering the Eucharist and in baptizing, as long as they were the bishop's only aids. They also performed a great number of other functions. Although they were inferior in rank to the presbyters, their position was one of much greater influence. The Didascalia (II, 44) calls them the bishop's "ears and mouth, heart and soul".

5. Other grades of the clergy were introduced after the times of the Apostles. As the congregations grew in numbers the work of the clergy naturally increased. A synod held at Neocaesarea in Cappadocia (between 314 and 325) speaks (can. 15) of the work of the clergy in large cities, yet deems it unbecoming to increase the original number of seven deacons in a church. Rome held to this tradition until the Middle Ages. Hence new offices, the so-called **minor orders**, were introduced to relieve the burden. There were the offices of *subdeacons* (ὑποδιάκονοι) the immediate assistant of the deacon; *lectors* (ἀναγνῶσται) who read the Sacred Scriptures at divine services, a post which was highly regarded and to which only educated persons were promoted; *acolytes* (ἀκόλουθοι) who seem to have had the duty of assisting the subdeacons and performing similar services; *exorcists* (ἐπορκισταί) who took charge of the possessed or

---

[1] J. N. SEIDL, Der Diakonat, 1884. O. ZÖCKLER, Diakonen u. Evangelisten, 1894. P. A. LEDER, Die Diakonen der Bischöfe u. Presbyter u. ihre urchristl. Vorläufer, 1905. R. SCHUMACHER, Der Diakon Stephanus, 1910. RHE. 1926, 513/37 (institution of deacons and widows). ST. BIHEL, Antonianum 1928, 129/50 (AG 6, 1—7). H. W. BEYER, διάκονος in Theol. Wörterb. z. N.T. II, 88/93.

the mentally afflicted and epileptics (ἐνεργούμενοι, χειμαζόμενοι); and finally *ostiarii* or porters, (πυλωροί) who guarded the church doors. They are all mentioned in a letter of Pope Cornelius (in Eus. VI, 43) about the middle of the third century as functioning in the church of Rome (seven deacons, 42 acolytes and 52 exorcists, lectors and porters). Some of these offices were introduced in the third and some (lectors) even in the second century. The development of minor orders in the East never kept pace with their introduction in the West; for example, the order of acolyte was never known in the East. In larger congregations the instruction of catechumens was commited to special *teachers*, mostly priests or deacons, although sometimes laymen were assigned to the task (Tertullian, Clement of Alexandria[?] Origen διδάσκαλοι, doctores audientium). In Alexandria this arrangement led to the foundation of the famed catechetical school (§ 39, 1). — *A. Harnack*, Ursprung des Lektorats u. der übrigen nied. Weihen, TU 2, 5, 1886; Sb. Berlin 1910, 551/55 (Ostiarius). — *H. Reuter*, Der Subdiakonat, 1890. — *F. Wieland*, Die genetische Entwicklung der sog. Ordines minores in den ersten 3 Jhh., 1897 (RQ Suppl. 7).

6. To perform certain services for females, especially at baptism, in illness and in want, **deaconesses** were *appointed*. In the East since the third century, it seems that they were given the same status as men in minor orders. They are mentioned by St. Paul in the Epistle to the Romans 16:1 (Φοίβη διάκονος in Cenchrae). About the same time devout *widows* (χῆραι) were given a certain ecclesiastical status. St. Paul (1 Tim. 5:9—13) gave detailed instructions for their guidance. Their duties were similar to those of the deaconesses, besides which they were expected to devote themselves to prayer and ascetical practices. If the two groups were actually different the distinction was never very great, since widows were often, and in the early Church regularly, chosen as deaconesses. — *Jos. Mayer*, Monumenta de viduis, diaconissis virginibusque tractantia, 1938 (Floril. patrist. 42). — A. J. Pankowsky, De Diaconissis, 1866. — L. Zscharnack, Der Dienst d. Frau in den ersten Jhh. d. christl. Kirche, 1902. — E. v. d. Goltz, Der Dienst d. Frau in der christl. Kirche, 2 vols. ²1914. — C. Robinson, The Ministry of Deaconesses, London 1898. — *A. Kalsbach*, Die altchristl. Einricht. der Diakonissen, 1926 (RQ Suppl. 22). — A. Rosembert, La veuve en droit canonique, Paris 1923. — *L. Bopp*, Das Witwentum als organ. Gliedschaft im Gemeinschaftsleben der alten Kirche, 1950. — P. Ketter, Christus u. die Frauen II, 1949.

The learned Oratorian *John Morinus* (Commentarius de sacris ecclesiae ordinationibus, Antwerp 1695, 143 ff.), *K. H. Schäfer* (Die Kanonissenstifter im deutschen MA., 1907, 46 ff.; RQ 1910, 68 ff.) and *A. Ludwig* (Weibl. Kleriker in der altchristl. und frühmittelalt. Kirche, Passauer Theol.-prakt. Monatsschrift 1910, 548/57, 609/17; cfr. 1911, 141/9) hold that the deaconess received a true clerical character similar to that of the deacons by the imposition of hands and the prayers of the bishop. But Morinus goes too far when he asserts that even in the East they were classed with the clergy in major orders. Only in the Gnostic sect and among the fanatical Montanists were women allowed to preach or perform priestly functions. — Cfr. *P. de Labriolle*, Mulieres taceant in ecclesia, BullLA 1911, 1 ff. 103 ff.

# § 19.
## Training, Selection, Maintenance and Qualifications of the Clergy.

1. Christ instructed His Apostles by *personal association* with them; and the Apostles trained their disciples in the same way. This method of training, generally followed in ancient times, was continued in the Church long after the days of the Apostles. The distinction of orders in the ranks of the clergy was recognized at a very early date and clerics of a lower order were prohibited from advancing to a higher one unless they had proved themselves competent in the one and qualified for the other. This arrangement lent itself admirably to proper training in their duties. The *catechetical schools*, in existence since the end of the second century, were originally established to instruct converts, but they also served at times as training schools for the lower clergy. Still earlier, the *charismata* (1 Cor. 12:28 ff.) supplied for any deficiencies in the knowledge or training of those whose office it was to instruct others. — Cfr. *H. R. Nelz*, Die theol. Schulen der morgenländ. Kirchen in ihrer Bedeutung f. die Ausbildung des Klerus (to 700), 1916.

2. Originally *admission* to the ranks of the clergy depended upon the Apostles and their disciples; but they did not ignore the wishes of the *congregation* in the matter (1 Clem. 44, 3). Later, the right to appoint a bishop rested with the congregation and the bishops of the province. According to Cyprian (Ep. 55, 8; 59, 5. 6; 67, 3—5; cfr. Hippolyt. Traditio Apostol. 31), the congregation had the right to elect (suffragium): the bishops of the province had the right to approve or to decide whether the election had been conducted properly (consensus, judicium) and finally to consecrate the one validly elected. According to the Synods of Arles 314 (can. 20) and Nicaea 325 (can. 4) at least three bishops were to be present on the occasion, and according to Nicaea it was the special prerogative of the metropolitan to approve of what had taken place. — On *the election of bishops*: *Funk*, AU I, 23 ff.; *H. Leclercq*, DictAC IV, 2618 ff.; *E. Göller*, Ehrengabe f. J. G. von Sachsen, 1920, 603 ff.; *K. Müller*, ZntW 1929, 274 ff.

3. According to Sacred Scripture (Matt. 10:10; 1 Cor. 9:13) the servants of the altar should live from the altar. A portion of the gifts (oblations) offered by the faithful at divine service went toward the maintenance of the clergy. Tertullian (Apolog. 39) also speaks of monthly contributions of money to a treasury (arca) of the congregation. The Didache (c. 13) demanded, moreover, the offering of the *firstlings* and the Didascalia (II, 25) speaks of giving *tithes* in as far as the words of Numbers 18, apply to the New Testament. Free will *offerings* and *legacies* in favor of the congregation were often quite *considerable*. From the end of the second century some congregations, especially at Rome, were able to acquire property for cemeteries and for the erection of places of worship (§ 23, 5). Rossi, Mommsen, Allard, Boissier and others believe that this was possible by taking advantage of the laws of Septimius Severus regarding Collegia funeraticia or tenuiorum (funeral guilds, burial associations for people of small means). But it is more probable that the property was acquired during the intervals when individual emperors were not enforcing existing laws against Christians or when officials were otherwise exceptionally tolerant

(the opinion of Duchesne, Waltzing, N. Müller et al. — Cfr. *Gerda Krüger,* Die Rechtsstellung d. vorkonstantin. Kirchen 1935; *G. Bovini,* La proprietà ecclesiastica e la condizione giuridica della chiesa in eta preconstantiniana, Milan 1949). However, it is not to be supposed that the congregations of this period were in a position to provide full support for the clergy. Many clerics lived from their patrimony or, after the example of St. Paul (Acts 20:34), from the work of their hands, farming, trades or commerce. In fact some bishops devoted themselves to secular pursuits to such an extent that Cyprian felt called upon to complain (De laps. 6) and the Synod of Elvira about 306 (can. 19) passed corrective measures.

4. Since it is the duty of the clergy to govern the Church of God, St. Paul demanded that the candidate for orders have certain moral and mental *qualifications* (1 Tim. 3:2—13; Tit. 1:5—9). To become a bishop or a deacon the candidate must be a man of one wife, i. e. he must not have married more than once. And just as the *digamus* was declared unfit for the clerical state, so the *neophyte,* i. e., the newly baptized, was excluded lest he be puffed up with pride (1 Tim. 3:6). Further, those who had performed *ecclesiastical penances* (§ 24:68), those who had been *baptized in illness* (baptismus clinicorum, Novatian) and those who had castrated themselves (Origen) were also disqualified. Those chosen for the episcopacy were to be 50 years of age and for the priesthood at least 30 years (Didasc. II, 1; Con. Neocaes. can. 11) .— C. Richert, Die Anfänge der Irregularitäten, 1901. — V. Fuchs, Der Ordinationstitel bis auf Innocenz III, 1930. — J. Blockscha, AdKR 111, 1931, 31/83 (Age requirement for major orders). — P. Browe, Zur Gesch. der Entmannung, 1936.

5. *Celibacy* was not imposed on the clergy. For the first three centuries there was no ecclesiastical legislation on this matter and still less an apostolic ordinance. If a married man entered the clerical state he was permitted to continue marital relations. But this privilege was allowed only to those who had married *before* ordination. A custom of long standing prohibited the higher clergy, that is bishops, priests and deacons from marriage *after* ordination under penalty of deposition. An exception was made in case of a deacon who before ordination protested that he reserved the right to marry and was ordained in spite of the protest (Council of Ancyra 314, can. 10). Since, according to the words of Christ (Matt. 19:12) as well as of St. Paul (1 Cor. 7:7, 25 ff.), celibacy is a more excellent state than marriage and more befitting the service of God, many Christians practised voluntary continency (§ 26, 3); and it is easily understood that clerics were chosen from this group whenever possible. At a very early date **celibacy** was widely practised by bishops and priests as the form of life more becoming their office. Toward the end of this period it became a law in Spain. The Synod of *Elvira* about 306 (can. 33) peremptorily commanded all clerics dedicated to the service of the altar (deacons, priests and bishops) to abstain from marital relations under pain of deposition. — *Funk,* AU I, 121/55; ThQ 1900, 157/60; *É. Vacandard,* Études de critique et d'hist. relig., Paris [5]1913, 69/120; *H. Leclercq,* DictAC II, 2802/32; *Chr. Knetes,* JThSt 1910, 348 ff., 481 ff.; *H. Böhmer,* Geschichtl. Studien, A. Hauck dargebracht, 1916, 6/24. — See also § 26.

## § 20.
## Dioceses and Provinces[1].

1. The first Christian congregations were established in the *cities*. They were called *parishes* (παροικίαι), i. e., groups of sojourners or pilgrims (Hebr. 11:13—16), and were presided over by *bishops*. In the course of time the number of Christians in larger cities required several churches. In Rome, suitable private homes donated or bequeathed to the Church were fitted out as residences of the presbyters (later also of other clerics) and became the centers of their activities. By about the year 300 there were fifteen to twenty such *titular churches* (originally the titulus meant the name of the owner, but eventually came to mean the name of a renowned martyr or saint to whom the place was dedicated). Pope Fabian (236—250) is said to have divided the city into seven districts (regions) each entrusted to the care of a deacon. After the third century, *churches* began to appear in *country places*. We hear of presbyters and doctors in the villages of Egypt (Eus. VII, 24, 6), of diaconus regens plebem in Spain (Council of Elvira, can. 77) and in Syria we first hear of village bishops (ἐπίσκοποι τῶν ἀγρῶν, Eus. VII, 30, 10: χωρεπίσκοποι, Council of Ancyra [314] can. 13). This development, however, did not affect the presidency of the bishop of the city. He remained the superior of the various churches of the city (§ 23, 1) as well as those in the city's environs.

2. As the faithful of a city formed a parish, so a number of parishes formed an *ecclesiastical province*, whose limits were coterminous with the borders of the civil provinces. As a rule the ecclesiastical head of a province was the bishop of the capital city. Since the fourth century the ecclesiastical superior of a province was called a *metropolitan*. The concurrence of ecclesiastical with

---

[1] E. STOLZ, ThQ 1907, 424/48; 1926, 1/8; P. DE LABRIOLLE, RechSR 1928, 60/72; U. STUTZ, ZRGkan 1935, 342 f.; 1936, 485/88 (parochia, parochus). J. P. KIRSCH, Die röm. Titelkirchen im Altertum, 1918; cfr. A. HARNACK, Sb. Berlin 1918, 954/87 = Mission II⁴, 836/66; U. STUTZ, ZRGkan 1919, 288/312; F. LANZONI, RivArchChrist 1925, 195/257. W. BIEDER, Ecclesia und Polis im N.T. u. in der alten Kirche, Diss. 1941. K. LÜBECK, Reichseinteilung und kirchl. Hierarchie des Orients (to 400), 1901. H. LINCK, Zur Übersetz. u. Erläuterung der Kanones 4, 6, 7 von Nicäa, Diss. 1908. P. WAGNER, Die geschichtl. Entwicklung d. Metropolitangewalt bis z. Dekretalgesetzgebung, Diss. 1917. K. MÜLLER, Beiträge usw., see § 18; Festgabe Ad. Jülicher, 1927, 190/202; ZntW 1929, 296/305. P. BATIFFOL, Le Primae Sedis Episcopus en Afrique, RechSR 1923, 425/32 (also d'Alès, ib. 1924, 160/64). K. V. SCHWARZ, Die Entstehung d. Snyoden in der alten Kirche, Diss. 1898. P. BATIFFOL, BullLA 1913, 3/19 (order of business in the African synods). G. ROETHE, Zur Gesch. der röm. Synoden im 3. u. 4. Jh., Diss. 1937.

political divisions was based on geographic and historic reasons, but was usually not without a religious reason, too, since the churches of a province were ordinarily established from the capital city and were regarded as daughter churches of the older church in the province. Except for Egypt, the church of the East was divided into provinces as early as the third century. In the West this did not take place until somewhat later.

Since the second half of the second century, the bishops of a province assembled in *synods* to discuss important problems. As far as we know this practice began in Asia Minor about the time the Montanists appeared. There was a political precedent for these synods in the conventions (κοινόν, conventus) of Asia Minor. Synods proved an important means for preserving and strengthening ecclesiastical unity and were soon held annually in Asia Minor.

3. But even the ecclesiastical province was not an independent unit. There were dignitaries who might be called *chief metropolitans* whose position the Council of Nicaea 325 (can. 6) says was of long standing. The Council expressly mentions the bishops of *Rome*, *Alexandria* and *Antioch*, whose jurisdiction respectively included the West, Egypt with the neighboring provinces and the political diocese of the East (Syria, Cilicia, Mesopotamia and Palestine as far as Sinai). Here we have the *beginnings* of the later *patriarchal organization*. In the same canon the Council seems to indicate that there were other metropolitans of high rank with special privileges and evidently refers to the bishops of *Ephesus* (Asia proconsularis), *Caesarea* in Cappadocia, *Caesarea* in Palestine and Heraclea in Thrace. Of similar high rank, if not by law at least in fact, was the bishop of *Carthage*, who exercised general supervision over northwest Africa. Here the relationship of mother church and daughter churches was the deciding factor and the bishops of Carthage claimed as an ancient right the privilege of consecrating and of deposing, for sufficient reasons, the bishops of the dependent churches.

## § 21.
### The Unity of the Church and the Primacy of Rome[1].

**The Popes** to 313: *Peter* (67?); Linus (67—79?); Anacletus (79—90?); *Clement* (90—99?); Evaristus (99—107?); Alexander (107—116?); Xytus or

---

[1] FR. TILLMANN, Jesus und das Papsttum, 1910. P. DAUSCH, Kirche u. Papsttum — eine Stiftung Jesu? ³1921 (Bibl. Zeitfr. IV, 2). P. BATIFFOL,

§ *21. The Unity of the Church and the Primacy of Rome.*

Sixtus (116—125?); Telesophorus (125—136?); Hyginus (136—140?); Pius (140—154/55?); Anicetus (154/55—166); Soter (166—174); Eleutherius (174—189); *Victor* (189—198); Zephyrinus (198—217); *Callistus* (217—222); Hippolytus (217—235) Anti-Pope; Urban (222—230); Pontianus (230—235); Anterus (235—236); *Fabian* (236—250); *Cornelius* (251—253); Novatian (251—258?) Anti-Pope; Lucius (253—254); *Stephen* (254—257); *Xystus* or *Sixtus II* (257—258); *Dionysius* (260—268); Felix (269—274); Eutychian (275—283); Cajus (283—296); Marcellinus (296—304); Marcellus (307—308); Eusebius (308); *Militiades* or *Melchiades* (311—314).

RevSR 1924, 440/53; RechSR 1928, 31/59 (Peter, Prince of the Apostles and first pope); these articles combined in Cathedra Petri, Paris 1938. J. GEISELMANN, Der Petrin. Primat, 1927 (Bibl. Zeitfr. XII, 7). M. BESSON, S. Pierre et les origines de la Primauté romaine, Geneva 1929. G. GLEZ-M. JUGIE, Primauté du pape, DictThC XIII, 247/391. H. LECLERCQ, Art. Pape, DictAC XIII, 1111/345. K. PIEPER, Jesus u. die Kirche, 1932. J. HOLLNSTEINER, Jb. der österreich. Leogesellschaft 1933, 87/127 (studies on the legal history of the primacy). Textus antenicaeni ad primatum Romanum spectantes, ed. G. RAUSCHEN, 1914; ed. H. VOGELS, 1937 (Floril. patrist. 9). J. T. SHOTWELL and L. R. LOOMIS, The See of Peter, New York 1927 (collection of texts to 400). F. X. SEPPELT, Gesch. der Päpste I, ²1939. J. A. MÖHLER, Die Einheit in der Kirche, 1825; new ed. by E. J. VIERNEISEL, 1925. H. HAGEMANN, Die röm. Kirche u. ihr Einfluß auf Disziplin u. Dogma in den ersten 3 Jhh., 1864. G. BARDY, RechSR 1924, 255 ff. 385 ff. (authority of the Roman See in the third century); La théologie de l'Église 2 vol. Paris 1945/7, (from Clement of Rome to Nicaea). K. ADAM, ThQ 1928, 161/256 (origen of the Church's teaching on the primacy); also in Ges. Aufsätze zur DG. etc., 1936, 123/85. TH. KLAUSER, ZThS 1931, 193/213 (lists of Roman bishops). J. HADZEGA, ThGl 1937, 431/40 (Origen on the primacy of Peter). L. HERTLING, Communio u. Primat, 1943. M. MACCARONE, Rev. di storia d. Chiesa in It. 1948, 1/32 (Vicarius Christi vioarius Petri) H RAHNER ZkTh 1947, 1/35 (Navicula Petri). Protestant and modernist literature: ER. CASPAR, Gesch. des Papsttums I (to Leo I), 1930 (standard); Die älteste röm. Bischofsliste, 1926; Primatus Petri, Untersuchung über die Ursprünge der Primatslehre, 1927 (also K. ADAM, op. cit.). JOH. HALLER, Das Papsttum, Idee u. Wirklichkeit I, ²1951 (violently anti-Roman). J. TURMEL (Modernist), Histoire du dogme de la Papauté, (to 400), Paris 1908, Histoire des dogmes, t. III: La Papauté, ib. 1933. W. E. BEET, The Early Roman Episcopate to 384, London 1913. A. HARNACK, Sb. Berlin 1904, 1044/62 = Mission II⁴, 817/32 (Nationality of the first forty-eight popes); Sb. Berlin 1927, 139/52 (Ecclesia Petri propinqua in Tert. De pud. 21); id. 415/46 (Christus praesens — Vicarius Christi). H. KOCH, Cathedra Petri, Neue Untersuchungen über die Anfänge der Primatslehre, 1930 (also K. ADAM ThRev 1931, 193/200, and in Ges. Aufsätze, 1936, 186/95 and B. POSCHMANN, infra. p. 117). E. KOHLMEYER, Festgabe JOH. FICKER, 1931, 3/16 (Ideology of the early papacy). K. D. SCHMIDT, ZKG 1935, 267/75 (Papa Petrus ipse). K. GUGGISBERG, ib. 276/300 (Mt 16 f. in Church History). K. J. KIDD, The Roman Primacy to A. D. 461, London 1936. L. BRUN, Z. f. systemat. Theol. 1937, 86/127 (concept of ecclesiastical unity). K. STOECKIUS AkKR 1937, 24/126 (Ecclesia Petri Propria bei Tertullian). W. KÖHLER, Omnis ecclesia Petri proprinqua, Sb. Heidelberg 1937/38, 3 (also B. ALTANER, ThRev 1939, 129/38). U. GMELIN, Auctoritas, röm. Princeps u. päpstl. Primat, 1937 (also B. ALTANER, ThRev 1938, 329/33). H. A. MORSTON, Rome et l'Église primitive, Paris 1938 (also E. AMANN, RevSR 1938, 459/65). FR. HEILER, Die kath. Kirche des Ostens u. Westens I—II, 1, 1937/41. H. E. SYMONDS, The Church Universal and the See of Rome, London 1939. T. G. JALLAND, The Church and the Papacy, London 1944. E. STAUFFER, ZKG 1943/4, 3/34 (prehistory and early history of the primacy).

1. The strong tendency toward unity under a monarchical government which is clearly seen in the organization of parishes, dioceses and metropolitan sees reached its culmination in the unity of the whole Church under a supreme head, the pope of Rome. However, this achievement, was not the result of purely natural effort; it resulted from the functioning of a principle that had been given the Church by Her Divine Founder. Just as Christ had preached *one* God and *one* faith (Eph. 4:5) so He founded but *one* Church and gave to her, in *Peter*, the chief of the Apostles, one visible head and center of unity (Matt. 16:18 f.; John 21:15 ff.; 10, 1). Nor was this arrangement to be restricted to apostolic times; it would be even more important and more necessary in the centuries to come. The primacy and the task given to Peter must descend upon his successors. The flock which had been committed to him was to be governed by this legitimate successors from the spot where Peter went to martyrdom. *Irenaeus* (Adv. haer. III, 3, 3) gives the list of Roman bishops from Peter to Eleutherius, and it is worthy of note that even non-Catholic research acknowledges this oldest list to be "an ancient document of genuine tradition" (E. Caspar).

2. The *primacy* of the *Church of Rome* naturally did not appear all at once and in its full external development. It developed organically and as need required. The testimony of the first three centuries forges a chain of conclusive evidence to the faith of those times in the Petrine-Roman primacy. One of the strongest indirect proofs consists in the fact that heretics and schismatics (§ 30; 32; 34) earnestly endeavored to be recognized by the Roman Church, because as Irenaeus and Tertullian (Adv. Prax. 1) say, communion with Rome was regarded as communion with the whole Church. From the beginning Rome was the "center and source of the 'orthodox' movement within the Church" (W. Bauer). Especially important is the authoritative tone with which the Roman Church about the year 96 exhorts the congregation of Corinth to restore peace (*Clement* of Rome, 1 Cor. 1, 59; 62—65)[1]; with which Pope *Victor* speaks to the churches of Asia Minor during the Easter controversy about the year 190 (§ 25, 3); with which Pope *Stephen* (256) forbids the Africans to repeat baptism in the case of heretics

---

[1] F. R. VAN CAUWELAERT, RHE 1935, 267 ff. 765 ff. sees in Rome's action only a fraternal solidarity and not a consciousness of authority; for opposite opinions see J. ZEILLER, ib. 762/64; B. ALTANER, ThRev 1936 41/45; ST. LÖSCH, in Studi dedicati alla memoria di P. Ubaldi, Milan 1937, 186/88.

(§ 22, 3); and with which Pope *Dionysius* (ca. 260) calls Bishop Dionysius of Alexandria to account for using heterodox expressions in speaking of the Logos (§ 32, 5). All of these incidents show clearly that the Roman bishops were aware that they occupied a position of supreme authority in the Church. The same is true of the Roman synods since the end of the second century. The Roman bishops appear in them not only as *primus inter pares*, but as taking precedence over the assembled bishops and empowered to make independent and authoritative decisions.

Direct testimony to the primacy of Rome is furnished in a number of authentic documents of the period. Bishop *Ignatius* of Antioch[1] in the address of his letter to the Romans written about 110 says that the Roman Church is "presiding in love" or is administratrix of the "bond of love" (προκαθημένη τῆς ἀγάπης). The exact meaning of this passage is much disputed. Taken by itself it can be understood in an ethical sense of a primacy of charitable sentiment and activity. But in connection with the words which immediately precede: "which also presides in the chief place of the Roman territory" (ἥτης καὶ προκάθηται ἐν τόπῳ χωρίου 'Ρωμαίων) it evidently refers to a special primacy in faith and charity. Although the primacy is not further described, Ignatius knew that the Romans would understand the allusion. The famous inscription on the tomb of *Abercius* (Bishop?)[2] of Hieropolis (ca. 180—200), which can not be interpreted as pagan or syncretic, says that he was sent to Rome by the "holy shepherd" to behold a "queen with a golden robe and golden sandals." *Irenaeus,* Bishop of Lyons[3], writing about the year 185 against the innovations of

---

[1] Cfr. FUNK, AU I, 2/12; A. HARNACK, Sb. Berlin 1896, 111/31; J. CHAPMAN, RevBén 1896, 385/400; J. THIELE, ThGl 1927, 701/9; O. PERLER, Divus Thom. Greib. 1944, 413/51.

[2] H. LECLERCQ, DictAC I, 66/87. W. LÜDTKE, and TH. NISSEN, Die Grabschrift des Aberkios, 1910. F. J. DÖLGER, Ichthys II, 1922, 454/507. A. ABEL, Byzantion 1926, 321/411; H. GRÉGOIRE, ib. 1933, 89/91. A. GREIFF, ThGl 1926, 78/88; ThQ 1929, 247 ff. 447 ff. H. STRATHMANN and TH. KLAUSER in RLAntChrist I, 12/7. A. FERRUA, RivArchCrist 1943, 279/305; Civ Catt 1943, IV, 39/45.

[3] Adv. haer. III, 3, 2: Ad hanc enim ecclesiam (sc. Romanam) propter potentiorem principalitatem necesse est omnem convenire ecclesiam, hoc est eos qui sunt undique fideles, in qua semper ab his qui sunt undique conservata est ea quae est ab apostolis traditio. Cfr. FUNK, AU I, 12/23; HARNACK, Sb. Berlin 1893, 939/55; G. ESSER, Kath. 1917 I, 289 ff., II, 16 ff. and ThGl 1922, 344/62 (versus H. KOCH, ThStKr 1921, 54/72); L. SALTET, BullLE 1920, 179/206; L. SPIKOWSKI, La doctrine de l'Église dans S. Irénée, Diss. Strassb. 1926; J. FORGET, EphThLov 1928, 437/61. P. GALTIER, RHE 1949, 411/28; R. JACQUIN, RevSR 1950, 72/87; H. HOLSTEIN, RechSR 1949, 122/35.

---

the Gnostics ascribes to the Roman Church a plenitude of power (potentior principalitas) because of her foundation by the glorious Apostles Peter and Paul. And he goes on to say that every individual church which would preserve the apostolic tradition must necessarily conform in belief with the Roman Church. And finally, *St. Cyprian*, Bishop of Carthage, in a letter to Pope Cornelius, designates the Roman Church as the "chair of Peter and the principal church from which issues priestly (= episcopal) unity" (Ep. 59, 14: Petri cathedra atque ecclesia principalis, unde unitas sacerdotalis exorta est; cfr. Ep. 58, 8; De cath. eccles. unitate, 4). The idea, originating in the East, and frequently repeated by Protestant scholars (Harnack, Haller, etc.) that the political influence of Rome as capital of the Empire was the basis of the special prerogatives of the Roman Church, (can. 3 of the Council of Constantinople 381; can. 28 of Chalcedon 451; Theodoret, Ep. 113), was unknown in this period. Later on such an argument was used as the main reason for the bishop of Constantinople assuming higher rank (§ 63, 1; 64, 2).

3. The position of authority occupied by the Roman Church and her bishops was thus a firmly established fact in the first centuries. From the third century a precise doctrine of primacy began to be enunciated. However, the Roman primacy was then far from the development it attained in the Middle Ages and the popes of this period were known by the same title as other bishops. Its function at this time consisted chiefly in *preserving ecclesiastical unity*. So long as faith or morals was not involved, the individual churches and provinces enjoyed full liberty in the management of their own affairs.

St. Cyprian's teaching on the primacy is much discussed by modern scholars and several divergent opinions have resulted. However, this much is certain: Cyprian acknowledged the primacy of Rome as based on Peter and not merely a symbol of the bond of charity established by Christ, but as the real source and lasting foundation of ecclesiastical unity precisely because Peter is and remains the rock on which the Church was founded. But Rome's role as the visible embodiment of the principle of unity was conceived by Cyprian to be a passive (static) and not an active (dynamic) function. For he stresses the equality of the other Apostles with Peter; insists that they partook of the same honor and were endowed with the same power of orders (De cath. eccles. unit. 4) and that bishops are responsible to God alone for the administration of their dioceses (Ep. 59, 14). And although personally he places the greatest importance on constant and close union with Rome and for all practical purposes acknowledges the primacy of the pope (Ep. 68), he nowhere recognizes the right of the Roman bishops to govern the whole Church or to issue binding decrees. The position he takes on the question is notably inconsistant and, for those times, quite unusual. For Cyprian's anti-Roman attitude in the controversy over the rebaptism of heretics cfr. § 22, 3. — *J. Ernst,* Cyprian und das Papsttum, 1912. — *K. Adam,* ThQ 1912, 99 ff. 203 ff.; 1928, 203 ff.; also in Ges. Aufsätze, 1936, 70/185. — *A. d'Alès,* La théologie de S. Cyprien, Paris 1922. — *B. Poschmann,* Ecclesia principalis, ein krit. Beitrag zur Frage des Primates bei Cyprian, 1933 (also K. Adam, ThQ 1933, 439/42 and B. Altaner, ThRev 1933, 425/32). — *H. Koch,* Cyprian und der röm. Primat, TU 35, 1, 19, endeavors to prove that Cyprian is a genuine Episcopalian, who rejects the Roman primacy absolutely.


# CHAPTER III

## WORSHIP, DISCIPLINE AND MORALS[1]


### § 22.

### Baptism, Profession of Faith and the Controversy over the Rebaptism of Heretics[2].

1. In apostolic times baptism was administered immediately after the profession of the Christian faith (Acts 2:41; 8:37 et pass.).

---

[1] L. DUCHESNE, Origines du culte chrétien, Paris ⁵1925 (standard). F. PROBST, Sakramente u. Sakramentalien in den 3 ersten christl. Jhh., 1872, Kirchliche Disziplin in den 3 ersten christl. Jhh., 1873. TH. SCHERMANN, Die allg. Kirchenordnung, frühchristl. Liturgien u. kirchl. Überlieferung, 3 parts 1914/6. J. LEBRETON, RechSR 1934, 129/64. J. H. SRAWLEY, The Early History of the Liturgy, Cambridge ²1947. TH. KLAUSNER, Abendländ. Liturgiegesch., 1949. C. CLEMEN, Der Einfluß der Mysterienreligionen auf d. älteste Christent., 1913; Die Reste der primitiven Religion im ältesten Christent., 1916; Religionsgesch. Erklärung des N.T., ²1924. J. DE GHEL-LINCK, E. DE BACKER etc., Pour l'histoire du mot Sacramentum I, Paris 1924. A. KOLPING, Sacramentum Tertullianeum, 1948. K. PRÜMM, ZkTh 1937, 391/425 ("Mysterion" from Paul to Origen). F. J. DÖLGER, Antike u. Christentum, kultur- u. religionsgesch. Studien, 1929 ff. Cfr. literature in § 5, 6 and 18.

[2] H. WINDISCH, Taufe u. Sünde im ältesten Christent. bis Origenes, 1908; ZntW 1929, 107/42 and A. OEPKE, ib. 1930, 81/111 (infant baptism). W. KOCH, Die Taufe im N.T., ³1921 (Bibl. Zeitfr. III, 10). A. V. STROMBERG, Studien z. Theologie u. Praxis d. Taufe in der christl. Kirche der ersten 2 Jhh., 1913. TH. SCHERMANN, Frühchristl. Vorbereitungsgebete zur Taufe, 1917; Kath. 1915 II, 263/80 (christian baptimal names). P. DE PUNIET, Baptême, DictAC II, 251/346; Catéchumenat, ib IV, 2579/621. H. LECLERCQ, Catéchèse, Caté-chisme, Catéchumène, ib. IV, 2530/79; Noms propres des chrétiens, ib. XII, 1481/1553. A. D'ALÈS et M. COPPENS, Baptême, Dict. de la Bible, Suppl. I, 1928, 852/924. P. DREWS, Taufe, RE XIX, 424/50. F. J. DÖLGER, Der Exorzismus im altchristl. Taufritual, 1909; Ichthys, Der hl. Fisch in den antiken Religionen u. im Christentum vols. I—V, 1910/43; Sphragis, eine altchristl. Taufbezeichnung, 1911; Die Sonne der Gerechtigkeit u. der Schwarze, Religionsgesch. Studien zum Taufgelöbnis, 1918; Sol salutis, Gebet u. Gesang im christl. Altert., ²1925; AntChrist 1930, 117/41 (Baptism of blood). J. LEI-

Later, but still as early as the second century, it was preceded by a period of instruction and trial, lasting from two to three years (Hippol., Trad. apost. 42; Council of Elvira, can. 4). Those who were undergoing this preparation were called *catechumens* (κατηχούμενοι, audientes) since they were being instructed in the saving truths of Christianity. The name is first found in Tertullian; but the arrangement was known as early as Justin (Apol. I, 61); and Hippolytus (Trad. apost. 40—50) speaks of an organized catechumenate in Rome about 220. Except in case of necessity, baptism was administered twice a year: on the vigils of *Easter* and *Pentecost*. At first, the catechumens were baptized in "living" (i. e. flowing) water (Did. 7, 1), in springs, rivers or the sea; later, in buildings erected especially for this purpose, (baptisteries, piscinae) by the *bishop*, or with his permission, by presbyters and deacons, and, in case of necessity, also by lay persons (Tert. De Bapt. 17). Baptism was usually administered by a threefold *immersion*, but in the case of the sick (baptismus clinicorum) or when immersion was imposible, by pouring or sprinkling water. Besides the baptismal formula, Holy Scripture and the Didache (c. 7) mention only the use of water. But since the beginning of the third century Tertullian and Hippolytus speak of various symbolic acts accompanying or rather preceding the ceremony: signing with the cross, renunciation of Satan, exorcism, exorcistic anointing, profession of *faith*, baptismal vows and anointing with the "oil of thanksgiving." Immediately after baptism called "enlightening," "sealing," or "rebirth," *confirmation* was administered and the baptized took part in the *Eucharistic* liturgy. After Communion the neophytes were given a mixture of milk and honey, the food of new-born children (Tert. De cor. 3; Adv. Marc. I, 14; Hippol. Trad. apost. 46, 9), a custom not derived from pagan mystery cults but based on Scripture (Exod. 3:8, 17 et passim; 1 Peter 2:2 and 3). For the eight days

POLDT, Die urchristl. Taufe im Lichte der Religionsgesch., 1928. R. REITZEN-STEIN, Die Vorgesch. der christl. Taufe, 1929 (a radical study of comparative religion). K. WEIDINGER, Die Haustafeln, ein Stück urchristl. Paränese, 1928. H. RAHNER, ZkTh 1931, 239/73 (Pompa diaboli). B. CAPELLE, RechThAM 1933, 129/54 (introduction of the catechumenate at Rome). J. THOMAS, Le mouvement baptiste en Palestine et Syrie 150 av. à 300 Après J. Christ, Diss. Louvain 1935. J. JEREMIAS, Hat die Urkirche die Kindertaufe geübt? ²1949. B. WELTE, Die postbaptismale Salbung ... der alten Kirche, 1939. E. DICK, ZkTh 1939, 1/49 (sponsors at baptism). TH. KLAUSER, in Pisciculi, Festschrift F. J. Dölger, 1939, 157/64 ("living" water). G. BARDY, La conversion au christianisme durant les premiers siècles, Paris 1949. O. CULLMANN, Le baptême des enfants ..., Neuchâtel 1948.

during which the baptimal festivities were kept, the newly baptized wore a *white* robe. Because this robe was laid aside on the Sunday after Easter, that day was known in the West as Dominica in albis (viz. depositis) while in the Greek Church it was called "New Sunday." *Sponsors* are mentioned as early as Tertullian (De bapt. 18). The bestowal of a special *Christian name* in baptism became customary about the middle of the third century. If the catechumen was martyred, the sacrifice of his life for Christ or the *baptism of blood* (baptismus sanguinis) supplied for the baptism of water (Tert. De bapt. 16; Cypr. Ep. 73, 72). Irenaeus (Adv. haer. II, 22, 4), Hippolytus (Trad. apost. 46, 1) and Origen (Hom. in Ep. ad Rom. V, 9) speak of *infant baptism* as being of apostolic tradition.

2. The **profession** of faith[1] made at baptism, which had constituted the basis of the instructions during the catechumenate, contained the chief truths of the Christian faith delivered by the Apostles. Hence Irenaeus and Tertullian call it κανὼν τῆς πίστεως, regula fidei or veritatis; later it became known as the symbol σύμβολον. The wording varied slightly in different places. From Tertullian and Hippolytus it can be proved with certainty that the profession of faith was given a permanent form in the West, more specifically at Rome, about the turn of the second century. This is the so-called *Apostle's Creed* in its oldest form, which became the

---

[1] For Hahn, Denzinger and other collections of creeds see § 2, 6. F. KATTENBUSCH, Das apost. Symbol, 2 vols. 1894/1900. B. DÖRHOLT, Das Taufsymbolum der alten Kirche, 1898. W. DIEKAMP, Über den Ursprung des Trinitätsbekenntnisses, 1910. W. M. PEITZ, Liber diurnus I, Sb. Vienna 185, 4, 1918; SZ 94, 1918, 553/66. K. HOLL, Harnack and Lietzmann, Sb. Berlin 1919, 2 ff. 112 ff. 269 ff. H. LIETZMANN, Die Anfänge des Glaubensbek., Festgabe Harnack 1921, 226/42; Symbolstudien, ZntW 1922, 1923, 1925, 1927. J. HAUSSLEITER, Trinitarischer Glaube u. Christusbek. in der alten Kirche, 1920. A. NUSSBAUMER, Das Ursymbol nach der Epideixis des hl. Irenäus u. dem Dialog Justins, 1921. P. FEINE, Die Gestalt des apost. Glaubensbek. in der Zeit des N.T., 1925. F. J. BADCOCK, The History of the Creeds, London [2]1938. E. V. DOBSCHÜTZ, Das Apostolicum in bibl. theol. Beleuchtung, 1932. D. VAN DEN EYNDE, Les normes de l'enseignement chrétien dans la littérature patristique des trois premiers siècles, Dissertation, Louvain, 1933 (also B. Reynders, RechThAM 1933, 155/91). J. RANFT, Der Ursprung des kath. Traditionsprinzips, 1931. K. PRÜMM, Der christl. Glaube u. die altheidnische Welt, 2 vols., 1935. W. MAURER, Bekenntnis u. Sakrament I, 1939. J. DE GHELLINCK, Patristique et Moyen Age I, Paris [2]1949. O. CULLMANN, Les premiers confessions de foi chrétiennes, Paris [2]1949 (also J. DE GHELLINCK, RHE 1946, 407/16). P. NAUTIN, Je crois à l'Esprit S. . . . ., ibid. 1947. J. N. D. KELLY, Early Christian Creeds, London, 1950. Cfr. also the studies of J. BRINKTRINE, ThQ 1921, 156/90; R. SEEBERG, ZKG 1922, 1/41; F. J. BADCOCK, JThSt 1922, 362/89; RevBén 1933. 3/9; R. H. CONNOLLY, JThSt 1924, 131/39; B. CAPELLE, RevBén 1927, 33/45; RechThAM 1930, 5/20; J. LEBRETON, RechSR 1930, 97/124; F. J. DÖLGER, AntChrist 1933, 138/46; J. CARPENTER, JThSt 1942, I ff., 1943, I ff.; H. HOLSTEIN, RechSR 1947, 454/61.

the common basis for all other creeds in the West (cfr. Tert. De praescript. 36). The present, somewhat expanded form, is encountered in southern Gaul about 450. It is possible that the Roman formula was composed and made permanent by Pope Zephyrinus (198—217) to counteract the heretical Monarchians (§ 32) (a combination of a Trinitarian and Christological formula ?). Its previous development is obscure. Allusions in the New Testament and in post-apostolic literature give good grounds for assuming that even the infant Church had a formula comprising the chief points of the Apostle's preaching as commanded in Matthew 28:19. This formula was then amplified at Rome in the second century during the conflict with the Gnostics, especially with Marcion (§ 29, 5; 30 B 1). It includes belief in God, the Father Almighty, in Jesus Christ, His only begotten Son, our Lord, and in the Holy Ghost, the forgiveness of sin and the resurrection of the flesh (§ 27, 1).

3. As heresies and schisms multiplied, it frequently happened that persons baptized in a sect sought admission into the Catholic Church. The question naturally arose as to whether baptism administered by a heretic or by those outside the Church was valid. Conflicting opinions led to the so-called **baptismal controversy**[1]. In a work (De baptismo) written in Greek and Latin, *Tertullian* denied the validity of baptism by a heretic. Undoubtedly it was the high esteem in which he was held that influenced three synods to favor the same opinion. The first of these synods was held at Carthage about 220 and the other two at Synnada and Iconium in Asia Minor about 230. Two synods held at Carthage under the presidency of Bishop *Cyprian* (255/56) to discuss the Novatian schism, renewed the pronouncements regarding the invalidity of baptism by heretics; and the controversy assumed greater importance. Pope *Stephen*, informed of the synodal decisions, forbade the Africans, under threat of being excluded from communion with the Church to rebaptize heretics, asserting that such procedure was an innovation. Those baptized by heretics were obliged merely to submit to

---

[1] J. ERNST, Die Ketzertaufangelegenheit in der altchristl. Kirche nach Cyprian, 1901; P. Stephan I u. der Ketzertaufstreit, 1905; studies in ZkTh 1903, 1905, 1906; ThQ 1911. A. D'ALÈS, RQH 1907 I, 353/400. H. V. SODEN QFItalAB 12, 1909, 1/42. H. BRUDERS, ZkTh 1911, 301/46. G. RAUSCHEN, ThGl 1916, 629/38. J. B. BORD, RHE 1922, 445/68. H. KOCH, IntkZ 1923, 73/104 (on the Carthaginian Synod of 256; cfr. § 40, 3 for the literature on the Liber de rebaptismate). K. MÜLLER, ZntW 1924, 235/47. F. J. DÖLGER, AntChrist 1929, 79 f., 319 (nihil innovetur); also H. KOCH, Philologus 1930, 128/32 (nisi = sed). F. DE ST. PALAIS D'AUSSAC, La réconciliation des hérétiques dans l'Église latine, Paris 1943.

penance (Cypr. Ep. 74, 1; si qui ergo a quacumque haeresi venient ad vos, nihil innovetur nisi quod traditum est, ut manus illis imponatur in poenitentiam). He addressed a similar letter to Asia Minor when he learned that the bishops Firmilian of Caesarea and Helenus of Tarsus held with the Africans. On September 1, 256 another synod of eighty-seven bishops was held in Africa which repeated the opinion of the previous meetings. It is not certain whether Pope Stephen's decision had reached them at this time; but Stephen broke off relations with them at once. Feeling ran high and there were harsh words on both sides. Bishop *Dionysius* of Alexandria, who inclined toward the Roman view, endeavored to make peace and to secure toleration of the contrary opinion. The controversy ceased temporarily when the persecution of Valerian began, especially since death soon removed the two principal contestants: Pope Stephen died in 257 and Cyprian was martyred in 258 (§ 16, 2). Sixtus II, Stephen's successor, appears to have resumed relations with the Africans, many of whom clung to their practice for some time. The Synod of Arles in 314 (can. 8) said of them propria lege sua utuntur, ut rebaptizent.

For Cyprian and the Africans, the *controversy* was not only a disciplinary but also a *dogmatic* question. Under the spell of Tertullian's concept of the sacraments and a spiritual Church, they made the validity of the means of grace depend on the orthodox faith and morals of the minister. According to this concept, one who is outside the Church or not in the state of grace can not validly baptize or consecrate. The personal and ethical factors were overemphasized. Rome, on the other hand, held fast to the principle of the objective efficacy of the sacraments which was later made clear by Augustine during the contest with the Donatists (§ 52, 4).

## § 23.

## The Eucharist. The Disciplina Arcani and the Agape[1].

1. The principle parts of divine worship in the infant Church are mentioned in the Acts of the Apostles 2:42: The teaching of the

---

[1] F. CABROL et H. LECLERCQ, Monumenta ecclesiae liturgica, see § 2, 5. G. RAUSCHEN, Monum. eucharistica et liturgica vetustissima, [2]1914, new ed. by J. QUASTEN, 7 parts 1935/37 (Floril. patrist. 7); Eucharistie und Buß-sakrament in den ersten 6 Jhh. der Kirche, [2]1910. F. PROBST, Die Liturgie der 3 ersten christl. Jhh., 1870; Lehre und Gebet in den 3 ersten christl. Jhh., 1871; Sakramente, etc., see literature in § 27. E. VON DER GOLTZ, Das Gebet in der ältesten Christenheit, 1901; Tisch- und Abendmahlsgebete, TU 29, 2 vols. (1905). A. SCHEIWILER, Die Elemente der Eucharistie in den ersten 3 Jhh., 1903 (opposes A. Harnack in TU 7, 2, 1891; cfr. also FUNK, AU I, 278/92). F. CABROL, Les origines liturgiques, Paris 1906. G. BAREILLE et F. BOUR, Eucharistie, DictThC V, 1121/1209. H. LECLERCQ, Communion

Apostles, the breaking of bread and prayers (cfr. also Acts 20:7—11, Paul at Troias). Conformably to Christ's command (Luke 22:19; 1 Cor. 11:24 f.), the Christian community celebrated the Eucharistic

DictAC III, 2427/65; Messe, ib. XI, 513/774. RUCH, GAUDEL et autres, Messe, DictThC X, 796/1402. J. COPPENS, Eucharistie, Dict. de la Bible, Suppl. II, Paris 1934, 1146/1215. P. GLAUE, Die Vorlesung hl. Schriften im Gottesdienst I, 1907. E. BAUMGARTNER, Eucharistie u. Agape im Urchristent., 1909. M. GOGUEL, L'Eucharistie des origines à Justin Martyr, Paris 1909. F. E. BRIGHTMAN, JThSt 1909, 497/528 (common prayer). TH. SCHERMANN, Ein Weiherituale d. röm. Kirche am Schluß des 1. Jh., 1913; Die allg. Kirchenordnung usw., see § 22; Der liturg. Papyrus v. Dêr-Balyzeh, TU 36, 1 b, 1910; Bibl. Z. 1910, 33 ff. 162 ff. ("Breaking of bread"); Philologus 1910, 375/410 ("Eucharistia"). W. KOCH, Das Abendmahl im N.T., 1911 (Bibl. Zeitfr. IV, 10). FR. DIBELIUS, Das Abendmahl, 1911. P. BATIFFOL, Études d'histoire et de théologie positive II: L'Eucharistie, Paris ⁹1930; Études de liturgie et d'archéologie chrét., Paris 1919. O. CASEL, Die Eucharistielehre des Justinus Martyr, Kath. 1914 I, 153 ff. et passim. — Passim J. BRINKTRINE, Der Meßopferbegriff, 1918; Die hl. Messe, ³1950. F. HEILER, Das Gebet, eine religionsgesch. u. religionspsychol. Untersuchung, ³¹⁵1923. J. LEBRETON, La prière dans l'Église primitive, RechSR 1924, 6 ff. 97 ff. P. CAGIN, Les origines de la messe, Paris 1921 (also BATIFFOL, Rev. bibl. 1916, 23/32). J. KROLL, Die christl. Hymnodik bis zu Klemens v. Alex., 2 parts 1921/22 (Progr. Braunsberg); idem in HENNECKE, Neutest. Apokryphen, ²1924, 596 ff. G. P. WETTER, Altchristl. Liturgien, 2 vols. 1921/2 (radical). F. J. DÖLGER, Die Eucharistie nach Inschriften frühchristl. Zeit, 1922 (≐ Ichthys II, 448 ff.). J. A. JUNGMANN, Die Stellung Christi im liturg. Gebet, 1925; Gewordene Liturgie, 1941; Missarum solemnia, 2 vols. ²1949. W. O. E. OESTERLEY, The Jewish Background of the Christian Liturgy, Oxford 1925. W. E. BARNES, Early Christians at Prayer, London 1925. H. LIETZMANN, Messe u. Herrenmahl, 1926 (important); Die Entstehung der christl. Liturgie nach den ältesten Quellen, in Vorträge der Bibliothek Warburg 1925/6 (1928) 45/66. J. SCHOUSBOE, RevHR 96, 1927, 193/256 (earliest form of the Mass). DE PUNIET, La liturgie de la messe, ses origines et son histoire, Avignon 1928. R. HARRIS, Eucharistic origins, London 1928. G. H. C. MACGREGOR, Eucharistic origins, London 1929. K. G. GOETZ, Der Ursprung des christl. Abendmahls, Basel Univ.-Progr. 1929. W. BAUER, Der Wortgottesdienst der ältesten Christen, 1930. W. GOOSSENS, Les origines de l'Eucharistie, sacrement et sacrifice, Diss. Louvain 1931. J. M. FROCHISSE, RHE 1932, 594/604 (the Eucharistic fast). O. CASEL, JbLW 12, 1934, 299/346 (literature on ancient christian liturgy to the reign of Constantine). R. HUPFELD, Die Abendmahlsfeier, ihr ursprüngl. Sinn etc., 1935. J. M. NIELEN, Gebet u. Gottesdienst im N.T., 1937. A. ARNOLD, Der Ursprung des christl. Abendmahls im Lichte der neuesten liturgiegesch. Forschung, ²1939. J. LEIPOLDT, Der Gottesdienst der ältesten Kirche jüdisch? griechisch? christlich? 1937. L. C. MOHLBERG, RivArchCrist 1937, 93/123 (Christian worship according to PLINY Ep. X, 96). K. M. HOFMANN, Philema hagion (the liturgical kiss), 1938. O. CULLMANN, Urchristent. u. Gottesdienst, ²1950. G. DIX, The Shape of the Liturgy, Westminster 1945. H. ENGBERDING, Misc. L. C. Mohlberg, I, Rom 1948, 47/71 (Trad. ap. not of the third century); D. VAN DEN EYNDE, ib. 407/11 (traces of the Trad. apost. in Roman liturgy); E. DEKKERS, ib. 231/57 (evening Mass in the Church of Antiquity). B. BOTTE, RechThAM 1947, 241/51; C. C. RICHARDSON, ib. 1948, 357/9. R. D. RICHARDSON, HarvThR 1949, 125/48 (origin of the Eucharist). G. DIX, A Detection of Aumbries, Westminster 1944 (Reservation of the Eucharist). R. H. CONNOLLY, JThSt 1938, 350/69 (the Eucharistic prayer in Hippolytus). E. LOHMEYER, Theol. Rundschau 1937, 168 ff. 195 ff.; 1938, 81 ff. (account of researches). H. STRATHMANN and R. MEYER, Art. im Theol. Wörterb. zum N.T. IV, 221/38. Cfr. literature in § 2, 5 and § 67.

liturgy as a community banquet and as a memorial of the sacrificial death of Jesus. At first this took place in the *evening* and was preceded by the agape (vide infra). But because of abuses censured by Paul (I Cor. 11:20 ff.), this arrangement was changed toward the end of the apostolic age or perhaps in the beginning of the second century as a result of Trajan's edict against hetairae (§ 15, 3) and the Eucharistic celebration was joined with the sermon in the morning. A detailed description of the service is given by *Justin* in the first Apology about 150 (c. 65—67). The celebration began with reading from the Scriptures. Then followed the homily by the "president", and after the catechumens (and penitents) had been dimissed, there was prayer in common (cfr. I Clem. 59—61). The faithful then exchanged the kiss of peace. Thereupon bread and wine mixed with water was presented to the bishop who pronounced over them "several *prayers* and a *thanksgiving*" (εὐχα-ριστία Matt. 26:27, hence the name of the rite), after which the deacon presented the consecrated gifts to those present as the "Flesh and Blood of the Incarnate Jesus." Justin's account does not mention that *psalms* were sung; yet the singing of the psalms together with prayer, lessons from Scripture and a homily consti-tuted the worship of the Jews in the diaspora and was incorporated into Christian worship from the beginning. At a very early date, *hymns* expressing Christian truths were also introduced. *Hippolytus'* Traditio apostolica written about 220 at the latest, describes the Eucharistic liturgy in even greater detail. When Hippolytus wrote, the form had become fixed, but in essentials goes back to older Roman traditions. Fundamentally, the Eucharistic liturgy was the same everywhere; although in the beginning the celebration in congregations of pagan converts differed slightly from the rites of Jewish Christians. Nowhere was the relation of the ceremony to the Last Supper and the sacrificial death of Jesus ever lost sight of. The Didache (14, 1) and Justin (Dial. c. Tryph. 4) expressly call the Eucharist a sacrifice.

*Sunday* appears to have been the usual day for the Eucharistic celebration (Did. 14, 1; Barn. Ep. 15, 8; Just. Apol. I, 67; cfr. also § 25, 1). Tertullian (De orat. 19) says that it was also celebrated on station days (§ 25, 1) and Cyprian (De orat. dom. 18; Ep. 57, 3; 63, 16) speaks of a *daily* sacrifice. This was no doubt the case in the first congregation at Jerusalem since the Christians there came together every day for the agape (Acts 2:46; cfr. § 8, 2).

The service was conducted by the *bishop* assisted by the presbyters and the other clergy. A presbyter could officiate only when commissioned by the bishop. Where there was more than one church in a city, the consecration took place in the bishop's church and the Eucharist under the Species of Bread was brought to the other churches by acolytes. In Rome this practice was a symbol of ecclesiastical unity and at the same time a means of preserving it, and was continued even after this period.

2. **Communion**, which Ignatius of Antioch (Eph. 20, 2) calls the "medicine of immortality" was received under *both Species* and, as is clear from *Justin's* account, every time the Eucharistic liturgy was celebrated. Besides this the consecrated Bread was given to the faithful to take home with them for daily reception (Cypr. De laps. 26) and in this practice as well as in bringing the Eucharist to sick and imprisoned, Communion was received under but *one* Species. The custom of receiving Communion *fasting* is mentioned as early as Tertullian (Ad uxoram 2, 5); and probably dates back to the time when the liturgy began to be celebrated in the morning. In distributing Communion, the sacred Host was placed on the open hand of the recipient and each one drank from the same chalice.

3. Only the baptized were permitted to receive Communion. Catechumens were debarred from the reception as well as from the common prayer and the offering of the sacrificial gifts at the beginning of the principal part of the liturgy. They were allowed to be present only at the *instruction*; after which they, with the energumenoi (18, 5) and one class of penitents (§ 24, 4) were obliged to withdraw. The Eucharist was considered as being above their comprehension. Neither were they thoroughly acquainted with the Creed (doctrine of the Trinity) nor the Our Father until ready for baptism. This practice of the early Church in guarding her chief mysteries can be traced back to the second century. The expression, **disciplina arcani**[1] or "discipline of the secret", which now designates the custom, was first used by the Protestant Theologian Jean Daille († 1670). Justin is the first to refer to it and Tertullian describes it more clearly. At any rate it was closely connected with the introduction and development of the catechumenate and was probably influenced, at least to some extent, by a similar usage in some of the pagan mystery cults. The Fathers seem to think that the injunction of Matthew 7:6 gave rise to it. But besides safeguard-

---

[1] G. ANRICH, Das antike Mysterienwesen in s. Einfluß auf das Christent., 1894. H. GRAVEL, Die Arkandisziplin I, Diss. 1902. FUNK, AU III, 42/57 (vs. P. BATIFFOL, Études d'hist. I⁷, Paris 1926, 1/41). L. SCHINDLER, Die altchristl. Arkandisz. u. die antiken Mysterien, Progr. Tetschen 1911. E. VACANDARD, DictHE III, 1497/513.

ing Christian teachings and customs from the pagans, the practice was favored rather for pedagogical reasons: it permitted the catechumens to be introduced gradually and systematically into the truths of Christianity. This explains why it was most highly developed in the fourth century (§ 66, 2). After the fifth century when most adults were Christian, the catechumenate no longer served a purpose; and with its disappearence the disciplina arcani also ceased.

4. As was mentioned above, the Eucharistic celebration was originally preceded by a special *love-feast*, the **agape**[1]. Even after the Eucharistic liturgy became a separate ceremony, the agape continued as a religious feast. It was made possible by donations of food and the meal was accompanied with prayer, the singing of psalms and possibly also with a suitable address by the presiding cleric. Its purpose was to foster fraternal charity and harmony and to aid the poor, widows and orphans. Relief of the poor eventually became the main purpose. The bread blessed at the agape was called *Eulogia*, not Eucharistia (Hippolyt, Trad. Apost. 47, 8). Since the fourth century, it was repeatedly forbidden to hold the agape in churches because of the abuses connected with it, and finally the Synod in Trullo held in 692 by a special canon (74) forbade such assemblies in church. After being excluded from church buildings, the agape was gradually discontinued, although traces of it are still found in some of the Eastern Rites.

*Batiffol* (Études d'hist. I[1], Paris 1926, 281/368) denies that the agape ever existed as a separate ceremony. He is of the opinion that passages which have been accepted as proving its existence actually refer to the Eucharistic celebration, to the distribution of alms and to funeral or memorial banquets. But even if 1 Cor. 11: 17—27 and other citations are not convincing, the locus classicus, Tertullian, Apolog. 39 (cfr. Ad ux. II, 4) may not be ignored (cfr. *Funk*, AU III, 1/41; *H. Koch*, ZntW 16, 1915, 139/46). The newly discovered Epistola Apostolorum (§ 38) c. 15 (26) knew of the agape, and the Traditio apostolica of Hippolytus (c. 47, 3—52) gives the formal rubrics to be observed during the repast.

5. The assemblies for divine worship were first held in suitable rooms of private houses (Acts 2:46). But from the end of the second century there were also special *buildings for religious purposes*, usually connected with cemeteries (§ 19, 3). Their ruins may still be seen at Rome, in Syria-Mesopotamia and in Palestine. Excavations in the old Roman garrison of *Dura-Europos*

---

[1] E. BAUMGARTNER, vide supra. A. STEINMANN, ThGl 1913, 715/23. H. LECLERCQ, DictAC I, 775/848. L. THOMAS, Dict. de la Bible, Suppl. I, 1926, 133/53. K. VÖLKER, Mysterium u. Agape, 1927. J. HANSSENS, Ephemerides liturgicae 1927, 525 ff.; 1929, 177 ff. 520 ff. B. STEPHANIDES, ZKG 1933, 610/3 (the artoclasia in the Greek Church a relic of the agape).

(1931—1932) brought to light the ruins of a Christian basilica with frescoes from the beginning of the third century. (The ruins of a synagogue with frescoes were found in the same place). Mention is made of a Christian church at *Edessa* in 201 (§ 12, 9). On the anniversary of a martyr the liturgy was celebrated above or on the grave (confessio) in crypts originally established as family burial places and in which the Christians of **Rome** found their last resting place. They were called cemeteries (κοιμητήρια) and since the ninth century were generally called *catacombs* (in or ad Catacumbas originally applied to the locality above the cemetery of St. Sebastian on the Via Appia). The narrow galleries of the cemeteries did not permit the holding of divine service for the congregation. The oldest and most renowned of these cemeteries in Rome are the Coemeterium *S. Callisti* from the second century on the Via Appia with the crypt of St. Cecilia and the graves of the popes of the third century, and the Coemeterium *S. Sebastiani* (ad Catacumbas,) also on the Via Appia, with the crypt of the Apostles (§ 10, 3). Very early, but hardly before 200, the Christians began to decorate the walls of the catacombs with *frescoes*. The subjects were mostly symbolic (sepulchral — eschatological), directing attention to trust in God, immortality and the joys of Paradise. The most frequently repeated figures are those of the Good Shepherd and the Orans. Christian plastic art began to develop in the third century (§ 71, 2). — *P. Lemmerle*, Bull. de l'Acad. R. de Belgique, Lettres 1948, 306/28; Rev. Archéol. 1949, 167/94 (origin of buildings for christian worship). — A. Badawy, Kyrilliana, 1944, 319/80 (the first church buildings in Egypt). — J. Lassus, Sanctuaires chrétiens en Syrie, Paris 1947. — *J. B. de Rossi*, Roma sotteranea cristiana, and other works, see § 2, 1. — *F. X. Kraus*, Roma Sotteranea, die röm. Katakomben,[2]1879. — *Fr.Wieland*, Mensa u. Confessio, 2 vols. 1906/12. — *N. Müller*, RE X, 794/877; F. E. Becker, ib. XXIII, 788/93. — *H. Leclercq,* DictAC II, 2376/486. — *W. Neuss*, Die Kunst der alten Christen, 1926. — *P. Styger*, Die altchristl. Grabeskunst, 1927; Die römischen Katakomben, 1933; Röm. Martyrergrüfte, 2 vols. 1935 (standard); Pisciculi, Festschrift F. J. Dölger, 1939, 266/75 (pagan and Christian catacombs). — *Th. Klauser,* Die Cathedra im Totenkult, 1927. — *E. Freistedt*, Altchristl. Totengedächtnistage, 1/28. — *J. P. Kirsch*, RQ 1928, 1/20 (ideas in back of the frescoes in the catacombs); 1930, 107/31 (sepulchres of the Roman martyrs and devotion to martyrs); 1933, 15/28 (pre-Constantinian places of worship in Rome and in the East). — *H. Lother*, Realismus u. Symbolismus in der altchristl. Kunst, 1931. — *A. B. Schuchert*, RQ 1931, 7/22 (frescoes of the catacombs in the history of art). — *O. Casel*, JbLW 12, 1932, 1/86 (early Christian art and Christology). — *H. Chéramy*, Les Catacombes romaines, Paris 1932. — *O. Marucchi*, Le Catacombe Romane, Rome 1934. — *W. Elliger*, Zur Entstehung u. frühen Entwicklung der altchristl. Bildkunst, 1934. — *F. Wirth*, Röm. Wandmalerei vom Untergang Pompejis bis ans Ende des 3. Jh., 1934. — *H. Achelis*, Die Katakomben von Neapel, 1935/36. — *G. Wilpert*, La fede della Chiesa nascente secondo i monumenti dell' arte funeraria antica, Rome 1938. — E. Dinkler, Die ersten Petrusdarstellungen, 1939 (versus Wilpert). — *F. Gerke*, Die christl. Sarkophage der vorkonstantinischen Zeit, 1940; ZKG 1940, 1/102 (history of the concepts in early christian art). — *J. Quasten*, Misc. G. Mercati, 1946, I, 373/406 (the Good Shepherd in early Christian burial services and in sepulchral ornamentation). — G. Leonardi, Ampelos. Il simbolo della vite nell' arte pagana e paleocristiana, Rome 1947. — E. Kirschbaum, Misc. C. Mohlberg, Rome 1948, I, 221/9 ("Petri in Catacumbas"). — On the excavations in **Dura-Europos**: *P. V. C. Baur* and *M. J. Rostovtzeff*, The Excavations at Dura-Europos, Preliminary Report, 6 vol. New Haven 1929/36; Dura-Europos and its Art, Oxford 1938. — Cfr. J. P. Kirsch, Oriens christ. 1933, 201/8; A. v. Gerkan, RQ 1934, 219/32; G. Wodtke, ZntW 1935, 51/62. Supplement see p. VII.

# § 24.
## The Penitential Discipline[1].

1. As the "Community of the Saints" the ancient Church demanded a high moral conduct of her members. Because the Lord was expected to return soon in judgment, the seal of baptism was to be kept "holy and inviolate" (II Clem. 6, 9; 8, 6). Hence sinners were treated with great severtiy. Toward the close of the second century there were individual bishops who punished the so-called *capital sins* by permanent exclusion from the Church. The capital sins (peccata capitalia, mortalia) were especially idolatry or denial of the faith (idolatria), murder, and sins of the flesh (adulterium and fornicatio). But from the beginning even those guilty of grave sins were admitted to ecclesiastical penance and after its performance were forgiven and received again into the Church. The "Shepherd" of Hermas, written at Rome about 140 (§ 38, B 1) announces ecclesiastical penance as the last opportunity for clemency in the present life,

---

[1] J. MORINUS, Commentarius hist. de disciplina in administratione sacramenti paenitentiae XIII primis saeculis, Paris 1651. O. D. WATKINS, History of Penance (to 1215), 2 vol. London 1920 (sources and explanation). B. POSCH-MANN in Handb. der Dogmengesch., ed. M. SCHMAUS et al., IV, 3, 1951. F. PROBST, Sakramente etc. (see § 22), 244/373. FUNK, AUI, 155/209. P. BATIFFOL, Études d'hist. et de théol. positive I⁷, Paris 1926, 43/224. G. RAUSCHEN, Eucharistie u. Bußsakrament, see § 23. H. WINDISCH, Taufe u. Sünde, see § 22. E. VACANDARD, Études de critique et d'hist. relig. II, Paris 1910, 51/125. A. D'ALÈS, L'édit de Calliste, Paris 1914. K. ADAM, Das sog. Bußedikt des P. Kallistus, 1917. A. D'ALÈS et P. GALTIER, Pénitence, DictApol III, 1922, 1756/856. F. CAVALLERA, BullLE 1929, 19 ff. 49 ff. (penitential discipline of the first three centuries). E. GÖLLER, RQ 1931, 79 ff. (development of the penitential discipline). P. GALTIER, L'Église et la rémission des péchés aux premiers siècles, Paris 1932; RHE 1934, 517 ff. 797 ff. J. HOH, Die kirchl. Buße im 2. Jh., 1932. J. A. JUNGMANN, Die latein. Bußriten in ihrer geschichtl. Entwicklung, 1932. B. POSCHMANN, Poenitentia secunda, 1940 (cfr. B. ALTANER, ThRev 1940, 193/200); id. ThRev 1933, 257/72 (HOH, GALTIER and JUNGMANN); cfr. A. GAUDEL, RevSR 1934, 419/43. E. AMANN, Pénitence, DictThC XII, 1933, 748/845 (antiquity); 845/948 (Middle Ages). C. B. DALY, Irish Eccles. Record 1947, 1948, 1950 (penance in Tertullian). Cyprian's idea of penance: B. CAPELLE, RechThAM 1935, 221/34; J. KÖHNE, ThGl 1937, 245/56. M. C. CHARTIER, Antonianum 1939, 17 ff. 135 ff.

before the structure of the Church is entirely complete. But Irenaeus of Lyons and Clement of Alexandria recognize penance as the second means of salvation (the first is baptism) without any restrictions. In his De poenitentia, written before he became a Montanist, Tertullian seems to admit that reconciliation with the Church is possible at least in the hour of death. The intercession of confessors and especially those about to be martyred in favor of a repentant sinner (libellus pacis) generally had the effect of reducing the period of penance and hastening his reception into the Church. For the rest, the sources are so meagre and imperfect that it is impossible to trace with certainty the development of the penitential discipline before the third century. It seems quite certain, however, that it was not the same everywhere. There were local and provincial variations. Thus the system was much more rigorous in Africa, overrun with Montanists (§ 34, 2) than in Rome (Cypr. Ep. 55, 21) and Cyprian himself took a milder view only after long deliberation.

It can not be shown that martyrs and confessors, if they were lay persons, had a right to reconcile sinners and remit their penance. Certainly their entreaty in the sinner's behalf carried great weight; but ordinarily it was the bishop who pronounced final judgement.

2. During the course of the third century a rigoristic attitude prevailed. Pope *Callistus* (217—220) was accused by his rival, the learned priest *Hippolytus* (§ 32, 4; 39, 4) who had even set himself up as anti-pope, of being guilty of laxity, because he remitted every sort of sin (without penance). At the same time, *Tertullian*, who had gone over to the Montanists, wrote the work De pudicitia, in which he embraces extreme rigorism and argues that adultery and fornication can never be forgiven. It is quite possible that it was he who first conceived the notion that the three *peccata capitalia* could not be forgiven. A generation later a dispute arose regarding the reconciliation of the lapsi. Even many bishops were confused because they had no clear tradition to guide them in the matter. However, a synod at Rome under the presidency of Pope Cornelius (251—253) and another at Carthage decreed that the lapsi were to be reconciled with the Church, not only on their deathbed, but also after undergoing a long period of penance. The priest *Novatian* (§ 35, 1; 40, 4) had earlier opposed a too hasty pardon of the lapsi, out of zeal for the antiqua severitas; but when Cornelius was elected to the office which Novatian had ambitioned, it was no longer zeal, but envy, which caused the priest to denounce bitterly

the new pope's decision. About the same time *Cyprian*, who followed a practice similar to that of Cornelius, was obliged to censure a too lax tendency on the part of confessors and among the clergy (cfr. § 35 for the schism of Felicissimus and also for the controversy in Egypt and at Rome in the early fourth century). In the East, *Origen* was at first somewhat hesitant (De oratione c. 28 written about 233) but later (C. Cels. III, 50, written about 248) held that a lapsus could be pardoned once. The Synod of *Elvira* in Spain about 306 punished a number of grave sins (18 or 19) with lifetime exclusion from the Church. But this is the only example of such extreme severity in this period; in general the practice of the Church of Rome was adopted everywhere. Absolution and Communion were denied to guilty persons who had refused to submit to penance until the hour of death. The pardon of the Church could be obtained but once; no leniency was shown to those who relapsed into the capital sins after doing penance. They were simply left to the mercy of God. There was *but one penance* after baptism.

In De pudicitia, *Tertullian* mentions an 'edictum peremptorium' of a bishop who is ironically called 'Pontifex Maximus', 'episcopus episcoporum,' 'benedictus papa,' 'apostolicus.' The person thus alluded to is severely criticised and represented as saying: "Ego et moechiae et fornicationis delicta poenitentia functis dimitto." The passage was usually understood as referring to Pope *Callistus*, who, according to Hippolytus (Philos. 9, 12) issued a decree mitigating the severity of the penances heretofore imposed. In more recent times, however, a number of scholars incline to the opinion that the reference is to Bishop *Agrippinus* of Carthage (ca. 215). They believe that the Bishop legislated in favor of leniency and that Tertullian, as the mouthpiece of the African rigorists, protested. Cfr. especially *K. Adam*, Das sog. Bußedikt des P. Kallistus, 1917; ThQ 1928, 168 ff.; *G. Bardy*, RevSR 1924, 1/25; *K. Graf Preysing*, ZkTh 1926, 143/50; *P. Galtier*, RHE 1927, 465/88; 1934, 545/8; *A. Ehrhard*, Die Kirche der Martyrer, 1932, 361 ff.; *B. Altaner*, ThRev 1939, 132 ff. — *B. Poschmann*, Handb. (vide supra), 20/3. — Callistus the author of the decree: cfr. *H. Koch*, Sb. Heidelberg 1919, 22; *H. Stoeckius*, AkKR 1937, 24/126; *W. Köhler*, Sb. Heidelberg 1937, 3; ZKG 1942, 124/35. Still another opinion seeks to harmonize the two preceding ones. *D. Franses*, Studia catholica 1924/25, 248/59, and *A. de Vellico*, Antonianum 1930, 25/56 hold that Tertullian had in mind both the edict of Callistus and its republication by the Bishop of Carthage.

3. In order to be readmitted to membership in the Church, the sinner guilty of a capital sin was obliged to confess his fault and for a long time, often as long as he lived, to do penance by wearing sackcloth and ashes, by fasting, praying and giving alms. During the time his penance lasted, the other members of the congregation

encouraged him by praying for him. The acknowledgement of guilt was considered of the utmost importance as is seen from the fact that the word ἐξομολόγησις, meaning the same as our English word, *"confession"*, was used throughout the East and West to designate the entire procedure. If the offense was public, the confession as a rule was made *publicly* before the clergy and people. If the offense was of a private nature, a secret confession was made to the bishop or a priest, after which the penances and absolution were generally imposed publicly, at least as late as the fourth century. Very often the secret confession would be followed by a public one, especially in cases where no scandal might be given. Absolution was given by the bishop or a priest imposing hands on the penitent in the presence of the assembled congregation. This was not looked upon as an efficient cause, but rather as a requisite for God's forgiveness. Holy Communion could not be received until the entire penance had been performed. An exception to this rule was made in favor of those grievously ill.

Public penance under the direction of the Church and the obligation of public confession were imposed only for the three capital sins. However, other sins could be brought under this classification as was actually done in the fourth century (Synod of Elvira, Pacianus, Ambrose). Other less grievous sins could be pardoned more than once, and it was generally recognized that other remedies such as almsgiving, fasting and prayer (the Our Father) helped to obtain their remission.

4. The system of penance was under the direction of the bishop. In the larger congregations of the East it seems that as early as the third century several *priests* were *specially chosen to assist the bishop* in this work. In the East, too, especially in Asia Minor during the third and fourth centuries, the penitents were divided into *classes* or *grades* so that their admission into the bosom of the Church would be a gradual process.

The lowest class of penitents, the *flentes* (προσκλαίοντες) is first mentioned by St. Basil the Great († 379) but the division is probably older. They stood at the door of the church and pleaded for the prayers of those who entered. The Synod of Ancyra 314, canon 17, speaks of the χειμαζόμενοι, who have been erroneously identified with the flentes, but who were without doubt energoumeni (§ 18, 5). The *Audientes* (ἀκροώμενοι) and the *prostrati* or *substrati* (ὑποπίπτοντες) are mentioned in the Epistola canonica of St. Gregory Thaumaturgus about 254. The Audientes, like the catechumens were obliged to leave after the sermon. It is not certain whether the prostrati were permitted to remain for the entire liturgy (Funk) or whether they remained until they had received the bishop's blessing just before the Communion (Rauschen et al). The *Consistentes* (συστάντες and similar expressions) are first mentioned by the Synod of Ancyra 314, can. 25. They were allowed to remain standing with the rest of the faithful throughout the service (§ 25, 1) but naturally were not admitted to Holy Communion. Cfr. *Funk*, AU, 189/209; *E. Schwartz*, Bußstufen u. Katechumenatsklassen, 1911. *E. Seeberg*, Die Synode v. Antiochien 324/25 (1913) 32 ff. — The *West* had no such classification, but evidently treated all penitents like the highest class of penitents in the East; that is, they were permitted to remain in a separate place near the entrance until the end of the service; but could not receive Communion. (Cfr. H. Koch, ThQ 1900, 481/534; 1903, 254/70; and for an opposite opinion, A. d'Alès, Limen ecclesiae, RHE 1906, 16/26; L'edit de Calliste, 409/21).

# § 25.
## Feasts and Fasts. The Easter Controversy[1].

1. Under the Old Law every Saturday was kept as a day of special worship, besides which there were various festival days throughout the year. The more zealous Jews also fasted twice a week (Luke 18:12) on Monday and Thursday (Did. 8,1). The Christian Church adopted a similar arrangement. Christians also dedicated one day a week to special worship; but instead of Saturday, the seventh day, they observed the first day as the day of the Lord's Resurrection and the day on which His second coming was to be expected (§ 23,1). In the language of the Church, **Sunday**[2] was known as the "day of the Lord" κυριακή (ἡμέρα), dies dominica, and was signalized as a day of joy by *standing* during *prayer*. The observance of Sunday can be traced back to the days of

---

[1] F. PROBST, Kirchl. Disziplin in den 3 ersten christl. Jhh., 1873. II. KELL NER, Heortologie, ³1911. J. DOWDEN, The Church Year and Calendar, Cambridge 1910. TH. SCHERMANN, Die allg. Kirchenordnung etc. II, 471 ff. F. CABROL, Fêtes, DictAC V, 1403/52. A. HOLLARD, Les origines des fêtes chrétiennes, Paris 1936. R. N. BONET LLEACH, De sanctificatione festorum... a primordiis ad saec. VI incl., Ripoll 1945. E. SCHWARTZ, Osterbetrachtungen, ZntW 1906, 1/33. H. KOCH, Pascha in der alten Kirche, ZkTh 1914, 289/313. P. CORSSEN, Das Osterfest, N JklA 39, 1917, 170/89. H. LECLERCQ, Pâques, DictAC XIII, 1521/74. O. CASEL, JbLW 14, 1/78. A. W. WATTS, Easter, London 1950. On the Easter controversy: K. BIHLMEYER, Kath. 1902 I, 314/27 (Polycarp and Pope Anicetus); C. SCHMIDT TU 43, 1919, 577/725; F. E. BRIGHTMAN, JThSt 1924, 254/70. A. LINSENMAYER, Entwicklung der kirchl. Fastendisziplin (bis 325), 1877. J. SCHÜMER, Die altchristl. Fastenpraxis, 1933. FUNK, AU I, 241/78 (the Easter fast). J. BON-SIRVEN, RechSR 1925, 258/66 (the station-day fasts); cfr. J. SVENNUNG, ZntW 1933, 294/308. K. HOLL, Sb. Berlin 1916, 847 ff. (also in Ges. Aufsätze zur KG. II, 1928, 373 ff.): Samstagsfasten.

[2] TH. ZAHN, Geschichte d. Sonntags, 1878 (also in Skizzen, ³1908, 160/208). H. MEINHOLD, Sabbat u. Sonntag, 1909. H. DUMAINE, Dimanche, DictAC IV, 858/994. J. BOEHMER, Der christl. Sonntag nach Ursprung u. Gesch., 1931. P. COTTON, From Sabbath to Sunday, Bethlehem Pa. 1933. E. SCHÜRER, ZntW 1905, 1/66 (the seven day week in the early Church). C. CALLE-WAERT, EphThLov 1938, 34/73 (Sunday and the feast of Easter in Jerusalem).

the Apostles (Apoc. 1:10; Acts 20:7; 1 Cor. 16:2). Besides Sunday, the Jewish Christians also observed Saturday.

At a very early date, the Christians kept *Wednesday* and *Friday* of every week as **fast-days**. These are mentioned in the Didache (8, 1) as corresponding with the Jewish fasts and in the West were given the military term, *dies stationis*, days of watching with the suffering Lord. A half-fast was kept on these days, that is, until the ninth hour or three o'clock in the afternoon; divine service was held on these days. In Alexandria, the service did not extend beyond the didactic part; in West Africa, the entire liturgy was carried out (§ 23, 1). The Synod of Elvira in Spain about 306 (can. 26) also speaks of a fast on *Saturday*, which most probably was also known in the Roman Church at this time.

2. Two annual feats of the Old Law were celebrated by the Christian Church because two of the principal events in the history of the Redemption occurred on these days. **Passah** (πάσχα) was kept by the Jews in memory of their liberation from the slavery of Egypt when God spared their first-born; by the Christians to commemorate the Crucifixion and Resurrection of Christ. **Pentecost** (πεντεκοστή), the Jewish feast of weeks or Harvest feast coincided with the day on which the Holy Ghost descended upon the Apostles. Thus these feasts came to have a new and peculiar meaning. Not only were the Jewish names retained, but also the Jewish method of reckoning their recurrence by the *lunar year*. Their connection with the Old Testament is evidence that these feasts date back to the very beginning of the Church. For a long time they remained the only feasts celebrated annually. While the Basilidians (§ 30 A 2) of Egypt celebrated the Baptism of Christ on January 6 since the beginning of the third century, it seems that the feast of **Epiphany** was not introduced until the next period. Individual congregations commemorated the *death* (birthday) of their *martyrs* by holding divine service at the martyr's graves (§ 14, 4; 23, 5).

The word **Passah** comes from the Hebrew פסח or from the Aramaic פסחא = a passing over, especially the Lord passing over the first-born in Egypt, and not from πάσχειν, as some of the Fathers thought. The word eventually found its way into all languages except High German and English. The English word *"Easter"* is very probably derived from the name of the Teutonic goddess of the spring season and of light, (Austro, Ostara). At least Venerable Bede (De temp. rat. 13) tells us that Eostrae, the word Easter in the Anglo-Saxon dialect was so derived. — Cfr. K. J. Hefele, Beiträge z. KG, II, 1864, 285 f. — W. Braune, BeitrGdSL 43, 1918, 409.

It was perhaps an effort to suppress a popular pagan feast that led to the introduction of the *feast of Epiphany*. Epiphanius relates (Haer. 51, 22) that on January 6, the Alexandrians celebrated the birth of the god Aion of a virgin *(Core)*. On the eve of the feast they drew water from the Nile which was supposed to have curative powers and which the people believed would turn into wine. — *K. Holl*, Sb. Berlin 1917, 402/38 (= Ges. Aufsätze zur KG.II, 1928, 123/54); the opposite opinion is held by *A. Ehrhard*, Die Kirche d. Martyrer, 1932, 332/34. — Cfr. *M. P. Nilsson*, ArchRelW 1918, 50/150. —

§ 25. Feasts and Fasts. The Easter Controversy.

B. Botte, Les origines de la Noël et de l'Épiphanie, Louvain 1932.— K.Prümm, StZ 135, 1939, 207/25.

3. The time of the **Easter celebration** was not the same everywhere. In the greater part of the Church, especially at Rome and throughout the West, it was always celebrated on Sunday, and specifically on the *Sunday* which fell on or followed the fourteenth *Nisan* of the Jews (the first full moon after the spring equinox), because Christ arose on Sunday. In *Asia proconsularis* the Christians, basing themselves on the tradition of St. John, kept the feast on the very day of the fourteenth *Nisan* (Luna XIV) regardless of the day of the week on which that date occurred, (but see § 7, 1). This practice, called *Quartodecimanism*, was not entirely incongruous since originally the feast was not a commemoration of the Resurrection alone, but of the Redemption as such. However, in proconsular Asia the date was nearly always different from the one observed by the rest of Christendom; and the divergence became all the more confusing as the solemnity of the feast increased. Repeated attempts were made to secure uniformity. The aged Bishop *Polycarp* of Smyrna travelled to Rome about 155 to confer with Pope Anicetus on the matter. No agreement was reached, but the bond of union remained intact. However, Pope *Victor* (189—198) ordered synods to be held in various provinces of the East and West to discuss the problem. All of the synods disapproved the custom of the Asiatics, who under the leadership of the Metropolitan *Polycrates* of Ephesus, clung stubbornly to their Quartodecimanism. Victor excommunicated them; but through the intervention of *Irenaeus* of Lyons peace was again restored. Finally, in the third century, the Asiatics, with few exceptions, abandoned their inconsistancy; at the Council of Nicaea 325 they appeared together with bishops of provinces which kept the "right" feast (Eus. H.E. V, 24; Vita Constant. III, 18—20).

However, *uniformity* was *by no means* achieved. For whereas the date of the Easter full moon had previously been based on Jewish reckoning, in the third century some of the principal churches, especially *Alexandria* and *Rome* began to compute the dates for themselves. They had probably observed that the Jews were no longer exact in their calculations and had frequently set the date of Easter before the first full moon of the spring equinox. At the same time these churches were not inclined to remain dependent on the Jews in such a matter. But even this arrangement failed to produce the desired result, for Rome used an eighty-four year Easter cycle, while Alexandria followed one of nineteen years. The bishop of Alexandria notified the other congregations of Egypt of the date, whence arose the custom of the *Paschal letter* (§ 39, 3). In some parts of the East the feast continued to be kept on a Sunday, but the date set by Jews was adhered to, which was the method strictly prescribed by the Didascalia *(Protopaschitism* (§ 39, 5). These divergencies led to repeated discussions in the following period (§ 69, 6).

The expressions Πάσχα σταυρώσιμον (Pasch of the Crucifixion) and Πάσχα ἀναστάσιμον (Pasch of the Resurrection), frequently used to designate the practice of Asia Minor and of Rome respectively, originated with the learned philologist Gerhardt John Voss († 1649); cfr. *E. Schürer*, Z. f. hist. Theol. 1870, 276 ff.

4. From the earliest times, Easter was preceded by a *fast*. It was based on the words of Christ (Matt. 9:15) and according to Tertullian (De jejun. 2) was observed generally on the days "in quibus ablatus est sponsus" that is, from the death to the resurrection of the Lord. But it was not the same everywhere. As Irenaeus (in Eus. V, 24) relates, in some places it lasted only *one* day, in others, *two* days, in still others, *several* days and in a few places the fast was for forty hours. Hippolytus of Rome (Trad. apost. c. 55) speaks of a two-day fast. Although this was relatively brief, the fast itself was very strict; for the entire day or even several days no food or drink of any kind was taken. The Didascalia expressly prescribes a complete fast for Friday and Saturday of Holy Week and a fast on bread, salt and water only for the first four days of that week, therefore an Easter fast of six days. Dionysius of Alexandria speaks of this practice as obtaining about the middle of the third century.

# § 26.
## Moral and Religious Life[1].

1. The author of the *Letter to Diognetus* (§ 38 A 6) c. 5 and *Tertullian* (Apolog. 42) both remark that Christians did not differ from

---

[1] W. DURANT, The History of Civilization III. 1949. J. CARCOPINO, Das Alltagsleben im alten Rom zur Blütezeit des Kaisertums, 1950. HARNACK, Mission I[4], see § 12. A. NEANDER, Denkwürdigkeiten aus der Gesch. des christlichen Lebens, 2 vols. [2]1845/6. K. J. HEFELE, Beiträge z. KG. II, 331/81. G. UHLHORN, Die christl. Liebestätigkeit I[2], 1884. H. J. BESTMANN, Gesch. d. christl. Sitte, 2 vols. 1880/5. E. V. DOBSCHÜTZ, Die urchristl. Gemeinden, sittengesch. Bilder, 1912. A. BIGELMAYR, see § 14. W. LIESE, Gesch. der Caritas, 2 vols. 1922. H. LECLERCQ, Charité, DictAC III, 598/653. O. DITTRICH, Gesch. der Ethik I—II, 1923/6. F. HEILER, Das Gebet, see § 23. C. J. CADOUX, The Early Church and the World, Edinburgh 1925. J. LEBRETON, La vie chrétienne au premier siècle de l'Église, Paris 1927. J. LORTZ, Tertullian als Apologet, 2 vols. 1927/8. JOH. KLEIN, Tertullian, Christl. Bewußtsein u. sittl. Forderungen, 1941. M. DIBELIUS, Urchristentum u. Kultur, 1928 (address). A. BAUDRILLART, Moeurs païennes, moeurs chrétiennes, La famille, 2 vol. Paris [2]1936. P. RICHTER, Die Liebestätigkeit in der alten Kirche, 1930. FR. WAGNER, Der Sittlichkeitsbegriff in der Heiligen Schrift u. in der altchristl. Ethik, 1931 (Gesch. des Sittlichkeitsbegriffs II). J. STELZENBERGER, Die Beziehungen der frühchristl. Sittenlehre zur Ethik der Stoa, 1933. H. SCHUMACHER, Kraft der Urkirche, 1934. G. KRÜGER, ZKGkan 1935, 113/40 (charitable work in the Church before Constantine). A. VOEGTLE, Die Tugend- u. Lasterkataloge im N.T., 1936. O. KARRER, Urchristl. Zeugen, 1937. H. BOLKESTEIN, Wohltätigkeit u. Armenpflege im vorchristl. Altert., Utrecht 1939. H. PREISKER, Das Ethos des Urchristentums, 1949. K. PIEPER, Urkirche u. Staat, 1935. E. STRATMANN, Die Heiligen u. der Staat II, 1950. A. HARNACK, Militia Christi, 1905; cfr. E. VACANDARD, Études de critique etc. II, Paris 1910, 129/68; H. LECLERCQ, Militarisme, DictAC XI, 1108/81. F. X. FUNK, Gesch. d. kirchl. Zinsverbots, 1876; Klemens v. Alex. über Familie u. Eigent., AU II, 45/60; Handel u. Gewerbe im christl. Altert., ib. 60/77. O. SCHILLING, Reichtum u.

other people in food, clothing or shelter, but followed the customs of the country in which they lived. The new religion, therefore, did not alter the ordinary conditions of life. But its religious and moral principles effected a deep and immediate change in their spiritual life. The Letter continues (c. 5, 8—6, 1): "Christians live in the flesh, but not according to the flesh; they live on earth, but their conversation is in heaven . . . They love all men and are persecuted by all. Men know them not, yet judge them; they are put to death and thereby find life. They are poor, yet they enrich many; they suffer the need of all things, yet enjoy a superfluity of all things . . . They do good, yet they are punished as evil doers; when condemned to death, they rejoice as though awakened to new life . . . To put it briefly: what the soul is to the body, that the Christians are to the world." *Theophilus*, Bishop of Antioch (§ 38 A 5) in his work Ad Autolychum III, 15 says: "Among Christians is to be found prudent self-control, sobriety is practised, monogamy observed, chastity preserved, injustice abolished, sin with its root destroyed, justice is practised, the law is kept, and piety is in evidence all the day long. God is recognized and truth is considered the greatest good. Grace preserves them, peace shelters them, the holy Word guides them, wisdom teaches them and (eternal) life directs them. God is their King." *Aristides* (§ 38 A 1) uses similar expressions (c. 15—16 in praising the morals of the early Christians. Nor do these testimonials (see also § 13, 2) lose their force because not every Christian lived up to the high ideals or because sin and imperfection were entirely unknown among them.

Besides attending the religious services held in common (§ 23), the early Christians also practised *private* prayer in their *homes*. They prayed especially in the morning and evening, before meals, before bathing, at the third, sixth and ninth hours (Tert. De orat. 25; Cypr. De dominica orat. 35; cfr. Didache 8, 3), even at midnight and at cockrow (Hippol. Trad. apost. 62, 32—33). Tertullian, Origen

Eigent. in d. altkirchl. Lit., 1908. E. TRÖLTSCH, Die Soziallehren der christl. Kirchen u. Gruppen, 1912 (Ges. Schriften I). FR. HAUCK, Die Stellung des Urchristentums zu Arbeit u. Geld, 1921. H. GREEVEN, Das Hauptproblem der Sozialethik in der neueren Stoa u. im Urchristent., 1935. R. LÖWE, Kosmos u. Aion, 1935. H. LARMANN, Christl. Wirtschaftsethik in der spätröm. Antike, 1935. K. PRÜMM, Christent. als Neuheitserlebnis, 1939. H. HOLZAPFEL, Die sittl. Wertung der körperl. Arbeit im christl. Altert., Diss. 1941. A. T. GEOGHEGAN, The Attitude towards Labour in Early Christianity and Ancient Culture, Washington 1945. J. GIORDANI, Il messaggio sociale di Gesù, 4 vol. Milan 1946. R. H. BAINTON, HarvThR 1946, 189/212 (Early Christianity and war). Cfr. literature in § 5.

and Cyprian composed beautiful works on prayer, especially the
Lord's Prayer. Tertullian (De corona 3; Ad ux. II, 5) and Hippolytus (Trad. apost. 62, 31—33) mention the custom of Christians
*frequently signing themselves with the sign of the Cross* as a protection
against demons. The constant direction of their thoughts toward
heaven naturally influenced their moral life the more thoroughly
the more sensual their pagan surroundings became. They avoided
*spectacles, gladiatorial combats, fights between wild beasts* and all
other such amusements because of the immorality and cruelty
connected with them (Tert. De spectaculis; Apolog. 38; Theophilus
Ad Autol. III, 15; Lact. Instit. VI, 20). Some refused to be present
at the execution of criminals (Athenag. Leg. 35). A few rigorists like
Tertullian, Hippolytus, and to some extent, Origen, went so far as
to say that Christians were not allowed to hold *public office* or
render *military service*. But, as a matter of fact, since the end of
the second century not a few Christians held office and were found
in the army. *Scandalous* or dangerous *trades* and *professions* were
forbidden. Those employed as painters, sculptors, actors, school
teachers (because of the pagan myths which had to be taught),
prize fighters, gladiators, temple watchmen, magicians, sooth sayers
and so forth were obliged to abdandon such occupations before
they could be admitted into the catechumenate (Hippol. Trad.
Apost. 41).

2. The whole striving of the Christian was directed not to this
perishable world, but to the *"future eon"* (II Clem. 6, 3). The expectation of the *parousia* gave to their world-view and their *asceticism*[1] a severity which in some instances was unduly exaggerated.

---

[1] M. J. ROUËT DE JOURNEL et J. DUTILLEUL, Enchiridion Asceticum;
J. DE GUIBERT, Documenta, see § 2, 9 f. H. KOCH, Quellen zur Gesch. der
Askese u. des Mönchtums in der alten Kirche, 1933. JOS. MÜLLER, Die
Keuschheitsideen in ihrer geschichtl. Entwicklung, [2]1912. F. MARTINEZ,
L'ascétisme chrétien pendant les trois premiers siècles, Paris 1913. H. STRATH-
MANN, Gesch. der frühchristl. Askese I, 1914. H. KOCH, Virgines Christi,
TU 31, 2, 1907. J. FEUSI, Das Institut der gottgeweihten Jungfrauen, sein
Fortleben im MA., Diss. Freiburg (Switzerland) 1917. P. POURRAT, La
spiritualité chrétienne I[6], Paris 1921. K. MÜLLER, Die Forderung der Ehe-
losigkeit für alle Getauften in der alten Kirche, 1927; also in "Aus der akade-
mischen Arbeit", 1930, 63/79. H. PREISKER, Christentum u. Ehe in den
ersten drei Jhh., 1927. E. BUONAIUTI, Le origini dell ascetismo cristiano,
Pinerolo 1928 (on the Index). K. GRAF PREYSING, ThQ 1929, 85/110
(Marriage according to Athenagoras). M. VILLER, La spiritualité des premiers
siècles chrétiens, Paris 1930; Germ. transl. by K. RAHNER, Aszese u. Mystik
in der Väterzeit, 1939 (standard). W. VÖLKER, Das Vollkommenheitsideal
des Origenes, 1931. J. KÖHNE, Die Ehen zwischen Christen u. Heiden in den
ersten christl. Jhh., 1931. H. SCHUMACHER, Das Eheideal des Apostels

With a view to storing up treasure in heaven, they refused to amass earthly goods, but spent whatever they had in *works of charity*. The great commandment of *love of God* and *love of neighbor* headed the teaching of their catechism, the Doctrine of the Twelve Apostles (Did. 1, 2). *Almsgiving* was considered of equal value with prayer, or, even more meritorious (Did. 15, 4; II Clem. 16, 4; Cypr. De opere eleemosynis); but indiscreet almsgiving was discouraged (Did. 1, 6). "We, who once loved to make money more than anything else," says Justin (Apol. I, 14; cfr. Tert. Apolog. 39), "now share everything we own with everyone and give to every needy person." The *care of the poor* was highly organized and was the chief concern of deacons and deaconesses (§ 18, 4, 6). After the example set in apostolic times (Acts 11:28—30; Rom. 15:26) needy congregations at a distance were often given generous aid. Widows and orphans, the sick and the weak, slaves and captives were all given solicitous attention; strangers and travellers were given hospitality and provided with opportunity to earn a living (Did. 12). According to Tertullian (De praescript. 20), all Christendom was a "brotherhood of hospitality" (contesseratio hospitalitatis). Loans were made without interest. The *taking of interest* was looked upon as the exploitation of the neighbor's need and was therefore condemned; the Synod of Elvira ca. 306 (can. 20) even threatened with excommunication any one who took interest, while Nicaea 325 (can. 17) and the other synods of antiquity decreed such penalties for clerics only. *Corporal needs* were reduced to a minimum, fancy dress and adornment, pomp and luxury were disdained.

The wearing of *earrings*, painting the *cheeks* or pencilling the *eyes*, dyeing the *hair*, wearing false hair, *cultivating the beard* and the like were considered particularly obnoxius (Clem. Alex. Paed. II, 8, 2; III, 2, 11; Tert. De cultu fem.; Cypr. De lapsis 6). To Christians these things were voluptuous, a means

---

Paulus, 1932. G. BARDY, La vie spirituelle d'après les Pères des trois premiers siècles, Paris 1935. A. KOCH, StZ 130, 1936, 457/71 (Woman in early Christianity). D. FRANSES, Radicalisme en de eerste eeuwen der Kerk, Hertogenbusch 1936. J. MARTY, RevHPhR 1939, 288/97 (duty of hospitality). F. QUATEMBER, Die christl. Lebenshaltung des Klemens v. Alex. nach seinem Pädagogus, 1946. M. R. NUGENT, Portrait of the Consecrated Woman in Greek Christian Literature of the First Four Centuries, Washington 1941. TH. CAMELOT, Virgines Christi, Paris 1944. H. V. CAMPENHAUSEN, Die Askese im Urchristentum, 1949. F. DE B. VIZMANOS, Las virgines cristianas en la Iglesia primitiva, Madrid 1949. CH. GUIGNEBERT, RevHR 88, 1923, 65/102 ("half Christians"). J. ZELLINGER, Bad u. Bäder in der alten Kirche, 1928. F. J. DÖLGER, AntChrist 1933, 1/61 (abortion in antiquity). A. DEKKER, Kenntnis u. Pflege des Körpers bei Clemens v. Alexandria, 1936. K. BAUS, Der Kranz in Antike u. Christent., 1940.

for seduction and an insult to the Creator as if He had not sufficiently adorned man or had not known how to order nature. The opposition to paganism often caused the rejection of practices that were susceptible of a more reasonable interpretation. To wear *wreaths* on the head or to adorn graves with *flowers* was sometimes considered sinful because such practices were thought to be contrary to nature or could be interpreted as dedicatory gifts to the gods (Clem. Alex. Paed. II, 8; Tert. De corona militis; Min. Fel. Oct. 12, 38). But as severely as these things were generally condemned, not every *luxury* was prohibited and some allowances were made for the wealthier class, as discoveries in the Roman catacombs have proved. As caustically as Clement of Alexandria censures luxury and display, he is less opposed to the use of gold ornaments and fine dress than to the unbridled desire for these things (Paed. II, 11), and he admits that there is such a thing as proper recreation in gymnastics, hunting, fishing, etc. (l. c. III, 10). Games of chance were strictly forbidden (Adv. aleatores [see § 40, 3] Council of Elvira can. 79). — Christians never adopted the practice of *cremation*, then quite common among pagans; they preferred the "nobler and more venerable" custom of *burying* the dead (Min. Fel. Oct. 11, 4; 34, 10) and decorated the graves with pictures and symbols that expressed a sure hope in a blessed life beyond (§ 23, 5). Since the third century in Africa and at Rome, a banquet at the grave was a reminder of communion with the dead and the grave of a martyr imparted a special blessing to the food (T. Klauser, ThGl 1928, 599/608).

3. Christians had a high concept of *marriage* and *family life* (Tert. Ad ux. II, 9). The bond was entered into "with the sanction of the bishop" (Ign. ad Polyc. 5); and marriages with pagans were discouraged (Tert. Ad ux. II; Cypr. De laps. 6; Conc. Illib. can. 15). Premarital chastity, monogamy and marital fidelity were Christian ideals preserved by severe penalties as we have seen (§ 24). The crime then common in the pagan world of killing the child in the womb or exposing it after birth was condemned and punished as murder; and the apologists often remark that such a crime is unknown among true Christians (Did. 2, 5; Ep. Barn. 19; Ep. ad Diogn. 5; Athenag. Leg. 35; Tert. Apolog. 9; Min. Fel. Oct. 30). A *second marriage* was not absolutely forbidden; in fact, St. Paul (1 Tim. 5:14) advises young widows to remarry. Yet second marriages were discouraged and considered an impediment to Holy Orders (§ 19, 4). They were even punished with ecclesiastical penances and the clergy were forbidden under penalties to take part in the festivities accompanying them (Conc. Ancyr. can. 19; Neocaes. can. 3, 7; Laodic. can. 1). The apologist Athenagoras, possibly influenced by Stoicism, goes as far as to call a second marriage "respectable adultery" (εὐπρεπὴς μοιχεία). The Montanists and Tertullian (§ 34) go even further.

## § 26. Moral and Religious Life.

The excellence which Sacred Scripture ascribed to *virginity* as a higher state, caused many Christians, men and women, to forego marriage voluntarily. The apologists constantly appeal to these as a proof of the purity of morals in the Church (Justin Apol. I, 15; Athenag. Leg. 33; Min. Fel. Oct. 31; Tert. Apolog. 9; Orig. Contra Cels. I 26). Bishop Methodius of Olympus (§ 39, 6) enthusiastically praises virginity in his "Symposium". Since the third century there were *virgins dedicated to God* (virgines sacrae, virgines Christi) who obliged themselves by *vow* to ascetical practices, although the vow was not always solemn nor for life. (Tert. De vir. vel. 10; Cypr. De habitu virg.; Conc. Illib. can. 13; Ancyr. can. 19). The two Pseudo-Clementine Letters Ad Virgines (§ 37, 3) written in Syria in the third century, consist of admonitions addressed to ascetics (ἐγκρατεῖς) of both sexes. The Letters also mention the very *peculiar arrangement* whereby a male ascetic or cleric lived with a consecrated virgin or widow in a sort of *spiritual marriage* for the mutual fostering of their religious life.

The passage in 1 Corinthians 7:36—38 is most probably not a reference to this strange institution (cfr. J. Sickenberger, Bibl. Z. 1905, 44 ff.; H. Koch, ib. 401 ff.; A. Jülicher, Protest. Monatshefte 1918, 97/119). The term συνείσακτος (scil. γυνὴ or ἀδελφή, translated into Latin, since the fifth century, by the word, subintroducta, cfr. F. Quadt, ZkTh 1910, 227/33) is found for the first time, and then in a reproachful sense, in the history of the Bishop of Antioch, Paul of Samosata (Eus. H. E. VII, 13, 12; cfr. § 32, 3) although the custom is older. In itself the custom is an indication of the high idealism in the Church of antiquity. But since such an arrangement could be dangerous in individual cases, it was suspected and discouraged since the third century (Pseudo Clem. Ad Virg.; Cypr. Ep. 4). Synods of the next period following the lead of Ancyra 314 (can. 19) forbade spiritual marriages; but they disappear in the East only in the next era (§ 60, 6) and reappear in the West especially in Ireland (conhospitae, agapetae; cfr. K. Meyers, Sb. Berlin 1918, 362/74), Constantinople, Rome and Gaul as Chrysostom and Jerome testify. In these places wealthy ladies would sometimes give permanent residence in their homes to a cleric or a monk to act as spiritual adviser and to serve at the same time as a protector and manager of the estate. Cfr. *H. Achelis*, Virgines subintroductae, 1902; RE 19; 123/7; *G. Ficker*, Amphilociana 1906, 273 ff.; J. Feusi, vide supra; *P. de Labriolle*, Rev. Hist. 137, 1921, 204/25; *G. Morin*, Rev. Ben. 1935, 101/13 (Agapetae).

As we have seen (§ 13, 2) the moral conduct of Christians was not lost on pagans. The pagan physician *Galen* († ca. 200) enthusiastically praises Christian virtue, especially their contempt for death, their sexual purity and sobriety, and declares that there are among the Christians those who in self-mastery and zeal for what is noble are not inferior to the true philosophers. — Cfr. Harnack, Mission I⁴ 232 f.; R. Walzer, Galen on Jews and Christians, London 1949.

## CHAPTER IV
## DEVELOPMENT OF DOCTRINE. HERESIES AND SCHISMS[1]

### § 27.
### Principal Points of Christian Faith. Heresy and Schism in General. Simon Magus and Menander.

1. At a very early date the doctrines of Christianity were summarized in a *Creed*. The candidates for baptism were taught that they would henceforth be obliged to hold this Creed as their rule of faith (§ 22, 2). In the first place it demanded belief in *one* God, the Father and almighty Creator and Ruler of the world. This strict *monotheism* was common to Jews and Christians and distinguished both from the polytheistic pagans. But entirely new and peculiar to Christians alone was the doctrine of the *Trinity*, i. e., of one God in three Persons, as expressly commanded in the commission to baptize (Matt. 28:19). It demanded belief in the only begotten *Son of God*, who appeared in *Jesus Christ* of Nazareth for the redemption of mankind, the Messias promised and foretold by the prophets.

---

[1] Heresiologies: IRENAEUS, Adv. haereses; HIPPOLYTUS, Refutatio omnium [haeresium (Philosophumena)]; PS.-TERTULL., Adv. omnes haereses (= Tert. De praescr. c. 45—53); EPIPHANIUS, Panarium s. Haereses; Theodoretus, Fabularum haereticarum compendium; FILASTRIUS (Philastrius), Liber de haeresibus; AUGUSTINUS, De haeresibus. H. HAGEMANN, see § 21. J. SCHWANE, Dogmengesch. I², 1892. J. TIXERONT, Hist. des dogmes I¹¹, Paris 1930, English: Handb. der Dogmengesch., ed. M. SCHMAUS, et al., 1951 ff. J. LEBRETON, Hist. du dogme de la Trinité, 2 vol. Paris 1927/8. J. RIVIÈRE, Le dogme de la Rédemption, Paris 1931. J. RANFT, Der Ursprung des kath. Traditionsprinzips, 1931. K. PRÜMM, Der christl. Glaube u. die altheidnische Welt, 2 vols. 1935. J. BROSCH, Das Wesen der Häresie, 1936. J. BARBEL, Christos Angelos, 1941. J. GROSS, La divinisation du Chrétien d'après les Pères grecs, Paris 1938. P. PALAZZINI, Il monoteismo nei padri apostolici e negli apologisti del II secolo, Rome 1946. J. GEWISS, see § 8. G. WELTER, Hist. des sectes chrét. des origines à nos jours, Paris 1950. Protestant Works: CH. W. F. WALCH, Historie der Ketzereien, Spaltungen etc., 11 vols. 1762/85. AD. HILGENFELDT, Die Ketzergesch. des Urchristentums, 1884. R. KNOPF, Das apost. Zeitalter, 1905. AD. HARNACK, Lehrb. der Dogmengesch. I⁴, 1909, reprinted 1931; Grundriß der DG., ⁶1922; Die Entstehung der christl. Theologie u. des kirchl. Dogmas, 1927. R. SEEBERG, Lehrb. der DG. I—II³ 1922/23; Grundriß der DG., ²1936. F. LOOFS, Leitfaden z. Studium der DG., ⁵1950 ff. N. BONWETSCH, Grundriß der DG., ²1919. F. WIEGAND, DG. der alten Kirche, 1912; DG. I, 1928 (Samml. Göschen). J. K. MOZLEY, The Beginnings of Christian Theology, Cambridge 1931. W. BAUER, Rechtgläubigkeit u. Ketzerei im ältesten Christentum, 1934 (extremely critical). G. L. PRESTIGE, God in Patristic Thought, London 1936. W. KOEHLER, DG. als Gesch. des christl. Selbstbewußtseins, Zürich 1938. E. MOLLAND, see § 39. 1. R. ASTING, Die Verkündigung des Wortes im Urchristentum, dargest. an den Begriffen „Wort Gottes", „Evangelium" u. „Zeugnis", 1939. M. WERNER, Die Entstehung des christl. Dogmas problemgeschichtl. dargestellt, 1941. W. NIGG, Das Buch der Ketzer, 1949.

He was truly man, born of the Virgin Mary, suffered under the Procurator, Pontius Pilate, died on the cross, and was buried. But on the third day He arose from the dead, ascended into heaven and there rules as "Lord" (κύριος) in power and glory and will soon come again as Judge of the world. The spurious Second Letter of Clement to the Corinthians (§ 37, 3) begins with the words: "Brethren, we must think of Jesus Christ as we think of God, as Judge of the living and the dead." Christians also believed in the *Holy Ghost*, the third Person of the Trinity (τριάς, first used by Theoph. Ad Autol. II, 15 or by Clem. Alex. Excerpta ex Theodoto 80, 3; Trinitas used by Tert. Adv. Prax 2 ff.), the Paraclete, who will remain always with the disciples of Jesus (John 14:16). And they believed in the *Holy Church* which Paul represented as the Mystical Body of Christ; in *penance* for the remission of sin, which is realized in *baptism*, the bath of regeneration; in the *resurrection of the flesh* which will take place at the end of the world when the Lord comes again; and in an *eternal life of bliss*, the reward of the just.

2. But not all to whom the Gospel was preached recognized it as the saving word of God which must be accepted without any addition or alteration. Some ventured to select from the Apostles' preaching only such doctrines as suited them and mingled with these all sorts of strange notions. Thus **heresy** (αἵρεσις) arose. The first heresies were of either Jewish or pagan origin. *Jewish* converts could not easily reconcile themselves to the thought that the Old Covenant had been superseded by the New; and some of them believed that the Mosaic Law still obliged everyone as a means of salvation. The more they emphasized the importance of the Mosaic Law the less they regarded the Founder of the New Law whose divine nature they denied wholly or in part. Many *pagans* could only with difficulty or not at all accept the Christian teaching regarding creation and the problem of evil. Since creation out of nothing seemed to them an impossibility, they substituted for Christian monotheism their own **dualism** (God and eternal matter). Hence heresy took two different directions: one resulting from the Church's contact with Judaism, the other from her contact with paganism, that is, with Greek philosophy and the Hellenic-Oriental systems of religion. But this antithesis is not always clear. Some heretics appear to have been influenced equally by Judaism and paganism. However, the heresies proved of the greatest importance in the

*development of the Church's doctrines.* They became the principal reasons for the truths of faith being explained more clearly, established more firmly and formulated more exactly (§ 1, 1).

St. Augustine (De vera relig. 8, 15) says: haeretici ... cum foris sunt plurimum prosunt, non verum docendo quod nesciunt, sed ad verum quaerendum carnales et ad verum aperiendum spirituales catholicos excitando. Similarly in De civ. Dei 16, 2, 1; 18, 51; De genesi c. Manich. 1, 2; Ennarr. in ps. 22, 2—9.

3. As heresy is a departure from Christian doctrine, so **schism** (σχίσμα from σχίζειν) is a separation from the communion of the Church because of disagreement with her discipline or organization. During this period the chief cause of schism was the Church's *system of penance.*

4. The early Fathers called **Simon Magus** of Gitta in Samaria, the "patriarch of heretics." According to the account in the Acts of the Apostles, 8:9 ff., he deceived many by his witchraft and gave himself out as "the great power of God." Converted by the preaching of the Deacon Philip, he was baptized, whereupon he offered the Apostles money in return for the power to communicate the Holy Ghost by the imposition of hands (simony). Peter indignantly rejected his offer. According to the apochryphal Acts of Peter, Simon is supposed to have met Peter later at Rome where Simon came to a miserable end. The importance he acquired in the minds of the Fathers was evidently due to the fact that he was the first known opponent of the Gospel. Actually there is very little trace of anything Christian in his religion, which was rather Syrio-Phoenician mythology and Oriental syncretism. It does, however, show the beginnings of Gnostic speculation (§ 29). Simon himself pretended to be the apparition of a theretofore unknown deity. Creation was merely the emanation of this god. Simon's countryman and successor, **Menander**, taught a similar doctrine of creation and although he did not pretend to be God, he did pose as the redeemer sent from a supersensible world for the salvation of mankind.

F. C. Baur and others are mistaken in believing that *Simon* was a mythical person or the personification of Gnosis. *Irenaeus* (Adv. haer. I, 23) gives the principal doctrines taught by Simon and his school: from the highest God (= Simon) proceeds His first creative "thought" *Ennoia*, the mother of all, from whom in turn emanate the *demiurges* who created the world. But in order to conceal their parentage, they imprisoned Ennoia in matter. As the lost sheep of the Gospel (Matt. 18:12) she assumed various female forms until finally she took the form of the prostitute, Helen of Tyre, Simon's companion. To set her free and to redeem mankind, Simon came down to earth and appeared as the *Son* to the Jews among whom he apparently (Docetism) suffered; to the Samarians he appeared as the *Father* and to other peoples as the *Holy Ghost*. All that is required for salvation is belief in him (Simon) and Helen; the value of good works is denied absolutely. As late as the fourth century a sect calling themselves Simonians continued to teach a similar doctrine, and like Simon, whom they considered their founder, dealt in witchcraft and magic. — Cfr. *H. Waitz*, RE 18, 351/61; 24, 518/20. — *A. Redlich*, Archiv f. Gesch. d. Philos. 1910, 374 ff. 537 ff. — *K. Pieper*, Die Simon Magus-Perikope (Acts 8:5—24), 1911. — *L. Cerfaux*, RechSR 1925, 1926, 1937.

## § 28.

### Judaistic Heresies: The Ebionites; Cerinthus; The Elchasaites; The Pseudoclementines[1].

1. The origin of Judaistic heresy was nothing more than the stubborn adherence of the *Jewish converts* to the Mosaic Law. From the beginning this heresy took two forms accordingly as the Law was considered binding only on Jewish Christians or was held to oblige pagan converts as well. It was this more *rigorous* group which first became heretical. They had received a mild rebuke at the Council of the Apostles and after the martyrdom of James the Younger in 62 or 63 (§ 8, 3), they left the Church. The occasion was a dispute over the succession in the episcopacy: Simeon, son of Cleophas and kinsman of the Lord (§ 15, 3) was validly elected, but was opposed by Thebutis and his partisans (Eus. IV, 22). At the outbreak of the Jewish war in 66 the Christian community of Jerusalem withdrew to Pella in Peraea, east of the Jordan, where in seclusion they came under the influence of Jewish sects such as the Essenes (§ 6, 1). But even the *milder* party in the course of time began to mingle dangerous ideas with Christian teachings. As early as the time of Justin (Dial. 47) about the middle of the second century, many Catholics (pagan converts) refused to associate with them, although Justin himself believed that it was still possible for them to be saved. After Justin's time they are nowhere mentioned as belonging to the Church. Now it was no longer their views on the Law which distinguished the two groups; it was rather their divergent opinions regarding *faith in Christ* (Orig. C. Cels. V, 61; Eus. III, 27). The rigorous group declared

---

[1] Cfr. literature in § 6 and 27. H. J. SCHOEPS, Theologie u. Gesch. des Judenchristentums, 1949. G. HOENNICKE, Das Judenchristent. im 1. u. 2. Jh., 1908. A. WURM, Die Irrlehren im 1. Johannesbrief, 1903. A. BLUDAU, Die ersten Gegner der Johannesbriefe, 1925. W. LÜTGERT, Die Irrlehrer der Pastoralbriefe, 1909. AD. SCHLATTER, Die Tage Trajans u. Hadrians, 1897. G. HÖLSCHER, Gesch. d. Juden in Palästina seit 70 n. Chr., 1909. J. EL-BOGEN, Gesch. der Juden seit d. Untergang des jüd. Staates, 1919. A. SCHMIDTKE, Neue Fragmente u. Untersuch. zu den judenchristl. Evangelien, TU 37, 1, 1911; ZntW 1936, 24/44; cfr. H. WEITZ, ZntW 1913, 38/64; 1937, 60/81. H. WAITZ, in Hennecke, Neutest. Apokryphen, ²1924, 39 ff. 422 ff. A. HARNACK, Judent. u. Judenchristent. in Justins Dialog, TU 39, 1, 1913. G. BAREILLE, Docétisme, DictThC IV, 1480/501. L. MARCHAL, Judéo-Chrétiens DictThC VIII, 1681/709. J. THOMAS, Le mouvement baptiste en Palestine et Syrei 150 av. — 300 après J.-Chr., Diss. Louvain 1935 (cfr. W. GOOSSENS, EphThLov 1937, 467/76); RHE 1934, 257/96 (Ebionites and similar sects). M. SIMON, Verus Israel, Paris 1948. H. BLETENHARD, ThLZ 1948, 174/92 (Church and Synagogue in the first centuries). G. QUISPEL, ib. 1949, 429/36 (Philo and the early Christian heresies). W. BOUSSET, Kyrios Christos, see § 7, 1. K. PIEPER, see § 12, 10.

that Christ was a mere man, while the milder party at least acknowledged His miraculous birth of the Virgin and the Holy Ghost. Both groups favored *Chiliasm* (§ 33). It was only since the end of the second century that these heretics were known by a special name. Irenaeus calls them **Ebionites** and says that they rejected the Apostle *Paul* as an apostate and enemy of the Mosaic Law. The sectaries themselves derived the name from the Hebrew word for poverty (cfr. Matt. 5:3; Acts 4:34 f.). The Fathers who say that the name is derived from their founder Ebion, are evidently mistaken. Epiphanius calls the members of the milder party **Nazarenes**; but Jerome is more correct when he makes little distinction between them and uses the terms indiscriminately. The Jewish Christians had their own Gospel written in the Syrochaldaic or Aramaic language. It was a revision of the canonical Gospel of St. Matthew and was referred to by the Fathers as the *Hebrew Gospel* (Evangelium secundum Hebraeos). As has been said, the sects established themselves east of the Jordan whence they spread into Syria. They abode there until the fifth century or possibly even until the Arab invasion (637).

2. **Cerinthus**, who lived in Asia Minor toward the end of the first century, was not a member of the rigorous Judaistic party (Epiph. Haer. 28) but according to Irenaeus (Adv. haer. I, 26, 1), Hippolytus (Philos. VII, 33) and the Epistola apostolorum (§ 38 B2) was also a *Gnostic*. He taught that the world was not created by God, but by an angelic being (demiurge), and that Jesus was a mere man. At baptism the divine Christ descended upon him in the form of a dove so that he could make the unknown Father known to men and could work miracles, but left Him before He began His passion *(Docetism)*. Cerinthus was also a Chiliast (§ 33). According to Irenaeus it was to combat Cerinthus that St. John wrote his Gospel. The attempt to prove (E. Schwartz, ZntW 1914, 210/19) that Cerinthus was a fictional and not a real person did not succeed. — *H. Gladder*, Bibl. Z. 1917, 317/32; *C. Schmidt*, TU 43, 1919, 403/52; *G. Bardy*, Bev. Bibl. 1921, 344/73.

3. The **Elchasaites** present a wild medley of Judaism, Christian doctrines and pagan superstitions. Epiphanius (Haer. 53) called them *Sampaeans* (= people of the Sun) while they were also known as Sabiai, *Sabaeans* (= baptizers) and to the Arabs as *Moghtasilah*. Several thousand of them are found today in southern Mesopotamia where they are known as **Mandaeans** (i. e., Gnostics, from mandâ = knowledge). They still trace their origin to a certain *Elchasai* or Elcai (= sacred power) who lived east of the Jordan during the reign of Trajan (101). He is supposed to have given the sect its sacred book which was brought to Rome about 220 by Alcibiades of Apamea (Syria). The Elchasaites observed the Mosaic Law (circumcision, the Sabbath, ceremonial laws) but without bloody sacrifices. To this was joined Chaldean astrology and magic with baptism for the remission of sins, similar to that of Christians, and frequent ritualistic ablutions probably adopted from the Essenes. They abstained from flesh meat and wine. Their doctrine contains very little that is Christian and that little badly distorted. They assume two primal principles, a male, ("Lord of Greatness," "King of Light") and a female ("Holy Ghost", "Rucha") and declare that the Redeemer Christ, the first ambassador of the most high God, was a spirit (eon) of fantastic

proportions who appeared in various forms, but first of all in Adam (Hippol. Philos. IX, 13—19; Epiph. Haer. 19; 30, 17; 53, 1). To the latter Mandaeans at least Jesus was a pseudo-messias and a deceiver. The Mandaeans pay special honor to *John the Baptist.* Hence some modern scholars (Reitzenstein and others) assume that they are somehow related to the *disciples of John.* But *Lietzmann* (vide infra) has proved conclusively that John the Baptist does not appear in a major role among them until after the revision of the Mandaean scriptures in the seventh or eighth century and that their baptismal ritual was derived from the Nestorian liturgy (§ 54, 5) of East Syria. *Drower* has also shown the influence of Parsiism and Islamism on Mandaean liturgy. Mandaeism is, therefore, nothing more than a slightly Christianized, Judaistic, Gnosticism which may have been organized as a sect in Palestine, but its tenets go back to pre-Christian times. — *S. A. Pallis*, Essay on Mandaean Bibliography 1560—1930, Copenhagen 1933. — *W. Brandt*, Die mandäische Religion, 1889; Elchasai, 1912; Die Mandäer, Abh. d. Akad. d. Wiss. zu Amsterdam 16, 3, 1915. — *K. Kessler*, RE 12, 155/83. — *M. Lidzbarski*, Das Johannesbuch der Mandäer, 2 vols. 1905/15; Mand. Liturgien übers. u. erklärt, Abh. Gött. NF. 16, 1, 1920; Ginza, der Schatz, oder das große Buch der Mandäer übers. u. erkl., 1925. — *R. Reitzenstein*, Das mandäische Buch des Herrn der Größe, Sb. Heidelberg 1919, 12; Das iran. Erlösungsmysterium, 1921; Die Vorgesch. der christl. Taufe, 1929. — *J. Behm*, Die mand. Religion u. das Urchristentum, 1927. — *L. Tondelli*, Il Mandeismo e le origini cristiane, Rome 1928. — *R. Stahl*, Les Mandéens et les origines chrétiennes, Paris 1930. — *H. Odeberg*, Die mand. Religionsanschauung, Uppsala 1930. — *A. Loisy*, Le Mandéisme et les origines chrét., Paris 1934. — *J. Thomas*, Le mouvement baptiste (vide supra) 140 ff. (Elchasaites), 186 ff. (Mandaeans). — *E. S. Drower*, The Mandaeans of Iraq and Iran, Oxford 1937. — *G. Bardy*, DictThC IX, 1812/24. — *E. Percy*, Untersuchungen über d. Entstehung des Joh.-evangeliums. Zugleich ein Beitrag z. Frage nach der Entsteh. des Gnostizismus. Diss. Lund 1939. — Ed. Schweizer, Ego eimi, 1939. — Various essays on the Mandaeans: *R. Reitzenstein*, ZntW 1921, 1/23; 1927, 39/70. — *E. Peterson*, ib. 1926, 236/48; 1928, 225/35. — *H. Lietzmann*, Sb. Berlin 1930, 596/608. — *J. Schmid*, Bibl. Z. 1932, 121 ff. 247 ff. — *H. Schlier*, Theol. Rundschau 1933, 1 ff. 69 ff.

4. A distinct form of Judaistic Gnosticism is encountered in the **Pseudo-clementines**, or more specifically in the twenty books of *homilies* (PG 2; ed. P. de Lagarde, 1865) which contain the "Preaching of the Apostle Peter." This work declares that the original revelation made at the time of creation had been obscured by sin, but had been renewed by the true prophets who appeared in the persons of Adam, Moses and Jesus. Christianity is nothing more than Judaism purged of all ambiguity and error. Jesus was a prophet greater than Moses, but not the Redeemer and neither true God nor true man. The world exists by emanation. In order to overcome sensuality one must abstain from flesh meat, must marry early and practise poverty. This doctrine is clothed in the form of a romance which represented *Clement of Rome*, the companion of St. Peter and later bishop of Rome, in his quest for truth. Peter's conflict with Simon Magus is also portrayed in detail. The same material is found in still another work of ten books called the *Recognitions*

(ἀναγνωρισμοί, or Clement's meeting with his long lost parents and brethren) which has been preserved in the Latin version of Rufinus (P. G. 1). In this version the Jewish elements are considerably toned down to give more prominence to Christian ideas. These works, together with two Greek epitomes of the homilies and a Syrian version of the Recognitions (this latter published by *W. Frankenberg* TU 48, 3, 1937), in the form in which they have been handed down, date back to the fourth century. They are probably based on a work written in Syria (Palestine) or east of the Jordan, about 220—230, which made use of older material from Ebionite circles of Syria (Κηρύγματα Πέτρου?) The entire collection is still a great literary-historical puzzle. — *J. Langen*, Dic Klemensromane, 1890. — *H. Waitz*, Die Pseudoklementinen, TU 25, 4, 1904. — *W. Heintze*, Der Klemensroman und seine griech. Quellen, TU 40, 2, 1914. — *C. Schmidt*, Studien zu den Pseudoklementinen, TU 46, 1, 1929. — *O. Cullmann*, Le problème littéraire et historique du roman pseudo-clémentin, Paris 1930. — Recent *studies*: *L. Cerfaux*, RechSR 1928, 143/63; *H. Waitz*, ZntW 1929, 1931, 1933; ZKG 1940, 304/41; *A. Siouville*, Rev HR100, 1929, 142/204 (by the same: a french translation of the pseudo-Clementine homily with commentary and introduction, Paris 1934); *R. Cadiou*, RechSR 1930, 506/28; *Ed. Schwartz*, ZntW 1932, 151/99; *W. Frankenberg*, Zeitschr. der Deutschen Morgenländ. Gesellsch. 1937, 577/604 (on the Syrian text). — *B. Rehm*, ZntW 1938, 77/184 (origin of the pseudo-Clementines); Philologus 1938, 218/47 (the pseudo-Clementine and Bardesanes).

## § 29.
### Gnosticism in General; Its Origin and Character[1].

1. The main tenets of Gnosticism as a religious system had been formulated before the birth of Christ and were not unknown to the Jews (§ 28, 2, 4). Gnosticism was an offspring of the syncretism of Oriental religions and Hellenic mysticism; but it began to assume

---

[1] Gnostic works, see § 30. Antignostic ecclesiastical writers, see § 27. W. VÖLKER, Quellen zur Gesch. der christl. Gnosis, 1932. W. SCHULTZ, Dokumente der Gnosis, 1910. J. A. MÖHLER, Versuch über den Ursprung des Gnost., 1831 (= Ges. Schriften I, 403 ff.). F. CHR. BAUR, Die christl. Gnosis, 1835. R. A. LIPSIUS, Der Gnostizismus, 1860. A. HILGENFELD, Die Ketzergesch. des Urchristentums, 1884; ZwTh 1890, 1/63. W. ANZ, TU 15, 4, 1897 (origin of Gnosticism). E. DE FAYE, Introd. à l'étude du gnosticisme, Paris 1903 (RevHR 45/46); Gnostiques et gnosticisme, Paris ²1925 (cfr. BATIFFOL, Rev. bibl. 1913, 597 ff.). W. BOUSSET, Hauptprobleme der Gnosis, 1907; RE Pauly-Wissowa VII, 1503/47. E. BUONAIUTI, Lo Gnosticismo, Rome 1907; Frammenti gnostici, Rome 1923. J. P. STEFFES, Das Wesen des Gnost. u. s. Verhältnis z. kath. Dogma, 1922. L. FENDT, Gnost. Mysterien, 1922. H. LEISEGANG, Die Gnosis, ²1936. F. C. BURKITT, Church and Gnosis, Cambridge 1932. A. EHRHARD, Die Kirche der Martyrer, 1932, 122/227. H. JONAS, Gnosis und spätantiker Geist, 1934. H. LECLERCQ, DictAC VI, 1327/67. G. BAREILLE, DictThC VI, 1434/67. L. CERFAUX, Dict. de la Bible, Suppl., 1936, 659/701. R. P. CASEY, JThSt 1935, 45/60 (investigation of Gnosticism). F. TORM, ZntW 1936, 70/75 (the expression "Gnostic"). S. PÉTREMENT, Le dualisme chez Platon, les gnostiques et les manichéens, Paris 1947. E. PERCY, see § 28, 3.

importance only after it had come face to face with Christianity. By tampering with Christian dogma in the general attempt at syncretizing all religions, Gnosticism created a serious crisis in the bosom of the Church which endured for the greater part of the second century. Gnosticism attracted the minds of men by promising them a higher "knowledge" (γνῶσις, cfr. 1 Tim. 6:20 ψευδώνυμος γνῶσις) than was offered in the simple truths of the Gospel and a more satisfactory solution to the questions which had always puzzled the human mind regarding the existence of evil, the origin of the world, the redemption and salvation of man (Clem. Alex. Strom. VI, 12:96; Tert. De praescript. 7; Eus. H.E. V, 27; Epiph. Haer. 24, 6). Certain Christian teachings, especially the acceptance of redemption through *Jesus Christ*, were merely grafted externally on Gnosticism and never actually affected its essential structure. The Gnostics explained the truths of faith by allegorical interpretations of the Sacred Scriptures and by mingling these distortions with concepts and ideas taken from Platonic-Pythagorean and Stoic philosophy and especially with elements of Asiatic religions: the Parsiism of Zoroaster (with its crude dualism of God and world, light and darkness), and the Babylonian-Chaldaic astrology (worship of the stars). Thus there arose a number of rainbow-colored and fantastic systems which professed to be able to satisfy the longing of the pagan world for salvation and to be able to reconcile the religion of Christ with the culture and philosophy of the times. Actually, however, they completely undermined the foundations of the faith, especially by distorting the Christian teaching regarding creation and redemption. For the most part the Gnostics appealed to a secret tradition handed down by the prophets and Apostles and preserved only in their ranks. They gathered in secret conventicles and in their religious services made use of all sorts of superstitious rites and magic formulas. Their organization and cult was taken partly from the Church and partly from pagan mystery cults.

2. In spite of the great variety of the Gnostic systems there are certain *concepts common to all* of them. This is true especially of *dualism* or the opposition between God and eternal matter (ὕλη). The latter is sometimes conceived, as in Platonism, as having neither essence nor form (μὴ ὄν), sometimes, as in Parsiism, as animated by an evil principle. In the more highly developed systems, it was held that the most high, hidden God (βυθός, ἀρχή) gives being by *emanation* (προβολή) to numerous *Aeons* or spirits (as many as three hundred and sixty-five) whose nature is less perfect the farther they are from the divine source. As the divine essence thus unfolds a point is reached where the elements of the

kingdom of light πλήρωμα *mingle* with elements of the kingdom of darkness and evil (κένωμα). This provides the matter for the *formation of the world* which is the work of the lowest aeon or of several of the lower aeons. The creator of the world *(demiurge)* is identified with the wrathful Jahve and the Law-giver of the Old Covenant. To effect *redemption*, that is, the liberation of the elements of light from the matter in which they are held captive and restore them to Pleroma, there comes a higher aeon, the Nous or Λόγος, *Christ* — and this is the turning point in the Gnostic world-drama — who makes known to men the hitherto unknown God and the world of light above them and teaches them how to conquer matter and disengage themselves from it. The Redeemer is either a man only in appearance *(Docetism)* or descends upon the man Jesus, who is the Messias sent by the demiurges, and remains with Him until He begins His passion. But only the *Pneumatici* or Gnostics share in the Redemption because only in them does the element of light preponderate. The *Hylicoi*, that is, the great majority of mankind, will be destroyed like other matter; the *Psychici*, that is, the simple faithful (Catholics) who were considered by some to constitute an intermediate group, will attain to a low degree of happiness. The goal and end is the return of all things to the place corresponding with their nature (ἀποκατάστασις πάντων).

3. As the above summary of Gnostic doctrines shows, the heresy was utterly *un-Christian* and *naturalistic*. It rejected the unity of God and the identity of Christ with the Messias and resolved all religion and morality into a purely natural process entirely independant of the free will of man. Redemption becomes only a step in the general evolution of the world and not a free act of the love of God. Hence ethics and asceticism are purely external — a mere physical conquest of matter. Originally the Gnostics embraced a very severe, even *unnatural* asceticism. But as is always the case, they soon went to the opposite extreme. Especially since they classified the demiurges who made the world with the Law-Giver of the Old Covenant, it was but a step to the rejection of all law, to unbridled libertinism and antinomism. Their claim to a higher knowledge naturally led to a minimizing of the value of external acts. Hence they considered it permissible for Christians to take part in pagan worship, and denied the necessity of confessing one's faith when brought before a magistrate, since true profession of faith or martyrdom consisted in Gnosis.

4. The beginnings of Gnosticism may be traced back to *Simon Magus* (§ 27, 4), *Cerinthus* and the *Elchasaites* (§ 28); but it was not until about 130 to 180 that it really developed and flourished. A number of gifted leaders contributed greatly to its spread and

influence. To propagate their ideas they created a copious literature, partly scholarly and partly of an edifying nature: philosophic, dogmatic and ethical treatises, commentaries on the Scriptures, Gospels, Acts of the Apostles (§ 11, 3), Epistles, Apocalypses, Psalms and hymns, of which but a few have been preserved (§ 30 A 3, 4). Among approximately thirty different Gnostic groups or schools it is possible to distinguish those of a strong *Oriental* tendency with a well-developed cosmogony and astrology from the more moderate groups who leaned rather toward *Hellenistic philosophy.* Their principal centers were in *Egypt* (Alexandria) and *Syria* (Antioch) and, for a time, at *Rome.* Their most important leaders were *Basilides, Valentinus* (both belonging to the Hellenic school) and *Marcion.* In many respects Marcion occupies a unique position in that he came closer to Christian teaching than the others and was more interested in practical reform measures than in mere speculation.

5. To meet the challenge of such insidious error, the Church was obliged to offer heroic resistance. And in doing so she revealed her divine institution and divine guidance scarcely less convincingly than in her victory over the brute force of the pagan State. The danger was obviated partly by the apologetic writings of the Fathers and other ecclesiastical authors (Justin, Irenaeus, Tertullian, Hippolytus, etc.) and partly, but most especially, by the closer unity of the bishops as the heirs and guardians of apostolic tradition. Rome, the center of ecclesiastical unity, where the leaders of the false Gnosis endeavored to establish themselves, gained particular merit in this respect. Several distinct benefits accrued to the Church as the result of the contest; chief of which was a clearer recognition of a *monarchical episcopate* based on apostolic succession (§ 18, 3); besides this, ecclesiastical *literature* and *learning* developed simultaneously. To build up a permanent defense against the unbridled speculation of the Gnostics and against their appeal to a secret tradition, the Church fixed the *"canon"* of the inspired works of the New Testament. Furthermore, she officially expressed in the *Creed for baptism* (§ 22, 2; 27, 1) the doctrines that had been attacked: the unity of God, Father and Creator, and the earthly life of Jesus, the only begotten Son, the Savior. Naturally, the Church's victory did not mean the end of Gnosticism; its ideas lived on in *Manicheism* (§ 31), in *Mandaeism* and in the *Pseudo-clementines* (§ 28, 3, 4) and later on showed up or were revived in various sects of the Middle Ages as the Paulicians, the Bogomils and the Cathari.

## § 30.
## The Chief Tendencies of Gnosticism. Related Sects.

### A. The True Gnostics.

1. According to Irenaeus (Adv. haer. I, 24), the real leaders of the Gnostics were *Saturnilus* and *Basilides*, both of whom were disciples of Menander, the successor of Simon Magus (§ 27, 4). **Saturnilus** lived at *Antioch*. He taught that all mankind was divided into two classes: the good and the bad, and that Christ, the Redeemer, had only an apparent body. The followers of Saturnilus rejected marriage as an institution of the devil and many abstained from flesh meat.

2. **Basilides** lived at *Alexandria* under Hadrian and Antoninus Pius about 120—145 A. D. He wrote an exposition of the Gospel (Exegetica) in twenty-four books. Two versions of his teaching have been given: according to Irenaeus (Adv. haer. I, 24, 3—7) he held an emanation from higher to lower grades of being (the Pleroma, with three hundred and sixty-five aeons, or world of spirits expressed by the mystical word Abrasax or Abraxas); while Hippolytus (Philos. VII, 14—27) says that he taught an evolution from lower to higher form. But the two accounts are otherwise fundamentally the same. Both Hippolytus and Irenaeus say that Basilides was a dualist and not a pantheist (cfr. *Funk*, AU I, 358/72; and for the opposite view, *A. Ehrhard*, Die Kirche der Martyrer p. 163). Although the Basilidians professed belief in Jesus, they held that it was not only permissible but even obligatory to reject belief in the Crucified. They permitted the use of meat offered to idols because they attached no importance to external acts. However, the leaders of this school, Basilides and his son, *Isidore*, followed a rigid code of morals. The sect survived until about the year 400. — *P. Hendrix*, De Alexandr. haeresiarch Basilides, Diss. Amsterdam 1926. — *M. Pieper*, Mitteil. des Deutschen Inst. f. ägypt. Altertumskunde 5, 1934, 119/43 (Abraxas-gems). — *G. Quispel*, Eranos Jb. 1948, 90/139 (the teaching of Basilides). — *J. H. Waszink*, RLAntChr I, 1217/25.

3. Other adherents of the heresy were simply called Gnostics or were given a name expressive of some peculiarity of their doctrine — such as **Barbelo-Gnostics,** the Ophites and other groups of Oriental tendency. The Barbelo-Gnostics or *Barbeliolae* believed that with the Father of All in the kingdom of light there was a never-aging female spirit called Barbelo (בארבצ אלוה = in the four is God). The product of each new emanation was a fourfold being or tetras, the members of which were called syzygies (συζυγία, a pair or team) and in which a female tetras is invariably followed by one of the masculine gender. — Cfr. C. Schmidt in Philotesia 1907, 315/36. — The **Ophites** constituted a widespread sect originating in Syria. They taught that the efforts of the demiurge, Jaldabaoth (= son of the desert), to withhold knowledge of the highest God from mankind were frustrated by the *serpent* (ὄφις) which appears in Genesis 3 : 5 as the first intermediary of Gnosis (Iren. I, 19, 30). Closely related to the Ophites were the *Naassenes* who honored the serpent (נהש) as the first being. An excerpt from a Naassene treatise and a hymn to the soul are found in Hippolytus (Philos. V, 6—10). The Fathers

mention a number of other Gnostic groups. The *Cainites* were an immoral sect who believed that all the wicked persons of the Old Testament branded by God were the true Pneumatici and martyrs of whom Cain was the first. The *Sethians* on the other hand considered Cain and Abel the progenitors of the Hylici and Psychici, while Seth was the father of the Pneumatici (Iren. I, 28, 31). This sect was fairly widespread in Egypt during the fourth century. The *Peratae* claimed that they alone could cross (περᾶν) the sea of death. A certain *Justin* and his followers mixed Christian and Jewish beliefs with Grecian mythology to form a strange medley in which even Hercules is considered a prophet (Hippol. Philos. V, 12—22; ib. 23—28, excerpts from Justin's Book of Baruch). Original Gnostic (Ophitic) texts of the four books of *Pistis Sophia* and two books of *Jeû* in Coptic transcription in Cod. Brucianus at Oxford were published in German by *C. Schmidt* in 1905 and again in 1925. They were also published in English by H. Horner, London 1924 and by C. A. Baynes, Cambridge 1933. A Greek fragment of a Gnostic Gospel of Mary (Magdalene) of the third century appeared in the Catalogue of the Greek and Latin papyri of the John Rylands Library 3, Manchester 1938 (No. 463). Other Gnostic writings in Coptic have been discovered quite recently. Among them a Sethian Gospel of the Egyptians, a letter of the Gnostic leader Gogessos surnamed Eugnostos, a dialogue of the Redeemer and lastly the Gospels of Philip and Thomas, the Ascension of Paul, the Tradition of Matthias, etc. — *H.-Ch. Puech* et *J. Doresse*, Comptes rendus de l'Acad. d. Inscript., Paris 1948, 87/95; *J. Doresse*, Bull. de l'Acad. R. de Belgique, Lettres 1949, 435/49; VC 1948, 137 ff., 1949, 129 ff. Cfr. also F. C. Burkitt, JThSt 1922, 271/80; 1925, 391/99; 1926, 148/57. C. Schmidt, ZntW 1925, 218/40. — R. P. Casey, JThSt 1926, 374/87. — R. Eisler, Angelos 1930, 93/110. — H.-Ch. Puech, RLAntChr I, 633/43 (Archonticites).

4. The high point in *speculative* Gnosticism was reached by **Valentinus** and his disciples. He came to *Rome* from *Alexandria* during the pontificate of Pope Hyginus (ca. 136) and remained there until the time of Pope Anicetus (ca. 160). Epiphanius relates that he died in Cyprus (Epiph. Haer. 31, 7). He was a highly talented man whose genius and eloquence were recognized by Tertullian (Ad Valentinianos 4). Only a few fragments of his sermons, psalms and letters have been preserved. Irenaeus (I, 11, 1) says that he revised and elaborated the teachings of his predecessors and became the founder of a new system in which the *doctrine of the aeons* is *highly developed*. Because of the strong influence of Platonism in the system, dualism is not stressed. The Pleroma comprises thirty aeons, an Ogdoas, a Decas, and a Dodecas, or fifteen pairs of aeons, since all the aeons emanate in *syzygies*. The highest of these is the Πατήρ or Βυθός and ῎Εννοια or Σιγή while the lowest aeon is called Σοφία. Valentinus divided the human race into three classes: Pneumatici, Psychici and Hylici (§ 29, 2). The details of this system can no longer be determined with certainty; but it is known that numerous *disciples* preached it; some of them as Valentinus organized it, and some with their own modifications. There were two general trends in Valentinianism: a *western* (Italian) trend, represented by *Secundus, Ptolemaeus* (whose letter to the noble Christian lady, Flora, expresses aversion to the Mosaic Law, in Epiph. Haer. 33, 3—7; published by Harnack in Kleine Texte 9, 1912; G. Quispel, Paris 1949;

VC 1948, 17/56) and *Heracleon* (fragments of his commentary on St. John in Origen); and an *Oriental* (Anatolic) trend represented by *Axionicus, Theodotus* and *Marcus*. The disciples of the latter, known as Marcosians, spread the heresy as far as Gaul. Marcus himself is said to have performed tricks of magic during the Eucharistic ceremony and to have lived a most immoral life. The *Valentinians* closely imitated the terminology of the Church for which reason they were considered particularly dangerous (Iren. I, 13—21). For *Bardesanes* see below, B 3. — *G. Bardy*, DictThC XV, 2497/519. — *F. Sagnard*, La gnose valentinienne et le témoignage de saint Irénée, Paris 1947; Clément d'Alexandrie. — Extraits de Théodote, Paris 1948. — *C. Barth*, TU 37, 3, 1911 (the New Testament of Valent.). — *W. Foerster*, Von Valentin zu Herakleon, 1928. — *A. Harnack*, Sb. Berlin 1902, 507/45 (the letter to Flora). — *O. Dibelius*, ZntW 1908, 230 ff. 329 ff. — *K. Müller*, Nachr. Gött. 1920, 179/204. — G. Quispel, VC 1947, 43/73. — R. P. Casey, HarvThR 1930, 275/98; The Excerpta ex Theodoto of Clement of Alex., London 1934.

5. **Carpocrates** of Alexandria, a Platonist, taught the creation of the world by lower aeons and the transmigration of souls. Redemption is accomplished by faith and charity: nothing else matters. Doubts which once were raised regarding the existence of this sect are without foundation. The *Carpocratians* were given to the worst forms of licentiousness. They made and kept images of Christ which they honored in pagan style together with images of Pythagoras, Plato, Aristotle and other philosophers. A woman named *Marcellina*, a member of the sect, came to Rome during the pontificate of Pope Anicetus (ca. 145—166) and deceived many (Iren. I, 25). *Epiphanes*, the son of Carpocrates, died at the age of 17 and was given divine honors on the island of Cephalonia, the birthplace of his mother. According to Clement of Alexandria (Strom. III, 2) he taught community of property and of women. — *H. Liboron*, Die karpokratinische Gnosis, 1938.

6. Antinomism led the Carpocratians and other sects into the grossest excesses. Thus the **Antitactae** followed the principle that the law must be broken ἀντιτάσσεσθαι (Clem. Strom. III, 4). The **Nicolaites** of Asia Minor who seem to be related to the Cainites (no. 3 above) were said to have been founded by the Deacon Nicholas at Jerusalem (Acts 6:5). They taught that lust could be overcome only be sexual excesses (cfr. Apoc. 2:6,15; Iren. I, 26,3; Clem. A. Strom. II, 20; A. von Harnack, Journal of Religion 1923, 413/21; M. Goguel, Rev. HR 115, 1937, 5/36. The **Prodicians**, disciples of a certain Prodicus, claimed that they, as sons of the King, were above the law which was given to servants (Clem. Strom. III, 4).

## B. Sects and Visionaries Related to Gnosticism.

1. Modern research has devoted quite some attention to **Marcion**[1] as the most important of the religious "Reformers" of this period of Church

---

[1] A. V. HARNACK, Marcion, das Evangelium vom fremden Gott, eine Mg. zur Gesch. der Grundlegung der kath. Kirche, TU 45, [2]1924; Neue Studien zu Marcion, TU 44, 4, 1923. Cfr. J. RIVIÈRA, RevSR 1921, 185 ff., 297 ff.; 1925, 634/42; A. D'ALÈS, RechSR 1922, 137/68; R. DRAGUET, RHE 1926, 537/50. E. BOSSHARDT, Essai sur l'originalité et la probité de Tertullien dans son traité c. Marcion, Lausanne 1921. H. RASCHKE, Abh. u. Vorträge

History. He can not be called a Gnostic in the strict sense of the word; for he rejected the fantastic doctrine of aeons and wild allegory and emphasized *practical religious* problems. But his system bears a close resemblance to Gnosticism in its dualism, its disdain of matter, its complete rejection of the Old Testament and its rigoristic ethics. All the ecclesiastical writers who opposed Marcion and his disciples, from Justin, Theophilus of Antioch, Rhodon, Tertullian, etc., down to Ephraem and Eznik of Golp, considered him the most important and dangerous enemy of the Church in this period. Irenaeus (III, 3, 4) says that Polycarp of Smyrna called him the "firstborn of Satan". He was born at Sinope in Pontus about 85 A. D., the son of the bishop of that place. Excommunicated by his father for immorality (heresy?), Marcion, then the wealthy owner of a ship, came to Rome about 139. He affiliated with the Catholic congregation to which he made a generous donation of money. But about five years later, under Pope Pius ('sub Pio impius', Tert.), he began to propose his *"reform ideas"* and broke with the Church. He gathered about him a number of disciples who honored him as "sanctissimus magister" and founded a *church of his own* to which he gave a more rigid and permanent organization than any of the Gnostics had succeeded in doing. The intense zeal of the Marcionites caused the sect to spread surprisingly fast and far until it soon surpassed all other Gnostic groups in numbers and influence. The Marcionite church consisted of a great many closely knit congregations with their own bishops, priests and even martyrs; and in spite of the laws against heresy enacted by Christian emperors, were able to exist for several centuries. In fact, many modern scholars see in the Paulicians of the Middle Ages (§ 91, 3) a continuation of the Marcionites. *Lucanus* and *Apelles* became the most prominent disciples of the founder. Apelles preached energetically at Rome and Alexandria, but soon deviated from the master's teachings by professing belief in *one* God and conforming more closely with Catholic doctrine. He was joined by a prophetess and visionary named *Philumena* whose pretended revelations he accepted as genuine.

Marcion's doctrine is fundamentally *anti-Judaistic*. His main objective was to make Christianity a religion entirely independent of Jewish influence and to restore it to its original purity. Hence he rejected all allegorical interpretations of the Old Testament. It seems quite certain that the Gnostic elements in Marcion's system were due to pressure exerted by *Cerdo*, a Syrian Gnostic who attached himself to Marcion at Rome. *Paul* was the only Apostle who had understood the Lord correctly. By adopting a one-sided interpretation

der Bremer Wissenschaftl. Gesellschaft I, 1926 128/201 (the Epistle to the Romans according to Marcion). H. KAYSER, ThStKr 1929 (Nature and God according to Marcion). E. BARNIKOL, Die Entstehung der Kirche im 2. Jh. u. die Zeit Marcions, ²1933. F. LOOFS, Theophilus v. Antiochien, Adv. Marcionem u. die anderen theol. Quellen bei Irenäus, TU 46, 2, 1930. R. S. WILSON, Marcion, London 1933. V. NAUMANN, ZkTh 1934, 311 ff., 533 ff. (The problem of evil in Tert. Adv. Marc. II). J. KNOX, Marcion and the New Testament, London 1943. E. C. BLACKMANN, Marcion and His Influence, London 1949.

of Pauline texts regarding the Law and the Gospel, divine justice and grace, Marcion reached the conviction that the Old Testament and the New Testament are diametrically opposed and do not even contain revelations of the *same* God, but are revelations of *two* different *divine beings*. The wrathful God of the Old Testament is the demiurge who created the world, while the God of love and mercy is the God of the Gospel. This good and highest God was unknown to men until revealed by *Christ*. In the fifteenth year of Tiberius, Christ descended from heaven and after assuming an apparent body began to tell of the God of love and mercy in the synagogue of Capharnaum and to work miracles. But because He was an enemy of the Law, the adherents of the demiurge, whose kingdom He endeavored to destroy, apparently nailed Him to the cross. To these strange articles of faith, Marcion added a strict code of morals. The full-fledged members of his sect were obliged to renounce all the works of the demiurge, especially marriage and the use of meat and wine. In his "Antitheses" which became the Creed of his followers and which has since been lost, he endeavored to prove that there is an irreconcilable opposition between the demands of the two Testaments. Marcion then proceeded to write a *New Testament conformable to his own opinions*. It consisted of the Gospel of St. Luke, without any reference to the childhood of Jesus, and the "Apostolicon" or the first ten Epistles of St. Paul, omitting the pastoral Epistles and the Epistle to the Hebrews. All quotations from the Old Testament and all "Judaizing forgeries" were deleted from Marcion's Bible. — Adolph von *Harnack* sees in Marcion a second St. Paul and the Luther of antiquity. He professes to believe that it was opposition to Marcion that brought the "Catholic" Church into existence, with her fixed canon of the Bible, her doctrine of Redemption and her monarchical episcopacy. But von Harnack idealizes his hero too ardently and overestimates his importance. With clear vision, the Church recognized the devastating character of the heresy, authoritatively condemned it and resolutely warred against it, especially by defending the divine inspiration of the Old Testament. Naturally during such a struggle the Church's form of organization was strengthened and her doctrine clarified and more exactly formulated (§ 22, 2; 29, 5).

2. The **Encratites** were either founded by or at least promoted by the apologist *Tatian* (§ 38 A 3) after his return to the East about 172. As the name indicates they were men of great self-denial and austerity. They renounced marriage and the use of flesh meat and wine, even using water in place of wine in the Eucharistic ritual. For this reason they were later known as Hydroparastates or Aquarians. They taught that Adam was eternally lost and seemed to have held a doctrine of aeons similar to the Valentinians (Iren. I, 28, 1; Clem. Strom. III, 13, 92; Eus. IV, 29). Besides Tatian, a certain *Julius Cassianus* played an important role in the sect (at Antioch or Alexandria?). Some modern scholars (Batiffol, Dobschütz et al), think that the Encratites were not really heretics, but a group of rigorists within the Church and that only later did they adopt some Gnostic ideas.

3. According to Epiphanius (Haer. 56, 1) and others, **Bardesanes** also taught a doctrine of aeons similar to the Valentinians and held that Christ had only an apparent body. Bardesanes (Bar Daisan) of Edessa († 222) was a Syrian of noble birth, a friend of King Abgar IX, and a most prolific writer.

154

Together with his son, *Harmonius*, he embodied his doctrine in beautiful hymns by means of which he attracted many followers. As late as the fourth century, St. Ephraem of Edessa (§ 75, 8 and literature) endeavored to counteract the errors of Bardesanes by writing hymns of truly Catholic sentiment. Recent research seems to indicate that Bardesanes did not teach a Gnostic dualism but rather a sort of strange astrology. Cfr. *F. Haase*, TU 34, 4, 1910; Oriens christ. N. S. 12/14, 1925, 129/40; *H. H. Schaeder*, ZKG 1932, 21/73; L. Cerfaux, RLAnt Chr I, 1180/6; B. Rehm, Philologus 1938, 218/47 (Bardesanes in the Pseudoclementines). — In 1909 a Syrian version of the forty-two Odes of Solomon was rediscovered and is thought by some to be the work of Bardesanes. The Odes show the influence of St. John's Gospel and have a slight Gnostic coloring. — Edition of A. Harnack and J. Flemming, TU 35, 4, 1910; of R. Harris and A. Mingana, 2 vol. Manchester 1916/20. — H. Gressmann in Hennecke, Neutest. Apokr.[2] 437/73. — W. Bauer in Kleine Texte 64, 1933. — R. Abramowski, ZntW 1936, 44/69 (Christ in the Ode of Solomon). — H. Leclercq, DictAC XII, 1903/21. — B. Rehm, see § 28, 4.

4. The artist **Hermogenes**, who migrated from Syria to Carthage toward the end of the second century, was not a true Gnostic. During the time he lived in Syria, his teaching was opposed by the apologist, Theophilus of Antioch (Eus. IV, 24) and when he moved to Carthage he was attacked by Tertullian (Adv. Hermogenem; De censu animae, now lost). Hermogenes approaches Gnosticism by assuming eternal matter as the substratum of creation and shows Gnostic influence in his Christology. Monograph by E. Heintzel, Dissertation 1902.

# § 31.
## Manicheism or Persian Gnosis[1].

1. By the end of the second century primitive Gnosticism had lost its importance and its appeal to the Hellenic-Roman

---

[1] Sources: Serapion of Thmuis against the Manichees, ed. R. P. CASEY, Cambridge Mass. 1931. F. CUMONT et A. KUGENER, Recherches sur le Manichéisme, 3 vol. Brux. 1908/12. A. V. LE COQ, Sb. Berlin 1908, 1909; Abh. Berlin 1911, 1922. P. ALFARIC, Les écritures manichéennes, 2 vol. Paris 1918/19 (from RevHR 67/68); BHLR 1920, 62/98. E. WALDSCHMIDT and W. LENTZ, Abh. Berlin 1926, 1933; Sb. Berlin 1933. F. C. ANDREAS and W. HENNING, Sb. Berlin 1932, 1934; Nachr. Gött. 1932, 1933. W. HENNING, Abh. Berlin 1936, 10. C. SCHMIDT, Neue Originalquellen des Manichäismus aus Ägypten, ZKG 1933, 1/28; SCHMIDT and H. J. POLOTZKY in Sb. Berlin 1933, 3/89; cfr. POLOTSKY, Muséon 1933, 247/71; F. C. BURKITT, JThSt 1933, 258/65; A. GHILAIN, Muséon 1946, 535/45. Manichaean manuscripts in the collection of Chester Beatty and of the Berlin Museum: Homilien, ed. H. J. POLOTSKY, 1934; Kephalaia I, ed. H. J. POLOTSKY, and C. SCHMIDT, 1935/40; A. Manichaean Psalm-Book, Part II, ed. by C. R. C. ALLBERRY and H. IBSCHER, Stuttgart 1938. Literature: F. CHR. BAUR, Das manich. Religionssystem, 1831, reprinted 1928. K. KESSLER, Man I, 1889; RE XII, 192/228. E. DE STOOP, Essai sur la diffusion du Manichéisme dans l'empire Romain, Gand 1909. I. SCHEFTELOWITZ, Die Entstehung der manich. Religion, 1922; ArchRelW 1930, 212/40. O. G. V. WESENDONK, Die Lehre des Mani, 1922;

world. But a few decades later there arose in Babylon and Persia a new form of the Gnostic religion known as *Manicheism* which rapidly assumed the proportions of a world religion and threatened to become a serious rival of Christianity. Its basis was the old Iranian (Persian) dualism of Zoroaster to which was added various elements of Mandaeistic (§ 28, 3), Babylonian-Chaldean, Buddhistic (morals and asceticism), Judaistic and Christian teachings. The Christian elements, which seem to have been supplied by Marcion and Bardesanes, amounted to little more than names, external forms, and usages. The founder of the new religion was *Mani* (Manes, Manichaeus) who was born of Persian parents at Babylon in 216 and was raised in the religion of the Sabians or Mandaeans. At one time information regarding Manicheism was drawn almost entirely from the very unreliable accounts of Christian and Mohammedan opponents. But in 1902 and 1903 important fragments of the writings of Mani and his disciples were found in Chinese Turkestan (Turfan); and in 1930 there were discovered in Egypt important original works in Coptic containing Mani's lectures (Kephalaia) and circular letters together with psalms and sermons of the founder and his disciples, as well as an account of Mani's death. In these works Mani acknowledges his dependence on the "Fathers of Justice," Jesus, Zoroaster, and Buddha, and expresses the aim and hope to be able to preach their religions to the *whole* world. After having preached in *India*, he appeared in *Persia* as the "Apostle of the true God" sometime after 242. For a while he enjoyed the favor of King *Sapor I* (241-272) in whose campaigns he took part. But under King *Bahram* in 277, Mani became the object of the hatred of the Zoroastrian priests and was crucified. A bitter and protracted persecution of his disciples then broke out, not only in Persia, but for political

Acra Orientalia 10, Leyden 1932, 336/63. R. REITZENSTEIN, Nachr. Gött. 1922, 249/60; 1931, 28/58. H. GRESSMANN, ZKG 1922, 154/65. H. H. SCHAEDER, Vorträge der Bibliothek Warburg 1924/25 (1927) 65/157; Z. f. Missionskunde 1935, 65/85. F. C. BURKITT, The Religion of the Manichees, Cambridge 1925. G. MESSINA, Biblica 1929, 313/31 (Manichaeism and Christianity); Cristianesimo, Buddhismo, Manicheismo nell' Asia antica, Rome 1947. A. V. W. JACKSON, Researches in Manichaeism, New York 1932. G. BARDY, DictThC IX, 1841/95. H. LECLERCQ, DictAC X, 1390/441. H. J. POLOTSKY, Art. Manichäismus in RE Pauly-Wissowa Suppl. VI, 1935, 240/71. H. CH. PUECH, Der Begriff d. Erlösung im Manichäismus, Zürich 1937; Le Manichéisme, son fondateur, sa doctrine, Paris 1949. C. R. C. ALLBERRY, Manichaean Studies, JThSt 1938, 337/49; ZntW 1938, 2/10 (the feast of Bema). T. SÄVE-SÖNDERBERGH, Studies in the Coptic Manichaean Psalm-book, 1950.

reasons, in the whole Roman Empire. Diocletian issued an edict against the Manicheans in 296 and the same policy was continued under the Christian Emperors. Sisinnius, Mani's successor as head of the sect, was also crucified and Manichean literature was burned. But in spite of this the sect spread as far as China in the East, to North Africa in the West (where Augustine belonged to it for nine years, § 76, 3) and to Italy and Spain: although its numerical gains were not so great as the territorial expanse would seem to indicate. From the fourth century synods mention the heresy frequently and it engrossed the attention of the Fathers and ecclesiastical writers. Until well into the Middle Ages it remained the fruitful soil from which sprang the Neo-Manichean heresies of the Paulicians, the Bogomils and the Cathari (§ 91, 3; 113).

2. As a religious system Manicheism combined creation and redemption in a great *cosmological* process which Oriental phantasy elaborated into an intricate myth. Two underived beings, a good one (the "Father of Greatness") and a bad one, the kindom of *light* and the kingdom of *darkness*, are eternally and irreconcilably opposed. Both of them develop by emanation into a kingdom of aeons in which the *first man* and the *first devil* play the principal rôles. A mingling of light with darkness gave rise to the present evil world. To free the element of light (which the western Manicheans called the Jesus patibilis), from the matter in which it is imprisoned, and thus effect redemption from the evil of existence, the (lower) heavenly aeon (or the *Jesus* impatibilis) came to earth with an apparent body to teach man the truth about his origin and end. Manichean hymns enthusiastically hail the Jesus impatibilis as the guide of souls. Since, however, His doctrine was misunderstood and falsified, *Mani* himself came as the *Paraclete* promised by Jesus. To accomplish the further liberation of the element of light, Mani taught the *three seals*: the signaculum oris = the prohibition of impure words and the use of flesh meat and wine; the signaculum manus (manum) = the prohibiting of menial work, which is an offense to the world of light; and signaculum sinus = the prohibition of marriage. When the liberation is finally accomplished the visible world will be destroyed in a conflagration which will last fourteen hundred and sixty-eight years. Both kingdoms will then be separated forever. The seals which help to free the element of light are only for the *elect*, that is, the members of the higher class, who were also called the "pure" (catharistae, Aug. Haer. 46). The far larger class of *catechumens* or "hearers" (auditores) were obliged only to the observance of the Ten Commandments. *Prayer* and *fasting* constituted an important part of the cult. It appears that the higher class also had esoteric practices consisting of a sort of *baptism* and a *Lord's Supper*. So far as is known, they kept only one feast, that of the "cathedra" (βῆμα), a memorial celebration of *Mani's* execution and ascent into heaven. Augustine says (l. c.) that the Manichean hierarchy consisted of the head of the sect, the successor of Mani, twelve teachers, seventy-two bishops, and an undetermined number of priests and deacons.

## § 32.
### Trinitarian Controversies. The Monarchians[1].

1. The central point of Christian belief was the doctrine of *one* God in three Persons, Father, Son (Logos), and the Holy Ghost (§ 27, 1). The oldest writings of the patristic period speak of the relationship of the three divine Persons to one another, especially of the Son to the Father; but the expressions used are by no means clear. The Redeemer was believed to be God and the Son of God, but no attempt was made to explain His nature and His relation to God the Father. It was only during the course of the second century when Judaistic and Gnostic heresies made their appearance and falsified Christian doctrine that the matter became the subject of serious concern. And then the principal question was: how belief in the *divinity of the Son* could be reconciled with the *unity of God*. The apologists and some of the ecclesiastical writers of the third century sought to solve the problem by following the theosophy of *Philo*, the Alexandrian Jew (§ 6, 2). Accordingly they distinguished a Logos within and a Logos outside the Godhead (λόγος ἐνδιάθετος and προφορικός). And while they held that He was eternal they thought that His hypostatization, that is, His distinction in personality from the Father depended on the creation of the world. In other words, they assumed that the Logos was originally the wisdom of the Father, but, in order to create and govern the world, was released from the inner life of the Godhead or begotten and thus became a distinct Person (Justin Apol. II, 6; even more clearly

---

[1] See the histories of Dogma, etc. (PRÜMM, PRESTIGE etc.) in § 27. J. KUHN, Kath. Dogmatik II, 1857. H. HAGEMANN, see § 21. G. KRÜGER, Das Dogma von der Dreieinigk. u. Gottmenschheit, 1905. A. HARNACK, Monarchianismus, RE 13, 303/36. J. LEBRETON, Les théories du Logos, Paris 1906; Hist. du dogme de la Trinité des origines au concile de Nicée I⁶, Paris 1927, II, 1928; RHE 1923, 481/506; 1924, 5/37 (the break between popular belief and theology in the third century). CH. E. RAVEN, Apollinarism. Essay on the Development of Christian Doctrine, Cambridge 1923. L. CHOPPIN, La Trinité chez les Pères Apostoliques, Lille 1925. Art. Monarchisme by G. BARDY, DictThC X, 2193/2209; by H. LECLERCQ, DictAC XI, 1947/64. R. ARNOU, Platonisme des Pères, DictThC XII, 2258/392; id. De „Platonismo" Patrum, Rome 1935. H. STORK, Die sog. Melchisedekianer (= Theodotianer), 1928. F. J. DÖLGER, AntChrist 1929, 271/90 (theology of the Logos) M. KRIEBEL, Studien zur älteren Entwicklung der abendländ. Trinitätslehre bei Tertullian u. Novatian, Diss. 1932. V. A. S. LITTLE, The Christology of the Apologists, London 1934. E. PETERSON, Der Monotheismus als polit. Problem, 1935. C. W. LOWRY, JThSt 1936, 225/40 (Origen's teaching on the Trinity). B. CAPELLE, RechThAM 1937, 109/24 (Hippolytus on the Logos). H. SCHÖNE, in Pisciculi, Festschrift. F. J. DÖLGER, 1939, 252/65 (anonymous pamphlete against the Theodotians in Eusebius). G. QUISPEL, see § 28, 1.

Theoph. Ad Autol. II, 10—22; Hippol. Philos. X, 33; Tert. Adv. Prax. 6, 7; Orig. De princ. I, 3, 5; C. Cels. III, 34; VIII, 15; In Joan. t. II, c. 2). These views subordinated the Son to the Father because they questioned the eternity of His subsistence as a Person and made His generation not so much an eternal and necessary act as a temporal and free act of God. On the other hand, however, since the unity of God as well as the divinity of the Son was preserved, this so-called *Subordinationism* did no particular harm at the time; although the theory was faulty. But another theory emerged about the same time which did seriously threaten the faith and hence had to be eradicated.

2. Some Christians overemphasized the *unity* of God and held that the Redeemer was but a *man*, although born miraculously of the Virgin Mary and the Holy Ghost and endowed with the power (δύναμις) of God. Others thought that He was actually the *Father* appearing in that particular way (modus). But either view did violence to the Trinity; the one denied the divinity of the Son, the other the distinction of Persons. Tertullian (Adv. Prax. 3) tells us that those who held either of these views adopted the slogan 'Monarchiam tenemus,' wherefore they were called Monarchians. Depending on which view was held they were distinguished as *Dynamic* or *Ebionitic* (§ 28, 1) *Monarchians* (Adoptionists) and *Modal* Monarchians or *Patripassians*. The attack on these errors was led principally by the Roman Church.

3. As far as we know, the founder of the **Dynamic Monarchians** was **Theodotus** the Tanner (σκυτεύς) of Byzantium, a man of more than ordinary learning. He taught that Christ, a mere man (ψιλὸς ἄνθρωπος) was filled with the power of God on the occasion of His baptism. About 190 Theodotus went to Rome where his error drew upon him the excommunication of Pope *Victor* (189—198). His disciples, *Asclepiodotus* and *Theodotus* the Younger, or the Money Changer, endeavored to found their own congregation over which they placed the confessor *Natalis* as bishop (first anti-pope). After a short time Natalis returned to the Church. A few decades later the same error was defended by a certain *Artemon* (Artemas) apparently also at Rome. But after the middle of the third century the error attracted still more attention due to the efforts of **Paul of Samosata**[1], Bishop of Antioch. The synodal letter issued by the

---

[1] M. J. ROUTH, Reliquiae sacrae III², Oxford 1846, 300 ff.   G. BARDY, Paul de Samosate, Louvain ²1929.   F. LOOFS, Paulus v. Samosata, TU 44, 5.

bishops who condemned him characterize him as an avaricious and vain man of the world, who was more interested in the position he held as regent for Queen Zenobia of Palmyra than in his office as bishop. Insisting on the unity of God in nature and person, Paul declared that Jesus was a mere man, born of the Virgin Mary; and that the impersonal Logos or wisdom of God, which had been given to Moses and the prophets in a lesser degree, dwelt in Him "as in a temple." The union between the Redeemer and God existed, not because it was natural for the Redeemer to be so united, but because God willed it. The first meeting of bishops to discuss Paul's teaching (264) was without result. But in a second great synod at Antioch 268 in which the learned priest Malchion exposed the heresy, Paul was excommunicated and *Domnus* was named to succeed him. Paul, however, refused to quit the see until the conquest of Antioch by Emperor Aurelian in 272 (§ 16, 3). His followers, called Paulians or Paulianists, were quite numerous and the General Council of Nicaea 325 (can. 19) was obliged to take cognizance of them. The renowned priest, *Lucian* of Antioch, the founder of the exegetical school of Antioch (§ 39, 5; 74, 2), was probably of their number. Lucian, who was an extreme Origenist, taught a strict subordinationism which he endeavored to prove from Scripture. As a follower of Paul, he was under excommunication for a long time (Theodoret, H. E. I, 3) but appears to have been reconciled during the Diocletian persecution. He died as a martyr in 312. The sources now available contain very little information regarding Lucian. Some few scholars (Loofs, Bardy et al.) think that Lucian, the excommunicated follower of Paul of Samosata is not the same person as Lucian, the exegete and martyr. The school in which he taught *(Syllucianists)* became very influential in the East and produced a number of learned bishops as well as the heretic *Arius* (§ 47, 2).

Formerly it was thought that the earliest exponents of Ebionitic Monarchianism were those Christians of Asia Minor, and later of the West, to whom Epiphanius (Haer. 51) refers sarcastically as *Alogi* (i. e. without reason). But this can scarcely have been the case. The Alogi did oppose the fanatical

---

1924 (differs widely from Bardy in his views on the person and teaching of Paul of Samosata). On the views of Bardy and Loofs: HARNACK, Sb. Berlin 1924, 130/51; LOOFS, ThLZ 1924, 457/62; 1925, 227/32; F. DIEKAMP, ThRev 1925, 201/10; E. AMANN, RevSR 1925, 328/42; H. V. SODEN, ZKG 1925, 161/70. ED. SCHWARTZ, Sb. München 1927, 3 (supposed correspondence between Dionysius of Alexandria and Paul of Samosata). G. BARDY, Lucien d'Ant., DictThC IX, 1024/31; RechSR 1932, 437/62 (Lucian and his school); Recherches sur Saint Lucien d'Antioche et son école, Paris 1936.

Montanists (§ 34) and questioned the genuinity of the Joannine writings which the Montanists were misusing. It is quite possible that the rejection of those writings led Epiphanius to conclude that they also denied the divinity of Christ. Cfr. *Th. Zahn*, Gesch. des neutest. Kanons I, 1888, 220 ff.; II, 1892, 967 ff. — *P. de Labriolle*, La crise Montaniste, Paris 1913, 190 ff. 283 ff. — *C. Schmidt*, TU 43, 1919, 420 ff. 726 ff. — *A. Bludau*, see § 28.

The Synod of Antioch 268 refused to accept the proposition that the Son is equal to the Father (ὁμοούσιος τῷ πατρί) which Nicaea (325) later raised to a dogma (§ 47, 3). The reason for Antioch's attitude was probably, as Hilary (De sym. 81, 86) says, because Paul ascribed to God and the impersonal Logos the same substance (eadem vel una substantia). Epiphanius (Haer. 65, 1) gives the same reason, but puts it more clearly. He says that Paul denied that the Logos had its own subsistence, but was the same substance and person as the Father. Other less probable explanations are found in Athanasius (De syn. 45) and Basil the Great (Ep. 52, 1). Cfr. P. Galtier, RechSR 1922, 30/45; Bardy, Paul de Sam., 251 ff.; Loofs 148 ff.

4. The first known proponent of **Modal Monarchianism**[1] was **Noëtus** of Smyrna, very likely the bishop of a city in Asia Minor, who was condemned by a synod about 190. The confessor *Praxeas* also of Asia Minor transplanted the error to Rome at the time of Pope *Victor* (189—198). From there he passed over to Carthage where Tertullian confronted him in public discussion as well as in a special treatise (Adv. Prax.) and forced him to retract. Shortly afterwards *Epigonus*, a deacon and disciple of Noëtus endeavored to spread the heresy at Rome and succeeded in forming a Patripassian party with *Cleomenes* and *Sabellius* (vide infra no. 6) at its head. These manuevers caused great consternation among the Christians at Rome. The chief opponent of the Modalists was the learned and contentious priest, *Hippolytus* (C. Haeresim Noeti; Philos. IX, 7—10; X, 27; cfr. 39, 4), who himself taught a form of subordination of the Logos (Philos. IX, 12; X, 33). Pope *Zephyrin* (198—217), a man of little theological learning, endeavored to settle

---

[1] V. MACCHIORO, L'eresia Noetiana, Napoli 1921 (cfr. H. KOCH, ThLZ 1923, 86). G. ESSER, Wer war Praxeas?, Progr. Bonn 1910 (also P. DE LABRIOLLE, BullLA 1911, 228/33). J. DÖLLINGER, Hippolytus u. Kallistus, 1853. A. D'ALÈS, La théologie de S. Hippolyte, Paris 1906. ANONYMUS im Kath. 1905 II, 1 ff. 112 ff. et passim. K. GRAF PREYSING, ZkTh 1914, 421/45; 1917, 595/97; 1918, 177/86; 1926, 604/8; 1928, 225/30 (Hippolytus and Callistus). A. HARNACK, Sb. Berlin 1923, 51/7 (Zephyrin's dogmatic declaration). K. MÜLLER, ZntW 1924, 231/4 (Schism of Hippolytus). G. LA PIANA, HarvThR 1925, 201/77 (the Roman Church at the end of the second century). B. CAPELLE, RevBén 1926, 321/30 (Zephyrin not a Modalist). ATHANASIUS, Epistola de sententia Dionysii ep. Alex., in Athanasius Werke, ed. H. G. OPITZ (see § 47) II, 1, 46/67. A. ANWANDER, ThQ 1921, 190/219 (Alexandrian teaching on the Trinity after Origen). K. MÜLLER, ZntW 1925, 278/85 (Dionysius of Alex.). H. G. OPITZ, in Studies presented to K. Lake, London 1937, 41/53 (Dionysius and the Libyans).

the controversy. So also did his adviser and successor, the confessor and deacon *Callistus*, who had risen from the condition of a slave to the highest ecclesiastical dignity. It is by no means correct to assert (as Harnack and some others do), that Modalism was sanctioned by the Roman Church during the reign of three popes (Victor, Zephyrin and Callistus). Rather all three strove earnestly to defend a position midway between Modalism and Subordinationism, although there was not as yet an exact and accepted terminology. In an official declaration Zephyrin stressed the divinity of Christ and the oneness of nature in God, but, to the delight of the Patripassians, he did not make a clear distinction of persons. The controversy was still raging when *Callistus* became pope (217—222). He excommunicated Sabellius and accused Hippolytus of Ditheism (δίθεοί ἐστε, Philos. IX, 12, 16). Hippolytus, envious of Callistus' elevation to the papacy, began to attack him bitterly and set himself up as bishop of his own partisans. The group comprised only a small minority of the Christian community of Rome, but due to the high rank of some of the rebels, they were able to exert an influence out of proportion to their number. The schism continued during the two following pontificates (*Urban* 222—230 and *Pontian* 230—235). In the persecution of Maximinus Thrax both Pope Pontian and Hippolytus were banished to Sardinia 235, where they soon died (§ 15, 17). The fact that Hippolytus has since been honored by the Church as a martyr is good reason for believing that he was reconciled with the Church before his death.

5. Besides being active at Rome and in North Africa, the Patripassians played a conspicuous rôle in *Arabia* and in the Libyan *Pentapolis*. Bishop *Beryllus* of Bostra inclined toward the heresy, but renounced it at the Synod of Bostra 244 after Origen had succeeded in convincing him of his error. Bishop *Dionysius* the Great of Alexandria (§ 39, 3) combatted the heresy in Libya by means of pastoral letters, but was not always fortunate in the use of terms. In accusing the Patripassians of identifying the persons, he stressed the distinction between Father and Son in such a way as to deny their essential unity. He referred to the Son as a creature of the Father and as something that had been given being (ποίημα καὶ γενητόν). The Egyptian priests, therefore, reported him to Pope Dionysius (260—268) who censured him severely. This clash of the two Dionysiuses (260—261) was a prelude to the later Arian controversy. The Egyptian Dionysius was able to

vindicate himself and accepted fully the teaching of Rome that Father and Son are one in nature (Athanasius, Ep. de sententia Dionysii). Irenaeus and Tertullian deserve credit for their early defense of the true doctrine in the West.

6. Before reaching Egypt, the controversy had been concerned only with the relation between the Father and Son. But now a similar question arose regarding the *Holy Ghost*. The same **Sabellius**, who was mentioned above, first directed attention to the problem. According to later accounts, he was a native of Libya, but began to expound his idea at *Rome*. He assumed that God had revealed Himself in three ways: as the Father in creation and in giving the Commandments; as the Son in the Redemption; and as the Holy Ghost in the work of sanctification. He represented these various ways of revelation as πρόσωπα (= masks worn by actors in playing different rôles) and succeeded in deceiving many as to the true nature of his doctrine. The error persisted for a long time and was generally known as Sabellianism. In fact, from the end of the third century *Sabellianism* was the only term used in the East to designate Modal Monarchianism.

## § 33.
## Eschatological Notions. Chiliasm[1].

1. The first Christians, indeed, the Apostles themselves, believed that Christ would soon return for the final judgment of mankind *(parousia)*. It was only gradually that they began to understand that Christ's second coming was not so imminent and that they began to adapt themselves to the idea that the Church was to endure for a long time. But the *expectation of the impending Judgement* lent a deep earnestness to the thought and life of the early Christians and induced them to practice the greatest austerities (§ 24, 1; 26, 2). At the same time it opened the way to some unhealthy fantasy. Such was **Chiliasm** (or Millenarianism), the belief in a thousand-year reign of the Messias on earth. This notion had its roots in the apocalyptics of late Judaism where the Messianic prophecies of the Old Testament were given a very realistic interpretation. Many Christians thought that the Kingdom of

---

[1] P. VOLZ, Die Eschatologie der jüd. Gemeinde im neutest. Zeitalter, 1934. L. ATZBERGER, Gesch. d. christl. Eschatologie in der vornicän. Zeit, 1896. F. TILLMANN, Die Wiederkunft Christi nach d. paulin. Briefen, 1909. L. GRY, Le Millénarisme, Paris 1904. H. WINDISCH, Der messian. Krieg u. das Urchristentum, 1909. J. ROHR, Bibl. Zeitfr. IV, 5, ³1922. B. RIGAUX, L'Antéchrist et l'opposition au Royaume Messianique dans l'Ancien et le Nouveau Test., Diss. Louvain. 1932. F. ALCANIZ, Ecclesia patristica et Millenarismus, Granada 1933. M. GOGUEL, RevHR 1946, 124/69; 1947/8, 103/61; (Pneumatism and Eschatology in the Early Church). B. BOTTE, RechThAM 1948, 5/17 (Traces of Chiliasm in western liturgy).

Glory referred to the Lord's second coming and put this construction on the most abstruse passages of St. John's Apocalypse (chapters 20 and 21) where it is said that after a time Satan shall be bound for a *thousand years* during which time the just shall arise and reign with Christ (χίλια ἔτη, hence the name). After Satan has been loosed and overcome there will be a second general resurrection followed by the General Judgement and there will be a new heaven and a new earth. The intense and protracted sufferings of the persecutions disposed many Christian confessors to look for such an outcome just as the oppression of Roman rule had disposed the Jews to look for a Messias. Hence we find Chiliasm in the Judaistic-Christian sects of Cerinthus and the Ebionites as well as among Christians otherwise orthodox. The first proponents of Chiliasm were the unknown author of the *Epistle of Barnabas* and *Papias* of Hieropolis (§ 37, 2, 6). Later it was embraced by *Justin, Irenaeus* and temporarily by *Hippolytus,* who was opposed on this point by the Roman priest *Caius.* Victorinus of Pettau and Lactantius (§ 38—40) also inclined toward Chiliasm. But it was to the fanatical *Montanists* and *Tertullian,* as one of them, that Chiliasm made the strongest appeal.

2. In the beginning Chiliasm was confined chiefly to *Asia Minor;* but about the middle of the third century it became notably strong in *Egypt.* Bishop *Nepos* of Arsinoe defended it in a work called "Refutation of the Allegorizers," directed against the Alexandrian theologians (Clement and Origen) whose allegorical interpretation of the Apocalypse destroyed the basis of the Chiliasts' argument. After the death of Nepos, the Egyptian Chiliasts left the Church; but *Dionysius* the Great of Alexandria, in a three-day disputation with *Korakion,* then the head of the sect, succeeded in convincing them of their error and restoring them to the fold. However, it was not debate that caused Chiliasm to decline; it was rather the improved fortunes of the Church under Constantine. And while the notion ceased to annoy the early Church, it appeared during the Middle Ages and continues to crop up in various sectarian movements down to the present day.

## § 34.

## Montanism[1].

1. While Gnosticism preached a form of Christianity with a cosmology accommodated to Hellenic culture, there were groups within the Church

---

[1] N. BONWETSCH, Gesch. des Montanismus, 1881; RE 13, 417/26; Kleine Texte 129, 1914. A. ZISTERER, ThQ 1892, 475/82 (Cataphrygians). P. DE LABRIOLLE, La crise Montaniste, Paris 1913; Les sources de l'hist. du Montanisme, Fribourg-Paris 1913 (cfr. N. BONWETSCH, Gött. Gel. Anz. 1916, 411/9). W. M. CALDER, Philadelphia and Montanism, Bulletin of J. Rylands Library (Manchester) 7, 1923, 309/54. A. FAGGIOTTO, L'eresia dei Frigi, Rome 1924; La diasporà catafrigia, Rome 1924. W. SCHEPELERN, Der Montanismus u. die phryg. Kulte, transl. from Danish by W. BAUER, 1929. H. BACHT, ThQ 1944, 1/18 (Prophetical inspiration in pre-Montanist times). W. M. RAMSAY, Byzantion 1931, 1/35. A. EHRHARD, Die Kirche der Martyrer, 1932, 227/65.

who demanded an austerity of life so great as to amount to complete renunciation of the world. This tendency reached its culmination in *Montanism*, a strange admixture of eschatological ideas, unbridled religious enthusiasm and rigorism. This sect originated with *Montanus*, a recently baptized convert to Christianity, said to have been a priest of Cybele. Epiphanius says that he first appeared in 156 or 157; but Eusebius (Chronicle) is propably more correct in giving the date as 172. He began his work as prophet and reformer at Ardabau on the border between Phrygia and Moesia, by claiming to be the Paraclete promised by Jesus (John 14:16, 26) and announcing that the age of the Holy Ghost had begun. At the same time, two female companions, *Priscilla (Prisca)* and *Maximilla* were filled with the "Spirit." The fanatics soon had a large following, all of whom accepted the "new prophecy" enthusiastically. The burden of Montanus' preaching was the speedy approach of Christ's Kingdom when the heavenly Jerusalem would descend upon the Phrygian city of Pepuza. Preparation for this event was to be made by a strict life and by introducing into the Church a higher morality which would bring her to maturity and perfection. *Second* marriages were forbidden (in fact, even first marriages were discouraged), the *fast* made more rigorous, the station fasts (§ 25, 1) were extended until evening two weeks of the year, Saturday and Sunday excepted. During the fasts only xerophagiae (dry foods) could be taken. *Flight* from persecution was not allowed; rather Montanists were encouraged to seek martyrdom. Those *guilty* of any one of the *capital sins* (§ 24, 1) could never be reconciled with the Church, and during divine service *virgins* as well as married women were obliged to wear *veils*.

2. The Montanists were generally called *Phrygians* from their place of origin and sometimes, though erroneously, Cataphrygians. They themselves used the term *Pneumatici* to distinguish their members from Catholics who were known as Psychici. The movement spread rapidly in Asia Minor; at Thyatira the entire Christian congregation went over to it. In several of the first synods known to history, the Catholic bishops condemned Montanism and several apologists, especially Miltiades, Apollonaris and Melito (§ 38 A 8) wrote against it. When these efforts proved fruitless, a rupture with the Church became inevitable. The Church of Asia Minor was the first to exclude them from its communion. During the reign of Pope Victor or Pope Zephyrin, the Monarchian Praxeas (§ 32, 4) called the attention of the Romans to the true nature of Montanist teaching; whereupon the Church of Rome condemned the sect although previously it had regarded the Montanists as a group of innocuous zealots. The Roman priest *Caius* (§ 10, 2; 33, 1) wrote against and publicly disputed with Proclus the Roman Montanist. But in spite of every effort made to check it, Montanism continued to grow. It reached *North Africa* in the first years of the third century and about 205 it struck a responsive chord in the heart of the great *Tertullian*.

J. ZEILLER, RHE 1934, 845/51 (Montanism in Illyrica 340/83). G. BARDY, DictThC X, 2355/70. R. A. KNOX, Enthusiasm, Oxford 1950.

From then on he became its most renowned proponent. He went so far as to hold that ecstacy is the proper form of revelation and defended all the principal tenets of the sect in a series of special treatises (De ecstasi [lost] De exhortatione castitatis, De monogamia, De virginibus velandis, De fuga in persecutione, De jejunio adversus psychicos, De pudicitia). All of these works exhibit a growing bitterness against the "Psychici", the members of the Church he once defended so valiantly. The sect was long-lived. In the land of its origin, it seems later to have incorporated many customs of the orgiastic cults of Phrygia. In other places it split into groups variously known as Aeschinists, Proclians, Quintillians, Priscillians, Tertullianists, etc. Many of its adherents adopted additional errors, as, for example, the *Aeschinists*, who accepted the beliefs of the Patripassians (§ 32, 4), while others joined the Novatianists. Constantine the Great issued several severe decrees against the Montanists in the fourth century; but they are still mentioned in the seventh and eighth centuries in measures taken against the sect by the Council of Constantinople in 682 (can. 95) and by Leo the Isaurian in 722.

## § 35.

## Disputes Regarding Penance:
## The Schisms of Novatian, Felicissimus and Melitius.

1. The question of penance which had caused such serious dissension in the Roman Church under Pope Callistus (§ 24, 2) eventually led to a schism which lasted several centuries. The vacancy in the Roman See caused by the death of Pope Fabian (§ 16, 1) was not filled until the spring of 251 when the majority of the Christian community elected the priest *Cornelius* (251—253), while a minority favored the learned priest **Novatian**[1]. (§ 40, 4). As one of the more prominent members of of the presbyteral college of Rome, Novatian had expected to be chosen and in a spirit of wounded pride allowed the minority to proclaim him bishop of Rome. A few priests and a large number of confessors supported him in his claim. Immediately the situation became grave. For while Cornelius promised ecclesiastical pardon to those who had *lapsed* during the persecution, Novatian refused it and to express his opposition went so far as to deny pardon to the dying lapsi to whom it had always been granted. Later the same severity was extended to the other capital sins. The *Novatians* demanded nothing less than a Church of "the pure", of "saints", and hence in the East were later known as *"cathari."* Catholics who went over to them were *rebaptized* (§ 22, 3). In a synod of 60 Italian bishops held at Rome 251 they were excommunicated. Cyprian of Carthage and Dionysius also took action against them. Due to their feverish zeal, the Novatians spread rapidly, especially in the East (in Syria, Asia Minor, Palestine, etc.) where many Montanists

---

[1] A. D'ALÈS, Novatien, Paris 1925. E. AMANN, DictThC XI, 816/49. R. JANIN, Échos d'Orient 1929, 385/97 (Novatians in the East).

joined them. Groups of Novatianists were to be found in the East until well into the seventh century. In the fourth century they possessed three churches in Constantinople. Toward the end of the fourth century a group of Novatianists called *Sabbatians* after Sabbatius, a converted Jew of Constantinople, followed the teaching of the Protopaschites in keeping the date of Easter (§ 25,3).

2. About the same time that the Novatian schism began at Rome, the Church of Carthage had difficulty of a similar nature. The lapsi who had obtained libelli pacis from the confessors (§ 24, 2) unreasonably demanded immediate reconciliation with the Church, while *Cyprian*, basing himself on older canons, insisted upon delaying it until the penitents had proved themselves. A group of ambitious clerics led by the priest *Novatus*, contested Cyprian's episcopal authority and chose *Fortunatus* as antibishop. This schism, however, was named after **Felicissimus**, a deacon, who led the rebel forces. It lasted but a short time. It was at this time that Cyprian wrote his splendid work De catholicae ecclesiae unitate (§ 40, 3).

3. In the beginning of the fourth century a schism arose in Egypt, occasioned, it appears, by Bishop **Melitius** (Melerius) of Lycopolis in the Thebaid. Because of the varying accounts found in the sources it is now difficult to determine the exact cause. Epiphanius (Haer. 68) thinks that it was a question of the penitential discipline and says that a quarrel ensued between Archbishop *Peter* of Alexandria († 311 as a martyr) and Bishop Melitius over the milder practice of the former and the severity of the latter. However, those documents dating from the beginning of the schism speak only of irregular ordinations of Melitius in dioceses other than his own and of his undue interference in the affairs of Alexandria while Peter was in prison. Athanasius (C. Arian. 59) and Socrates (H. E. I, 6) relate that Melitius denied the faith during the Diocletian persecution, but their only authority for such a statement seems to be a later biased rumor. The account of Epiphanius and the three documents may be reconciled by assuming that Melitius undertook the ordinations to extend his influence and spread his strict views. The schism spread over a great part of Egypt and lasted for a century. The Melitians made common cause with the Arians (§ 47, 3; 48, 2) and set up their own bishop in opposition to Athanasius. Recently discovered papyri reveal that Athanasius proceeded against them with the support of the secular arm (334—335). — Cfr. *H. Achelis*, RE 13, 558/62; 24, 83. — *E. Schwartz*, Nachr. Göttingen 1905, 164/87. — *K. Müller*, Abh. Berlin 1922, 3. — *H. Idris Bell*, Jews and Christians in Egypt, Oxford 1924; also E. Schwartz, DLZ 1924, 2096 ff.; *K. Holl*, Sb. Berlin 1925, 18/31 (and in Ges. Aufsätze z. KG. II, 1928, 283/97); *A. d'Alès*, RHE 1926, 5/26. — *F. H. Kettler*, Der melitian. Streit in Ägypten, Diss. 1934; ZntW 1936, 155/93.

4. During the *Diocletian persecution* the Roman Church was again disturbed by the problem of penance. Pope *Marcellus* (307—308) was obliged to contend with lapsi who claimed the right to receive Communion without submitting to the customary penance. His successor *Eusebius* (308) was accused of laxism (rigorism ?) by a certain *Heraclius* and his adherents. We derive our information regarding these disturbances from inscriptions composed by Pope

Damasus (§ 76, 6), who indicates that they became so violent that the Emperor Maxentius banished Heraclius and both popes. Cfr. Liber Pontif. ed. Duchesne I, 164/7. *E. Schwartz,* Nachr. Gött. 1904, 531 f.; *E. Caspar,* ZKG 1927, 321/33.

# CHAPTER V
## ECCLESIASTICAL LITERATURE AND LEARNING[1]

### § 36.
### The Development
### of Ecclesiastical Literature during the First Three Centuries.

Excepting the books of the New Testament, the earliest Christian literary productions began to appear, as far as we know, in

---

[1] Collections of works of the Fathers § 2. 9. HIERONYMUS u. GENNADIUS, De viris illustribus, see § 76, 2. 9. R. CEILLIER, Histoire générale des auteurs sacrés et ecclésiastiques, 23 vol. Paris 1729/63; nouv. éd., 16 vol. 1858/69. J. A. MÖHLER, Patrologie I, 1840. O. BARDENHEWER, Gesch. der altkirchl. Literatur, 5 vols. 1902/32; I ²1913, II ²1914, III ²1923; Patrologie, ³1910. G. KRÜGER, Gesch. der altchristl. Lit. in den 3 ersten Jhh., 1895; Nachträge 1897. A. HARNACK, Gesch. der altchristl. Lit. bis Eusebius I (tradition and present state), 1893, II (Chronology), 1897/1904. P. BATIFFOL, La litt. grecque, Paris ⁴1905 (Anciennes littératures chrét. I). A. EHRHARD, Die altchristl. Lit. u. ihre Erforschung 1880—1900, 2 parts 1894/1900. G. RAUSCHEN, Grundriß der Patrologie, 1903, revised by B. ALTANER, ¹⁰/¹¹1931; a more thorough revision was made by B. ALTANER, Patrologie, ²1950 (good presentation and bibliography). H. KIHN, Patrologie, 2 vols. 1904/8. H. JORDAN, Gesch. d. altchristl. Lit., 1911. O. STÄHLIN, Die altchristl. griech. Lit., in W. V. CHRIST-W. SCHMID, Gesch. d. griech. Lit. II, 2 ⁶1924. J. TIXERONT, Précis de Patrologie, Paris ⁵1923; Mél. de Patrologie et d'hist. des dogmes, Paris 1920. H. EIBL, Augustin u. die Patristik, 1923. E. NORDEN, Die antike Kunstprosa II, 1898. F. CAYRÉ, Précis de patrologie, 2 vol. Paris 1927/30, English transl. by H. HOWITT, Manual of Patrology, 2 vols. Paris 1936. A. PUECH, Histoire de la litt. grecque chrétienne (to c. 400), 3 vol. Paris 1928/30. G. BARDY, Litt. grecque chrét., Paris 1928; En lisant les Pères, Paris 1933. U. MANNUCCI-A. CASAMASSA, Istutizioni di patrologia, 2 vol. Rome ⁶1948/50. B. STEIDLE, Patrologia, 1937; Die Kirchenväter, Einführung in ihr Leben u. Werk, 1939. J. DE GHELLINCK, Patristique et moyen-âge II: Introduction et complément à l'étude de la patrist., Brüssel 1947. J. QUASTEN, Patrology I, Utrecht 1950 II, ib. 1952. O. KARRER, Urchristl. Zeugen, 1937. E. AMANN, Pères de l'Église, DictThC XII, 1192/1215. H. LECLERCQ, Lettres chrétiennes, DictAC VIII, 2683/2885. H. FUCHS, Antike 1929, 107/19 (early Christian Church and ancient culture). G. BARDY, RevSR 1932, 1/28 (the Church and instruction in the first three centuries). CH. N. COCHRANE, Christianity and Classical Culture, New York 1940. É. GILSON and PH. BÖHNER, Gesch. der christl. Philosophie I: patrist. Philosophie, 1936. H. MEYER, Gesch. der abendländischen Weltanschauung II, 1947. A. SIEGMUND, Die Überlieferung der griech. christl. Literatur in der latein. Kirche bis zum 12. Jh., 1949. D. VAN DEN EYNDE, see § 22, 2. J. DE GHELLINCK, Gregorianum 1933, 185/218; Mél. F. Cavallera, Toulouse 1948, 55/85 (Progress and problems of of patrology). G. KRÜGER, HarvThR 1933, 173/321 (research in ancient Christian literature 1921/30). B. ALTANER, ThRev 1948, 11/6 (Patristic research in the U.S.A.). SPECIAL works on ancient Christian Latin literature, see below §§ 40 and 74. For further literature in the patristic section (§§ 36 ff.

the last decade of the first century. Since the seventeenth century the authors of such works have been known as *Apostolic Fathers* because they themselves had been disciples of the Apostles or at least had received their knowledge of Christianity from men who had known the Apostles personally. In form and content these writings resemble the Scriptures, especially the Pauline Epistles. The early Church esteemed such writings highly as may be judged from the fact that they were often included in manuscripts of the Bible and were read publicly at divine services. Thus the Codex Sinaiticus contains the Epistle of Barnabas and the Shepherd of Hermas, while Codex Alexandrinus contains the Epistles of Clement. Both of these MSS are now in the British Museum, the former having been acquired in 1934.

About 125, a new type of Christian literature — the *apologies* — began to appear. The *apologists* defended Christianity against the attacks of pagans and Jews and later against heretics and schismatics, especially against Gnosticism. Alongside of the apologists there sprang up another class of writings, called forth not by attacks from without, but rather by the peculiar *inner* needs of the Church herself.

Finally about 200, even before apologetic literature had ceased to be necessary, the Hellenic East, specifically *Alexandria*, became the birthplace of *theology properly so called*. The new science owed its origin to a lively interest in matters of faith and undertook a more systematic exposition of the truths of faith, together with an explanation of the Scriptures and an application of Christian teaching to Christian life. Up to this time the Fathers and ecclesiastical writers had used the *Greek* language almost exclusively, but now, especially in North Africa, *Latin* also became a vehicle of Christian literature.

## § 37.

## The Apostolic Fathers[1].

The earliest Christian works were written to edify and instruct; to confirm, explain and intensify oral instruction. As the oldest

---

and 74 ff.) the reader is referred to BARDENHEWER and ALTANER. On the meaning of * and ** see § 2, 9d and e.

[1] O. GEBHARDT, A. HARNACK, TH. ZAH, Patrum apostolicorum opera, 3 Fasc. 1875/77, I ²1876/78; Editio minor, ⁶1920. F. X. FUNK, Patres Apostolici, 2 vol. ²1901, vol. II³ par F. DIEKAMP, 1913; small edition: Die Apostol. Väter, ²1906, revised by K. BIHLMEYER I, 1924. J. B. LIGHTFOOT, The

sources, after the New Testament, they are of inestimable value for the history of dogma, as well as for the history of the organization, piety and customs of the early Church. Although they were but brief treatises of little or no erudition, they were evidently intended to be of more than passing interest for a large circle of readers. They were originally written in Greek very much in the style of the Epistles.

1. In 1833 Metropolitan Bryennios of Constantinople discovered and published the **Didache**[1] or Doctrine of the Twelve Apostles (Διδαχὴ τῶν δώδεκα ἀποστόλων). This work by an unknown author, is a sort of religious manual in two parts. The first part is a moral catechism (c. 1—6) or instruction on the Two Ways: one of Life and one of Death. The second part is a ritual, treating of baptism, fasting, prayer and the Eucharist, with prescriptions regarding the reception of apostles (i. e., itinerant preachers), prophets and brethren from other congregations; it also lays down rules for the proper observance of Sunday and for the election of bishops and deacons. The little work bears the stamp of great antiquity and was probably composed about 150 in Syria or Palestine. (For its relationship to the Epistle of Barnabas, see below). It was held in high esteem and many considered it on a par with the Scriptures. During the

---

Apostolic Father (Clement, Ignatius, Polycarp), 5 vols. London 1886/90 (vol. III—V ²1889). H. HEMMER, G. OGER, A. LAURENT, A. LELONG, Les Pères Apostoliques, 4 vol. Paris 1907/12, I—II ²1926 (in Textes et documents, see § 2, 9 f.). G. BOSIO, I Padri Apostolici, 2. vol. Turin 1940/2. Die Apostol. Väter, Germ. tr. by FR. ZELLER, 1918 (BKV 35); in E. HENNECKE, Neutest. Apokryphen, ²1924; with commentary by R. KNOPF, W. BARUER, H. WINDISCH, M. DIBELIUS, in Handb. zum N.T., ed. H. LIETZMANN, suppl. 4 parts 1920/23. W. ROSLAN, Die Grundbegriffe der Gnade nach der Lehre der Apostol. Väter, 1938. A. HEITMANN, Imitatio Dei. Die eth. Nachahmung Gottes nach der Väterlehre der ersten 2 Jhh., Rome 1940. J. KLEVINGHAUS, Die theol. Stellung der Apost. Väter zur alttestamentl. Offenbarung, 1948. T. F. TORRANCE, The Doctrine of Grace in the Apostolic Fathers, Edinburgh 1949.
[1] Recent editions of the Didache (and the Epistle of Barnabas) by TH. KLAUSER, 1940 (Floril. patrist. 1). German translations with introduction and explanations by H. LILJE, 1938; L. WINTERSWYL, 1939. J. SCHLECHT, Die Apostellehre in der Liturgie der kath. Kirche, 1901. L. WOHLEB, Die lat. Übersetzung der Did., 1913. A. GREIFF, Das älteste Pascharituale der Kirche, Did. 1—10, u. das Johannesev., 1929. J. MUILENBURG, The Literary Relations of the Epistle of Barnabas and the Teaching of the Twelve Apostles, Diss. Yale Univ. (Marburg) 1929; also R. H. CONNOLLY, JThSt 1932, 237/53, and J. A. ROBINSON, ib. 1934, 113 ff. 225 ff. (the Didache dependent on the Epistle of Barnabas). F. E. VOKES, The Riddle of the Didache, London 1938. J. M. CREED, JThSt 1938, 370/87 (holds it was composed in the first half of the second century). W. TELFER, ib. 1939 and 1944. On the Didache c. 9—10: M. DIBELIUS, ZntW 1938, 32/41; E. PETERSON, Ephem. Lit. Rom 1944, 1/13.

following centuries it served as a guide and a source for various liturgical and canonical works. (Cfr. § 39, 5 for the Didascalia and § 75, 5 for the Apostolic Constitutions).

2. The **Epistle of Barnabas**[1] is a didactic devotional treatise in the form of a letter which the MS itself and the early Fathers ascribed to St. Barnabas, the companion of St. Paul (§ 8, 2; 9, 1—3). But the author's attitude toward the Old Testament differs entirely from that of the Apostles. He desires that the traditional observances of the Old Law obliged in the sense in which the Jews understood them. The precepts of fasting, sacrifice, distinction of foods, circumcision, the Sabbath observance and the temple services which Jews had interpreted in a grossly material sense were to be understood in a purely spiritual way. Moreover, the letter was composed after the time of the Apostle Barnabas who did not long survive the destruction of Jerusalem (Barn. 16, 4). The author was most probably a pagan convert who wrote to show that Christianity was a religion radically different from Judaism and to warn Christians against the efforts of the Judaizers. It contains (c. 18—21) the discourse on the Two Ways as in the Didache. While it is generally believed that this was copied from the Didache and while there are several scholars (Muilenberg, Connolly, Robinson et al.) who advance weighty reasons for the opposite opinion, there is still the possibility that both authors took it from a common source. Attempts to fix the date of composition have resulted in slightly different theories: Funk thinks it was composed between 96 and 98; Harnack places it between 130 and 131, while Lietzmann puts it definitely in 138.

3. The ancient Church also regarded highly the rather lengthy and certainly genuine letter of **Clement of Rome**[2], the third successor

---

[1] PH. HÄUSER, Der Barnabasbrief neu unters. u. erklärt, 1912. KLAUSER, MUILENBURG, CONNOLLY and ROBINSON, see preceding note. A.L. WILLIAMS, JThSt 1934, 337/46. P. MEINHOLD, ZKG 1940, 253/303 (history and exegesis in the Ep. of Barnabas). K. THIEME, Kirche u. Synagoge. Der Barnabasbr. u. der Dialog Justins d. M., Olten 1944. KLEVINGHAUS, vide supra.

[2] Recent pocket editions, Greek and Latin, by TH. SCHÄFER, 1941 (Floril. patrist. 44). German translations by L. A. WINTERSWYL, 1941. W. SCHERER, Der 1. Klemensbrief an die Korinther nach s. Bedeutung f. d. Glaubenslehre, 1902. W. PRAETORIUS, ZKG 1912, 347 ff. 501 ff. A. HARNACK, Einführung in die alte KG.: 1. Clemensbrief übers. u. erklärt, 1929; Sb. Berlin 1909, 38/63. FR. GERKE, Die Stellung des 1. Klemensbriefes usw., see § 18. W. K. L. CLARKE, First Epistle of Clement to the Corinthians, London 1937. ST. LÖSCH, in Studi ded. alla memoria di P. Ubaldi, Milano 1937, 177/88 (problems of the Ep. of Clement). L. LEMARCHAND, RevSR 1938, 448/57 (interpolations?). P. MEINHOLD, ZKG 1939, 82/129 (officials vs. the pneumatici

of St. Peter. The letter was written in the name of the Roman Church and addressed to the congregation at *Corinth* in an effort to restore order that had been disturbed by some of the younger members rebelling against the clergy. It was written toward the end of or shortly after the Domitian persecution (95—96). The author incorporates in his letter an instruction on Christian belief and speaks as one conscious of the authoritative position he occupies (§ 21, 2). He draws a comprehensive picture of Christian ideals and quotes Sacred Scripture as well as Stoic philosophy. Besides bearing witness to Christian belief, he proves the existence of the liturgical organization of the Church (§ 18, 1). The letter closes (c. 59—61) with a beautiful prayer of praise and petition which everyone agrees is a part of the old Roman liturgy (§ 23, 1). The Epistle of Clement has been preserved in the Greek original and in very old Latin, Syrian and Coptic translations.

A **Second Epistle to the Corinthians**, falsely ascribed to the same Clement is actually a homily, the oldest sermon to a congregation that we possess. It was written between 140 and 150 in Corinth (Funk, Krüger et al.) and not at Rome (Harnack: Pope Soter). Cfr. Funk, AU III, 261/75; H. Windisch, in Harnack-Ehrung, 1921, 119/34; ZntW 1926, 258/62 (against J. Rendel Harris, ZntW 1924, 193/200); G. Krüger, in "Studies in Early Christianity" ed. by S. J. Chase, New York 1928, 419/39. — Likewise ungenuine are the two letters preserved in Syrian, **Ad virgines**, i. e. to ascetics of both sexes. The entirely different way of using Scripture, the language and the contents, especially the references to virgines subintroductae prove conclusively that these letters are not the work of Clement of Rome and were composed at a later date. They probably originated in the first half of the third century in Palestine or Syria. Cfr. L. T. Lefort, Muséon 1927, 249/64. — To Clement of Rome, whom legend made a consul and member of the imperial house of Flavian (§ 15, 2), was also ascribed the so-called *Clementine Homilies* and *Recognitions* (§ 28, 4) as well as the *Apostolic Constitutions* (§ 75, 5). The Greek Passio S. Clementis (in *Funk-Diekamp II*³, 50/80) of the fourth or fifth century, is entirely legendary. Cfr. E. Hosp, HpBl 169, 1922 I, 312/8; P. Franchi de' Cavalieri, Studi e Testi 27, Rome 1915, 3/40.

4. By all means the most important of the Apostolic Fathers was **Ignatius**[1], Bishop of Antioch, surnamed ὁ Θεοφόρος, the God-

---

in Clement). L. SANDERS, L'Hellénisme de S. Clément de Rome et le Paulinisme, Löwen 1943. G. BARDY, see § 21. Clement and the Gospel of St. John: C. C. TARELLI, JThSt 1947, 208/9; M. E. BOISMARD, Rev. Bibl. 1948, 376/87.

[1] Recent editions of the letters of Ignatius with explanations by P. G. CRONE, 1936; with French transl. by TH. CAMELOT, Paris 1945; Germ. transl. by L. WINTERSWYL, ³1942. Monogr. on Ignatius by TH. ZAHN, 1873; E. V. DER GOLTZ, TU 12, 3, 1894. E. BRUSTON, Paris 1897. H. DE GENOUILLAC, see § 18. M. RACKL, Die Christologie des hl. Ignatius v. Ant., 1914 (cfr. supplementary articles in Kath. 1917 I, 33 ff. 107 ff.). G. BAREILLE, DictThC

bearer. He was a man of deepest spirituality, immersed in the sublime thoughts of Paul and John, and filled with a lively Christian faith and mystic ardor. He was condemned under the Emperor Trajan about 110 and was thrown to the wild beasts in Rome (§ 15, 3). On his way to martyrdom he wrote or dictated seven *letters* of surpassing beauty. While at Smyrna he composed four of them addressed to the Churches of *Ephesus, Magnesia, Tralles* and *Rome*; of the three written at Troas, two were for the Churches of *Philadelphia* and *Smyrna* and one was addressed to *Polycarp*, the bishop of Smyrna. The letters contain an expression of his gratitude for the kindness shown him and the greetings sent to him by the various congregations as he passed through Asia Minor. Then he takes occasion to warn them against the errors of the Judaistic Docetae (§ 28, 1, 2) and to admonish the congregations to maintain a close bond of unity under their bishops. The unique letter to the Romans breathes an ardent longing for his coming martyrdom. (Cfr. § 21, 2 for the special title he uses in addressing the Roman Church). The Ignatian letters are the first irrefutable witnesses to the monarchical episcopacy and the division of the hierarchy into bishops, priests and deacons. For that reason their genuinity has been contested in the past and chiefly for that reason they are of inestimable value.

Thanks to the brilliant defense of their genuinity by *Th. Zahn, F. X. Funk* (Die *Echtheit* der Ign.-Briefe, 1883), *Lightfoot* and others, no scholar today would dare question them. Polycarp, Irenaeus, Origen and Eusebius testify to their authenticity and their inimitable originality of language and content give ample assurance that they were written by the martyr-bishop of Antioch. About 400 an adherent of *Apollinaris* of Laodicea (§ 53), who was possibly also the compiler of the Apostolic Constitutions (§ 75, 5), revised and altered the Ignatian Epistles and added six others of his own composition. Then, during the Middle Ages four other forged letters in Latin were added. All this spurious material can be found in *Funk-Diekamp* II³, 83 ff. — Among the various extant versions of the *Acts of the Martyrdom* of St. Ignatius, none is original or genuine, not even the so-called Martyrium Colbertinum or Antiochenum which at one time was thought to have some claim to genuinity. Eusebius knew nothing about it and it contradicts the letters in several important details. Cfr. Funk AU II, 338/47; ThQ 1903, 159; Funk-Diekamp II³, LXIV ff.

VII, 685/713. J. LEBRETON, RechSR 1925, 97 ff. 393 ff. (Trinitarian doctrines). H. SCHLIER, Religionsgeschichtl. Untersuchungen zu den Ignatiusbriefen, 1929. C. CH. RICHARDSON, The Christianity of Ignatius of Antioch, New York 1935. J. MOFFAT, HarvThR 1936, 1/38 (explanations and amended text). H. W. BARTSCH, Gnostisches Gut u. Gemeindetradit. bei Ign. v. Ant., Diss. 1940. O. PERLER, see § 21, 2 and RivArchCrist 1949, 47/72 (account of the Martyrdom).

5. Shortly after the death of Ignatius, Bishop **Polycarp** (martyred February 22, 156; cfr. § 15, 3), a disciple of St. John the Apostle and a friend of Ignatius, wrote to the Church in *Philippi*, which had requested him to send the letters of Ignatius. Polycarp's epistle contains admonitions to Christians of various states of life to hold fast to the faith and to practise Christian virtues. As the most ancient witness for the Epistles of St. Ignatius it is of special value. Jerome says (De vir. ill. 17) that even in his day it was read during divine services in the churches of Asia Minor. (On Polycarp's journey to Rome in the affair of the Easter controversy, see § 25, 3).

The English scholar *P. N. Harrison* (Polycarp's Two Epistles to the Philippians, London, 1936) has shown that it is very probable that Polycarp's epistle actually contains two different letters: a brief one (c. 13—14) written about 110 while Ignatius was still journeying toward his death and which was sent along with Ignatius' letters to Philippi; and a longer one (c. 1—12) written later (ca. 135) which supposes that Ignatius had been martyred (c. 9) and speaks of the heretic Marcion (c. 7; cfr. § 30 B 1). Cfr. also G. Krüger ThLZ 1937, 401/3; E. Amann, RevSR 1937, 344/8.

The **Martyrium Polycarpi** (text newly revised in Funk-Bihlmeyer, Die Apost. Väter I, 120/32; ib XI ff.; German transl. by H. Rahner, Die Martyrakten des 2. Jh., 1941, 23/37) in the form of a letter from the Church of Smyrna to the Church of Philomelium in Phrygia, is the oldest account we possess of the passion of a martyr from the age of the persecutions. In spite of doubts that have been cast upon its genuinity, it is essentially trustworthy and is a most touching document (Lipsius, Keim, H. Müller). Cfr. *W. Reuning*, Zur Erklärung des Polykarpmartyriums, Diss. 1917; *H. Delehaye*, Les passions des martyrs (§ 14, 4) 11 ff., 37 ff.; *W. M. Ramsay*, Jahresh. d. Österreich. Archäol. Instituts 1932, 245/8. — The Vita et Conversio S. Polycarpi (in Funk-Diekamp II³, 402/50) written by a certain Pionius about the end of the fourth century is purely legendary.

6. Bishop **Papias**[1] of Hieropolis in Phrygia was another disciple of St. John the Apostle and not, as Eusebius (H. E. III, 39) would have it, of the imaginary "Presbyter" John of Ephesus (§ 11, 1). About 130 Papias compiled five books entitled *"Explanations of the Sayings of the Lord"* (Λογίων κυριακῶν ἐξηγήσεις), that is, a collection of traditions regarding the words and acts of Christ. Unfortunately only a few fragments of this work have been preserved. Some of these which speak of the origins of the Gospels of Matthew and Mark are very valuable, while others are unimportant, even crassly chiliastic.

---

[1] TH. ZAHN, Forsch. 6, 1900, 109/57. K. L. LEIMBACH, RE 14, 642/54. J. DONOVAN, The Logia in Ancient and Recent Literature, Cambridge 1924; Irish Eccles. Record 1928, 337/50; 1931, 124/37. C. LAMBOT, RevBén 1931, 116/23. E. GUTWENGER, ZkTh 1947, 385/416 (Papias before 110).

# § 38.
## The Apologetic, Anti-heretical
## and Theological Literature of the Second Century[1].

A. The Apologists defended the Christian religion against the attacks of *paganism* and *Judaism* which partly caused and greatly intensified the persecutions. Their works are serious discussions (called diatribes) with their opponents in the form of *conversation* or *dialogue*. They make full use of late Platonic and Stoic philosophy and are always addressed to pagan audiences, sometimes to the emperors themselves. They take particular pains to refute the popular calumnies against Christianity and endeavor to prove its truth from the prophecies of Christ and the prophets, by appealing to the great age of Sacred Scripture (archaeomania), but especially by showing its moral effect on the lives of Christians. While defending the Christian cause, they often sharply attack pagan mythology and immorality. The theological concepts of the apologists are often immature and faulty.

1. Marcian **Aristides**[2] was a Christian "philosopher" of Athens. His apology was addressed to Antoninus Pius (138—161) or possibly, as Eusebius thinks (H. E. IV, 3, 3), to Hadrian (117—138). It attempts to prove that the idolatry of the barbarians and Greeks

---

[1] J. C. TH. DE OTTO, Corpus apologetarum christianorum saec. II, 9 vol. 1847/72, I—V (Justin) ³1876/81. A. HARNACK, Die Überlieferung der griech. Apologeten des 2. Jh., TU I, 1/2, 1882. E. J. GOODSPEED, Die ältesten Apologeten (exc. Theophilus), 1915; Index apologeticus s. clavis Iustini etc., 1912. Frühchristl. Apologeten, deutsch übers. v. G. RAUSCHEN u. a., BKV 12, 14, 33, 1913/7. K. WERNER, Gesch. der apolog. u. polem. Lit. der christl. Theologie, 5 vols. 1861/7. G. SCHMITT and J. ZAHN, the § 17. J. GEFFCKEN, Die altchristl. Apologetik, NJklA 15, 1905, 625/66; Zwei christl. Apologeten (Arist. and Athenag.), 1907. J. RIVIÈRE, S. Justin et les apologistes du II⁰ s., Paris 1907. W. KOCH, Die altkirchl. Apologetik, ThQ 1908, 7/33. A. PUECH, Les apologistes grecs du II⁰ s., Paris 1912. A. CASAMASSA, Gli apologisti greci, Rome 1944. M. PELLEGRINO, Studi su l'antica apologetica, Rome 1947. H. MEYER, Gesch. der Lehre v. den Keimkräften bis z. Ausgang, der Patristik, 1914. F. ANDRES, Die Engellehre der griech. Apologeten des 2. Jh., 1914. W. BOUSSET, Jüdisch-christl. Schulbetrieb in Alexandrien u. Rom, 1915. A. WAIBEL, Die natürl. Gotteserkenntnis in der apolog. Lit. des 2. Jh., Diss. 1916. A. HAUCK, Apologetik in der alten Kirche, 1918. J. LORTZ, Das Christentum als Monotheismus in den Apologien des 2. Jh., Festgabe A. Ehrhard, 1922, 301/27. J. GIORDANI, La prima polemica cristiana, Brescia ²1943. V. A. S. LITTLE, The Christology of the Apologists, London 1934. H. ROSSBACHER. Die Apologeten als politischwissenschaft. Schriftsteller, 1937. H. RAHNER, Griech. Mythen in christl. Deutung, 1945. For other literature see § 14 and 26 (LORTZ, STELZENBERGER, etc.).

[2] F. HAASE, ThQ 99, 1917/8, 422/9 (the apology addressed to Hadrian). PH. FRIEDRICH, ZkTh 1919, 31/77 (Aristides' doctrine). R. L. WOLFF, HarvThR 1937, 233/47 (tradition of the Apology). W. HUNGER, Scholastik 1949, 390/400 (the Apologia written to promote Conversions).

can not be reconciled with the true concept of religion; that idolatry promotes immorality and that the religion of the Jews consists in the worship of angels and mere external observances. On the contrary truth and purity of morals are to be found among the new race of Christians whose edifying conduct is then described in glowing terms.

The original Greek text of the apology was largely incorporated into the tenth century legend of Barlaam and Josephat. But this fact first became known in 1889 when Rendel Harris discovered the apology in a Syrian translation in the monastery of St. Catherine on Mt. Sinai. More recently two papyri were found containing fragments of the apology in Greek. Cfr. G. Krüger, ThLZ 1924, 47 f.; J. de Zwaan, HarvThR 1925, 109/11.

2. **Justin**[1], the "philosopher and martyr," (according to Tertullian, Adv. Valent. 5) was born of a pagan Greek family at Flavia Neapolis (Sichem) in Samaria and was beheaded for the faith at Rome under Marcus Aurelius about 165 (§ 15, 4). He is the most important apologist of the second century although his reputation as a writer is not high. He defends the Christian religion earnestly and enthusiastically while endeavoring to do good to those whom he addresses. He attempts to harmonize Christianity with the teachings of Plato and Philo, in which attempt he frequently falls into error particularly regarding the doctrine of the Logos (§ 32, 1). Eusebius knew of eight works written by Justin, but of these only three have come down to us: two apologies addressed to pagans and one to Jews. The earlier and longer apology was addressed to

---

[1] Editions of the works of Justin by OTTO und GOODSPEED vide supra. Editions of the Apologists by G. KRÜGER, [4]1915, G. RAUSCHEN, [2]1911 (Floril. patrist. 2), J. M. PFÄTTISCH, 2 small volumes with commentaries 1912); cfr. the Dialogue by G. ARCHAMBAULT, 2 vol. Paris 1909 (also HARNACK, TU 39, I, 1913). W. SCHMID, ZntW 1940, 87/138 (text tradition). Monographs on Justin by K. SEMISCH, 2 vols. 1840/2; M. J. LAGRANGE, Paris 1914 (cfr. BullLa 1914, 3/15). G. BARDY, DictThC VIII, 2228/77. TH. WEHOFER, Die Apologie Justins in literarhist. Beziehung, RQ Suppl. 6, 1897 (opposite views held by G. RAUSCHEN, ThQ 1899, 188/206). L. FEDER, Justins Lehre von Jesus Christus, 1906. J. M. PFÄTTISCH, Der Einfluß Platos auf die Theol. Justins, 1910. K. HUBIK, Die Apologien des hl. Justin, 1912. W. JEHNE, Die Apologie Justins, Diss. 1914. E. R. GOODENOUGH, The Theology of Justin Martyr, Jena 1923. R. STAHLER, Justin Martyr et l'apologétique, Diss. Genf. 1935. G. BARDY, RechSR 1923, 491 ff.; 1924, 33 ff. (Justin and Stoicism). C. HÜNTEMANN, ThGl 1933, 410/28 (Justin's technique of composition). B. SEEBERG, ZKG 1939, 1/81 (Justin's history of theology). O. PERLER, Div. Thomas 1940, 296/316 (the Logos and the Eucharist according to Apol. I, 66). On the Dialogue with Tryphon: E. PREUSCHEN, ZntW 1920, 102/27; G. SCHLÄGER, Nieuw Theol. Tijdschrift 1924, 117/43 (both hold that the work is spurious); L. FONCK, Biblica 1921, 342/7 (versus Preuschen); K. THIEME, see § 37, 2. S. ENSLIN, Jewish Quarterly Review 1943, 179/205.

Antoniuns Pius about 150. In the form in which it has been preserved, this apology begins by refuting the accusations of atheism, immorality and Thyestean banquets (§ 14, 2), goes on to prove the divinity of Christ from the Old Testament prophesies and adds a most valuable description of the religious services of the Christians (§ 23, 1). The shorter apology is a sort of supplement to the first, although it is an entirely independent work. It was occasioned by the execution of three Christians in Rome (§ 15, 3). It answers the questions asked by the pagans: why Christians do not commit suicide to reach their God the sooner and why God, their Protector, allows them to be slain. The apology addressed to the Jews, Dialogus cum Tryphone Judaeo, whose authenticity has recently been questioned, deals with the Old Testament, Jesus as Son of God and Messias and the call of the pagans to the true religion.

3. **Tatian**, a native of Assyria (East Syria), a disciple of Justin and later the head or founder of the Encratites in the East (§ 30 B 2), unlike his mild and prudent master was a fiery character inclined to extremes. About 170 he wrote an Oratio adversus Graecos which is a fierce attack on mythology, philosophy and Greek culture in general rather than an apology for Christianity. It answers the charge that Christianity is a new religion by showing the great antiquity of the books of the Old Testament. (On Tatian's Diatesseron see below, B 5).

4. **Athenagoras**[1] was a "philosopher" of Athens. His Legatio seu Supplicatio (Πρεσβεία) pro Christianis, composed about 177 and addressed to Marcus Aurelius and his son Commodus, refutes the three principal charges made against Christians. It is marked by clarity, a pleasing presentation and a dignified treatment throughout. In his work, De resurrectione, he ably establishes the reasonableness of Christian belief in the resurrection of the body and seeks to show that the scandal which pagans profess to take from this belief is utterly groundless.

5. **Theophilus**[2], Bishop of Antioch during the reign of Commodus (180—192), wrote three books dedicated to Autolycus, his pagan

---

[1] J. GEFFCKEN, see p. 178.  G. BARDY, Athénagore (French transl. with introduction and explanation), Paris 1943.

[2] Editions by E. RAPISARDA, Turin 1939; G. BARDY et J. SANDER (with French transl. and explanation), Paris 1948.  FR. LOOFS, Theophilus v. Ant. Adv. Marcionem u. die anderen theolog. Quellen bei Irenäus, TU 46, 2, 1930; also F. R. M. HITCHCOCK, JThSt 1937, 130 ff. 255 ff.  E. RAPISARDA, in Studi ded. alla memoria di P. Ubaldi, Milano 1937, 381/400.  F. OGARA, Gregorianum 1944, 74/102 (Aristides, the letter to Diognetus and Theophilus). R. M. GRANT, HarvThR 1947, 227/56; 1950, 179/96.

friend. The first book contains a striking treatment of the nature of the true God; the second shows the folly of idolatry and contrasts the teachings of paganism with those of Holy Scripture concerning the origin of the world; and the third deals with Sacred Scripture, especially its antiquity. A commentary on the Gospels, a work against Marcion, another against Hermogenes, and a few other books of Theophilus, mentioned by Eusebius and Jerome, have been lost except for a few fragments.

6. The **Letter to Diognetus**[1], whose contents closely resemble the work of Aristides, is an apology addressed to a man named Diognetus, a pagan in high office. It contains a refutation of paganism and Judaism and explains why Christianity did not appear sooner. The noble language and the beautiful delineation of Christian life led many to ascribe this work to one of the Apostolic Fathers. In fact, the author says in chapter 11 that he was a disciple of the Apostles. But it is now generally agreed that the two last chapters, 11 and 12, are probably fragments of a work of Hippolytus of Rome (§ 39, 4).

The only extant MS of this apology bears the name of Justin. Actually, however, it was written by an unknown author toward the end of the second or beginning of the third century. Some recent scholars incline to the belief that it is the work of the oldest known apologist **Quadratus**, who wrote it for presentation to Hadrian during the Emperor's stay in Asia Minor in 123—124. The passage in Eusebius IV, 3 fits well in the break which occurs in Diognetus VII, 6—7. It is not likely that the apology of Quadratus was used in the metaphrastic legend of St. Catherine of Alexandria (Rendel Harris). Cfr. E. Klostermann and E. Seeberg, Die Apologie der hl. Katharina, 1924. — G. Bardy, Mél. H. Grégoire I, Brussels 1949, 75/86; P. Andriessen, Sacris erudiri 1949, 44/45 (Was Quadratus in Asia Minor?).

7. The Christian "philosopher" **Hermias** composed an Irrisio philosophorum gentilium. It is a witty, but superficial derision of pagan philosophy, especially of its psychology and metaphysics, based on 1 Cor. 3:19 and Tatian Orat. 25. It was probably written in the beginning of the third century. Cfr. *A. v. Di Pauli*, Die Irrisio des Hermias, 1907; ThQ 1908, 523/31.

8. Besides the above-mentioned works, a number of others have been *lost* entirely or are known only in brief fragments: the apologetic and other works of Bishop Claudius *Apollinaris* of Hieropolis in Phrygia; the works of the gifted and energetic Bishop *Melito* of Sardis (see below B 5); three apologies of the otherwise unknown *Miltiades*, composed during the reign of

---

[1] Recent editions of the letter to Diognetus by J. GEFFCKEN, 1928; E. H. BLAKENEY, London 1943; H. G. MEECHAM, Manchester 1950. H. KIHN, Der Ursprung des Briefes an D., 1882. N. BONWETSCH, Nachr. Göttingen 1902, 621/34. E. MOLLAND, ZntW 1934, 289/312. R. H. CONNOLLY, JThSt 1935, 347/53; 1936, 2/15. P. ANDRIESSEN, RechThAM 1946, 5 ff. 125 ff. 237 ff. 1947, 121 ff.; VC 1947, 129/36.

Marcus Aurelius; and the Altercatio Jasonis et Papisci of *Aristo* of Pella, an apology against the Jews, written about 140.

B. A number of works of the second century were written against the *heresies* and *schisms* of the time, while others were called forth by some *internal* needs of the Church and served the purpose of instructing or edifying. Unfortunately, only a few have been preserved in their entirety.

1. The **Shepherd** (Ποιμήν) **of Hermas**[1], so-called because an angel of penance appears in the guise of a shepherd, is a lengthy admonition to Christendom to do penance and practise good works. It is in the form of an apocalypse and is divided into five visions, ten commandments and ten parables. It was written at Rome and was evidently intended for popular consumption. The oldest part (Vis. I—IV) was probably composed during the time of Pope Clement (§ 37, 3) for the author claims (Vis. II, 4, 3) to have been a contemporary of Clement. The composition of the latter part (the "Book of the Shepherd") and the redaction of the entire work very likely took place during the pontificate of Pius I (140—154) for according to the Muratorian Fragment (see below) Hermas was a brother of Pius I. The work was held in high esteem and was widely read as may be judged from the discovery of many very old papyrus fragments in Egypt and numerous translations into Latin (second century), Coptic and Ethiopian. In fact, many (Irenaeus, Tertullian, Origen et al.) regarded it as belonging to the Sacred Scriptures and it was incorporated in the Codex Sinaiticus. It is of special value as reflecting the religious and moral views of the Roman Church in the second century (*one* pardon after Baptism [§ 24, 1], the value of good works, etc.).

2. Not long ago an apochryphal **Epistola Apostolorum** was found in a Coptic and Ethiopian translation (published by *C. Schmidt*, TU 43, 1919; German by H. Duensing, Kleine Texte 152, 1925; English in James, cfr. § 11, 3). It contains an encyclical letter of the Apostolic College to Christendom

---

[1] See the literature on the Apostolic Fathers § 37; Germ. transl. with commentary by M. DIBELIUS, 1923; cfr. in „Harnack-Ehrung", 1921, 105/18 (the shepherd angel). C. BONNER, A Papyrus Codex of the Shepherd of Hermas (Simil. 2—9), Ann Arbor (Mich.) 1934. C. H. TURNER, JThSt 1920, 193/209 (Latin transl.). G. BAREILLE, DictThC VI, 2268/88. H. LECLERCQ, DictAC VI, 2265/90. A. BAUMEISTER, Die Ethik des Pastor Hermae, 1912. W. J. WILSON, HarvThR 1927, 21/62. R. VAN DEEMTER, Der Hirt des H. Apokalypse oder Allegorie?, Diss. Amsterdam 1929. A. V. STRÖM, Der Hirt des H. Allegorie oder Wirklichkeit?, Leipzig 1936. L. TH. LEFORT, Muséon 1938, 239/76; 1939, 223/8 (the Pastor Hermae coptic-sahid.). G. D. KILPATRICK, JThSt 1947, 204/5. E. PETERSON, OrChrPer 1947, 624/35 (the interpretation of the visions).

with supposed conversations and revelations of Christ after His Resurrection. In content, it closely resembles the "Testament of the Lord" (§ 75, 5). The author is a Quartodeciman (§ 25, 3) and wrote in Asia Minor about 160—170 (Schmidt) or possibly as early as 140 (Ehrhard). Although he vehemently attacks the errors of Simon Magus and Cerinthus (§ 27, 28) he himself was influenced by Gnosticism. Cfr. A. Ehrhard, HpBl 165, 1920 I, 645 ff. 717 ff.; G. Bardy, Rev. bibl. 1921, 110/34; J. Delazer, Antonianum 1928, 369 ff. 1929, 257 ff., 369 ff.

3. The most important theologian of the second century, in a sense, the "Father of Catholic Dogma", was **Irenaeus**[1], Bishop of Lyons. He was born in Asia Minor and as a youth was a disciple of Polycarp of Smyrna (§ 156). Later he became a priest in Lyons and about 177 succeeded the martyred bishop Pothinus (§ 15,4) in that see. It is not certain whether he himself suffered martyrdom in the persecution of Septimius Severus (ca. 202). He distinguished himself by zealous missionary work in Gaul (§ 12, 2) by an indefatigable defense of Catholic doctrine against Gnosticism and by acting as "peacemaker" in the Easter controversy (§ 25, 3). Besides a few brief fragments found in Eusebius (H. E. V, 20, 24) only two of Irenaeus' works have been preserved: the five books of The Detection and Overthrow of the False Gnosis (Ἔλεγχος καὶ ἀνατροπὴ τῆς ψευδωνύμου γνώσεως), now generally known as Adversus Hae-

---

[1] IRENAEUS, Adv. haereses, ed. R. Massuet, PG 7; ed. A. STIEREN, 2 vols. 1848/53; ed. W. HARVEY, 2 vol. Cambridge 1857, reprinted 1949. E. KLOSTERMANN, ZntW 1937, 1/34 (die latein. Irenäushss.). S. LUNDSTRÖM, Neue Studien zur latein. Irenäusübersetzung, Lund 1948. Armenian Fragments ed. in TU 35, 2, 1910 u. 36, 3, 1913; cfr. A. MERK, ZkTh 1926, 371 ff. 481 ff. German transl. by E. KLEBBA, 2 vols. 1912 (BKV 3/4). Epideixis Germ. tr. in TU 31, 1, ²1908, by S. WEBER, 1912 (BKV 4), and Latin, 1917, Armenian and French in Patrologia Orientalis 12, Paris 1919, 655 ff. CH. MARTIN, RHE 1942, 143/52 (Fragments of letters). Novum Test. S. Irenei edd. W. SANDAY et C. H. TURNER, Oxford 1923. Monographs on Irenäus by A. DUFOURCQ, Paris 1904; F. R. M. HITCHCOCK, Cambridge 1914. F. VERNET, DictThC VII, 2394/533. E. KLEBBA, Die Anthropologie des hl. Ir., 1894. J. HOH, Die Lehre des hl. Ir. über das N.T., 1919. A. NUSSBAUMER, Der Grundriß der Epideixis des Ir., Diss. 1921. G. N. BONWETSCH, Die Theologie des Ir., 1925. J. LAWSON, The Biblical Theology of S. Ir., London 1948. On the doctrine of Irenaeus: A. D'ALÈS, RechSR 1916, 185/211; 1924, 497/538; H. KOCH, ThStKr 1925, 183/214; J. LEBRETON, RechSR 1926, 385/406; H. D. SIMONIN, Angelicum 1934, 3/22; A. VERRIELE, RevSR 1934, 493/524; P. GÄCHTER, ZkTh 1934, 503/32; W. HUNGER, Scholastik 1942, 161/77; J. DANIELOU, RechSR 1947, 227/31; H. HOLSTEIN, ib. 1947, 454/61; 1948, 282/8; 1949, 229/70. L. SPIKOWSKI, La doctrine de l'Église dans S. Irénée, Thèse Strassb. 1926. W. SCHMIDT, Die Kirche bei Irenäus, Diss. Helsingfors 1934. FR. LOOFS, Theophilus v. Ant. etc. see above. D. B. REYNDERS, RechThAM 1935, 5/27; 1936, 225/52 (Method of polemics used by St. Irenaeus). W. X. SPIKOWSKI, Die Polemik des hl. Ir. gegen die Gotteslehre der Gnostiker, Lwów 1935. K. PRÜMM, in Pisciculi, Festschrift F. J. Dölger, 1939, 192/219 (Christianity an innovation). E. SCHERL, Recapitulatio mundi, 1941.

reses, written about 180—190 and existing in a Latin translation made about 300; and the Demonstratio praedicationis apostolicae (Ἐπίδειξις τοῦ ἀποστολικοῦ κηρύγματος) in an Armenian translation rediscovered in 1904. Since the loss of Justin's "Syntagma Against All Heresies," Irenaeus' Adversus Haereses is the oldest extant work on heresy. For a history of Gnosticism and the positive development of dogma, the work is of inestimable value. Irenaeus not only brilliantly proves ecclesiastical authority and the principle of tradition (§ 18, 2 the episcopal office; § 21, 2, the primacy of Rome; § 22, 2 the rule of faith), but he also clarifies the doctrine of the Trinity and the Logos which had often been presented faultily by previous apologists. His favorite thought is the constant rejuvenation of the human race in Christ its Head (recapitulatio). If the passages in V, 32—35 are genuine, Irenaeus inclined toward Chiliasm (§ 33, 1). The Demonstratio is an apologetic-catechetic treatise which gives the plan of salvation and proves the truth of the Gospel from the prophecies of the Old Testament.

4. The **Muratorian Fragment**[1] or Canon, named after its discoverer and first publisher, Luigi Muratori (1740), is a fragment of a list of the *canonical books of the New Testament*, with some valuable facts about the authors and origin of the individual books. It is written in poor Latin and is probably a translation of a Greek original written at Rome about 200. Many scholars (Lightfoot, Robinson, Lagrange et al.) think that Hippolytus of Rome (§ 39, 4) was the author of the original.

5. Among the works of the second century which have been *lost*, first place must be given to a work of the Jewish convert, *Hegesippus*, entitled Memoirs (Ὑπομνήματα), comprising five books written about 180. It is not, as Jerome would have it (De vir. ill. 22), a coherent history of the Church but rather a collection of the traditions of the principal churches for the purpose of refuting the Gnostics. To gather his matter Hegesippus travelled to Rome, where he made a *list*, also lost, *of the popes* down to Anicetus (155—166) (Eus. IV, 8 1, 2; Funk AU I, 373/90. Other authors of note whose works have been lost are: Bishop *Dionysius* of Corinth, composer of numerous letters to various churches (Eus. IV, 23); Rhodon, a disciple of Tatian, opponent of Marcion and author of a Commentary on the work of creation (Eus. V, 13); *Apollonius*, opponent of Gnosticism (Eus. V, 18); the Roman priest Caius,

---

[1] TH. ZAHN, Gesch. des neutest. Kanons II, 1, 1890, 1/143; NkZ 1922, 417/36. G. RAUSCHEN, Floril. patrist. 3, 1905, 24/35. H. LIETZMANN, Kleine Texte I, ²1921, reprinted 1933. A. HARNACK, ZntW 1925, 1/16. H. KOCH, ib. 1926, 154/60. S. RITTER, RivArchCrist 1926, 215/63. M. J. LAGRANGE, Rev. bibl. 1926, 83/91; 1933, 161/86. H. LECLERCQ, DictAC XII, 543/60 with facsimile).

opponent of Montanism (§ 10, 2 f.; 33, 1; 34, 2); Bishop **Melito** of Sardis, the apologist mentioned in A 8, who, Eusebius says (H. E. IV, 26), wrote about twenty other books on Easter, the Church, Sunday observance, faith, creation, etc. A recently discovered papyrus contains a beautiful sermon of Melito's (originally Syrian?) on the Passion of Christ (εἰς τὸ πάθος) in which he convincingly proves Christ's divinity. — Ed. C. Bonner, London 1940; also in Mél. Fr. Cumont, Brux. 1936, 107/19; HarvThR 1938, 175/90; 1939, 140 f.; 1943, 316/9; VC 1948, 184 f. — P. Kahle, ThSt 1943, 52/6; E. J. Wellesz, ib. 41/52; P. Nautin, RHE 1949, 429/38 (denies Melito's authorship). The loss of Tatian's (above A 3) famed **Diatesseron** (Τὸ διὰ τεσσάρων scil. εὐαγγέλιον) is particularly regrettable. It was a harmony of the Gospels used in divine service in Syria down to the fifth century. It appears to have exercised a strong influence on the text of the Gospels throughout Christendom. It was probably composed in Syria after *Tatian's* break with the Church and return to the East (ca. 172). St. Ephraem quotes it, and comments on it in Armenian; and versions in Arabic, Persian, Latin, Italian and Dutch make it possible to reconstruct the greater part of this work. The Dutch version is a thirteenth century translation from the Latin which is supposed to stem directly from the Syrian. A Greek fragment of the Diatesseron was found in 1933 during excavations at Dura-Europos (§ 23, 5). (Ed. C. H. Kraeling, London 1935; cfr. A. Merk, Biblica 1936, 234/41; A. Baumstark, Oriens Christ. 1939, 111/5; *C. Peters*, Biblica 1940, 51/5). — C. Peters, Das Diatessaron Tatians, Rome 1939 (summary with earlier literature; Biblica 1942, 68/77 (recent discoveries and researches). — A. J. B. Higgins, JThSt 1944, 187/99 (Arabic translations of the eleventh century and also Syrian). — *G. Messina*, Notizie su un Diatessaron persiano, Rome 1943 (vgl. H. Vogels, ThRev 1943, 106/8); Biblica 1949, 10/27; 356/76 (Persian translation of the thirteenth century with Gnostic tendency).

§ 39.

## Greek Writers of the Third Century. Development of Theology.

The turn of the second century saw a notable progress in ecclesiastical literature in the Greek Orient. There now began to develop a *science of theology* which manifested itself in exegesis or the explanation of Holy Writ and in an attempt to present systematically the entire content of faith. Highly gifted men like Clement of Alexandria and Origen analyzed the most important problems of Hellenic philosophy and utilized the worth-while elements of that philosophy to establish and uphold the dogmas of the Church. This process which had begun with the apologists of the second century may well be called the *Christianization of Hellenism* and not, as some have tried to see it, the *Hellenization of Christendom*. The nascent *theological schools* were located at *Alexandria, Caesarea* in Palestine and *Antioch*. Rome, too, was represented by a theologian of note in the person of Hippolytus, although he wrote in Greek.

1. From very obscure beginnings, there early developed at **Alexandria**[1], the second largest city of the Roman world and the center of intellectual life, a flourishing *catechetical school* (τῆς κατη-λχήσεως διδασκαλεῖον). Since this school was open not only to children, but also to adults, many of whom were men of learning, it was necessary, if this latter group were to be attracted to Christianity, to provide a course of studies extending from the profane sciences (philosophy) to the heights of theology (exegesis). The first known director of this "Christian Academy," which was under the supervision of the bishop of Alexandria, though probably not from the beginning, was the former Stoic philosopher, *Pantaenus* of Sicily (ca. 180—200). Notwithstanding the assertion of Eusebius, it is doubtful whether he published any works (§ 12, 10). Under the next two directors the school reached the peak of fame and influence — an influence felt in Christian circles far beyond the confines of Alexandria. Titus Flavius **Clemens**\*\*[2] of Athens († before

---

[1] CII. BIGG, The Christian Platonists of Alexandria, Oxford ²1913. A. HECKEL, see § 12, 7. A. ANWANDER, see § 12, 11. H. R. NELZ, see § 19, 1. W. BOUSSET, Jüdisch-christl. Schulbetrieb in Alexandrien u. Rom, 1915. R. ARNOU, Platonisme etc., s. § 32. R. CADIOU, La jeunesse d'Origène, Histoire de l'école d'Alexandrie au début du IIIe siècle, Paris 1936. G. BARDY, RechSR 1937, 65/90; Vivre et penser 1942, 80/109 (the beginnings and history of the Alexandrian School). E. MOLLAND, The Conception of the Gospel in the Alexandrian Theology, Oslo 1938 (valuable).

[2] Works of Clement of Alexandria ed. O. STÄHLIN, 3 Bde u. 1 Reg.-Bd. 1905/36; I/II², 1936/9. CLEMENS ALEX., Excerpta ex Theodoto (cfr. § 30 A 4), ed. R. P. CASEY, London 1934. Extraits de Théodote, ed. F. SAGNARD, Paris 1948 (with French translation). H. A. ECHLE, Traditio 1945, 365/8 (Fragment of the Hypotyposis in Moschus). Selected writings of Clement of Alex., Germ. transl. by O. STÄHLIN, 5 vols. 1934/38 — BKV 2. R. 7, 8, 17, 19, 20 (with excellent introduction). T. FL. CLEMENS, Die Teppiche, Germ. by F. OVERBECK, 1936. Monographs on Clement by E. DE FAYE, Paris ²1906; J. PATRICK, London 1914; R. B. TOLLINTON, 2 vol. London 1914; G. BARDY, Paris 1926. W. SCHERER, Klemens v. Alex. u. seine Erkenntnisprinzipien, 1907. TH. RÜTHER, Die Lehre von der Erbsünde bei Kl. v. Alex., 1922. A. MAYER, Das Gottesbild im Menschen nach Cl. v. Alex., Rome 1942. J. MEIFORT, Der Platonismus bei Clemens Alex., 1928. M. POHLENZ, Kl. v. Alex. u. sein hellen. Christentum, Nachr. Göttingen 1943, 3. E. TENGBLAD, Syntaktisch-stilist. Beiträge z. Kritik u. Exegese des Kl. v. Alex., Lund 1932. J. MUNCK, Untersuchungen über Kl. v. Alex., 1933. J. M. TSERMOULAS, Die Bildersprache des Kl. v. Alex., Diss. 1934. W. DEN BOER, De Allegorese in het werk van Clemens Alexandrinus, Leyden 1940. J. FRANGOULIS, Der Begriff des „Geistes" bei Cl. Alexandrinus, Diss. 1935. A. DECKER, Kenntnis u. Pflege des Körpers bei Cl. v. Alex., 1936. G. LAZZATI, Introduzione allo studio di Clemente Alessandrino, Milano 1939. F. BURI, Clemens Alex. u. der paulin. Freiheitsbegriff, 1939. C. MONDÉSERT, Clément d'Al., Introduction à l'étude de sa pensée religieuse, Paris 1944. TH. CAMELOT, Foi

215) a renowned teacher (though probably not a priest) and a brilliant, progressive thinker, endeavored from about 190 to 202 or 203 to formulate a *Christian theology*. In a great work divided into three parts which clearly reveal that it originated from his lectures, Clement subjects Christianity to a comprehensive examination as a doctrine and as a way of life. In the first part, Protrepticus or Cohortatio ad gentes, he refutes idolatry and exhorts pagans to abandon their errors and accept Christianity. In the second part, called the Paedagogus, he shows how to lead a moral, Christian life. Most probably Clement intended to add a third part, which some scholars think would have been called Didascalos or Master, a complete exposition of Christian dogma; but it was never written. The incomplete and somewhat planless Stromata (Στρωματεῖς = a tapestry or colorful collection) is intended to be an introduction to the faith of a true Christian. In the homily Quis divus salvetur?, based on the Gospel story of the rich young man (Mark 10:17—31), he refutes the notion that wealth as such is evil, but he points out very logically that it imposes many social obligations. Among the works of Clement preserved only in fragments, the Hypotyposes (sketches) is the most important. It contains allegorical explanations of passages from Holy Scripture. Clement was a real teacher who had mastered the entire body of Greek learning; and he wrote fluently, sometimes with Attic eloquence. Thoroughly convinced that Greek philosophy was a gift of God to man (§ 5, 4). he sought with its help to penetrate the problems which religion poses and in doing so attained a remarkable depth and originality. But in his eagerness to bridge the gap between Hellenism and Christianity, he comes dangerously near to Plato, the Stoics and false Gnosis, although in everything else he is the declared foe of heretical

---

et gnose. Introduction à l'étude de la connaissance mystique chez Cl. d'Alex. ib. 1945. F. QUATEMBER, see § 26, 2, Articles on Clement of Alexandria: H. KOCH, ZntW 1921, 43/48 (he was not a priest). R. P. CASEY, HarvThR 1925, 39/101 (Christian Platonism in Cl. of Alex.). F. PRAT, RechSR 1925, 234/57 (literary plan of Clement). F. ANDRES, RQ 1926, 13 ff. 129 ff. 307 ff. (teaching on angels and demons). TH. CAMELOT, RechSR 1931, 38 ff. 541 ff. (Clement and profane learning); Rev. Bibl. 1946, 242/8 (Clement and H. Scripture); J. RUWET, Biblica 1948, 77 ff. 240 ff. 391 ff. (canon and apocryphal works in Cl). H. G. MARSH, JThSt 1936, 64/80 (Mysterion bei Kl.). C. MONDÉSERT, RechSr 158/80 (Symbolism in Clement). H. SEESEMANN, ThStKr 1936, 312/46 (St. Paul in Cl.). K. PRÜMM, Scholastik 1937, 17/57 (Faith and knowledge in Strom. II). A. C. OUTLER, Journ. of Relig. 1940, 217/40 (Platonism of Clem.). J. LEBRETON, RechSR 1947, 55 ff. 142 ff. (the Trinity in Cl.). W. VÖLKER, Theol. Z. Basel 1947, 15/40 (historical sequence of the idea of perfection in Clement). J. MOINGT, RechSR 1950, 195/251 (Gnosis bei Kl.).

Gnosticism. His theology (especially on the nature of God, the Trinity and the Logos) is, at times, seriously faulty.

2. Still more famous than Clement is his great disciple and successor **Origen**[1]. He was born at Alexandria about 185, the son of the Christian catechist and martyr, Leonidas (§ 15, 5). At the age of 18 (202 or 203) Origen was appointed by Bishop Demetrius as

[1] Origen's works ed. CH. DE LA RUE, 4 fol. Paris 1733/59 = PG 11—17; von C. H. E. LOMMATZSCH, 25 vols. 1831/48; in der Sammlung „Griechische christl. Schriftsteller" von P. KOETSCHAU, E. KLOSTERMANN u. a., 1899 ff. (12 vols. published) Fragmente der Hexapla, ed. F. FIELD, 2 vol. Oxford 1867/75; G. MERCATI, Studi e Testi 5, Rome 1901. O. GUÉRAND, RevHR, 131, 1946, 85/108 (Papyrus discovered at Toura 1945). Separate editions C. CELSUM (1899), De Oratione u. Exhortatio (1899), De principiis (1913), by P. KOETSCHAU; Origenis Philocalia (of Basil. Gregory of Naz.), ed. J. A. ROBINSON, Cambridge 1893 (also J. B. COLOU RevSR 1940 1/27). Homilies on Genesis, French by L. DROUTELEAU, Paris 1944; on Exodus by FORTIER, ib. 1947. J. SCHERER, Entretiens d'Or. avec Héraclide, ib. 1949. R. CADIOU, Commentaires inédits des Psaumes, ib. 1936. ORIGENES, selections, Germ. transl. by P. KOETSCHAU, 3 vols. 1926/7 (BKV 48, 52/3). H. U. V. BALTHASAR, Or., Geist u. Feuer, ein Aufbau aus s. Schriften, [2]1951. W. BAEHRENS, TU 42, 1, 1916 (text tradition of homilies on A.T.). E. KLOSTERMANN u. E. BENZ, Tu 47, 2, 1931; 47, 4, 1932 (Commentary on St. Matthew). M. RAUER, TU 47, 3, 1932 (homilies on St. Luke). G. BARDY, Recherches sur l'hist. du texte et des versions latines du De principiis d'Origène, Paris 1923; cfr. K. MÜLLER, Sb. Berlin 1919, 616/31; B. STEIDLE, ZntW 1941, 236/43. Monogr. on Origen by E. R. REDEPENNING, 2 vols. 1841/6; E. DE FAYE, 3 vol. Paris 1923/8 (also A. D'ALÈS, RechSR 1930, 224/68); Esquisse de la pensée d'Origène, Paris 1925. J. DANIÉLOU, ib. 1948; M. T. ANTONELLI, Brescia 1946; G. BARDY, Paris 1931; Origène in DictThC XI, 1489/1565. G. FRITZ, Origénisme, ib. XI, 1565/88. H. KOCH, RE Pauly-Wissowa XVIII, 1940, 1036 ff. A. D'ALÈS, Origénisme, DictApol III, 1228/58. F. PRAT, Origène, le théologien et l'exégète, Paris 1907. C. CAPITAINE, De Origenis ethica, 1898. A. HARNACK, Der kirchengesch. Ertrag der exeget. Arbeiten des Orig., Tu 42, 3/4, 1918/9. FR. SCHEMMEL, Philol. Wochenschr. 1925, 1277/80 (School of Caesarea). H. KOCH, ZntW 1926, 278/82 (Orig. and Heraclas). A. MIURA-STANGE, Celsus u. Or., 1926. C. VERFAILLIE, La doctrine de la justification dans Origène, Thèse, Strasb. 1926. W. VÖLKER, Das Vollkommenheitsideal des Or., 1931. R. CADIOU, Introduction au système d'Origène, Paris 1932; La jeunesse d'Origène, ib. 1936 (valuable); RevSR 1936, 474/83 (the library of Caesarea and the Catenae). HAL KOCH, Pronoia u. Paideusis, Studien über Orig. u. s. Verhältnis z. Platonismus, 1932. H. CH. PUECH, RevHPhR 1933, 508/33 (Mysticism of Orig.). W. SESTON, RevHR 108, 1933, 197/213 (Origen and the beginnings of Monasticism). H. U. V. BALTHASAR, RechSR 1936, 513 ff.; 1937, 38 ff. (Mysteries in Orig.). C. W. LOWRY, JThSt 1936, 225/40 (Trinitarian doctrine of O.). A. LIESKE, Die Theologie der Logosmystik bei Orig. 1938. C. VAGAGGINI, Maria nelle opere di Origene, Rome 1942. J. RUWET, Biblica 1944, 143/66; 311/34 (O's. use of apocrypha). ST. BETTENCOURT, Doctrina ascetica Origenis, Rome 1945. J. DANIÉLOU, RevAM 1947, 126/41 (scriptural sources of mysticism in O.). R. P. C. HANSON, JThSt 1948, 17/27 (Tradition in Orig.). H. CHADWICK, ib. 1947, 34/49 (Orig., Celsus and the Stoa); HarvThR 1948, 83/102 (Origen and resurrection of the body). J. F. BONNEFOY, Mél. F. Cavallera, Toulouse 1948, 87/145 (Theol. method of Orig.). H. JONAS, Theol. Z. Basel 1948. 101/19; 1949, 24/25 (Gnosis and mysticism). J. LEBRETON, AB 1949, 55/62 (Mysticism). H. RAHNER, Eranos-Jb. 1947, 197/248 (human nature). H. DE LUBAC, Histoire et esprit. L'intelligence de l'Écriture d'après Origène,

teacher in the catechetical school to succeed Clement who had been obliged to flee during the persecution of Septimius Severus. He loved Christianity most ardently, led a life of strict asceticism and interpreted literally the text of Matthew 19:12. His earliest philosophical training had been in moderate Platonism, but to ground himself more thoroughly in philosophy he attended the lectures of the celebrated Neo-Platonist Ammonius Saccas (§ 17, 2) and devoted himself to the study of Hebrew. About 212 he journeyed to Rome "to see the most ancient Church" (Eus. VI, 14, 10) on which occasion he probably made the acquaintance of the learned priest Hippolytus. After teaching for some times he summoned Heracles to assist him so that he could devote his time to the more advanced students. For twenty-eight years the catechetical school continued to make progress under his direction, when he was charged with having received Holy Orders irregularly and possibly also accused of heterodox teaching. At any rate, two synods in 231 and 232 condemned him and Bishop Demetrius of Alexandria deposed him from the priesthood and from his position in the school and banished him from the city. He betook himself to *Caesarea* in Palestine where his deposition was not recognized and there he founded a new theological school and began to preach in public. About 232 the Empress Julia Mamaea, who was well-disposed toward Christians, summoned him to Antioch (§ 15, 6). In Arabia he opposed the errors of the Patripassians (§ 32, 5). During the persecution of Decius in 250, Origen, then an old man, was imprisoned and subjected to torture which he bore bravely. He died soon thereafter at Caesarea or Tyre.

Origen was a man of brilliant gifts, of prodigious learning and was by far the most prolific writer of the pre-Nicene period. From an early date his numerous admirers endeavored to express his powers of mind and indefatigability by surnaming him Ἀδαμάντιος, man of steel or Χαλκέντερος, man of brass. He is the *most influential theologian of the Greek Church* and the most important theologian of the entire Church before Augustine. His influence on the history of Christian thought and learning in the East can not be overestimated. His contemporaries considered him a teacher without equal and posterity for some time concurred in the judgement. On the other hand while he still lived he was charged with many errors

Paris 1950. J. DANIÉLOU, RevSR 1948, 27/56 (unity of the two Testaments in O.).

and these charges grew in number and vehemence after his death. Finally in 543 Justinian condemned him as a heretic as did the Council of Constantinople in 553 and the Church approved the sentence. Later generations judged him less rigorously.

Origen's literary activity extended over all the fields of ecclesiastical learning. By far the greater number of his works are *exegetical*, consisting partly of exhaustive commentaries (τόμοι) on practically every book of Sacred Scripture; partly of brief notes (σχόλια) on difficult or obstruse passages; and partly of lectures or sermons (ὁμιλίαι, tractatus) on certain portions of the Scriptures which were recorded by stenographers. In spite of the fact that most of these works have been lost, the number of Origen's works that have been preserved is considerable. Many of the homilies have come down to us through the Latin translations of Jerome and Rufinus. The gigantic work called the *Hexapla*, containing the Hebrew text of the Old Testament and several Greek translations has been preserved only in fragments. Of scarcely less importance are Origen's *apologetic* and *dogmatic* writings. The eight books Contra Celsum written in 248 consist of a refutation of the attack made on the Church by the pagan philosopher Celsus (§ 17, 1) and is by all means the best apology produced before the reign of Constantine. *De principiis* (Περὶ ἀρχῶν) which exists only in a free and faulty Latin version by Rufinus, is a comprehensive presentation of Christian dogma. In four books it treats of God, the Trinity and Angels (I), of creation, man and Redemption (II), of freedom of the will and the conflict between good and evil (III), of Holy Scripture and its threefold sense, somatic, moral and mystical (IV). In spite of the errors which crept into this work, it was a trailblazing accomplishment. Finally Origen's *practical theology* and *asceticism* are to be found in the tract De Oratione (on prayer in general with an explanation of the Lord's Prayer), and in the Exhortatio ad martyrium written during the persecution of Maximinus Thrax (235).

Origen was an *enthusiastic* and *pious Christian*, an ascetic and a mystic, who took his religious obligations seriously and was ready to lay down his life for the faith. As a "Man of the Church" he held fast to the rule of faith and stressed much more forcibly than Clement the authority of Holy Scripture and the teachings of the Church. His concept and understanding of the mystery of the Incarnation and of the indwelling of the Logos in the soul of man are truly remarkable. Christian piety, mysticism and monasticism owe him much. On the other hand, his unquenchable thirst for learning and his tendency to overrate Gnosis at the expense of Pistis led him to a certain Spiritualism which was sometimes Hellenic rather than Christian, as even the pagan polemicist Porphyrius (§ 17) could see (Eus. VI, 19, 7). But Bishop Epiphanius of Salamis (§ 51, 2) is certainly overstating the case when he says (Ep. 51, 3) that Origen is "the father of Arius and the root of every other heresy." Origen's *errors* are found chiefly in the fields of *exegesis, cosmology, eschatology* and in the *doctrine of the Trinity*. They are the result of his opposition to Gnosticism and his too great dependence on Platonism. To meet the objections which Gnostics made to certain passages of Scripture, Origen, like Philo, stretched his *allegorical* interpretation to the danger-point. According to Origen there are very many passages in Scripture which can be interpreted only morally (psychic) or mystically (pneumatic) but not literally or historically (somatic). Hence he gave rein to a purely subjective trend in exegesis. Furthermore, to meet the objection that God is unjust in not creating all creatures equal, Origen drew on Plato and taught the *pre-existence of souls* and their *fall before the beginning of time*. The present visible world was preceded by a world of equally perfect spirits (naturae rationabiles) who abused their free will by turning away from God and were therefore exiled in matter created just for this purpose. The angels were given very refined bodies of spherical shape (the stars), men were given animal bodies and demons were given invisible bodies indescribably hideous. *Creation* itself is conceived as an *external act* since God's omnipotence and goodness must constantly be manifested. The purpose of the visible creation is to restrain and purify spirits. The purification will be universal and all fallen spirits, even Satan, will eventually return to God. The material world will then come to an end and the body of man will rise as a pure spirit so that its end will be as its beginning. But this *restoration of all things* (ἀποκατάστασις πάντων) according to Origen, is only a preliminary to further evolution, for world will follow world in endless succession. In *writing of the Trinity*, Origen sees the three Persons in a relationship of *subordination*. The Logos is less than the Father (not ὁ θεός, or αὐτόθεος like the Father, but only θεός, δεύτερος θεός) and the Holy Ghost is of lesser rank than the Son (De prin. I, 3, 5; C. Cels. V, 39). Still Origen's views on this point were no less faulty than many of his contemporaries (§ 32, 1), although it was always to Origen that the Arians later appealed. He always held unswervingly to the divinity of the Logos or the God-Man (θεάνθρωπος) and to the dignity of Mary as θεότοκος.

3. Another teacher in the school of Alexandria was **Dionysius**[1], whom Eusebius (H. E. VII praef.) surnames **the Great**. Dionysius was a disciple of Origen and later (ca. 247) became bishop of the city († ca. 264). He was a man of action rather than of letters and while he engaged in nearly all the ecclesiastical controversies of his day (§ 22, 3; 32, 5; 33, 2) he exhibited remarkable moderation and prudence. Only a few fragments of his writings have been

---

[1] PG 10. Best edition by CH. L. FELTOE, Cambridge 1904; English transl. by the same, London 1918. Monogr. by F. DITTRICH, 1867; J. BUREL, Paris 1910.

preserved. The practice of issuing an annual Easter letter from Alexandria (§ 25, 3) probably originated with Dionysius.

When Origen was teaching at Caesarea, he had among his disciples **Gregory Thaumaturgus**[1] a zealous and successful missionary bishop of Neocaesarea in the Pontus († ca. 270). A life of Gregory written by Gregory of Nyssa is largely legendary. From the pen of the Thaumaturgus we have a panegyric in which he thanks Origen and praises his teaching; an Epistola canonica with prescriptions for penitents guilty of various sins; a Paraphrase of Ecclesiastes; a Creed, and a Syrian version of a work entitled The Passibility and Impassibility of God.

4. The priest **Hippolytus**[2] has been mentioned before; but he also belongs in this section because he wrote in Greek and was

---

[1] PG 10. Gregors Dankrede, ed. P. KOETSCHAU, 1894; German in BKV 2. Monogr. by RYSSEL, 1880. L. FROIDEVAUX, RechSR 1929, 193/247 (Gregory's creed). W. TELFER, JThSt 1930, 142 ff. 354 ff. (the Latin Vita Gregorii); HarvThR 1936, 225/344 (Gregory's cult). Cfr. also § 75, 6 on Apollinaris.

[2] The Philosophumena of H.: PG 16, 3; ed. P. CRUICE, Paris 1860; ed. P. WENDLAND, 1916; German in BKV 40; French with commentary by A. SIOUVILLE, 2 vol. Paris 1928. Exegetical and homiletic works ed. G. N. BONWETSCH and H. ACHELIS, 1897. Chronicle, ed. A. BAUER u. R. HELM, 1929. L. MARIÈS, Hippolyte de Rome, Sur les bénédictions d'Isaac, de Jacob et de Moïse, Paris 1935. ED. SCHWARTZ, Zwei Predigten Hippolyts, Sb. München 1936, 3; also CH. MARTIN, RHE 1941, 5/23. Commentary on Daniel with French transl. ed. G. BARDY et M. LEFÈVRE, Paris 1947. CH. MARTIN, Mél. F. Cumont I, Brux. 1936, 321/63; RHE 1937, 255/76 (PG 59, 735/46 en Easter sermon of Hippolytus); opposite view R. H. CONNOLLY, JThSt 1945, 192/200. P. NAUTIN, RechSR 1947, 100/7, 347/59 (Ann index to the works of Hippolytus); Hippolyte, Contra les hérésies, Paris 1950. J. DÖLLINGER, Hipp. u. Kallistus, 1853. G. FICKER, Studien zur H.-frage, 1893. H. ACHELIS, H.-Studien, TU 16, 4, 1897. K. J. NEUMANN, H. in seiner Stellung zu Staat und Welt, 1902. A. D'ALÈS, La théologie de S. Hippolyte, Paris 1906. A. BAUER, NJklA 33, 1914, 110/24. Monogr. on Hippolytus by A. DONINI, Rome 1925; G. BOVINI, Rome 1943; E. AMANN, DictThC VI, 2487/2511; F. CABROL et H. LECLERCQ, DictAC VI, 2409/83. H. NAUTIN, Hippolyte et Josipe, Paris 1947 (Josipus an unknown Roman cleric author of the Philosophumena and other works: Hippolytus wrote contra Noetum, in the East ca. 250; Traditio apostolica etc., the opposite view G. BARDY, MSR 1948, 63/88; B. CAPELLE, RechThAM 1950, 145/74). A. HAMEL, Der Kirchenbegriff Hippolyts, Diss. 1929. C. WENDEL, ThStKr 1938, 362/69 (the statue of Hippolytus). Studies: FUNK, AU II, 161/97 (the Refutatio); G. N. BONWETSCH, Nachr. Gött. 1919, 347/60 (commentary on Daniel); cfr. ib. 1923, 27/32, 63 f.; TH. ZAHN, NkZ 1922, 405/16 (forgotten fragments); K. GRAF PREYSING, s. § 32, 4). On the Traditio apostolica: ED. SCHWARTZ, Über die pseudoapostol. Kirchenordnung, 1910. R. H. CONNOLLY, The So-called Egyptian Church Order and Derived Documents, Cambridge 1916 (Texts and Studies 8, 4). B. S. EASTON, The Apostolic Tradition of Hippolytus translat., Cambridge 1934. G. DIX, S. Hippolytus, The Treatise of the Apostolic Tradition translat., London 1937. B. BOTTE, Hippolyte de Rome, La Tradition apostolique, Paris 1946 (French transl. with commentary). H. DUENSING, Der äthiop. Text der Kirchenordn. des H., ed. and transl., 1946. Deutsche Übersetzung der Apostolischen Überlieferung des hl. Hippolytus, Klosterneu-

probably a Greek by birth. He was a disciple of Irenaeus of Lyons, but whether he actually sat at Irenaeus' feet or merely studied his writings, is not known. Hippolytus is renowned as an exegete, a vigorous opponent of the Gnostics and Modalists, a brilliant scholar and versatile writer, and was antipope from the pontificate of Callistus to that of Pontian (§ 15, 7; 32, 4). During the persecution of Maximinus Thrax he was banished to Sardinia where he died in 235 or 236. His body was brought back to Rome and interred in the cemetery which bears his name. It was here in 1551 that the beautiful marble statue was found which his partisans had erected in his honor. Inscribed on the statue is a copy of the Paschal cycle he computed together with a catalogue of his numerous works. It is now almost universally accepted by scholars that the *Philosophumena* or Refutatio omnium haeresium, which was discovered in the nineteenth century, is actually the work of Hippolytus. Of the ten books into which the work was divided, the second and third and part of the fourth are missing. The first four books deal with Greek philosophy, mystery cults and astrology while the remaining six books contain the refutation of every heresy from Simon Magus down to the date of composition, after 222. Special attention is given to Gnosticism. In general, the plan of the work is admirable. Among the other extant works of Hippolytus we have a dogmatic monograph on the Antichrist, a commentary on Daniel, a homily (?) against Noëtus and his followers (§ 32, 4), a Chronicle or compendium of profane and sacred history down to the year 234 and finally, numerous exegetical and homiletic fragments in various Oriental languages. In the explanation of Scripture Hippolytus is much more restrained than the Alexandrians, although he does not scorn allegory altogether. His Syntagma contra omnes haereses has been lost. A genuine work of Hippolytus, the *Traditio apostolica* (Ἀποστολικὴ παράδοσις) has recently been recognized. Formerly it had been known as the Egyptian Church Ordinance because it was extant only in Coptic, Ethiopian and Arabic translations; but in

---

burg 1932 (Liturg. Lesebücher 5). ED. HENNECKE, Harnack-Ehrung, 1921, 159/82. P. GALTIER, RechSR 1923, 511/27. K. MÜLLER, ZntW 1924, 226/31; 1929, 273 f. J. A. JUNGMANN, ZkTh 1929, 579/85. A. HAMEL, ZntW 1937, 238/50. C. C. RICHARDSON, Angl. theol. Rev. 1948, 38/44 (Trad. ap. um 197). The following question H's. authorship: R. LORENTZ, De Egypt. Kerkordening en Hippolytus van Rome, Diss. Harlem 1929; H. ENGBERDING, Festschrift L. K. Mohlberg I, Rome 1948, 47/71. H. ELFERS, Die Kirchenordnung Hippolyts v. R., 1938 (vs. LORENTZ). B. BOTTE, RechThAM 1949, 177/85 (vs. ENGBERDING); 1947, 241/51 (Epiklesc bei H.). K. PRÜMM, ZkTh 1939, 207/25 (Mysterion in H.). Cfr. also § 75, 5.

1916 Dom Connolly, O.S.B., proved that the Ordinance is none other than the Traditio and many scholars agree. The Traditio was written about 220 or possibly as early as 197 and is an important and abundant source for a knowledge of ancient Roman liturgy, organization and discipline. It is the basis for the eighth book of the Apostolic Constitutions and later similar works (§ 75, 5).

5. The other Greek writers belong almost exclusively to *Palestine* and *Syria*. In point of time, Sextus **Julius Africanus**[1] comes first. He was a lay theologian born at Aelia Capitolina (Jerusalem) and later lived at Nicopolis (Emmaus) († after 240). He had been instructed by Heracles of Alexandria, was acquainted with Origen and was a friend of King Abgar IX of Edessa (§ 12, 9). He compiled the *first Christian world chronicle* (Χρονογραφίαι, to 221) with dates based on Daniel's seven weeks of years (each week a thousand years). This work became the basis of all later Byzantine historiography. Another work of purely secular, even superstitious, nature called Κεστοί (= Embroideries) was dedicated to the Emperor Septimius Severus (§ 15, 6). Both of these works exist only in fragments. We have, however, two letters of Julius on exegetical problems. In the one, written to Origen about 240 and preserved in its entirety, he denies the authenticity of the story of Susanna.

The **Didascalia** *Apostolorum*[2] was written in Syria probably in the first half of the third century. It is one of those pseudo-apostolic works which enlarges on the matter in the Didache (moral, liturgical, and canonical prescriptions). The Greek original exists only in revised form in the first six books of the Apostolic Constitutions (§ 75, 5). It has, however, been completely preserved in a Syriac translation and partly in a Latin version. Very probably the work was compiled by a bishop.

Toward the end of the third century a theological school began to develop at *Antioch*, the capital of Syria. Subsequently the

---

[1] H. GELZER, S. Julius Afrikanus und die byzant. Chronographie, 2 vols. 1880/98. W. REICHARDT, Die Briefe des S. Julius Afrik., TU 34, 3, 1909. J. R. VIEILLEFOND, Jules Africain, Fragments des Cestes, Paris 1932; Rev. des études grecq. 1933, 197/203 (recent fragments). G. BARDY, Rev. apolog. 1933, 257/71.

[2] Didascalia et Constitutiones Apost., ed. F. X. FUNK, 2 vol. 1905. Die Didask. Germ. transl. from Syrian by H. ACHELIS and J. FLEMMING, TU 25, 2, 1904. R. H. CONNOLLY, Didasc. apostolorum, the Syriac Version Translated with the Latin Fragment, Oxford 1929. E. TIDNER, Sprachl. Kommentar zur lat. Didasc. Apostolorum, Stockholm 1938. F. C. BURKITT, JThSt 1930, 258/65. H. LECLERCQ, DictAC IV 800/12. P. GALTIER, RHE 1947, 315/51. K. RAHNER, ZkTh 1950, 257/81 (Doctrine and practice of Penance in the Did.).

*Antiochian School* adopted the grammatical-historical *interpretation of Scripture* in opposition to the caprices of the allegorical method (§ 74, 2). **Lucian** of Samosata, a priest and martyr († 312) is considered the founder and first director of this exegetical school and is further looked upon as the continuator of the subordinationism of Paul of Samosata (§ 32, 2 with literature). None of his works are extant.

6. Toward the close of the period there lived two men, both of whom suffered martyrdom under Maximinus Thrax (§ 16, 5), but who differed widely in their theological opinions. They were **Methodius** of Olympus**[1] and Pamphilus of Caesarea. Methodius († 311) was bishop of Olympus in Lycia or, as some think (Diekamp) of Philippi in Macedonia and is known as one of Origen's most resolute opponents. He composed a famous work entitled Symposion (The Banquet), modelled on Plato's work of the same name, in which he enthusiastically extols Christian virginity (§ 26, 3). The Greek text is extant. Other works of Methodius On the Resurrection and On the Will have been found in fragmentary form in Old Slavonic translations. **Pamphilus**, the virtuous and learned priest of Caesarea in Palestine († 310) on the other hand, was one of Origen's most fervent admirers. Ecclesiastical learning owes to him a debt of gratitude not only for enriching the magnificent library founded by Origen, and for his efforts to provide a good text of Scripture, but also for the defense of Origen which he wrote in prison while awaiting martyrdom. This work written with the help of his devoted disciple Eusebius (ὁ τοῦ Παμφίλου § 75, 1) was originally in six books of which only one remains in a faulty Latin translation by Rufinus.

7. Finally mention must be made of the so-called **Sibylline Oracles**** so highly regarded by the Church of Antiquity as well as of the Middle Ages. Of the original fourteen books, two — the ninth and tenth — have been lost. The Oracles are cast in hexameter verse of varied origin and still more varied content: stories and prophecies about peoples and kingdoms; about the coming

---

[1] PG 18. Best edition by N. BONWETSCH, 1917. METHODIUS, Über den freien Willen (De autexusio), slavisch u. griech. mit französ. Übers. v. A. VAILLANT, Patrol. Orientalis XXII, 5, 1930, 631/889. Méthode, Du libre arbitre, trad. par. J. FARGES, Paris 1929. Symposion Germ. tr. in BKV 2. N. BONWETSCH, Die Theologie des Methodius, Abh. Gött. 1903. J. FARGES, Les idées morales et relig. de Méthode d'Ol., Paris 1929. F. DIEKAMP, ThQ 1928, 285/308 (Methodius, bishop of Philippi). J. MARTIN, Symposium, Gesch. einer literar. Form, 1931, 285 ff. On the Symposion cfr. also: P. HESELER, Byzantinisch-Neugriech. Jbb. 1928, 95/118; 1935, 325/40; G. LAZZATI, in Studi ded. alla memoria di P. Ubaldi, Milano 1937, 117/24; M. MARGHERITIS, ib. 401/12.

of the Messias; admonitions and exhortations to penance. The work is basically of Jewish origin (from about 200 B.C. to 400 A.D.), although most of the books were revised by a Christian hand in the third century. Books VI and VII, alone are evidently of Christian origin. — Best edition by *J. Geffcken*, 1902; Germ. tr. in E. Kautzsch, Apokryphen und Pseudepigraphen des A.T. II 1900, 177 ff.; excerpts in E. Hennecke, Neutest. Apokryphen, [2]1924, 399 ff. — — Cfr. *J. Geffcken*, TU 23, 1, 1902. — *W. Bousset*, RE 18, 265/80. — A. Rzach, RE Pauly-Wissowa, 2nd series II, 2117/83. — *K. Prümm*, Scholastik 1929, 54 ff. 221 ff. 498 ff. (the Sibyls in eccl. literature). — *A. Kurfess*, ThQ 1936, 11 ff. 351 ff.; Hermes 1939, 221/3; Symbola Oslo. 1939, 99/105.

# § 40.
# Latin Literature[1].

Christian works written in Latin first appear in the last quarter of the second century especially in the Romanized part of West Africa. It was probably here that the first Latin translation of the Bible was made — and this in spite of the fact that all Latin translations of the Bible before Jerome came to be known as *Itala*[2]. At this time the Church of *Carthage* held the primacy in Christian literature in the West, and here the great spokesmen *Tertullian* and *Cyprian* created a new ecclesiastical and theological language. At Rome, on the contrary, Greek was used in the liturgy and in theological writings (Hippolytus) as late as the beginning of the third century. It was only during the course of this century that

---

[1] BARDENHEWER, HARNACK, ALTANER etc., see § 36. A. EBERT, All-gemeine Gesch. der Lit. des MA.s im Abendland I[2], 1889 (to Charlemagne). M. SCHANZ, Gesch. der röm. Lit. III[3], 1922 (christl. Lit., neubearb. v. G. KRÜGER). A. KAPPELMACHER u. M. SCHUSTER, Die Lit. der Römer bis zur Karolingerzeit, 1934. E. BICKEL, Lehrbuch der Gesch. der röm. Lit., 1937. P. MONCEAUX, Hist. littéraire de l'Afrique chrétienne, 7 vol. Paris 1901/23; Hist. de la littérature latine chrét., Paris 1924. P. DE LABRIOLLE, same title, Paris [3]1947 (revised by G. BARDY). A. GUDEMAN, Gesch. der altchristl. lat. Lit. vom 2.—6. Jh., 1925 (Samml. Göschen). U. MORICCA, Storia della letteratura latina cristiana I—III, 2, Torino 1925/34. A. G. AMATUCCI, Storia della letteratura latina cristiana, Bari 1929. G. BARDY, Littérature latine chrét., Paris 1929; RHE 1932, 501/32 (Christian schools of Rome in second cent.). La question des langues dans l'église ancienne I, Paris 1948. M. PELLEGRINO, La poesia cristiana latina, Turin 1947 (to Ambrose). J. MARTIN, HJG 1921, 201/14 (popular, written and eccl. Latin). J. SCHRIJNEN, Charakteristik des altchristl. Latein, Nymwegen 1932. H. JANSSEN, Kultur u. Sprache, Zur Gesch. der alten Kirche im Lichte der Sprachenentwicklung von Tertullian bis Cyprian, Nymw. 1938. J. DE GHELLINCK, Études class. 1939, 440/78 (Christian Latin). C. MOHRMANN, see § 3, 5. Cfr. the Bulletin of Latin Christian literature in the RevBén 1921 ff. and in RechThAM 1929 ff.
[2] F. STUMMER, Einführung in die lat. Bibel, 1928. Itala, Das N.T. in altlat. Übersetzung, ed. A. JÜLICHER (†) and W. MATZKOW I (Matthew), 1938; II (Mark), 1940. B. BISCHOFF, Misc. G. Mercati I, Rome 1946, 407/36. B. BOTTE, Dict Bible, Suppl. IV, 1948, 777/82 (Itala). Vetus latina, Die Reste der altlatein. Bibel, ed. by the Archabbey of Beuron, 1949 ff.

Greek was displaced by Latin. And it should be noted that both in matter and form the Latins and Greeks (Orientals) exhibit a striking dissimilarity. While the latter by preference dealt with the speculative problems of theology, the former applied themselves to *positive* and *practical* questions of Christian morality and ecclesiastical organization. While the Orientals turned to the favorite philosophical school to seek light in their religious problems, the Latins either flouted the schools or were at most eclectics.

1. The first work of a Christian writer to be produced in the Latin language seems to have been the dialogue *Octavius* composed by the Roman lawyer **Minucius Felix**\*\*1, who was a native of Africa. Jerome, it is true, says (De vir. Ill. 53): Tertullianus presbyter primus post Victorem (pope) et Apollonium (martyr) Latinorum ponitur. But the age-old discussion as to how to explain the similarity of style and content of the Octavius and Tertullian's Apology (written in 197) can best be settled by admitting the priority of the former. Octavius is an apology which was probably occasioned by the inflammatory speech of Fronto (§ 15, 4) against Christians. It is in the form of an animated debate between Octavius, the author's friend and countryman, and Caecilius Natalis, a pagan. In the course of the debate, polytheism is denounced, the charges made against Christians are refuted and an inspiring picture of Christian life is drawn. Since the work was intended primarily for educated pagans, the author gives more prominence to questions

---

1 Editions of Octavius by C. HALM, 1867; J. P. WALTZING, Louvain 1903, Bruges 1909 (with commentary), Leipz. ²1926 (also a Lexicon Minucianum, Liège 1910); A. SCHÖNE, 1913; J. MARTIN, 1930 (Floril. patrist. 8); C. SCHNEIDER, 2 parts 1934 (Text and commentary); A. D. SIMPSON, New York 1938; G. QUISPEL, Leyden 1949; M. PELLEGRINO, Turin 1950. German in BKV 14. A. ELTER, Prolegomena zu Minucius Felix, Progr. Bonn 1909. M. SCHUSTER, Wiener Studien 1934, 163/7 (Min. Felix and popular christian philosophy). H. LECLERCQ, DictAC XI, 1388/1412. J. J. DE JONG, Apologetie en Christendom in den Octavius van Min. Felix, Diss. Leyden 1935. F. WOTKE, Commentationes Vindobonenses 1, 1935, 110/28. R. BEUTLER, Philosophie und Apologie bei Min. Felix, Diss. 1936. A. KURFESS, ThGl 1938, 546/52 (to Oct. 12—25). W. DEN BOER, Mnemosyne 1943, 161/90 (Clement of Alex. and Min. Felix). On the priority of Octavius, recent works: J. STIGLMAYR, ZkTh 1913, 221/43; G. HINNISDAELS, Mémoirs de l'Acad. R. de Belgique, Lettres II, 19, Brux. 1924; W. A. BAEHRENS, ZntW 1924, 110/22; J. G. P. BORLEFFS, De Tertulliano et Min. Felice, Diss. Groningen 1925; A. GUDEMAN, Philologus 1926, 353 ff.; 1927, 25 ff.; H. J. BAYLIS, Min. Felix and His Place Among the Fathers of the Latin Church, London 1928; JOHANNA SCHMIDT, Min. Felix oder Tert. ? Diss. 1932. On the priority of Tertullian: R. HEINZE, Abh. Leipzig 62, 1910, 279/490; G. GOETZ, ZntW 1924, 161/73; G. MEYER, Philologus 1926, 67/83; H. DILLER, ib. 1935, 98 ff. 216 ff. J. LORTZ, Tertullian als Apologet I, 1927, 14 f. 395 ff.; B. AXELSON, Das Prioritätsproblem Tertullian—Min. Felix, Lund 1941.

of Weltanschauung than to any specific Christian doctrine or to
Holy Writ. He uses Cicero's De natura deorum to good advantage
and draws heavily on Stoic thought. In skill of composition and
beauty of language Octavius surpasses all other apologies of the
period.

2. Quintus Septimius Florens **Tertullianus**\*\*[1] is, without question
the greatest of the early Latin writers. He was born at Carthage

---

[1] Opera omnia: PL 1—2; ed F. OEHLER, 3 vols. 1851/4 and Ed. minor
1854; in CSEL 4 vols. thus far. ed. A. REIFFERSCHEID et al., 1890/1942.
Germ. transl. by H. KELLNER, 2 vols. 1882; selections H. KELLNER and
G. ESSER in BKV 7 v. 24. E. ROLFFS, Tertullian (selections), 1930. Separate
works: Apologeticum, ed. J. E. B. MAYOR and A. SOUTER, Cambridge 1917
(with English transl. and commentary); J. P. WALTZING, (with French transl.
and commentary). 2 vol. Paris 1930; A. SOUTER, Aberdeen 1926; J. MARTIN,
1933 (Floril. patrist. 6); H. HOPPE, 1939 (CSEL 69). De testimonio animae,
ed. W. A. J. C. SCHOLTE, Amsterd. 1934 (with transl.); German by M. HAIDEN-
THALLER, 1942 (with Ad nationes L. 2). De praescriptione haeret., ed. E.
PREUSCHEN, ²1910; P. DE LABRIOLLE, Paris 1907 (with French transl.);
J. MARTIN, 1930 (Floril. patrist. 4); J. N. BAKHUIZEN VAN DEN BRINK, Den
Haag 1946 (with Adv. Praxean). De baptismo, ed G. RAUSCHEN, 1916 (Floril.
patrist. 11); J. W. P. BORLEFFS, Leyden 1931 (from Mnemosyne 1931, 1/102
and with De patentia and De poenitentia, Den Haag 1948; A. D'ALÈS, Rome
1933 (Textus et documenta). De anima, ed. J. H. WASZINK, Amsterd. 1933
(with Germ. transl. and commentary; also an Index verborum . . ., Bonn 1935;
on the sources cfr. H. KARPP, ZntW 1934, 31/47 ) and English, ib. 1948. Adv.
Praxean, ed. E. KROYMANN, 1907; E. EVANS, London 1948. De oratione,
ed. R. W. MUNCEY, London 1926; G. F. DIERCKS, Bussum 1947. De poenitentia
ed. J. W. P. BORLEFFS, Mnemosyne 1932, 41 ff. 254 ff. (with Index verborum).
De poenitentia and De pudicitia, ed. G. RAUSCHEN, 1915 (Floril. patrist. 10);
E. PREUSCHEN, ²1910; P. DE LABRIOLLE, Paris 1906 (with French transl.),
De spectaculis, ed. A. BOULENGER, Paris 1933; J. BÜCHNER, Tert. De spec-
taculis, Kommentar, Diss. 1935. De cultu feminarum, ed. W. KOK, Dokkum
1934 (with commentary). De fuga in persecutione, ed. J. J. THIERRY, Hilver-
sum 1941. De pallio, ed. A. GERLO, Wetteren 1940. Both works ed. J. MARRA,
Torino 1932. Monographs on Tertullian by A. HAUCK, 1878; E. NÖLDECHEN,
1890; Monceaux (see above) I; CH. GUIGNEBERT, Paris 1901; F. RAMORINO,
Milano 1923; J. LORTZ, 2 vols. 1927/8 (standard); J. BERTON, Paris 1928;
B. NISTERS, 1950; H. KOCH, RE Pauly-Wissowa 2. R. V. 822/44; M. S. ENS-
LIN, Journal of Rel. 1947, 197/212; G. BARDY, DictThC XV, 130/71. A. NEAN-
DER, Antignosticus, Geist des Tert., ²1849. G. ESSER, Die Seelenlehre
Tertullians, 1893. H. HOPPE, Syntax u. Stil des Tert., 1903; Beiträge zur
Sprache u. Kritik Tertullians, Lund 1932. A. D'ALÈS, La théologie de Tert.,
Paris 1905. K. ADAM, Der Kirchenbegriff Tertullians, 1907. G. THOERNELL,
Studia Tertullianea, 4 parts, Upsala Univ.-Schriften 1917/26. E. BOSSHARDT,
see § 30 B. 1. E. R. ROBERTS, The Theology of Tert., London 1924. P. VIT-
TON, I concetti giuridici nelle opere di Tertulliano, Roma 1924. AL. BECK,
Röm. Recht bei Tert. u. Cyprian, 1930 (also J. J. VÖGTLE, AkKR 1932, 693/7).
J. K. STIRNIMANN, Die Praescriptio Tertullians im Lichte des röm. Rechts
u. der Theologie, 1949. ST. W. J. TEEUWEN, Sprachl. Bedeutungswandel
bei Tert., 1926. J. MORGAN, The Importance of Tert. in the Development of
Christian Dogma, London 1928. TH. BRANDT, Tertullians Ethik, 1929.
L. BAYARD, Tertullien et S. Cyprien, Paris 1930 (Moralistes chrét.). J. KLEIN,
T. Christl. Bewußtsein u. sittl. Forderungen, 1940. B. B. WARFIELD, Studies
in Tert. and Augustine, Oxford 1930 (Trinitarian doctrine). M. KRIEBEL,
Studien etc. see § 32. C. DE L. SHORTT, The Influence of Philosophy on

about 160, the son of a centurion. A pagan until middle life, he accepted Christianity about 197 or earlier after having followed for some years the profession of a lawyer, and died after 220. Jerome (De vir. ill. 53) says that Tertullian was a priest, but the general opinion seems to be that he was never ordained. He was a man of exceptional mental gifts, thoroughly conversant with rhetoric and law. Although he was possessed of a ready wit, lively phantasy and forceful eloquence and originality which did not hesitate to coin new words and expressions, his style is often somber and obscure. Of a fiery, harsh and bitter disposition (ardens vir — Jerome, Ep. 84, 2), he was inclined to be excessively severe in judgement and action. Hence, it is not difficult to understand why he later (ca. 205) embraced Montanism whose views were so like his own. But even after becoming a Montanist he continued to defend the rule of faith with characteristic force and skill, — and invented words and phrases which most aptly expressed the Church's teaching especially regarding the Trinity and Redemption. He was a bitter foe of pagan philosophy which he considered the root of all heresy; yet he himself was strongly influenced by later Stoicism. Thirty-one of his works, known to be genuine, have been preserved. Some of them were written in defense of Christianity against pagans and Jews, some are controversial and some explain Christian (Montanist) morality and discipline. The most important of the apologetic works are the Ad nationes, probably dependent on Minucius Felix, and the smaller, but excellent De testimonio animae. The dogmatic-polemic works are usually considered Tertullian's best productions.

the Mind of Tert., London 1933. R. HÖSLINGER, see § 12, 6. A. M. VELLICO, La rivelazione e le sue fonti nel 'De praescriptione haereticorum' diTertulliano, Rome 1935. G. ZIMMERMANN, Die hermeneut. Prinzipien Tertullians, Diss. 1937. H. JANSSEN, Kultur u. Sprache etc., see above. E. DEKKERS, Tertullianus en de geschiedenis der liturgie, Amsterd. 1947. A. KOLPING, Sacramentum Tertulianeum, 1948. Separate studies: H. KOCH, HJG 1907, 95 ff.; ZntW 1912, 59 ff.; ZKG 1914, 1/8 (Tertullian a layman); P. DE LABRIOLLE, BullLA 1913, 161/77 (T. a priest). H. KOCH, IntkZ 1920, 45/61 (Tert. and Cyprian); ThStKr 1930, 458 ff.; 1931, 95 ff.; 1932, 127 ff.; 1933, 39 ff. P. GUILLOUX, RHE 1923, 5 ff. 141 ff. (religious development of Tertullian). H. V. CAMPENHAUSEN, Theol. Blätter 1929, 193/200 (early church and tradition in T.). F. J. DÖLGER, AntChrist 1929, 143 ff. 174 ff.; 1930, 117 ff. 142 ff. 222 ff.; 1934, 138 ff. (De baptismo). J. H. WASZINK, Mnemosyne 1936, 165/74 (Tertullianea); VC 1947, 137/49; 1948, 224/42. A. D'ALÈS, Revue des études grecques 1937, 329/62 (Tert. a Hellenist). V. MOREL, RHE 1944/5, 5/46 ('disciplina' in Tert.). G. D. SCHLEGEL, Downside Rev. 1945, 125/8 (Ad martyres). A. J. FESTUGIÈRE, RevSPhTh 1949, 129/61 (De anima). On the Apologeticum see lit. on Minucius Felix (especially R. HEINZE); also H. SCHRÖRS, TU 40, 1, 1914; E. LÖFSTEDT, Lund Univ.-Schriften 1915, 1918, 1920.

Among these must be mentioned De praescriptione haereticorum which presents a brilliant defense of the Church's principle of tradition (c. 45—53 are not genuine, but probably a redaction of the Greek); De baptismo (§ 22, 3); and De anima which is a sort of Christian psychology and borrows from the Greek physician Soranus of Ephesus; Adversus Marcionem and Adversus Praxean. The best practical ascetical works are from the period when Tertullian was still a Catholic. They are: De oratione; De poenitentia; De spectaculis; De cultu feminarum and Ad uxorem. For the others, written while a Montanist and attacking the Psychici (Catholics) see § 34, 2.

3. The third Latin writer and second in importance is Caecilius **Cyprianus**\*\*[1], surnamed Thascius. Before his conversion he was a rhetorician, but shortly after baptism became a priest and bishop of Carthage (249—258). He read and admired Tertullian's writings (Da magistrum) but prudently refrained in his own works from

---

[1] S. Cypriani Opera, rec. G. HARTEL, 3 vols. 1868/71 Opuscula, ed. S. COLOMBO, Torino 1935 (with Italian transl.). L. BAYARD, S. Cyprien, Correspondance. Texte et trad., 2 vol. Paris ²1933. De lapsis, ed. J. MARTIN, 1930 (Floril. patrist. 21); also H. KOCH, ThLZ 1930, 439/41. De cath. ecclesiae unitate, French transl. by P. DE LABRIOLLE, Paris 1942. Both works in German: Cyprians Hirtenbriefe über die Kirche, v. B. STEIDLE, 1940. Cyprians Schriften deutsch v. J. BAER, BKV 34 u. 60. Monogr. by J. PETERS, 1877; B. FECHTRUP, 1878; E. W. BENSON, London 1897; Monceaux (see above) II, condensed, Paris 1914 (Les Saints); J. H. FICHTER, St. Louis 1942. L. NELKE, Die Chronologie der Korrespondenz Cyprians, 1902. H. V. SODEN, Die Cyprian. Briefsammlung, TU 25, 3, 1904; Das lat. N.T. in Afrika zur Zeit Cyprians, TU 33, 1909. B. MELIN, Studia in Corpus Cyprianeum, Upsala 1946. B. POSCHMANN, Die Sichtbarkeit der Kirche nach der Lehre des hl. C., 1908. A. D'ALÈS, La théologie des S. Cyprien, Paris 1922. H. KOCH, Cyprian. Untersuchungen, 1926; IntkZ 1920, 45/61 (C.'s personality); ib. 229/47 (zu Ep. 8 u. 9); Ricerche religiose 1929, 137 ff.; 1930, 304 ff. 492 ff.; 1934, 502 ff. (C. and early Christian Lit.). S. COLOMBO, Didaskaleion 1928, 1/80 (C. the man and the writer). AL. BECK u. L. BAYARD, see above under Tertullian. F. SCHUBERT, Weidenauer Studien III, 1909, 253/97 (C.s pastoral principles). CH. FAVEZ, Rev. de Etudes Lat. 1941, 191/202 (C.s flight). R. B. DONNA, Traditio 1946, 399/407 (on De habitu virginium). M. P. NILSSON, HarvThR 1947, 167/76 (Greek mysteries in C.). J. SCHRIJNEN ed. CH. MOHRMANN, Studien zur Syntax der Briefe des hl. C., 2 parts. Nymwegen 1936/7. H. JANSSEN, Kultur u. Sprache etc., see above. M. BÉVENOT, St. Cyprian's De unitate 4 in the Light of the Manuscripts, London 1939. Further studies on De cath. eccles. unit. 4: D. VAN DEN EYNDE, RHE 1933, 5/24; J. LEBRETON, RechSR 1934, 456/67; O. PERLER, RQ 44, 1936, 1 ff. 151 ff.; cfr. O. GRADENWIT, Z. f. Rechtsgesch., Roman. Abt. 1930, 170/83. On the Martyrdom and the Acta Cypriani: R. REITZENSTEIN, Sb. Heidelberg, 1913, 46/69; Nachr. Gött. 1919, 177/219; P. FRANCHI DE CAVALIERI, Studi Romani 2, 1914, 189/215; P. CORSSEN, ZntW 1914/18; H. DELEHAYE, Les passions litt. des martyrs, Brux. 1921, 82 ff.; F. C. CONYBEARE, ZntW 1922, 169/77. On the Vita Cypriani by Pontius: A. HARNACK, TU 35, 3, 1913; J. MARTIN, HJG 1919, 674/712; A. D'ALÈS, RechSR 1918, 319/78; REITZENSTEIN, CORSSEN, noted above.

the latter's narrowmindedness and crudeness. He was a Roman in every fibre of his being, noble, sincere and sympathetic. During the persecutions of Decius and Valerian, as well as in the internal disturbances in the Church, he proved himself a faithful shepherd of his flock and a staunch defender of the faith and of ecclesiastical discipline. Augustine (De bapt. III, 3, 5) calls him "catholicus episcopus" and "catholicus martyr". And such he certainly was, in spite of the fact that his opinions regarding the rebaptism of heretics did not, for the time, coincide with the decisions of the bishop of Rome (§ 22, 3). Cyprian was martyred during the Valerian persecution in 258 (§ 16, 2). His writings reflect his calm, equable temperament, his grasp of the Holy Scriptures and his purpose to benefit his readers. His style was admired and imitated in the following centuries. The main idea which appears in all that Cyprian wrote was the unity of the Catholic Church as the source of salvation; (for his theory of the Roman primacy see § 21, 3). Foremost among the works of Cyprian must be placed the two treatises De catholicae ecclesiae unitate and De lapsis. There is still a question whether c. 4 of the former work was revised by Cyprian himself or by another hand. Both works were written in 251. De unitate was directed against the schisms of Felicissimus and Novatian (§ 35) and De lapsis is a pastoral letter bitterly lamenting the fall of so many Christians during the persecution and energetically upholding the penitential discipline of the Church. Besides these moral treatises he wrote an apology Ad Donatum shortly after his conversion, De habitu virginum, De dominica oratione and De moralitate. His collection of *letters* (65 written by him and 16 addressed to him) are an important source for the ecclesiastical history of his day. The Acta of his martyrdom and a biography written by his deacon Pontius have been preserved. The Vita bears the distinction of being the oldest known Christian biography and while it lacks historical value, it does give a highly idealized picture of Cyprian the Bishop.

A number of *writings* composed about this time were eventually circulated under *Cyprian's* name and *erroneously* included in manuscript collections of his works. (Almost all such spurious works are to be found in the third volume of Hartel's edition). Due to the lack of any accepted tradition it is now impossible to determine the authorship of these works. Recently the tracts De bono pudicitiae, De spectaculis and De laude martyrii have been thought, because of internal evidence, to be from the pen of *Novatian*; but this certainly can not be so in the case of De laude martyrii (cfr. H. Koch,

ZKG 1919, 86/95). — Harnack believed that the Latin sermon *Adv. aleatores* was the work of Pope Victor and *Ad Novatianum* the work of Pope Sixtus II (257—258) but in neither case are the reasons for thus assigning them very convincing. (On Adv. aleatores cfr. Funk, AU II, 209/36; H. Koch, Festgabe K. Müller 1922, 56/67; on Ad Novatianum cfr. H. Koch, Cyprian. Untersuchungen 1926, 358/420). It is impossible to make even a sound conjecture regarding the authorship of the *Liber de rebaptismate* (ed. G. Rauschen, Floril. patrist. 11, 1916). It definitely upholds the validity of baptism conferred by heretics (§ 22, 3), therefore the very opposite of Cyprian's view. It was probably written by an African bishop about 256. — (Cfr. *H. Koch*, Die Tauflehre des Liber de reb., 1907; ZntW 1907, 190 ff.; IntkZ 1924, 134 ff.; J. Ernst, ThQ 1908, 1909; ZhTh 1917.) — An imperfectly preserved homily *De centesima, sexagesima, tricesima* (Matt. 13:8) i. e. on the threefold reward of martyrs, ascetics and good Christians (publ. by *R. Reitzenstein*, ZntW 1914, 60/90) was composed in North Africa in the third or fourth century. — Cfr. J. M. Heer, RQ 1914, 97/186; H. Koch, ZntW 1932, 248/72.

4. At the same time that Cyprian was writing at Carthage, the ambitious priest **Novatian**[1], who gave his name to the schism he began, (§ 35, 1) was displaying considerable literary activity at *Rome*. He was a man of extensive learning, a trained philosopher, and an elegant stylist. Only a few of his works have been preserved. Two letters in the Cyprianic collection (nos. 30 and 36) were evidently written by Novatian. Of the treatises ascribed to him, De bono pudicitiae and De spectaculis are probably from his pen, while De cibis judaicis and De trinitate are certainly authentic. The latter is a dogmatic monograph of some importance, written to combat the Monarchians, but itself not entirely free from Subordinationism. The Church historian Socrates (H.E. IV, 28) says that Novatian died a martyr in a persecution (of Valerian?). An inscription discovered in a Donatist catacomb at Rome in 1932, Novatiano beatissimo martyri Gaudentius diaconus fecit, could possibly refer to the Roman presbyter and antipope.

K. Weyman and H. Jordan have erroneously ascribed to Novatian the twenty *Tractatus de libris SS. Scripturarum* (ed. P. Batiffol, Paris 1900) previously accepted among the works of Origen. Most probably these works were written by Bishop *Gregory of Elvira* in the fourth century (§ 76, 6).

---

[1] Novat., De trinitate, ed. W. Y. FAUSSET, Cambridge 1909; De cibis iud., ed. G. LANDGRAF and K. WEYMAN, Archiv f. lat. Lexikographie 1900, 221/49. A. D'ALÈS and E. AMANN, see § 35. 1. H. KOCH, Art. Novatian, RE Pauly-Wissowa S VII, 1138/55; AntW 1935, 303/6 (on Cyprian Ep. 30); Religio 1937, 278/94 (Novatian's language and style). B. MELIN, Studia in Corpus Cyprianeum, Upsala 1946. M. KIREBEL, see § 32 (Trinitarian doctrina). F. J. DÖLGER, AntChrist 1930, 258/67 (Novatian's baptism). C. MOHLBERG, Ephemerides Liturgicae 1937, 242/49 (Novatian a martyr); cfr. D. VAN DEN EYNDE, RHE 1937, 792/4 and A. FERRUA, CivCatt 1944, IV, 232/9.

It is difficult to determine whether the Christian poet **Commodianus** wrote in the third or fifth century. We shall speak of him among the writers of the later date § 76, 8.

**Victorinus**\*\*[1] Bishop of Poetovio, the present city of Pettau in Styria, died a martyr under Diocletian († 304). He is the *oldest exegete* among the Latin Fathers and wrote a number of commentaries on Scripture in which he drew strongly on Origen. These are preserved only in a few fragments. Of his other writings there is extant the entire text of De fabrica mundi (on creation). His Commentary on the Apocalypse, discovered in 1895, was known and used by Jerome. And while Jerome was favorably disposed toward Victorinus as a countryman, he did not excuse the chiliastic ideas (§ 33) evident in his writings.

5. The list of Christian latin writers of this period conclude with the names of two apologists, both laymen and both Africans. **Arnobius the Elder**\*\*[2] was a rhetorician at Sicca in Numidia. On the occasion of his conversion about 305, he wrote a treatise (incomplete) Adversus nationes in seven books. However, the work is a vigorous attack on paganism rather than a defense of Christianity and gives evidence of a superficial and often inexact understanding of Christian doctrine. According to Jerome (De vir. ill. 80) Lucius Caecilius Firmianus **Lactantius**\*\*[3] was a pupil of Arnobius. During the reign of Diocletian he went to Nicomedia as a rhetorician and later (ca. 316) was called to Trier as tutor to Crispus, son of Constantine the Great. His classical style caused the Humanists to surname him the "Christian Cicero." Besides two small philo-

---

[1] V's works ed. by J. HAUSSLAITER, 1916; cfr. id. in RE 20, 614/19.

[2] Editions of Arnobius by A. REIFFERSCHEID, 1875; G. MARCHESI, Torino 1934. F. GABARROU, Arnobe, Thèse Toulouse 1921; Le latin d'Arnobe, Paris 1921. H. KOCH, Zu Arnobius u. Laktantius, Philologus 1924, 467/72. S. COLOMBO, Didaskaleion 1930, 1/241. F. TULLIUS, Die Quellen des Arn. im 4.—6. Buch seiner Schrift Adv. nationes, 1934. H. HAGENDAHL, La prose métrique d'Arnobe, Goeteborg 1937. G. WIMAN, Eranos 1947. 129/52.

[3] Editions of the writings of Lactantius by S. BRANDT and G. LAUBMANN, 2 vols. 1890/7. Selections in BKV 36. R. PICHON, Lactance, Paris 1901. MONCEAUX (see above) III. E. AMANN, DictThC VIII, 2425/44. H. LECLERCQ, DictAC VIII, 1018/41. G. MOLIGNONI, Didaskaleion 1927, 117/54. L. ROSSETTI, ib. 1928, 115/200 (sources of De opif. Dei). G. KUTSCH, In Lactanti de ira Dei librum quaestiones philologae, 1933. M. SCHUSTER, Wiener Studien 54, 1936, 118/28 (De ave Phoenice); Commentationes Vindobonenses 2, 1936, 55/70 (the phoenix myth). A. HUDSON-WILLIAMS, VC 1949, 237/43 (Orientius and L.). On De mortibus persecutorum (genuinity formerly questioned): J. BELSER, ThQ 1892, 246 ff. 439 ff.; 1898, 547 ff. K. JAGELITZ, Über den Verfasser der Schrift De mort. pers. Gymn.-Progr., Berlin 1910. A. MÜLLER RQ Suppl. 19, 1913, 66/88. H. KOCH, ZntW 1918, 196/201. J. G. P. BORLEFFS, Mnemosyne 1929, 427/36; 1930, 223/92.

sophical essays (De opificio Dei, De ira Dei), there are extant from his pen two larger and more important works, Divinae institutiones and De mortibus persecutorum. Both are apologetic, but De mortibus is also historical and as such is of interest and value for the history of the persecutions. Lactantius himself later abridged the Divinae institutiones in an edition called Epitome also still extant. The Institutiones were intended to be an apology against paganism and at the same time a summary of Christian teaching (the first Christian Weltanschauung in the West). However, his theology is quite ordinary and Lactantius proves himself a much better apologist than theologian. De mortibus gives dramatic and passionate expression to the indignation felt by the author as an eyewitness to the Diocletian persecution and dwells on the miserable fate that befell the persecutors. De ave Phoenice, a poem of eighty-five distichs, which relates the legend of the phoenix (the symbol of immortality) is sometimes ascribed to Lactantius, but his authorship is as frequently denied since the poem contains scarcely an idea capable of Christian interpretation.

## SECOND PERIOD
## FROM THE EDICT OF MILAN
## TO THE COUNCIL IN TRULLO (313—692)

### Retrospect and Survey

The Fathers of the fourth and fifth centuries often express their astonishment at the rapid spread of Christianity during the persecutions. *Eusebius* the historian (H.E. II, 3) says: "Of a sudden the saving Word, like a ray of sunshine illumines the whole world with heavenly light and power." And Bishop *Niceta* of Remesiana in Dacia, the author of the Te Deum, writing about 410 in the midst of the confusion caused by the Migration of Nations, expressed Christendom's confidence of victory with the words: "Te per orbem terrarum sancta confitetur ecclesia . . . in Te domine speravi, non confundar in aeternum!" The history of Christianity in the first three centuries presents even to the more critical modern gaze a marvelous picture of an almost uninterrupted *growth* of the institution founded by Christ for the world's salvation; and this in spite of external and internal hindrances and opposition, in spite of all the weakness, sins and misdeeds of the Church's own children. The mustard seed had become a tree in whose branches the birds of the air could dwell (Matt. 13:31 f.). The *persecutions* had at first been more or less sporadic efforts on the part of emperors, governors and the pagan populace; but from Decius to Diocletian, all the might of the State had been employed to eliminate Christianity from the Empire. And while these efforts had convulsed the Church, neither the bloodiest nor the most prolonged had succeeded in destroying her. Her host of martyrs strengthened by the power of God's Spirit continued to triumph over brute force. No less striking is the manner in which the Church was able to *assert herself* against religious syncretism (Gnosticism), heresy, schism and the other *internal dangers* which threatened her existence. Basing herself on the certain criteria of the inspired Scriptures and the "Rule of Faith", the great society which formed but one body throughout the Roman Empire, the "great Church" (as the pagan polemist Celsus called it, Orig. C. Cels. V, 59), was able to recognize what was false and reject it authoritatively. Like the persecutions, the controversies over truths of faith often cost the Church dearly, but in spite of them she kept her unswerving course, guided by the hierarchy of bishops descending in direct line from the Apostles. And at the head of the hierarchy stood the successor of Peter in whom all Christendom recognized the necessary embodiment of ecclesiastical unity. Even in the heat of battle she proceeded vigorously and uncompromisingly to develop the fundamental truths of faith committed to her by Christ and to build up the organization willed for her by the same divine Founder. The sentiments of *St. Cyprian*: "Salus extra ecclesiam esse non potest" (Ep. 73, 21) and "Habere non potest Deum patrem, qui ecclesiam non habet matrem" (De cath. eccl. unit. 6 and Ep. 74, 7) were the firm convictions of all believing Christians. An harmonious relationship existed between clergy and laity; and both clerics and laics drank deep of the fonts of salvation which they possessed in the dogmas, the worship and the Sacraments of the Church. And throughout the Church there was a conscious development of a specific Christian morality and a Christian theology which as early as the third century far surpassed in depth and life the profane productions of a later period. "Everything which was the common possession of Christianity in the field of ecclesiastical organization, of Christian dogma, of worship and religious moral life in the East, down to the present day and in the West until the sixteenth century was given its essential content and direction in the second and third centuries." (A. Ehrhard, Die Kirche der Martyrer, p. 268).

The last vain attempt of Diocletian and his co-regents to uproot Christianity as a sect dangerous to the State made the Church's power and importance evident to the world. The act of *Constantine the Great* (313) in granting her liberty and official recognition not only freed her from the oppression she had suffered for centuries, but also placed her in a position she had not theretofore held. The period of her first missionary activities was over and she faced a period of transformation which was to have far-reaching consequences. The State now allied itself with the Church, granted her special privileges and promoted her interests. But at the same time the State sought to control her as the *universal Church of the Empire*. Henceforth the Church could preach and teach publicly her sublime doctrines and ideals and direct the currents of her doctrine and means of salvation toward the regeneration of the ancient world.

The glad tidings of the Gospel were soon being preached on the most distant frontiers of the Empire; and before long these same tidings were heard by Germanic and Celtic tribes and were re-echoed from the plains of Central Asia to the rim of the Sahara. Paganism began gradually to disappear, although its suppression by secular force or by mass conversion to the Church was attended with disastrous results which affected Christian life for centuries. In the meantime the Church, especially in the East, was often shaken to her foundations by serious *controversies* over the most important points of belief. The great quarrels known as Arianism, Nestorianism, Monophysitism, Monotheletism, Origenism, Donatism and Pelagianism were frequently intensified and prolonged by the interference of court officials. But they were finally settled in the great *ecumenical councils* which decreed dogmatically what was to be held regarding the questions involved and thus firmly laid the immutable foundations of all subsequent theology. As a result of these quarrels the Church of the East saw whole nations (Syria, Persia, Egypt, Abyssinia, Armenia) permanently separated from her communion. Yet the fourth and fifth centuries mark the classical period of *Christian theology*, the period of the great *teachers of the Church* from Athanasius to Cyril and Theodoret, from Hilary to Jerome down to Augustine, the greatest of them all. *Monasticism* which had its beginning in the East opened up a new and abundantly flowing spring from which all subsequent generations could draw a deeper religiosity and a more pervading spirit of ecclesiastical unity.

The *Latin Church* of the West, conscious of the differences between the Western and Eastern mind, had begun during this period to go more and more her own way. Yet her history is no less turbulent than that of the Greek-Oriental Church. For the most part, however, it was storms from without that brought the Church of the West to the brink of ruin. The old Roman Empire of the West had not been able to withstand the impact of invading *Germanic tribes*, and collapsed. The same fate threatened the Church. Some of the Germanic tribes succeeded in setting up permanent kingdoms in the territory of the Empire and in place of the orthodox religion of the Empire introduced religious differences with disastrous results. For the Germanic tribes which had accepted Christianity, accepted it corrupted by *Arianism* and only after long and bitter struggle did they renounce the heresy for Catholicism. When the *Franks* under Clovis became Catholics, the first step was taken toward the restoration of ecclesiastical unity, the principle on which medieval civilization was based. During the confusion of the Migration of Nations the *popes*, especially the two who have merited to be called Great, *Leo I* and *Gregory I*, upheld the old traditions, defended Rome as the center of the Empire's spiritual unity and delivered to the Germans and Celts the blessings of Christianity and the most precious heritage of the ancient culture. The Order of *St. Benedict* became the nursery of a noble religious spirit and a genuine civilization. Since the days of the Emperor Justinian, the Byzantine Empire and the *Eastern Church* had become more indelibly stamped with their own peculiar characteristics and more completely estranged from the West. In the seventh century the East again suffered terrific losses by the victory of *Islam*. Syria, Egypt and North Africa, provinces which for centuries had been the scenes of flourishing Christian life were overrun by the disciples of Mohammed who in the beginning of the eighth century crossed the Strait of Gibraltar and entered Spain. Then the stage of World and Church History gradually shifted from East to West and from South to North. Grecian-Roman antiquity was at an end and the future belonged to the young Germanic and Romanic nations. However, much time and a tedious process of education, carried out by the Church or under her guidance, was still needed before these nations could take over the civic and cultural leadership of Central Europe. But the beginning of the process marks the birth of the Middle Ages in the proper sense of the term.

# CHAPTER I

## SPREAD OF CHRISTIANITY
## AND OBSTACLES ENCOUNTERED[1]

### § 41.

### Constantine the Great and His Successors.
### Suppression and Gradual Decline of Paganism in the Roman Empire.
### The Church[2].

1. The epoch-making *Edict of Milan* of 313 (§ 16, 6) gave the
Christian Church in the Roman Empire full and unconditional public

---

[1] Cfr. literature in § 4, 6—8 and preceding § 5. Also: O. SEECK, Regesten der Kaiser u. Päpste 311—476, 1919. The Cambridge Ancient History XII (193—324), Cambridge 1939. The Cambridge Medieval History, ed. by GWATKIN and WHITNEY I—II (to 800), ib. 1911/3. F. LOT, La fin du monde antique et le début du moyen âge, Paris 1928. B. MOSS, The Birth of the Middle Ages (395—814), Oxford 1935. M. BESNIER et A. PIGANIOL, Le Bas-Empire jusqu'en 395, Paris 1937/47 (Hist. générale, publ. p. G. GLOTZ, Hist. Romaine IV); F. LOT, CH. PFISTER et F. L. GANSHOFF, Les destinées de l'Empire en Occident (395—888), Paris 1928/35 (Hist. générale . . . Moyen âge I); CH. DIEHL et G. MARCAIS, Le monde oriental de 395—1081, Paris 1936 (Hist. générale . . . Moyen âge III). PH. HILTEBRANDT, Ideen u. Mächte, Der Aufstieg des Abendlandes seit dem Untergang der antiken Welt, 1937 (biased). H. PIRENNE, Geburt des Abendlandes, deutsch v. P. HÜBINGER, 1939. C. SILVA-TAROUCA, Fontes historiae ecclesiasticae medii aevi I (see V—IX), Rome 1930; Ecclesia in Imperio Romano-Byzantino, Rome 1933. L. DUCHESNE, Hist. ancienne de l'Église II—IV (4./6. Jh.), Paris 1908/25. P. BATIFFOL, Le Catholicisme des origines à S. Léon, 4 vol. Paris 1909/24. H. V. SCHUBERT, Gesch. der christl. Kirche im Frühmittelalter (c. 480—900), 1921. A. DUFOURQ, Hist. de l'Église III—V, Paris ³1930/1. G. SCHNÜRER, Kirche u. Kultur im MA. I, ³1936; Die Anfänge der abendländ. Völkergemeinschaft, 1932. A. FLICHE, La chrétienté médiévale (395—1254), Paris 1929. E. CASPAR, Gesch. des Papsttums I—II (to 750), 1930/3. J. HALLER, Das Papsttum I, ²1951. F. X. SEPPELT, Geschichte der Päpste I (to 590), 1931; II (590—1250), 1934. Histoire de l'Église, publ. p. A. FLICHE et V. MARTIN, vol. III (313—395), Paris 1936; vol. IV (395—590), Paris 1937; vol. V (590—757), Paris 1938 (standard). A. EHRHARD, Die kath. Kirche im Wandel der Zeiten u. der Völker I, 2, 1: Die altchristl. Kirchen im Osten u. Westen, 1937. H. LIETZMANN, Gesch. der alten Kirche III—IV, 1938/44. K. MÜLLER, Kirchengeschichte I, 1, ³1941. E. M. PICKMAN, The Mind of Latin Christendom (373—496), Oxford 1937. F. HEILER, Die kath. Kirche des Ostens u. Westens I—II, 1, 1937/41.

[2] Cod. Theod. XVI tit. 10 (cfr. § 2, 4). V. SCHULTZE, Gesch. des Untergangs des griech.-röm. Heidentums, 2 vols. 1887/92; Altchristl. Städte u. Landschaften I—III (Constantinople, Asia Minor and Antioch), 1913/30. G. BOISSIER, La fin du paganisme, 2 vol. Paris ⁶1909. O. SEECK, Gesch. des Untergangs der antiken Welt, 6 vols. 1895/1921; I⁴ 1922 (rationalistic). P. BATIFFOL, La paix Constantinienne et le Catholicisme (303—359), Paris 1914. G. FERRERO, Der Untergang der Zivilisation des Altertums, deutsch v. E. KAPFF, 1922. J. GEFFCKEN, Der Ausgang des griech.-röm. Heidentums, ²1929. P. DE LABRIOLLE, La réaction païenne, see § 17. H. LECLERCQ, Art. Déclin du paganisme, DictAC XIII, 241/375. K. S. LATOURETTE, A History

recognition and placed it on an equal footing with the pagan cults. The high regard which **Constantine the Great**[1] continued to have

of the Expansion of Christianity II, New York 1939. G. BARDY, L'année théol. 1943, 457/507 (christianity and paganism c. 400). L. HERTLING, ZkTh 1938, 92/108 (number of Catholic Christians c. 600). J. MILLER, Jahresbericht über die Fortschritte der klass. Altertumswiss. 246, 1935, 43/130 (röm. Kaisergesch. 284—395). H. RICHTER, Das weström. Reich, besonders unter Gratian, Valentinian II u. Maximus, 1865. A. GÜLDENPENNING, Gesch. des oström. Reiches unter Arkadius u. Theodosius II, 1885. J. B. BURY, History of the Later Roman Empire from Arcadius to Irene (395—800), 2 vol. London 1889; Hist. of the Later Roman Empire (395—565), 2 vols. London 1923. CH. DIEHL, Histoire de l'Empire byzantin. Paris [10]1934. C. JULLIAN, Hist. de la Gaule, vol. VII bis VIII: Les empereurs de Trèves, Paris 1926. E. STEIN, Gesch. des spätröm. Reiches I (284—476), 1928; Hist. du Bas-Empire II (476—565), Paris 1949. G. OSTROGORSKY, Gesch. des byzant. Staates, 1940. CH. CLERCQ, Dix siècles d'histoire byzantine (476—1461), Paris 1946. L. BRÉHIER, Le monde byzantin, 2 vol. ib. 1947/9. N. H. BAYNES and B. MOSS, Byzantium, Oxford 1949. FR. KAMPERS, Vom Werdegang der abendländ. Kaisermystik, 1924. M. VOGELSTEIN, Kaiseridee-Romidee u. das Verhältnis von Staat u. Kirche seit Konstantin, 1930. W. REHM, Der Untergang Roms im abendländ. Denken, 1930. H. WERNER, Der Untergang Roms. Studien zum Dekadenzproblem, 1939. J. A. STRAUB, Vom Herrscherideal in der Spätantike, 1939. F. BERTOLINI, Storia di Roma (bis 476), Milano 1934. A. SOLARI, Il rinnovamento del Impero romano I (363—476), Rome 1938. R. PARIBENI, L'Italia imperiale da Ottaviano a Teodosio, Milano 1938. L. SALVATORELLI, L'Italia medioevale (c. 395—1000), Milano 1938. K. VOGT, Staat u. Kirche von Konstantin d. Gr. bis zum Ende der Karolingerzeit, 1936 (also W. ENSSLIN, Gnomon 1938, 211/7). H. LIETZMANN, Das Problem Staat u. Kirche im weström. Reich, Abh. Berlin 1940, 11. H. BERKHOF, Kirche u. Kaiser, 1947. Cfr. lit. in § 15 (LINSENMAYER, DURUY-HERTZBERG, POEHLMANN, WOLF etc.) and § 16, 6 (Sesan).

[1] EUSEBIUS, Vita Constantini, ed. I. A. HEIKEL, 1902. H. G. OPITZ, Byzantion 1934, 535/93 (anonymous Vita Constantini); cfr. P. HESELER et J. BIDEZ, ib. 1935, 399/442. I. DANIELE, I documenti Constantiniani della "Vita Constantini" di Eusebio di Cesarea, Diss. Rom Univ. Greg. 1938. J. BURCKHARDT, Die Zeit Konstantins d. Gr., 1853, [6]1949. L. SEUFFERT, Konstantins Gesetze u. das Christentum, 1891. J. MAURICE, Numismatique Constantinienne, 3 vol. Paris 1908/12; Constantin le Grand, Paris 1925. V. SESAN, see § 16, 6. E. SCHWARTZ, K. Konstantin u. die christl. Kirche, [2]1936. H. KOCH, Konstantin d. Gr. u. das Christentum, 1913. Konstantin d. Gr. u. seine Zeit, ges. Studien, ed. F. J. DÖLGER, 1913 (RQ Suppl. 19). P. BATIFFOL, La paix Constantinienne. J. D'ELBÈE, Constantin le Grand, Paris 1947; K. HÖNN, Konstantin d. Gr., [2]1945. J. VOGT, Constantin d. Gr. u. sein Jh., 1949; Festschr. L. Wenger II, 1945, 118/48 (Christian influence on Constantine's legislation). A. H. M. JONES, Constantine and the Conversion of Europe, London 1948. V. SCHULTZE, RE X, 757/70; ZKG 1925, 321/37 (Christian emblems on coins under Constantine). H. LECLERCQ, Constantin, DictAC III, 2622/95. F. X. FUNK, Konstantin d. Gr. u. das Christentum, AU II, 1/23. L. WRZOL, Weidenauer Studien I, 1906, 227/69. V. BURCH, Myth and Constantine the Great, Oxford 1927. L. SALVATORELLI, Costantino il Grande, Rome 1928 (also CivCatt. 1929 III, 412/22); Ricerche religiose 1928, 289/328 (Constantine's religious policy). G. P. BAKER, Constantine the Great and the Christian Revolution, London 1930. N. H. BAYNES, Const. the Great and the Christian Church, London 1931; Mél. J. Bidez II, Paris 1933/4, 13/18 (Eusebius and the Christian Empire). A. PIGANIOL, L'empereur Constantin, Paris 1932 (also A. D'ALÈS, Études 213, 1932, 429/44 and N. H. BAYNES, Byz. Z. 1934, 118/23). K. MÜLLER, HZ 140, 1929, 261/78 and again in „Aus der akad. Arbeit", 1930, 80/100 (Constantine the Great and the christian

for the Church soon obtained for her further privileges, especially those which had been enjoyed by the old State-religion. These privileges enabled the Church to become a corporate part of the State. In 313 the clergy were granted immunity, i. e., were exempted from military and other public duties; in 318 and 333 (§ 60, 4; 61, 1, 3) the Church was permitted to receive legacies, bishops were publicly recognized as possessing civil jurisdiction; and in 321 Sunday was made a public holiday. Numerous and generous donations of money and property were made to the Church and to the clergy. As the new religion advanced under the favor of the State, the old religion proportionately declined. But since the great part of the population, especially in the West and in the rural districts still professed paganism, a policy of temporary toleration had to be followed. At first only private haruspicy (sacrifice accompanied by divination) was forbidden (319) and this for political reasons. But Constantine took cognizance of the situation by retaining for himself the title and office of Pontifex Maximus and continued to issue coins bearing the customary pagan symbols. However, Christian emblems (the cross and the monogram of Christ) soon became the chief ornaments of public coinage.

Thus the conqueror of the West openly declared himself on the side of the new religion. Shortly after his victory over Maxentius, Constantine had publicly professed his belief in the God of the Christians. And although he was not baptized until just before he died, he was considered a catechumen in the broader sense of the

Church). CHR. BAUR, AkKR 111, 1931, 99/113 (beginning of caesaropapism). H. G. OPITZ, ZntW 1935, 1/19 (Eusebius of Caesarea as a theologian). H. EGER, ZntW 1939, 97/115. (Emperor and Empire in theology according to Eusebius). E. GERLAND, Konstantin d. Gr. in Geschichte u. Sage, Athen 1937 (aus Byzant.-Neugriech. Jbb. 1937). H. LIETZMANN, Der Glaube Konstantins d. Gr., Sb. Berlin 1937, 29; Die Anfänge des Problems Kirche u. Staat, ib. 1938. F. STÄHELIN, Konstantin d. Gr. u. das Christentum, Zeitschr. f. schweiz. Gesch. 1937, 385/417 (also separately); 1939, 396 ff. J. STRAUB, Das neue Bild der Antike II, 1942, 374/94 (Constantine's consciousness of his Christian mission). A. KANIUTH, Die Beisetzung Konstantins d. Gr., 1941. H. GRÉGOIRE, Byzantion 1938, 561/83 (Constantine's "conversion"). A. ALFOLDI, Journal of Roman Studies 1932, 9/23 (the monogram on Constantine's shield 317); PISCICULI, Festschr. F. J. Dölger, 1939, 1/18 (Hoc signo victor eris); The conversion of Constantine and Pagan Rome, English transl. by H. MATTINGLY, Oxford 1948; A. GRAF SCHENK V. STAUFFENBERG, Festschr. J. Haller, 1940, 70 ff. (Constantine's idea of Empire). J. GAUDEMET, RevHEFRance 1947, 25/61 (religious legislation). H. KARPP, ZntW 1942, 145/51 (laws forbidding the haruspices 319—21); Theol. Rundschau, 1951, 1/21. Cfr. lit. in § 16, 6. On the year of the decisive battle with Licinius (324, not 323!). Cfr. E. STEIN, ZntW 1931, 177/85; H. G. OPITZ, ib. 1934, 132/42.

word. His brother-in-law **Licinius**[1], Emperor of the East, gradually adopted a different attitude. This was due, no doubt, to political rivalry; for as early as 314 their rivalry had resulted in armed conflict. Licinius did not formally abrogate the law of 313, but from 320 the Christians in his part of the Empire were subject to various sorts of oppression. They were dismissed from the army and from the court; many were deprived of their freedom and their property; synods were forbidden; it was made unlawful for men to give religious instructions to women; obstacles were placed in the way of holding religious services and in some cases the governors of provinces even inflicted the death penalty (the martyrdom of forty soldiers at Sebaste in Armenia). But this situation did not last long. The jealousy of the two rulers, aggravated by religious differences, led to another war in 324 in which Licinius was defeated. He was imprisoned at Thessalonica and in 325 was executed for alleged conspiracy.

2. The restoration of monarchical government in the Empire definitely favored the cause of Christianity. Thenceforth Constantine was able to give freer expression to his religious policy. Although his moral conduct was often reprehensible (unbridled ambition, cruelty) and his religious notions were a strange admixture of syncretism and superstition, yet he was convinced of the superiority of Christianity over the pagan cults. And since he himself had witnessed the insuperable vitality of the Christian Church in the persecutions, he resolved to use the Church as the firm support of the State. Henceforth the Christian religion was to take the place of effete paganism as the one bond uniting all the peoples of the Roman Empire. In a manifesto to his new subjects in the East, issued in 324 (Eus. Vita Const. II, 48—60), he expressed the wish that everyone forsake "the temples of deceit" and enter "the radiant house of truth". But at the same time he forbade anyone to be molested because of religious convictions. The highest offices in the State were given preferably to Christians, magnificent Christian basilicas were erected at Rome, Jerusalem, Constantinople, etc., pagan temples were allowed to decay, or, as in the case of those devoted to immoral rites of Venus, were destroyed, and marriage and family

---

[1] F. GÖRRES, Krit. Untersuchung über die Licin. Christenverfolgung, 1875; Philologus 1913, 260/62. CH. ANTONIADES, Kaiser Licinius, 1884. H. GRÉGOIRE, Byzantion 1938, 551/60 (religious policy of Licinius). On the martyrdom at Sebaste: Sozom. H. E. IX, 2; P. FRANCHI DE' CAVALIERI, Studi e Testi 22, 1909, 64/70; 49, 1928, 155/84; W. WEYH, Buz. Z. 1912 76/93.

life according to the Christian ideal were protected by law. (On this point see also § 73, 3, 4). The new imperial city, *Byzantium-Constantinople* or New Rome was dedicated in 330; and unlike Old Rome, which was still strongly pagan, was given an essentially Christian character. The materials of former pagan temples were used largely in its construction and gold and silver idols and votive offerings were melted down for its ornamentation.

After a long and successful reign during which he had proved himself a capable general and statesman, Constantine died at Ancyrona, a suburb of Nicomedia, on Pentecost 337. Shortly before his death he was baptized by Eusebius, the Arian bishop of Nicomedia (§ 47, 3, 4; 48, 2). The Greek Church later honored him as a saint together with his mother Helena (§ 70, 6), compared him with the Apostles and called him "the thirteenth Apostle." The West was satisfied to bestow on him the surname "Great". Few men deserved the title more than he: he brought about a change in world history of the most far-reaching importance by divorcing the Roman Empire from the pagan religion and introducing Christian ideas and ideals into public life and that without disrupting the organization of the Empire. Understandably, political considerations played a large part in the move. But no one is justified in asserting as Gibbon, Burkhardt and others have done, that Constantine was totally insincere and was nothing more than a religious hypocrite. It is true that at first he valued the Christian religion because of the results he had seen it accomplish; but his later life and actions prove that he allowed himself to be more and more influenced by Christian thought and that he sincerely rejoiced in the moral conquests of the Gospel. This is evident from his words and deeds down to the instructions he gave regarding his burial. He believed that he had been given a special mission by God and that it was necessary for the Church and State to work together harmoniously. His favorite title was "Servant of God" and while showing the Church due reverence, he felt that he was her master as the former emperors had been masters of the old pagan State religion. His biographer Eusebius tells us (Vita Const. IV, 24) that Constantine called himself "Bishop of those outside the Church" (ἐπίσκοπος τῶν ἐκτός) and in another place (I, 44) Eusebius goes so far as to recognize him as a "sort of universal bishop" (οἷά τις κοινὸς ἐπίσκοπος). In his endeavor to protect the Church against heresy and schism, Constantine interfered unduly in purely ecclesiastical affairs. He convoked synods to deal with Donatism and Arianism, sought to influence the decisions of those synods and proclaimed the decisions as laws of the Empire. He banished Arius; but he also exiled Athanasius (§ 52; 47; 48). Thus he not only laid the foundations for a Christian State but he also laid the foundations for a *State-Church*, for *Caesaropapism* (Byzantinism). At a later date the Caesaropapism which Constantine introduced became the accepted norm of the Greek Orient.

The legend that *Constantine* was *baptized* by Pope *Sylvester*, on which occasion the emperor was cured of leprosy, was accepted throughout the Middle Ages and down to the seventeenth century. However, the story has not the slightest historical basis. It probably originated at Rome during the second half of the fifth century and may have had some connection with the so-called Baptistry of Constantine near the Lateran. The legend was popularized by the Vita Silvestri. — Cfr. *J. Döllinger*, Papstfabeln, ²1890, 61 ff.; *F.J.Dölger*, Konstantinsfestschrift (see above), 377/447; *W. Levison*, Misc. F. Ehrle II, Rome 1924, 159/247; ZRGkan 1925, 501/511; V. Burch, Myth (see above) 26 ff.; *G. B. Giovenale*, Il Battistero Lateranense, Rome 1929. (On the *Donation of Constantine*, a forgery of the eighth or ninth century, see § 85, 3).

Constantine's sons endeavored to carry on the work of Christianizing the Empire, but instead of proceeding with the patience and tolerance of their father they resorted to violence and force. After the early death of *Constantine II* (337—340), *Constantius* in 341 appealed (erroneously?) to a law of his father and prohibited all pagan sacrifice. In 346 in conjunction with *Constans* (337—350), the ruler of the West, he renewed the prohibition under penalty of death and confiscation of property and at the same time ordered that all pagan temples be closed. (Cod. Theod. XVI, 10, 2: Cesset superstitio, sacrificiorum aboleatur insania!). The apologist Firmicus Maternus (§ 76, 5) urged the emperors to extirpate paganism by force. After Constans had defeated and murdered Magnentius the Usurper in Gaul (351) the law was renewed (353—356), a proof that it had not been enforced everywhere. In 351 Constantius became sole ruler of the Empire. He was a Christian, but favored Arianism and a State-Church in which his will would be the only law (§ 48). He was baptized on his deathbed by the Arian Bishop Euzoïus.

3. The fortunes of the Church now suffered a sharp reversal. **Julian**[1] (361—363), the son of a step-brother of Constantine the

---

[1] Iuliani imp. libros c. Christianos coll. C. J. NEUMANN, 1880; Germ. transl. by the same 1880. Iuliani Epistulae, leges, poëmatia edd. J. BIDEZ et F. CUMONT, Paris 1922. L'empereur Julien, Oeuvres complètes, ed. J. BIDEZ, Paris 1924 ff. (with French transl.). R. ASMUS, Julians Galiläerschrift,

Great, although raised a Christian, had long inclined toward paganism, encouraged by his tutor, the Neoplatonist and theurgist, Maximus of Ephesus. The army in Gaul admired Julian's qualities as a leader and in 360 proclaimed him Augustus, whereupon he openly renounced Christianity (hence his sobriquet — Apostate) and declared himself in favor of the old religion. He zealously promoted sun worship and other forms of paganism, especially theosophy and magic. Since the Emperor Constantius died in November 361 Julian at once became undisputed ruler. Immediately he restored to paganism its ancient rights and privileges, while he revoked all privileges of the "Galileans", as he scornfully called the Christians, and removed them from all public offices. He forbade Christians to teach the classics (362) evidently to force Christians to attend pagan schools or to deprive them of all higher learning. As a matter of fact, this edict proved most troublesome to Christians. Julian furthermore encouraged heresy and schism within the Church (Arianism, Donatism, § 48, 6; 52, 3) and to please the Jews as well as to flout the prophecy of Christ (Matt. 24:2), planned to rebuild the Temple at Jerusalem. However, due to earthquakes and fire, the undertaking never succeeded. He wrote several works against Christianity, only parts of which have been preserved in their refutation by Cyril of Alexandria (§ 75, 7). Julian, unlike earlier emperors, did not favor open persecution of the Church, but the overzealousness of officials and the fanaticism of the pagan populace resulted, at times, in bloody riots. On the other hand, obsessed with the notion of founding a State-Church according to the ideals of Neoplatonism, he strove to reform the old pagan religion. He built almshouses, orphanages and hospices, prescribed religious instruction for the people, insisted on the

Gymn.-Progr. Freib. 1904; Julians philos. Werke übers. u. erklärt, 1908. Monogr. on Julian by A. MÜCKE, 2 vols. 1867/9; P. ALLARD, 3 vol. Paris 1900/3; J. GEFFCKEN, 1914; E. J. MARTIN, London 1919; F. DOLDINGER, 1926; G. NEGRI, Milano ⁴1928; J. BIDEZ, Paris 1930 (standard), Germ. by H. RINN, ⁵1947; also J. WOLF, StZ 1941, 219/25; W. D. SIMPSON, Aberdeen 1930; F. A. RILEY, London 1937. H. GOLLANCZ, Julian the Apostate, Oxford 1928 (the legendary Syrian Vita). E. V. BORRIES, RE Pauly-Wissowa X, 26/91. J. VITEAU, DictThC VIII, 1942/71. H. LECLERCQ, DictAC VIII, 305/99. G. MAU, Die Religionsphilosophie K. Julians, 1907. W. KOCH, Revue belge de philol. et d'hist. 1927, 123 ff.; 1928, 49 ff. 511 ff. 1363 ff. (Julian's religious reform). K. LATTE, Antike 1928, 325/41. P. REGAZZONI, Didaskaleion 1928, 1/114 (Julian's work contra Galilaeos). P. DE LABRIOLLE, RQH 113, 1930, 257/303; La réaction païenne (see § 17), 369/436. B. K. WEIS, Das Restitutionsedikt K. Julians, Diss. 1933. C. H. HENNING, De eerste schoolstrijd tussen Kerk en Stat onder Julianus, Diss. Nijmwegen 1937. J. VOGT, K. Julian u. das Judentum, 1939.

moral conduct of pagan priests and introduced a sort of penitential discipline. These reform measures — a tribute to Christianity, since they were modelled for the most part on Christian ideas — had but little success. When Julian died in the Persian campaign, his work of restoration, though scarcely begun, came to an end.

The account of Theodoret (H. E. III, 25) that the dying emperor exclaimed: "Galilean, Thou hast conquered!" is a later Christian invention. Julian was a visionary who lacked all sense of reality. Even the pagans were indifferent toward his reform measures which were doomed to failure from the beginning. Thus the threat to Christianity "Passed like a white cloud" (Athanasius). Cfr. R. v. Nostiz-Rieneck, Vom Tode des Kaisers J., Progr. Feldkirch 1907; N. H. Baynes, Journal of Roman Studies 1937, 22/9.

4. The succeeding emperors, although Christians, wisely refrained from taking stern measures against paganism. *Jovian* (363—364) restored to his co-religionists the rights of which Julian had deprived them and relegated paganism to the position it had held under Constantine, but did not molest it otherwise. This same policy was followed by *Valentinian I* (364—375) in the West and by his brother, the Arian *Valens* (364—378) in the East. Early in their reigns they prohibited nocturnal sacrifices, and later on when a general decree forbidding all sacrifices was issued, an exception was made allowing the offering of incense.

The word *"pagani"* to designate idolaters came into use shortly after 350. It appears in the law of 370 (Cod. Theod. XVI, 2, 18) and since the time of Baronius this has been taken as a proof that paganism had declined so as to be found only in rural districts (pagani from pagus = rustics, peasants). Thus *J. Zeiller* (Paganus, Collectanea Friburg., Fribourg 1917). But *A. Harnack* (Mission [§ 12] I[4], 430 ff.) and *B. Altaner* (ZKG 1939, 130/41) are perhaps more correct in tracing the usage back to Tertullian and other early writers where the meaning of the word is "civilian" (= non-soldier, in contradistinction to a Christian who is a "miles Christi").

**Gratian**[1] (375—383), Emperor of the *West*, renounced the title and insignia of Pontifex Maximus, discontinued State subsidy for pagan worship, confiscated the revenue of pagan priests and Vestal virgins together with the landed property of the temples, restricted

---

[1] H. RICHTER, E. STEIN, et al. See lit. at the beginning of § 41. H. V. CAMPENHAUSEN, Ambrosius v. Mailand als Kirchenpolitiker, 1929. J. R. PALANQUE, S. Ambroise et l'Empire romain, Paris 1933, 41/7; Byzantion 1933, 41/7 (Gratian and the title Pontifex Max). F. H. DUDDEN, The Life and Times of St. Ambrose, 2 vol. Oxford 1935. J. WYTZES, Der Streit um d. Altar der Viktoria (text with transl. and commentary), Amsterd. 1936. V. HAERINGEN, Mnemosyne 1937, 157 ff. 229 ff. (Valentinian II and Ambr. 386). W. WILBRAND, MissWRelW 1938, 195 ff.; 1941, 97 ff. (paganism and the mission in Ambr.).

the immunity of pagan priests and removed the altar of the goddess *Victoria* from the Senate Chamber (382). This last enactment created great consternation among the pagans. The pagan party among the Roman nobility sought to avert the blow. A deputation headed by Symmachus, a senator and renowned orator, went to the court at Milan to ask the emperor to reconsider his edict; but Gratian refused to grant them audience. After his death at the hands of the usurper *Maximus* at Lyons, the petition was made in writing to Gratian's brother and successor, the thirteen-year-old *Valentinian II* (383—392). The imperial council was in favor of granting the request; but *St. Ambrose*, the great bishop of Milan, prudently but energetically advised the young emperor to reject the petition (Relatio Symmachi) and not allow the ara Victoriae to be restored (384). According to Ambrose (Ep. 17, 9. 10), the majority of the Senate was, by this time, Christian.

5. Similar severity toward paganism was also being shown in the *East*. **Theodosius I the Great**[1] (379—395), a capable and firm ruler, had been appointed by Gratian to succeed Valens. In February 380 he issued the decree De fide catholica in which he called upon all his subjects to accept the Nicene Creed as their rule of life (§48,6). By this decree he may be said to have established the Catholic Church as the **Church of the Empire.** Although he had been somewhat lenient in the beginning of his reign, it was not long before he proceeded to extreme measures. By 388 numerous temples had been closed and where pagans offered resistence, they merely made matters worse. In Alexandria, Bishop Theophilus led a popular campaign against paganism during which a number of old pagan sanctuaries were destroyed, including the renowned Serapeion (391). In other places the people and especially the monks carried out a similar program. Where the temples were not destroyed, they where seized for Christian worship. In vain did the aged rhetorician *Libanius* address to the emperor his Oratio pro templis (388). An edict of Theodosius and Valentinian II forbade all forms of pagan worship; not only sacrifice, but also the visiting of temples and honoring of idols (391). A later law of Theodosius made the offering of sacrifice and haruspicy the equivalent of high treason punishable by heavy fines (392). The assassination of Valentinian II by the

---

[1] G. RAUSCHEN, Jahrbücher der christl. Kirche unter Theodosius d. Gr., 1897. J. MISSON, Recherches sur le paganisme de Libanios, Louvain 1914. G. V. BESELER, Byzant.-Neugriech. Jbb. 1938, 1/40 (Libaniana). G. BARDY, L'église et les derniers Romains, Paris 1948.

Frankish general Arbogast and the accession of the usurper *Eugenius* (392—394), himself a Christian, gave paganism in the West a short respite, during which its practice was permitted at Rome and the ara Victoriae was restored. But the decisive victory of Theodosius on the banks of the Isonzo near Aquileia in 394 ended all hopes of a further pagan revival. (On the penance imposed by Ambrose on Theodosius for the blood-bath at Thessalonica, 390, see § 76, 1).

6. Now that pagan worship in all its forms had been forbidden by imperial decree and under penalties, it remained only to enforce the laws. Yet further laws were enacted. In the *East, Arcadius* (395—408) deprived pagan priests of the privileges and incomes they still retained, and caused the temples in rural districts to be destroyed (396, 399). His son, *Theodosius II* (408—450), who, during his minority was under the regency of his politically-wise and pious sister, *Pulcheria*, and who, even later, relied on her advice, excluded pagans from all public offices in 416 and in 448 ordered the anti-Christian works of Porphyrius to be burned (§ 17). An imperial edict of 423 seems to imply that there were no pagans left (quamquam jam nullos esse credamus). About this time (415) there occurred the brutal and most reprehensible murder of the famed Neoplatonist, Hypatia (§ 75, 7), by a mob of Christians in the city of Alexandria. As late as the sixth century it was still found necessary to enact laws against pagans. Emperor *Justinian I* (527—565) closed the school of philosophy at Athens (529), the chairs of which had been until then occupied almost exclusively by pagan Neo-Platonists. He also ordered under penalty of deprivation of civil rights and property that all pagans receive baptism. It is said that as a result of this edict 70,000 were baptized in Asia Minor.

In the *West*, which had suffered greatly since the fifth century from the inroads of Germanic tribes, and which had been seriously depopulated (§ 43), the process had taken longer. The Christian Vandal, Stilicho[1], minister and father-in-law of the young emperor Honorius (395—423), ordered the Sibylline books to be burned. Yet, in the West, care was taken to preserve the ornaments of the public buildings, even the statues of the gods. And after the temples had been stripped of all pagan objects, the buildings themselves were not subject to further defacement. By a law of 407/8 all revenue was withheld from pagan temples and after the altars had

---

[1] S. MAZZARINO, La politica religiosa di Stilicone, Milan 1938.

been removed the buildings were used for public purposes. But paganism was by no means dead. In rural districts and in out-of-the-way places it actually lasted longer than in the East. Toward the end of the sixth century Pope Gregory the Great was still concerned about its existence in the islands of Sardinia, Corsica and a few other places. In the Latin West where the total population had declined to about ten million by the year 600, the number of Catholic Christians was probably between seven and eight million.

7. While the State had been concerned about the complete conquest of the pagan religion, the Church had not been idle. It had become her task to supplement State legislation so that the many who were now nominally her members, some only because of pressure from the civil authorities, be transformed into true Christians by learning her doctrine and making use of her means of grace. Naturally she did not always succeed in this task to the extent she desired. Remnants of pagan belief and pagan immorality were not soon nor easily eradicated (§ 73). At the same time the Church continued as before to preach the Gospel to the heathens inside and outside the Empire (§ 42—44). Among the great missionaries, or rather as foremost promoters of the Church's missions, must be mentioned *St. Martin*, Bishop of Tours († 397) (§ 72, 6), who worked for the conversion of the pagan population of Gaul; and *St. John Chrysostom*, Bishop of Constantinople († 407) (§ 75, 3) who showed a like interest in the pagan and Arian Goths[1]. But as yet we know very little about this chapter of mission history.

## § 42.

### The Spread of the Church in Asia and Africa[2].

1. Christianity had found its way into **Persia**[3] as early as the third century (§ 12, 9) and appears there in a flourishing condition

---

[1] P. ANDRES, Der Missionsgedanke in den Schriften des hl. Johannes Chrysostomus, 1935.

[2] L. DUCHESNE, Autonomies ecclésiastiques, Églises séparées, Paris, ²1904; K. S. LATOURETTE, see § 41.

[3] J. LABOURT, Le christianisme dans l'empire perse (224—632), Paris 1904. W. A. WIGRAM, Introduction to the History of the Assyrian Church (100—640), London 1910. E. SACHAU, Abh. Berlin 1919, 1/80. O. BRAUN, Akten pers. Martyrer, BKV 22, 1915. K. LÜBECK, Die altpers. Missionskirche, 1919. P. PEETERS, AB 1925, 261/304 (Martyrs of Adiabene). The Cambridge Ancient History IV: The Persian Empire and the West, Cambridge 1926; A. CHRISTENSEN, L'Iran sous les Sassanides, Paris 1936. J. ORTIZ DE URBINA, ORChrPer 1937, 456/85 (origin of the Persian schism). P. DEVOS, AB 1946, 87/131 (Martyrdom of St. Sirinus c. 570).

during the fourth century. But government officials became suspicious of Christians and agitated for the suppression of their religion. The first persecution began during the reign of King *Schapur* (Sapor) II (310—380) and lasted for forty years. Since 337 Persia had been at war with Emperor Constantius and this circumstance made the lot of the Persian Christians most distressful. In general, however, they proved most loyal to the faith. The Church historian Sozomen (II, 9—14) speaks of 16,000 Persian martyrs known by name. Succeeding rulers were less severe. Under *Jezdedscherd* (Jezdijird) I (399—420) Christians even enjoyed royal favor. But the imprudent action of Bishop Abdas of Susa in destroying a pagan temple provoked a new persecution in 420. It became very severe under *Bahram V* (420—438) and lasted, with brief lulls, until 450. About this time Persia became the headquarters of *Nestorianism* (§ 54, 5) which established here a *national Church* under the Metropolitan of Seleucia-Ctesiphon. The Catholic congregations still existing in the country soon merged with the heretical group.

2. Christianity was introduced into the kingdom of **Armenia**[1] during the third century. For some time the country had been subject to Christian influence from Syria and eastern Asia Minor (§ 12, 8). The apostle of the country was a native Armenian, *Gregory*, surnamed the *Illuminator*. In flight from the Persians, he was baptized at Caesarea in Cappadocia and upon his return to the homeland, converted the king Trdat (Tiridates). The king immediately destroyed all pagan places of worship and made Christianity the State religion. The nobility followed the king in his conversion and Gregory lived to baptize a large part of the population, the remainder being converted shortly after his death. Gregory's successors governed the *national Church* of Armenia with the title of Catholicos (= chief bishop, patriarch) and were originally under the jurisdiction of the See of Caesarea. The position of catholicos became hereditary in

---

[1] S. WEBER, Die kath. Kirche in Armenien vor der Trennung, 1903. F. TOURNEBIZE, Hist. politique et relig. de l'Arménie, Paris 1910; DictHE IV, 290/391. M. ORMANIAN, L'Église arménienne, Paris 1910. J. B. AUFHAUSER, ZMW 1918, 73 ff. 166 ff.    J. SANDALGIAN, Histoire documentaire de l'Arménie (to 305), Rome 1917.    J. DE MORGAN, Hist. du peuple arménien, Paris 1919.    R. GROUSSET, Histoire de l'Arménie (to 1071), Paris 1947.    H. PASDERMASJIAN, Hist. de l'Arménie . . ., ib. 1949. L. ARPEE, A History of Armenian Christianity, New York 1946.    J. MARKWART, OrChr 27, 1932, 141/236 (first dioceses in Armenia).    S. LYONNET, RechSR 1935, 176/87 (Armenian translation of the Bible).    N. AKINIAN, AB 1949, 74/86 (series of Armenian bishops 219—439).

Gregory's family. The catholicos *Nerses I* (339?—373) did much to deepen the religious life of Armenia. During the fifth century *St. Mesrob* and his disciples established an important school of Christian literature. When the country became a Persian province in 428, the conquerors endeavored to introduce Parsiism, but the Christians remained steadfast. However, the Armenian Church went over to *Monophysitism* when it accepted the Henoticon of the Emperor Zeno at the Synod of Walarschapat in 491 and rejected the Council of Chalcedon (§ 55, 4. 5). The decision was repeatedly confirmed during the sixth century and from that time the Armenian Church was separated from the Church of the Empire.

3. **Iberia** or **Georgia** situated in the northern part of Armenia, south of the Caucasus, is said to have accepted Christianity during the reign of Constantine the Great, about 325. The king (Mirian?) was the first convert and he in turn converted his people. According to Rufinus (H. E. X, 10) the conversion of the land was due to the virtues and miracles of a Christian woman named *Nino* or Nune who had been a prisoner of war. But several scholars (Kekelidse, Peradse, Peeters) consider this account legendary and place the evangelization of the country about 30 years later (under Emperor Constantius). An Iberian bishop named Jeremias is known to have lived in 431. From Iberia Christianity pressed eastward into *Albania* and in the beginning of the sixth century, westward to the *Colchians* and the *Abasges*. All the countries evangelized from Armenia followed the example of that Church in accepting Monophysitism. Cfr. *H. Leclercq*, Géorgie, DictAC VI, 1029/33. — *M. Tamarati*, L'Église géorgienne, Rome 1910. — *E. Amélineau*, RevHR 69, 1914, 143 ff. 289 ff. — *K. Lübeck*, Georgien u. die kath. Kirche, 1919. — *P. Peeters*, AB 1917/19 (Georgian monasteries); ib. 1932, 5/58; 1933, 5/33 (beginnings of Christianity in Georgia). — *K. Kekelidse*, Die Bekehrung Georgiens z. Christentum, 1928 (also Th. Hermann, Theol. Blätter 1 31, 121/6; *J. Markwart*, Caucasia 1931, 111/67). — *G. Paradse*, ZKG 1927, 34/75 (Georgian monasticism); Oriens christ. 1930/3 (Georgian Christian literature).

4. The Emperor Constantius sent a Bishop *Theophilus* to preach the Gospel to the **Homerites** (Himjarites) or *Sabaeans* in southern Arabia (Yemen). Apparently his work was attended by some success, for as late as the sixth century the people remained faithful during the persecution of King Dhû Nuwâs who had become a convert to Judaism. However, later in the same century and early in the seventh Christianity was practically annihilated by the Persians and Mohammedans. The few remaining Christians eventually became Nestorians. Cfr. *W. Fell*, Z. der Deutschen morgenl. Gesellsch. 35, 1881, 1/75. The Book of Himyarites ed. *A. Moberg*, Lund 1924. — *R. Aigrain*, Arabie, DictHE III, 1158/339. — *H. Charles*, Le Christianisme des Arabes nomades, Paris 1936.

5. Central Asia as far as **Turkestan, India, China** and **Mongolia** received knowledge of Christianity from *Nestorian* missionaries from Persia. Hundreds of Christian gravestones have been discovered in Russian Turkestan, some

of them dated as late as 1345. In 1625 Jesuit missionaries at Si-ngan-fu (province of Schensi) discovered a Syrian-Chinese inscription of the year 781 (according to Mingana the date should be 779), which speaks of the missionary activities of a monk named Olopen and the building of a Nestorian monastery in the year 635 or 638. Cfr. *P. Y. Saeki*, The Nestorian Monument in China, London 1916, reprinted 1928 (also F. Haase, ThRev 1917, 102/5). — *H. Leclercq*, Chine, DictAC III, 1353/85. — *F. Nau*, L'expansion nestorienne en Asie, Paris 1914, 189 ff. — *A. Mingana*, Bulletin of J. Rylands Library Manchester 1925, 297/371; 1926, 127/33. — *J. Stewart*, Nestorian Missionary Enterprise, Edinburgh 1928. A. C. Moule, Christians in China before 1550, London 1930. — *H. Bernard*, La découverte des Nestoriens mongols aux Ordas et l'histoire ancienne du christianisme en Extrême-Orient, Paris 1937. — *G. Rosenkranz*, Die älteste Christenheit in China in den Quellenzeugnissen der Nestorianer Texte der Tangdynastie (635—845), 1938 (from AMW 1937). — H. Klett, Aufstieg u. Untergang einer christl. Missionsarbeit, Diss. 1942.

6. About the middle of the fourth century the Gospel was preached in the highlands of **Abyssinia**[1] (Ethiopia). *Frumentius* and *Edesius*, two young men of Tyre, were captured by barbarians on their return from a trip to India and were sold as slaves to the court at Axum. There they took advantage of the favor they enjoyed to explain Christianity and soon succeeded in converting the king *Aizanas*. The king's desire to establish relations with Byzantium played a part in his conversion. Frumentius remained to work among the people and became known as the "Apostle of Abyssinia". Edesius returned home, but was later consecrated bishop of Axum by Athanasius of Alexandria. The conversion of the entire country progressed rapidly. In 356 Emperor Constantius wrote to the king to induce him to accept Arianism; but the Emperor's effort failed. Later, because of its dependence on Alexandria, the Abyssinian Church went over to *Monophysitism*. At the present time, the greater part of the people hold that form of Christianity, now interspersed with Jewish and Mohammedan practices.

[1] H. LUDOLF, Historia aethiopica, Frankf. 1681; Commentarius in historiam aethiop., ib. 1691. I. GUIDI, Abyssinie, DictHE I, 210/27. H. LECLERCQ, Éthiopie, DictAC V, 584/624. E. LITTMANN, in „Deutsche Aksum-Expedition", 4 vols. 1913; also A. RAHLFS, Oriens christ, 1916, 282 ff. M. CHAÎNE, La chronologie des temps chrétiens de l'Égypte et de l'Éthiopie, Paris 1925. A. KAMMERER, Essai sur l'histoire antique de l'Abyssinie, Paris 1926. C. CONTI ROSSINI, Storia d'Etiopia I, Milano 1928. E. A. W. BUDGE, History of Ethiopia, Nubia and Abyssinia, 2 vol. London 1928; The Book of the Saints of the Ethiopian Church transl., 4 vol. Cambridge 1928. J. B. COULBEAUX, Histoire politique et relig. de l'Abyssinie, 3 vol. Paris 1929. W. TILL, Koptische Heiligen- und Martyrerlegenden, 2 vols. Rome 1935/6 (OrChrAn 102, 108). DE LACY O'LEARY, The Ethiopian Church, London 1936. ED. SCHWARTZ, Philologus 1936, 355/7 (an Abyssinian bishop at Chalcedon 451). R. HENNING, Terrae incognitae II, 1937, 4 ff. (Axum).

7. During the sixth century the **Nubians** in the northern part of Abyssinia accepted Christianity apparently in its orthodox form. During the reign of Justinian I, the priest Julian of Alexandria worked among the tribe of *Nabataeans* and was followed by Bishop Theodore of Philae (until 551). Somewhat later Bishop Longinus interested himself in the same people and also succeeded in converting the *Alodaeans*. In the beginning of the eighth century the Nubians appear as Monophysites and in the tenth century they show the influence of Islamism. Since the thirteenth century they ceased entirely to be Christian and are now Mohammedans. Cfr. *J. Maspéro*, RevHR 59, 1909, 299/317. — *G. Röder*, ZKG 1912, 364/98. — *E. L. Griffith*, Nubian Texts of the Christian Period, Abh. Berlin 1913; Proceedings of the British Academy vol. 14, London 1928. — *H. Junker*, Z. f. ägypt. Sprache u. Altertumskunde 60, 1925, 111/48 (Christian grave stones in Nubia). — *J. Kraus*, Die Anfänge des Christentums in Nubien, Diss. 1930. — *Chaîne* and *Budge*, see under Abyssinia. — *U. Monneret de Villard*, Storia della Nubia cristiana, Rome 1939 (OrChrAn 118). E. Stein, RHE 1940, 131/42.

# § 43.

# Christianity Among the Germans During the Migration of Nations[1].

1. The *Migration of Nations* brought a number of Germanic tribes into contact with Christianity. For a century these warlike

---

[1] **I. General:** See literature preceding § 41. Also: Germanenrechte, Texte u. Übersetzungen, ed. H. FRANK, 15 vols. 1935 ff. BR. GEBHARDT, Handbuch d. deutschen Geschichte I, 1891, revised by R. HOLTZMANN I[7], 1930. W. SCHULTZE, Deutsche Gesch. von der Urzeit bis zu den Karolingern, 2 vols. 1894/6. FED. SCHNEIDER, Mittelalter bis z. Mitte des 13. Jh., 1929. JOH. BÜHLER, Deutsche Geschichte I (to 1100), 1934. G. KURTH, Les origines de la civilisation moderne, 2 vol. Paris [7]1923. G. GRUPP, Die Kultur der alten Kelten u. Germanen, 1905; Kulturgesch. des MA.s I[2], 1907. A. DOPSCH, Wirtschaftl. u. soziale Grundlagen der europ. Kulturentwicklung von Cäsar bis Karl d. Gr., 2 vols. 1923/5. G. STEINHAUSEN, Gesch. der deutschen Kultur I[4], 1936. Handbuch der Kulturgeschichte, ed. H. KINDERMANN, Abt. I vol. 1: G. NECKEL, Kultur der alten Germanen; P. KLETLER, Deutsche Kultur zwischen Völkerwanderung u. Kreuzzügen, 1934. CH. DAWSON, The making of Europe, New York 1945. E. VAHLE, et al., Der Aufstieg des Germanentums u. die Welt des MA.s, 1940 (Neue Propyläenweltgesch. II). W. SCHUBART, Christentum u. Abendland, 1947. C. D. BURNS, The First Europe (400—830), London 1948. H. AUBIN, Vom Altertum zum MA., 1949. **II. Migration of Nations:** J. BÜHLER, Die Germanen in der Völkerwanderung (select sources), 1922. W. CAPELLE, Die Germanen der Völkerwanderung, 1940. J. FISCHER, Die Völkerwanderung im Urteil der zeitgenössischen kirchl. Schriftsteller usw., Diss. 1948. P. COURCELLE, Histoire littéraire des grandes invasions germaniques, Paris 1948. F. DAHN, Die Könige der Germanen, 12 vols. 1861/1909, Reg. 1911; I—II[2], 1910/11; VI[2], 1885. E. V. WIETERSHEIM-F. DAHN, Gesch. der Völkerwanderung, 2 vols. [2]1880/81. L. SCHMIDT, Allg. Gesch. der german. Völker (to 550), 1909; Gesch. der dtsch. Stämme bis zum Ausgang der Völkerwand., 2 vols. in 8 parts 1904/18; revised under the titles, Die Ostgermanen (Vandalen, Burgunder, Goten, Langobarden), [2]1934; Die Westgermanen (Alamannen, Bayern, Thüringer, Franken, Friesen, Sachsen usw.) I—II, 1, [2]1938/40; Gesch. der germanischen Frühzeit (to 481), [2]1934. TH. HODGKIN, Italy and Her Invaders, 8 vol. London [2]1892/1916. L. M. HARTMANN, Gesch. Italiens im MA. I—II,

peoples had been settling within the confines of the Empire filling the native population with fear, sometimes causing great suffering and always creating confusion and chaos. But at the same time,

[1]897/1902; I[2], 1923. P. VILLARI, Le invasioni barbariche in Italia, Milano [4]1928. G. ROMANO, Le dominazioni barbariche in Italia (395 to 1024), Milano 1909. N. ABERG, Die Franken u. Westgoten in der Völkerwanderung, Uppsala 1922; Die Goten u. Langobarden in Italien, ib. 1923. L. HALPHEN, Les Barbares des grandes invasions etc., Paris [5]1948 (Peuples et civilisations V). J. B. BURY, The Invasion of Europe by the Barbarians, London 1928. I. R. PALANQUE, et al., Le christianisme et l'Occident barbare, Paris 1945. R. LATOUCHE, Les grandes invasions et la crise de l'Occident en 5[es]., ib. 1946. A. SCHENK V. STAUFFENBERG, Das Imperium u. die Völkerwanderung, 1947. H. LECLERCQ, Germanie, DictAC VI, 1187/222; Invasion germanique, ib. VII, 1272/396; Italie, ib. VII, 1612/814; Lois des barbares, ib. IX, 1947/2186. T. E. KARSTEN, Die Germanen, Gesch. ihrer Sprache u. Kultur, 1928. J. DE VRIES, Die Welt der Germanen, 1935. F. LOT, Les invasions germaniques, 2 vol. Paris 1935/7. J. HALLER, Der Eintritt der Germanen in die Geschichte, 1939 (Sammlung Göschen). **III. Germanic peoples and Christianity:** TH. HÄNLEIN, Die Bekehrung der Germanen zum Christentum (sources), 2 parts 1919. H. TIMERDING, Die christl. Frühzeit Deutschlands in Berichten über die Bekehrer, 2 parts, 1929. O. CLEMEN, Fontes historiae religionis germanicae, 1928. F. R. SCHRÖDER, Quellenbuch zur germ. Religionsgesch., 1933. G. MÜLLER, Zeugnisse german. Religion, 1935. W. BAETKE, Die Religion der Germanen in Quellenzeugnissen, [2]1938. W. BOUDRIOT, Die altgerm. Religion in d. amtl. kirchl. Literatur des Abendlandes v. 5. bis 11. Jh., 1928. K. HELM, Altgerman. Religionsgesch. I—II, 1, 1913/37; Die Entwicklung der german. Religion, in "Germanische Wiedererstehung", ed. N. NOLLAU, 1926, 292/422. FR. JOSTES, Sonnenwende Bd. II (Religion of the Germans), 1930. C. CLEMEN, Altgerman. Religionsgesch., 1934. J. DE VRIES, Altgerman. Religionsgesch., 2 vols. 1935/7 (excellent). W. BAETKE, Art u. Glaube der Germanen, [2]1935. A. HEUSLER, Germanentum, [2]1936. H. HOFMEISTER, Germanenkunde, 1936. F. PFISTER, ArchRelW 1936, 1/14 (the Germanic religion and the problems it presented). II. SPEIIR, Archiv f. Kulturgesch., 1936, 227/63 (Literaturbericht über die germ. Religionswiss.). W. GRÖNBECH, Kultur u. Religion der Germanen, aus dem Dän. v. E. HOFFMEYER, 2 vols. 1937/9. H. GÜNTERT, Altgerman. Glaube nach Wesen u. Grundlage, 1937. F. V. D. LEYEN, Die Götter der Germanen, 1938. H. SCHNEIDER, ders. Titel, 1938. H. SCHNEIDER u. a., German. Altertumskunde, 1938. AL. CLOSS, Das Heidentum d. Altgermanen, [2]1939. JOH. FRIEDRICH, KG. Deutschlands, 2 vols. 1869. A. HAUCK, KG. Deutschlands I[3/4], 1904 (standard). G. UHLHORN, Kämpfe u. Siege des Christentums in der german. Welt, [2]1905. G. SCHNÜRER, Kirche u. Kultur im MA. I[3], 1936. H. V. SCHUBERT, Gesch. der christl. Kirche im Frühmittelalter, 1921; Das älteste german. Christentum, 1909; Staat u. Kirche in den arian. Königreichen u. im Reiche Chlodwigs, 1912; Festgabe Harnack 1921, 389/404. H. BÖHMER, Das german. Christentum, ThStKr 1913, 165/280. W. CLASSEN, Die Germanen u. das Christentum, 1921. F. W. SCHAAFHAUSEN, Der Eingang des Christentums in das deutsche Wesen I, 1929. H. RÜCKERT, Die Christianisierung der Germanen, [2]1934 (lecture). I. HERWEGEN, Antike, Germanentum u. Christentum, 1932. K. ALGERMISSEN, Germanentum u. Christentum, [5]1935 (apologetic). W. BAETKE, Arteigene german. Religion u. Christentum, [2]1936; Religion u. Politik in der Germanenbekehrung, 1937; Die Welt als Gesch. 1943, 143/66 (Germanization of Christianity). A. STONNER, Germanentum u. Christentum, [2]1934. H. BECHER, Germanisches Heldentum u. christl. Geist, 1934. A. HERTE, Die Begegnung des Germanentums mit dem Christentum, 1935. W. DEINHARDT, Die german. Völker u. das Christentum, 1935 (lecture). G. FLADE, ZKG 1935, 301/22 (German mission). K. D. SCHMIDT, Die Bekehrung der Germanen zum Christentum, 1935 ff. (standard); German.

the invaders were observing the culture, the morals and the lives of the people into whose midst they had come. Gradually they saw the advantages of the ancient civilization and culture and began to contemplate the possibility of forming their own tribes into permanent states. By the year 500 Germanic tribal chieftains were the rulers at Ravenna, Paris, Toulouse and Carthage. When the Germans became Christian they were a people with high physical and mental endowments and with all the unspoiled vigor of youth. They possessed a notable culture all their own, and, as Tacitus describes them in his Germania, they had, besides the usual human failings, a number of noble characteristics: they viewed life earnestly had a deep sense of honor, a love of liberty and justice, were loyal to the family and the tribe, were brave, hospitable and chaste, and recognized monogamy as the ideal form of marriage. These qualities provided a natural soil for the seed of the Gospel. At least the Church had no need to suppress these natural virtues, but rather to purify and spiritualize them. Almost all the German tribes originally believed in the same three higher gods: Ziu, the highest god of heaven; Donar or Thor, the god of Thunder; and Woden or Odin, the god of storm and death. But by the time they met the Romans, in battle or otherwise, along the Rhine, the Limes and the Danube (first to the fourth century) their original beliefs and practices had suffered somewhat from long wanderings and contacts with other peoples, and their religion had become a rather gloomy fatalism and fear of demons. Like all the peoples of antiquity, the Germans recognized the insufficiency of their faith and longed for something better. Their gods no longer had any meaning as far as justice and morality were concerned. Hence, their paganism surrendered almost without resistance to a superior religion. It is quite certain that the Germans did not consider Christianity strange or unnatural. On the contrary, the doctrine of one God, the Creator of heaven and earth, the all-wise Ruler of the world, the Lord even of demons and fate, the just Rewarder of good and Punisher of evil came to them as a light in their darkness and a firm foundation

Glaube u. Christentum, 1948. K. VOIGT, Staat u. Kirche von Konstantin d. Gr. bis zum Ende der Karolingerzeit, 1936, 114 ff. (German states). H. LO-THER, Die Christusauffassung der Germanen, 1937. H. E. GIESECKE, Die Ostgermanen u. der Arianismus, 1939 (also B. ALTANER, ThRev 1940, 63/5). H. KUHN, ZfdA 1940, 1/15 (king and people in the history of the conversion of the Germans). J. A. JUNGMANN, ZkTh 1947, 36/99 (repression of Germanic Arianism). TH. FRINGS, Antike u. Christent. an der Wiege der deutschen Sprache, 1949.

for the natural virtues they practised. Details of the conversion of the Germans are few and by no means clear. But it was not accomplished, as in the first centuries, by individuals accepting the faith from purely spiritual motives. It was rather mass conversion effected through some external circumstances or from temporal motives. As a rule, the chieftain of a clan or the prince of a tribe would first become a Christian and all his retainers would imitate his example. An important circumstance in the conversion of the Germans was the fact that there had always been among them a close connection between their tribal life and their religion. Hence their conversion to Christianity was not only a religious event, but a practical one as well. So far as we know, during the period of migration, the Germans were never subjected to force to effect their conversion. But some of the pagan and Arian Germans (Visigoths and Vandals) did resort to extreme cruelty to coerce Christians to apostatize. It is worthy to note that beginning with the conversion of the Visigoths, almost all the Germanic tribes first accepted Christianity in the form of Arianism, a form later condemned by the Church of the Empire. Part of them held fast to *Arianism* until their extinction (Ostrogoths and Vandals) and part of them eventually accepted Catholic orthodoxy (Visigoths, Suevi, Burgundians, etc.). The Germans themselves suffered from these religious differences and the conquered Romans suffered more because of them.

2. The first Germanic tribe to be converted as a group was the **Visigoths**[1]. In the third century they settled along the lower Danube

---

[1] JORDANES, De origine actibusque Getarum, ed. M. PETSCHENIG, 1881; Germ. transl. by W. MARTENS, [3]1913. Isidorus Hispal., Historia de regibus Gothorum, Vandalorum et Suevorum, ed. TH. MOMMSEN, MG Auct. antiq. XI, German by D. COSTE, [3]1910. Gesetze der Westgoten, ed. and transl. by E. WOHLHAUPTER, 1936 (Germanenrechte XI); Altspanisch-got. Rechte, ed. and transl. by the same, 1936 (Germanenr. XII). M. SCHÖNFELD, Goti RE Pauly-Wissowa Suppl. III, 797/845. H. LECLERCQ, Goths, DictAC VI, 1430/48. F. DAHN, Könige (see above) V—VI. GAMS, LECLERCQ, G. VILLADA, see § 12, 3. F. GÖRRES, ThStKr 1893; ZwTh 1898, 1899 (Eurich 466 to Sisibut 620). F. MARTROYE, Goths et Vandales, Paris 1904. E. MAGNIN, L'Église Wisigothique au VIIe siècle, Paris 1912. H. DELEHAYE, AB 1912, 161/300 (Gothic Martyrs); cfr. G. MORIN, HJG 1932, 178/84. J. MANSION, AB 1914, 5/30 (beginnings of Christianity among the Goths). E. STOCQUART, L'Espagne politique et sociale sous les Visigoths (412—711), Brux. 1915. J. ZEILLER, Les origines chrét. dans les provinces Danubiennes, Paris 1914. 407 ff.; Mél. Schlumberger, Paris 1924, 3/11; Misc. Isidoriana, Rome 1936, 287/92. A. K. ZIEGLER, Church and State in Visigothic Spain, Diss. Wash. 1930. J. SAUER, Oriens Christ. 1932, 188/202 (christian monuments in the Crimea). A. A. VASILIEV, The Goths in Crimea, Cambridge 1936. W. STACH, HistVS 1935, 417/45 (foundation of the Visigothic kingdom). J. MARTINEZ SANTA-OLALLA, Necropolis Visigoda de Herrera de Pisuerga (Palencia),

and on the west and north shores of the Black Sea. A few of them had been converted early. A bishop of "Gothis" (probably in the Crimea) named Theophilus and possibly a Greek by birth, attended the Council of Nicaea 325. But the greatest progress in the evangelization of the Goths was made by *Wulfila*[1] or Ulfila. He was the grandson of Christian Cappadocians who had been taken as prisoners of war. For forty years (341—383) he devoted himself to preaching the Gospel north and south of the Danube. After he had taught for a time, the Arian bishop, Eusebius of Constantinople, (§ 48, 2) consecrated him "bishop of the Christians in the land of the Goths" (341). Ulfila's *translation of the Bible* into Gothic, a linguistic and cultural monument of the first order, very considerably aided his work. The chieftain Fritigern was converted, while his rival Athanarich persecuted the Christians (348, 370—372) and caused many Christian Goths to be put to death. When the Huns began to threaten the Empire (376) Emperor Valens made Fritigern and his tribe allies of the Empire (Foederati) and assigned them their own territory in Thrace. Here Ulfila and other missionaries completed the work of Christianizing the Goths, that is to say, in making them Arians. For the emperors Constantius and Valens not only favored *Arianism,* but sought by force to make it the State religion (§ 48, 3—6). Ulfila was among the first to sign the homoiousion creed at the Synod of Constantinople in 360 in which the Catholic doctrine was designated as "odibilis et execrabilis, prava et perversa confessio." Ulfila's Goths became the mission center of the East Germanic world. From this time on all the *Germanic tribes from the East* that crossed the borders of the Empire accepted Christianity in the form of Arianism. Although the universal or Catholic Church was to be found within the boundaries where the individual tribes

---

Madrid 1935 (cfr. W. NEUSS, ThRev 1936, 24 f.). B. STEIDLE, BenMS 1936, 425/34 (Isidore of Seville and the Visigoths). K. F. STROHEKER, Eurich, König der Westg. (466 to 84), 1937; Die Welt als Gesch. 1939, 446/83 (Leovigild). ST. MCKENNA, Paganism and Pagan Survivals in Spain up to the Fall of the Visigothic Kingdom, Diss. Wash. 1938. A. MICHEL, DictThC XV, 1176/208 (Synode of Toledo). J. MADOZ, RHE 1938, 5/20 (Creed of the Synod of Tol. 633). J. A. JUNGMANN, ZkTh 1947, 36/99 (repression of Germanic Arianism).

[1] Monogr. on Wulfila by G. WAITZ, 1840; W. BESSEL, 1860. F. KAUFFMANN, Aus der Schule des Wulfila I, 1899. H. BÖHMER, RE 21, 548/58. G. BARDY, DictThC XV, 2048/57. H. BÖHMER-ROMUNDT, ZwTh 1903, 233 ff. 361 ff. (W's. literary legacy). C. MÜLLER, ZfdA 1914, 76/147 (Wulfila's death). B. CAPELLE, RevBén 1922, 226/33 (Ep. Auxentii de fide, vita et obitu Wulfilae). W. STREITBERG, Die got. Bibel, 2 vols. ²1919/28. K. D. SCHMIDT, Die Bekehrung der Germanen (see above) 231 ff. H. E. GIESECKE, see above.

lived or settled, the Goths zealously guarded and stubbornly adhered to *their own Arian Church* as their *national treasure*. And this even after the Emperor Theodosius I endeavored to make the Catholic (Nicene) Church the Church of the Empire (§ 41, 5). The Church of the Goths possessed several distinctive characteristics: it held to the *homoiousion creed* (the Son is only similar to the Father and not eternal); it rejected all speculation regarding the Trinity or the Logos; it used the Germanic language in divine services, influenced in this by Ulfila's translation of the Bible; the *tribal Church* was governed by the king, who appointed bishops, called synods and divided the clergy in military fashion according to the organization of the tribe into hundreds and clans, and finally, the church buildings were erected on the domains of landowners who were considered the *owners of the buildings*.

The Visigoths soon came into conflict with their Greek masters. Ill-treatment on the part of the imperial officials led to a revolt. Emperor Valens was defeated and lost his life in the battle of Adrianople in 378. The attempt of his successor Theodosius I the Great as well as the later attempt of St. John Chrysostom, Bishop of Constantinople, to induce the Goths to accept Nicene orthodoxy met with little success. Even after their devastating migration through Greece and *Italy* (Rome taken and sacked under Alarich in 410) and their conquest of *Southern Gaul* and *Spain* (419) which was to be their new home, the first Germanic kingdom on Roman soil, the Visigoths for a long time clung tenaciously to Arianism. But toward the end of the sixth century a far-reaching change occurred. King *Leovigild* (568—586) began a policy of great severity, even cruelty, toward his Catholic subjects. His sons, on the other hand, were strongly inclined to the Roman Church. The older son, *Hermenegild*, married a Frankish princess, Ingunde, who induced him to accept the Catholic faith. A revolt against his father produced little result, since Hermenegild was defeated and cast into prison where he was executed (murdered?) in 585. The second son, *Recared*, in the first year of his reign, declared that he felt obliged by "grave heavenly and earthly reasons" to profess the Catholic faith. Thanks to the zealous endeavors of *Leander*, the archbishop of Seville, († c. 600), the greater number of the Arian bishops, nobles and people followed the king's example. The Synod of Toledo in 589 consolidated the conversion of the Visigoths. During the seventh century Catholic life in Spain reached a high degree of development, as may be seen from the numerous national synods convoked by the king and held in the royal residence at Toledo. Many parishes were established in rural districts and monasteries were erected. Yet for a long time pagan practices continued, such as magic, fortune telling, the worship of stones, trees, springs and other natural objects and required the closest vigilance of the Catholic bishops. *Isidore*, Archbishop of Seville (c. 600—636), brother and successor of Leander, was the most important figure in the hierarchy. His vast knowledge and his numerous writings, so highly appreciated during the Middle Ages, lent lustre and fame to the Spanish Church (§ 78, 4). Among his works is a popular history of the Visigoths. An intimate union existed between Church and State. But the Catholic Church in Spain continued to be the State and National Church and in its government little was left to the authority of the pope. Weakened by internal dissensions, the Visigoth kingdom collapsed on the invasion of the Arabs (711).

When the **Suevi** settled in *Galicia* in northwestern Spain (409), most of them were still pagans. They were converted to the Catholic faith about the middle of the fifth century. But due to the marriage of their king Remismund to a Visigoth princess and the efforts of the Visigoth Bishop Ajax they soon became Arians. King *Chararic* (550—559) returned to the Catholic Church. Archbishop *Martin* of Braga (Bracara) († 580) (§ 78, 4) further evangelized the country. We still have a list of the parishes from his time. The subsequent history of the Suevi merges with that of the Visigoths to whose rule they were subjected under Leovigild (585). F. Görres, ZwTh 1893, 542 ff.; RE 19, 128/32; *P. David*, Études historiques sur la Galice et le Portugal du 6 au 12 s., Paris, 1947.

3. Due to their close relations with the Visigoths, the **Ostrogoths**[1] became Arians in the fourth century and remained so until the collapse of their kingdom. After the middle of the fifth century they settled in Pannonia, but withdrew to *Italy* in 489. This move was the result of an agreement between Emperor Zeno and the Ostrogoth chieftain **Theodoric the Great** (471—526) who became the

---

[1] Cfr. literature preceding § 43 and in no. 2 above. DAHN, Könige II—IV. M. SEIDLMAYER, Gesch. des italien. Volkes u. Staates vom Zusammenbruch des Röm. Reiches bis zum Weltkrieg, 1940 (Die große Weltgesch. Bd. 9). E. CASPAR, Theoderich d. Gr. u. das Papsttum, 1931 (Kleine Texte 162). G. PFEILSCHRIFTER, Theoderich d. Gr., 1910. L. SCHMIDT, HJG 1927, 727/29 (Cassiodorus and Theodoric). W. VON DEN STEINEN, Theod. u. Chlodwig, 1934. G. VETTER, Die Ostgoten u. Theod., 1938. W. ENSSLIN, Theoderich d. Gr. 1947. A. NAGL, RE Pauly-Wissowa 2, R. V, 1745/73 (Theod.); ib. XVII, 1888/96 (Odoacer). H. GRISAR, Gesch. Roms und der Päpste im MA. I, 1901. FED. SCHNEIDER, Rom u. Romgedanke im MA., 1926. On the end of the Roman Empire see lit. in § 41.

most renowned of all the Germanic kings. The condition of Italy at this time was most deplorable. With the murder of the incompetent Valentinian III (455) the Roman Empire of the West began its death struggle. The commander of the German mercenary troops was the actual ruler of the land. One of these, *Odoacer*, an Arian of the tribe of the Scirri had himself proclaimed king of Italy in 476 and deposed the last nominal Roman emperor *Romulus* who was mockingly called Augustulus. This marked the inglorious *end* of the once glorious *empire* of the West. Zeno recognized Odoacer as a regent and gave him the honorary title of Patrician (479). After a reign of thirteen years Odoacer was conquered by Theodoric (489—490) and was finally murdered at Ravenna (493). The Ostrogoth ruler then created for himself an empire that included Italy, Sicily, Dalmatia, Pannonia, Noricum, Rhaetia and Provence. With the help of Clovis, to whom he was related by marriage, Theodoric dreamed of extending his rule over the Franks and eventually of uniting all the Germanic nations under the hegemony of the Ostrogoths. But his ambitious project came to naught. Emperor Anastasius recognized Theodoric as ruler of Italy and, in general, his regime was commendable. He showed an understanding and appreciation of Roman culture which he endeavored to protect. The noble Roman *Cassiodorus* (§ 78, 2) was his sectretary and as such was the chief officer of administration. Although Theodoric himself was an Arian, he was tolerant (religionem imperare non possumus, Variae II, 27) and allowed his Catholic subjects the free practice of their religion. They in turn placed great confidence in him. In 498 when the papal election was contested (Symmachus vs. Lawrence) the Catholics called upon Theodoric to act as arbiter (§ 64, 6). When Monophysitism spread throughout the East and was favored by the Byzantine court (§ 55, 4) the Catholics of Italy for a time found a strong support in their Arian king. However, toward the end of his reign when after the settlement of the Acacian Schism (519) the Romans began to be more favorably disposed toward Byzantium, Theodoric became suspicious and changed his policy. The noted philosopher and statesman *Boethius* (§ 78, 2) and his father-in-law, Symmachus, who was the ranking senator, were executed on charges of high treason (524—525); and Pope *John I* upon returning from an unsuccessful mission to Constantinople, was cast into prison where he died (526). But Theodoric was never the bloody persecutor of Catholics which later legend pictured him to be. His imposing tomb is still preserved at Ravenna. After his death (526) the Ostrogoth kingdom did not long endure. Weakened by internal dissensions and external wars waged for almost twenty years, it succumbed under the last two kings, Totila and Teja, to the superior force and military skill of the Byzantines (552—553).

4. But the Empire of the East did not long enjoy the fruits of its victory over the Ostrogoths. In 568 the **Lombards**[1] (Langobards) under king Alboin left Pannonia and invaded the Apennine Peninsula. With the exception of Ravenna (later the residence of the exarch), the duchy of Rome and few stretches of land in the south, they conquered the greater part of Italy. Spoleto and Benevento became Lombard dukedoms. Some of the Lombards were pagans, but most of them were Arian, the result of their contact with other Germanic tribes along the Danube. They established their capital at Pavia. The Lombards had little regard for Roman culture and were unfriendly, sometimes openly hostile, to the Catholic Church. Hence they were dangerous neighbors for Rome. When their King Authari married *Theodelinda*, daughter of the Duke of Bavaria in 589, the Lombards had a Catholic queen whose influence long supported the missionary efforts of Pope Gregory the Great. After Authari's death Theodelinda married Duke *Agilulfus* of Turin, likewise an Arian; but as Authari's successor (590—616) he offered no opposition to the spread of Christianity. Adelwald, the son of this marriage, was baptized a Catholic. During his minority, Theodelinda († 628) held the regency. After Adelwald was deposed in 625 several Arian kings inherited the sovereignty, but by 680 the victory of Catholicism was assured. The monastery of *Bobbio* which St. Columban (§ 72, 8) founded in the valley of the Trebbia in 614 became a center of asceticism and learning for the kingdom of the Lombards. By intermarriage and the adoption of Roman culture the Lombards gradually merged with the Romans.

---

[1] Paulus Diaconus, Historia Langobardorum, ed. G. WAITZ, 1873; German by O. ABEL, ³1939. A. PONTONI, Introduzione agle studi su Paolo Diacono, Neapel 1946. L. SCHIAPARELLI, Codice diplomatico longobardo I (620—754), Rome 1929. Gesetze der Langobarden, ed. and transl. by F. BEYERLE, 1947. H. FEHR, Schweiz. Beiträge z. allgem. Gesch. 1948, 37/49 (Spirit of the Langobard laws). O. BERTOLINI, Roma di fronte a Bisanzio e ai Langobardi Rome 1943. DAHN, Könige XII. K. BLASEL, Die Wanderzüge der Langobarden, 1909. K. VOIGT, Die königl. Eigenklöster im Langobardenreiche, 1909. F. SCHNEIDER, Die Reichsverwaltung in Toskana (568—1268) I, 1913. FR. TARDUCCI, L'Italia dalla discesa di Alboino alla morte di Agilulfo (568—616), Città di Castello 1914. Other literature (L. SCHMIDT, L. M. HARTMANN etc.) § 43, 1.

The **Rugii** (Rugians) an East Germanic tribe, like the Goths and the Lombards, were also Arians; but when or under what circumstances they adopted that religion, we do not know. When the kingdom of the Huns collapsed after the death of Attila (453) the Rugii were then settled in Noricum (Upper and Lower Austria). Due to the withdrawal of the legions, the Roman citizenry of that territory were left defenseless against the invasion of barbarians. However, those in Noricum ripense, along the Danube, found a protector and comforter in *St. Severin* († 482), an ascetic of unknown nationality (African?) whose marvelous life was written by his disciple Eugippius. He was highly respected by Odoacer as well as by the Arian Germans. Other tribes closely related to the Rugii, such as the *Scirri*, were also Arians. — Vita S. Severini, editions: Th. Mommsen, 1918; P. Becker, 1935; R. Noll, 1947 (with transl.); German by E. Rodenberg, [3]1912; N. Hovorka, 1925. — M. Schuster, 1946. — Monogr. by *A. Baudrillart*, Paris 1908; *F. Kaphahn*, Zwischen Antike u. MA., 1947. — *W. Bulst*, Die Welt als Gesch. 1950, 18/27 (hagiographic character of the "vita" S. Severini). — *Th. Sommerlad*, Die Lebensbeschreib. Severins als kulturgesch. Quelle, 1903. — *R. Tomanek*, Weidenauer Studien II, 1908, 351/418. — *R. Egger*, Frühchristl. Kirchenbauten im südl. Noricum, 1916. — W. Scherer, Theol.-prakt. Quartalschr. 1926, 326/30; 1927, 95/108.

5. The **Burgundians**[1] who settled along the Rhine (near Worms), the Main and the Neckar in the beginning of the fifth century are described by the historians Orosius (VII, 32) and Socrates (VII, 30) as Catholic Christians. But this can scarcely be correct. They had most likely adopted the Arian faith from the Visigoths and retained it until, after a serious defeat by the Huns (435, 437), they sought a new home in Savoy along the Rhone between the Jura and the Vosges Mountains. There they were soon quite thoroughly Romanized. With the death of King Gundobad and the accession of his Catholic son *Sigismund* (561), the people began to be converted to the Catholic Church. Archbishop *Avitus* of Vienne (§ 78, 4) contributed greatly toward this work. Arianism disappeared rapidly when the Burgundians came under the rule of the Franks (532).

6. The **Vandals**[2] were Arians when they left Pannonia. Together with the Suevi and Alani they devastated Gaul in 409 and settled

---

[1] Gesetze der Burgunden, ed. and transl. by F. BEYERLE, 1936 (Germanenrechte X). H. FEHR, Schweiz. Beiträge z. allgem. Gesch., 1945, 5/21 (spirit of the old Burgundian laws). DAHN, Könige XI. A. JAHN, Gesch. der Burgundionen, 2 vols. 1874. H. V. SCHUBERT, Die Anfänge des Christentums bei den Burgundern, Sb. Heidelberg 1911, 34. G KÖLLER, ZKG 1938, 237/43 (conversion of the Burgundians). P. N. FRANTZ, Avitus von Vienne als Politiker u. Hierarch, Diss. 1908. P. E. MARTIN, Étude critique sur la Suisse à l'époque mérovingienne, Genève 1910. A. COVILLE, Recherches sur l'histoire de Lyon 450—800, Paris 1928. H. LECLERCQ, DictAC X, 149 ff. (Lyons).

[2] Isidorus Hispal., Historia Wandalorum (see above no. 2). Victor Viten-

for a time in *Spain*. They crossed over to *North Africa* (429) where their capable leader *Genseric* (428—477) crushed the Roman power and founded an important kingdom. Wherever the Vandals went they strove to eradicate the Catholic religion. This group exhibited a fanatical intolerance unlike the other Germanic peoples and under their kings Genseric and Huneric (477—484) directed several severe persecutions against Catholics which have been graphically described by Bishop Victor of Vita (484). Bishops and the nobility were the special objects of their fury. Finally in 534 Belisarius, the general of Justinian, put an end to the Vandal kingdom. Salvianus (De gubernatione Dei VII, 6 ff.) lauds these "barbarians" because of their chaste lives and proposes them as models to the licentious Romans. But the climate of Africa and the luxury they there enjoyed soon ennervated them morally and physically.

The taking of Africa by the land-hungry Vandals was attended with much suffering and great cruelty. After a siege lasting a year, *Genseric* in 431 took Hippo, the see-city of St. Augustine († 430). The struggle which then ensued between the Arian Vandals and the Catholic Romans was most bitter. When Genseric finally subdued *Carthago* (439) he banished the Bishop Quodvultdeus (cfr. Franses, Die Werke des hl. Q., 1920) together with a large number of his clergy and gave the churches with the property belonging to them to the Arians. In 455 the Vandals under Genseric attacked and plundered defenseless Rome and brought back to Africa many noble prisoners of war. With the exception of a three-year lull (454—457) the persecution in Africa lasted for thirty years. *Hunseric* began his reign with a show of leniency toward Catholics, but after 483 he proved more severe than his father. The religious dispute at Carthage on February 1, 484 seemed only to deepen the hatred of the Arian bishops and all Catholic Churches were turned over to the Vandals. The oppressive laws which the emperor had enacted against the "homoousians" (Catholics) were enforced and three hundred and forty-eight bishops were banished. As under Genseric, so now, there were many martyrs. A favorable change occurred when *Gunthamund* (484—496) ascended the throne: the bishops were allowed to return and religious services were permitted. But his brother *Thrasamund* (496—523) again closed the churches and banished sixty bishops to Sardinia; among them Fulgentius of Ruspe (§ 57,3; 78, 1). *Hilderic* (523—530) was friendly toward Catholics; but he was succeeded by *Gelimer* (530—534) a rabid Arian bent on persecution. Only his overthrow by Belisarius prevented him from carrying out his plans.

sis, Hist. persecutionis Africanae provinciae, ed. M. PETSCHENIG, 1881. F. GÖRRES, Kirche u. Staat im Vandalenreich, Deutsche Z. f. GW. 10, 1893, 14/70; ZwTh 1893, 494 ff.; HJG 1911, 323 ff. CH. DIEHL, L'Afrique byzantine (533—709), Paris 1896. L. SCHMIDT, Gesch. der Vandalen, ²1942. F. MARTROYE, L'Occident à l'époque byzantine, Goths et Vandales, Paris 1904; Genséric, Paris 1907; DictAC VI, 1004/14. E. F. GAUTIER, Genséric, Paris 1932, German by J. LECHLER, 1934. H. LECLERCQ etc., see § 12, 6.

7. The **Franks**[1], who eventually became the most influential of all the Germanic tribes, were introduced to the Gospel when they settled in a land that had already been Christianized. After the middle of the fifth century, the Salian Franks moved from the Lower Rhine toward the southwest. Their young and energetic king, **Clovis**[2] (481—511), defeated the governor Syagrius near

[1] MOLINIER, Les sources de l'histoire de France, 6 vol. Paris 1901/6. GREGORIUS TURONENSIS, Historia Francorum, ed. W. ARNDT, MGSS rer. Merov. I, 1884; Historiarum libri, ed. II cur. B. KRUSCH, 1937 ff.; edd. H. OMONT et G. COLLON, 2 vol. Paris ²1913; ed. O. M. DALTON, 2 vol. Oxford 1927 (with English transl.); German by W. GIESEBRECHT and S. HELLMANN, 3 vols. 1911/3. J. W. LOEBELL, Gregor v. Tours u. seine Zeit, ²1869. Cfr. S. HELLMANN, HZ 107, 1911, 1/43. B. KRUSCH, HistVS 1932, 674/757; 1933, 1/21; MIÖG 1931, 486/90. Fredegarii Chronicon, ed. B. KRUSCH, MGSS rer. Merov. II; Vol. IV Germ. transl. O. ABEL, ³1888. Diplomata Imperii, Capitularia regum Francorum, Concilia aevi Merovingici, Passiones vitaeque Sanctorum, Epistolae Merov. aevi in MG, see § 2, 10 c. K. A. ECKHARDT, Die Gesetze des Merowingerreiches (481—741) lat. u. deutsch, 1935 (Germanenrechte I). Pactus Legis Salicae, ed. H. F. W. D. FISCHER, Leyden 1948. General literature preceding § 43, especially GEBHARDT I, DAHN VII bis VIII, L. SCHMIDT, HAUCK I, H. V. SCHUBERT. L. DUCHESNE (Fastes épiscop.), LAUNAY, LECLERCQ, see § 21, 2. Also: J. BÜHLER, Das Frankenreich nach zeitgenöss. Quellen (selections), 1923. G. RICHTER, Annalen des fränk. Reiches im Zeitalter der Merowinger, 1873. J. HAVET, Questions mérovingiennes, Paris 1885. M. PROU, La Gaule mérovingienne, Paris 1897. G. KURTH, Études Franques, 2 vol. Brux. 1919. E. LAVISSE, Histoire de France II, 1, Paris 1903. H. LECLERCQ, Monarchie franque, DictAC XI, 2034/2182. W. WIERUSZOWSKI, Bonner Jbb. 1922, 1/83 (the Gallic and Frankish episcopate to 843). G. LÖHLEIN, Die Alpen- u. Italienpolitik der Merovinger im 6. Jh., 1932. L. UEDING, Gesch. der Klostergründungen der frühen Merowingerzeit, 1935. E. WINHELLER, Die Lebensbeschreibung der vorkaroling. Bischöfe von Trier, 1935. R. BARROUX, Dagobert, roi des Francs (623—39), Paris 1938. F. STEINBACH and F. PETRI, Zur Grundlegung der europ. Einheit durch die Franken, 1939. C. POULET, Histoire de l'église de France, I (496—1516), Paris 1946. L. DUPRAZ, Le royaume des Francs et l'ascension politique des maires du palais (656—80), Freiburg Schw., 1948. E. LOENING, Gesch. des deutschen Kirchenrechts, 2 vols. 1878. N. D. FUSTEL DE COULANGES, Histoire des institutions politiques de l'ancienne France, 5 tom. Paris ²⁄³1901/14. R. WEYL Das fränk. Staatskirchenrecht zur Zeit der Merowinger, 1888, reprinted 1935. C. DE CLERCQ, La législation religieuse franque de Clovis à Charlemagne (507—814), Louvain 1936. K. VOIGT, Staat u. Kirche von Konstantin d. Gr. bis zum Ende der Karolingerzeit, 1936, 236/306. A. MARIGNAN, Études sur la civilisation française, 2 vol. Paris 1899. C. A. BERNOULLI, Die Heiligen der Merowinger, 1900. S. DILL, Roman Society in Gaul in the Merovingian Age, London 1926. TH. ZWÖLFER, St. Peter, Apostelfürst u. Himmelspförtner, s. Verehrung bei d. Angelsachsen u. Franken, 1929. K. WEBER, StMBenO 1930, 347/403 (cultural-historical problems in the lives of Merovingian saints). G. ZENKER, German. Volksglaube in fränk. Missionsberichten, 1939; R. F. MULLER, L'époque mérovingienne, New York 1945. J. B. GAI, La vie spirituelle 1942, 366/89 (Columban's influence on Merovingian society). E. SALIN La civilisation mérovingienne I, Paris 1950.

[2] G. KURTH, Clovis, 2 vol. Brux. ³1923; Sainte Clotilde, Paris ⁸1905 (Les Saints). M. M. GORCE, Clovis, Paris 1935. H. LECLERCQ, Clovis DictAC III, 2037/74. W. VON DEN STEINEN, Theoderich u. Chlodwig, 1934. H. RAHNER, Die gefälschten Papstbriefe aus dem Nachlaß von Jérôme Vignier, 1935

Soissons in 486 and thus put an end to Roman rule in Gaul. He then conquered the territory as far as the Loire, pushed back the Visigoths, and continued his conquests southward to the Garonne (507). Up to this time only a few of the Franks had accepted Christianity, but soon the people as a whole became *Christian* and *Catholic*. This was due chiefly to the example of Clovis. He had married Clotilda, a Catholic princess of the royal house of Burgundy and at her persuasion had permitted their two sons to be baptized. Gregory of Tours in his history of the Franks (II, 31) relates that during a battle with the Alemanni on the left bank of the Rhine, Clovis was hard pressed. Like another Constantine, he vowed to become a Christian if he won the day. He was victorious; and on Christmas day, probably in the year 496, he and 3 000 of his retainers were baptized at Reims by Bishop *Remigius*. No doubt political as well as religious motives influenced the king's conversion; especially the desire and the hope of securing the support of the Church and her distinguished bishops for the young Merovingian kingdom. The rest of the Franks followed the king's example. As in the case of the other Germans, the religion of the king was the religion of the people and force or undue pressure was unnecessary. Indeed, Clovis' example was imitated beyond the confines of his own realm (King Chararic and his son). It was not long before Clovis had succeeded by force and fraud in uniting all of the Franks into *one* kingdom. His victory over the Alemanni and the extention of Frankish rule over the Burgundians, Thuringians and Bavarians under his sons, was a powerful factor in the christianization of these nations (see above no. 5 and § 79).

----

(pp. 67/128 on the forged letter of Pope Anastasius II to Clovis). On Clovis' conversion and baptism: G. KURTH, Etudes Franques II.   L. LEVILLAIN, Bibliothèque de l'École des Chartes 67, Paris 1906, 472/88.   E. VACANDARD, RClFr 76, 1913, 143/56.   A. STRACKE, Over bekeering en doopsel van Clodovech, Antwerpen 1931.   L. SALTET, BullLE 1932, 97/113.   B. KRUSCH, MIÖG 1893, 427/48;   NA 1932, 457/68; HistVS 1932, 560/67 (Clovis baptized at Tours in 501!); contrary opinion W. VON DEN STEINEN, HJG 1933, 51/66; MIÖG Erg.-Bd. 12, 1933, 417/511.  Cfr. also L. LEVILLAIN, RevHEFrance 1935, 161/92; 1937, 149/56 (defeat of the Alemanni 497, Clovis baptized at Reims 498 or 499); also L. SALTET, BullLE 1936, 171/90; 1937, 49/66.   A. VAN DE VYVER, Revue belge de philologie et d'hist. 1936, 859/914; 1937, 35/95; Le Moyen Âge 1947, 177/96 (victory and conversion of Clovis 506);   J. CAL-METTE, Comptes rendus de l'Acad. des inscr. et belles-lettres 1946, 193/202. B. KRUSCH, Sb. Berlin 1933, 1060/7 ("coronation" of Clovis at Tours 508!); also L. SCHMIDT, HJG 1934, 221 f.; H. GÜNTER, ib. 468/75, and again Krusch, Sb. Berlin 1937, 15.   R. BARROUX, St. Rémi et la mission de Reims, Paris 1947.

8. The conversion of the Franks to the Catholic faith was an event of exceptional importance. This was recognized even by contemporaries. Archbishop *Avitus* of Vienne in congratulating Clovis, wrote: "Vestra fides nostra victoria est." (A similar letter purporting to be from Pope Anastasius II is a forgery of the seventeenth century). The dissension over religious belief between conqueror and conquered was thus avoided in the kingdom of the Franks and the merger of all *into a corporate state* was thus facilitated. The Franks moreover, had immediate access to the treasures of antiquity which the Church alone had preserved. A definite check was put to the spread of Arianism which the Ostrogoth Theodoric was endeavoring to advance. The renunciation of their errors by the Arian Burgundians, Visigoths and Suevi in the sixth century may be viewed as a result of the action of the Franks. After its extinction in the Roman Empire, Arianism persisted for some time among the Germans, but its doom was sealed. Since all the other German princes at the time were either pagans or Arians, it fell to the lot of the Frankish king to appear in the rôle of protector and champion of the orthodox religion. Thus at that early date the way was prepared for the position of leadership to be assumed by the Carolingian monarchs and at the same time the possibility suggested itself of uniting all the Germans on the basis of a common religion. And the identification of the Germans with Catholic Christianity, with ancient culture and Roman statecraft gave to Central and Northern Europe a cultural and political ascendency.

The conversion of the Frankish king and people was at first scarcely more than an external change of religious form and by no means meant an immediate flowering of fine Christian life and virtues. The Franks were indeed proud of their faith. The Prologue of the Lex Salica of about 555 begins: Vivat qui Francos diligit Christus! Numerous pious foundations were made and the veneration of saints and their relics flourished. The central point of the Frankish kingdom, divided into Nuestria, Austrasia and Burgundy, was the tomb of *St. Martin of Tours* (§ 72, 6) the great national patron. On the other hand there was still evidence of immorality, superstition and pagan practices. The rapidly decaying Merovingian dynasty and the licentious nobility disgraced themselves by crimes and misdeeds of all sorts: treachery, perjury, murder and lechery. The nadir was reached in the last quarter of the sixth and beginning of the seventh century (the strife between

Queen Brunhilde and Fredegunde, the concubine of Chilperic I). The Church was rich and powerful; the bishops as the mainstays and advisors to the throne occupied positions of great honor. But the Frankish Church was entirely dependent on the king — a *State-Church*, on which the pope could exert little influence — although the form was truly Roman (Lex Ribuaria 58, 1: Ecclesia vivit lege Romana). Bishops were appointed by the will of the king or the influence of nobles without regard to the merits or abilities of appointees and at times the sees were simoniacally purchased (§60, 3). Literature and learning were at a low ebb. Yet during the sixth century synods were held frequently. Between 511 and 614 more than 30 national synods are known and even in the worst days, some of the monasteries never ceased to be nurseries of piety and learning. During the sixth century there was a long line of excellent bishops such as *Avitus* of Vienne († 518; § 78, 4), *Remigius* of Reims († 535), *Caesar* of Arles († 542; § 78, 4), *Nicetius* of Trier († 566), *Germanus* of Paris († 576), *Gregory* of Tours († 594), and *Venantius Fortunatus* of Poitiers († 601; §78, 4). Toward the end of the sixth and the beginning of the seventh century, Gaul and Burgundy were blessed for twenty years by the presence of the Irish monk and abbot *Columbanus* (§ 72, 8) a powerful preacher of penance and founder of monasteries. His principal monastery at Luxeuil in Burgundy was a focal point whence spread the rays of asceticism, learning and missionary zeal. Many renowned women[1] worked in convents and in the world, such as *St. Genevieve*, Patroness of Paris († 512), Queen *Clotilda* († 545), *St. Radegunde* († 587) of the royal house of Thuringia, first the wife of the brutish king Clotaire I and afterwards a nun at Poitiers, *St. Burgundofara* († 657) Abbess of Faremoutier, *St. Bathilde* († ca. 680) wife of Clovis II and many others. The spiritualizing and civilizing power of the Church never failed. Still in the eighth century there was need of a thorough reform within and powerful impetus from without to save the Church of the West Frankish kingdom from collapse and to make it an active and healthy member of the Church Universal.

---

[1] Vita S. Genovevae, ed. B. KRUSCH, MGSS rer. Merov. III, 204 ff.; ed. C. KÜNSTLE, 1910. Cfr. also G. KURTH, RHE 1913, 5/80; 1914/20, 437/42; E. VACANDARD, Études de critique IV, Paris 1923; B. KRUSCH, NA 1916, 131 ff. 265 ff.; H. LECLERCQ, DictAC VI, 960/90; C. JULLIAN, Mél. Schlumberger II, Paris 1924, 372 ff. P. CROIDYS, St. Geneviève et les barbares, Paris 1946. Monogr. on St. Radegunde by J. BERNHART, 1915; R. AIGRAIN, Paris 1918; M. ALANIC, Paris 1930; J. F. GÖRRES, ³1942. Monog. on St. Bathilde by M. J. COUTURIER, Paris 1909.

# § 44.

## The Church Among the Celts and Anglo-Saxons in the British Isles[1].

1. Christianity became known to the **Britons**[2], the inhabitants of the Roman province of Britannia about the turn of the second century (§ 12, 5). By the fourth century it had been generally accepted and had penetrated northward toward Scotland. But its progress among the people was not maintained. When the Romans withdrew from the province in the beginning of the fifth century, the mastery of the land was contested by the heathen Picts and Scots, that is, the inhabitants of Scotland and Ireland. The British prince Vortigern, a Christian, called on the help of the German tribes, the *Angles, Saxons* and *Jutes* on the mainland, who after 428 swarmed over the island in great numbers. But instead of being friendly allies, they soon became the conquerors, and the greater part of the island reverted to paganism. Political independence and the Christian faith were maintained only by those Britons in the mountainous West, Cambria (Wales) and Cornwall, or who crossed over to the shores of northwest Gaul (Armorica, Bretagne). Because of their island position and lack of communication with the rest of Christendom they gradually developed *customs at variance* with the Church in continental Europe, such as the retention of the eighty-four year Easter cycle, the form of clerical tonsure, the ceremonies of baptism, etc. These practices then spread to the mission churches of Ireland and Scotland and only after long discussion did the British Church in the seventh and eighth centuries conform to the Roman practices (§ 69, 6). But the assertion (Ebrard and many others) that the Church in Britain was "free from Rome",

---

[1] HADDAN-STUBBS, Councils etc., see § 2, 2.   J. ZWICKER, Fontes historiae religionis Celticae, 1934/5.   L. GOUGAUD, Les chrétientés celtiques, Paris [2]1916; transl. and augmented in: Christianity in Celtic Lands, London 1932. H. ZIMMER, Kelt. Kirche, RE X, 204/43.   G. SCHNÜRER, Kirche u. Kultur im MA. I, 1924, 216 ff. 260 ff.   J. C. MACNAUGHT, The Celtic Church and the See of Peter, Oxford 1927.   A. WILMART, Anal. Reginensia, in Studi e Testi 59, Rome 1933, 29/112 (old Celtic catechesis); cfr. P. GROSJEAN, AB 1936, 113/36.
[2] BEDA H. E. (see no. 4 below) I, 8—22).   F. CABROL, H. Williams etc., § 12, 5.   TH. HODGKIN, History of England to the Norman Conquest, London 1906.   E. WINDISCH, Das kelt. Britannien, Abh. Leipzig 29, 1912.   R. W. CHAMBERS, England before the Norman Conquest, London 1926.   E. RIEMAN, Germanen erobern Britannien, 1939.   D. JERROLD, An Introduction to the History of England from the Earliest Time to 1204, London 1949.   G. SHELDON, The Transition from Romain Britain to Christian England (368/664), London 1932.   F. LOOFS, Antiquae Britonum Scotorumque ecclesiae quales fuerint mores etc., 1882.   FUNK, AU I, 412/59 (early Church in Britain vs. Ebrard).   A. W. WADE-EVANS, Welsh Christian Origins, Oxford 1934.

"an evangelical *church of Culdees*" (Ceile-De = servant, companion, or even, spouse of God) without an episcopacy, without clerical celibacy and entirely beyond papal jurisdiction, has no historical basis.

2. While Christianity was being suppressed in Britain, it began to spread in neighboring lands. **Ireland**[1] (Hibernia, Scotia, Scotia major) which had never been conquered by the Romans and had been entirely unaffected by the Migration of Nations, probably first heard of Christianity from Britain (Wales) and West Gaul. Pope Celestine I in 431 sent *Palladius* as first bishop 'ad Scottos in Christum credentes'. But he did not remain long (in southern Ireland)

---

[1] J. F. KENNEY, The Sources for the Early History of Ireland I, New York 1929. L. GOUGAUD, Modern Research with Special Reference to Early Irish Ecclesiastical History, Dublin 1929. Libri S. Patricii, ed. N. J. D. WHITE, Dublin 1904/5 and London 1918, English transl., London 1920. Das Bekenntnis des hl. Patrick u. dessen Brief an die Gefolgsleute des Coroticus, transl. by F. WOTKE, 1940. Liber Ardmachanus, The Book of Armagh, ed. J. GWYNN, Dublin 1913; Fascimile, Dublin 1937. C. PLUMMER, Vitae Sanctorum Hiberniae, 2 vol. Oxford 1910; Lives of Irish Saints, 2 vol. Oxford 1922; Misc. hagiographica hibernica, Brux. 1925. Monogr. on St. Patrick by J. B. BURY, London 1905; RIGUET, Paris 1911; F. R. M. HITCHCOCK, London 1916; N. J. D. WHITE, London 1920; H. CONCANNON, London 1931; W. M. LETTS, London 1932; C. F. HAMILTON, Dublin, 1932; E. MACNEILL, Dublin 1935. H. DE BLACAM, Milwaukee 1941; L. BIELER, Dublin 1949; P. GROSJEAN, Patriciana, AB 1925, 241/60; 1932, 346/57; 1944, 42/73. K. MULCHRONE, Z. f. keltische Philol., 16, 1926, 1/94 (Vita of St. Patrick); The Tripertite Life of S. Patrick, Dublin 1939. K. MÜLLER, Nachr. Göttingen, 1931, 4, 62/116 (St. Patrick). G. H. WHEELER, English Historical Rev. 1935, 109/13 (Patrick's birthplace: Banna = Bewcastle). D. S. NERNEY, Irish Eccl. Record 1949 (sources of Patrick's spiritual principles). H. LECLERCQ, Irlande, DictAC VII, 1461/552. K. GREITH, Gesch. der altir. Kirche, 1867. A. BELLESHEIM, Gesch. der kath. Kirche in Irland, 3 vols. 1890/1. G. TH. STOKES, Ireland and the Celtic Church (to 1172), London ⁷1928. H. ZIMMER, Sb. Berlin 1909, 543 ff. 582 ff. (Gaul and Ireland). L. GOUGAUD, L'oeuvre des Scotti dans l'Europe continentale, RHE 1908, 21 ff. 255 ff.; 1933, 253/71; Gaelic Pioneers of Christianity (VI—XII Cent.), Dublin 1923; Les Saints irlandais hors d'Irlande, Louvain 1936. W. LEVISON, Die Iren u. die fränk. Kirche, HZ 109, 1912, 1/22; cfr. NA 1914, 167 ff. (Palladius and Patrick). Were there two Patricks? cfr. G. MURPHY and in Studies 1943, 297/326. F. KATTENBUSCH, Irland in der KG., ThStKr 1921, 1/27. H. GRAHAM, The Early Irish Monastic Schools, Dublin 1923. J. P. FUHRMANN, Irish Medieval Monasteries on the Continent (600/1500), Diss. Wash. 1927. W. G. HANSON, The Early Monastic Schools of Ireland, Cambridge 1927. J. SNIEDERS, RHE 1928, 596 ff. 828 ff. (Irish hagiography). P. W. FINSTERWALDER, ZKG 1928, 203/26 (Irish and Anglo-Saxon missions). ST. J. D. SEYMOUR, Irish Vision of the Other World, London 1930. J. RYAN S.J., Irish Monasticism, Dublin 1931. W. S. KERR, The Independence of the Celtic Church in Ireland, London 1931. A. M. TOMMASINI, I santi Irlandesi in Italia, Milano 1932. H. FRANK, Die Klosterbischöfe des Frankenreiches, 1932. W. DELIUS, ThStKr 1935, 356/75 (introduction of Christianity into Ireland). R. A. S. MACALISTER, Ancient Ireland, London 1935. A. MAHR and J. RAFTERY, Christian Art in Ancient Ireland, 2 vol. Dublin 1932/41. F. HENRY, Irish Art in the Early Christian Period, London 1940.

unless we hold that Palladius is merely another name for Patrick. The conversion of the island was the work of *St. Patrick* and his disciples. He was a native Briton, son of the Deacon Calpurnius of Banna in Cumberland. As a youth of sixteen years he was captured by pirates and brought to Ireland where, as a slave, he herded sheep and developed a deep religious spirit. After six years he escaped and returned home where he was admitted among the clergy. He studied in Gaul (Lérins, Auxerre), embraced the monastic life and was consecrated bishop. Called in a dream to return to Ireland (Confessio S. Patricii), he took up the work which Palladius had begun and in 30 years (432?—461) succeeded in making the Emerald Isle a thoroughly Catholic land. Patrick's life and apostolic labors have been surrounded by a fund of beautiful legend. He is said to have established his see at *Armagh* in North Ireland, which later became the metropolitan see of the country. Monasteries became so numerous — every clan had at least one — that the whole Irish Church took on a *monastic* character. These monasteries were not only schools of strict asceticism ("Isle of saints") but were also seats of classical learning. Especially renowned was the monastery of *Bangor* near Belfast, founded by *St. Comgall* in 558. The monks of Ireland were also the pastors of souls. Ecclesiastical jurisdiction was exercised by abbots. In some cases the abbot of a monastery was himself a bishop, in other cases one of the monks received episcopal consecration. Either a natural tendency to wander or an ascetical desire to sever the ties of home and kindred induced many Irish monks (Scotti peregrinantes, peregrini) to go to Scotland, Gaul, Germany and Italy where they preached the Gospel and established monasteries. Beginning with St. Columbanus and continuing from the sixth to the eleventh century these wandering Irish monks (peregrinari pro Deo amore) became an important factor in the mission and monastic history of the continent. Many of these missionaries lacked talent for organization and their missionary methods and piety were all too individualistic. But in general they accomplished much for the Kingdom of God and the cultural development of the West.

3. Toward the end of the fourth century, the Briton, *St. Ninian*, preached the Gospel in southern *Scotland*[1] which the Romans called

---

[1] M. B. MACGREGOR, The Sources and Literature of Scotish Church History, Glasgow 1934. ADAMNANUS, Vita S. Columbae, ed. J. T. FOWLER, Oxford ²1920; cfr. G. BRÜNING, Adamnans Vita Col., Diss. 1917. T. H. WAL-

Caledonia and which was known in the Middle Ages as Scotia (minor). The northern part of the land was Christianized by the Irish abbot *St. Columba* (or Columbanus the Elder † 597) who preached throughout the north for thirty-four years. The center of the mission was the monastery he had founded on Iona (Eo, Io, I, Hy), one of the islands of the Hebrides. Like the Church of Ireland, the newly founded Church of Scotland long had a *monastic organization* and followed the peculiar customs of the British Church. At first the abbots of Iona governed the Scottish Church although, according to the prescriptions of Columba, they were only priests. It was only in the eighth century, when closer relations with Rome were established, that secular priests were introduced and only in the twelfth century that the country was divided into dioceses.

4. A revival of Christianity took place in **England**[1] toward the end of the sixth century. In 590 Pope *Gregory the Great* (§ 64, 7) sent

KER, S. Columba, London 1923. W. D. SIMPSON, The Historical Saint Columba, Aberdeen [2]1927; On Certain Saints, ib. 1928; The Celtic Church in Scotland, ib. 1935. H. LECLERCQ, DictAC VII, 1423/61 (Iona). A. O. ANDERSON, Early Sources of Scottish History (500—1286), 2 vol. Edinb. 1922. A. BELLESHEIM, Gesch. der kath. Kirche in Schottland, 2 vols. 1883. W. F. SKENE, Celtic Scotland, 3 vol. Edinb. [2]1887. J. DOWDEN, The Celtic Church in Scotland, London 1894; The Bishops of Scotland, London 1912.— A. R. MACEWEN, History of the Church in Scotland I (to 1560), London 1913. G. A. F. KNIGHT, Archaeological Light on the Early Christianizing of Scotland, 2 vol. London 1933. A. B. SCOTT, St. Ninian, London 1917; The Pictish Nation, Edinb. 1918. K. STRECKER, NA 1922, 1/26 (Ninian). W. D. SIMPSON, S. Ninian and the Origins of the Christian Church in Scotland, Edinb. 1940.

[1] CH. GROSS, The Sources and Literature of English History to 1485, London [2]1915. HADDAN-STUBBS, Councils etc., see § 2, 2. Beda Venerabilis, Historia Ecclesiastica gentis Anglorum, ed. A. HOLDER, [3]1890; ed. C. PLUMMER, 2 vol. Oxford 1896; ed. J. E. KING, 2 vol. London 1930 (with English transl.). P. F. JONES, A Concordance to the Historia Eccles. of Bede, Cambridge Mass. 1929. H. BLASCHE, Angelsachsen u. Kelten im Urteil der Hist. eccl. gentis Anglorum des Beda, 1940. VITA S. WILFRIDI, ed. W. LEVISON, MGSS rer. Merov. VI; ed. B. Colgrave, London 1927 (with English transl.). B. HOLTHEUER, Die Gründung der angelsächs. Kirche, 1897. A. BROU, S. Augustin de Cant., Paris [4]1900. H. HOWORTH, S. Augustine of Cant., London 1913. A. CARDINAL GASQUET, The Mission of S. Augustine, London 1924. M. MÜLLER, ThQ 1932, 94/118 (Gregory's reply to Augustine Reg. XI, 56a not genuine); opposite opinion F. WASNER, Jus Pontificium 1938, 174 ff. 293 ff. S. BRECHTER, Die Quellen zur Angelsachsenmission Gregors d. Gr., 1941. K. OBSER, Wilfrid d. Ältere, 1884. A. HUMBERT, Angleterre (5./10. Jh.), DictHE III, 156/73. E. WINKELMANN, Gesch. der Angelsachsen bis z. Tode K. Alfreds (901), 1884. G. F. BROWNE, The Conversion of the Heptarchy, London [2]1906. W. HUNT, The English Church from its Foundation to the Norman Conquest, London [2]1907. TH. HODGKIN, R. W. CHAMBERS and D. JERROLD, see no. 1 above. F. CABROL, L'Angleterre chrétienne avant les Normands, Paris 1909. CH. OMAN, England before the Norman Conquest., London 1910. A. HAUCK, Deutschland u. England in ihren kirchl. Beziehungen, 1916. F. KATTENBUSCH, England in der KG.,

the Roman Benedictine Abbot *Augustine* and fifty of his monks as missionaries to the *Anglo-Saxons.* King *Ethelbert* of Kent, then the Bretwalda, or overlord of the Anglo-Saxon heptarchy, had married Bertha, a Frankish princess, who acquainted her husband with the fundamentals of the faith. He not only permitted the newly arrived missionaries to preach, but he himself and several thousand of his people received baptism (at Pentecost?) in 597. Upon receiving the news of this great success, the pope sent more missionaries to England (Mellitus, Justus and others) and ordered the erection of two metropolitan sees each with twelve suffragans (601). The metropolitan sees were to be located in the two cities which had already been the seats of bishops: *London,* for the south; and *York* for the north. But eventually *Canterbury* the capital of Kent was chosen in place of London because it was from here that the mission had started and Augustine had already taken up residence there. According to the prudent instructions which the pope had given to the missionaries, they were to conform as far as possible to the customs and practices of the people (use old pagan temples for Christian worship, convert pagan festivals into Christian feasts, etc.). Augustine († 604) endeavored to establish contact with the British Church in Wales (see above no. 1), but because of the hatred of the Britons for the Anglo-Saxon conquerors, the western Christians did not at once show a friendly spirit. However within fifty years, five other Anglo-Saxon kingdoms had become Catholic, especially *Essex* with London its capital (a bishopric in 604) and powerful *Northumbria.* The conversion of the latter kingdom was the work of *Paulinus,* Bishop of York, who baptized King *Edwin* (627), the son-in-law of Ethelbert of Kent. But later on, due to a reaction of pagans, King Oswald called in missionaries from the monastery of Iona who introduced the old customs of

ThStKr 1920, 1/53. E. A. PHILIPSON, German. Heidentum bei den Angel-sachsen, 1929. J. L. GOUGH MEISSNER, The Celtic Church after the Synod of Whitby (664), London 1929 (weak). TH. ZWÖLLER, St. Peter, Apostelfürst u. Himmelspförtner, s. Verehrung bei den Angelsachsen u. Franken, 1929. S. CRAWFORD, Anglo-Saxon Influence of Western Christendom (600—800), Oxford 1933. G. BAESECKE, Der Vocabularius S. Galli in der angelsächs. Mission, 1933. J. R. SALA, Preaching in the Anglo-Saxon Church, Thesis Chicago 1934. H. WÜRDINGER, ZRGkan 1935, 105/30 (Christianity and Anglo-Saxon law). R. H. HODGKIN, A History of the Anglo-Saxons, 2 vol. Oxford 1935. K. TH. STRASSER, Sachsen u. Angelsachsen, [3]1941. F. M. STEN-TON, Anglo-Saxon England, Oxford 1943. E. S. DUCKETT, Anglo-Saxon Saints and Scholars, London 1947. O. JENSEN, Der engl. Peterspfennig, 1903. C. DAUX, Le denier de S. Pierre, Paris 1909. W. J. MOORE, The Saxon Pilgrims to Rome and the Schola Saxonum, Diss. Freiburg (Switz.) 1937.

the Irish-Scotch Church (635). *St. Wilfred*, Bishop of York, worked hard for unity and in 664 a synod was held at Streaneshalch or Whitby in which conformity with Rome was decreed, especially regarding the date of Easter (§ 69, 6). The organization of the Anglo-Saxon Church was completed under Pope Vitalian, who at the request of the English, sent *Theodore*, a highly educated Greek (Part II, §89, 2) to be archbishop of Canterbury (669—690). Nowhere among the Germanic peoples did the seed of the Gospel take stronger root, spread more rapidly or become the source of a nobler culture than in England. Ecclesiastical and national life were intimately and happily united. Numerous monasteries and convents under the rule of St. Benedict produced saintly and learned men and women who contributed greatly to the cultural progress of the nation. The gratitude of the Anglo-Saxons toward the papacy and their veneration for the successor of Peter "Prince of the Apostles" and "Gatekeeper of heaven" found expression in pilgrimages "ad limina apostolorum" and in the custom of an annual donation to Rome. It is certain that King Offa of Mercia († 796) promised a *Peter's pence* (denarius S. Petri). Like the Irish-Scottish Church, the Anglo-Saxon Church in the second half of the seventh century began active missionary work on the continent. The Anglo-Saxons possessed the qualities which the Irish missionaries had lacked: adaptability, talent for organization and an appreciation of the hierarchical order in the Church. They aided in the reform of the Frankish Church and transmitted to it their own love of learning and literary endeavor.

## § 45.
### Christianity Impeded by Islam[1].

1. While the Gospel was making steady progress in the West, there arose in the East a powerful obstacle in the form of *Islamism*.

---

[1] Monogr. on Mohammed by H. GRIMME, 2 vols. 1892/5, condensed 1904; H. RECKENDORF, 1908; R. F. DIBBLE, London 1927; F. BUHL, German by H. SCHAEDER, 1930; T. ANDRAE, 1932; E. DERMENGHEM, Paris 1950. O. PRETZL, HZ 161, 1940, 457/76. A. HARNACK, DG. II¹, 1909, 529/38. Chantepie de la Saussaye, Lehrb. der Religionsgesch. I¹, 1925, 648/756. P. CASANOVA et L. GARDETTE, Mahomet, Mahométisme, DictThC IX, 1572 to 1650. H. GRÉGOIRE, Mél. Ch. Diehl I, Paris 1930, 107/19 (Mohammed and Monophysitism). H. LAMMENS, RechSR 1930, 416/38 (Charakter of Mohammed according to the Koran). A. BAUMSTARK, ZMW 1932, 319/32 (M's. tragic lot). W. RUDOLPH, Die Abhängigkeit des Quorans von Judentum u. Christentum, 1922. R. BELL, Origin of Islam in the Christian Environ-

## § 45. Christianity Impeded by Islam.

Arabia was the birthplace of this new religion and its founder was *Mohammed*, a deeply religious Arabian merchant, who was born at Mecca in 570 and died at Medina in 632. It is to his credit that he extirpated idolatry from his native land and introduced *monotheism* with which he had become acquainted from his frequent contacts with Jews and Christians as well as with Judaizing Christian sects. He recognized Moses and Christ as prophets and held to belief in the resurrection of the body and eternal life. Basing himself on revelations he claimed to have received in dreams and visions, he began in 610 to proclaim himself a messenger of God and the greatest of the prophets specially chosen by God to announce the rediscovery of the true faith and to prophesy the immediate and severe judgement of God. Hence he felt himself called to make war on the other two religions. The definite turning point came in 622 when his reform program at Mecca failed and he and his disciples were obliged to flee (Hegira, hedschra = flight — 622 the

ment, London 1925. T. ANDRAE, Der Ursprung des Islam u. das Christentum, Uppsala 1926. K. AHRENS, Muh. als Religionsstifter, 1935. O. JÄSCHKE, MissWRelW 1949, 16/28 (M. and Christianity). J. SCHACHT, Der Islam, ²1931 (Religionsgesch. Lesebuch 16). R. AIGRAIN, Arabie, DictHE III, 1158/1339. H. LECLERCQ, Invasion arabe, DictAC VII, 1220/72. AUG. MÜLLER, Der Islam im Morgen- u. Abendland, 2 vols. 1885/7. The Cambridge Medieval History II, Cambridge 1913. CL. HUART, Gesch. der Araber, German by S. BECK and M. FÄRBER, 2 vols. 1914/6. K. GÜTERBOCK, Der Islam im Lichte der byzant. Polemik, 1912. H. LAMMENS, Le berceau de l'Islam I, Rome 1914; L'Islam, croyances et institutions, Beyrouth 1926; L'Arabie occidentale avant l'Hégire, ib. 1928. T. MANN, Der Islam einst u. jetzt, 1914. J. HELL, Die Religion des Islam I, 1914 (selections); Die Kultur der Araber, ²1919; R. HARTMANN, Palästina unter den Arabern (633—1516), 1915. G. SIMON, Der Islam u. die chiistl. Verkündigung, 1920. CARRA DE VAUX, Les penseurs de l'Islam, 5 vol. Paris 1921/6. J. Lippl, Der Islam, 1922 (Samml. Kösel). C. H. BECKER, Islamstudien, 2 vols. 1924/32. I. GOLDZIHER, Vorlesungen über den Islam, ²1925. G. PFANNMÜLLER, Handbuch der Islam-Literatur, 1923. TH. W. ARNOLD, The Caliphate, Oxford 1924. JUL. RICHTER, Der Islam als Religion, 1927. M. D'HERBIGNY, L'Islam naissant, Rome 1929 (Orientalia christ. XIV, 2). F. W. HASLUCK, Christianity and Islam under the Sultans, 2 vol. Oxford 1929. A. J. WENSINCK, The Muslim's Creed, Cambridge 1932. G. BERGSTRÄSSER, Grundzüge des islam. Rechts, 1935. M. M. ALI, The Religion of Islam, London 1936. P. K. HITTI, History of the Arabs, London ⁴1948. C. KOPP, ThGl 1938, 255/80 (Christianity and Islam). C. BROCKELMANN, Gesch. der islam. Völker u. Staaten, ²1943; Gesch. der arab. Literatur, 2 vols. Leyden ²1943/9. A. DIEZ, Glaube u. Welt des Islam, 1941. ABU'S SU'UD, Rapporti tre l'Islam e il cristianesimo, Rome 1942. E. KELLERHALS, Der Islam, 1945. H. PIRENNE, see § 41. L. E. BROWE, The Eclipse of Christianity in Asia from Muhammed til the 14th Century, Cambridge 1933. F. NAU, Les Arabes chrétiens de Mésopotamie et de Syrie du VIIᵉ au VIIIᵉ siècle, Paris 1933. H. CHARLES, Le christianisme des Arabes nomades, Paris 1936. E. L. ISELIN, Der Untergang der christl. Kirche in Nordafrika, 1918; cfr. G. BARDY, Revue apolog. 1930, 513/30; W. SESTON, MélAH 1936, 101/24. G. MARÇAIS, La Berbérie musulmane et l'Orient au moyen âge, Paris 1946.

beginning of the Moslem era). From that time he began to approve polygamy which was permitted among the Arabians. He accused the Jews and Christians of having falsified the Scriptures, the Christians especially by introducing the doctrine of the Trinity. He also rejected several Jewish customs and ordained that instead of turning towards Jerusalem to pray, his disciples must turn toward Mecca.

Islam (i. e. unconditional surrender to Allâh, God) is a *syncretic* religion composed of elements taken from Judaism, Christianity and Arabic paganism. Its three chief dogmas are: belief in one invisible God, in Mohammed as the greatest prophet and in a divine judgement. The doctrine of predestination becomes a crude sort of determinism (kismet = fate), and the future life is conceived as a life of sensual pleasures. The five principal duties or "pillars" of Islam are: Profession of faith, prayer five times a day with ritualistic purifications, a fast during the month of Ramadan, almsgiving, and a pilgrimage to Mecca at least once in a lifetime. Further prescriptions include circumcision, abstinence from wine and pork, destruction of pictures or statues, etc. The holy book of Islam, the *Koran* (= to read), contains the words and supposed revelations of the prophet which were collected and edited after his death. It regulates religion, morals and justice. (An Arabic and German edition by Sadr-ud-Din, 1939; German by L. Ullmann, ⁹1897; L. Goldschmidt, 1923; selections by H. Grimme, 1923). The Sunna (= custom, tradition) is an explanation of the Koran. The *Shiah* (schismatic) faction of Persia and neighboring lands, numbering about 15 million, reject most of the Sunna and recognize only the successors of Ali, Mohammed's nephew and son-in-law, as rightful heads of Islam. The *Sunni* (orthodox) accept both books and uphold the legitimacy of the succession of the first three caliphs. The total number of Mohammedans at the present time is estimated at between 250 and 280 million.

2. In the later years of his life Mohammed became more occupied with dreams of political power and envisioned how his religion could be used to that end. And so the dreamer, the preacher of penance and prophet became the powerful military leader, lawgiver and grafty politician, who with undeniable genius formed a new commonwealth according to his own principles. His character shows definite strains of cruelty and lust. By means of the new revelation he foisted on his followers, he committed them to a holy war, a systematic and ceaseless attack on all "unbelievers" that is, all non-Mohammedans. The war began in Arabia. In 630 he recaptured *Mecca* and after destroying all idols, proclaimed the ancient Arabic Kaaba (lit., square building or cube) the chief sanctuary of the new religion. After Mohammed's death his successors the *caliphs* (= representatives) under whom the Mohammedan theocracy developed, began to conquer and plunder the countries border-

ing on Arabia *(Arabian Migration of Nations)*. Conquest after conquest tore from the Byzantine Empire some of its richest provinces and threatened to destroy every vestige of Grecian culture in them. "Islam became the executioner of Hellenism" (Mommsen). But it was not only Hellenic culture that suffered; Christianity was practically annihilated in the East. The first two caliphs, Abu Bekr (632—634) and Omar (634—644) took *Palestine, Syria, Egypt* and *Persia.* Thus the patriarchates of Antioch (637), Jerusalem (638) and Alexandria (642) were brought under Mohammedan rule. The dissensions among Christians, especially the bitter Christological controversies made the conquest easier. The Monophysites of Egypt rejoiced that the Arabs had liberated them from Byzantium. Under Caliph Othman (644—656) *Armenia* and *Cyprus* were taken and an attempt was made on the territory around Carthage. The *Omaijad* dynasty which established the hereditary caliphate at *Damascus* (661—750) pushed eastward as far a *India* and *Turkestan,* and westward to *Carthage* which they took in 698, to *Barbary* and the northwest coast of Africa and in 711, crossed into *Spain.* Even Constantinople was beseiged (717—718) but not taken. The dynasty of the *Abbasides* established the caliphate at *Bagdad* (750—1258) and made that city the capital of the *Islamic world-empire.*

3. As a rule the Mohammedans did not immediately molest the Christian religion in the countries they conquered beyond imposing certain restrictions on public worship. They did, however, expel all Christians and Jews from Arabia. But Christianity suffered greatly nonetheless. As a result of the long religious controversies, some of the countries which at one time had been flourishing Christian nations, declined in faith and discipline. The new Mohammedan masters welcomed apostate Christians into their religion and did everything possible to induce them to join. Those who became Mohammedans were exempt from poll taxes and Christian slaves or bondmen who embraced Islamism were freed; but a Mohammedan who abandoned his faith was put to death. This effectively prevented any missionary work among them. Under such circumstances there were numerous defections among the Christian population so that the Churches in those countries dwindled into insignificance. In northwest Africa where the Church had once been so strong, it ceased to exist altogether and the population became savage and uncivilized. In 1053 there were still five cathedrals, but the last of them, the great cathedral of Carthage, was a shapeless ruin by 1160.

## CHAPTER II

### DEVELOPMENT OF DOCTRINE
### THEOLOGICAL CONTROVERSIES, HERESIES AND SCHISMS[1]

### § 46.

**Theological Controversies and Development of Doctrine in General.**

1. The theological controversies of this period were more numerous and more important than those of the preceding period. They lasted from the beginning to the end of the period and, at least in the East, gave the period its specific character. They were concerned with the most essential doctrines and revealed the most widely divergent points of view. All classes of Christian people took part in them. But what made them particularly intensive was the fact that the civil power in the now Christian Empire, took sides and endeavored to influence the decisions (§ 41, 2). Frequently, a theological dispute was at the same time a political contest for power. A series of *general councils* or *synods of the Empire* usually convoked by imperial decree were held at which the points at issue were thoroughly examined and decided. Then all the latent powers within the Church were aroused and the best minds came to her defence in clarifying, expounding and developing her dogma as the need arose. The Golden Age of patristic literature closely coincides with the period of dogmatic quarrels (§ 74—76).

2. According to the subject matter, we may distinguish three principal controversies.

a) The first was a recurrence of the *question concerning the Trinity* which had attracted some attention in the preceding period.

---

[1] J. SCHWANE, Dogmengesch. der patrist. Zeit (325—787), [2]1895. J. TIXERONT, Histoire des dogmes II (318—430), III (430—800), Paris 6./7. éd. 1922/4. HEFELE, Conc.-Gesch. and HEFELE-LECLERCQ (see § 2, 2) I—III. A. HARNACK, Lehrbuch der DG. II—III, [4]1909/10, reprinted 1932. R. SEEBERG, Lehrb. der DG. II[3], 1923. RIBIÈRE, LOOFS et al., see § 27. W. NIGG, Das Buch der Ketzer, 1949. E. CASPAR, Gesch. des Papsttums I—II, 1930/3. R. DEVREESSE, Le patriarcat d'Antioche depuis la paix de l'Église jusqu'à la conquête arabe, Paris 1945. F. MARIN-SOLA, L'évolution homogène du dogme catholique, 2 vol. Fribourg 1924. J. DE GHELLINCK, RHE 1930, 5/42 (Dialectics and Aristotle in the Trinitarian controversy of the fourth c.); Patristique et moyen âge III, Paris 1948. G. L. PRESTIGE, God in Patristic Thought, London 1936. A. SPINDELER, Cur Verbum caro factum? Das Motiv der Menschwerdung in den Glaubenskämpfen des 4. u. 5. Jahrhunderts, 1938. K. PRÜMM, ZkTh 1939, 311 ff. et passim (the theology of the Fathers). E. V. IVÀNKA, Hellenisches u. Christliches im frühbyzantin. Geistesleben, 1948.

In the beginning the dispute concerned only the relation of the Son to the Father, that is, it dealt with the theology, in the narrower sense, by which the false teachings of the *Arians* and the *Semiarians* were to be combatted. Later, when the *Pneumatomachi* arose, it was necessary to settle the question of the nature of the Holy Ghost. Both these questions were authoritatively settled by the first two ecumenical councils at Nicaea in 325 and Constantinople in 381.

b) The *Christological* controversy arose naturally from the Trinitarian error, and passed through four stages. First it was necessary to combat the teachings of the *Arians* and *Apollinaris* of Laodicea that the Logos had not assumed complete human nature. Then came the question as to the relation of the two natures in Christ. The faulty notions on this point held by the *Nestorians* and the *Monophysites* were condemned in the third and fourth General Councils: at Ephesus in 431 and at Chalcedon in 451. These disputes resulted in the East in the separation of the *schismatic national churches* from the Church of the Empire, a separation which exists to the present day. Lastly, the error known as *Monothelitism*, which held that the Logos had but one will, was condemned by the sixth General Council at Constantinople in 680—681.

c) About the same time that the great Christological controversies were raging in the East, the West, whose religious interests had always been concerned with the practical, was disturbed by an *anthropological* or *Soteriological* problem. This resulted from an inquiry into the original state of man, the consequences of original sin and the relation between grace and free will. The errors on these points were known as *Pelagianism* and *Semipelagianism* and were combatted chiefly by *St. Augustine*, whose writings in defence of the Church's doctrine earned for him the title "Doctor gratiae".

Accompanying the theological quarrels in point of time, sometimes related to them and sometimes of entirely independent origin, were a number of lesser disturbances on the Church — lesser in the sense that their implications were not so serious, but grave enough to convulse the Church in large areas and for a long time. Such was *Donatism* (§ 52; 66, 4) which ended with the Vandal invasion of Africa; and such was the *quarrel over the Three Chapters*, settled by the fifth General Council at Constantinople in 553.

# § 47.

## Arianism and the First General Council at Nicaea in 325[1].

1. By excluding both the Dynamic and Modal Monarchians from her communion (§ 32) the Church had acknowledged Christ to be divine and yet distinct from the Father. But nothing was decided authoritatively regarding the relation of the Son's divinity to that of the Father. Quite a few, without actually denying the divinity of the Son, held that He was more or less *subordinate* to the Father. Of those who inclined to such an opinion, some thought that His generation was somehow related to the creation of the world and thus denied His eternity or at least the eternity of His subsistence

---

[1] S. Athanasii Opera, PG 25—28. Athanasius' Werke, hg. im Auftrag der Kirchenväter-Kommission der Preuss. Akad. der Wiss., 3 vols. 1934 ff.; of which vol. III, 1 contains Urkunden zur Gesch. des Arian. Streites 318—28, hg. v. H. G. OPITZ, 1934/5. Also H. G. OPITZ, Untersuchungen zur Überlief. der Schriften des Ath., 1935; ZntW 1934, 131/59 (chronology of Arianism to 328). W. TELFER, JThSt 1946, 129/42 (beginning of Arianism); AB 1949, 117/30. G. BARDY, RHE 1930, 253/68 (fragments of A's. writings). J. DE GHELLINCK, Misc. A. de Meyer 1946, 159/80 (lost works). P. NAUTIN, AB 1949, 131/41 (interpolation in the letter of A.). W. ELLIGER, ThStKr 1931, 244/51 (theology of Ar.). Gelasius Cyzicenus, Acta Concilii Nicaeni s. Historia Ecclesiastica (c. 475), hg. v. G. LOESCHKE u. M. HEINEMANN, 1918. J. KUHN, G. KRÜGER, et al., § 32. P. BATIFFOL, La paix Constantinienne et le Catholicisme (303—359), Paris 1914. E. CASPAR, Gesch. des Papsttums I, 1930, 118 ff. 137 ff. 220 ff. H. LIETZMANN, Gesch. der alten Kirche III, 1938, 80 ff. F. LOOFS, Arianismus, RE II, 6/45; XXIII, 113/15. G. GENTZ, Arianer, RLAntChrist I, 647/52. ED. SCHWARTZ, Zur Gesch. des Athanasius I—IX, Nachr. Gött. 1904/5, 1908, 1912. S. ROGALA, Die Anfänge des arian. Streites, 1907; also V. HUGGER, ThQ 1909, 66/86. E. SEEBERG, Die Synode v. Antiochien 324/5, 1913. G. BARDY, Recherches sur Saint Lucien d'Antioche et son école, Paris 1936. On the Council of Nicaea: HEFELE, Conc.-Gesch. I², 252 ff.; HEFELE-LECLERCQ I, 335 ff. 1125 ff. F. HAASE, Die kopt. Quellen z. Konzil v. Nicäa, 1920. L. FEDER, ZkTh 1906, 172/8 (number of bishops); cfr. ib. 382/4. C. A. KNELLER, StML 1909 II, 503/22 (the papacy at Nicaea). A. E. BURN, The Nicene Creed, London 1909; The Council of Nicaea, London 1925. M. WEIS, Die Stellung des Eusebius v. Cäs. im arian. Streit, Diss. 1920. F. LOOFS, Das Nicänum, Festgabe K. Müller 1922, 68/82; cfr. H. LIETZMANN, ZntW 1925, 193/202. A. D'ALÈS, Le dogme de Nicée, Paris 1926. G. FRITZ, Concile de Nicée, DictThC XI, 399/417. H. LECLERCQ, Nicée, DictAC XII, 1179/1232. A. MICHEL, Hypostase, DictThC VII, 370/437. H. G. OPITZ, ZntW 1935, 1/19; D. S. BALANOS, ThQ 1935, 309/22 (Eusebius of Caesarea as theologian). H. BERKHOF, Die Theologie des Eusebius von Caes., 1939; J. BARBEL, see § 77, 1. F. ERDIN, Das Wort Hypostasis, 1939; cfr. K. RAHNER, ZkTh 1940, 159 f. CH. HAURET, Comment le „Défenseur de Nicée" [S. Athanasius] a-t-il compris le dogme de Nicée? Thèse Bruges 1936 (cfr. B. ALTANER, ThRev 1937, 490/2). J. ORTIZ DE URBINA, El simbolo niceno, Madrid 1947; OrChrPer 1936, 330/50 (text of the N. Creed). TH. CAMELOT, ib. 1947, 425/33 (creed of N.). On the lists of bishops from Nicaea 325 to Chalcedon 451; E. HONIGMANN, Byzantion 1936, 429/49; 1939, 17/76; 1942/3, 20/80; E. SCHWARTZ, Abh. München NF. 13, 1937. G. BARDY, Irénikon 1939, 385/424; RevSR 1940, 26/83 (the West in the Arian controversy). H. YABEN, Osio, obispo de Cordoba, Barcel. 1945.

as a person; others considered the Son less than the Father because they believed that He had received His divine being from the Father and hence His divinity was derived from the Father (Origen; § 39, 2). Yet we find, especially in the Roman Church, the firm conviction that Father and Son are *co-equal*. This doctrine based on Holy Scripture became constantly clearer in the consciousness of the Church and was officially and authoritatively declared to be the true doctrine. The occasion for the declaration was the Arian controversy.

2. **Arius**, a distinguished priest of Alexandria, had been educated in the school of Antioch under the renowned exegete *Lucian* (§ 32, 3; 39, 5). While some of the earlier Fathers, due to lack of definition and exact language seemed to teach subordinationism, Arius espoused it deliberately and taught it boldly. Not only did he subordinate the Son to the Father in nature, but he denied that the Son had a divine nature or any of the divine attributes, especially eternity. He asserted: "There was a time when he (the Logos) did not exist" (ἦν ποτε, ὅτε οὐκ ἦν) and "He began to exist out of nothing" (ἐξ οὐκ ὄντων ἐστίν). According to Arius, the Logos is a creature of the Father (ποίημα, κτίσμα τοῦ πατρός), the first and noblest of creatures, but created out of nothing to serve as a sort of instrument in the rest of creation, because according to the Stoic philosophy of Philo, the absolute, transcendent God can not come in direct contact with what is wholly material. The Logos, said Arius, is subject to change and development, and in essence is quite different from the Father to whom He is united only by will. By a special act of grace He was accepted as the Son of God because of His foreseen merits. He may be called God, not in the proper sense of the word, but only metaphorically or morally (μετοχῇ). These shocking notions which would debase the Logos to a sort of demigod and inevitably cause a reversion to paganism were preached by Arius, from about 315. He expressed the same notions in letters and hymns and later wrote a work called Θάλεια by means of which he won a surprisingly large number of clergy and people to his views. Bishop *Alexander* of Alexandria opposed the error, which he considered a form of Ebionitic Monarchianism. But when all efforts to induce Arius to abandon his teaching proved futile, he and his clerical adherents (2 bishops, 6 priests and 6 deacons) were excommunicated. This took place at a great synod attended by about 100 Egyptian bishops at *Alexandria* in 318. (The date of the synod

has been variously given as 320, 321 or 323; but Opitz has now established the date as 318. See literature above). Alexander then announced the decision of the synod to Pope Sylvester and the other bishops and forced Arius to leave the city.

3. The quarrel assumed greater proportions when Arius gained new and able adherents to his cause. These he found not only among the *Melitians*, a schismatic group which had been separated from the Alexandrian Church since the beginning of the century (§ 35, 3) and to which Arius himself had once belonged, but also among Catholic bishops who had studied at the school of Antioch and who were known as Syllucians (§ 32, 3). One of these, *Eusebius*, the pliant but influential bishop of Nicomedia, to whom Arius fled, took the heretic under his protection. All the Christian people of the East became interested in the controversy and were divided over it. Emperor *Constantine the Great*, who, after the defeat of Licinius in 324, had become ruler of the East, felt himself called upon to restore the unity of the Church as rapidly as possible. First he sent his friend *Hosius*, the eminent bishop of Corduba to Alexandria to try to compose the differences between Alexander and Arius; but nothing was accomplished. Early in 325 Hosius presided at a rather well attended synod at *Antioch*, which declared in favor of Alexander and against Arius. At this synod three bishops, including Eusebius of Caesarea (§ 75, 1), the church historian, were severely censured, but the controversy was not ended. Since there were other matters also calling for attention, especially the date of Easter (§ 69, 9), Constantine resolved to summon a *general council* to settle the dispute. It was first decided to hold the council at Ancyra, but actually it met at **Nicaea** in Bithynia from May until July 325 and was attended by some three hundred bishops (Athanasius and Gennadius say 318) from all parts of the Christian world. Only seven representatives of the West were present, among them the two Roman priests (Victor and Vincent), delegates of the aged Pope Sylvester. The most ardent and capable champions of the orthodox faith, besides Hosius and Alexander, were bishops *Eustathius* of Antioch (§ 50, 1) and *Marcellus* of Ancyra (§ 50, 4). *Athanasius* of Alexandria attended the council as companion and secretary to Bishop Alexander, and although he was but a deacon at the time he took an active and important part in the defense of orthodoxy. It appears that Hosius presided, assisted by the two papal legates (§ 65, 2).

4. Because of the opposing views, the debate in the synod frequently waxed warm and sometimes bitter so that, it is said, the emperor was obliged at times to intervene and admonish the bishops to greater moderation and harmony. Eusebius of Nicomedia presented a creed which was summarily rejected as Arian, after which the Fathers endeavored to find expressions in Scripture which would safeguard the faith. Especially did they oppose the Arian idea that the Logos was "made from nothing" and stressed that He is "of God" (ἐκ τοῦ θεοῦ). *Eusebius of Caesarea*, the leader of a compromise party, the members of which, like himself, were followers of Origen, proposed the baptismal symbol in use in his diocese. Had it been accepted, it would have been complete vindication for him. It was favored by the emperor; but upon examination it was found to be too indefinite and capable of being interpreted in an Arian sense, since according to 1 Cor. 8:6, everything is of God. Finally, in full agreement with the theology of the Roman West and with the consent of the emperor, a *creed* was drawn up (June 19, 325) which expressed clearly that the Son of God is "of the essence of the Father" (ἐκ τῆς οὐσίας τοῦ πατρός), that He is "God of God, Light of Light, true God of true God, begotten, not made, *consubstantial* with the Father (ὁμοούσιος τῷ πατρί) through whom all things in heaven and earth are made." Then the main teachings of Arius were listed and anathematized: that there was a time when the Son of God did not exist; that He was made from nothing; that He is a different substance (ὑπόστασις) or essence (οὐσία) than the Father; that He was created (κτιστός); that He is subject to change or variation (τρεπτὸς ἢ ἀλλοιωτός). The symbol was almost unanimously accepted by the assembled Fathers. Only two Libyan bishops, *Secundus* of Ptolemais and *Theonas* of Marmorica, who had favored Arius from the beginning, refused to subscribe. They were excommunicated and banished together with Arius. Soon afterward Constantine also banished Bishop *Eusebius* of Nicomedia and *Theognis* of Nicaea who persisted in maintaining relations with some of the Alexandrian Arians. The writings of Arius and his friends were condemned and ordered to be burned and the penalty of death was threatened on anyone who would attempt to conceal these writings. The Council completed its work by regulating the date of Easter and passing twenty disciplinary canons (election of bishops § 20, 3 and 63, 1, 2; the organization of patriarchates, § 60, 6; the discipline of penance § 26, 2; taking of interest § 32, 3;

the Paulianists § 60, 6; celibacy § 25, 3 and 69, 6). This was the first of a series of *ecumenical* councils, and a landmark in the history of Christian dogma and of the Church of the Empire. As the "great and holy synod composed of 318 teachers" the Nicene Council was given an almost religious veneration throughout the East.

## § 48.
### Further Controversy and Final Defeat of Arianism[1].

1. The decision of the Council of Nicaea did not effect the peace of the Church. On the contrary, there were long and eventful struggles before the decision was finally accepted universally. Arianism had been condemned, but its spirit was by no means broken. It found powerful support in court circles and many *Origenists* whose ideas on the subject were confused and vacillating claimed to find a trace of Sabellianism (§ 32, 6) in the word ὁμοού-σιος which the Council had stressed. The Arians united and succeeded in driving from their sees the bishops of the Nicene party. Eustathius of Antioch and Marcellus of Ancyra were deposed and banished. But the one who was made to feel the full impact of Arian wrath was *Athanasius*, the most courageous champion of orthodoxy. In 328 he became bishop of Alexandria and devoted his life and heroic efforts to the conquest of heresy. With the aid of Emperor *Constantius* (337—361) Arianism gained the upper hand

---

[1] S. Athanasii Opera, see § 47. Especially important are: Apologia c. Arianos (335/58); Ep. de decretis Nicaenae synodi (c. 350); Ep. ad Serapionem de morte Arii (c. 356); Apologia ad Constantium (357); Apologia de fuga sua (357); Historia Arianorum ad monachos (358); Ep. de synodis Arimini et Seleuciae celebratis (359). Lit. § 46, 47 and 75. Also: J. GUMMERUS, Die homöusian. Partei (356—61), 1900. A. LICHTENSTEIN, Eusebius v. Nikomedien, 1903. M. ALBERTZ, ThStKr 1909, 205/78 (early Arians). L. FEDER, Studien zu Hilarius, Sb. Wien 162, 166, 169 (1910/2). P. STIEGELE Der Agennesiebegriff in der griech. Theol. des 4. Jh., 1913. P. ZÖPFL, ThQ 1923, 170/201 (Eustathius). B. NIEDERBERGER, Die Logoslehre des hl. Cyrill v. Jerusalem, 1923. H. I. BELL, etc. see § 35, 3 (Athanasius and the Melitians 334/5). G. BARDY, RevSR 1928, 516/51 (Constantine's religious policy after Nicaea); RHE 1928, 809/27 (Aëtius); RechSR 1933, 430/50 (no second C. of Nicaea in 327). P. PEETERS, AB 1945, 131/44 (Tyrus 335). J. CHAPMAN, Studies on the Early Papacy, London 1928, 51/61 (Athanasius and Pope Julius I). J. ZEILLER, RechSR 1928, 73/86 (spread of Arianism in the R. Empire). A. GAUDEL, RevSR 1929, 524 ff.; 1931, 1 ff. (Athan's theology of the Logos). R. SEILER, Athanasius' Apologia c. Arianos, ihre Entstehung u. Datierung, Diss. 1932. K. FR. HAGEL, Kirche u. Kaisertum in Lehre u. Leben des Ath., Diss. 1933. ED. SCHWARTZ ZntW 1935, 129/213 (the confusion 325/81). S. GONZÁLES, La formula μία οὐσία τρεῖς ὑποστάσεις en S. Gregorio de Nisa, Rome 1939. W. TELFER HarvThR 1950 31/92 (Paul of Constantinople at Sardica 342).

in the East and long threatened to become the State religion. A series of new creeds, especially the four *Antiochian* formulas of 341 and the *Sirmian* formulas of 351 to 359, all of which rejected or weakened the idea of ὁμοούσιος, added to the confusion. The entire Church suffered greatly. Two attempts were made on the part of the civil rulers to restore the unity of the Church: at *Sardica* in 343 and at *Rimini-Seleucia* in 359—360, but by that time the Arians were irreconcilable. By 360, thanks to imperial favor, the heresy seemed completely triumphant; but in the period (361—381) after the death of Constantius there were signs that the storm was abating even though *Valens*, (364—378), emperor of the East, was a fanatical Arian. Split into various sects (Eunomians, Homoeans, Semiarians), deprived of official support by the death of Valens (378) and interiorly vanquished by the superior theology of a *younger generation of Nicene* champions, especially *Basil* of Caesarea, *Gregory* of Nazianzus and *Gregory* of Nyssa, Arianism was finally defeated after a struggle which had lasted more than half a century. Emperor *Theodosius the Great* (379—395) now became the powerful protector of Catholic orthodoxy, the victory of which was sealed by the Council of *Constantinople* in 381.

2. The zeal of Constantine the Great for the Nicene Creed did not last long. He soon came under the influence of his step-sister Constantia, the widow of Licinius, who was a confirmed Arian and all-powerful at court. The account of a second synod at *Nicaea* in 327 at which *Arius, Eusebius* of Nicomedia and Theognis were rehabilitated is not deserving of credence. However, in 328 the emperor permitted the three exiles to return and reinstated the two bishops in their dioceses. Encouraged by this success, the Arians proclaimed war on the champions of Nicaea. In 330 Bishop *Eustathius* of Antioch was deposed by a synod on grounds of tyranny, Sabellianism and disrespect toward Helena, the Emperor's mother. His banishment occasioned a lengthy schism in Antioch (§ 50, 1). **Athanasius**, the successor of Alexander in the see of Alexandria (328) was long persecuted by the *Eusebians* and the Melitians. He was even accused of having murdered the Melitian Bishop Arsenius, and although the charge was clearly proved false, he was deposed by a synod held at *Tyre* in 355 under the presidency of an imperial officer. The emperor would never have believed the story of murder, but he did believe a new accusation brought against Athanasius that he had threatened to stop the shipment of Egyptian grain to Constantinople; and toward the end of 335 banished the maligned bishop to Trier. Athanasius' friend, *Marcellus* of Ancyra, whose writings on the Trinity if not unorthodox are at least lacking in clarity and accuracy of expression, was deposed by a synod at Constantinople in 335. But the emperor's plan to have Arius solemnly reinstated in the Church

of Constantinople was frustrated by the sudden death of the heresiarch (336).

The death of Constantine the Great on May 22, 337 brought Athanasius' exile to an end. Constantine II (337—340), ruler of Gaul, Spain and Britain, acting, it is said, out of deference to his father's wishes, permitted him to return to Alexandria (337). But the Eusebians would not allow the courageous advocate of the Nicene faith to possess his see in peace. They found a compliant friend in *Constantius*, emperor of the East, and soon their ambitious and crafty leader, *Eusebius* of Nicomedia, was elevated to the see of Constantinople (338). Athanasius was again deposed and in a synod at Antioch (339) a notorious Arian, Gregory the Cappadocian, was appointed in his place. Like Marcellus of Ancyra, Athanasius went to Rome and appealed to Pope *Julius I* (337—352). A Roman synod in 341 declared his deposition unwarranted. But on the occasion of the dedication of the so-called Golden Church at *Antioch* in 341, the Eusebians held a synod (in encaeniis) in which they drew up three formulas. They purposely avoided the use of the word ὁμοούσιος but stressed the eternity of Christ's kingdom against Marcellus and pronounced excommunication on anyone who refused to accept their decision. Eusebius died soon thereafter and with his death his followers seem to have undergone a slight change of heart. In a fourth formula which was sent to the court at Trier, they condemned the very proposition of Arius which had been condemned by Nicaea. But they still refused to use the word ὁμοούσιος.

3. The lack of unity was deeply regretted especially in the West. Hence, *Constans* (337—350) the emperor of the West, who was favorably disposed toward the Nicene Creed, suggested to his brother Constantius that another *general council* be held. It met in the fall of 343 (342?) at **Sardica** in Moesia (the present city of Sofia in Bulgaria) a city on the border between the two empires. But even this did not effect the desired peace. When the supporters of Nicaea about 90 in number and mostly Westerners, admitted Athanasius and Marcellus to the Council, the 80 Eusebians withdrew and held their own council (in Sardica and not as Socrates H.E. II, 20 says, at Philippopolis [Plovdiv]). They not only excommunicated Athanasius and Marcellus, but also anathematized Pope Julius, Bishop Hosius and all other bishops who "favored heresy." They then drew up a formula similar to the fourth Antiochian formula and adjourned. The orthodox under the presidency of Hosius, pronounced excommunication on the leaders of the Eusebians and reaffirmed the Nicene Creed. The twenty canons decreed at Sardica are important, especially canons 3 to 5 which ordain that *Rome* is the court of *highest appeal* for the entire Church. In spite of the unfavorable outcome of the synod, which marks the beginning of the cleavage between East and West, Constans was able to stop the persecution of the Nicenes in the East. Athanasius returned to his see in 346.

The peace lasted for a few years. But when *Constantius* became sole ruler (350—361) the quarrel broke out anew. In a synod held at *Sirmium* in Pannonia (the present city of Mitrovitz) where the emperor then resided, Bishop *Photinus*, a disciple of Marcellus, was deposed (351) for teaching a doctrine similar to the dynamic Monarchians. The creed which was adopted at this synod, the *first Sirmium formula*, was a redaction of the fourth Antiochian formula. At the same time the attack on *Athanasius* was renewed. Intimidated by the emperor who was present, almost all of the bishops at the synod of *Arles* in 353 and of *Milan* in 355 agreed to Athanasius' deposition. Those who refused to concur in the unjust sentence were banished as Paulinus of Trier in 353, Eusebius of Vercelli in 355, *Lucifer* of Cagliari (§ 50, 3), Pope *Liberius* (on the Roman Schism 355—358 see § 50, 2), the centenarian *Hosius* of Corduba and *Hilary* of Poitiers (in 356). Athanasius was obliged to flee to the monks of the Egyptian desert to save his life (356) and this time his see was given to another Cappadocian named George.

4. The Anti-Nicene party was now the victor. They owed their success partly to imperial support, but chiefly to their own tactics in concentrating their attack on the ὁμοούσιος as a form of Sabellianism, in which they presented a united front. But they soon began to split into *several parties*. The question on which they divided was whether the Son was *unlike* the Father (ἀνόμοιος) or *similar* to the Father (ὅμοιος). The *Anomoeans* were led by the Deacon *Aëtius* of Antioch and *Acacius* of Caesarea in Palestine, the successor of Eusebius the historian. The *Homoeans*, descendants of the old Eusebians, were further divided: some of them wished to restrict the similarity between the Father and Son to the will and operation, while others insisted that the Son was similar to the Father in essence or in all things (ὁμοιούσιος, ὅμοιος κατὰ πάντα). These later were called *Homoiousians* or, less correctly, *Semiarians* ('Ημιάρειοι in Epiphanius). These parties persisted in their principles for a long time and were really nothing more than the old radical and more moderate parties opposed to Nicaea appearing under new forms and new names. But when they began to quarrel among themselves they sealed their own fate.

Led by the ambitious court bishops, *Valens* of Mursa in Pannonia and *Ursacius* of Singidunum (Belgrade) in Moesia, both of whom had long been fanatical opponents of Nicaea, the various groups of stricter Arians drew up a new formula at a synod held at *Sirmium* in 357 — the *second Sirmium formula*. It rejected both expressions ὁμοούσιος and ὁμοιούσιος as un-Scriptural and simply subordinated the Son to the Father. The more moderate groups, with the bishops *Basil* of Ancyra and *George* of Laodicea at their head, objected to this Arianizing formula at the synod of *Ancyra* in 358 and declared that Father and Son are essentially similar. The emperor approved their decision, so that now the Homoiousians were triumphant. In a synod at Sirmium later in the same year 358, they drew up still another formula which 70 Anomoeans refused to approve and were banished. This *third Sirmium formula* is a compilation of previous synodal decrees among which is the decree of the Antiochian synod of 268 against Paul of Samosata (§ 32, 3). It also rejected ὁμοούσιος, but is otherwise anti-Arian.

Sozomen (H.E. IV, 15) relates, and in the main facts is corroborated by other deponents, that Pope *Liberius*, broken by his long banishment to Beroea in Thrace, signed the *third Sirmium formula* and was permitted to return to Rome (358). However, Liberius saved his orthodoxy by appending the remark that anyone who denies that there is *similarity of essence* between the Father and Son and in *all things* excludes himself from the Catholic faith. This formula comes very close to Nicaea. Hence there is no question of heresy nor can this instance be used as an argument against papal infallibility. By agreeing to exclude Athanasius from the communion of the Church and by subscribing to a formula, however orthodox, which abandoned the word for which the Nicenes had fought and sacrificed, Liberius showed great weakness. The four compromising letters of Liberius (best text in the Vienna edition of Hilary, Vol. IV, ed. A. L. Feder, 1916) are certainly genuine. According to the second one (Pro deifico timore) the pope in exile also accepted the *first* Sirmium formula. Cfr. *L. Duchesne*, MélAH 1908, 31/78. — *L. Saltet*, BullLE 1907, 279 ff.; 1909, 128 ff. — *A. L. Feder*, Sb. Wien 162, 1910, 153 ff. 325 ff. — *J. Zeiller*, BullLA 1913, 20/51. — P. Glorieux, MSR 1944, 7/34 (Hilary and Liberius). — A. d'Alès, DictApol II, 1842/51. — *E. Amann*, DictThC IX, 631/59. — *H. Leclercq*, DictAC IX, 497/530.

5. In the meantime, the strict Arians had not given up the cause as lost. When Constantius arranged for another *council* to restore the peace of the Church in 359, they suggested to him that he divide the episcopacy into two groups and have the Westerners meet at *Rimini* (Ariminum) and the Easterners at *Seleucia* in Thrace. This was to prevent a union of the orthodox Westerners with the Homoiousians of the East, which seemed quite possible. As a further precaution, Valens, Arsacius and their adherents met with the Homoiousians at Sirmium and drew up a *fourth Sirmium formula* (359) in which the term οὐσία was rejected as unscriptural and confusing and simply said that according to the Scriptures the Son is *similar* to the Father and *in all things* (ὅμοιος τῷ πατρὶ κατὰ τὰς γραφάς ... κατὰ πάντα). The emperor approved this compromise formula and relied on his authority to force it on **Rimini**. In July 359, the Western synod composed of about 400 bishops — Pope Liberius did not take part — reaffirmed the Nicene Creed by a large majority and pronounced excommunication on the Arian leaders. But Constantius was not to be frustrated. At *Nice* in Thrace a new formula was adopted which deleted κατὰ πάντα and merely said that "according to the Scriptures there is a similarity between Father and Son." This formula was then proposed to the Fathers at Rimini who were unwilling to accept it. However, threats and force were used to such an extent that all present eventually signed it. Some subscribed with their names only; others to satisfy their consciences added a note in which they anathematized Arius and declared that the Son is like the Father, without beginning and is not a creature.

A similar farce was being enacted in the East. The synod at **Seleucia** in the fall of 359 accomplished nothing because the members could not agree. However, the emperor forced the delegates to sign the formula of Nice so that now there was a Creed of Nice instead of the Creed of

Nicaea (symbolum *Nicenum* instead of symbolum *Nicaenum*). This formula was approved by a synod at *Constantinople* in January 360 and sent to all the bishops of the Empire for signature under penalty of banishment. Only a few bishops refused to sign, among them Pope *Liberius*. *Hilary* of Poitiers (§ 76, 1) whom the Emperor had sent home from exile in Asia Minor, worked fearlessly and successfully for orthodoxy in Gaul and Italy. But the greatest confusion reigned in the Church throughout the Empire. Jerome (Dial. adv. Luciferianos) trenchantly characterized the situation: Ingemuit totus orbis et Arianum se esse miratus est. For the time being the *Homoeans* were victorious. For the Synod of Constantinople had been controlled by *Acacius* and his followers, who had separated from the Anomoeans at Seleucia, and excommunicated the Homoiousians as well as Aëtius. Actually, however, it was *Arianism* that had triumphed. It now began, in the form of Homoiousionism, to win the Germanic tribes, and first of all the Visigoths (§ 43, 2— Ulfila had taken part in the synod of Constantinople).

6. But Arianism's triumph was a brief one. When Constantius died in November 361, the Nicene Creed prevailed throughout the West. Emperor Julian (361—363) the Apostate and foe of Christianity, to increase the confusion in the Church permitted all deposed bishops, even Athanasius, to return to their sees. In 362 *Athanasius* held a synod at *Alexandria* in which the Nicene Creed was reaffirmed, the errors of Arius, of the Pneumatomachi (§ 49) and of Apollinaris were condemned and, much to the dislike of *Lucifer* of Cagliari and other old champions of Nicaea (§ 50,3), the way was made easy for the Homoiousians to return to the communion of the Church. At the same time many misunderstandings which had arisen from the inexact use of words were cleared up (even at Nicaea [§ 47, 4] ὑπόστασις had been used as synonomous with οὐσία = substantia; from now on it was used to mean person). Arianism had begun to decline. While *Valentinian* I (364—375), emperor of the West, prudently refrained from interfering in ecclesiastical affairs, his brother *Valens* (364—378) openly supported the strict Arians in the East and both orthodox Christians and Semiarians were subjected to cruel persecution. The Semiarians held a synod at Lampsacus on the Hellespont in 364 at which they repudiated the synod of Constantinople (360). Valens again banished all the bishops whom Julian had permitted to return and Athanasius, then seventy years old, was obliged to leave his see for the fifth time, but returned after four months. The action of Valens induced many of the Semiarians to accept ὁμοούσιος and seek union with Pope Liberius (366). When the persecution was over some of them relapsed into their old errors. Pope *Damasus*[1] (366-384), Liberius' successor, endeavored by a policy of friendliness and leniency to win the Semiarians of the East and to reunite the Church in the two parts of the Empire (§ 50, 1). *Gratian* (375—383), emperor of the West,

---

[1] J. WITTIG, Die Friedenspolitik des P. Damasus und der Ausgang der arian. Streitigkeiten 1912. J. SCHÄFER, Basilius d. Gr. Beziehungen zum Abendland, 1909. G. RAUSCHEN, H. V. CAMPENHAUSEN and J. R. PALANQUE, see § 41, 4. 5. E. CASPAR, Gesch. des Papsttums I, 1930, 196 ff.

was a Catholic, and after 374, *Ambrose*, the saintly and capable bishop of Milan, devoted his life to the cause of orthodoxy. After the death of Valens (378) the Nicene Creed became more widely and firmly established in the East. The three great Cappadocians: *Basil* the Great of Caesarea, *Gregory* of Nazianzus (Bishop of Constantinople 380—381) and *Gregory* of Nyssa were worthy successors of Athanasius († 373) in its defense and were at the same time the leaders of a younger generation of *adherents of Nicaea*. In writing of the Trinity, they constantly used the expression "one nature, three Persons" (μία οὐσία τρεῖς ὑποστάσεις) and this succeeded in clarifying the concept. Valens' successor, *Theodosius* the Great (379—395), became the powerful protector and promoter of Nicene orthodoxy (§ 41, 5) and thus established the *Catholic Church as the Church of the Empire*. Shortly after ascending the throne he issued an edict to all inhabitants of the Empire urging them to accept the faith "professed by Damasus of Rome and Peter of Alexandria," and ordered that all the churches of Constantinople be given over to the Catholics. In order to strengthen the faith, he called a great council of the East which met at **Constantinople** in 381 and which later was known as the *second General Council*. It reaffirmed the Nicene Creed and condemned Arianism and all related heresies (§ 49, 2; 53). After interdicting the Arians of Constantinople, Theodosius forbade them to hold services in the other cities of the Empire. But this by no means proved the death blow to the heresy. It persisted for a long time as the national religion of the Germanic tribes (§ 43). **Justina** († 388), widow of Valentinian I and regent for her son Valentinian II, endeavored to reestablish it in the West and would, perhaps, have succeeded had it not been for the resolute opposition of *Ambrose* of Milan. But once the power of Arianism had been broken in the Roman Empire, it gradually expired, especially after the Franks, the most influential of the Germanic tribes, had accepted Catholic Christianity (§ 43, 7. 8).

§ 49.

## The Pneumatomachian Controversy and the Council of Constantinople 381. The Filioque[1].

1. The Church's teaching regarding the Holy Ghost had been no more clearly or exactly expressed during the first centuries than

---

[1] HEFELE II², 1/33; HEFELE-LECLERCQ III, 1/48. C. H. TURNER, JThSt 1914, 161/74; E. HONIGMANN u. ED. SCHWARTZ, see § 47 (list of bishops at the Synod of 381). H. B. SWETE, The Holy Spirit in the Ancient Church, London 1912. TH. SCHERMANN, Die Gottheit des Hl. Geistes nach den griech. Vätern des 4. Jh., 1901. G. GALTIER, Le Saint Esprit en nous d'après les Pères grecques, Rome 1946. J. GUMMERUS, see § 48. F. LOOFS, Macedonius RE XII, 41/8; Sb. Berlin 1914, 526/51; Geschichtl. Studien A. Hauck dargebr. 1916, 64/76. G. BARDY, Macédonius et Macédoniens, DictThC IX, 1464/78. A. PALMIERI, Filioque, DictThC V, 2309/43. J. A. DE ALDAMA S.J. El simbolo Toledano I, Rome 1934 (also B. ALTANER, ThRev 1935, 337/41). M. JUGIE, De Processione Spiritus Sancti ex fontibus revelationis et sec.

had been the doctrine of the Logos. The repeated condemnation of Sabellianism (§ 32, 6) had indicated the belief of the Church that there are three distinct Persons in the Holy Trinity; but there was, especially among the Origenists, a tendency to subordinate the second and third Persons. For the Arians, who held that the Son was a creature of the Father and the creator of all things else, it was but logical to see the Holy Ghost as a creature of the Son. At first, theological interest was so wholly concentrated on the question of the Logos, that it was not until the middle of the fourth century that attention began to be given to erroneous teachings regarding the Holy Ghost. But when not only the strict *Arians*, but also the *Semiarians* began to teach that the Holy Ghost was but a ministering spirit (Hebr. 1:14) differing from the angels only in rank, *St. Athanasius* wrote four letters to Bishop Serapion of Thmuis in 359 in which he maintained that the Holy Ghost is a divine Person. A synod at *Alexandria* in 362 under the presidency of Athanasius, declared that the third Person of the Trinity is of the same substance and divinity as the other two. The chief representative of the heretical view was the Semiarian bishop of Constantinople *Macedonius*, who was deposed in 360. After 380 the Pneumatomachi were generally called *Macedonians*.

2. Soon other synods at Alexandria (363), Rome (369, 373, 380) and in Asia Minor also condemned the heresy. The three Cappadocians were particularly clear in explaining the consubstantiality of the Holy Ghost. It was, however, the General Council of **Constantinople** in 381 which pronounced the official and authoritative condemnation of the Pneumatomachian heresy. After 36 Macedonians had withdrawn from the Council, the remaining 150 orthodox bishops anathematized "the Semiarians or Pneumatomachi." As the synodal profession of faith, they adopted with slight modification, the baptismal symbol which Epiphanius, Bishop of Constantia (Salamis) on the island of Cyprus (§ 75, 4) had recommended in his work Ancoratus (chap. 118), written about 374. The first and second articles which treat of the Father and Son are almost the same as the Nicene Creed, while the third article "And (we believe) in the Holy Ghost", contains the doctrines which the Council stressed: "the *Lord* and *Giver of Life*, who proceedeth from the Father (John 15:26), who together with the Father and the Son

Orientales dissidentes, Rome 1936 (Lateranum N. S. II, 3/4); RevSPhTh 1939, 369/85 (rise of the controversy over Filioque).

is to be adored and glorified, who spoke by the Prophets." When the synod of Constantinople was recognized as a *General* Council — in the East at the synod of Chalcedon in 451, and in the West in the beginning of the sixth century — the *Niceno-Constantinopolitan Creed* was given the rank of an ecumenical Symbol. Later on, it was the only creed permitted in the Greek Church for the rite of baptism and the Eucharistic liturgy.

The Symbol of Epiphanius is not, as some (Franzelin, Jungmann and E. Schwartz) have thought, an interpolation inserted in the Ancoratus after 381. In all probability it originated at *Jerusalem* and was the one used by Bishop *Cyril* (§ 75, 4) in his catechetical instructions shortly after 362. It was, therefore, the old baptismal symbol of Jerusalem revised to accord with Nicaea and amended to include the beliefs which the Macedonians denied. There is also a widespread theory that the Niceno-Constantinopolitan Creed was not adopted at the Council of 381, but was later mistakenly ascribed to it (thus *J. F. A. Hort*, Two Dissertations, Cambridge 1876; *A. Harnack*, RE XI, 12/28; *G. Rauschen*, Jahrbücher [§ 41, 5] 477 ff.; *J. Kunze*, Das nicän-konstan. Symbol, 1898, and others). But this theory lacks historical basis. The silence of the old Church historians, especially in view of their very brief accounts of the synod, can not be pressed as an argument. In the synodal letter of 382 in Theodoret (V, 9. 13) and also in Gregory Nazianzus (De vita sua 1754 f.; Ep. 102 ad Cledon.) there is at least an allusion to the adoption or the revision of a creed (Cfr. *F. X. Funk*, RE Kraus II, 810/3; ThQ 1900, 611; *W. Schmidt*, NkZ 1899, 935/85. In the acta of the General Council of Chalcedon in 451 (Sess. V) the Creeds of Nicaea (325) and Constantinople (381) do not appear in their authentic form; but are partly abbreviated and partly amplified. Cfr. *E. Schwartz*, ZntW 1926, 38/88, also J. Lebon RHE 1936, 537/47; 809/76; A. d'Alès, RechSR 1936, 579/84; *J. Ortiz de Urbina*, OrChrPer 1936, 330/50.

3. By declaring that the Holy Ghost proceeds from the Father, the Arian theory was rejected; but this did not entirely settle the relation of the Hagia Pneuma to the Trinity. There remained the question of His relation to the *Son*. The difference of solution given in the East and West was rather in the form than in the sense. As early as the fourth century, the Greek Church taught a procession from the Father *through the Son* (ἐκ τοῦ πατρὸς διὰ τοῦ υἱοῦ); while the Latin Church held that the procession was from the Father *and the Son*. The word **Filioque** (Spiritus sanctus ... a Patre Filioque procedens) was used in the creed composed by Bishop *Pastor* of Palencia in Spain in 447 and the synod of Toledo (§ 50, 8) in 589 officially ordered that throughout Spain the word be inserted in the Niceno-Constantinopolitan Creed.

It is not likely that the Filioque originated at Rome before the year 400 and was introduced into Spain from there (*W. M. Peitz*, Das vorephesin.

Symbol der Papstkanzlei, Rome 1939, 46 ff. maintains that it was). The Filioque was also used in the *Symbolum Quicumque* (vult salvus esse etc.), which is a statement of the Church's Trinitarian and Christological doctrine in 40 rhythmic verses. Since the seventh century the Quicumque has been generally ascribed to St. Athanasius and therefore called the *Symbolum Athanasianum*; but it is certainly later and was originally composed in Latin. The actual time of its composition as well as its authorship is still disputed. Some maintain that it was directed against the Priscillians (§ 50, 8) and suggest that it may have been written by *St. Ambrose* toward the end of the fourth century (Brewer, Burn, Schepens) or by a theologian of southern Gaul, probably of Lérins, or Spain in the first half of the fifth century (Künstle and others). *Caesar* of Arles or one of his disciples (Morin) and *Fulgentius* of Ruspe (Stiglmayer) in the sixth century are also mentioned as possible authors of the Symbolum. — Critical text by *C. H. Turner*, JShSt 1910, 401/11. — *F. Loofs*, RE II 177/94; XXIII, 125 f. — *H. Brewer*, Das sog. Athan. Glaubensbek. ein Werk des hl. Ambrosius, 1909. — *A. E. Burn*, JThSt 1911, 161 ff. 337 ff.; RevBén 1932, 207/19. — *J. Stiglmayr*, ZkTh 1925, 341/57. — *P. Schepens*, RHE 1936, 548/69. — *J. Madoz*, Exerpta Vincentii Lir., Madrid 1940, 65/90 (terminological parallels).

## § 50.
## Other Controversies and Heresies of the Fourth Century.

1. **The Schism of Antioch.** When Bishop *Eustathius* of Antioch was deposed in 330 (§ 48, 2) a small part of the congregation remained loyal to him, while the majority recognized the new Arian bishop. In 360 *Eudoxius*, the Arian incumbent, was transferred to Constantinople and was replaced by *Meletius* of Sebaste in Armenia (361). Whereupon, a second orthodoxy party was formed distinct from the Eustathians. For while Meletius was orthodox, he had been elected by the Arians; hence the Eustathians refused to acknowledge him and he was forced to leave the see within a month. Succeeding bishops of the Eustathian party were *Paulinus* (362—388), consecrated by Lucifer of Cagliari (see no. 3 below) and *Evagrius* (388—393). Both of these were recognized in the West (Paulinus was also recognized in Alexandria) while in the East Meletius and his successors were looked upon as the legitimate bishops. Pope *Damasus* also, who relied on St. Basil for his information inclined to favor the Meletians and in the synod of Antioch in 379 general agreement was reached. At least the strength of the schism was broken and the Eustathians elected no successor to Evagrius. The majority of them were reconciled about 415 and the remainder about 482. — *F. Cavallera*, Le schisme d'Antioche, Paris 1905. — *J. Wittig* and *J. Schäfer*, see § 48, 6. — *C. B. Armstrong*, JThSt 1921, 206 ff. 347 ff. *F. Zoepfl*, ThQ 1923, 170/201 (teaching of Eustathius). — *R. V. Sellers*, Eustathius of Antioch, Cambridge 1928. — *M. Spanneut*, Recherches sur les écrits d'Eustathe, Lille 1948. — *G. Bardy*, RevBén 1933, 196/213 (Synod of Antioch 379). — *Ed. Schwartz*, ZntW 1935, 163 ff. — H. Chadwick, JThSt 1948, 27/35 ( (deposal of Eustathius in 326). — P. Galtier, RechSR 1936, 385 ff. 563 ff. (the Tomus Damasi and the Roman Synod of 382).

2. **The Roman Schism.** When Constantius banished Pope **Liberius** in 355, the tyrannical emperor caused the deacon *Felix* to be consecrated bishop of Rome (*Felix II*). The majority of the clergy, under the influence of the Arian court, supported Felix. But when Liberius returned in 358 (§ 48, 4), the people, who had always been loyal to him, rose against Felix († 365) and forced him to retire. Later legend (Liber Pontificalis, see § 78, 3) distorted these facts — made Liberius a heretic bent on persecution and Felix the orthodox and legitimate bishop. In fact, by confusing Felix with the Felix who had been martyred on the road to Porto, the antipope Felix began to be honored as a martyr. — *G. Krüger*, RE XI, 450/6; XXIV 16; *J. Döllinger*, Papstfabeln, ²1890, 126/45; *Funk*, AU I, 391/420; *L. Saltet*, BullLe 1905, 222/36; *J. P. Kirsch*, RQ 33, 1925, 1/20; *E. Caspar*, Gesch. des Papsttums I, 1930, 166 ff. — Upon the death of Liberius (366) the schism was revived. The majority of the Roman clergy elected the deacon **Damasus** (366—384) while an intransigent minority chose the deacon *Ursinus*. The contested election resulted in riots and bloodshed and although Ursinus was repudiated and exiled to Gaul (367) by Valentinian I, almost the entire pontificate of Damasus was disturbed by the malcontents.

3. **The Luciferian Schism.** *Lucifer*, Bishop of Cagliari (Calaris) on the island of Sardinia († 371) was one of the most ardent advocates of the Nicene Creed. He was banished (355—361) by Constantius (§ 48, 3) but continued during that time to assail the emperor with his vigorous pen (PL 13; ed. W. Hartel, 1886). The lenient policy adopted by Athanasius in the Alexandrian synod of 362 toward the Semiarians (§ 48, 6) was imitated by other Catholic bishops. Lucifer showed his intense displeasure at this action by treating these bishops as if they themselves were heretics. His precipitate action in consecrating Paulinus during the Antiochian schism was not approved by the synod. The schism which he then began was confined chiefly to *Sardinia* and *Spain*, but did not last long. After Lucifer's death, it was headed by Bishop *Gregory* of Elvira (§ 76, 6). Cfr. *G. Krüger*, Lucifer v. C. u. das Schisma der Luciferianer, 1886. — *L. Saltet*, BullLE 1906, 300/26. — A. Merk, ThQ 1912, 1/32. — A. Wilmart, RevBén 1921, 124/35. — E. Amann, DictThC IX, 1032/45. — *G. Thoernell*, Studia Luciferiana, Uppsala 1934.

4. The teachings of Bishop **Marcellus of Ancyra** († ca. 374) gave rise to a number of disputes (§ 48, 2, 3). At Nicaea and afterward he was a zealous opponent of Arianism. But his own teaching on the Trinity shows the influence of pre-Origenist speculation on the Logos (§ 32, 1) and smacks strongly of *Sabellianism*. According to him, the Deity is simply a monad which in the economy of salvation, developed into a Trinity. In the creation of the world, the Logos evolved as the "efficient power" of God; in the Incarnation He became a person and the Son of God and when the Spirit was given to the Apostles (John 20:22) the Holy Ghost evolved from the Father and the Son. At the end of time both the Logos and the Holy Ghost will return into the Father. The synod held at Antioch in 341 on the occasion of the dedication of the Golden Church (§ 48, 2), declared that Christ's kingdom is eternal and about 350 A. D. the words of Luke 1:33: "And of his kingdom there shall be no end," were inserted in the Creed to counteract Marcellus' error.

Eusebius of Caesarea wrote against him (§ 75, 1). Fragments of Marcellus' polemic writings against the Arian Asterius are found in the Berlin edition of the works of Eusebius, vol. IV, published by E. Klostermann 1906, 183 ff. Cfr. also M. Richard, MSR 1949, 5/28; *Th. Zahn*, Marcellus, 1867; W. Gericke 1940 (Dissertation); *F. Loofs*, RE XII 259/65; Sb. Berlin 1902, 764/81; *Chenu*, DictThC IX, 1993/8; *G. Bardy*, RHE 1926, 221/72 (Asterius).

5. Bishop **Photinus of Sirmium**, a disciple of Marcellus, taught a form of dynamic Monarchianism (§ 32, 3). He held that Christ is merely a man, born in a marvelous manner and endowed with divine power, who, because of His miracles and virtues was adopted by God. After being condemned several times, Photinus was deposed and banished by the Synod of Sirmium in 351 (§ 48, 3). The heresy persisted after his death († 376). It was still being taught by the **Bonosians** in the seventh century, although the founder of this sect, Bishop *Bonosus* of Sardica (end of fourth and beginning of fifth century) probably only denied the virginity of the Blessed Virgin (§ 70, 3). Cfr. *F. Cavallera*, BullLE 1920, 141/7.

6. **Audius** of Mesopotamia was excommunicated because of his strictures on the failings of the clergy. About 325 he founded his own monastic communities, whose members were Protopaschites (§ 25, 2; 69, 6), and held anthropomorphic notions of God. When Audius was banished to Scythia, he endeavored to spread his ideas among the Goths. The sect he founded, known as **Audians**, ceased to exist in the fourth century or was partly absorbed by the Gnostics. — Epiph. Haer. 70; E. L. Iselin, Jb. f. prot. Theol. 1890, 298/305; K. D. Schmidt, Die Bekehrung der Germanen z. Christ. I, 1939, 228/30; H.-Ch. Puech, RLAntChr I, 910/15.

7. The **Messalians**, also known as *Euchites* and *Adelphians*, from their leader *Adelphius*, were a fanatical sect with a sort of monastic organization and Manicheistic tendencies, who appeared about 350 in Mesopotamia and Syria whence they spread to Asia Minor. They urged constant prayer as the only means of overcoming the demon which every individual has from birth and which is not expelled even by baptism. Sacraments were held to be useless since the "Pneumatici" are already sinless and see God. They had no possessions, refused to work, lived from begging and practised a crude form of Quietism. They were condemned at the synods of Side and Antioch about 390 and again by the General Council of Ephesus in 431. Although many efforts were made by the civil authorities to suppress them, they continued to exist, and appear to be the direct ancestors of the medieval Paulicians and Bogomili (§ 91, 3). The "Spiritual Homilies", long circulated under the name of *Macarius* the Great, are now thought, with good reason, to be the work of a talented member of the sect named Symeon of Mesopotamia. — Epiph. Haer. 80. Zeugnisse über die Messalianer, zusammengestellt v. *M. Kmosko* in Patrologia Syriaca I, 3, Paris 1926. — *G. L. Mariott*, HarvThR 1926, 191/8. — E. Peterson, ZntW 1932, 273/88 (Marcus Eremita vs. the Messal.); Oriens Christ. 1932, 172/9 (Acts of Philip). — *M. Wellnhofer*, Byz. Z. 1930, 477/84. — *I. Hausher*, OrChrPer 1935, 328/60. — *K. Rahner*, ZkTh 1937, 258/71 (a Messalian Fragment on baptism). — M. Rothenhäusler, see under Diadochus (§ 72, 6). — *H. Dörries*, Symeon v. Mesopotamien 1941 (TU 55, 1). — *A. M. Burg*,

Messal. Schriften u. Leben um 400, Diss. 1943. — *E. Klostermann*, Sym. u. Makarius, Abh. Berlin 1943, 11; ThLZ 1948, 687/90. — *A. Kemmer*, see under John Cassian (§ 72, 6).

8. **Priscillianism** created a great disturbance in the West. **Priscillian**, the founder of the sect, a wealthy and gifted layman of ascetical life, appeared in southern Spain about 375. He gathered his admirers into conventicles devoted to Montanistic practices and the reading of apocryphal writings. Priscillian is said to have learned Gnostic dualism from a certain Mark of Memphis; but his eleven tracts which have been rediscovered show him to have been a thoroughgoing Manichean. After he had been consecrated *bishop of Avila*, Priscillian began to work in earnest to spread his ideas in Spain and Aquitania and won over the bishops *Salvianus* and *Instantius* and many women. The synod of Sargossa in 380 excommunicated Priscillian and all his followers. In 385 Emperor *Maximus* the Usurper of Gaul, ordered Priscillian and six companions to be put to death for "criminal magic" (maleficium) (after torture?) at Trier — the *first instance* of the death penalty being inflicted for *heresy*. A few bishops approved the sentence while *St. Martin* of Tours (§ 72, 6) futily endeavored to save the lives of the condemned. When news of the execution had spread, Pope Siricius, Ambrose of Milan and many other bishops denounced Maximus. However, in spite of the execution, the sect continued to increase. The whole of Galicia with all the bishops of the province went over to it. The invasion of Spain by the Germans favored the proselytizing efforts of the heretics. It was not until the sixth century after the synod of Braga in Galicia in 561, that the sect began to decline. A creed which appears in the acta of the council of Toledo of the year 400, but which was actually composed by Bishop Pastor of Palencia in 447 (§ 49, 3) and approved by a synod of Toledo in the same year (cfr. J. A. de Aldama), is directed against the Priscillianists. According to this creed, they taught Sabellianism and Docetism, used apocryphal writings, practised astrology, denied the creation of the world by God, denied that the God of the Old Testament is the same as the God of the New Testament, denied the resurrection of the body and rejected marriage and the use of flesh meat. — Priscilliani quae supersunt, ed. *G. Schepss*, 1889. — *K. Künstle*, Eine Bibliothek der Symbole, 1900; Antipriscilliana, 1905. — *E. Ch. Babut*, Priscillien et le Priscillianisme, Paris 1909; Paulin de Nole et Priscillien, RHLR 1910, 97 ff. 252 ff. (vs. Babut: *A. Puech*, BullLA 1912, 81 ff. 161 ff.). — *G. Morin*, RevBén 1909, 255/80; 1913, 153/72 (Instantius the author of the eleven tracts); opposite opinion *M. Hartberger*, ThQ 1913, 401/30, and *J. Martin*, HJG 1927, 237/51. — *M. Hartberger*, Priscillianea, Diss. 1922. — *A. v. Harnack*, Sb. Berlin 1925, 180/213 (the apocryphal epistle of Titus De dispositione sanctimonii a Priscillian sermon). — *E. Suys*, RHE 1925, 530/38 (Execution of Priscillian). — *Z. Garcia Villada* (see § 12, 3) I, 1929, 91 ff. 357 ff. — *J. A. Davids*, De Orosio et S. Augustino Priscillianistarum adversariis commentatio, Diss. Haag 1930. — *A. d'Alès*, RechSR 1933, 1 ff. 129 ff. (Priscillian and his doctrine); id., Priscillien et l'Espagne chrétienne, Paris 1936. — *G. Bardy*, DictTHC XIII, 391/400. — *J. Madoz*, RHE 1939, 530/93 (Creed of the Synod of Toledo 675 vs. Prisc.); opposite opinion *J. de Pérez*, La cristologia en los Símbolos Toletanos IV, VI y XI (633, 638, 675), Rome 1939.

## § 51.

### Origenism[1] in the Fourth and Beginning of the Fifth Century.

1. During the Trinitarian controversy, the name of *Origen* frequently recurred. The Arians never failed to appeal to the renowned theologian and to quote his works in support of their doctrine. Generally speaking, the orthodox felt that the heretics had exploited the great writer to their own advantage. Some of the keenest minds, later the three great Cappadocians, continued to esteem Origen and to use the wealth of thought he offered without being blind to the temerity of his speculation (§ 39, 2). But not all churchmen were able to dicriminate. Some repudiated Origen as the father of Arianism as well as for his teachings regarding the pre-existence of soul and other errors and endeavored to prohibit the reading of his works. The leaders of this strict traditionalistic trend toward the end of the fourth and beginning of the fifth century were the bishops *Epiphanius* († 403) of Constancia (Salamis) (§ 75, 4) and *Theophilus* of Alexandria († 412).

2. **Epiphanius**, a saintly and learned, but narrow-minded and brusque individual, not only listed Origen among the heretics in his Panarion (Haer. 64) but spoke openly against all of Origen's adherents. In 392 (393 ?) he preached against Origen in the Church of the Resurrection at Jerusalem which precipitated a quarrel with Bishop *John* of Jerusalem. Two famous men who had theretofore been close friends were drawn into the quarrel: *Jerome* (at Bethlehem) on Epiphanius' side, and *Rufinus* (on Mt. Olivet near Jerusalem) on the side of John, who was an admirer of Origen. Jerome himself had at one time been a close adherent of Origen — even afterward in his exegetical works Jerome leaned heavily on him; but when Aterbius, a monk, in 392, accused him of being an Origenist, Jerome felt obliged to vindicate himself by openly expressing a dislike of Origen and his works. Shortly before Rufinus returned to the West (397) Bishop Theophilus of Alexandria succeeded in reconciling the former friends. But in the introduction to his translation of Origen's περὶ ἀρχῶν (398) Rufinus quoted Jerome's earlier eulogy on Origen and the quarrel was renewed with great bitterness on both sides. Even after Rufinus' death Jerome continued to speak caustically of him. — Cfr. § 76, 2 and 7 (*Grützmacher, Cavallera, Brochet, Trzcinski, Murphy*). — *K. Holl*, Sb. Berlin 1916, 226/55 (chronology); also *A. Jülicher*, ib. 256/75; both articles also in *K. Holl*, Ges. Aufsätze zur KG. II, 1928, 310/50. — *M. Villain*, RechSR 1937, 5 ff. 165 ff.

3. While this quarrel was going on, a more serious one arose in Egypt. It assumed grave importance when it occasioned the deposition of one of the most distinguished and learned bishops of the period. Bishop **Theophilus**

---

[1] See § 39,2 for bibliography.

of Alexandria (385—412), an ambitious and astute man, had offended the ignorant monks of the Desert of Scete, by condemning their anthropomorphism. They in turn demanded that he condemn Origen, and although he himself had been an ardent Origenist, he actually did condemn Origen in a synod held in 399 or 400. He then proceeded to persecute the learned monks of Nitria among whom were the *four "Tall Brothers,"* men as distinguished for piety and learning as for their size. Almost 300 of the Nitrian monks, driven from their monastery, went to Palestine, whence about 50 of them moved on to Constantinople. The great bishop of Constantinople, **John Chrysostom,** gave them shelter and protection. But a series of circumstances caused John's kindness to work his ruin. When Emperor Arcadius summoned Theophilus to answer the charges of the monks, Theophilus urged the aged Epiphanius to go to Constantinople and accuse John of heresy. Epiphanius the "Hammer of Heretics" soon saw he had been deceived, left Constantinople and died before reaching Salamis. Theophilus awaited a favorable moment to answer the Emperor's summons. When he heard that John's reform measures had made him unpopular in Constantinople, especially with Empress *Eudoxia,* he appeared in the city not as the accused to answer to the bishop of the capital, but as that bishop's accuser. The so-called *"Synod of the Oak"* (Ad quercum, held on an estate called Drys near Chalcedon) attended by 36 bishops, of whom 29 were Egyptians, under Theophilus' presidency, deposed Chrysostom, (403) and the emperor banished him to Bithynia. To still the popular outcry John was quickly recalled; but the very next year (404) his criticism of the empress' conduct caused him to be banished again, this time to Armenia. Since his loyal people were able to correspond with him, he was ordered to be transferred to Pityus in Colchis, but died on the way at Comana, September 14, 407. The people of Constantinople refused to recognize his first two successors, Arsacius and Atticus. It was only after his remains had been solemnly interred in the capital during the reign of Emperor Theodosius II and Bishop Proclus (438) that the *"Joannine Schism"* ended. — Cfr. *Funk,* AU II, 23/44. — *F. Ludwig,* Der hl. Joh. Chrysost. in s. Verhältnis zum byzant. Hofe, 1883. — *V. Schultze,* Altchristl. Städte I, 1913, 117 ff. — *Chr. Baur,* Der hl. Joh. Chrysost. II, 1930, 166 ff. — *G. Lazzati,* Teofilo d'Alessandria, Milano 1935; cfr. *H. G. Opitz,* RE Pauly-Wissowa 2. R. V. 2149/65. — *M. Richard,* RHE 1937, 46/57 (homily of Theophilus on the Eucharist); Muséon 1939, 33/50 (writings of Theophilus). — *Ed. Schwartz,* ZntW 1937, 169 ff. (the Origenist confusion).

## § 52.

### Donatism[1].

1. The Donatist rebellion which seriously disturbed West Africa for more than three centuries and led the emperor to intervene for

---

[1] Optatus Milevitanus, De schismate Donatistarum, ed. C. ZIWSA, 1893. S. Augustini scripta c. Donatistas, ed. M. PETSCHENIG, 3 vol. 1908/9; cfr. A. WILMART, RevBén 1912, 148/67. H. V. SODEN, Urkunden zur Entstehungsgesch. des Donatismus, 1913 (Kleine Texte 122). LECLERCQ, Mes-

the first time in ecclesiastical affairs, was, in a sense, a continuation of the quarrel over the baptism of heretics (§ 22, 3). Underlying the whole trouble was the old question whether the sacraments (Baptism, Orders) are of themselves efficient means of grace or whether they depend on the worthiness of the minister. The Africans had been influenced by Tertullian's and Cyprian's sub-jective-spiritual concept of the Church and the sacraments and held to that concept in opposition to Rome. The external occasion for the outbreak of the schism was a contested election after the death of *Mensurius,* Bishop of Carthage (311). The majority vote was for the Archdeacon *Caecilian.* But he met strong opposition from the congregation because during the Diocletian persecution, he and the deceased bishop had forbidden unauthorized honor to all those who had been put to death as well as undue veneration of confessors. Lucilla, a wealthy and pietistic widow, whom Caecilian publicly reprimanded, became a rallying point for all his opponents. Added to this was the rumor that Bishop *Felix* of Aptunga, who consecrated Caecilian, had surrendered the Scriptures during the persecution and hence was a traditor (§ 16, 4). The rigorists, there-fore, maintained that the consecration of Caecilian was invalid. The Numidian bishops, offended because they had not been consult-ed, and prejudiced by false reports, came to Carthage, seven in number, and held a synod in which Caecilian was deposed. They then consecrated (312) as bishop of Carthage the lector *Majorinus,* a favorite of Lucilla. When Majorinus died in 315, he was succeeded by *Donatus* (of Casae Nigrae?) surnamed *the Great,* from whom the movement took its name (pars Donati).

---

nage et al. § 12, 6. FUNK, AU I, 352/8 (Synod of Arles 314). O. SEECK, ZKG 1889, 505/68; 1909, 181/127; Gesch. des Untergangs der antiken Welt III, 1909, 313 ff. 501 ff. L. DUCHESNE, Le dossier du Donatisme, MélAH 1890, 589/650. W. THÜMMEL, Zur Beurteilung des Donatismus, 1893. F. MAR-TROYE, Circumcellions, DictAC III, 1692/170; H. LECLERCQ, Donatisme, ib. IV, 1457/505. P. MONCEAUX, Histoire litt. de l'Afrique chrét. IV—VII, Paris 1912/23. O. R. VASALL-PHILLIPS, The Work of St. Optatus against the Donatists, London 1917. P. BATIFFOL, Le catholicisme de St. Augustin, 2 vol. Paris 1920. H. SCHRÖRS, 3 Aktenstücke z. Konzil v. Arelate, ZRGkan 1921, 429/39; also K. MÜLLER, ZntW 1925, 28/90. J. H. BAXTER, JThSt 1924/5, 21/37 (Donatist martyrs); N. H. BAYNES, ib. 37 ff. 404 ff. (documents in Optatus); Constantine the Great and the Christian Church, London 1931, 11 ff. 75 ff. G. H. TURNER, JThSt 1926, 283/96 (Optatus). S. BLOMGREN, Eranos 1939, 85/120 (Optatus). E. CASPAR, ZKG 1927, 333/46 (Roman Synod of 313); Gesch. des Papsttums I, 1930, 108 ff. F. J. DÖLGER, AntChrist 1932, 245/52 (Lucilla). FR. HOFMANN, Der Kirchenbegriff des hl. Augustinus, 1933, 124 ff. J. P. BRISSON, RechSR 1946, 280/316 (social tension in Christian Africa).

2. The schism was not confined to its place of origin. The position of the Church of Carthage as primatial see lent the schism a significance it would not otherwise have had and the fanaticism of the Donatists made all of them apostles, so that soon the greater part of North Africa was drawn into the quarrel. *Constantine* the Great, who had begun to take an active interest in the Christian Church (§ 16, 5) was annoyed by dissension in the Church on which be based his hopes for unity in the Empire. The Donatists placed before him their complaints about Caecilian and in 313 he requested Pope *Miltiades* and three bishops of Gaul to arbitrate. The pope further invited fifteen Italian bishops for consultation and together they declared Caecilian to be the rightful bishop. When the Donatists refused to accept this decision, Constantine summoned a *general synod* of the Church to meet at *Arles* in August 314. The decision which had been reached in Rome was confirmed and canon 13 of Arles declared consecration by a traditor to be valid. In canon 8 of the same synod the African practice of repeating baptism after it had been conferred by a heretic was condemned (§ 66, 4). The Donatists were still not satisfied and appealed directly to the emperor. In 315 he appointed the proconsul of Africa, Aelianus to make an official investigation, which proved that Felix of Aptunga was not a traditor. (The acts of the synod of Cistra in 305, on the other hand, clearly prove that there were actually several traditores among the Donatists). Constantine made a lengthy and personal investigation of the whole affair at *Milan* and in 316 again decided against the Donatists. But they submitted to this decision no more than to the ones previously given. The emperor then resorted to stronger measures; the leaders of the sect were banished and the churches were restored to the Catholics. However, this procedure served only to increase the fanaticism of the sectaries. Although they themselves had appealed to the emperor, they now questioned the right of civil authority to interfere in ecclesiastical affairs (Quid est imperatori cum ecclesia?). And basing themselves on the Novation concept, they declared their church alone to be the pure congregation of the saints, the "immaculate church of martyrs" in contrast to the Catholic Church "the defiled church of traditores." They alone could administer the sacraments validly; so they rebaptized all who joined them.

3. Some time later (321) Constantine revived the laws against schismatics, but to no avail. The Donatists continued to increase in

number and to organize. About 336 they held a synod at Carthage attended by 270 bishops. Social conditions of the country which had long imposed hardship on the lower classes favored the spread of the sect. Fanatical ascetics (agonistici or milites Christi) popularly known as *Circumcellions* because they roamed about living in abandoned huts, terrorized the Catholic population. These were joined by hosts of peasants and escaped slaves who committed every sort of crime. Emperor *Constans* (337—350) attempted to restore peace, at first by kindness, and when that failed, by severity. Again the Donatist churches were closed and their leaders banished. But Julian the Apostate (362) revoked these laws and encouraged the schism. Succeeding emperors were unable by old or new measures to effect peace. Donatus the Great († c. 355 in exile) was succeeded by *Parmenian* (c. 355—391), who wrote quite extensively in defense of the sect. He was answered (c. 365) by Bishop *Optatus* of Mileve in a work later called De schismate Donatistarum which traces the origin and history of the schism. But it was *Augustine*, the great bishop of Hippo, who proved to be the strongest and most capable antagonist of the Donatists. After being consecrated auxiliary to Valerius in 394, he wrote a series of treatises in which he pointed out the errors of Donatism and convincingly proved the objective efficacy of the sacraments. When the schismatics became bolder in their violence toward the Catholics, the Catholic bishops, assembled in a synod at Carthage in 404, petitioned Emperor *Honorius* (395—423) to apply the laws of Theodosius against heresy and the emperor acceded to their request. Augustine hesitated for a long time before agreeing to this move; but finally he became convinced that the text of Luke 14:23 (cogite intrare) and the duty of the State toward the Church justified it. However, he did not approve of the death penalty for heresy alone. A three-day conference (collatio) held at Carthage in 411, in which 286 Catholic and 279 Donatist bishops took part did not effect the desired union, in spite of Augustine's noble efforts. The laws were more rigorously applied; the Donatists were deprived of civil rights and were forbidden to assemble under penalty of death (414—415). During the Vandal occupation of North Africa (§ 43, 6) the schism began to decline; but it was not until the country was conquered by the Saracens that it disappeared entirely.

## § 53.

## Apollinaris of Laodicea
## and the Beginning of the Christological Controversies[1].

The *Arians* not only denied the divinity of the Logos, they also mutilated His humanity by asserting that He inhabited a human body without a human *soul*. What seemed to be manifestations of a soul in Christ were actions of the Logos and go to prove that He was created and is subject to change. For a long time this error did not attract particular attention. But when it was seriously noted and condemned, first at Alexandria in 362 (§ 48, 6), later by Pope Damasus (377 and 382 )and especially by the General Council of *Constantinople* in 381 (can. 1) it was seen that the quarrel was not so much with the Arians as with another adversary. And this other was Bishop *Apollinaris* (Ἀπολινάριος) of Laodicea († c. 390), a gifted and versatile theologian (§ 75, 6), a friend of St. Athanasius and a zealous defender of Nicaea against the Arians; but since 352 he had begun to hold with them regarding the human nature of Christ. When he was shown that such a doctrine is untenable according to Scripture, he restricted himself to teaching that Christ did not have the higher, intellectual soul (ψυχὴ λογική) or mind (νοῦς). As a Platonist he held the trichotomy of man. Hence he declared that Christ had assumed our flesh (σάρξ) and an animal soul (ψυχὴ σαρκική) but that the Logos took the place of the higher soul or spirit.

He argued that unless Christ's human nature be considered thus, it would not be possible to uphold His *unity* and *sinlessness*. For two perfect beings or substances (God and man) can never become one (δύο τέλεια ἐν γενέσθαι οὐ δύναται). Further: where there is a perfect man there is sin and sin exists in the human will, i. e., higher soul; therefore Christ could not have had such a soul. Apollinaris appealed to John 1:14 where he interpreted the word "flesh" in the narrow sense, and not as meaning complete human nature. Since he believed nature to be identical with person, hence that two natures are the same as two persons, he held that there could be but *one* nature (μία φύσις) in Christ. This idea is expressed in his treatise "On the Incarnation

---

[1] G. VOISIN, L'Apollinarisme, Paris 1901. H. LIETZMANN, Apollinaris v. Laodicea u. seine Schule, 1904. J. FLEMMING and H. LIETZMANN, Apollinarist. Schriften (Syrian), Abh. Gött. 1904. E. WEIGL, Untersuchungen zur Christologie des hl. Athanasius, 1914; Christologie vom Tode des hl. Athan. bis zum Ausbruch des Nestorian. Streites (373—429), 1925. CH. E. RAVEN, Apollinarism, Cambridge 1923; cfr. A. D'ALÈS, Rev. apologétique 1926/7, 131/49. F. DIEKAMP, ThQ 1904, 497/511 (Vitalis). W. RICHARD, MSR 1945, 5/32; 243/70 (the word "hypostase" in Christology); 1947, 5/54 (the psychology of Christ in Athanasius). S. GONZÁLEZ, § 48.

of the Word of God," a profession of faith handed to Emperor Justin and which his disciples later circulated under the name of Athanasius (§ 54, 1).

This portentous Christological error was condemned by several synods and was attacked by *Gregory of Nyssa* (Antirrheticus), the Antiochians and other theologians. Emperor Theodosius decreed banishment for all who taught or held it (388); yet it found numerous adherents. An Apollinarian congregation was formed at *Antioch* under Bishop *Vitalis*. They reunited with the orthodox Church about 420, but not all of them forsook the heresy. The heresy attained larger proportions and much more prestige in *Monophysitism*.

## § 54.
### Nestorianism and the Third General Council at Ephesus 431[1].

1. Official declarations of the Church had upheld the divinity of the Logos against the Arians and the perfect humanity of Christ

[1] HEFELE II[2], 141/288; HEFELE-LECLFRCQ II 218/422. Acta conciliorum oecumen. ed. ED. SCHWARTZ tom. I: Concilium universale Ephesinum, 5 vol. 1922/30 (survey in B. ALTANER, Patrologie, [2]1950, 214 f.). ED. SCHWARTZ, HZ 112, 1914, 237/63 (antecedents to the Council); Konzilstudien, 1914, 1/17 (Cassian and Nestorianism); Neue Aktenstücke z. ephes. Konzil, Abh. München 30, 8, 1920; Die sog. Gegenanathematismen des Nest., Sb. München 1922, 1; Misc. Fr. Ehrle II, Rome 1924, 56/72 (list of bishops at Ephesus); Cyrill u. der Mönch Viktor, Sb. Wien 208, 4, 1928. R. DEVREESSE, RevSPhTh 1929, 223 ff. 408 ff. (on E. Schwartz: Acta Conciliorum). B. NISTERS, ThQ 1932, 119/47 (Collectio Palatina). W. KRAATZ, Kopt. Akten zum ephesin. Konzil, TU 26, 2, 1904; also P. BATIFFOL, Mél. G. Schlumberger, Paris 1924, 28/39. I. RUCKER, Ephesin. Konzilsakten in armen.-georgischer Überlief., Sb. München 1930, 3; Studien zum Concilium Ephesinum I—IV, 1930/6. E. CASPAR, Geschichte des Papsttums I, 1930, 389/420. **Nestorius:** F. LOOFS, RE XIII, 736/49; XXIV, 239/44; Nestoriana, 1905; Nestorius and his Place in the History of Christian Doctrine, Cambridge 1914. J. LEBON, Muséon 1923, 47/65 (Nestorian fragments). E. AMANN, Nestorius, DictThC XI, 76/157; RevSR 1949, 1950. I. RUCKER, Nestorius, RE Pauly-Wissowa XVII, 126/37. R. ABRAMOWSKI, ZKG 1928, 305/24. R. H. NORWOOD, The Heresy of Antioch, New York 1929. History of the **Theotokus:** V. SCHWEITZER, Kath. 1903 I, 97/113. P. CLEMENT, EphThLov 1928, 599/613. F. J. DÖLGER, AntChrist 1929, 118/23. E. KREBS, Gottesgebärerin, 1931. E. JOLY, Theotokos après le Concile d'Ephèse, Paris 1932. H. RAHNER, ZkTh 1935, 73/81; 1936, 577/90 (Theotokos in Hippolytus). NILIS A S. B., De Maternitate div. B. Mariae V. Nestorii et Cyrilli sententia, Rome 1944. **Cyril and Ephesus:** M. JUGIE, DictThC V, 137/63. E. WEIGL, Christologie etc., § 53. J. MAHÉ, RHE 1906, 505/42 (Cyrill's anathemas); cfr. A. DENEFFE, Scholastik 1933, 64 ff. 203 ff.; P. GALTIER, RechSR 1933, 45/57 (the anathemas not approved at Chalcedon 451). F. NAU, S. Cyrille et Nestorius, RevOC 1910, 365 ff.; 1911, 1 ff. 167 ff. F. X. BAUER, Proklos, B. v. Konstantinopel (436—46), 1919. P. BATIFFOL, Le Siège Apostolique 359—451, Paris 1924, 337 ff. A. D'ALÈS, Le dogme d'Ephèse, Paris 1931. Aufsätze z. Konzil v. Ephesus: P. GALTIER, RechSR 1931, 169 ff. 269 ff.; J. LEBON, EphThLov 1931, 393/412; E. BÖMINGHAUS, StZ 121, 1931, 284/92; M. JUGIE, R. DEVREESSE et al., in Échos d'Orient 1931, 271 ff. H. DU MANOIR, Gregorianum 1931, 104/37; RechSR 1935, 441 ff. 531 ff. A. DENEFFE, Scholastik 1931, 588/92 (literature). G. NEYRON in Kyrilliana, Kairo 1947, 37/59. M. JUGIE, Theologia dogmatica

against the Arians and Apollinaris. Now it became necessary to define more clearly the relation between the *divine* and *human nature*. The contemporaries of Apollinaris had expressed themselves very inexactly on this point, in fact, some of them used expressions which were intentionally ambiguous. This is clearly seen in the teachings of the theological schools (§ 74). The *Alexandrian* School, stressing the union of the two natures, calls it a "mingling" (σύγ-κρασις). By circulating Apollinaris' profession of faith (§ 53) under the name of Athanasius, it was made to appear that Athanasius held *one* nature instead of two in the Logos (μία φύσις τοῦ θεοῦ λόγου σεσαρκωμένη). Since such expressions endangered the doctrine of the two natures, the moderate and critical *Antiochian* School did everything possible to safeguard the two natures and keep them separate. Two leaders of this school, *Diodorus* of Tarsus and *Theodore* of Mopsuestia (§ 75, 5) went too far in this endeavor. Diodorus speaks of the indwelling (ἐνοικεῖν) of the Logos in human nature like a person in a temple or a man in the garments he wears; and he speaks of two Sons of God, one by nature and one accepted as a son by grace. The latter can be called son only figuratively. Theodore, too, maintained that there was not an incarnation in the proper sense of the word, since this would mean the change of the Logos into a man; but there is merely the *indwelling* (ἐνοί-κησις) of the Logos in the man Jesus. His acceptance of Aristotle's notion that no substance (nature) is perfect without a person, led him to hold that there were *two Persons* in Christ. He does, indeed, speak expressly of only *one* Person, but the unity he understood was not a physical or substantial union (ἕνωσις φυσική) but a rela-tive or moral union (ἕνωσις σχετική) a union of the will (σχέσις τῆς γνώμης), an external bond (συνάφεια) such as exists between man and wife or between a temple and the idol in it. He saw union only when two natures were viewed simultaneously; when viewed separately they were persons. Hence Theodore argued that the Son of God was not born, but a man Christ, in whom God dwelt, and hence also he did not call *Mary* "Mother of God" (θεοτόκος)

christianorum orientalium t. V: Nestoriani et Monophysitae, Paris 1935. R. ARNOU, Gregorianum 1936, 116/31 (Nestorianism and Neoplatonism). G. BARDY, RevSR 1938, 20/44 (Acacius of Beröa and the Nestorian. quarrel). A. SPINDELER, Cur Verbum caro factum? Das Motiv der Menschwerdung, usw., 1938. W. M. PEITZ, Das vorephesin. Symbol der päpstl. Kanzlei, 1939. J. VAN DER DRIES, The Formula of St. Cyril of Alex. μία φύσις etc., Diss. London 1939. J. GUILLET, RechSR 1947, 257/302 (exegesis of Alexandria and Antioch). See below and § 75, 5. 7 (Diodorus, Theodore, Cyril, Theodoret).

(as Hippolytus of Rome probably did, certainly as Origen and the Alexandrians had done since the third century) but only "mother of Christ" (χριστοτόκος).

2. Antiochian Christology was at first a subject of interest only to theologians; **Nestorius** gave it wider publicity. He had been a monk at Antioch, most probably one of Theodore's disciples, and a renowned preacher; imperial favor elevated him to the see of Constantinople in 428. He was not without virtue and inclined toward solitude, but he was disputatious and impetuous and a foe of heretics and Jews. Nevertheless he took under his protection the Pelagians (§ 56, 4) who had been forced to withdraw from the West, an action which merited for him the strong disapproval of Rome. The priest Anastasius who had followed Nestorius to the capital, rebuked the people in his sermons for using the ancient and cherished title "Mother of God" in their devotions to the Blessed Virgin. The indignation of clergy and people was increased when Nestorius defended Anastasius and preached several sermons in which he told the people that the expression was "an innovation" and that the proper term was "Mother of Christ". (Later, he admitted that he could accept the term θεοτόκος if it were properly understood, i. e., as he would have it understood). When the report of Nestorius' utterances reached other parts of the Empire, the reaction of the clergy and people was the same as in the capital city, As early as 429 Bishop *Cyril* of Alexandria (§ 75, 7) attacked him in his Easter letter to the Egyptian bishops and in an encyclical to the Egyptian monks. Without impugning Cyril's sincere concern for the orthodox faith, it can not be denied, that other considerations played a part in his censure of Nestorius. There was the old rivalry of the two great theological schools, but more telling was the ecclesiastical-political rivalry of the two sees. Since 381 the see of Constantinople had been given precedence in the East over the much older patriarchate of Alexandria. Cyril's uncle, Theophilus, had shown his resentment by his attack on John Chrysostom (§ 51, 3; 63, 1). Both parties now appealed to Pope *Celestine I* and in a Roman synod held in August 430, the opinion of Nestorius was condemned. Cyril ordered Nestorius to retract within ten days under threat of deposition. At the same time he sent Nestorius twelve "anathemas" which had been drawn up at a synod at Alexandria and ordered Nestorius to abjure all of the heresies thus *anathematized*. Nestorius was not inclined to humble himself before his rival. He knew he

could rely on the support of the emperor and the numerous disciples of the Antiochian School, especially Bishop *John of Jerusalem* and the learned Bishop *Theodoret of Cyrus* (§ 75, 7), who considered Cyril's concepts identical with those of Apollinaris, or at least, as being a form of Monophysitism. With such support Nestorius replied to Cyril with a set of twelve contra-anathemas, some of which had no bearing on the point at issue. Although the patriarch of Antioch sided with Nestorius from the beginning of the quarrel, he pleaded earnestly with him to accept θεοτόκος as the teaching of the Fathers and of the orthodox faith.

In the third anathema, *Cyril* speaks of an ἕνωσις φυσική, as did the other members of the Alexandrian School including St. Athanasius, and opposes this to the συνάφεια of the Antiochians. (He also uses the expression ἕνωσις καθ' ὑπόστασιν or κατὰ φύσιν). He endeavored to indicate that the union of the two natures is most intimate and real, but not a mingling or change of one into the other. And although his notion is correct, his language is ambiguous especially since he sometimes, though not frequently, uses the phrase μία φύσις τοῦ θεοῦ λόγου σεσαρκωμένη of Apollonaris which had falsely been attributed to Athanasius. It must also be borne in mind that at the time he wrote, φύσις and ὑπόστασις as applied to Christ were used interchangeably, sometimes as meaning nature and sometimes person.

3. At the instigation of Nestorius, Emperor **Theodosius II** called a **general council** (the third) to meet at **Ephesus** at Pentecost in 431. But things did not augur well from the beginning. Nestorius appeared first with 16 bishops, later Cyril came with 50 of his suffragans. *John* the Patriarch of Antioch intentionally postponed his arrival and the papal legates were delayed by storms at sea. In spite of the remonstrances of Candidian, the imperial commissary, and numerous bishops (68), Cyril, under the impression that he represented the pope, opened the synod in the church of the Blessed Virgin at Ephesus on June 22, 431. One hundred and fifty-three bishops were then present. In the first session proofs were adduced from the early Fathers justifying the use of θεοτόκος and the belief in the real union of two natures in Christ. Nestorius, who absented himself from the council and refused to answer the citations, was deposed and stigmatized as "another Judas" because of his "godless sermons" and his "disobedience to the canons." The Council of Ephesus did not compose a new creed, but was satisfied to reaffirm the Nicene Creed. Four days after the synod had opened John with his Syrian bishops entered the city; but instead of taking part in the council, they held their own conciliabulum of 43 members in the presence of the imperial commissary, in which

272

they decreed the deposition of Cyril and Bishop Memnon of Ephesus. The three papal legates arrived about the same time and recognized the legitimacy of the sessions over which Cyril had presided. In the fifth session held on July 17, John and his followers were excommunicated. The Emperor faced a dilemma. At first he confirmed the decisions of both assemblies, but later he invited representatives of both parties to his court at Chalcedon. When they were unable to agree the emperor took matters in his own hands and decided against Nestorius. To gain such a victory it had been necessary for Cyril to conciliate the court even to the extent of distributing expensive gifts. He had a powerful ally in *Pulcheria,* the emperor's pious and influential elder sister. Nestorius was sent back to his monastery in Antioch and was succeeded at Constantinople by Maximian, a bishop agreeable to Cyril's party. The Synod of Ephesus was then adjourned and Cyril and Memnon were permitted to return to their sees.

However, the schism among the bishops of the East continued. The Antiochians were indignant at the outcome and accused Cyril of Arianism and Apollinarianism. As soon as they returned home they again passed sentence of excommunication on Cyril and his followers. A semblance of *union* was reached in 433. Cyril accepted the Creed which the Antiochians had proposed at Ephesus (hence called symbolum Ephesinum). It was probably composed by Theodoret. John, on his part, was obliged to recognize the decisions of Cyril's synod of 431 and agreed to the deposition of Nestorius. But even this did not effect general peace. The symbol which Cyril accepted was correct in that it professed faith in *one* Christ, *one* Son and Lord and gave Mary the title ϑεοτόκος. But it speaks of the human nature of Christ as the "temple" of the Logos. Hence Cyril was charged with having compromised on expressions that favored Nestorianism. A majority of John's followers held out against the excommunication of Nestorius. But when the emperor threatened them with deposition, all but a few reluctantly agreed.

4. The *"Nestorian tragedy"* as it was called even by contemporaries, ended when the emperor in 435 banished the deposed patriarch to Arabia, then to Libya and finally to the desert of Upper Egypt and ordered his writings to be burned. After spending about 15 years in exile, Nestorius died just before the General Council of Chalcedon (451). A short time before his death he composed *a work* in which he endeavored *to justify himself.* This work, entitled "The Bazar (= treatise) of Heraclides of Damascus" (a pseudonym) was recently discovered in a Syrian translation. (ed. *P. Bedjan,* Paris

1910; French trans. by F. Nau, Paris 1910; English trans. by G. R. Driver
and L. Hodgson, Oxford 1925; cfr. F. Loofs, ThLZ 1926 193/201). In this
work Nestorius severely criticizes the decisions of Ephesus and insists that
his teaching agreed perfectly with that of Pope Leo I and Patriarch Flavian
of Constantinople (§ 55, 2). — The *person* and *doctrine* of *Nestorius* are still
*subjects of discussion* among historians. Some scholars, like *Bethune-Baker*
and *Duchesne* (see below), hold that he was perfectly orthodox and that
his condemnation was the result of rivalry, misunderstandings, slander and
ignorance. I. Rucker, in his work Studien zum Concilium Ephesinum (III
and IV, see below) also defends the unfortunate Patriarch of Constantinople,
but with better balance. Nestorius was certainly not altogether in bad faith.
The concluding lines of the "Bazar" express the true Christian spirit of forgiveness and charity. But his ideas were far from orthodox even though they
did not go to the extremes reached by Diodorus and Theodore. It was his
misfortune that he held so stubbornly to the erroneous Christological opinions
of the Antiochian School and that he refused to accept the faith of the Church
as explained by Cyril and the Cappadocians. His concept of two natures
(prosopa) in Christ united by a third πρόσωπον (Rucker) can never be understood as a real, physical, not even moral, union of natures. Nestorius definitely
*rejected* the *communicatio idiomatum*, especially the θεοτόκος and held to the
old Antiochian idea that Christ *merited* divine attributes and honor by His
moral victories and His passion and death. — *J. F. Bethune-Baker*, Nestorius
and his Teaching, Cambridge 1908. — *L. Duchesne*, Hist. ancienne de l'Église
III³, Paris 1910, 313 ff. 446 ff. — *L. Fendt*, Die Christologie des Nest., 1910. —
*F. Nau*, Nest. d'après les sources orientales, Paris 1911; Patrologia Orient.
XIII, 2, 1919. — *J. P. Junglas*, Die Irrlehre des Nest., 1912. — *M. Jugie*,
Nest. et la controverse nestorienne, Paris 1912. — Ch. Pesch, Nest. als Irr-
lehrer, 1921. — L. T. J. Lohn, Collectanea Theol. 1933, 1/37. — *A. Deneffe*,
Scholastik 1935, 548/60; 1938, 522 f. (vs. Rucker).

5. The stern measures adopted by the civil authorities caused Nestorianism
to decline in the Roman Empire. But when the Nestorians were deprived
by imperial decree of the works of Nestorius, they turned to the works of
*Diodorus* and *Theodore*, the real fathers of Nestorianism. Bishop *Rabulus*
of Edessa († 436) called attention to this fact and proscribed the reading
of these works. (Cfr. P. Peeters, RechSR 1928, 170/204; F. Nau, RevHR 103,
1931, 97/135; E. R. Hayes, L'école d'Édesse, Paris 1930). Rabulus was
succeeded by *Ibas* (436—457) who was an ardent disciple of Theodore (cfr.
A. d'Alès, RechSR 1932, 5/25 — on the letter of Ibas to Bishop Maris).
In 489 Emperor Zeno closed the theological school at *Edessa*, then the
nursery of Nestorianism. Attempts to suppress the error in the Empire caused
many of its adherents to migrate to *Persia* where Bishop *Barsumas* (Barsauma)
of Nisibis (c. 450—495) worked for the spread of the heresy and founded
a new theological school at *Nisibis* (Cfr. T. Hermann, ZntW 1926, 89/122). In
498 *Babaeus* (Babai), Archbishop of *Seleucia-Ctesiphon* (497—503) assumed
the title Catholicos (Patriarch), declared himself independent of the Patriarch
of Antioch, and formed the *national Nestorian Church of Persia*. During the
course of the next several centuries, zealous Nestorian missionaries penetrated
far into Asia with notable success (§ 42, 5; § 127, 4). The so-called Thomas-

Christians on the west coast of India (§ 12, 11) were Nestorians. After the Mongol invasions during the fourteenth century, the sect began to decline rapidly. But as late as 1915 more than 100,000 Nestorians were still to be found in Kurdistan on the borders between Turkey and Iraq, with a patriarch (Catholicos) as their ecclesiastical superior. After World War I, the new boundary treaties brought them (they were then classified as "Assyrians") under the civil rule of Iraq. Due to persecution by the Mohammedans between 20,000—30,000 of them migrated to Syria and Cyprus; the remainder eventually were allowed a restricted practice of their religion. At various times, groups of Nestorians to the number of about 150,000 united with Rome. These are known as "Chaldean Christians" and have their own patriarch who resides at Mosul, sometimes at Bagdad. About a million "Thomas Christians" also united with Rome. The remaining "Thomas Christians" have been Monophysites (Jacobites) since the seventeenth century. — *Duchesne, Labourt, Wigram etc.*, § 42. — *K. Kessler*, Nestorianer, RE XIII, 723/36. — *E. Tisserant* et *E. Amann*, Église nestorienne, DictTh CXI, 157/325. — *W. Barthold*, Zur Gesch. des Christent. in Mittelasien bis z. mongol. Eroberung, German by *R. Stübe*, 1901. — *A. Fortescue*, The Lesser Eastern Churches, London 1913. — *E. Roz* et *I. Hausherr*, Orientalia Christ. XI, 1, Rome 1928 (Nestorianism in India). — *R. Strothmann*, ZKG 1936, 17/82 (Nestorians-Assyrians today). — *B. Spuler*, Die Gegenwartslage der Ostkirchen, 1948. — *A. R. Vine*, The Nestorian Churches, London 1937. — *G. Messina*, CivCat 1945 II, 243/53 (organisation of the Nest. Church), 1946 II, 116/27 (Nestorian propaganda in Asia). — *W. de Vries*, Sakramententheologie bei den Nestorianern, Rome 1947.

# § 55.

# Monophysitism and the Fourth General Council at Chalcedon 451[1].

1. The Nestorians separated the natures of Christ in such a way that He was made to be two distinct persons. Their opponents,

---

[1] HEFELE II², 313/578; HEFELE-LECLERCQ, II 499/880. Akten der Räubersynode v. 449 (Bruchstück), syrisch u. deutsch, hg. von J. FLEMMING and G. HOFFMANN, Abh. Gött. 15, I, 1917. Acta conciliorum oecum., ed. ED. SCHWARTZ, tom. II: Concilium Chalcedonense, 6 vol. 1932/38 (Survey in B. ALTANER, Patrologie, ²1950, 215). P. PEETERS, AB 1936, 143/59; H. V. CAMPENHAUSEN, Theol. Blätter 1938, 162/66 (on the Documents of Chalcedon). Leo M., Epist. dogmatica ad Flavianum, ed. E. H. BLAKENEY, London 1923; rec. C. SILVA-TAROUCA, Rome 1932; S. Leonis M. Epistolae c. Eutychis haeresim, rec. C. SILVA-TAROUCA, 2 parts, Rome 1934/5. C. SILVA-TAROUCA, in Studi ded. alla memoria di P. Ubaldi, Milano 1937, 151/70 (manuscript tradition of the Tomus Leonis). L. WINTERSYL, Das Lehrschreiben des Papstes Leo d. Gr. über die Menschwerdung Christi, German transl. 1938. I. RUCKER, Florilegium Edessenum (syriace a. 562), Sb. München 1933, 5. W. H. P. HATCH, HarvThR 1926, 377/81 (Fragments of Dioscurus). J. B. CHABOT, Documenta ad origines Monophysitarum illustr., Louvain 1933 (Corpus SS. Christ. Orient. SS. Syri II, 37). G. KRÜGER, Monophysitische Streitigkeiten im Zusammenhang mit der Reichspolitik, 1884; Art. Monophysiten, RE XIII, 372/401; XXIV, 187 f. M. JUGIE, Eutyches, DictThC V, 1582/1609; Monophysisme, ib. X, 2217/2306. F. LOOFS, Eutyches, RE V, 635/47; XXIII, 438. A. AMELLI, Leone Magno e l'Oriente, Montecassino

especially the Alexandrians went to the opposite extreme. They overemphasized his divinity to the point of denying His humanity and held that there was a *commingling* of natures in which the human nature was wholly absorbed by or *transformed* into the divine. According to them, Christ had indeed two natures; but *after* the Incarnation there was only one (μία καὶ μόνη φύσις). The body of Christ, they held, was not essentially the same as our bodies (ὁμοούσιος ἡμῖν) but was divine. The doctrine of two natures in Christ, according to the Monophysites, could mean only a return to Nestorianism, to heresy. Their Platonic philosophy which induced the conclusion that the human nature of Christ had lost its identity in the divine, led logically to the conclusion that all human nature is divine. It was this idea that made Monophysitism the most popular heresy of Christian antiquity. The controversy began when **Eutyches**, the aged archimandrite of Constantinople, a pious, but superficial theologian attacked Bishop *Eusebius* of Dorylaeum in Phrygia, for teaching Diophysitism. In a synod at Constantinople in 448 (§ 65, 3) under the presidency of Patriarch *Flavian*, Eutyches was deposed and excommunicated.

2. This was the prelude to a major conflict. Flavian informed Pope *Leo I* (§ 64, 6) and other bishops of the decisions of the synod. But Eutyches scorned the decisions and complained that they were unjust. He succeeded in winning the court to his views which gave him the advantage from the beginning. *Dioscurus*, the ambitious patriarch, who succeeded Cyril in the see of Alexandria in 444, and who held the same views as Eutyches, induced Theodosius II in 449 to call a general synod at *Ephesus*, the site of Cyril's triumph. The emperor appointed Dioscurus to preside. Backed by his monks and the emperor's soldiers Dioscurus intimidated the assembled

[2]1890. P. BATIFFOL, Le Siège Apostolique 359—451, Paris 1924, 493 ff. E. CASPAR, Gesch. des Papsttums I, 1930, 462 ff.; II, 1933, 10 ff. F. HAASE, Dioskur nach monophysit. Quellen, in Kirchengeschichtl. Abhandl., hg. v. M. SDRALEK 6, 1908, 145/233. A. WILLE, B. Julian v. Kios, Nuntius Leos d. Gr. in Konstant. (449—60), 1910. Separate studies: ED. SCHWARTZ, Abh. München 32, 2, 1925 (from the Acta of Chalcedon); Festgabe Ad. Jülicher, 1927, 203/12 (Pulcheria at Chalc.); Sb. München 1929, 5 (trial of Eutyches). R. DRAGUET, Byzantion 1931, 441/57 (Christology of Eutyches). COSTANTINO DA MAZZARINO, La dottrina di Teodoreto di Ciro sull' unione ipostatica..., Rome 1941. J. MONTALVERNE, Theodoreti Cyrensis doctrina antiquior de verbo ,,inhumanato'' (423—35), Rome 1948. J. LEBON, Muséon 1946, 515/28 (Dioscurus). M. JUGIE and A. SPINDELER, § 54. ED. SCHWARTZ, J. LEBON, et al., (on the Creeds of Nicaea and Constantinople in the Acta of Chalcedon), § 49, 2. V. LAURENT, Bull. de la section hist. de l'Acad. roumaine 1944, 152/73; 1945, 33/46 (attendance at the Council). ED. SCHWARTZ and E. HONIGMANN (list of bishops at Chalcedon), § 47, 1.

bishops. The papal legates were not allowed to preside nor were the papal briefs allowed to be read. Pope Leo I had sent to the council a letter, later known as the *Epistola dogmatica*, in which he defined the faith of the Church regarding the two natures in Christ. In this letter, Leo explained that the union of the two natures was not a mingling of the two, but that each retained its own identity and one cooperated with the other in perfect harmony. This decision of Rome meant a break with the Alexandrian School. The outcome was obvious. Eutyches was declared orthodox, since he accepted Nicaea and Ephesus and rejected the heresies of Nestorius and Apollinaris. The doctrine of two natures after the Incarnation was rejected as an innovation. Flavian and Eusebius were deposed because it was said they had gone too far in their attempts to explain the Creeds of Nicaea and Ephesus. The same fate befell other bishops who opposed Eutyches and who were therefore accused of Nestorianism. Among these were *Theodoret* of Cyrus, *Domnus* of Antioch and *Ibas* of Edessa. Flavian was so mistreated that he died three days later on his way to exile. But he, as well as Eusebius and Theodoret, had in the meantime appealed to the pope against the unjust sentence.

Soon, however, the Monophysites were deprived of the emperor's help on which they had relied. In a letter to Augusta Pulcheria (451) Pope *Leo I* called the synod a *"Robber Synod"* and there was a general demand for another council. After the sudden death of Theodosius II (July, 450) *Pulcheria* (§ 54, 3) married *Marcian*, the head of the imperial army, who thus became Emperor (450—457). Rome wanted the council to meet in Italy, but because of the invasion of the Huns in Gaul, it was impossible to hold it there. Marcian called it to meet at Nicaea, but later decided on **Chalcedon** on the Bosphorus across the strait from Constantinople. The Fourth General Council at Chalcedon in 451 was the largest gathering of bishops up to that time. More than 600 bishops were present, including two from North Africa and three papal legates who presided. The Emperor and Empress attended all the sessions and in the sixth session on October 25, 451 in which the declaration of faith was solemnly proclaimed, the Empress Pulcheria was given the honor of presiding. The assembly declared the synods of 325, 381 and 431 to have been ecumenical councils and reaffirmed the Nicene and the Niceno-Constantinopolitan Creeds (§ 49, 2). After a long and stormy debate the "Robber Synod" was condemned and Dioscurus was deposed, while Theodoret and Ibas were reinstated and Domnus was indemnified. Leo's dogmatic letter was hailed enthusiastically and was used as a basis for a Creed in which the errors of Nestorius and Eutyches were repudiated in the words: "We teach and believe *one and the same Christ . . . in two natures* (ἕνα καὶ τὸν αὐτὸν Χριστόν . . . ἐν δύο φύσεσιν) unmixed and unchanged (ἀσυγχύτως, ἀτρέπτως) undivided and unseparated (ἀδιαιρέτως, ἀχωρίστως) since the distinction of natures is by no means destroyed in the union, but rather the qualities of each nature are preserved and both are united in *one* Person (πρόσωπον) and *one* hypostasis." For further important decisions regarding the Patriarchates of Constantinople and Jerusalem, see § 63, 1. 2.

3. The Council of Chalcedon by no means ended the history of Monophysitism[1]. In 452 Emperor Marcion banished Dioscurus and Eutyches and passed stringent laws regarding their followers. But the condemnation met with more stubborn resistence than the condemnation of the Nestorians. The opposition party was not united. Besides some who were crude Monophysites (Eutychians), there were some, like Severus of Antioch and the Severians, who held the view which Cyril had held before 433 and refused to accept Chalcedon because they thought it was nothing more than a concealed form of Nestorianism. These were schismatics rather than heretics. But the Monophysite quarrel proved highly dangerous to the Empire since many of its adherents in *Syria* and *Egypt* mixed national and political tendencies with their religion and threatened the rule of Byzantium.

The situation rapidly became menacing. The opponents of Chalcedon were able to take possession of the Eastern Patriarchates. The see of *Jerusalem*

---

[1] Cfr. literature above. L. DUCHESNE, L'Église au VIe siècle, Paris 1925. A. A. LUCE, Monophysitism Past and Present, London 1920. W. A. WIGRAM, The Separation of the Monophysites, London 1923. J. MASPÉRO, Hist. des patriarches d'Alexandrie 518—616, Paris 1923; also A. JÜLICHER, ZntW 1925, 17/43. M. CHAINE, § 42, 6. A. FORTESCUE, The Lesser Eastern Churches, London 1913; The Uniate Eastern Churches, ib. 1923. R. JANIN, Les Églises orientales et les rites orientaux, Paris ³1935. B. J. KIDD, The Churches of Eastern Christendom (431—1927), London 1927. CH. DIEHL, L'Égypte chrétienne et byzantine, Paris 1933. S. SALAVILLE, Échos d'Orient 1918, 255 ff.; 1920, 49 ff. 415 ff. (Henoticon). W. T. TOWNSEND, Journal of Religion 1936, 78/86 (Henoticon and Rome). ED. SCHWARTZ, Abh. München 32, 6, 1927 (an anti-Chalcedon collection from the time of Emp. Zeno); also R. DRAGUET, RHE 1928, 51/62; FR. DIEKAMP, ThRev 1928, 311/2; R. DEVREESSE, RevSPhTh 1930, 251/65. ED. SCHWARTZ, Sb. München 1934 (collection of pamphlets on the Acacian schism). TH. SCHNITZLER, Im Kampf um Chalcedon, Gesch. u. Inhalt des Cod. Encyclius v. 458, Rome 1938. Severus Antioch., Philalethes, ed. A. SANDA, Beirut 1928; Liber c. impium Grammaticum, oratio I—III; Orationes ad Nephalium, ed. J. LEBON, Corpus SS. Christ. Oriental., SS. Syri, 4. Ser. t. 4—7, Paris 1929/49 (also H. G. OPITZ, ThLZ 1940, 130/6; F. DIEKAMP, ThRev 1939, 387/9). J. LEBON, Le Monophysisme Sévérien, Louvain 1909; RHE 1908, 677/702 (Timotheus Älurus). W. DE VRIES, Sakramententheologie bei den syr. Monophysiten, Rome 1940. See below under no 5 (R. DRAGUET etc.).

for a time was governed by the Monophysite monk *Theodosius* (452—453). In *Alexandria*, Proterius, the orthodox successor of Dioscurus, was murdered in an uprising of the people and *Timothy Aelurus* (457—460) was made patriarch, while *Peter Fullo* became patriarch of *Antioch* (c. 470—471; cfr. also § 58, 2). Due to the intervention of Emperor *Leo I* (457—474) none of these interlopers reigned long; but they made their presence felt, especially in Egypt where Monophysite bishops were appointed to almost all the sees. When Leo I died Aelurus and Peter Fullo were reinstated. The Usurper *Basiliscus* (475—476) who restored them also wrote an encyclicon in which he anathematized Pope Leo's dogmatic letter and the Symbol of Chalcedon and threatened severe penalties on all who adhered to either. More than 500 Eastern bishops signed this encyclicon.

4. When Emperor Zeno (474—491) defeated Basiliscus in 476, orthodoxy was again endangered. The Monophysite Patriarch of Alexandria *Peter Mongus* joined with Patriarch *Acacius* of Constantinople in drawing up a new symbol in which Nestorius and Eutyches were condemned, but which also indirectly anathematized the Council of Chalcedon and declared that the only norms of faith were the Niceno-Constantinopolitan Creed, the 12 anathemas of Cyril and the decisions of Ephesus. Zeno published this formula as a religious law in 482 under the name of **Henoticon.** It was intended to bring about religious unity in the Empire, but it actually served only to strengthen the schism. Not only many Catholics, but also the stricter Monophysites rejected the Henoticon as a partial measure. In Alexandria, those who rejected it were called *Acephali* because they had broken with their bishop, Peter Mongus, and were now without a head. When Pope *Felix II* (III) excommunicated and deposed the bishop of Constantinople in 484, the breach between East and West was completed. This **Acacian Schism** lasted 35 years (484—519). In the meantime Monophysitism made great progress in the East. Emperor *Anastasius I* (491—518) began to negotiate with Rome, but his favoritism toward the Monophysites annulled his efforts. The confusion in the East became worse with the outbreak of the *Theopaschite controversy* (§ 58, 2). Emperor *Justin* (518—527) was urged by his gifted nephew and successor Justinian to seek union with the Apostolic See (519) and Pope *Hormisdas* did not rebuff him. He sent legates to Constantinople with a *formula for union* (Formula or libellus Hormisdae) which recognized Chalcedon and the dogmatic letter of Leo, and reaffirmed the excommunication of Nestorius, Eutyches, Dioscurus and all other Monophysite leaders. The formula further declared that by reason of Christ's promise: Thou art Peter etc. (Matt. 16:18) the Catholic religion in the Apostolic See at Rome had always been preserved immaculate, hence it was necessary to submit to and obey Rome's decisions. (This letter or formula was quoted in the Constitutio de Ecclesia Christi chap. 4 of the Vatican Council). The Greek bishops, headed by the court patriarch John II of Constantinople were obliged to subscribe to this formula. As far as appearances were concerned, the schism was at an end. Rome had gained a decisive victory; but in Egypt Monophysitism still held sway. — W. Haacke, Die Glaubensformel des P. Hormisdas (Dissertation) Rome, 1939. — P. Choranis, The Religious Policy of Anastasius I (491—518) Madison, 1949. — A. A. Vasiliev, Justin I, Cambridge 1950.

5. Emperor *Justinian I* (527—565) exerted every effort to induce the Monophysites of his Empire to accept Chalcedon; but at the same time his wife *Theodora* was secretly favoring the heresy (§ 58). Since the sixth century especially in *Egypt*, the Monophysites had broken up into several parties and had begun to quarrel among themselves. The most important of these divisions were the *Severians* and the *Julianists*, who owe their origin to Bishop *Severus of Antioch* (512—518) and Bishop *Julian* of Halicarnassus. These two bishops had been deposed by Justin in 518 after which they lived at Alexandria. Severus (§ 77, 2) was a theologian of some ability. But he adopted a form of mitigated Monophysitism in which he taught that there was only one nature in Christ "put together" somewhat after the manner of the union of soul and body in man. Before the Resurrection the body of Christ was subject to corporal infirmities and was corruptibile. Hence the Severians were called *Phthartolatrae* by their enemies while they called the Julianists *Aphthardocetae* or *Phantasiasts* because they held that after the Incarnation the body of Christ was paradisaical and incorruptible. (The attempt of R. Draguet to prove that Julian merely held that Christ was free from the consequences of original sin was not successful). After the death of the Monophysite Patriarch of Alexandria, Timothy III in 535, the Severians and Julianists elected Theodosius and Gaianus as their ecclesiastical superiors from which fact they were later known as *Theodosians* and *Gaianites*. Both parties eventually split into still smaller groups. Some of the Julianists (Gaianites) held that the incorruptible body of Christ was not created (*Actistetae* — to whom were opposed the *Ctistolatrae*) and some of the Theodosians, following the deacon Themistius of Alexandria, held that in certain matters Christ's knowledge was defective. These were called *Themistians* or *Agnoëtae*. But they were not Monophysites strictly speaking. Nor were they heretics. — *R. Draguet*, Julien d'Halicarnasse et sa controverse avec Sévère d'Antioche, Louvain 1924 (cfr. RHE 1937, 92/5); also *F. Loofs*, ThLZ 1925, 320/6; *M. Jugie*, Échos d'Orient 1925, 129 ff. 257 ff.; *Fr. Diekamp*, ThRev 1927, 89/93; *Th. Hermann*, Theol. Blätter 1928, 32 ff. — *Severi* Antioch. Antiiulianistica I, ed. A. Sanda, Beirut 1931; see also § 56, 3. — *R. Draguet*, Muséon 1932, 255/317 (writings against and by Julian of Halicarnassus). — On the *Agnoëtae*: *J. Marič*, De Agnoëtarum doctrina, Zagreb 1914. — *E. Schulte*, Die Entwicklung der Lehre vom menschl. Wissen Jesu, 1914. — *F. Diekamp*, ThRev 1915, 97/108. — *Th. Hermann*, ZntW 1933, 287/93.

About the sixth century the Monophysites of Egypt revived the *Trinitarian* controversy. The Aristotelian *John Philoponus* of Alexandria and *Stephen Gobarus* (§ 77, 3) began to teach that each of the divine Persons had a special nature or hypostasis *(Tritheists)*. They were opposed by the *Tetradists* or *Damianists* (after the Patriarch Damian of Alexandria) who held a sort of quaternity in the Godhead, and by the *Niobites* (after Stephen Niobes) who later accepted the Catholic teaching and were reunited with the Church. — *Joh. Philoponus: G. Furlani*, Patrologia Orientalis XIV (1920), 675 ff. — *A. Sanda*, Joannis Philoponi opuscula monophysitica syr. et lat., Beirut 1930. — *Th. Hermann*, ZntW 1930, 209/64 (John Phil. as Monophysite). — *A. Gudeman* and *W. Kroll*, RE Pauly-Wissowa IX, 1764/95. — *G. Bardy*, DictThC VIII, 831/39. — *Stephanus Gobarus: A. v. Harnack*, HarvThR 1923, 205/34.

In spite of all the efforts made later to convert the Monophysites, the heresy persisted especially after Palestine, Syria and Egypt were invaded by the Mohammedans in the seventh century and these countries were cut off from the Byzantine Empire (§ 45, 2). In *Armenia* (§ 42, 6), *Syria, Meso-potamia, Egypt* and *Abyssinia* they formed *national churches*: the Armenian, the Jacobite-Syrian, the Coptic-Egyptian and Abyssinian churches which gradually developed a culture entirely foreign to the old Greek culture. These churches exist today. In Egypt they are called *Copts*, i. e., old Egyptian Christians, while the Orthodox of Egypt and Syria, mostly Greeks, are known as *Melchites*, i. e., imperial or belonging to the Church of the Empire. Today in Egypt there are about 1 million schismatic and 60,000 uniate Copts. In Syria, Palestine and Egypt there are about 320,000 schismatics, and about 150,000 uniate Melchites. In Syria and neighboring countries the Monophysites are known as *Jacobites* after Bishop *James of Edessa* (541—578) called *Baradai* because in his poverty he wore a horse blanket. James organized the Monophysite Church and in 544 appointed Sergius of Antioch as its head. The Patriarch (Catholicos) of the Syrian Monophysites formerly lived at the monastery of Zapharan in Northern Mesopotamia, but now resides at Jerusalem; while the head of the Armenian Monophysites since 1443 makes his home at Etschmiadz in the Caucasus. — *The Coptic Church*: Cl. Kopp, ThGl 1929, 305/15; Orientalia Christ. 30, 1, Rome 1932. — *Jacobites*: E. Nestle, RE VIII, 565/71; XXIII, 666 f. — A. Baumstark, Das Festbrevier u. Kirchen-jahr der syr. Jakobiten, 1910. — R. Abramowski, Dionysius v. Tellmatre, jakobit. Patriarch (814—45), 1940. — Spuler, § 54, 5.

# § 56.
## Pelagianism in the West[1]. Augustine, Doctor Gratiae.

1. While the Trinitarian and Christological disputes were ab-sorbing the attention of the East, a heresy made its appearance

---

[1] The most important documents are to be found in PL 45 and in A. BRUCKNER, Quellen zur Gesch. des pelag. Streites, 1906. Augustine's anti-Pelagian works in CSEL 42 and 60, 1902/13. The Commonitoria of Marius Mercator against the Pelagians in PL 48 and better in Acta concil. oecum., ed. ED. SCHWARTZ t. I vol. V, 1, 1924. Pelagius, Expositiones in Ap. Pauli epistolas, edd. A. SOUTER et A. ROBINSON, Texts and Studies IX, 1—3, Cambridge 1922/31. J. J. DEMPSEY, Pelagius' Commentary on St. Paul, Diss. Rome Univ. Greg. 1937. G. DE PLINVAL, Pélage, ses écrits, sa vie et sa réforme, Lausanne 1943 (standard); Essai sur le style et la langue de Pélage, Freiburg Schw. 1947 (with the tract De induratione cordis Pharaonis); RHE 1939, 5/21 vs. I. KIRMER, Das Eigentum des Fastidius (British bishops in the fifth century) im pelagian. Schrifttum, 1938. J. COMELIAN, RHE 1935, 77/89 ("prayer" of Pelagius). C. MARTINI, Antonianum 1938, 293/334 (four fragments of Pelag.). HEFELE II[2] 104 ff. HEFELE-LECLERCQ II, 168 ff. F. WÖRTER, Der Pelagianismus nach s. Ursprung u. s. Lehre, [2]1874. F. KLA-SEN, Die innere Entwicklung des Pelagianismus, 1882. F. LOOFS, Pelagius u. der pelag. Streit, RE XV, 747/74; XXIV, 310/22. R. HEDDE et F. AMANN, Pélagianisme, DictThC XII, 675/715. E. DINKLER, Pelagius, RE Pauly-Wissowa XIX, 226/42. H. ZIMMER, Pelagius in Irland, 1901. P. BATIFFOL, Le Catholicisme de S. Augustin, 2 vol. Paris 1920. E. JAUNCEY, The Doctrine

in the West, entirely unlike the ones heretofore known in the East. It involved the fields of Christian *anthropology* and *Soteriology* (§ 46, 2) and was known as Pelagianism, after **Pelagius**, a British monk, though not a priest. Pelagius came to Rome toward the end of the fourth century and succeeded in gaining the confidence and esteem of a large circle of pious persons. He was joined by another lay-monk, *Coelestius*, who had formerly been a lawyer. The two of them probably influenced by the theology of the Ambrosiaster, denied original sin and held that the will of man could be strengthened by ascetical practices so that even after the fall man was fully capable of performing good works and of achieving sinlessness (impeccantia). Pelagius proposed these views in his commentaries on the Epistles of St. Paul (except to the Hebrews). This work, later revised, was circulated as the work of St. Jerome; but the original text has been preserved in a manuscript of the monastery of Reichenau. When the Visigoths invaded Rome in 410, Pelagius went to Carthage, where his doctrine met with strong opposition. Pelagius then left Carthage and went to Palestine. Coelestius endeavored to be ordained priest; but the Deacon Paulinus of Milan, who had also gone to Africa, accused him of heresy and when Coelestius refused to retract he was excommunicated by a synod at *Carthage* in 411. He was accused of teaching seven erroneus propositions regarding *original sin* and the natural *capacity* of man to perform good works. The principal errors are contained in the first and fifth propositions: I. Adam was created mortal and would have died even if he had not sinned; V. Man can live without sin and easily observe all the commandments of God.

The other propositions merely support and explain these two. They are: II. The sin of Adam affected him alone and not other members of the human race. III. New-born children are in the same state in which Adam was before

---

of Grace (to 431), London 1925. J. GROSS, La divinisation du chrétien d'après les Pères grecs, Paris 1938. N. MERLIN, S. Augustin et les dogmes du péché originel et de la grâce, Paris 1931. A. GUZZO, Agostino contro Pelagio, Torino ²1934. K. ADAM, Festgabe A. Ehrhard, 1922, 1/23 (Causa finita est); also in Ges. Aufsätze, 1936, 216/36. J. CHAPMAN, Studies on the Early Papacy, London 1928, 133/83 (condemnation of Pelagianism). A. J. SMITH, JThSt 1929, 21/32 (Pelagius and Augustine). K. MÜLLER, Nachr. Göttingen 1931, 113/16 (Pelagius, a native of Ireland). K. JANSSEN, Die Entstehung der Gnadenlehre Augustins, 1936. PH. PLATZ, Der Römerbrief in der Gnadenlehre Augustins, 1937. J. RIVIÈRE, RHE 1946, 1/43 (the Pelagian concept of Redemption not heterodox). G. BARDY, BullLE 1948, 3/20 (Greeks and Latins in the first Pelagian controversy). A. BRUCKNER, Julian v. Eclanum, TU XV, 3, 1897; Die 4 Bücher Julians v. Aeclanum an Turbantius, 1910. A. LEPKA, RHE 1931, 573/79 (Marius Mercator vs. Julian).

the fall. IV. The whole human race does not die as a result of Adam's fall any more than the whole race rises as the result of Christ's resurrection (Children who die without baptism attain "eternal life." At least Marius Mercator said that Pelagius taught such a doctrine). VI. The Law, as well as the Gospel, leads to the Kingdom of Heaven. VII. Before the coming of Christ there were men who lived without sin. — Pelagius' ideas remained in the realm of the purely *natural*. They were a superficial, rationalized *moralism*. They denied to man an internal, enlightening and strengthening supernatural grace and hence denied a specific difference between pagan (natural) and Christian (supernatural) morality. The Redemption by Christ loses its essential meaning and the Sacrament of Baptism is a mere empty ceremony.

2. Immediately after the synod of 411 had rejected the erroneous doctrines of Pelagius, **Augustine** began to analyze the teaching scientifically. The great Bishop of Hippo (§ 76, 3) to whom an admiring posterity gave the title *"Doctor Gratiae"*, studied the question of sin and grace more thoroughly than any other theologian and thereafter devoted the exceptional powers of his mind and the experiences of his own heart to the settlement of the controversy.

In 412 he wrote the work De peccatorum meritis et remissione et de baptismo parvulorum, in which he refutes the teaching that Adam's sin affected his descendants only by imitation and not by propagation. He pointed out that according to the Scriptures, all men, with the single exception of Christ, are sinners, since no one observes the commandments perfectly and that in spite of the grace of God and the exercise of free will. In the work De spiritu et littera, written toward the end of 412, he showed that *grace* consists not only in the external fulfillment of the Law, as the Pelagians said, but in an inner *sanctification of the will*. And in the work De natura et gratia written in 415, Augustine attacked the now-lost work of Pelagius, De Natura. Herein he shows that for justification, man not only needs the means of grace, since by the sin of Adam he lost his original strength and innocence, but that grace itself is not dependent on man's merits, but is a free gift of God (non meritis, sed gratis), therefore *unmerited*.

3. While the African Church was thus engaged in detecting and refuting the errors of Pelagianism, the heretics had been able by denial and subterfuge to conceal the real consequences of their teaching and to soften the attacks that were being made upon them. The strained relations between East and West aided the cause of the heretics. Moreover, the influence of Socratic-Platonic ethics in the conflict with Gnostic-Manicheistic Dualism had caused the Greek ecclesiastics to stress free will and moral conduct over divine grace; thus they were not in a position to see the consequences of Pelagianism as the Westerners saw it. *St. Jerome* at Bethlehem (§ 76, 2) came out strongly against the heresy; but the diocesan synod of *Jerusalem* (§ 51, 2) under the presidency of Bishop *John*,

at which the priest Orosius, a disciple of Augustine, denounced the heresy, ended without rendering a verdict. The synod of *Diospolis* (Lydda) in December 415, called to hear the complaints of Bishops Heros and Lazarus, who had been expelled from Gaul after being deceived by Pelagius, ended by declaring him orthodox. In a letter to Augustine (Ep. 143, 2), Jerome complains bitterly about this synod and calls it "miserabilis synodus". When the news of these proceedings in the East had reached the West, two provincial synods at *Carthage* and *Mileve* in 416, condemned Pelagius and Coelestius and petitioned Pope *Innocent I* (402—417) to confirm the decisions. When the answer arrived, Augustine preached a sermon (Sermo 131, 10) in which he said: A rescript has been received from the Apostolic See. This settles the matter" *(Causa finita est)*. He thereby declared his conviction that the teaching authority of Rome definitely settled any dispute in matters of faith. In his sermon he went on to say: "Utinam aliquando finiatur error!" But this wish was not granted. Pope *Zozimus* (417—418), a Greek by birth, was approached by Pelagius and Coelestius, who succeeded in convincing him that they admitted the means of grace and that the Africans had been unjust in their condemnation. In May 418, the African Bishops again met at *Carthage* and again thoroughly examined the teachings of Pelagius with the same adverse conclusions. In the same year, Augustine wrote De gratia Christi et de peccato originali, in which he proved that Pelagius understood by grace only the Law, the teaching and example of Christ as an enlightenment to the human mind as to how the commandments were to be observed and not as an infusion of charity or a movement of the will (gratia interna) to fulfill the Law of God.

4. Pope Zozimus saw that he had been deceived. In May 418, he issued an encyclical (Epistola tractoria) in which he demanded that all bishops accept the decision of the Africans and condemn Pelagianism. The letter was obeyed by most bishops and the 18 Italian bishops who refused to abide by it were banished by Emperor Honorius in 419. As usual, there were repercussions. Bishop **Julian** of Eclanum in Apulia, one of the bishops who had objected to the Epistola tractoria, and a strong supporter of Pelagius, objected that Augustine's idea of original sin undermined morality and made marriage the immoral relation which the Manicheans conceived it to be. From then on the dispute was chiefly concerned with *original*

*sin* and *concupiscence*. Augustine defended his views (419—420) in his work De nuptiis et concupiscentia and continued to write on the same subject until his death on August 28, 430. He never completed the last work he undertook against Julian, hence it is called Contra Julianum opus imperfectum. Some of the Pelagians who were banished from the West were received with open arms by Theodore of Mopsuestia and Nestorius (§ 54, 1. 2). *Marius Mercator*, a friend of St. Augustine, and presumably an African, wrote his Commonitoria (429—431) most probably in a Thracian monastery. In 429 or 430 Emperor Theodosius II expelled all Pelagians from Constantinople. At the General Council of *Ephesus* in 431, the heresy was proposed for discussion. But beyond condemning it in canons 1 and 4, the decisions of the West were accepted.

# § 57.
## Augustine's Theory of Predestination. Semipelagianism[1].

1. The concepts of *St. Augustine* on grace and election underwent important changes in the course of his intensive study. Most worthy of note is his idea regarding *predestination*. Before he became bishop (i. e. before 396) he ascribed to God a *universal* salvific will and explained the fact that some men believe while others do not, by saying that this was due to their *will* to believe or their refusal to do so. Later, however, in a work addressed to Bishop Simplicianus of Milan (396—397) after he had studied more thoroughly the Epistle to the Romans, and had become more convinced of the

---

[1] E. PORTALIÉ, Augustinisme, DictThC I, 2501/61. J. SAINT-MARTIN, Prédestination, ib. XII, 2832/96. O. ROTTMANNER, Der Augustinismus, 1892. K. KOLB, Menschl. Freiheit u. göttl. Vorherwissen nach Augustin 1908. J. MAUSBACH, Die Ethik Augustins, 2 vols. 1909, ²1929. P. BATIFFOL, N. MERLIN, PH. PLATZ, § 56. A. CASAMASSA, Il pensiero di San Agostino nel 396/97. Roma 1919. T. SALGUEIRO, La doctrine de S. Augustin sur la grâce d'après le traité à Simplicien (396/97), Diss. Strassb. 1925. K. RAHNER, ZkTh 1938, 171/96 (Augustine and Semipelagianism). HEFELE II², 597 ff. 724 ff. HEFELE-LECLERCQ II, 908 ff. 1085 ff. F. LOOFS, Semipelagianismus, RE XVIII, 192/203; XXIV, 500 f. E. AMANN, Semi-pélagiens, DictThC XIV, 1796/1850. F. WÖRTER, Beiträge zur DG. des Semipel., 1898; Zur DG. des Semipel., 1899. J. CHÉNÉ, RechSR 1948, 566/88 (Initium fidei in Semipelagianism). A. HOCH, Lehre des Joh. Cassianus von Natur u. Gnade, 1895. M. JACQUIN, RHE 1904, 265 ff. 725 ff.; 1906, 169 ff. (the question of predestination in the fifth and sixth centuries. M. CAPPUYNS, RevBén 1927, 198/226 (Prosper the author of De vocatione gentium); RechThAM 1929, 309/37 (the Augustinism of Prosper); 1934, 121/42 (the capitula of Orange 529). P. PELLAND, S. Prosperi Aquitani doctrina de praedestinatione, Montreal 1936. J. GAIDIOZ, RevSR 1949, 270 ff. (Prosper and the letter to Flavian). G. FRITZ, DictThC XI, 1087/1103 (Synod of Orange). J. ERNST, ZkTh 1906, 650/70 (dogmatic force of the decrees of Orange).

omnipotence of the Divine Will, he expressed himself as being persuaded that God's will to save is a *particular* and not a universal will. The difference between the believer and the unbeliever, between the good and the bad, between the saved and the lost is to be ascribed, he said, to the *Divine* Will in their regard. In his later works Augustine taught that by Adam's sin the whole human race had become a massa perditionis. However, from all eternity and without any regard to their personal merits, God willed to be merciful to a certain number of the human race (certi) and elected them to salvation, while the others (ceteri) were committed to eternal perdition. Since the ceteri are guilty and no man has a claim to God's grace, His action in no wise offends against justice. The *irresistible* power of God's grace renders the elect immune to temptation and the final grace of *perseverance* (donum perseverantiae), which Augustine taught after 426, makes the salvation of the elect infallible. The non-elect, the reprobate, because they lack the necessary grace, are hopelessly lost. There can be no talk of a universal salvific will, since God is omnipotent and if He willed the salvation of all men, all men would be saved.

Augustine realized that his theory ran counter to 1 Tim 2:4: "Who will have all men to be saved," and he sought in a forced exegesis of this passage (De corrept. et gratia 14, 44; 15, 47; Enchir. 103, 27; Ep. 217, 6. 19) to justify his stand. He explained the passage as meaning: all who are saved, are saved because God wills it; or, God wills to save men of various classes: reges, privatos, nobiles, ignobiles; or, God desires that we wish all men to be saved. — Augustine never uses the term *gratia irrestibilis*, but he uses similar expressions when he speaks of voluntas Dei efficacissima, semper invicta (Enchir. 95, 102), of (voluntatem humanam) divina gratia indeclinabiliter et insuperabiliter agi, and Deo donante invictissime velle (De corrept. et gratia 12, 38).

2. These extreme ideas of Augustine, and "Augustinism" only in the narrower sense of the word, were attacked not only by Pelagius, but even by opponents of Pelagianism as being contrary to the *freedom* of the human *will* and as destructive of the Christian teaching that all men should strive to be virtuous and that sinners should be converted. The first attack came from the monastery at *Hadrumetum*. Augustine then wrote two works, De gratia et libero arbitrio and De correptione et gratia for the instruction of the monks; but these works occasioned a new controversy.

The monks of *Marseilles* and Lérins headed by Abbot John *Cassian* of St. Victor, who had organized monasticism in southern Gaul (§ 72, 6) objected to the stress which Augustine placed on predestination. They wished to take the via media between the Pelagian concept of grace which they repudiated and the more mature teachings of St. Augustine. They believed Augustine's teaching to be contrary to Scripture and gravely dangerous to morals since it led logically to fatalism. Cassian (Collat. Patrum XIII, 7) calls Augustine's notions 'ingens sacrilegium.' The Massilians, therefore, taught that *predestination* does not depend on the mere will of God, but rather on God's foreknowledge. That is, He elects to salvation those whom He foresees will make themselves worthy of it. Hence predestination is conditioned (praevisis meritis) and not absolute; but it is the will of God that all men be saved. However, the Massilians made the mistake of teaching that the initium fidei, the first step toward salvation, is man's own work. (Before 396 Augustine held the same notion, but later revised it; and a certain Vitalis of Carthage taught this idea — Ep. 217). However, they admitted that the work could not be perfected without grace. Furthermore, they held that a life of faith is a matter of individual will and the just do not need the gift of final *perseverance* to be saved. During the controversy over Molinism toward the end of the sixteenth century, the teaching of the Massilians was incorrectly referred to as *Semipelagianism*. Older writers speak only of the doctrine of the Massilians or Galli.

3. Augustine defended himself in the works De praedestinatione sanctorum and De dono perseverantiae (428—429). After his death which occurred on August 28, 430, his great admirer, *Prosper* of Aquitaine and his friend *Hilary*, both of them laymen, who had kept Augustine informed of the progress of the quarrel in Gaul, continued to defend Augustine against misinterpretation. In order to soften Augustine's teaching on predestination, *Prosper* (§ 463) began to stress God's foreknowledge of man's demerits. And the author of the work, De vocatione omnium gentium (written about 450, probably by Prosper himself), although in all else a follower of Augustine, expressly maintains the universal salvific will of God. At the request of Prosper and Hilary, who went to Rome, Pope *Celestine I* (422—432), wrote to the bishops of Gaul (431) praising Augustine as a "man of holy memory" who had been recognized by the popes as "among the best teachers." The pope also gave attention to combatting Pelagianism in the British Isles where it had been introduced by the disciples of Pelagius. Various forms of *Semipelagianism* continued to manifest themselves for another century.

The priest, **Vincent** of Lérins († 450), espoused a **Semipelagian** doctrine of grace in the Commonitorium adv. haereses (434). In the second chapter there is an excellent statement of the Catholic principle of authority and tradition: Magnopere curandum est, ut id teneamus, quod ubique, quod semper, quod ab omnibus creditum est; haec est enim vere proprieque catholicum. But for the rest, the work does not show much theological skill and throughout Vincent rather slyly criticizes Augustine and his Gallic friends. **Arnobius the Younger**, an African, who became a monk at Rome, wrote in the spirit of Vincent. He is probably the author of an anonymous pamphlet *Praedestinatus* which gives a distorted idea of Augustine's theory of predestination and a history of heresies based on Augustine's De haeresibus. The synods of Arles and Lyons about 473 also favored Semipelagianism. They condemned the priest *Lucidus* whose exaggerated Augustinism went so far as to deny the freedom of the will and to assert a positive predestination to damnation. The synods commissioned the highly esteemed Bishop **Faustus** of Riez (Reji) in the Provence, formerly abbot of Lérins, to present systematically the teachings of the Gallic theologians in his work De gratia, for which he was vehemently attacked by Augustine's followers. The Scythian monks who had supported the Theopaschite Creed (§ 58, 2) for several decades at Constantinople and Rome endeavored since 519 to induce Pope *Hormisdas* to condemn Faustus and his followers as 'inimici gratiae'. In general, Rome favored Augustine, but withheld a decision in the matter. However, the Scythians found allies in Bishop **Fulgentius** of Ruspe (§ 78,1) and other African bishops who had been driven out of Africa by Thrasamund, King of the Vandals (§ 43, 6) and were living in Sardinia. In an Epistola synodica they expressed their opposition to Faustus; and Fulgentius, a skillful theologian and an ardent supporter of Augustine's doctrine of grace, undertook a refutation of Semipelagianism in his work, De veritate praedestinationis et gratiae Dei and in his seven books Contra Faustum, now lost.— *Vincentius* of Lérins: PL 53.Commonitorium, ed. A. Jülicher, ²1925; ed. G. Rauschen, 1906 (Floril. patrist. 5); German in BKV 20. — F. Brunetière et P. de Labriolle, S. Vincent de Lérins, Paris 1906. — J. Madoz S.J., El concepto de la tradicion en S. Vicente de Lerins, Rome 1933.—Excerpta Vincentii Lirinensis, Madrid 1940; Gregorianum 1940, 75/94 (anti-Nestorian attitude of Vincent.). — A. d'Alès, RechSR 1936, 334/56 (on the Commonitorium). — *Arnobius* junior: PL 53. — H. Kayser, Die Schriften des sog. Arn. iunior, 1912. — G. Morin, Études textes etc. I, Maredsous 1913, 309/439; RevSR 1936, 177/84 (Arnobius an African). — H. v. Schubert, Der sog. Praedestinatus, TU 24, 4, 1903. — E. Amann, Art. Praedestinatus, DictThC XII, 2775/80. — *Faustus* of Reji: PL 58; better in CSEL 21, 1891. — J. Huhn, ThQ 1950, 176/83 (De ratione fidei a work of Faustus). — Monogr. by A. Koch, 1895; G. Weigel, Philadelphia 1938.— G. Morin, ZntW 1935, 92/115 (sermons of faustus). — A. G. Elg, In Faustum Reiensem studia, Upsala 1937. — Literature on *Fulgentius* of Ruspe § 78, 1.

4. Semipelagianism prevailed among the theologians of southern Gaul for a long time; but during the sixth century there was a gradual reaction against it, thanks to the zeal of Archbishop **Caesar** of Arles (§ 78, 4). Although he had been educated at the monastery

of Lérins, he showed himself "a cautious representative of genuine Augustinian thought" (F. Loofs). In opposition to the Semipelagian decisions of the synod of *Valence* (528), Caesar with 13 other bishops and 8 princes, held an important synod at **Orange** in July 529 (Conc. Arausicanum II). On the basis of capitula which had been sent from Rome and which were taken largely from Prosper, the synod in 25 canons rejected both Pelagianism and Semipelagianism and declared for a *modified form of Augustinism.* The incapability of the natural man to perform supernaturally goods works, the absolute necessity of grace even for the initium fidei and for perseverance in doing good to the end and the impossibility of meriting grace (ex condigno) were defined, while the particular salvific will and the unconditional predestination ad malum were rejected. Pope *Boniface II* (530—532) confirmed the decision which was soon accepted throughout the Catholic Church, thus bringing to a close the first great controversy in the West.

## § 58.

### Theopaschitism — Monophysitism — Origenism — The Three Chapters — The Fifth General Council at Constantinople 553[1].

1. During the reign of **Emperor Justinian I** (527—565) the Byzantine Empire once more witnessed days of splendor and glory. It

---

[1] Cfr. general literature preceding § 41, especially Histoire de l'Église, publ. p. A. FLICHE et V. MARTIN, vol. IV—V; The Cambridge Medieval History I—II; CH. DIEHL et G. MARÇAIS, Le monde oriental 395—1081; F. HEILER, Die kath. Kirche des Ostens u. Westens I; E. CASPAR, Gesch. des Papsttums II; J. HALLER, Das Papsttum I. Ferner: J. B. BURY, History of the Later Roman Empire from Arcadius to Irene (395—800), 2 vol. London 1889; History of the Later Roman Empire (395—565), 2 vol. London 1923. K. ROTH, Gesch. des byzant. Reiches, [2]1919. H. GELZER, Abriß der byzant. Kaisergesch., in K. Krumbachers Gesch. der byzant. Lit., [2]1897, 919/60; Byzant. Kulturgesch., 1909. CH. DIEHL, Histoire de l'Empire byzantin, Paris [12]1934; Choses et gens de Byzance, Paris 1926. N. H. BAYNES, The Byzantine Empire, London 1926. A. A. VASILIEV, History of the Byzantine Empire 324—1453, Madison, Wis., 1952. N. JORGA, Hist. de la vie byzantine (527—1453), 3 vol. Bukarest 1934. E. GERLAND, Das Studium der byzant. Gesch. vom Humanismus bis zur Jetztzeit, 1934. E. HONIGMANN, Die Ostgrenze des byzant. Reiches von 363—1071, Bruxellis 1935. F. DÖLGER, ZKG 1937, 1/42 (Rome in the intellectual world of the Byzantines). O. TREITINGER, Die oström. Kaiser- u. Reichsidee nach ihrer Gestaltung im höfischen Zeremoniell, 1938. W. ENSSLIN, Gottkaiser u. Kaiser v. Gottes Gnaden, Sb. München 1943. IR. HAUSHERR, Die großen Linien der morgenländ. religiösen Geistigkeit, 1939. J. PARGOIRE, L'Église byzantine (527—847), Paris [3]1923. W. H. HUTTON, The Church of the Sixth Century, London 1897. L. DUCHESNE, L'Église au VIe siècle, Paris 1925. S. H. SCOTT, The Eastern Churches and the Papacy (to Photius), London 1928. G. CRONT,

was Justinian's aim to rebuild a world empire on the foundation of a unified Christianity. It was this aim that motivated him in his victorious wars with the Vandals and Ostrogoths (§ 43, 3. 6), in his attempts to eradicate paganism (§ 41, 6) and heresy (see nos. 5 and 6 below; also § 55, 5), in his gigantic work of codifying the law (Corpus juris civilis § 2, 4), in his untiring efforts to organize State and Church and finally in building numerous churches, especially at Constantinople (Hagia Sophia) and Ravenna (§ 71, 1. 2). Seldom has a ruler done so much for religion and the Church as did Justinian. But he ruled the Church according to his principle: Regis voluntas, suprema lex, and even the pope was expected to submit to the imperial will. For although he recognized the pope's primacy over the whole Church in theory, he often rendered it ineffective in practice (§ 64, 1). Hence it is not too much to say that his reign marked the classical epoch of Byzantine *Caesaropapism*. As theocratic ruler and protector of orthodoxy, Justinian felt himself justified and obliged to regulate dogma and ecclesiastical discipline and thus make them serve the welfare of the State. He took a lively interest in questions of faith, even wrote on theological subjects and presided in person at religious assemblies. His interference in religious controversies occasioned new and disastrous disorders in the Empire and he failed in the task he had set for himself of reconciling the Monophysites with the Church.

2. **Theopaschitism** was being warmly debated when Justinian ascended the throne. It was probably Bishop Proclus of Constantinople († 446) who

La lutte contre l'hérésie en Orient jusqu'au IXᵉ siècle, Paris 1933. K. VOIGT, Staat u. Kirche von Konstantin d. Gr. bis z. Ende der Karolingerzeit, 1936, 44/113. R. M. HAACKE, Rom u. die Cäsaren, 1947. CH. DIEHL, Justinien et la civilisation byzantine au VIᵉ siècle, Paris 1901; Theodora, Impératrice de Byzance, Paris 1937. W. G. HOLMES, The Age of Justinian and Theodora, 2 vol. London ²1912. E. GRUPE, Justinian, 1923. H. STADELMANN, Theodora v. Byzanz, 2 vols. 1926. G. P. BAKER, Justinian, London 1932. W. SCHUBART, Just. u. Theodora, 1943. Art. Justinian von M. JUGIE, DictThC VIII, 2277/90; H. LECLERCQ, DictAC VIII, 506—604. Justinian's theological writings in PG 86, 1 and PL 69. ED. SCHWARTZ, Drei dogmat. Schriften Justinians, Abh. München N. F. 18, 1939. A. KNECHT, Die Religionspolitik Kaiser Justinians, 1896; System des Justinian. Kirchenvermögensrechtes, 1905. G. PFANNMÜLLER, Die kirchl. Gesetzgebung Justinians, 1902. H. S. ALIVISATOS, Die kirchl. Gesetzgebung Justinians, 1913; also in Atti del congresso internazionale del diritto romano II, Rome 1933, 79/87. G. GLAIZOLLE, Un empereur théologien, Thèse Lyon 1905. P. BATIFFOL, RechSR 1926, 193/264 (Justinian and the Apostolic See). W. SCHUBART, Antike 1935, 255/73 (Justinian's Corpus iuris). B. BIONDI, Giustiniano I principe e legislatore cattolico, Milano 1936; also D. LINDNER, ThRev 1936, 325/9. C. HOHENLOHE, Einfluß des Christentums auf das Corp. iuris civ., 1936. J. CROCE, Textus selecti ex operibus commentatorum Byzantinorum iuris ecclesiastici, Rome 1939.

introduced the *Trisagion* (ἅγιος ὁ θεός, ἅγιος ἰσχυρός, ἅγιος ἀθάνατος, ἐλέησον ἡμᾶς) into the Greek liturgy. About 470 the Monophysite Peter Fullo of Antioch added to this the words "who was crucified for us" (ὁ σταυρωθεὶς δι᾽ ἡμᾶς). Emperor Anastasius I (491—518) ordered that the additional words be used at the liturgical services in the capital city, which occasioned great dissatisfaction among the people. In 519 a number of Scythian (i. e. Gothic) monks under the leadership of *John Maxentius* and *Leontius* (§ 77, 2) came to Constantinople and demanded that there be added to the Trisagion the words "one of the Trinity suffered for us in the flesh" (ἕνα τῆς ἁγίας τριάδος πεπονθέναι σαρκί). This group known as **Theopaschites** endeavored thus to oppose the Nestorian tendencies of some bishops. Because of the communicatio idiomatum the formula in itself was correct. But because of its too ready acceptance by the Monophysites and especially because it was an innovation, many were scandalized at its use in the liturgy. The Roman legates at Constantinople declared it to be dangerous. The same monks who had invaded Constantinople went to Rome the same year (519), but Pope *Hormisdas* refused to give a decision. The noted monk Dionysius Exiguus (§ 78, 2), then in Rome, and himself a Scythian, lent a sympathetic ear to his countrymen. It was probably at this time that the learned statesman and lay-theologian Boëthius (§ 78, 2), wrote his treatise on the Trinity. Opinion regarding the formula began to change. *Justinian* approved it because it seemed to make easier the union of the Monophysite party of the *Severians* (§ 55, 5). In 533 he summoned a *conference at Constantinople* to arrange for the reconciliation of this group, but the conference proved a failure. At Justinian's request, Pope *John II* (533—535) approved the formula in 534 and later it was approved by the Fifth General Council in 553. — Libelli Johannis Maxentii in *Ed. Schwartz*, Acta concil. oecum, t. IV vol. II, 3/62. — B. *Marx*, Procliana, 1940 (80 homilies of Proclus among the homilies of Chrysostom). — G. *Krüger*, Theopaschiten, RE XIX, 658/62. — V. Schurr, Die Trinitätslehre des Boethius im Lichte der „skythischen Kontroversen", 1935, 108 ff.

3. Orthodoxy was even more seriously threatened from another side. The Empress *Theodora* († 548), Justinian's shrewd and energetic wife, was secretly devoted to Monophysitism, which she believed promoted piety. She succeeded in elevating to the see of Constantinople (535) Bishop *Anthimus* of Trebizond (the ancient Trapezus), who was also covertly a Monophysite. But when Pope *Agapetus* (535—536) appeared in Constantinople, Anthimus was obliged to resign and the patriarchal see was given to the orthodox *Mennas* (536). Agapetus died suddenly while a guest in the imperial palace (April, 536) and the designing empress now sought to plant Monophysitism in Rome where under the protection of the papacy it would become the world-religion. The ambitious and avaricious Roman deacon, **Vigilius** then apocrisiarius, or papal legate, at the Byzantine court, fell in with the empress' plans. Because Pope *Silverius* (536—537) had been friendly to the Goths, General Belisarius, who took Rome in 536, caused Silverius to be banished (537) and Vigilius was set up as antipope. (Cfr. P. Hildebrand, HJG 1922, 213/49; O. Bertolini, ArchSRom 1924, 325/43). Silverius soon died in exile on the island of Pontia (December, 537), after which Vigilius was generally

recognized as legitimate pope. However, he never declared in favor of Mono-physitism, one reason being the hostile attitude of the West toward the doctrine. In writing to the emperor and the Patriarch Mennas, Vigilius expressly asserted his firm adherence to Chalcedon (540). But all during Justinian's reign, Monophysitism played an important rôle in the East. Toward the end of his life, the emperor seems to have favored the heresy of the *Aphthardocetae* (§ 55, 5). (Cfr. F. Loofs, Harnack-Ehrung, 1921, 232/48; M. Janin, Échos d'Orient 1932, 399/402).

4. At the beginning of the sixth century, the monasteries of Palestine were again disturbed by **Origenism**[1], that is, the dispute over the orthodoxy of the man who had already occasioned so much serious dissension in the Church (§ 51). The new laura in the desert of Thecua (near Jericho) became a center of Origenists opposed by *St. Sabbas*, abbot of the old or great laura near Jerusalem and superior of all Palestinian monks. His efforts to have Justinian take action against Origen had no results. After Sabbas' death (532) the Origenists of Palestine became more powerful and their influence spread to other parts of the Empire. Two of their number, the learned monk, *Domitian* and Theodore *Askidas* were elevated (537) to the sees of Ancyra and Caesarea in Cappadocia. Soon, however, matters took a turn. The new Abbot-general, *Gelasius*, expelled more than 40 Origenists from the old laura. Both parties found support outside of Palestine; but for a time the Anti-Origenists or Sabbaites were victorious. They induced Patriarch *Ephraem* of Antioch to condemn Origenism, and Patriarch *Peter* of Jerusalem entered a complaint against the Origenists with the emperor in 542. Justinian now took action. In 542 he issued an *edict* in which nine sentences of Origen (from De principiis) were condemned and his name was added to the list of heretics which bishops and abbots were obliged to anathematize upon taking office. Thus Origen, the greatest theologian of the Greek Church, the son of a martyr and himself a confessor, was ranked with Sabellius, Arius and other heretics, and this in an age which was deploring the lack of theological fecundity and genuine piety. Since all the bishops of the empire, especially Mennas of Constantinople and Pope *Vigilius* of Rome (537—555) accepted the edict, this meant that Origen was being condemned in the most solemn manner three hundred years after his death.

5. The **quarrel over the Three Chapters**[2] was closely related to Origenism and affected the interests of the West and the papacy very

---

[1] Acta conciliorum oecumen., ed. ED. SCHWARTZ, t. III: Collectio Sabbaitica contra Acephalos et Origenistas, 1940. ED. SCHWARTZ, Kyrillos v. Skythopolis (lives of holy monks of the fifth and sixth centuries), TU 49, 2, 1939. F. DIEKAMP, Die origenist. Streitigkeiten im 6. Jh., 1899; HJG 1900, 743/57. G. BARDY, RechSR 1920, 224/52 (Origen's De principiis and Justinian). G. FRITZ u. A. D'ALÈS, Origénisme, § 39, 2.
[2] Acta concil. oecum., ed. ED. SCHWARTZ, t. IV vol. II, 1914; cf. t. I, vol. IV—V, 1922/6. Writings of the African theologians Facundus and Liberatus in PL 67 and 68; the Breviarium of the latter is best rendered in Acta concil. oecum. t. II vol. V, 1936, 98/141. Pelagius diaconus, In

deeply. In order to divert the emperor from further persecution of the Origenists and at the same time to take revenge on their opponents, the powerful court bishop *Theodore Askidas* (see above) directed imperial attention to other matters. The *Monophysites*, he told Justinian, could easily be reunited to the Church of the Empire if the leading theologians of the *Antiochian* School, so obnoxious to the Monophysites were condemned as Nestorians. Theodore, therefore, asked the emperor to condemn: 1. *Theodore* of Mopsuestia, his person and his works (§ 54, 1. 5; 75, 5); 2. The writings of *Theodoret* of Cyrus against Cyril and the Council of Ephesus (§ 54, 2; 55, 2; 75, 7); 3. The letter of the priest *Ibas*, later Bishop of Edessa (§ 54, 5; 55, 2) to Bishop Maris of Seleucia in which he defended Theodore and opposed the anathemas against Cyril. Justinian, proud of his theological knowledge, and eager to display it, accepted the suggestion and in 544 (543?) issued an *edict* which without prejudice to the Council of Chalcedon, condemned the *"Three Chapters"* (τρία κεφάλαια) and all who defended them.

There were indeed good and sufficient reasons for proceeding against the Three Chapters. For these partially falsified writings were in fact Nestorian and Theodore of Mopsuestia was the spiritual father of Nestorianism. At the religious conference at Constantinople (see above no. 2), the Severians had made the charge against Chalcedon that Theodoret and Ibas had been illicitly reinstated by the Council (§ 55, 2). But for the same reasons many Catholics saw in the condemnation of the Three Chapters a blow struck at the Fourth General Council which with the three preceding ones was considered a pillar of orthodoxy. Furthermore, the anathema touched the person of a man (Theodoret) who had died at peace with the Church and who had already been judged by God. Hence some considered such a sentence as exceeding human authority. In the West, too, there was a false notion that the letter of Ibas had been formally approved by Chalcedon.

6. The imperial decree against the Three Chapters, therefore, met with great dissatisfaction on all sides. An attempt to force its acceptance was bound to occasion conflict. But Justinian did not hesitate. The Oriental bishops, headed by the court patriarch *Mennas*, bowed, though somewhat reluctantly, to the imperial will. The Westerners were to be forced to do the same. The action of Pope *Vigilius* paved the way. By Justinian's order, he was brought to Constantinople to condemn the Three Chapters. In April, 548, more than a year after his arrival,

defensione trium capitulorum (554), ed. R. DEVREESSE, Studi e Testi 57, Rome 1932; also E. SLOOTS, De Diaken Pelagius en de verdediging der Drie Kapittels, Diss. Nijmegen 1936. HEFELE II², 787 ff. HEFELE-LECLERCQ II, 1182 ff.; III, 1 ff. J. PUNKES, P. Vigilius u. der Dreikapitelstreit, 1864. L. DUCHESNE, Vigile et Pélage, RQH 36, 1884, 369 ff.; 37, 1885, 579 ff. G. KRÜGER, Vigilius, RE XX, 633/40. E. AMANN, DictThC XV, 1868/924 (Trois Chapîtres); ib. 2994/3005 (Vigilius). R. DEVREESSE, RevSR 1931, 543/65 (beginnings of the quarrel over the Three Chapters); MélAH 1940, 143/66 (the African Church during the Byzantine occupation). ER. CASPAR, Gesch. des Papsttums II, 1933, 243 ff. W. PEWESIN, Imperium, Ecclesia universalis, Rom, Der Kampf der afrikan. Kirche um die Mitte des 6. Jahrh., in: Geistige Grundlagen röm. Kirchenpolitik, 1937, 3.

he presented his '*Judicatum*' in which he consented to the anathema of the Three Chapters, but expressly declared that he in no wise denied the full authority of Chalcedon. Yet this step created the greatest alarm in the West. It was looked upon as a triumph of Caesaropapism, an unlawful approval of Monophysitism and an implicit undermining of Chalcedon. The African bishops, who for some time had been acting rather independently of Rome, now met under the presidency of Bishop Reparatus of Carthage and declared Vigilius excluded from communion with the Church until he should do penance (550). Bishop *Facundus* of Hermiane and other African theologians (§ 78, 1; see also the sources given at the beginning of this section) began a sharp attack on Justinian's ecclesiastical policy and defended the Three Chapters. Under these circumstances, the pope and the emperor agreed in 550 that the only way in which the confusion could be composed was to summon a *general synod* and that until the synod met the matter was to remain in statu quo. But in 551, at the instigation of Theodore Askidas, Justinian issued *a new edict*, again condemning the Three Chapters. This led to a formal break between pope and emperor. In order to protect his person, Vigilius was obliged to seek refuge first in St. Peter's Church in Constantinople and later in the church of St. Euphemia at Chalcedon. He then proceeded to pronounce censure on Askidas, Mennas († 552) and their adherents. Since a council was considered of such great importance, it became necessary for the pope and emperor to discuss arrangements. But when no agreement could be reached, the council got under way without the pope's participation. It met during May and June of 553 under the presidency of Eutychius, the new patriarch of **Constantinople**. As was to be expected, it anathematized the Three Chapters and threatened excommunication on all, clerics and laics, who should defend them. The emperor also induced the assembled bishops, probably before the formal opening of the Council (Diekamp), to pronounce a final condemnation of *Origenism* in 15 anathemas. The condemnation also included *Didymus* of Alexandria (§ 75, 4) and *Evagrius Ponticus* (§ 75,6) because of their teaching regarding the preexistence of souls and the apocatastasis. Later generations have treated these theologians, especially Origen, more charitably.

7. In the meantime Vigilius through his deacon Pelagius presented another memorial on May 14, 553, called the 'Constitutum', in which he took the opposite position from that taken before, and strictly forbade the condemnation of the Three Chapters. In explaining his action, he gave the same reasons that the Westerners had advanced from the beginning (see above, no. 5). But Justinian was not to be contradicted. He refused to accept the Constitutum. And although he was not willing to break with the Apostolic See, he did order the Council to strike the pope's name from the diptychs because he wrongly maintained that Vigilius had shared in the godlessness of Nestorius and Theodore. Under extreme pressure, ill, and deprived of the presence of his counsellors, Vigilius yielded a second time. In December 553, he withdrew his Constitutum and approved the decisions of the Council of Constanti-

nople. In a second Constitutum, dated February 23, 554, the genuinity of which can not be doubted, he again explained his conduct. He was now permitted to return to Rome, but died on the way at Syracuse in June 555. His ambition and inconstancy had cost him dearly. However, succeeding popes, even his immediate successor Pelagius I (556—561), who as Roman deacon and secretary to Vigilius, had himself written bitterly against the condemnation of the Three Chapters, all recognized the synod of Constantinople as the *Fifth General Council*. But the rest of the Latin Church was not so easily brought into line. The authority and esteem of the pope had suffered; but the esteem of the emperor had suffered more. The *African* bishops submitted after a few years; but the ecclesiastical provinces of *Milan* and *Aquileia* separated completely from communion with Rome over the Three Chapters. The invasion of Italy by the Lombards in 568 (§ 43, 4) favored their schism since the emperor was unable to use force against them. It was only during the pontificate of Pope *Sergius I* (687—701) that the schism of Upper Italy was completely healed; although for a long time it was confined to a rather small group. Milan began to seek reunion after 570 and the region around Aquileja-Grado, which was still under Byzantine rule, was reunited about 607. It was at this time and as a result of the quarrel over the Three Chapters that the titular patriarchates of *Aquileia* and *Grado* came into being (§ 63, 3).

## § 59.

## Monotheletism
## and the Sixth General Council of Constantinople 680—681.
## The Synod in Trullo II 692[1].

1. In the beginning of the sixth century the Byzantine Empire was again seriously afflicted. The *Avars* and *Slavs* swarmed over the Balkans and threatened Constantinople, while the *Persians* devastated Syria and Egypt and invaded Asia Minor as far as the Bosphorus (Chalcedon). Emperor *Heraclius* (610—641) the courageous founder

---

[1] HEFELE III², 121/348; HEFELE-LECLERCQ III, 317/581. FR. DÖLGER, Regesten der Kaiserurkunden des oströmischen Reiches I (565—1025), 1924. OSTROGORSKY, § 41, 1. G. OWSEPIAN, Die Entstehungsgesch. des Monotheletismus, Diss. 1897. G. KRÜGER, Monotheleten, RE XIII, 401/13. M. JUGIE, Monothélétisme, DictThC X, 2307/23. G. FRITZ, Art. Quinisexte, Concile, DictThC XIII, 1581/97. L. DUCHESNE, L'Église au VIᵉ siècle, Paris 1925, 391/485. J. STIGLMAYR, Kath. 1908 II, 39/45 (Maximus Confessor and the two Anastasiuses). W. M. PEITZ, HJG 1917, 213 ff. 429 ff. (Martin I and Max. Confessor). A. JÜLICHER, Festgabe A. Harnack, 1921, 121/33 (chronology). V. GRUMEL, Échos d'Orient 1928, 6 ff. 257 ff.; 1929, 19 ff 272 ff.; 1930, 16 ff. (on the history of Monotheletism). J. MARIC, Pseudo-Dionysii formula de Christi activitate theandrica, Zagreb 1932 (from Bogoslovska Smotra 1932, 105/73). E. CASPAR, ZKG 1932, 75/137 (Lateran Synod of 649); Gesch. des Papsttums II, 530 ff. P. PEETERS, AB 1933, 225/62 (the Greek Vita Martini I); also R. DEVREESSE, ib. 1935, 49/80. See § 58 and 77, 2. 3 (Maximus Confessor and Sophronius).

of a new dynasty (610—717) succeeded after a nine-year campaign in subduing the Persians and recapturing the Cross of Christ (628—629). But toward the end of his reign he saw some of the most valuable provinces of the East surrender to the victorious armies of Islam (§ 45, 2). In spite of these difficulties, Heraclius became interested in new attempts to reunite the Monophysites of Syria and Egypt with the Church of the Empire and it appeared to the emperor that *Monotheletism* offered the best means. The question had arisen whether the Savior had a *twofold operation* (ἐνέργεια), that is, two principles of action and a *twofold will*, or only one principle of operation and *one* will. Chalcedon's definition (§ 55, 2) regarding two complete natures in Christ evidently demanded the admission of two wills. However, about 619 Patriarch **Sergius** of Constantinople (610—638) began to teach that, owing to the hypostatic union, there could be but *one will* and *one principle* of operation which was at the same time divine and human or theandric (The expression μία θεανδρικὴ is found in the fourth letter of the Pseudodionysius, § 77, 1). Cyrus of Phasis in Colchis, whom the emperor had elevated to the patriarchate of Alexandria (631) was soon persuaded to accept Sergius' views. By means of the Monotheleistic formula, Cyrus actually succeeded in reuniting the *Theodosians* (Severians) of Egypt with the Church of the Empire and the emperor's personal efforts to reunite the Monophysites of Armenia and Syria had achieved notable results.

2. In the meantime, however, the new doctrine was meeting determined opposition. The learned Palestinian monk *Sophronius* (§ 77, 3) attacked it as a revival of Monophysitism or Apollinarianism. When he became Patriarch of Jerusalem in 634, he issued the usual profession of faith in which he explained in detail the orthodox teaching of two wills. Faced with such opposition, Sergius agreed to abandon the use of the expression "one operation" although he still clung to the notion which seemed to be so acceptable to the Monophysites. By means of a shrewdly worded letter, he enlisted the support of Pope *Honorius I* (625—638). Unfortunately, Honorius, unskilled in speculation and with but little theological training, wrote two letters to Sergius in which he agreed that it would be advisable to refrain from objectionable expressions indicating one or two operations. He did not, however, explicitly approve the doctrine of one operation or one will (see below). Constantinople then took a further bold step. Heraclius issued as an

authoritative profession of faith the *Ecthesis* composed by Sergius (638) which intentionally disregarded the concept of one operation, but which stressed the *idea of one will* (ἐν θέλημα), a doctrine which had been taught by the Monophysite Patriarch Dioscurus of Alexandria (§ 55, 2). Most of the Oriental bishops accepted it; but the Western bishops, especially the susccessors of Honorius († 638), Severinus, John IV and Theodore I strenuously objected to it. Hence *Constans II* (641—668) the grandson of Heraclius, withdrew the Ecthesis and, at the instance of Patriarch *Paul* of Constantinople, issued (648) a new profession of faith — the *Typus* — which proved equally ineffectual in settling the quarrel. It forbade all controversy over one or two wills or operations and simply ordered that the old Creeds were to be regarded as the norm of faith. The threats of punishment contained in the new edict were by no means idle ones. In 649 Pope *Martin I* (649—653) held a synod in the Lateran which defined that there are "two natural wills and operations" in Christ, and pronounced excommunication on Sergius, Pyrrhus and Paul of Constantinople and Cyrus of Alexandria. Pope Martin, who was already in the emperor's bad graces for having received consecration without imperial assent (§ 60, 3) was now made to feel the full force of imperial wrath. He was taken prisoner, brought to Constantinople (653) where he was tried for "high treason", shamefully mistreated and banished to Cherson in the Crimea (654) where he died (September 16, 655, or possibly, not until April 13, 656). Other opponents of Monotheletism in the East were treated in similar fashion. The aged Abbot *Maximus* Confessor, Anastasius a monk, and another Anastasius, a Roman apocrisiarius, were first scourged, then had their tongues torn out and their right hands cut off, after which they were banished to Colchis, where Maximus died a martyr to orthodoxy in August 662.

3. Constans II was murdered at Syracuse in 668. His son and successor, *Constantine IV Pogonatus* (668—685) resorted to other means. After concluding a treaty with the Arabs and Avars in 678, he determined to summon a general council to restore unity in the Church and Empire, although at the time it appeared that Italy, too, would be lost to the Empire. Pope *Agatho* (678—681) was pleased at the suggestion of a Council and prepared the West to take part in it. He held a synod in the Lateran and sent legates to the East with letters clearly defining the doctrine of two wills

and two operations in Christ. The General Council, attended by about 170 bishops met from November 680 to September 681 in the great domed hall of the imperial palace (Τροῦλλος) and hence was called the Concilium Trullanum or in Trullo. From the beginning it was recognized as a *General* Council (the sixth) and succeeded fairly well in fulfilling the task that had been assigned to it. The stubborn defenders of Monotheletism, *Macarius* of Antioch, his disciple, the Abbot *Stephen* and others were deposed and excommunicated; the "originators and leaders of the Monothelistic heresy," Sergius, Pyrrhus, Paul and Peter of Constantinople and Cyrus of Alexandria were anathematized. The same sentence was also pronounced on *Honorius*, Bishop of Old Rome, because in his letter to Sergius, he adopted the latter's views and approved his godless teaching. The writings of all the above named were ordered to be burned as dangerous to the faith. A profession of faith was adopted which consisted in adding to the *Creed* of Chalcedon the words: "In keeping with the teachings of the Holy Fathers we confess two natural wills and two natural operations, undivided and unchanged, unseparated and unmixed (δύο φυσικὰς θελήσεις ἤτοι θελήματα . . . καὶ δύο φυσικὰς ἐνεργείας ἀδιαιρέτως, ἀτρέπτως, ἀμερίστως, ἀσυγχύτως), two wills, but not as if they were in opposition, but so that the human obeyed the divine and was subject to it[1]."

4. The case of Pope **Honorius** has long been the subject of much discussion. It was brought up at the Vatican Council as the principal objection to the declaration of papal infallibility as a dogma (Cfr. especially *C. J. Hefele*, Causa Honorii Papae, Naples 1870). Some scholars, following Baronius, have denied that the Sixth Council condemned Honorius; and maintain that a falsified copy of the acta substituted the name of Honorius for that of Patriarch Theodore of Constantinople. The expressions used by Honorius in the two letters to Sergius, which the synod condemned, can *not* be considered definitive or *official decisions*. Neither did he declare for *Monotheletism* or *Monergism*. This is seen from the following considerations: 1. Although, like Sergius, Honorius repeatedly appeals to the hypostatic union, he never goes so far as the latter and never draws the conclusion that there is but one will and one operation. 2. The expression, una voluntas, which he used once in agreeing with Sergius is, as the context shows, not to be understood in the physical, but only in the *moral* sense, that, is, it refers to the oneness of the will of Christ's complete human nature which always agreed with the divine will. Hence it implies rather that the pope believed in two wills. 3. Neither did Honorius accept the doctrine of two operations, as is clear from his second letter to Sergius, parts of which have been preserved. Here

---

[1] See FUNK I p. 165 for an English translation of this text.

as in the first letter, he agrees with Sergius that discussion about one or two operations should be abandoned as likely to cause objectionable innovations, but he then quotes from the Epistula dogmatica of Leo I and says that the two natures operate in the one Person of Christ, without commingling without division and without change, which is peculiar to these natures alone. Hence Constantinople was not justified in its condemnation of Honorius. Neither did Rome ever accept the condemnation as pronounced. It is true that Pope *Leo II* (682—683), who succeeded Agatho, wrote to Constantine Pogonatus and confirmed the decrees of the synod. But in referring to the guilt of Honorius, Leo gives it a much milder interpretation: Qui (Honorius) hanc apostolicam ecclesiam non apostolicae traditionis doctrina lustravit, sed profana pro traditione immaculatam fidem dari permittendo conatus est (i. e., permisit, equivalent to the Greek παρεχώρησε). In a letter to the Spanish bishops Leo wrote in a similar strain: Qui flammam haeretici dogmatis non, ut decuit apostolicam auctoritatem, incipientem extinxit, sed *neglegendo* confovit (Harduin, Acta concil. III, 1475, 1730). In the solemn profession of faith which the popes of the Middle Ages were for a long time obliged to take on the occasion of assuming office (Liber diurnus Romanorum Pontificum, ed. T. Sickel 1889, 100/2) Honorius is mentioned among the auctores novi haeretici dogmatis, as one qui pravis eorum adsertionibus *fomentum* impendit. At any rate, the guilt of his carelessness was considered so serious by Rome that he was mentioned along with heretics in the same, profession of faith. — Cfr. *Hefele* III², 145 ff. 289 ff.; *Hefele-Leclercq* III, 347/538. — *H. Grisar*, KL VI, 230/57; ZkTh 1887, 675 ff. — *B. Jungmann*, Diss. in hist. eccl. II, 1882, 382/458. — *J. Chapman*, The Condemnation of Pope Honorius, London 1907. — *W. Plannet*, Die Honoriusfrage auf dem Vat. Konzil, Diss. 1912. — *V. Crumel*, Échos d'Orient 1929, 272/82. — *K. Hirsch*, in Festschr. der 57. Versammlung deutscher Philologen und Schulmänner zu Salzburg, 1929, 158/79 (defense of Honorius). — *E. Amann* DictThC VII, 93/132. — *F. Cabrol*, DictApol II, 514/19. — *P. Galtier*, Gregorianum 1948, 42/61 (first letter of Honorius).

5. After the murder of Justinian II, the Usurper *Philippicus Bardanes* (711—713) attempted to revive Monotheletism and ordered a new synod in 712 to repudiate the decrees of the Sixth General Council. However, a year later Emperor *Anastasius II* (713—715) repealed the acts of his predecessor. From that time on, Monothelitism was held only by the *Maronites* on Lebanon and later on the island of Cyprus. This group derives it names from Maron a hermit and founder of a community of monks in the fourth or fifth century. According to the account of Archbishop William of Tyre, the historian of the first Crusade, a number (about 40,000) of the Maronites were reunited with the Church in 1181 and the remainder in 1445. These good people who have been able to retain their faith in spite of their Mohammedan masters, have come to believe in the course of time, that they never departed from strict orthodoxy and never, as a people, embraced Monotheletism. Unfortunately, the popular legend does not correspond with historical facts. On several occasions popes have felt it necessary to warn them not to fall back into heresy. — Cfr. Bullarium Maronitarum, ed. *T. Anaissi*, Rome 1911. — *P. Dib*, L'Église Maronite I, Paris 1930; the same in DictThC X, 1/142. — *K. Kessler*,

Maroniten, RE XII, 355/64. — *S. Vailhé*, Échos d'Orient 1900, 1901, 1906. — E. Drinkwelder, ZkTh 1912, 405/11. — G. Graf, Theol.-prakt. Monatsschr. 1917, 237/46. — *P. Raphael*, Le rôle des Maronites dans le retour des Églises orientales, Beyrouth 1935. — *J. B. Chabot*, Mémoires de l'Acad. des Inscriptions et Belles Lettres, Paris 1936, 1/19 (Vita of St. Maron apocryphal).

6. The Fifth and Sixth General Councils had considered questions of faith which had so absorbed time and attention that neither Council had passed disciplinary decrees. Emperor *Justinian II* (685—695 and 705—711), therefore, sought to supply this deficiency by another synod. It was held at **Constantinople** in 692 and its sessions were again conducted in the domed hall of the palace. Hence it has been called the Second **Synod in Trullo**. Because it met to supplement the two preceding Councils it is also often called Πενθέκτη or *Quinisextum* (concilium). It was intended to be an ecumenial council but actually took cognizance of Greek or Oriental conditions only; and in several of its 102 canons it shows a thinly disguised aversion or at times an open hostility toward the West. Thus, in canon 36 the precedence of the bishop of Constantinople is decreed, although the matter had been stricken from the canons (can. 28) of Chalcedon. In canon 13 the Western law of celibacy is rejected and priests and deacons are permitted to continue marital relations (§ 60, 6). Canon 55 forbids under penalties the Roman practice of fasting on Saturdays during Lent (§ 69, 1); canon 67 reinforces the ancient prohibition of using blood as food (Acts 15:29), while canon 82 forbids the practice, common in the West, of representing Christ as a lamb. It was evident that the Eastern Church was rapidly separating herself from the West. Pope *Sergius* (687 to 701), himself an Oriental by birth (Syrian) like several other popes of the period, steadfastly refused to sign the synodal acts. When the despotic emperor attempted to force him, the militia of Ravenna and neighboring domains came to the pope's aid and the emperor's men were obliged to flee from Rome. Justinian was overthrown in 695 but regained the throne in 705. The Greeks down to the present day hold the Quinisextum to be a General Council. The Latins, on the other, never recognized it as such, but constantly referred to it as the synodus erratica.

# CHAPTER III
## ECCLESIASTICAL ORGANIZATION[1]

### § 60.
### The Clergy. Training, Election, Maintenance and Qualifications of the Clergy[2].

1. The rapid spread of Christianity and the multiplication of congregations after the fourth century entailed many readjustments among the clergy. In the first place, the oldest or sometimes the most competent priest and deacon were given the titles respectively of *Archpriest* and *Archdeacon*. The former officiated at ecclesiastical functions in the bishop's absence; the latter assisted the bishop in his duties of supervision and administration. The office of archdeacon eventually became a most influential one so that very often, especially in Rome, the archdeacon succeeded the bishop. In the larger parishes of rural districts the archpriest held a unique position which will be described in § 62, 3.

Even greater changes were introduced among the *lower* clergy, although these changes were by no means uniform in all parts of the Empire. During the seventh or eighth century *Exorcists* and *Ostiarii* are less frequently mentioned in the East and the office of *Acolyte* seems never to have been introduced there. When infant baptism became the rule (§ 66, 1) there was no longer need for the services of *deaconesses*, although the office was retained in the Greek Church until the end of the seventh century. Synods of the fifth and sixth centuries abolished the office in Gaul and it seems to have disappeared elsewhere in the West during the course of the next few centuries. It is possible that the canonesses and other cloistered women (sanctimoniales) of the early

---

[1] Cfr. literature § 18; § 19 and § 58 (Justinian's ecclesiastical legislation). L. THOMASSINUS, Vetus et nova ecclesiae disciplina circa beneficia, 3 vol. Paris 1688. J. B. SÄGMÜLLER, Lehrb. des kath. Kirchenrechts I[4], 3—4, 1930/4 (extensive literature). B. KURTSCHEID, Historia Iuris canonici I: Hist. fontium et scientiae iuris can., Rome 1943. A. M. STICKLER, Hist. iuris can. I, Turin 1950. M. ROBERTI, Christianesimo e diritto Romano, Milan 1935. K. VOIGT, Staat u. Kirche von Konstantin d. Gr. bis z. Ende der Karolingerzeit, 1936 (valuable).

[2] M. ANDRIEU, RevSR 1925, 232/74 (the minor eccl. offices in the old Roman Ordo). B. FISCHER, ZkTh 1938, 37/75 (the lower clergy in the writings of Gregory the Great). AL. SCHEBLER, Die Reordinationen in der "altkath. Kirche" (with special reference to Sohms), 1936. B. BOTTE, RechThAM 1939, 223/41 (Ordination ritual of the Statuta Ecclesiae antiquae [cfr. § 65, 4]). A. HAUCK, Die Bischofswahlen unter den Merowingern, 1883. E. VACANDARD, Études de critique etc., Paris [5]1913, 123/87. H. V. SCHUBART, Staat u. Kirche in den arian. Königreichen u. im Reiche Chlodwigs, 1912. P. CLOCHÉ, Les élections épiscopales sous les Mérovingiens, Paris 1925. TH. MICHELS, Beiträge zur Gesch. des Bischofsweihtages im christl. Altert. u. MA., 1927. K. VOIGT, see above. G. BARDY, RHE 1939, 217/42 (ancestry of bishops in the first Christian centuries). J. A. EIDENSCHINK, The Election of Bishops in the Letters of Gregory the Gr., Wash. Cath. Univ., 1945. U. STUTZ, Gesch. des kirchl. Benefizialwesens I, 1895. A. PÖSCHL, Bischofsgut u. mensa episcopalis, 3 vols. 1908/12. E. LESNE, Hist. de la propriété ecclésiastique en France I—VI, Paris 1910/43.

Middle Ages or at least the abbesses were at one time looked upon as deaconesses.

A number of entirely *new ecclesiastical offices* were introduced, especially in the East. The *Cantors* (ψάλται, ψαλτῳδοι, cantores, confessores) were considered as constituting a distinct order, while other functions were performed by clerics in various orders or even by laymen. The *Hermeneutae* (interpreters) translated the Scriptures and the homily for the benefit of those not understanding the language used in the service; the *Parabolani* tended the sick; the *Copiatae* (fossores) buried the dead; the *Mansionarii* (custodes) acted as watchmen over church property; the *Syncelli* were the bishops' companions and advisers; the *Oeconomi* administered church property, and canon 26 of Chalcedon prescribed that every bishop appoint an oeconomus for his church. In the West, these officials were known as vicedomini and their duties were considered of great importance. The *defensores* (ἔκδικοι) attended to ecclesiastical trials, while the *notarii* (ὀξυγράφοι = exceptores) and the chartularii or *archivists* (χαρτοφύλαξες) drafted the official documents and filed them. The *apocrisiarii* (responsales, nuntii) were special representatives or business agents of patriarchs but especially the pope's representatives at the court of Constantinople, and, since the time of Pope Leo the Great, also at the Exarchate in Ravenna.

2. The manner of *training the clergy* described in § 19, 1 was generally followed. However, when Bishop *Eusebius* of Vercelli († 307) and *St. Augustine* introduced a form of common life among their clergy, they may be said to have instituted *seminaries* in which the younger clerics were more or less methodically instructed by the older and more experienced members of the community. Other bishops, especially *Caesar* of Arles, adopted the same plan. In Spain special institutions were established for the education of boys destined for the clerical state. In Italy, priests in rural districts took young clerics into their homes for day by day training in the duties of their state. This practice also spread. At the Synod of Vaison in 529, Caesar of Arles prescribed it for the entire province. Finally, many *monasteries*, like *Lérins* in southern Gaul, became training schools for the clergy and many of the most eminent bishops of the period received their training from the monks or at least had spent some time with them. (Cfr. *G. H. Hörle*, Frühmittelalterliche Mönchs- u. Klerikerbildung in Italien, 1914).

3. *Bishops continued to be chosen* as in the preceding period (§ 19,2), that is, the clergy and the people elected a candidate and the bishops of the province gave their approval. In the *East*, however, the participation of the people in the election of their bishop was soon limited. Justinian I (527—565) restricted the right to vote to the clergy and the nobility. They were permitted to propose three candidates and the metropolitan then had the privilege of naming the most worthy of the three. Later on the laity was entirely excluded from an episcopal election, and the right of nomination was reserved solely to the bishops of the province. In the case of the more important sees, especially in the *East*, the influence of the court played a large, often a decisive, part. From the time of Theodosius I, the incumbent of the see of Constantinople was invariably named by the emperor. After the fourth century,

various synods protested against bishops *designating* their own *successors*. When Pope *Felix III* (IV) (526—530) was dying, he named his Archdeacon, *Boniface*, a Romanized Goth (son of Sigiswult and the "first German pope") as his successor. And although he asked the approval of the Senate, the greater part of the Roman congregation proceeded to elect the Deacon *Dioscurus* as pope. The schism was of short duration, for Dioscurus died within a month and Boniface was generally recognized. Another attempt was made by Boniface II who in 531 named his Deacon, *Vigilius* (§ 58, 3), but he was obliged by the Ostrogoth ruler of Italy to withdraw his Constitutum as being contrary to the canons[1].

In the *West*, especially in the *Frankish* and *Visigothic kingdoms*, the *royal consent* was required before a bishop could be consecrated. The Synod of Orleans in 549 (canon 10) mentions this procedure as being of long standing. In the Merovingian Kingdom (§ 43, 8), in spite of repeated protests, the king very often simply appointed as bishop the man who was willing to pay the highest price for the office. Outside of the province of Rome, the influence of the pope in the election of bishops was scarcely felt. Yet under Gregory the Great the bishop of Milan, elected by the suffragans of that see, could not be consecrated until the pope had confirmed the election. Upon the death of Pope John I in 526, Theodoric the Great exerted his influence in the election of Felix III (IV) and from that time the *Ostrogoth* rulers claimed the right of approval. The *Byzantine* emperors claimed the same right since the pontificate of Pelagius I (556—561) and the reign of Justinian. But to obviate lengthy vacancies in the Roman See, Constantine Pogonatus in 684 permitted the imperial Exarch in Ravenna to give the approval — a privilege which the Exarch had been exercising in a measure even before 684.

4. Some of the clergy possessed a patrimony sufficient for their *support*, others were obliged to earn their livelihood. The latter group had the choice of a trade or agriculture. The privileges granted to the clergy under Constantine the Great made it possible for them to engage in commerce, but owing to abuses, Valentinian III (425—455) forbade clerics in the West to engage in business. But from the time (321) that Constantine permitted the Church to receive legacies, most congregations were richly or at least adequately *endowed*. According to Roman custom (Pope Gelasius 494) the income of cathedral churches was divided into *four parts*: one part for the bishop, one for the other clergy, one for the upkeep of the buildings and the costs of divine services, and one part for the relief of the poor. In Spain the income was divided three ways, and the usage varied in different parts of Gaul. At an early date even rural parishes had sources of income, and although the title of ownership of all ecclesiastical property was vested in the bishop, the parishes enjoyed a goodly share of the endowments. In Gaul and Spain, the rural parishes could claim at least one-third of the offerings of the faithful.

---

[1] K. HOLDER, Die Designation der Nachfolger durch die Päpste, 1892; AkKR 1894, 409 ff. J. B. SÄGMÜLLER, ThQ 1903, 235 ff. A. HARNACK, Sb. Berlin 1924, 24/42. E. CASPAR, Gesch. des Papsttums II, 1933, 194 ff.

5. A new *condition* for entrance into the *clerical state* was established in this period. It was required that the candidate be a *freeman*. A slave could not be ordained until his master had formally declared him free. The apostolic admonition (1 Tim. 3: 6) regarding the ordination of neophytes was extended by the Synod of Sardica in 343. Canon 10 decreed that a *layman* could not be advanced to the episcopacy without having proved himself by passing *some time* in each of the *lower orders*. It was forbidden under severe penalties for a cleric to return to the lay state or to assume a public office incompatible with the ecclesiastical vocation. Bishops, priests and deacons were obliged to remain in the service of the church for which they had been ordained. *Translation to another church* was *forbidden* by the canons of several synods, e. g., Arles 314 (canon 14), Nicaea (canon 15), Sardica (canon 1), Chalcedon (canon 5) and others. By way of exception, a cleric could transfer to another church if the apparent needs of the congregation demanded his special care. During the fifth century, the *tonsure* adopted from monasticism, came into use as the external badge of the clerical state. (cfr. *L. Ober*, Die Translation der Bischöfe im Altertum, AkKR 1908, 209 ff. et passim; 1909, 3 ff.; *P. Gobillot*, RHE 1925, 399/454 [The Tonsure]).

6. From the fourth century the East and West began to differ regarding a *married clergy*. The Synod of Elvira about 306 (§ 19, 5) forbade the higher clergy to marry and Leo the Great and Gregory the Great extended the prohibition to subdeacons. However, celibacy could not be enforced everywhere at once. According to the testimony of Pope Siricius (384—390) in the late fourth century there were still many married clerics in Spain where the prohibition was first given the force of law. And St. Ambrose (De offic. I, 50, written c. 391) says that in rural districts and small cities the majority of the clergy were married men. But with the enthusiastic support of all the leading churchmen of the West, especially men like Ambrose, Jerome and Augustine (§ 70, 3), *celibacy* was eventually made *obligatory* on all clerics in major orders. The Greek Church, however, retained its former practice which forbade deacons, priests and bishops to marry after ordination, but permitted those who had married before ordination to continue marital relations. The Council *of Nicaea* in 325 considered the enactment of a decree enforcing celibacy on the clergy of the Eastern Church, but refrained from doing so on the plea of the Egyptian Bishop *Paphnutius*, himself a celibate. However, a goodly number of the Eastern clerics voluntarily abstained from marriage and the bishops as a rule were chosen from among the unmarried. *Justinian I* passed a law that a married man could not be made bishop and this law is still strictly observed throughout the Greek Church. The *Quinisextum* of 692 (§ 59, 6) permitted married priests and deacons to live as married men (can. 13) but prescribed that bishops must separate from their wives (can. 12; 48). The same synod (can. 2) forbade a cleric to remarry after the death of his wife. A laxer discipline found acceptance among the *Nestorians*. Synodal decrees of 486 permitted priests to marry and in 497 the same privilege was extended to bishops. However in 544 a new law demanded that bishops must be celibate. (See § 19, 5 for bibliography).

In order to avoid scandal as well as possible occasion of sin, the Council of Nicaea (can. 3) decreed that an unmarried cleric might not keep in his house a female person (συνείσακτος, subintroducta) other than a close relative or one otherwise above suspicion. This decree was respected by later synods.

# § 61.
## Privileges of the Clergy[1].

1. Constantine the Great released Christian clerics from the obligation of holding civil office (munera civilia) so that they might devote themselves entirely to the duties of their state; and his son Constantius exempted them and their relatives from all assessments except the common tax. But since quite a few became clerics in order to enjoy these *immunities* and thus escape the duties incumbent on lay citizens, Constantine forbade *decurions* (municipal senators) and *wealthy* persons in general to become clerics. Later emperors, especially Theodosius I permitted decurions to receive orders only on condition that they renounce their property in favor of the whole Senate or one of its members and thus fulfill their obligations to the State. In *France*, ordination released a man from all military duty and wholly or partially from taxation. Hence the consent of the king was required for a man to enter the clerical state. An exception was made in favor of the sons of priests.

2. To the privilegium immunitatis there was soon added the *privilegium fori*. The Synod of Carthage in 397 (can. 9) decreed that clerics were to seek legal redress only in ecclesiastical courts and the Council of Chalcedon in 451 forbade (can. 9) recourse to the civil court if both of the contending parties were clerics. Other synods of the period forbade appeal to the civil courts without the permission of the bishop; but a layman was permitted to institute proceedings against a cleric in civil court if he so wished. Justinian in 530 advised that even in such cases the ecclesiastical court should conduct the trial. Thus the clergy were given special *privilege before the courts*. From this time, bishops were constituted judges of cases in which clerics were involved and metropolitans or patriarchs acted in the same capacity in cases involving bishops. A cleric accused of a serious crime was tried before his ecclesiastical superior. If found guilty he was degraded from the clerical state and surrendered to the civil courts which could them punish him in accordance with the extant laws. In the *West*, especially

---

[1] K. RIFFEL, Verhältnis von Kirche und Staat bis Justinian, 1836. E. LOENING, Gesch. des deutschen Kirchenrechts, 2 vols. 1878. K. VOIGT, § 60. F. LEIFER, ZRG roman. Abt. 1938, 185/202 (christianity and Roman law after Constantine). A. NISSL, Der Gerichtsstand des Klerus im fränk. Reich. 1886. L. GALTIER, Du rôle des évêques dans le droit public et privé du bas empire, Paris 1893. G. LARDÉ, Le tribunal du clerc dans l'Empire romain et la Gaule franque, Moulins 1920. G. VISMARA, Episcopalis audientia. L'attività giurisdizionale del vescovo... fino al sec. IX, Milano 1937. G. SCHUBERT, Der Einfluß des Kirchenrechts auf das weltl. Strafrecht der Frankenzeit, 1937. G. FERRARI DELLA SPADE, Immunità ecclesiastiche nel Diritto Romano Imperiale, Venezia 1939. E. MAGNIN, Immunités ecclés., DictThC VII, 1218/62. H. LECLERCQ, Immunité, DictAC VII, 323/90.

in *France*, the procedure was somewhat different. The civil court needed the permission of the bishop to proceed against a cleric; contentious cases involving clerics and laymen were to be tried in the presence of ecclesiastical judges and even in cases of serious crime the bishop had a voice in the final sentence. In the West, too, since the sixth century, bishops could be tried only before a provincial synod and punished only with ecclesiastical penalties (§ 68, 3).

3. Ecclesiastical courts had jurisdiction not only over clerics, but under certain circumstances, also over laymen. St. Paul (1 Cor. 6: 1 ff.) had told the early Christians to settle their differences among themselves and not before pagan judges. Thus it had become customary for Christians to call on the bishop to *arbitrate* their contentions. *Constantine the Great* decreed (318—333) that if either party desired to bring a case before the bishop, even if the other party objected, the bishop thereby became the judge with the same powers enjoyed by civil judges. One reason for this arrangement was, no doubt, the general corruption of the civil courts. Arcadius in the East (398) and Honorius in the West (408) limited the competence of the bishop to cases in which both parties agreed to submit to his judgment. In spite of restrictions such as this, bishops continued for a long time to exercise the office of civil judges, except among the German tribes and later kingdoms where the practice seems to have been unknown.

## § 62.
### Rise of Parishes. Ecclesiae Propriae in the West[1].

1. As early as the third century Christian *churches* were to be found in the rural regions surrounding the cities (§ 20, 1). They formed the

---

[1] Cfr. literature § 20. P. IMBART DE LA TOUR, Les paroisses rurales dans l'ancienne France, Paris 1900; also U. STUTZ, Gött. Gel. Anz. 1904, 1/86. ST. ZORELL, Die Entwicklung des Parochialsystems, Diss. 1901 (from AkKR 1902). J. AHLHAUS, Civitas u. Diözese, in Gedächtnisschrift G. v. Below, 1928, 1/16. K. MÜLLER, ZntW 1933, 149/85 (parishes and dioceses). W. SESTON, RevHPhR 1935, 243/54 (rise of rural parishes in the West). L. PFLEGER, Die elsäss. Pfarrei, ihre Entstehung u. Entwicklung, 1936 (from Archiv f. Elsäss. KG., Bd. 4/9, 1929/34). H. LECLERCQ, Art. Paroisses rurales, DictAC XIII, 2198/235. M. CHAUME, Rev. Mabillon 1937, 61/73 (rural parishes of Burgundy in Merov. times). O. MONACHINO, La cura pastorale a Milano, Cartagine e Roma nel sec. IV, Rome 1947. A. SCHROTT, Seelsorge im Wandel der Zeiten, 1949. F. GILLMANN, Das Institut der Chorbischöfe im Orient, 1903. H. BERGÈRE, Étude hist. sur les chorévêques, Thèse Paris 1905. TH. GOTTLOB, Der abendländ. Chorepiskopat, 1928. H. LECLERCQ, Chorévêques, DictAC III, 1423/52. On the history of Church property: U. STUTZ, A. PÖSCHL, E. LESNE, K. VOIGT, § 60; E. LOENING, § 61. On the system of patronage: U. STUTZ, Die Eigenkirche als Element des mittelalterlich-germanischen Kirchenrechtes, 1895; Art. Eigenkirche, RE XXIII, 364 ff. H. SCHUBERT, Staat u. Kirche in den arian. Königreichen u. im Reiche Chlodwigs, 1912. R. BIDAGOR S.J., La ,,Iglesia propria'' en España, Rome 1933 (also J. VINCKE, AkKR 1934, 308/19; E. WOHLHAUPTER, ZRGkan 1935, 367/77). H. E. FEINE, Z. der Akad. f. deutsches Recht 1939, 120/3 (origin and system of patronage in Germanic Eccl. law): ZRGkan 1941,

*parish* (παροικία = παρα, beside; οἰκία, house) of the bishop who resided in the city. In the West, since the fourth century, the territory over which a bishop presided was called a *diocese*, a term originally used to designate a unit of administration in the Roman Empire (§ 16, 4; 20, 3). When pagans began to enter the Church in large numbers, the number of rural churches increased proportionately. At first it was customary to appoint a bishop to each new church as is evident from the frequent reference to *chorbishops* (χώρα = land, country). But such an arrangement seems not to have proved practical. The Synod of Ancyra in 314 (can. 13) and a synod at Antioch probably in 341 (can. 10) forbade chorbishops to ordain priests and deacons without the permission of the bishop of the city to which the church belonged. The Synod of Sardica in 343 (can. 6) decreed that bishops should not be appointed in villages and small cities lest the authority and prestige of the episcopacy suffer. And the Synod of Laodicea held about 380, (can. 57) decreed that chorbishops be replaced by *Periodeute* (visitatores, circuitores) that is, by simple priests who were to function in the rural church under orders from the bishop of the city. As a result of such legislation the office of chorbishop became one of little importance and soon the title did not even imply episcopal consecration. By the eighth century both title and office had disappeared in the East except among a few sects who considered and still consider their chorbishops merely as priests. In the West, chorbishops were unknown, except in a few instances, before the eighth century, when the title was sometimes applied to auxiliary bishops.

2. The multiplication of churches outside of cities necessitated placing their administration in the hands of simple *priests*. At first priests were appointed temporarily to conduct services on certain days or for certain seasons in which case their authority in the congregation was naturally very limited. But eventually when permanent appointments were made, the appointees were invested with wider powers. Thus evolved the *"parish system"* known to all subsequent centuries — a number of churches under one bishop, but each church or parish with its own priest or priests empowered to conduct all the religious services not requiring episcopal consecration. This development took place more rapidly in the *East* than in the West. In larger cities, especially in Rome, the bishop continued to conduct all of the services with the priests merely assisting. While some forms of worship were permitted in the other churches of the city, the Consecration of the Species was restricted to the bishop's church (§ 23, 1).

In the *West*, especially in Gaul and Spain, during the fifth and sixth centuries, there were many rural churches with a permanently attached clergy, as is seen from the frequent use of the term parochia in documents of that time. The development of such a system was all the more necessary in these places since the new German States had fewer large cities than the Roman Empire. According to the old Christian concept as

---

I ff. 1942, 1ff. 1943, 64ff. (right of patronage in the Lombard-Italian church); ebd. 1944, 265/77 (patronage in Dalmatia).

well as according to Roman decrees, the bishop of the city was also superior of the country churches, with the indisputable right to administer their property and income (§ 60, 4) and to appoint or remove the clergy. It was his duty to visit these churches every year and to regulate worship and discipline. The newer dioceses were no longer a single city and its environs, but vast areas with many parishes. This circumstance naturally prevented close supervision and necessitated the delegation of authority with the consequent lessening of the personal authority of the bishop. But nothing so contravened episcopal authority as did the *ecclesiae propriae,* or churches over which laymen claimed the right of patronage. The arrangement developed among the Arian and Catholic Germans and later among the Slavs. It probably stemmed from the pre-Christian custom of wealthy pagans building a temple for private use and maintaining at their own expense a priest to offer sacrifice; but the idea was not altogether unknown among Roman Christians. As here understood, ecclesia propria meant that a wealthy person built a church or chapel on his estate, endowed it to assure its upkeep, but claimed it as his personal property and at the same time claimed the right to appoint to it a priest of his own choice without necessarily consulting the bishop. Such a system naturally opened the door to many and grave abuses. Yet the idea spread after the seventh century until such churches were common especially in *France,* where the right of patronage became a serious problem. The same system appears in Italy and Spain but in a much modified form since in these countries the rights of the bishop were safeguarded to some extent.

The term precaria (petition) was applied to grants of revenue-bearing ecclesiastical property made to clerics or laymen. The person receiving the grant had the right to the revenue for a specified time or for life. Later the word *benefice* (beneficium) was used to designate *precaria* granted to a cleric who was obliged to fulfill certain spiritual duties while drawing the revenue.

3. *Churches* or *chapels* were often erected within the geographic limits assigned to a parish. Some of these were chapels of ease to accommodate persons living at a distance from the parish church; sometimes they were oratories built to honor the Blessed Virgin or some saint. They were variously known as oratoria, basilicae, martyria, capellae ot tituli minores (§ 70, 1). Baptism was administered only in the parish church (ecclesia baptismalis). After the sixth century the priest who presided over a large parish and directed other priests in the parish or in the oratories within its limits, was given the title of *archpriest,* formerly reserved to the first priest of the bishop's cathedral (§ 60, 1).

## § 63.

## The Patriarchates[1].

1. During the course of the third century efforts were made to bind the metropolitan sees together into still larger units of organiza-

---

[1] Cfr. literature in § 20.  R. VANCOURT, Patriarcats, DictThC XII, 2253/97. H. LECLERCQ, Patriarcat, DictAC XIII, 2456/87.  FR. MAASSEN, Der Primat

tion known later as *patriarchates*. The General Council of Nicaea in 325 decreed in canon 6 that the "ancient privileges" of the Bishops of *Rome, Alexandria* and *Antioch* as well as of the other chief metropolitans be preserved (§ 20, 3). But five years later an event occurred which tended eventually to interfere with the order of precedence theretofore recognized in the Church. This event was the building of **Byzantium-Constantinople** or *New Rome* as the imperial residence (§ 41, 2). Since the metropolitan organization of the Church closely followed the political divisions of the Empire, it was to be expected that the bishop of the new capital which until then had been subject to the metropolitan see of Heraclea in Thrace, would claim a rank in keeping with the political importance of his see. The attempt was made at the Council of Constantinople in 381 when canon 3 prescribed that the bishop of "New Rome" be given the *precedence of honor* immediately after the bishop of Old Rome. Naturally this meant a deep humiliation for the see of *Alexandria* which had always been considered the most important see of the East. But by shrewd and often ruthless politics, the bishop of the capital city soon achieved a position of great power. From time to time Alexandria endeavored to check the ambitious aspirations of the bishops of Constantinople (§ 51, 3 Theophilus-Chrysostom; § 54 Cyril-Nestorius; § 55, 2 Dioscurus-

des Bischofs v. Rom u. die alten Patriarchalkirchen, 1853. P. BATIFFOL, Le Siège Apostolique 359—451, Paris 1924; also J. CHAPMAN, Studies on the Early Papacy, London 1928, 9/27 (rise of the Patriarchates). ED. SCHWARTZ, Sb. Berlin 1930, 611/40 (can. 6 of Nicaea at Chalcedon). Le Patriarcat Byzantin, Sér. I: Regestes, Fasc. 1—2 (381—1043), éd. p. V. GRUMEL, Istanbul 1932/6; Sér. II: Corpus notitiarum episcopatuum Ecclesiae orientalis graecae I, 1—2, ed. p. E. GERLAND et V. LAURENT, Istanbul 1931/6. G. EVERY, The Patriarchate 461—1204, London 1947. H. GELZER, Ausgew. kleine Schriften, 1907, 57/141 (Church and State in Byzantium). S. VAILHÉ, Art. Constantinople, DictThC III, 1307/1519; Échos d'Orient, 1908, 65 ff. 161 ff. (the title ecumenical patriarch). C. D. COBHAM, The Patriarchs of Constant., Cambridge 1911. V. SCHULTZE, Altchristl. Städte u. Landschaften I: Konstantinopel (324—450), 1913. P. BATIFFOL, RechSR 1926, 193/264 (Justinian and the Roman See). E. GERLAND, Byzant.-Neugriech. Jbb. 1932, 215/30 (antecedents of the patriarchate of Constantinople). H. GRÉGOIRE, Byzantion 1933, 570 f. (Ecumenical Patriarch = episcopus superior). J. FAIVRE, Alexandrie, DictHE II, 289 ff. J. MASPÉRO, Hist. des patriarches d'Alexandrie 518—616, Paris 1923. CHR. PAPADOPULOS, Ἱστορία τῆς ἐκκλησίας Ἀλεξανδρείας (62 to 1934), Alexandria 1935. M. TREPPNER, Das Patriarchat v. Antiochien bis 431, 1891. R. DEVREESSE, Le patriarcat d'Antioche, depuis la paix de l'Église jusqu'à la conquête arabe, Paris 1945. V. SCHULTZE, Altchristl. Städte u. Landsch. III: Antiocheia, 1930. C. KARALEVSKIJ, Antioche, DictHE III, 563 ff. T. E. DOWLING, The Orthodox Greek Patriarchate of Jerusalem, London ³1913. ED. SCHWARTZ, Abh. München 32, 2, 1925 (Patriarchate of Jerusalem 451). H. KOCH, ThLZ 1934, 219 (on can. 7 of Nicaea).

Flavian), but the matter was settled, at least temporarily, at the Council of Chalcedon in 451 when the privilege was conceded (canon 28) to the Bishop of Constantinople of consecrating the metropolitans of the political dioceses of *Pontus, Asia* and *Thrace.* This placed the Church of Constantinople on a par with the churches of Rome, Alexandria and Antioch; her bishops were given the status of *patriarchs* (a title not in general use until later) and the venerable primatial sees of *Ephesus, Caesarea* and *Heraclea* were subject to the new patriarchate. The legates of Pope Leo I immediately protested and the pope himself declared canon 28 invalid, but to no avail. It became all the easier for the bishop of Constantinople to maintain the usurped precedence when the other eastern patriarchates became largely heretical as Nestorians (Antioch) or Monophysites (Alexandria) and especially when in the seventh century they passed under the rule of Islam. During the Acacian Schism of the sixth century the title *"Ecumenical Patriarch"* began to be given to the bishop of New Rome. In 545 *Justinian* declared (Novellae 131, 2) that the Bishop of Constantinople ranked next to the Bishop of Rome and before all other bishops. When John Nesteutes (the Faster) began to use the term "Ecumenical Patriarch" as part of his official title, Pope *Gregory the Great* (590—604) protested vehemently and called it "disgusting presumption". However, with the approval of the emperor, the Constantinopolitan patriarchs continued to use the title.

2. The see of **Jerusalem** was also given special honor from purely ecclesiastical and not political reasons. The see had long been a suffragan see of *Caesarea* in Palestine although the Bishop of Jerusalem enjoyed certain marks of honor in the province. The Council of Nicaea (325, canon 7) recognized and confirmed the unique dignity of the Holy City without changing its dependence on Caesarea; it gave the bishop "succession of honor" (ἀκολουθία τῆς τιμῆς) within the province. Later bishops, however, were not satisfied with an empty honor and began to exert their efforts to obtain the patriarchal dignity. The ambitious Bishop *Juvenal* (421—458) succeeded. The Synod of Chalcedon gave him jurisdiction over the three *provinces of Palestine* after he had already deceived Emperor Theodosius II into recognizing his jurisdiction over Phoenicia and Arabia. These countries had been subject to the patriarchal see of Antioch to which see Juvenal was eventually obliged to return them.

3. As far as the organization of the *West* was concerned, the *Bishop of Rome* was and is *Patriarch* of the West and *Primate* of Italy. However, his primacy over the whole Church gave him a unique position so that these titles were seldom used in referring to him. Besides Rome, there were several other sees in the West which exercised a sort of primatial or patriarchal supervision over large territories. This was the case of *Carthage* in North Africa, of *Milan* in Upper Italy, of *Arles* in southern Gaul and of *Thessalonica* in Eastern Illyria, which belonged politically to the Eastern Empire. From the beginning of the fifth century the bishops of Arles (407) and Thessalonica were *Apostolic Vicars*, i. e., representatives of the pope in their territories. The jurisdiction of Illyria was disputed between Rome and Constantinople for a hundred years and was finally conceded to Rome. There was also friction between Rome and the metropolitan of Arles, especially during the pontificate of Leo the Great (§ 64, 4). — Literature on *Carthage*. § 12, 6. — On *Arles*: W. Gundlach, NA 1889, 251 ff.; 1890, 9 ff. 233 ff.; H. J. Schmitz, HJG 1891, 1 ff. 245 ff.; L. Duchesne, Fastes épisc. (§ 12, 2) I², 112 ff.; W. Völker, ZKG 1927, 355/69. — On *Thessalonica*: Epistularum Rom. Pontificum Collectio Thessalonicensis (531), rec. C. Silva-Tarouca, Rome 1937. — G. Pfeilschifter, Die Balkanfrage in der KG., 1913, 7 ff.; F. Streichhan, ZRGkan 1922, 330/84; 1928, 538/48; W. Völker, ZKG 1927, 370/80; Ed. Schwartz, Festschrift R. Reitzenstein, 1931, 145 ff. — S. L. Greenslade, JhTSt 1945, 17/30.

Two *titular patriarchates* came into being in the West as a result of the quarrel over the Three Chapters (§ 58, 1). When the diocese of Aquileia was dismembered and the metropolitan of **Grado,** or Aquileia-Grado, was reconciled with Rome, the metropolitan of **Old Aquileia** assumed the title of patriarch to express his independence of Rome. About 604 the Apostolic See permitted the metropolitan of Grado to use the same title so as not to appear of lesser dignity than his schismatic rival. In 1451 the patriarchate of Grado was transferred to *Venice*. When an earthquake destroyed Aquileia in 1348, the patriarchate was transferred to *Udine*, but the title was abolished in 1751. — Cfr. Hefele II², 922 ff. — W. Meyer, Abh. Göttingen 1898. — W. Lenel, Venezianisch-istrische Studien, 1911. — P. Richard, Aquilée, DictHE III, 1112/42. — A. Calderini, Aquileia romana, Milano 1930. — P. Paschini, Storia del Friuli, 3 vol. Udine 1934/6.

# § 64.
## The Papacy and Primacy of Rome.
## Leo I the Great and Gregory I the Great[1].
## Relations between Church and State.

Series of popes from 311 to 692, (Every pope until Pope Silverius [† 537] was given the title "sanctus", excepting John II and, of course, the Anti-

---

[1] **I. Sources:** Pontificum Romanorum Epistolae u. Regesta, § 2, 3; Liber Pontificalis, § 78, 3. Collectio Avellana (Collection of imperial and papal letters 367—553), ed. O. GUENTHER, CSEL, 35, 1895/8. Germ. transl. of papal briefs (to 498) by S. WENZLOWSKY, in BKV 1. Aufl., 7 vols. 1875/80. H. LECLERCQ, Lettres des Papes, DictAC VIII, 2942/82. C. SILVA-TAROUCA, ZkTh 1919, 467 ff. 657 ff.; Gregorianum 1931, 3 ff. 349 ff. 547 ff. (on papal

popes): Miltiades or Melchiades (311– 314); Sylvester (314—335); Marcus (336); *Julius I* (337—352); *Liberius* (352—366); Felix II (355—365), antipope; Damasus I (366—384); Ursinus (366—367), anti-pope; *Siricius* (384 to briefs from fourth to ninth cent.) H. GETZENY, Stil und Form der ältesten Papstbriefe bis auf Leo d. Gr., Diss. 1922. N. ERTL, Archiv f. Urkundenforsch. NF. 1, 1937, 56/132 (Dictatores of early medieval papal briefs from Leo I to John VIII). F. DI CAPUA, Il ritmo prosaico nelle lettere dei Papi etc. s. IV—XIV, 2 vol., Rome 1937/9; cfr. J. COCHEZ, EphThLov 1938, 526/34. A. MENZER, RQ 1932, 27/103 (dating of papal documents to 1100). M. KOPECZYNSKI, Die Arengen der Papsturkunden . . . bis Gregor VII, 1936. L. SANTIFALLER, Die Abkürzungen in den ältesten Papsturkunden (788 to 1002), 1939. Liber diurnus Romanorum Pontificum (book of formulas of the old papal chancery to the eleventh century), ed. TH. SICKEL, 1889; edd. L. Grammatica e G. Galbiati (Cod. Ambrosiano), Milano 1921. Cfr. W. M. PEITZ, Sb. Wien 185, 4, 1918; StZ 94, 1918, 486 ff.; 553 ff.; Das vorephesin. Symbol der päpstl. Kanzlei, 1939 (opposite opinions K. MOHLBERG and B. ALTANER, ThRev 1939, 297/305 and L. SANTIFALLER, HZ 161, 1940, 532/8); also in Misc. historiae pontificiae II, Rome 1940 (methods of research on the Liber diurnus). M. TANGL, NA 1919, 741 ff.; L. SANTIFALLER, Festgabe H. Finke 1925, 23/26; MIÖG 49, 1935, 225/366; also Anzeiger der phil.-hist. Klasse der Akad. . . . Wien 1946, 172/212. H. LECLERCQ, DictAC IX, 243/344. O. SEECK, Regesten der Kaiser u. Päpste 311—476, 1919. K. MIRBT, Quellen zur Gesch. des Papsttums und des röm. Katholizismus, [4]1924. SHOTWELL and LOOMIS, The See of Peter, § 21. L. BROEL-PLATER, De primatu Romanorum Pontificum ab Anastasio II ad Pelagium II (496—590), Rome 1930 (collection of texts). F. SCHNEIDER, Die Epitaphien d. Päpste v. 4.—12. Jahrh., 1933. L. SANTIFALLER, Saggio di un Elenco dei funzionari impiegati e scrittori della Cancelleria Pontificia I, Rome 1940. H. RAHNER, Abendländ. Kirchenfreiheit, 1943.

  II. **Monographs and Researches:** Cfr. literature § 21 (espec. P. BATIFFOL, Cathedra Petri; GLEZ et JUGIE, Art. Primauté; LECLERCQ, Art Pape; TURMEL, KIDD, GMELIN, HEILER). FR. MAASSEN, Der Primat u. P. BATIFFOL, Le Siège Apost., § 63. R. BAXMANN, Die Politik der Päpste v. Gregor I bis Gregor VII, I 1868. J. LANGEN (Old Catholic), Gesch. der röm. Kirche bis z. Pontifikat Leos I, 1881; von Leo I bis Nikolaus I, 1885. H. GRISAR, Gesch. Roms u. der Päpste im MA. I (to 590), 1901. W. E. BEET, The Early Roman Episcopate to 384, London 1913; The Rise of the Papacy 385—461, London 1910. ER. CASPAR, Gesch. des Papsttums I (to Leo I, † 461), 1930; II (to Zacharias, † 752), 1933; cfr. J. P. KIRSCH, HJG 1930, 534/44; H. KOCH, Gött. Gel. Anz. 1932, 1/21; PH. FUNK, Hochland 1933/4 II, 168/75; J. HOLLN-STEINER, Jb. der österreich. Leogesellschaft 1933, 87 ff.; zu Bd. II: E. STEIN, Cath. Hist. Review, 21, 1935/6, 129/63; G. STADTMÜLLER, Byz. Z. 1937, 428/35. J. HALLER, Das Papsttum, Idee u. Wirklichkeit I (to 788), [2]1951 (hypercritical and bitterly anti-Roman). F. X. SEPPELT, Gesch. des Papsttums I (to 590), [2]1939; II (to 1046), 1934; Papstgeschichte, [5]1949. Histoire de l'Église, publ. p. A. FLICHE et V. MARTIN, vol. III—V, see § 41. TH. HARAPIN, Primatus Pontificis Romani in Concilio Chalcedonensi et ecclesiae dissidentes, Quaracchi 1923. J. CHAPMAN, Studies on the Early Papacy, London 1928. S. H. SCOTT, The Eastern Churches and the Papacy (to Photius), London 1928. K. VOIGT, Staat u. Kirche von Konstantin d. Gr. bis z. Ende der Karolingerzeit, 1936. K. JÄNTERE, Die röm. Weltreichsidee u. die Entsteh. der Weltmacht des Papstes, Universität Abo 1936. J. W. JONES, Roman and Christian Imperialism, London 1939. H. E. SYMONDS, The Church Universal and the See of Rome (to 1054), London 1939. H. SMELIN, DAGM 1938, 509/31 (genesis of the idea of primacy). H. LIETZMANN, Die Anfänge des Problems Kirche u. Staat, Sb. Berlin 1938; Das Problem Staat u. Kirche im weström. Reich, Abh. Berlin 1940, 11. T. G. JALLAND, The Church and the Papacy, London 1944. M. LEITNER, Festschrift Hertling, 1913, 504/15

399); Anastasius I (399—402); *Innocent I* (402—417); Zosimus (417—418); Boniface I (418—422); Eulalius (418—419), anti-pope; *Caelestine I* (422—432); Sixtus III (432—440); **Leo I the Great** (440—461); Hilarus (461—468); Simplicius (468—483); Felix II (III) (483—492); *Gelasius I* (492—496); Anastasius II (496—498); Symmachus (498—514); Laurence (498—505), anti-pope; *Hormisdas* (514—523); John I (523 until 526); Felix III (IV) (526—530); Boniface II (530—532); Dioscurus (530), anti-pope; John II (Mercurius) (533—535); Agapetus I (535—536); Silverius (536—537); *Vigilius* (537—555); Pelagius I (556—561); John III (561—574); Benedict I (575—579); Pelagius II (579—590); **St. Gregory I** the Great (590—604); Sabinian (604—606); Boniface III (607); St. Boniface IV (608—615); St. Deusdedit (615—618); Boniface V (619—625); *Honorius I* (625—638); Severin (640) John IV (640—642); Theodore I (642—649); *St. Martin I* (649—653); St. Eugene I (654—657); St. Vitalian (657—672); Adeodatus (672—676); Donus (676—678); *St. Agatho* (678—681); St. Leo II (682—683); St. Benedict II (684—685); John V (685—686); Conon (686—687); Theodore (687) anti-pope; Paschal (687—692), anti-pope; St. Sergius I (687—701).

1. During this period the primacy of the Roman Church, i. e., of her bishops, was generally recognized in the East as well as in the West. Both Constantinople (381, can. 3) and Chalcedon (451, can. 28) when endeavoring to satisfy fully the demand of New Rome for honor, expressly state that its bishop was to have precedence only *after* the bishop of Rome (§ 63, 1). When Emperor *Justinian* approved this arrangement, he spoke of the Bishop of Rome as "the first" and "the chief of all the priests of God" (Cod. Just. I, 1, 7 of the year 553; Novellae 131, 2 of the year 545). And although he was, no doubt, sincere in these expressions, his policy of Caesaropapism often led him to subjugate the pope to the imperial will (§ 55). During the great Christological controversies in the East and the Soteriological disputes in the West, the Roman See had spoken authoritatively (§ 54, 2; 55, 2; 56, 3; 57, 3. 4; 59, 3). Her legates were given the first place in general councils (§ 65, 2). When the Oriental bishops subscribed to the formula of Pope Hormisdas in 519, which ended the Acacian Schism (§ 55, 1), they acknowledged their subjection to the teaching authority of Rome. The orthodox (Western) Synod of *Sardica* in 343 (§ 48, 3) declared the Bishop of Rome to be the *highest court of appeal* for the whole

(the papacy in Corp. iur. civ. Justiniani). A. M. KOENIGER, Festgabe A. Ehrhard, 1922, 273/300 (Prima sedes a nemine iudicatur). P. RICHARD, RHE 1924, 413/56 (development of the papal monarchy). P. BATIFFOL, RechSR 1926, 193/264 (Justinian and the Roman See). E. CASPAR, HZ 139, 1928, 229/41 (problems of papal history in the fourth cent.). F. DÖLGER, ZKG 1937, 1/42 (Rome as appraised by Byzantium). G. ROETHE, Zur Gesch. der röm. Synoden im 3. u. 4. Jh., 1937 (in: Geistige Grundlagen römischer Kirchenpolitik).

Church in important matters of discipline. An edict of Emperor *Gratian* of 378 issued at the request of a Roman Synod, appointed Pope *Damasus* the supreme judge of all other metropolitans of the West. It was this pope who first referred to the Roman Church as the Apostolic See. Pope *Gelasius I* declared (in 493 and 495) that it was the office of the Roman Church to judge other churches, but to be judged by no human tribunal and that it was the obligation of others to accept her decisions. The Roman synod of 501 (synodus palmaris, see below no. 6) and Ennodius, later bishop of Pavia (§ 78, 2) spoke in the same strain. Hence Canon Law of the Middle Ages and of modern times (CJC, can. 1556) enunciates the principle "Prima sedes a nemine judicatur".

*Canons* 3, 4 and 5 of *Sardica* have given rise to much discussion. Although their genuinity has been questioned (J. Friedrich) the supporting evidence leaves no room for doubt. However, the question is still undecided: which of the versions, the Latin (Turner, Schwartz, Lietzmann) or the Greek (von Hankiewicz and Caspar), is the original. The canons decree that a bishop deposed by a provincial synod may appeal to the Bishop of Rome. If he does not concur in the judgment of the synod, he has the right to order an investigation to be made by the bishops of a neighboring province. If the accused appeal to him from the court of second instance, he may himself render judgement or appoint a court of bishops under the presidency of his legates to give the final decision. Here was an official pronouncement that the Roman Bishop was considered the supreme judge over the entire Church. However, owing to the Arian Schism, the synod could not be considered ecumenical, nor was it practical at the time to follow such procedure in distant places especially in the East. But during the fifth century several appeals were made, to decide which the popes invoked the canons of Sardica. Such was the case of John Chrysostom in 404 (§ 55, 2); of Flavian of Constantinople in 449, of Eusebius of Dorylaeum and of Theodoret of Cyprus (§ 55, 2). In *North Africa* where an independent spirit had developed among the bishops, the canons of Sardica were not at first observed. The General Synod of Carthage in May 418 forbade priests, deacons and members of the lower clergy to appeal to transmarina judicia (i. e. to Rome). Nevertheless Pope Zozimus (417—418) received the appeal of the priest *Apiarius* of Sicca who had been deposed by his bishop. In justifying his action, the pope again invoked Sardica, which he mistakenly quoted as decisions of Nicaea because the collection of canons he used had simply added the Sardica canons after Nicaea without indicating where the legislation had been formulated. The case of Apiarius dragged on for a long time and was finally dropped during the pontificate of Celestine (422—432) when the Africans declared that all disciplinary cases involving Africans must be settled in Africa. However, as we know from St. Augustine (Ep. 209, 8) appeals were made from African dioceses to Rome; so that gradually the canons of Sardica were accepted throughout the Church. — *P. A. Leder*, Acht Vorträge über das älteste

Synodalrecht der päpstl. Gerichtshoheit, 1915 (also H. Lietzmann, ZRGkan 1916, 423 ff.). — *E. Heckrodt*, Die Kanones von Sardika aus der KG. erläutert, 1917. — *J. Friedrich*, Sb. München 1901, 417/76; 1902, 383/426; 1903, 321/43. — *F. X. Funk*, AU III, 159/217. — *C. H. Turner*, JThSt 1902, 370/98. — *Gr. v. Hankiewicz*, ZRGkan 1912, 44/99. — *E. Caspar*, ZKG 1928, 162/77. — *Ed. Schwartz*, Sb. Berlin 1930, 629 ff.; ZntW 1931, 1/35. — *P. Batiffol*, RHE 1925, 5/32 (appeals to Rome before 451). — *J. Chapman*, Studies on the Early Papacy, London 1928, 184/209 (Apiarius). — *R. Höslinger*, Die alte afrik. Kirche (§ 12, 6). — *W. Pewesin*, Imperium, Ecclesia universalis, Rome 1937.

2. Canon 3 of Sardica bases the primacy of Rome on the fact that the Roman Church was founded by St. Peter (sancti Petri apostoli memoriam honoremus, etc.). From the fourth century on, attempts were made in councils (381, 481) and otherwise to ascribe the primacy to the earlier political prestige of the city as the capital of the Empire. Such an interpretation contradicts the facts of history (§ 21, 2). It was evidently devised to justify the action of Constantinople in assuming precedence over the eastern patriarchates. But imperial decrees (Anastasius I, Justinian, Constantine Pogonatus) and innumerable letters of bishops furnish sufficient evidence that even in the East it was generally held that the Primacy of Rome was due to the foundation of the Roman Church by St. Peter.

During this period no one *title* was used exclusively to designate the incumbent of the See of Peter. The titles papa, apostolicus vicarius Christi, summus sacerdos, summus pontifex, sanctus, etc., were often used by other bishops. But in the sixth century some writers like Ennodius of Pavia and Cassiodorus (§ 78, 2) began to apply the title **papa** to the Bishop of Rome only, and their example was imitated. The formula, *Servus servorum Dei*, used by *Gregory the Great* was not, as some have thought, adopted as a result of his quarrel with John the Faster (§ 63, 1) over the title "Ecumenical Patriarch". He had known and used the form in the days when he was a simple monk. — On the title *Papa*: P. de Labriolle, BullLA 1911, 215/20; Bulletin Du Cange 1928, 65/75. — E. v. Dobschütz, TU 38, 4, 1912, 226 ff. — P. Batiffol, RivArchCrist 1925, 98/116 (Papa, Sedes Apostolica, Apostolatus). —H. Leclercq, Papa, DictAC XIII, 1097/111. —On the formula *Servus servorum Dei*: K. Schmitz, Ursprung u. Gesch. der Devotionsformel, 1913, 120 ff. — W. Levison, ZRGkan 1916, 384//86. — H. Delehaye, Strena Buliciana, Zagreb 1924, 377 f. — L. Levillain, Le moyen âge 1930, 5/7. — G. Tellenbach, Libertas. Kirche u. Weltordnung im Zeitalter des Investiturstreites, 1936, 199/201.

3. The transfer of the imperial *residence* from Rome to *Byzantium* (§ 41, 2) was an event of the greatest importance for the popes. It left them greater freedom of action and removed the danger of them becoming mere court bishops as the bishops of Constantinople eventually became. While the Emperors in the East ruled the

Church, the situation in the West, for the most part, was the reverse. The great *Ambrose* of Milan expressed the Christian concept of the relationship between Church and State: the emperor was not over the Church, but in it, and in matters of religion was subject to the bishop, especially the Bishop of Rome. It is true that the Ostrogoth and Byzantine rule proved at times most trying. The unsettled condition of affairs in the West often swept the popes into a position of great power and as quickly to one of helplessness. Two popes, both deserving of the surname Great, *Leo I* and *Gregory I*, notably increased the prestige of the papacy and secured it for the future. During the *Migration of Nations* it was the achievement of the papacy to preserve order and save the civilization of the West; and when the old Empire of the West declined, — more so after its total collapse — the popes became the sole defenders of the sorely afflicted population of Italy. In its unity and moral power the Catholic Church stood for what had been the greatness of Old Rome and transmitted to the nascent Middle Ages the idea of Empire. And ecclesiastical Rome inherited something of the authority and world power which had been the glory of imperial Rome.

Among the Popes of the fourth century, *Julius I* (337—352), *Liberius* 352—366), *Damasus I* and *Siricius* are especially noted. The first three took an active part in the Arian controversy. **Damasus I** (366—384) a native Roman (not a Spaniard), was obliged to defend himself during the greater part of his pontificate from the attacks and intrigues of the party of Ursinus and of the converted Jew Isaac (for the so-called Ambrosiaster see § 76, 1). The emperors Valentinian I and Gratian supported him by giving him full jurisdiction over ecclesiastical courts and lending him imperial officers to enforce his decisions (no. 1 above). Damasus endeavored to reconcile the East and the West torn asunder by Arianism (§ 48, 6). He also did much for the reform of liturgy (§ 67, 1) wrote many letters and poems and when he undertook the restoration of the catacombs, composed beautiful metric inscriptions for the tombs of the martyrs (§ 23, 5). St. Jerome was his secretary and theological advisor and it was at Damasus' suggestion and with his encouragement that Jerome undertook the revision of the Latin version of the Scriptures (§ 76, 2). Damasus' successor **Siricius** (384—399) contributed much to the consolidation of papal jurisdiction by issuing to the bishops of the West numerous *decretals* (decreta, constituta) on matters of liturgy and discipline. He also reorganized the papal chancery after the model of the late Roman imperial chancery (Getzeny, vide supra). **Innocent I** (402—417), one of the most capable popes of the period, showed energy and vision in administration. In a letter (Ep. 2, 6) to Bishop Victricius of Rouen (404) he demanded that in accordance with the canons of Sardica, all important cases brought before the provincial synod should be submitted to the Apostolic See for decision. The brief

316

pontificate of his successor *Zozimus*, a Greek by birth, was taken up almost entirely with the Pelagian controversy (§ 56, 3. 4), while the ten-year pontificate of *Celestine I* (422—432) was disturbed by Nestorianism (§ 54, 2). — On **Damasus**: M. Ihm, Damasi Epigrammata, 1895. — C. Weyman, Vier Epigramme des hl. P. Damasus, 1905. — *A. Ferrua*, Epigrammata damasiana, Rome 1942. — Monogr. by M. Rade, 1882; J. Wittig, 1902; J. Vives, Barcelona 1943. — *E. Caspar*, Gesch. des Papsttums I, 196/256; ZKG 1928, 178/202 (trial of Damasus etc.) — *J. Wittig* and *J. Schäfer*, § 48, 6. — *J. Vives*, Damasiana, in ,,Span. Forschungen der Görresgesellschaft" I, 1, 1928, 93/102. — *E. Schäfer*, Die Bedeutung der Epigramme des P. Damasus I für die Gesch. der Heiligenverehrung, Rome 1932. — *P. Galtier*, RechSR 1936, 385 ff. 563 ff. (Tomus of Damasus of 382). — On **Innocent I**: *H. Gebhardt*, Die Bedeutung Innocenz' I für die Entwicklung der päpstl. Gewalt, Diss. 1901. — *J. Wittig*, ThQ 1902, 388/439. E. Caspar, op. cit. I, 296/343.

4. **Leo I the Great** (440—441)[1] was not only the greatest pope of the fifth century, but will always rank among the great popes of all times. He was a true Roman of noble character, dignity and ability. In 452 he met *Attila*, King of the Huns, at Mantua and induced him to desist from his march on defenseless Rome. And in 455 with the same dauntless spirit, he met *Genseric*, the conquering leader of the Vandals. Genseric indeed entered Rome, but at Leo's entreaty did not carry out the work of devastation which marked the path of the Vandals elsewhere. Leo was motivated by the firm conviction that the Bishop of Rome, as the successor of Peter, endowed with the power and authority of the Prince of the Apostles, had the right and duty to guide and govern the Universal Church.

---

[1] Leonis M. Opera, edd. P. et H. BALLERINI, 3 fol. Venet. 1753/7 (= PL 54 to 56). Leonis I Epistulae, ed. ED. SCHWARTZ in Acta Concil. Oecumen. t. II vol. IV, 1932; ed. C. SILVA-TAROUCA, § 55 (cfr. Festschrift P. F. Kehr, 1926, 23/47). Leos sermons Germ. transl. in BKV 54/5, 1927. Leos Reden über Petrus ed. W. HAACKE, with Germ. transl. by TH. BREME, 1939. W. J. HALLIWELL, The Style of Pope St. Leo the Gr., Diss. Wash. 1939. Monogr. on Leo by E. PERTHEL, 1843; FR. BÖHRINGER (Leo I and Gregory I), 1879; A. REGNIER, Paris 1910; T. JALLAND, London 1941; P. BREZZI, Rome 1947. P. BATIFFOL, DictThC IX, 218/301. ER. CASPAR, Gesch. des Papsttums I, 1930, 423/564, 610/17. R. GALLI, Didaskaleion 1930, 51/235. PH. KUHN, Die Christologie Leos I, 1894. J. PSCHMADT, Leo d. Gr. als Prediger, Diss. 1912. W. KISSLING, Das Verhältnis von Sacerdotium u. Imperium nach den Anschauungen der Päpste von Leo d. Gr. bis Gelasius I, 1921. K. VOIGT, ZKG 1928, 11/17 (Leo and Eastern Empire). A. DENEFFE, Scholastik 1934, 543/54 (tradition and dogma in the writings of Leo). K. D. SCHMIDT, ZKG 1935, 267/75 (Papa Petrus ipse in Leo). P. SANTINI, Il primato e l'infallibilità del Romano Pontifice in Leone M. e gli scrittori Greco-Russi, Grottaferrata 1936. B. KOLON, Die Vita S. Hilarii Arelatensis, 1925. V. GLUSCHKE, Die Unfehlbarkeit des Papstes bei Leo . . ., Diss. Rome 1938. W. ENSSLIN, ZRG rom. Abt. 1937, 867/78 (constitution of Valentinian III of 445). M. JUGIE, Misc. P. Paschini I, Rome 1948, 77/94 (Leo and the internal affairs of the Oriental Church). GMELIN, see above. E. A. THOMPSON, A History of Attila and the Huns, Oxford 1948. Also literature § 55.

He stressed the fact (Ep. 14, 1) that the other bishops were called to share his solicitude for the Church, but not the plenitude of his power (in partem sollicitudinis, non in plenitudinem potestatis). The idea of the *Universal Episcopacy* of the pope was to him not merely a beautiful abstraction — but an essential factor of the Church's organization — and he, better than any of his predecessors, knew how to exercise it for the Church's welfare. Leo's legates interpreted canon 6 of Nicaea before the Council of Chalcedon in the form: Quod Ecclesia Romana semper habuit primatum, etc. In a sermon on the feast of SS Peter and Paul (Sermo 82) he very effectively contrasted the Pax Christiana which emanates from Christian Rome and the Chair of Peter with the old Pax Romana preserved by force of arms. The Monophysite controversy in the East absorbed his attention and he intervened with his Epistula dogmatica to Flavian (§ 55, 2) which clearly and authoritatively set forth the doctrine of the Church. Nor did he hesitate to speak with a voice of authority regarding the presumptuous claims of Constantinople. Leo's actions in the West were equally resolute. Archbishop Hilary of Arles, a former monk of Lérins (§ 72, 6), in his misguided zeal for discipline, arrogated to himself authority which would have made him the independent patriarch of southern Gaul. Leo revoked the title and delegation of Apostolic Vicar which had been granted to the bishops of Arles (§ 63, 3), suspended *Hilary* from the exercise of his office as bishop and thus forced him to submit. In this case Leo was supported by a rescript of *Valentinian III* (445) which forbade clerics of the West to do anything contrary to the authority of the Roman See. The emperor argued that the peace of the Church could be preserved only if everyone obeyed the head (rectorem suum). Thus the pope's primacy of jurisdiction was recognized although it was not always easily enforced. Leo's numerous letters, treatises on dogmatic and disciplinary subjects, and sermons earned for him the title of Doctor of the Church. (For the Sacramentarium Leonianum see § 67, 3).

5. During the pontificate of Leo's third successor, *Felix II* (III) (483—492), the Henoticon of Emperor Zeno caused serious trouble and resulted in the first *great schism* of the Greek Church — a schism which lasted 35 years (§ 55, 4). The pontificate of **Gelasius I**[1]

---

[1] PL 59, 13/190. E. CASPAR, op. cit. II, 1933, 44/81, 749/58. I. ROHR, ThQ 1902, 110/23 (Gelasius I. and the primacy). E. BERNHEIM, Mittelalterliche Zeitanschauungen in ihrem Einfluß auf Politik u. Geschichtsschreibung I, 1918, 150 ff. W. KISSLING, see above. H. KOCH, Gelasius im kirchenpolit.

318

(492—496) was brief but important. He was a theologian of more than ordinary ability, in which field he recognized Augustine and Leo I as his masters. His diplomatic training had been obtained as deacon (i. e., assistant and secretary) to his two immediate predecessors. E. Caspar calls him "one of the great architects of the idea of primacy." Theodoric, the new Arian ruler of Italy, admired and respected him. Gelasius strove energetically to heal the Acacian Schism, but to no avail. In writing to Emperor Anastasius I, he enlarges on Augustine's idea: "There are two chief (principalitates) factors by which this world is ruled, the sacred authority of bishops and the power of kings" (auctoritas sacrata pontificum et regalis potestas). Of the two the first is of the greater importance (gravius pondus) because it must give an account to God even for kings. On the other hand, in the realm of public order, that is, in secular affairs, even the heads of religion (antistites) must obey the laws of the emperor. These words of Gelasius were often quoted during the Middle Ages and became the norm for relations between Sacerdotium and Imperium (§ 111, 1). It was this same pope who declared that the See of Peter can be judged by no one (v. supra no. 1). Some liturgical reforms have been ascribed to him (§ 67, 1. 3).

The famous *decretum Gelasianum* de libris recipiendis et non recipiendis is erroneously said to have been issued by Gelasius I in a Roman Synod in 494. It contains a list of canonical books of Scripture, a disquisition on the Roman primacy, a list of general councils and a list of condemned apocryphal and heretical books. It was probably written by a cleric of Upper Italy or southern Gaul in the early sixth century, although it reflects Roman influence. The first three chapters may have been composed at the time of Pope Damasus. — (Cfr. E. v. Dobschütz, TU 38, 4, 1912; J. Chapman, RevBén 1913, 187 ff.; 315 ff.; H. Leclercq, DictAC VI, 722/47; E. Schwartz, ZntW 1930, 161/8).

6. When Pope Anastasius II (§ 43, 8) died in November 498 the so-called **Laurentian Schism** began. The Deacon **Symmachus** was chosen by the majority of electors to succeed Anastasius; but on the same day (November 22) a group friendly to Byzantium and led by the Senator Festus, chose the Archpriest **Laurentius** in the hope that by having a pope who would accept the Henoticon (§ 55, 4), the Acacian Schism would he healed. Both parties appealed to the Ostrogoth Theodoric at Ravenna, who decided in favor of Symmachus (499). Symmachus magnanimously appointed his rival bishop of Nuceria (Nocera in

Dienst seiner Vorgänger Simplicius und Felix III., Sb. München 1935, 6. L. KNABE, Die gelasianische Zweigewaltentheorie bis z. Ende des Investiturstreits, 1936. On the theory of the two powers: A. K. ZIEGLER, Cath. Historical Review 1942, 412/37. G. SORANZO, Rivista di storia della Chiesa in It. 1947, 3/21.

Campagna); but the party strife continued. In 501 the Senators Festus and Probinus charged Symmachus with grave dereliction and petitioned the king to call a synod of Italian bishops to investigate. In the fourth session (synodus palmaris) in October 501 the synod declared, as Gelasius I previously had done, that no one could judge the Apostolic See. The opponents of Symmachus were not satisfied and when Laurentius returned to the city, the schism was renewed. Ennodius of Pavia (§ 78, 2) defended the synod, but the Laurentians wrote bitterly against it and resorted to physical violence with much bloodshed. In 506 Theodoric ordered that all the churches seized by the Laurentians be restored to Symmachus. The schism came to an end under the next pope, Hormisdas. — *E. Caspar*, Theoderich d. Gr. u. das Papsttum (collection of sources), Kleine Texte 162, 1931; Gesch. d. Papsttums II, 87 ff. 758 ff. — *G. Pfeilschifter*, Theoderich d. Gr., 1896, 55/125. — L. Duchesne, MélAH 1915, 221/56; L'Église au VIᵉ s., Paris 1925, 113 ff. — R. Cessi, ArchSRom 1919, 5/230; 1920, 209/321; A. Alessandrini, ib. 1944, 153/207. — W. T. Townsend, Journal of Religion 1933, 165/74 (the so-called Symmachian forgeries); cfr. W. v. Pölnitz, RHE 1936, 81/8. — G. Westenburger, Der Sym.-Prozeß v. 501, Diss. 1940. — W. Ensslin, Theoderich d. Gr., 1947.

The popes from *Felix III* (IV) (526—530) to *Silverius* (536—537) were elected under the influence of the *Gothic* crown (§ 60, 3) and when Gothic rule collapsed, the Byzantine influence on papal elections was even more pronounced. During the greater part of the sixth and and seventh centuries, the popes were rendered helpless and dependent (§ 60, 3). The quarrel over the Three Chapters occasioned the humiliation of the papacy under *Vigilius* (§ 58, 4—7) and the Monothelite controversy had a similar result during the pontificates of *Martin I* and *Honorius* (§ 59, 2. 3).

7. On the threshold between Christian Antiquity and the Middle Ages stands the impressive figure of **Gregory I the Great**[1] (590—604).

---

[1] Gregorii M. Opera in PL 75—79. Gregorii I Registrum epistolarum, edd. P. EWALD et L. M. HARTMANN, 2 vol. 1891/9 (MG Epist. 1—2); also W. M. PEITZ, Das Register Gregors d. Gr., 1917; M. TANGL, NA 1919, 741/52; E. POSNER, ib. 1922, 243/315; D. NORBERG, In Registrum Gregorii M. studia critica, 2 vol. Uppsala 1937/9; G. DAMIZIA, Lineamenti di diritto canonico nel „Reg. epistolarum" di S. Gregorio M., Rome 1949. Gregorii M. Dialogorum libri IV, ed. U. MORICCA, Rome 1924. Selected works of Gregory in Germ. transl. in BKV 2. R. 3—4, 1933 (Regulae pastoralis liber and Dialogi). Homilien über die Evangelien Buch 1 u. 2 deutsch übertragen, 2 Teile Klosterneuburg 1931/2. Das Leben des hl. Benedikt übers. v. F. FAESSLER, 1949. H. GOLL, Die Vita Gregorii des Joh. Diaconus, 1940. Monogr. on Gregory by FR. BÖHRINGER (see under Leo I); C. WOLFSGRUBER, ²1897; A. SNOW, London ²1924; H. GRISAR, Rome 1904 (in Civ. Catt.), reprint 1928; F. H. DUDDEN, 2 vol. London 1905; F. TARDUCCI, Rome 1909; H. H. HOWORTH, London 1912; P. BATIFFOL, Paris 1928 (Les Saints). H. LECLERCQ, DictAC VI, 1753/76. BARDENHEWER, GeschAL V, 284/301. E. CASPAR, in "Meister d. Politik", ed. E. MARCKS and K. A. V. MÜLLER I², 1923, 325/56; Gesch. des Papsttums II, 306/514, 774/78. Histoire de l'Église, publ. p. A. FLICHE et V. MARTIN, vol. V: L. BRÉHIER et R. AIGRAIN, Grégoire le Grand etc. (590—757), Paris 1938. S. BRECHTER, StKBenO 1939, 209/24 (Gregory was not an abbot). J. ZEILLER, RHE 1949, 458/62 (Gregory and Dalmatia). E. H. FISCHER, ZRGkan 1949, 15/144 (Gregory and Byzantium). G. PFEILSCHIFTER, Die authentische Ausgabe der Evangelienhomilien Gregors d. Gr.,

Born of high Roman nobility, he held the office of Prefect of the city of Rome; but about 537 he retired to the Monastery of St. Andrew which he had founded under the Benedictine Rule. However, he was unable to enjoy the solitude he loved. He was appointed apocrisiarius or papal representative at the court of Constantinople and when he was about 50 years of age, much against his will was unanimously elected by clergy and people to succeed Pelagius II. His pontificate began when Italy was sorely tried by pestilence, famine, the inroads of the Lombards (§ 43, 4) and the schism of Milan (§58, 7). Yet in spite of failing health he carried on a farsighted program of ecclesiastical, social and political reform with such success that he was able to build the Church of the future on the ruins of the past. The inscription on his first tomb in St. Peter's called him the "consul Dei." By prudent administration of the Roman Church, the patrimony of Peter, Gregory laid the foundation of the States of the Church and the later political power of the popes in Italy. He recognized the importance of winning the *Germanic peoples* to the Church, worked zealously for the conversion of the Arians and Lombards, sought to bring the Visigoths and the Franks into closer relationship with the Church and the papacy, and took the initiative in sending missionaries to the *Anglo-Saxons*. This latter benefaction was repaid by centuries of true British loyalty to Rome and affection for the pope as successor of Peter, "the Gatekeeper of Heaven". Gregory also reformed the Roman *liturgy* (§ 67, 3) and *church music* (§ 67, 6), promoted Benedictine *monasticism* (§ 72, 7), endeavored to stamp out the remains of paganism in the islands off the coast of Italy, and vehemently protested the use of the title

1900. G. M. DREVES, ThQ 1907, 548/62; 1909, 436/45 (Gregory did not compose hymns). V. DIGLIO, La bassa latinità e San Gregorio M., Benevento 1912. W. STUHLFATH, Gregor I, s. Leben bis zur Wahl z. Papst, 1913. J. LEBON, RechThAM 1929, 177/201 (Christology of Gregory). J. STIGL-MAYR, Stella Matutina-Festschrift (Feldkirch) I, 1931, 493/512 (Gregory as revealed by this letters). M. B. DUNN, The Style of the Letters of S. Gregory the Great, Diss. Washington Cath. Univ. 1931. M. HAUBER, The Late Latin Vocabulary of the Moralia of St. Gregory the Gr., ib. 1938. K. BROZ-ZEL, The Clausulae in the Works of St. Gregory the Gr., ib. 1939. FR. LIEB-LANG, Grundfragen der myst. Theologie nach Gregor d. Gr. Moralia und Ezechielhomilien, 1934. H. SCHWANK, Gregor d. Gr. als Prediger, Diss. 1934. J. SPÖRL, R. Guardini-Festschrift, 1935, 198/211 (Gregory and the classics). L. KURZ, Gregors d. Gr. Lehre v. den Engeln, 1938. L. WEBER, Hauptfragen der Moraltheologie Gregors d. Gr., 1947. EIDENSCHINK § 60. Gesch. des Kirchenstaates unter Gregor d. Gr.: TH. MOMMSEN, Archiv f. Sozial- u. Wirtschaftsgesch. 1, 1893, 43 ff. K. BLASEL, AkKR 1904, 83 ff. 225 ff. E. SPEARING, The Patrimony of the Roman Church in the Time of Gregory the Great, Cambridge 1918.

"Ecumenical Patriarch" by the Bishop of Constantinople because he rightly considered it as a threat to the Roman Primacy (§ 64, 2). After the Lombard invasion, Gregory became the great protector of the Italian people and on several occasions (592 and 593) when the Lombards were before the walls of Rome, he succeeded in inducing them to spare the people. His *social* and *charitable works* made him especially beloved among the poor.

Since the eighth century Gregory the Great has been ranked with Ambrose, Jerome and Augustine as one of the four great *Doctors of the Western Church.* From the viewpoint of theologians and scholars, he scarcely belongs in such company. For Gregory was not a scholar. He was a conscientious and precise theologian, but with little talent for the speculative. His education coincided with a period of intellectual and cultural decline, when classical studies were neglected (Gregory knew no Greek) and attention was directed almost exclusively to the practical-ascetical duties of pastoral work, administration and the missions. In these fields he accomplished truly great results and his pastoral and exegetical works skillfully popularized the products of the Golden Age of the Fathers. His Liber regulae pastoralis, a manual of pastoral theology, was translated into Greek during Gregory's lifetime and in the ninth century was translated into Anglo-Saxon by Alfred the Great. During the Middle Ages the work was regarded with almost the same veneration as a book of the Scriptures. His Moralia is a work of practical wisdom in which the moral teaching of the Church is explained as the author comments on the book of Job. Besides these works, Gregory wrote homilies on the Gospels and on Ezechiel, and compiled a collection of popular legends of the saints called Dialogi de vita et miraculis patrum Italicorum. The second book of this work contains the life of St. Benedict. The hymns which are ascribed to Gregory are not of high quality. His Registrum Epistolarum (848 in all) is an important source for the history of the period.

## § 65.

### Synods.[1]

1. The many and important theological controversies of this period explain the frequency with which synods were held. Shortly

---

[1] For the most important collections see § 2, 2. Also: G. VOELLUS et H. JUSTELLUS, Bibliotheca iuris can. veteris, 2 tom. Paris 1661. H. TH.

after the beginning of the period, the first great assembly of bishops was called by Constantine the Great and met at *Nicaea* in 325. It was intended to serve as a sort of a supreme court to decide definitely and for the whole Church the matters proposed. Before the end of the seventh century five more *ecumenical*, that is, general synods, were held — all in the East: at *Constantinople* in 381, 553 and 680—681; at *Ephesus* in 431 and at *Chalcedon* in 451. The first and second synods of Constantinople were, strictly speaking, only general councils of the East (v. infra no. 3 and § 48, 6; 49, 2; 58, 5) but later were approved by the West and thus attained the character of general councils of the whole Church. The synods of Sardica in 343 (§ 48, 3), Ephesus in 449 (§ 55, 2) and Constantinople in 692 (§ 59, 6) were intended to be general councils (the schismatic Greeks still hold that the synod of 692 was a general council); but never received universal recognition. The ecumenical councils were at the same time *councils of the Empire* since they dealt not only with ecclesiastical matters, but affairs of State as well. Moreover, attendance at them was confined almost exclusively to bishops within the boundaries of the Empire, since up to this time few Christians, except Arians, Nestorians and Monophysites dwelt beyond.

---

BRUNS, Canones Apostolorum s. IV—VII, 1839. F. LAUCHERT, Die Kanones der wichtigsten altkirchl. Konzilien nebst den Apost. Kanones, 1896. C. H. TURNER, Ecclesiae occidentalis monumenta iuris antiquissima I II, 3, Oxford 1899/1930. F. SCHULTHESS, Die syrischen Kanones d. Synoden v. Nicäa bis Chalcedon, Abh. Gött. 1908. Corpus notitiarum episcopatuum Ecclesiae orientalis graecae I, 1—2: Les listes conciliaires, éd. p. E. GERLAND et V. LAURENT, Istanbul 1931/6. H. J. SCHROEDER, Disciplinary Decrees of the General Councils (325—1215), text, translat. and commentary, St. Louis 1937. Codificazione canonica orientale Fonti, Rome 1930 ff. FR. MAASSEN, Gesch. der Literatur u. der Quellen des kanon. Rechts im Abendland I, 1870. H. LECLERCQ, Liber canonum, DictAC IX, 85/159. C. J. v. HEFELE, Conciliengeschichte, und HEFELE-LECLERCQ, Histoire des Conciles, § 2, 2. J. FORGET, Art. Conciles, DictThC III, 636/76. C. A. KELLER, Papsttum u. Konzil im ersten Jahrtausend, ZkTh 1903/4; also F. X. FUNK, Die Berufung der ökum. Synoden des Altertums, AU I, 39 ff. 498 ff.; III, 143/9 (rejoinder of KNELLER in ZkTh 1908, 75/99). H. GELZER, Die Konzilien als Reichsparlamente, Ausgew. kleine Schriften, 1907, 142/55. ED. SCHWARTZ, Die Konzilien des 4. u. 5. Jh., HZ 104, 1909, 1/37; On the Councils of the Empire from Theodosius to Justinian, ZRGkan 1921, 208/54; Zweisprachigkeit (griechisch u. lateinisch) in den Konzilsakten, Philologus 1933, 245/53; Die Kanonessammlungen der alten Reichskirche, ZRGkan 1936, 1/114; ZntW 1936, 1/23 (collection of canones of the Cod. Veron. LX). B. STEPHANIDES, ZKG 1936, 127/57 (Development of the synods of the patriarchate of Constantinople). G. ROETHE, Zur Gesch. der röm. Synoden im 3. u. 4. Jh., Diss. 1937. J. A. EISELE, Die Rechtsstellung des Papstes im Verhältnis zu den allg. Synoden, 1938. M. GOEMANS, Het algemeen Concilie in de vierde eeuw, Nymwegen 1945.

---

2. The character of general councils as *synods of the Empire* is also clearly seen from their *structure*. The idea of a State Church which had prevailed since the time of Constantine the Great sanctioned the right *of the emperor to summon* a general council or, if necessary, transfer it to another place. The synods themselves and the popes conceded this right. Furthermore the emperor personally, or through his commissaries, made provision for external order, which in those turbulent times was a desirable if not highly necessary precaution. Theoretically, the discussions of purely ecclesiastical matters and the final decisions concerning them was left to the bishops; but under the circumstances it is not difficult to understand that the State's influence could easily be, and very often actually was, exerted. Finally, the emperors *confirmed* the decrees and gave them the force of law throughout the Empire.

All metropolitans were invited to the general councils and were required to bring at least some of their suffragans. It was considered essential that the *patriarchs* be present or send representatives with plenipotentiary powers. Owing to the fact that all the early councils were held in the East, western representation was always numerically weak. No *pope* was personally present at any of the general councils held during this period; but papal *legates* were present at all of them. Indeed it was the general conviction that without the participation of Rome general councils could not make definite decisions. Precedence was always given to papal legates in sessions of the synods, as well as in subscribing the protocol. The legates were previously instructed by the popes themselves or by Roman synods held for that purpose, so that the legates' approval of decisions was considered the same as *papal approval* (vide infra). When legates refused to subscribe, as in the case of canon 28 of Chalcedon (§ 63, 1), pressure was often brought to bear on them.

Since Constantine was present in person at Nicaea and Theodosius I at Constantinople (381), no protocol was drawn up at either of these councils. Only three fragments have been preserved: the Creeds, the disciplinary canons and the list of bishops who subscribed, arranged according to the provinces to which they belonged. But *Ephesus* (431) and *Chalcedon* (451) as well as the other general councils yield detailed *minutes of the sessions* and quite extensive official acta. In some cases the acta were drafted by the contending parties, in other cases they are the official reports provided by the imperial notaries. — The *lists of bishops subscribing* to the decrees of the general councils of antiquity are given in Harduin, Acta Conciliorum I, 312, 1527; II, 627; III, 1423. At *Nicaea* and *Ephesus* the names of Hosius of Corduba and Cyril of Alexandria appear before the names of the papal legates; but we know that Cyril represented the pope and it is probable that Hosius did also. The legates refused to sign the acta of *Chalcedon* because of their objection to canon 28. However, that they took precedence during the council is seen from the minutes of the individual sessions (Harduin II, 366, 383, 446, 458, 467, 502). This was not the case at the second and fifth general council (387 and 553) since these synods were not originally intended to be general (*E. Schwartz*, Die Kanonessammlungen, vide supra; idem, Über die Bischofslisten der Synoden von Chalcedon, Nicäa und Konstantinopel, Abh. München NF. 13, 1937. *E. Honigmann*, cfr. § 47, 1).

At this time it was *not* considered necessary that the pope issue a *special* proclamation confirming the decrees of the general councils. Under the circumstances in which the councils were held, it was possible for the emperor to approve as soon as the work of the council had been completed and long before a formal confirmation by the pope could be obtained. Cfr. Funk AU I, 87/121 (opposes the opinion of J. Blötzer, ZkTh 1886, 86 ff.).

3. The general councils were assemblies representing the entire Church and were called only to deal with extraordinary affairs. But there were also synods such as Constantinople in 381, Arles in 314 and Rome in 680 in which only the bishops of the East or West respectively participated. These were known as *general synods*. *Patriarchal, national, provincial, diocesan synods* were assemblies of bishops or priests of such ecclesiastical divisions under the presidency of the respective ecclesiastical superior. An assembly of all the bishops of West Africa was called a *Plenary Council*.

*Provincial synods* early became important institutions for systematizing and consolidating ecclesiastical law. Nicaea (can. 5) and Chalcedon (can. 19) prescribed that they be held twice a year. Orleans in 533 (can. 2) and other councils of the sixth century ordained that they be held at least once a year. Several synods of the West during the sixth and seventh centuries advised the holding of *diocesan synods* once every year.

A special type of synod called *endemusa* (σύνοδος ἐνδημοῦσα) became an important factor in the government of the Greek Church during the fifth century. It consisted of a meeting of the bishops who happened to be in the city of *Constantinople* and was called by the patriarch to discuss any weighty problems on which he desired advice. Later, a number of bishops took up residence in the city so that the endemusa synod might meet whenever the patriarch desired.

The right to *participate* in a synod belonged only to the *bishops* or in the case of diocesan synods, to the clergy. In Spain, however, since the middle of the seventh century, the right was granted to the nobility who were also permitted to sign the acta after the bishops and abbots. Such concilia mixta were later introduced into France.

4. The *agenda* at synods varied according to circumstances. Any problem or difficulty concerning the external or internal affairs of the Church which called for settlement became matter for synodal

discussion. The *decrees* (ὅροι) fall into two classifications: either matters of faith (δόγματα, σύμβολα) or matters of organization, discipline and worship (κάνονες). To facilitate reference to this latter and more extensive group, the practice was early adopted of making special *collections of canons*.

The most important collection in the Greek Church is the Συναγωγὴ κανόνων of *John Scholasticus* († 577) a priest of Antioch and later Patriarch of Constantinople. The collection was made about 550. In the Latin Church several collections were made: a) The Codex canonum ecclesiae Africanae of the Synod of Carthage in 419; b) the Dionysiana (scil. collectio) a collection of synodal canons and papal decrees from 384 to 498 of the Scythian monk, *Dionysius Exiguus* (§ 78, 2), made at Rome about 500. These two were later combined to form c) Corpus (codicis) canonum (PL 76; Strewe and Wurm, vide infra); d) *Statuta ecclesiae antiqua*, influenced by the Apostolica Traditio of Hippolytus. This collection was probably made in southern Gaul toward the end of the fifth century or the beginning of the sixth century (cfr. G. Morin, RevBén 1913, 334/42); e) *Hispana* (Isidoriana) *collectio* (PL 84) of the seventh century and for a long time erroneously ascribed to Isidore of Seville (§ 78, 4). The collections of John Scholasticus and Dionysius Exiguus contain the so-called *Apostolic Canons* with prescriptions regarding the election, ordination, conduct and duties of clerics. They form the conclusion to the Apostolic Constitutions (§ 75, 5) and are probably the work of the same author. They originated in Syria about the year 400. Some of the 85 canons have been taken from Oriental synods of the fourth century. The Synod in Trullo of 692 declared them to be genuine and binding. Dionysius Exiguus copied only the first 50 of them in his collection. For a long time the Latin Church doubted their authenticity, but when the Dionysiana attained wide circulation — Pope Hadrian I gave Charlemagne a copy in 774 — the canons were gradually accepted and copied in later collections. — *Ioannis Scholastici* Synagoga L titulorum ceteraque eiusdem opera iuridica, ed. *V. Beneševič I*, Abh. München NF. 14, 1937. — *Ed. Schwartz*, Die Kanonessammlung des Johannes Scholastikus, Sb. München 1933, 6. — *Ad. Strewe*, Die Canonessammlung des Dionysius Exiguus in ihrer ersten Redaktion, ed. 1931. — *H. Wurm*, Studien u. Texte zur Dekretalensammlung des Dionysius Exiguus, 1939. — *P. Séjourné*, Isidore de Seville, son rôle dans l'hist. du droit canonique, Paris 1929 (cfr. G. Le Bras, RevSR 1930, 218/57). — *H. Leclercq*, DictAC II, 1910/50 (the Apostolic Canons).

It is the opinion of Peitz, but as yet only an hypothesis, that all the known collections and translations of ancient canons, with the exception of a little known collection at Constantinople, are copies of Dionysius. It is also thought that Dionysius was called to Rome by Pope Gelasius I and made use of the original protocols in the papal archives. Peitz further believes that the disciplinary decrees of Nicaea and Chalcedon were not cast in their final form at the Councils, but were sent to the pope for revision; that a translation made by Dionysius about 515 was sent to the Spanish Church (the Hispana) and was approved by the synod of Tarragona in 516; that the Dionysiana was then taken over by the Eastern Church in 520 or 521 (Quesnelliana) and that the present Dionysiana does not go beyond 527, the date of Dionysius' death. — Cfr. *W. M. Peitz*, Dionysius Exiguus als Kanonist 1945; also H. Förster, Schweiz. Beiträge z. allg. Gesch. 1946, 282/8.

# CHAPTER IV
## WORSHIP, DISCIPLINE AND MORALS

### § 66.
### Baptism and the Catechumenate. Baptism of Heretics[1].

1. This period witnessed no great changes in the administration of baptism. Most of those to be baptized were *adults* converted from paganism. Even the children of Christian parents did not receive the Sacrament of Regeneration until adulthood and it was often postponed until the end of life (Constantine the Great, Constantius and others). Although there is ample evidence that the Church from the beginning taught that the Sacrament could be administered to infants, the practice of *infant baptism* did not become general until the fifth century. And then it seems to have been a reaction against Pelagianism (§ 56, 1).

2. The *catechumenate* was retained as long as the circumstances which gave rise to it continued. In the fourth century it appears fully developed. During Lent or some other time (see below) those who had decided to receive baptism and were found worthy of being admitted to the Church, were given a course of special instructions. They were called φωτιζόμενοι, βαπτιζόμενοι competantes (sc. baptismum), electi. The instructions were based on the *Creed* (§ 22, 2). In the East, the Niceno-Constantinopolitan Creed (§ 49, 2) was used for this purpose. The candidates were obliged to learn the Creed and the *Our Father* by heart and at an appointed time were called upon to recite them before the assembled congregation (traditio, redditio symboli). The process of preparation also included exorcisms, confession of sins, fasting and

---

[1] Cfr. literature in § 22. F. PROBST, Katechese u. Predigt vom 4. bis 6. Jh., 1884. F. WIEGAND, Stellung des apost. Symbols im kirchl. Leben des MA. I, 1899. J. KUNZE, Die Übergabe der Evangelien beim Taufunterricht, 1909. P. GLAUE, Zur Gesch. der Taufe in Spanien, Sb. Heidelberg 1913, 9; 1927/8, 2. F. J. DÖLGER, Die Taufe Konstantins u. ihre Probleme, RQ Suppl. 19, 1913, 429 ff. A. BLUDAU, ThGl 1924, 225/42 (the catechumenate in Jerusalem). A. DONDEYNE, RHE 1932, 5 ff. 751 ff. (the bapt. examination in the Latin Church). F. J. BADCOCK, RevBén 1933, 292/311 (the baptismal creed in the fourth century). H. SCHEIDT, Die Taufwasser-Weihegebete, 1936. E. STOMMEL, Studien zur Epiklese der röm. Taufwasserweihe, 1950. D. VAN DEN EYNDE, RechSR 1937, 196/212 (baptism and confirmation according to the Apost. Constitutions); Antonianum 1939, 257/76 (post-baptismal rites in the West). B. BUSCH, De initiatione christiana sec. doctrinam S. Augustini, Rome 1939. A. CHAVASSE, RechSR 1948, 325/81 (the scrutinium in Rome before the ninth cent.). O. HAGEMÜLLER, Hl. Gottesgeburt. Ein altsyr. Tauftraktat, 1947. M. C. DIDIER, MSR 1949, 232/46 (infant baptism in the fourth cent.). J. ERNST, ZkTh 1903, 759/67 (baptism by heretics in the Synods of Arles and Nicaea). W. SATTLER, Die Stellung d. griech. Kirche zur Ketzert., Diss. 1911.

prayer. At Rome and in Africa these preliminaries were called *scrutinia* and served the purpose of testing the disposition of the candidate as well as preparing him. It appears that the scrutinia were introduced in the church of France during the seventh century. After the catechumens had been baptized they were further instructed regarding the *sacraments*. For as long as the disciplina arcani prevailed, only the baptized were considered capable of receiving such instruction. The Greeks referred to the post-baptismal instructions as the mystagogical catecheses. The Catecheses of *St. Cyril* of Jerusalem are famous. They consist of five instructions on the sacraments to those who have been recently baptized and are preceded by nineteen instructions preparatory to baptism. A series of such instructions by Theodore of Mopsuestia has recently been discovered in a Syrian translation. *St. Augustine's* De catechizandis rudibus contains the theory rather than the practice of the catecheses. When infant baptism became general there was no longer place for the preparatory instructions; but all the elements of the catechumenate were retained in modified form in the rite of baptism.

Many scholars of past and more recent times have held that Origen (C. Cels. III, 51) distinguished two *classes of catechumens*, the κατηχούμενοι and the φωτιζόμενοι. But such is not the case. The *candidates for baptism*, in Christian antiquity did not constitute a subdivision of the catechumenate but were considered as belonging to a *special state* between the catechumens and the faithful. Still less correct is the belief that the catechumens were divided into *three classes*. It is true that canon 3 of the Synod of Neocaesarea (between 314 and 325) mentions ἀκροώμενοι, and γόνυ κλινόντες before the φωτιζόμενοι, but the reference is to classes of penitents and not to catechumens. Cfr. Funk AU I, 209/41; III, 57/64. (For the opposite cfr. E. Schwartz, Bußstufen u. Katechumenatsklassen, 1911).

3. During this period baptism was usually administered by a triple immersion and was conferred in special chapels called *baptisteries* (§ 71, 2) erected near the church. In Spain and among the Arian sects of the Eunomians and Aëtians (§ 48, 4) administration was by a single immersion. Among the heretics, the practice expressed their denial of the Trinity, whereas in Spain it had just the opposite purpose, viz., to profess belief in the Trinity by mentioning the three names during the one immersion. Besides the two days heretofore set aside for baptism, the vigils of Easter and Pentecost, the *feast of the Epiphany* (§ 25, 2) was also set apart in the East as a special day for administering baptism. In Spain the sacrament was conferred on other feast days as well, while Rome insisted on the ancient practice. When infant baptism became general, the same days were adhered to, except in case of necessity.

The Latin Church recognized *baptism of desire* as a substitute for baptism of water. In his famous funeral sermon over the murdered Emperor Valentinian II in 392 (§ 41, 5), *St. Ambrose* expressly said that the deceased emperor's piety and desire for baptism had cleansed him (hunc sua pietas abluit et voluntas). *Augustine* expresses the same idea in his work De baptis. c. Donat. IV, 22 n. 29. On the other hand we find the opinion that only martyrdom, or *baptism of blood*, can take the place of baptism of water. In fact, in the Greek Church this idea prevailed.

4. *Baptism administered by heretics* was no longer the subject of bitter dispute as in the third century, yet various opinions were still held. The Latin Church never altered her opinion. The General Synod of Arles in 314 (§ 52, 2) repudiated the opposite practice of the Africans and ordered that those who had been baptized by heretics in the name of the Trinity were not to be rebaptized but manus ei tantum imponatur ut accipiat spiritum sanctum. It was then that the adherents of the stricter view in Africa left the Church as Donatists. In the East the validity of baptism by heretics was disputed for some time. During the fifth century a distinction began to be made between the valid baptism of Arians, Macedonians, Novatians, Quartodecimans and Apollinarians and the invalid baptism of the Eunomians, Montanists and Sabellians. This view was adopted by canon 95 of the Synod of Trullo in 692.

## § 67.

### Liturgy, Preaching, Holy Communion.
### Chant and the Recitation of the Canonical Hours[1].

1. No longer fearful of persecution and with numerous large and beautiful buildings, the Church was free to expand her *liturgy* on a grand and solemn scale. The essential Eucharistic prayers (the Anaphora and the Canon) remained the same; but the non-essential

---

[1] Cfr. the sources and literature in § 2, 5, and § 22 (DUCHESNE etc.) and especially in § 23. Codificazione canonica orientale. FONTI, Rome 1930 ff. Jahrbuch für Liturgiewissenschaft (JbLW), ed. O. CASEL, 1921 ff. (extensive literature). Archiv f. Liturgiewissensch., ed. H. EMONDS, 1950. Liturg. Jahrb. ed. J. PASCHER, 1951. H. ENGBERDING, Ephem. Liturgicae 1940, 105/14 (bibliography of Oriental liturgies). F. PROBST, Liturgie des 4. Jh. u. deren Reform, 1893; Die abendländ. Messe vom 5.—8. Jh., 1896. L. EISEN-HOFER, Handb. der kath. Liturgik, 2 vols. 1932/3. PH. OPPENHEIM, Institutiones systematico-historicae in sacram liturgiam I, Turin [2]1945. M. RIGHETTI, Storia liturgica, Mailand 1945 ff. I. SCHUSTER, Liber sacramentorum. Note storiche e liturgiche sul Missale Romano, 9 vol. Torino 1919/28; Appendice (Reg.) by C. D'AMATO, ib. 1932; Germ. transl. R. BAUERSFELD, 9 vols. and index 1929/32. F. CABROL, Liturgie, DictAC IX, 787/845. P. DREWS, Messe, RE XII, 697/723; XXIV, 91 f. A. BAUMSTARK, Die Messe im Morgenland, 1906 (Samml. Kösel); Vom geschichtl. Werden der Liturgie, 1923; Liturgie comparée, Amay s. M. 1939. E. BISHOP, Liturgica historica, Oxford 1918. F. BATIFFOL, Leçons sur la Messe, Paris [8]1923. F. J. MOREAU, Les liturgies eucharistiques, Brux. 1924. F. J. DÖLGER, Sol salutis, Gebet u. Gesang im christl. Altertum, [2]1925. J. A. JUNGMANN, Die Stellung Christi im liturg. Gebet, 1925. I. EPHREM II RAHMANI, Les liturgies orientales et occidentales, Beyrouth. 1929. J. BRINKTRINE, Die hl. Messe, [3]1950. A. VILLIEN, Les sacraments, histoire et liturgie, Paris 1931. O. CASEL, Oriens Christ. 1932, 289/302 (Leiturgia = munus). C. CALLEWAERT, Sacris eruditi, Fragmenta liturgica, Bruges 1939. TH. KLAUSER, Misc. G. Mercati I, Rome 1946, 467/82 (the transition to Latin as the liturgical language). JUNGMANN, § 23.

elements underwent many and great changes. For example, it was felt necessary to make the doxology of the liturgy express fully the dogmatic concepts which had been so admirably clarified as a result of the religious controversies. Infant baptism (§ 66, 1) and the modification of the penitential discipline made it no longer necessary to dismiss catechumens and penitents before the Mass of the faithful. It is said that Basil the Great and John Chrysostom abridged the liturgy because they noted that as the people grew lukewarm, lengthy services, instead of increasing their devotion, only irked them. While the liturgical prayers in the *East* were always the same, the *West* developed a great variety in its prayers, especially after Greek was abandoned and Latin became the liturgical language (about 380). Liturgical *reforms* in the West are ascribed to popes *Damasus* (366—384), *Gelasius* (492—496), *Gregory I* (590—604) and to *St. Ambrose* of Milan († 397). But there is still much uncertainty and a great deal of discussion regarding the nature of these reforms (vide n. 3 infra). Certainly the introduction of feasts and festive seasons about the time of Pope Damasus, and the gradual arrangement of these feasts into liturgical cycles (§ 69, 2) had a far-reaching influence on liturgy. The lesson of Scripture, formerly read consecutively (the lessons of one day began where the previous day's reading had stopped and continued as long as the bishop desired), were now arranged in *Pericopes*. Even the orations (collects), prefaces and Communicantes of the Canon were also varied to correspond to the season or the feast. St. Jerome is said to have compiled the first Lectionarius or Comes.

2. Each of the principal churches had its own rite. The *Greek-Oriental*[1] liturgies were much more dramatic than those of the West

---

[1] Editions of the liturgy § 2, 5 and § 23. Maximilianus Princeps Saxoniae, Praelectiones de liturgiis orientalibus, 2 vol. 1908/13. R. JANIN, Les Églises orientales et les rites orientaux, Paris ²1926. J. M. HANSSENS, Institutiones liturgicae de ritibus orientalibus z. II—III, Rome 1930/32. S. SALAVILLE, Liturgies orientales, Paris 1932; An Introduction to the Study of Eastern Liturgies, London 1938; Studia Orientalia Liturgico-Theologica, Rome 1940. J. ZIADÉ, Messe orientale, DictThC XI, 1434/87. W. H. FRERE, The Anaphora or Great Eucharistic Prayer, London 1938. Greek Liturgies, Germ. transl. in BKV 5, 1912. FL. DE MEESTER, Grecques Liturgies, DictAC VI, 1591/1662; Liturgia byzantina Lib. II p. 6, Rome 1930; Die Lit. des hl. Joh. Chrysostomus, griech. u. deutsch. München 1932; Χρυσοστομικά Rome 1908, 245/357 (history of the Chrysostom liturgy). A. BAUMSTARK, Die konstantinopolit. Messe vor dem 9. Jh., Kl. Texte 35, 1909; Oriens Christ. 1927, 1/32 (beginnings of the Byzantine rite). F. MERCENIER et F. PARIS, La prière des Églises de rite byzantin I, Amay s. M. 1937. M. TARCHNISVILI, Die byzant. Lit. als Verwirklichung der Einheitsgemeinschaft im Dogma, 1939; Liturgiae ibericae antiquiores, Paris 1950 (CSCO 122/3). F. J. MOREAU, Les anaphores des

and stressed more forcefully the mysterious nature of worship. In Jerusalem and Antioch the prevailing liturgy was named after *St. James*, the "Brother of the Lord", while that of Alexandria was called after St. Mark. At Constantinople and throughout that patriarchate there were two liturgies: one called after *St. Basil the Great* and the other after *John Chrysostom*. The latter (shorter) was and is still used generally in the Greek Church, while the former and longer rite is reserved for use on certain days such as the Sundays of Lent, vigils and principal feasts. Older than these liturgies, and in a sense the model from which they were taken, is the so-called *Clementine liturgy* found in the eighth book of the Apostolic Constitutions (§ 75, 5), dependent in turn on *Hippolytus'* Ap. Traditio. It gives a complete formula for Sunday services. Also originating in Egypt is an old euchologion with the rite for the Eucharistic celebration, baptism and ordination. It bears the name of Bishop Serapion of Thmuis († after 362), the friend of St. Anthony and St. Athanasius.

The liturgies of the *West* or of the *Latin* Church[1] bear the name of the principal church in which they developed, e. g., *Rome* and

---

liturgies de S. Jean Chrysost. et de S. Basile, Paris 1927. H. ENGBERDING, Das eucharist. Hochgebet der Basileioslit., 1931; Oriens Christ. 1932, 32/48 (ancient Antioch liturgy). AD. RÜCKER, Ritus baptismi et missae quem descripsit Theodorus Mopsuestenus, 1933 (Opuscula et textus, ser. liturg. 2); also H. LIETZMANN, Sb. Berlin 1933, 915/36; M. JUGIE, Échos d'Orient, 1935, 257/71. Anaphorae Syriacae, edd. et latine vert. A. RAES, AD. RÜCKERT, H. W. CODRINGTON, Rome 1939 ff. A. BAUMSTARK, Festbrevier u. Kirchenjahr der syr. Jakobiten, 1910. AD. RÜCKER, Die syr. Jakobosanaphora, 1923. H. FUCHS, Die Anaphora des monophysit. Patriarchen Johanan I († 648), 1926. TH. SCHERMANN, Ägypt. Abendmahlsliturgien, 1912. Rituale Melchitarum, ed. and transl. M. BLAC, 1938. B. CAPELLE, Muséon 1946, 425/43 (Anaphora of Serapion). S. A. B. MERCER, The Ethiopic Liturgy, London 1915. J. M. HARDEN, The Anaphora of the Ethiopic Liturgy, London 1915. J. M. HARDEN, The Anaphora of the Ethiopic Liturgy, ib. 1927. S. EURINGER, Äthiop. Anaphoren hg. u. übers. in Orientalia Christ. 30, 33, 36, Rome 1933/4. P. DREWS, Untersuchungen über die sog. klementin. Liturgie I, 1906. H. LECLERCQ, DictAC III, 2748/95 (liturgy of the Apost. constitutions).

[1] Collections of sources (MURATORI, ASSEMANI, DANIEL etc.) § 2, 5. Liturgy of Milan: M. MAGISTRETTI, La liturgia della chiesa Milanese nel sec. IV, Milano 1899. P. LEJAY, Ambrosien rite, DictAC I, 1373/1442. W. C. BISHOP, The Mozarabic and Ambrosian Rites, London 1924. A. PAREDI, I Prefazi Ambrosiani, Milano 1937 (cfr. L. C. MOHLBERG, ThRev 1938, 41/47), ib. in S. Ambrogio nel XVI Centenario della nascità, Milano 1940, 69/157. Gallican liturgy: PL 72. A. WILMART, E. A. LOWE a. H. A. WILSON, The Missal of Bobbio (s. VII), London 1924. K. MOHLBERG, Missale Gothicum, ein gallikan. Sakramentar des 7./8. Jh., 1929. J. QUASTEN, Expositio antiquae liturgiae gallicanae Germano Paris. ascripta, 1934 (Opuscula et textus, ser. liturg. 3); Traditio 1943, 55/8 (Oriental influence on the Gallican liturgy). A. DOLD, Ein altgallikan. Lektionar des 5./6. Jh. aus d. Cod. Weissenb. 76, 1935 (Texte u. Arbeiten H. 26/28). J. B. THIBAUT, L'ancienne liturgie

*Milan*; or of the country in which they eventually prevailed, e. g., *Spain, Gaul,* Britain and Ireland. The Roman liturgy extended over southern Italy and Latin Africa while the Milanese or Ambrosian liturgy influenced Upper Italy. The *Gallic* or *Gallican* liturgy can be traced back to the fifth or sixth century through a palimpsest of the monastery of Weissenburg in Alsace (now in Wolfenbüttel). Spanish (Visigothic) liturgy is also called *Mozarabic* (cfr. § 84, 2; 98, 1) from the Arab rule in Spain (711).

3. **Roman liturgy**[1] is of special interest since it eventually superseded the other Latin liturgies. Most probably in the beginning it

---

Gallicane, Paris 1930; also F. CABROL, RHE 1930, 950/62.    H. LECLERCQ Liturgie Gallicane, DictAC VI, 473/593; IX, 1636/1729.   P. SALMON, Le Lectionnaire de Luxeuil, Rome 1944.   Mozarabic liturgy: PL 85.   W. C. BISHOP, see above.   W. CABROL, DictThC X, 2518/43; DictAC XII, 391/490.   A. W. S. PORTER, JThSt 1934, 266/86.   M. DIETZ, Gebetsklänge aus Altspanien (Illationes = Praefationes), 1947.

[1] H. LECLERCQ, Sacramentaires, DictAC 15, 242/85.   Sacramentarium Leonianum: PL 55: ed. CH. L. FELTOE, Cambridge 1897. P. BRUYLANTS, Concordance verbale du Sacramentaire Léonien, Louvain 1948.   F. CABROL, DictAC VIII, 2549/73; R. BUCHWALD, Weidenauer Studien 2, 1908, 187/252. M. RULE, JThSt 1908, 515 ff.; 1909, 54 ff. 467 f.; Ephemerides Liturgicae 1933, 3/12 (Cassiodorus, author of the Sacr. Leon.?)   Also G. DE JERPHANION, RechSR 1936, 364/6.   C. CALLEWAERT, S. Léon le Gr. et les textes du Léonien, Den Haag 1948.   A. STRUIBER, Libelli sacramentorum Romani, 1950.   F. L. CROSS, JThST 1949, 191/7 (pre-Leonine elements).   Sacram. Gelasianum: PL 74; ed. H. A. Wilson, Oxford 1894.   K. MOHLBERG, Das fränkische Sacram. Gelasianum in alemannischer Überlieferung, ²1939; Ein St. Galler Sacramentar-Fragment, 1939.   P. DE PUNIET, Le sacramentaire romain (Sacramentarium Gelas.) de Gellone, Rome 1938 (from Ephemerides Liturg. 1938, 104 ff.).   B. CAPELLE, RHE 1939, 22/34 (Pope Gelasius and the Roman Mass).   F. CABROL, DictAC VI, 747/77.   Sacram. Gregorianum: PL 78; ed. H. A. WILSON, 1915; ed. H. LIETZMANN, 1921; id. in Misc. F. Ehrle I, Rome 1924, 141/58 and in JbLW IX, 1929, 132/38; G. GASSNER, ib. VI, 1926, 218/23 (Gregory's testimony); H. HOHLWEIN, Ephemerides Liturg. 1928, 213 ff. 444 ff.; B. CAPELLE, RevBén 1937, 13/28; C. CALLEWAERT, RHE 1937, 306/26. F. CABROL, DictAC VI, 1776/96.   A. DOLD, Ein vorhadrian. Gregorian. Palimpsest-Sakramentar, 1919.   A. DOLD and A. BAUMSTARK, Das Palimpsest-Sakr. im Cod. Aug. CXII, 1925.   K. MOHLBERG and A. BAUMSTARK, Die älteste erreichbare Gestalt des Liber sacramentorum anni circuli der röm. Kirche, 1927.   J. BRINKTRINE, Sacramentarium Rossianum, 1930.   A. BAUMSTARK, Liturgia Romana e Liturgia dell'Esarcato, Rome 1904; Das Missale Romanum, s. Entwicklung, Nymwegen 1929.   ST. BEISSEL, Die Entstehung der Perikopen des röm. Messbuches, 1908; cfr. G. MORIN, RevBén 1910, 41 ff.; 1911, 296 ff.   A. FORTESCUE, The Mass. Study of the Roman Liturgy, London ²1917.   E. BISHOP, Liturgica historica, Oxford 1918, 77 ff.   H. GRISAR, Das Missale im Lichte röm. Stadtgeschichte, 1925.   J. P. KIRSCH, Die Stationskirchen des Missale Rom., 1926.   E. HOSP, Die Heiligen im Canon Missae, 1926. V. L. KENNEDY, The Saints of the Canon of the Mass, Rome 1938.   F. CABROL, Les livres de la liturgie latine, Paris 1930; La messe en Occident, Paris 1932; Missel Romain, DictAC XI, 1468/94.   P. ALFONZO, L'eucologia romana antica, Subiaco 1931.   G. NICKL, Der Anteil des Volkes an der Meßliturgie im Frankenreich von Chlodwig bis auf Karl d. Gr., 1930. W. H. FRERE, Studies in Early Roman Liturgy, vol. I: The Calendar; vol. II: The Gospel-Lectionary: vol. III: The Epistle-Lectionary, Oxford 1930/5.

was very much like the other liturgies since there was a basic resemblance among them all. But in the general development which was taking place and especially in the reforms under the popes from the fourth to the sixth century, it received a special character until in the sixth and seventh centuries it took the essential form it has today. At any rate, the *Canon*, the fixed part of the Roman Mass from the Sanctus to the Pater Noster, probably taken, at least in part, from the Greek, had assumed its definite form by the end of the sixth century. Unfortunately the sources, the old Roman *Sacramentaries*, i. e., collections of variable prayers and blessings, do not give the detailed information that might be expected of them. The reason is that with the exception of the Leonianum, they have all been revised several times. The oldest of them, the *Sacramentarium Leonianum*, is no doubt partly the work of Leo the Great. But it is a private collection of Roman Mass-prayers that was completed about the middle of the sixth century. The *Sacramentarium Gelasianum*, on the other hand, is an official collection, but belongs to the Frankish-Carolingian period (700—750). Finally the *Sacramentarium Gregorianum*, the basis of the later Roman Missal, is a book for use at the papal Mass and was introduced into France by Pepin in 754 on the occasion of his coronation (§ 98, 1). In its oldest form part of it can be traced back to Gregory the Great. It is worthy of note that the *Station Masses* of the Roman Missal contain many references to local history during the siege of Rome by the Ostrogoths and the Lombards.

The following *changes* in the *Roman liturgy* are to be noted. The **Canon** was revised and re-arranged probably by Pope Gelasius I (Drews) or Gregory the Great (Baumstark). It may be safely assumed that at one time the *epiclesis* was part of the Roman Mass. After the fourth century almost all of the Oriental and some of the Western liturgies placed this prayer after the words of Institution. It was an invocation of the Holy Ghost asking him to come

P. PUNIET, Le Pontifical Romain, historie et commentaire, 2 vol. Paris 1930/1; German, 2 vols. Klosterneuburg 1935/6. D. BUENNER, L'ancienne liturgie romaine; Le rite lyonnais, Lyons 1934. TH. KLAUSER, Das röm. Capitulare Evangeliorum I, 1935. H. W. CODRINGTON, The Liturgy of Saint Peter, Münster 1936. R. HIERZEGGER, ZkTh 1936, 511/54 (Collecta u. Statio in the Roman liturgy). B. CAPELLE, RHE 1938, 556/9 (Lectionarius Romanus before Gregory the Great). K. M. HOFMANN, Philema hagion (the holy kiss) 1938. B. BECK, Annotationes as textus quosdam liturgicos e vitis sanctorum aevi Merovingici selectos, Rome 1939. G. MORIN, RevBén 1940, 3/14 (part played by the popes of the sixth century in the development of the liturgy). E. DONCKEL, Außerröm. Heilige in Rome, 1946. See literature preceding § 67.

down upon the altar and change the bread and wine into the Body and Blood of the Lord. But in the course of reforms, the epiclesis disappeared from the Roman liturgy, probably under Gelasius I. Some liturgists think there are traces of the epiclesis still to be found in the Roman Mass, in the Supplices te rogamus or in the Quam oblationem. But neither of these prayers contain the real characteristic of the epiclesis. The *"Prayer of the Faithful"* in the form of a litany was taken from the East into the Roman liturgy by Gelasius I and is now found at the beginning of the Mass of the Catechumens. Gregory the Great abbreviated it to the present Kyrie. Otherwise, *intercessory prayers* were all said after Consecration (Constantinople) or before it (Alexandria, Gaul, Spain). But in the Roman liturgy the Memento vivorum precedes and the Memento mortuorum follows the Consecration. The names of those for whom special prayers were to be said during Mass were inserted on the *diptych*, a hinged wax tablet. Hence to strike a name from the diptych (§ 58, 7) meant to sever all relations with such a person. The insertion of a list of saints in the Communicantes and Nobis quoque peccatoribus dates from Gelasius I. The list was augmented by Gregory the Great (Kennedy). The *kiss of peace* in most liturgies appears in connection with the offertory; in the Orient, before, in the West, except at Rome, after the offertory. It was given place in the Roman Mass, before Communion, probably just before this period, since Innocent I (402—417) and Augustine were both familiar with it in this place. — On the Roman **Canon**: F. Cabrol, DictAC II, 1847/1905. — F. X. Funk, AU III, 85/134. — K. J. Merk, Der Konsekrationstext der röm. Messe, 1915; also A. Baumstark, ThRev 1916, 342/50. — B. Botte, Le Canon de la Messe romaine, Louvain 1935. — G. Morin, RevBén 1939, 101/8 (the Canon in Milan). — B. Capelle, RHE 1946, 417/21. — C. Callewaert, Sacris erudiri 1948, 123/62. — On the **Epiclesis;** S. Salaville, DictThC V, 194/300; Échos d'Orient 1941/2, 268/82. — F. Cabrol, DictAC V, 142/84. — J. Höller, Die Epiklese der griech.-oriental. Liturgien, 1912; HJG 1914, 110/26. — J. Brinktrine, ZkTh 1918, 301 ff. 483 ff.; RQ 31, 1923, 21/8; ThGl 1929, 434/52. — O. Casel, JbLW III, 1923, 100 ff.; IV, 1924, 169 ff. — R. H. Connolly, JThSt 1924, 337/64. — A. G. Hebert, G. Dix and E. G. Atchley, in Theology 1933 and 1934. — E. G. Atchley, On the Epiclesis of the Eucharistic Liturgy, Oxford 1935. — H. W. Codrington, JThSt 1938, 141/50 (the Epiclesis in Egypt). — M. *Jugie*, De forma Eucharistiae. De epiclesibus eucharisticis, Rome 1943. — A. Chavasse, MSR 1946, 197/206 (an attempt to explain the Epiclesis in the Orient). — B. Botte, RechThAM 1947, 241/51 and C. C. Richardson, HarvThR 1947, 101/8 (does Hippolytus treat of the Epiclesis?).

The word **Mass** to designate the entire Eucharistic liturgy has been used since the end of the fourth century. Ambrose is the first certain witness of the usage (Ep. 20, 4 written in 384; cfr. Funk AU III, 134/43; H. Koch, Kath. 1907 II, 239 f.; 1908 I, 114/28). In the Peregrinatio Silviae (c. 395; § 70, 5), Missa, dismissal, means religious service in general and the Eucharistic celebration in particular. As the liturgist Florens of Lyons explained (ninth century), the term is evidently taken from the formula, Ite missa est, which was used in ancient times to signify that a service had ended. There was a twofold dismissal in Christian antiquity: missa (vulgar Latin = missio) catechumenorum and missa fidelium. This led some writers of the Middle

Ages, like Ivo of Chartres († 1117) to believe that there were two Masses: a Mass of the Catechumens and a Mass of the Faithful, whereas, in antiquity the term was used only to indicate the dismissal. The formula Ite missa est was also used at the end of other religious services; hence we find the expressions missae matutinae et vespertinae in canon 30 of the Synod of Agde (506) in southern Gaul. — K. J. Hefele, Beiträge z. KG. II, 1864, 273/76. — O. Rott-manner, ThQ 1889, 531/57; 1890, 526 f. — F. Kattenbusch, RE XII, 66/9. — Fr. Zimmermann, Die Abendmesse in Gesch. u. Gegenwart, 1914. — F. J. Döl-ger, AntChrist 1934, 271/75; 1940, 81/132. — J. A. Jungmann, ZkTh 1940, 26/37.

4. The quality of **preaching**[1] as a regular feature of divine service improved greatly during this period. The simple homily which had formerly followed the Scripture reading became an artistic sermon (λóγος) in which every device was used to interest and instruct. The Golden Age of preaching coincides with the most flourishing period of Patristic literature (c. 325—451). Sermons were delivered not only on Sundays and feast days, but also during the week and daily during Lent. The bishop preached, seated on his cathedra, but after the fifth century, he would, on occasions, ascend the ambo (§ 71, 3). With his delegation, priests and deacons preached regularly in the rural churches. However, the form of the sermon, especially in the East, was often unduly influenced by contemporary rhetoric, and the conduct of the audience was not always in keeping with the sacredness of the place. Thunderous applause often gave the church the atmosphere of a theater. But the accomplishments of Basil, Gregory Nazianzus, Gregory of Nyssa and especially of *John Chrysostom* in the East; and of Ambrose, *Augustine*, Peter Chrysologus, Zeno of Verona, Maximus of Tours, Caesar of Arles, Leo the Great and Gregory the Great in the West, still evoke admiration and imitation.

5. As in the preceding period, the Eucharistic *liturgy* was celebrated in most places only on Sunday. Since the fourth century Saturday was kept in the East as a half feast (§ 69, 1) and from that time Mass was celebrated on Saturday as well as on Station days. In the West, especially in Africa, at Rome and Milan it very early became customary to offer the Sacrifice daily.

Holy *Communion* was received frequently. St. Augustine (Ep. 54, 2) speaks of daily Communion as well as of its reception every Sunday. But with the mass conversions after the fourth century which brought many merely nominal Christians into the Church (§ 73, 1) the old practice was no longer generally followed. Many of the Fathers, especially John Chrysostom, complained that the laity communicated so seldom. Under these circumstances, the synod of Agde (506) in Southern Gaul, under the presidency of Caesar of Arles, ordained (can. 18) that Holy Communion was to be received at least three times a year, at Christmas, Easter and Pentecost; and this legislation governed the practice for the next several centuries. The communicant remained

---

[1] F. PROBST, Katechese u. Predigt vom 4.—6. Jh., 1884. F. STINGEDER, Gesch. der Schriftpredigt, 1920. J. ZELLINGER, Festgabe Knöpfler, 1917, 403/15 (applause during the sermon). See the literature in § 75—78.

standing and received the Sacred Species in the palm of the extended right hand. In Gaul it was customary for women to cover the hand with a linen cloth. The deacon presented the Chalice to each communicant. Some particles of the Species were reserved in a special vessel suspended above the altar to provide Viaticum for the dying; but it was not until the eleventh century that the Blessed Sacrament was reserved for distribution at other times. — *P. Browe*, De frequenti communione in Occidente usque ad a. 1000, Rome 1932; ThQ 1921, 22 ff. 133 ff. (Communion in the Gallican Church); ZkTh 1936, 1 ff. 211 ff. (Viaticum in antiquity and in the Middle Ages); ThGl 1938, 388/404 (reservation of the Bl. Eucharist); Die Pflichtkomm. im MA., 1940. — *Funk*, AU I, 293/308 (the rubrics for the distribution of Holy Communion).

At the end of Mass, those who had not received communion were given particles of blessed bread called **eulogia** (§ 23, 4). It was a substitute for the true δῶρον and hence also called ἀντίδωρον and the bread presented by the faithful at the offertory was used for the purpose. The practice has been preserved in the Greek Church and in parts of France to the present day. In the course of time, the eulogia lost its original significance since it was not only consumed in Church, but given to the faithful to take home with them and was also presented to those who had received Communion. Cfr. *A. Franz*, Die kirchl. Benediktionen im MA. I, 1909, 229 ff.

6. **Chant**[1] originated from the early custom of singing psalms and hymns during divine service (§ 23, 1). During the liturgical reforms singing was further developed and encouraged. Naturally in the early Church all singing in connection with religious worship was homophonic. In the Eastern Church the cantores (ψάλται) constituted one of the minor orders (§ 60, 1). Pope Sylvester is said to have established a special school for chanters at Rome about 330. Somewhat later, *Ambrose* of Milan, who, like Hilary, wrote many beautiful hymns (§ 76, 1) created a special liturgical chant, based on ancient Greek music (cantus Ambrosianus), which combined melody with rhythmic accent. The schola cantorum which *Gregory* the Great founded became the model for all other such institutions. He is credited, with good reason, with being

---

[1] G. MORIN, Der Ursprung des Gregorian. Gesanges, German by TH. EL-SÄSSER, 1892. G. DREVES, Ambrosius, der „Vater des Kirchengesanges", 1893. P. WAGNER, Einführ. in die Gregor. Melodien, 2 vols. ³1910/3; Neumen-kunde, ²1912. A. MÖHLER, Die griech., griech.-röm. u. altchristl.-latein. Musik, 1908 (RQ Suppl. 9); Gesch. der alten u. mittelalt. Musik, 2 parts ²1907 (Samml. Göschen). A. GASTOUÉ, Les origines du Chant romain, Paris 1907; L'art grégorien, ib. 1910. E. NIKEL, Gesch. der kath. Kirchenmusik I, 1908. H. LECLERCQ et A. GATARD, Chant romain et grégorien, DictAC III, 256/321. E. WELLESZ, Aufgaben u. Probleme auf dem Gebiet der byzant. u. oriental. Kirchenmusik, 1923. O. FLEISCHER, Die german. Neumen, 1923. F. J. DÖLGER, Sol salutis, Gebet u. Gesang im christl. Altert., ²1925. R. AIGRAIN, La musique religieuse, Paris 1929. J. QUASTEN, Musik u. Gesang in den Kulten der heidn. Antike u. christl. Frühzeit, 1930. O. URSPRUNG, Die kath. Kirchenmusik, 1933 (Handb. der Musikwiss., supplement). K. WACHS-MANN, Untersuchungen z. vorgregorian. Gesang, Diss. Freiburg (Schw.) 1935. P. GENNRICH, Der Gemeindegesang in der alten u. mittelalt. Kirche, 1935. K. G. FELLERER, Der gregorian. Choral im Wandel der Jhh., 1936; Gesch. d. kath. Kirchenmusik, ²1949.

the one who gave to liturgical chant the fixed form which came to be known as cantus Gregorianus, Romanus, firmus, choralis; and is said to have composed many new melodies. In order to preserve these melodies, a method of writing music in numbers was employed. *Romanus* the Melodist (§ 77, 2) was the most noted composer of hymns in the Greek Church.

7. Besides the Eucharistic liturgy, the recitation or singing of the **Canonical Hours** assumed importance as a form of religious service. The Hours consisted of psalms, hymns, Scriptural readings and prayers. The usual hours of prayer, especially for monks, were the early morning, the third, sixth, and ninth hours (these even in pre-Christian times § 26, 1), the evening and midnight. Very early Completorium was separated from Vespers and served as a form of evening prayer. In addition to the *four vigils* customary among the Romans, the monks divided the night, including daybreak, or at least the nights before feasts and Sundays, into four periods of prayer: three nocturns and matins (originally Laudes, later, nocturni). Finally, another period of prayer, Prime, was inserted between Laudes and Tierce, thus completing the seven Canonical Hours of the later breviary. *St. Benedict* and his Order did much toward introducing the Office, as the canonical hours came to be known, as a form of worship in the Church. Not only the clergy and monks took part in this form of prayer, but from the sixth century, the laity, too, attended, at least for Matins and Vespers, since in many churches the Eucharistic service was not held on week days (cfr. canon 30 of the Synod of Agde 506). — S. Bäumer, Gesch. des Breviers, 1895. — P. Battifol, Histoire du Bréviaire romain, Paris [3]1911. — H. Lietzmann, Einführung in das röm. Brevier, 1917. — *J. Brinktrine*, Das römische Brevier, 1932; Italian edition and revision, Rome 1946. — G. Morin, RevBén 1932, 145/52 (the canonical hours in the monasteries of Cassiodorus). — H. Leclercq, Office divin, DictAC XII, 1962/2017. — J. Froger, Les origines de Prime, Rome 1946 (sixth cent.). — K. J. Merk, Das Brevier u. der Säkularklerus, 1950.

From the sixth century on, the beautiful prayer of praise, thanksgiving and petition, the **Te Deum laudamus**, was usually added to Matins. Hincmar of Reims in the ninth century repeated the then old, but erroneous legend that it had been composed by St. Ambrose or by Ambrose and Augustine together. In its present form the Te Deum was probably composed by Bishop *Niceta* of Remesiana in Dacia (§ 76, 7) who used phrases from older Greek prayers. — *A. E. Burn*, The Hymn Te Deum and its Author, London 1926. — G. Morin, RevBén 1907, 180/223. — *Cl. Blume*, StML 81, 1911, 274 ff. 401 ff. 487 ff. — M. Frost, JThSt 1933, 250/57; 1938, 388/91; 1942, 59 ff. 192/4. — *A. Baumstark*, Oriens Christ. 1938, 1/26. — Cfr. § 76, 7 (Niceta).

# § 68.

## Penance[1].

1. As may be seen from the canons of Ancyra (314), Neocaesarea (between 314 and 325) and Nicaea (325), as well as from the "canonical"

---

[1] Cfr. literature § 24. K. HOLL, Enthusiasmus u. Bußgewalt beim griech. Mönchtum, 1898; also H. KOCH, HJG 1900, 58/78. J. HÖRMANN, Unter-

letters of Basil the Great and Gregory of Nyssa, public *penance* was still a legally recognized institution in the *Greek* Church in the fourth century. To the classification of penitents then established throughout Asia Minor, a fourth class was added — the weepers (§ 24, 4). However, circumstances had brought about some mitigations. The Synod of Ancyra in 314 (can. 22) had permitted a murderer to be reconciled on his deathbed; Basil the Great (can. 56) permitted him to receive Communion after twenty years of penance. But toward the end of the fourth century an even more striking change occurred. The rapid increase of the number of Christians with a consequent decline in fervor necessitated a more indulgent treatment of the transgressor. A scandal connected with a public confession, induced Bishop *Nectarius* of Constantinople in 391 to abolish the discipline of public penance and the office of penitentiary, and permitted each individual to approach the sacred Mysteries as his conscience dictated. The example of the capital city was not without effect on other churches of the East. However, certain public crimes remained subject to ecclesiastical discipline in that they excluded the offender from public worship or at least from Communion (minor excommunication). But for the rest, the matter was left to the individual's own discretion. Thus penance became a private or, at least, a semipublic institution. Socrates, the Church historian (HE V, 29), writing about the year 440, complains, and not without reason, of a decline of morals.

During the fourth and fifth centuries the administration of penance in the *Greek* Church was assumed almost exclusively by *monks* and *hermits*. They were given a certain veneration, something like that given to martyrs and confessors in the preceding period (§ 24, 1), and were looked upon as as ἄνδρες πνευματικοί (spiritual men) endowed with special psychic gifts. Such a deviation can be accounted for only by the fact that in the East from very early times the therapeutic factor was stressed in the forgiveness of sin, whereas in the West the judicial function of the bishop or priest was properly recognized. As a result of Iconoclasm in the eighth century the influence of

suchungen z. griech. Laienbeicht, 1913. B. POSCHMANN, Die abendländ. Kirchenbuße am Ausgang des christl. Altertums, 1928 (also K. ADAM, ThQ 1929, 1/66 [and in Ges. Aufsätze, 1936, 268/312], and B. POSCHMANN, ZkTh 1930, 214/52); id. Die abendländ. Kirchenbuße im Frühmittelalter, 1930. J. A. JUNGMANN, Die latein. Bußriten in ihrer geschichtl. Entwicklung, 1932. E. GÖLLER, Papsttum und Bußgewalt in spätröm. u. frühmittelalterl. Zeit, 1933. P. GALTIER, RHE 1934, 797 ff.; 1937, 5 ff. 277 ff. (the history of private penance); Gregorianum 1948, 288/94 (the canons on penance of Nicaea). KL. JÜSSEN, Die dogmat. Anschauungen des Hesychius v. Jerusalem († after 451) II, 1934. R. SPILKER, StMBenO 1938, 281 ff. 1939, 12 ff. (penitential practices in the rule of St. Benedict). J. A. JUNGMANN, Misc. L. C. Mohlberg I, Rome 1948, 169/82 (the Pentecostal octave and penance in the Roman liturgy). J. GAUDEMET, RevSR 1949, 641/77 (Excommunication). S. G. RIVOS, La penitencia en la primitiva Iglesia española, Salamanca 1949. St. Augustine's teaching on penance: S. Augustini textus selecti de poenitentia, coll. B. POSCHMANN, 1934 (Floril. patrist. 38). F. HÜNERMANN, Die Bußlehre des hl. Augustinus, 1914. K. ADAM, Die kirchl. Sündenvergebung nach dem hl. Aug., 1917; Die geheime Kirchenbuße nach dem hl. Aug., 1921. B. POSCHMANN, ZkTh 1921, 208 ff. 405 ff. 497 ff.; Kirchenbuße u. correptio secreta bei Aug., Braunsberg 1923.

monks over the people was still further increased and remained dominant until the thirteenth century. Private penance and confession were never so perfectly organized in the East as in the West. Cfr. Hall (in literature above); also Hörmann; Vacandard, RClFr 42, 1905, 235/61; F. Diekamp, Festschrift J. Mausbach, 1931, 43 ff.

2. The discipline of Penance was maintained much longer in the *West* than in the East. The old law that a sinner could be admitted to public penance for capital sins only once in a lifetime remained in force and the Synod of Toledo in 589 insisted on its observance (can. 11). Because of the hardships it imposed, (see no. 3 below), many sinners postponed accepting the penance as long as possible, sometimes even until the hour of death. But as in the East, so here, too, the old severity was mitigated. Formerly, *those who relapsed* after performing public penance were forever excluded from the Church, but Pope Siricius (384—399) permitted such to attend divine service and admitted them to Communion before death. Formerly those who did not submit to penance before they became *seriously ill*, were never again admitted to the Church in case they recovered; now they could receive absolution and Communion. An order of Pope Leo I (Ap. 168, 2 of the year 459) practically abolished *public confession.* Public penance remained in force, but it was restricted more and more to particularly grave crimes which were generally known and on which the civil courts had pronounced sentence. Some of the newly converted peoples such as the *Celts* (Irish and Scotch) and the *Anglo-Saxons* were averse to public penance. Through the influence of their missionaries, especially St. Columbanus, the practice of penance as observed in their monasteries was promoted during the sixth and seventh centuries. Up to this time the Irish or Scottish monks and ascetics (conversi) practised *secret* and voluntary *penance* and *private confession* immediately followed by absolution which could be repeated any number of times.

Very few traces of a sacramental *private penance* directed by the Church can be discovered in the first three centuries. Even in the following period it was still but imperfectly organized in the Greek Church. In the Latin Church it was promoted and justified on dogmatic grounds especially by *St. Augustine.* In the case of grave sins (peccata mortifera) not publicly known, he was definitely opposed to public censure and exclusion from the Church. He pleaded rather for secret reprimand and secret penance (correptio secreta, satisfactio secreta) as an adequate substitute for the old canonical penances (Karl Adam). In this matter as in so many others Pope *Gregory the Great* followed in Augustine's footsteps. The Fathers of the fourth century (Pacianus, Ambrose, Jerome), especially when attacking the Novatians, brilliantly defend the *power of the keys* and its exercise through the priesthood.

3. Public penance began officially when the bishop or priest imposed hands on the penitent and gave him the cilicium (hairshirt). In general, public penance not only obliged one to the manner of life of the *ascetics* (§ 72, 1) but also involved a number of other extremely rigorous observances. Those who were enrolled in the Ordo penitentium were obliged to pray, fast, give alms,

shear their hair, wear a monk's garb or clothes of mourning and abandon any business or profession. If they were single, they might not marry, and if married, they might not continue marital relations. Hence a married person could not perform public penance without the consent of the other spouse. In the Roman Church the reconciliation took place on *Holy Thursday*; in the other churches on one of the three following days. — A. Pummerer, StZ 129, 1935, 62/8 (the name for the Thursday of Holy Week); H. Frank, Festschrift I. Herwegen, 1938, 136/73 (reconciliation of penitents in Milan).

During the first three centuries, *clerics* guilty of capital sins were treated the same as laymen. But from the fourth century, the Roman, African and Gallic Churches deposed such clerics without excommunicating them; that is, they were admitted to *lay Communion*, but not enrolled among the penitents. — H. Kellner, Das Buß- und Strafverfahren gegen Kleriker in den ersten 6. Jhh., 1863.

## § 69.
### Feasts and Fasts[1].

1. Any feasts which the Christians celebrated during the preceding period passed entirely unnoticed by the non-Christian world. But the changed circumstances now gave Christian feasts a public character. In 321 Constantine the Great decreed that on **Sunday**, the day of the Lord's Resurrection, courts be closed and all public work cease; and in 386 Theodosius I forbade theatrical performances and public spectacles on Sunday. Theodosius II (425) and several synods extended this prohibition to exclude the higher feasts and the time between Easter and *Pentecost* — the *Quinquagesima*, as it was called. Constantine the Great had permitted work in the fields on Sunday, but in the course of time various synods (Laodicea c. 380, can. 29; Orleans 528, can. 28, etc.), forbade this too, except in case of urgent necessity.

Since the fourth century, *Saturday* was kept in the East as a *half feast* with divine service. The practice in the West of fasting on Saturday was strictly prohibited in the East. The so-called Apostolic Canon (can. 64) and the Synod in Trullo (692, can. 55) forbade fasting on Saturday under penalties — excommunication for a layman, deposition for a cleric.

2. Many new annual feasts were observed throughout the entire Church and around these the *liturgical year* gradually developed. Among the **Feasts of the Lord**, *Epiphany* (§ 25, 2) was kept on January 6 in

---

[1] Cfr. § 2, 5 (N. NILLES etc.) and § 25 (H. KELLNER, Heortologie, et al.). E. STOLZ, ThQ 1924, 226/57 (beginning of an ecclesiastical calendar). J. P. KIRSCH, Der stadtrömische christliche Festkalender im Altertum, 1924. R. N. BONET-LLACH, De sanctificatione festorum ... ad s. VI incl., Ripoll, 1945. J. A. JUNGMANN, ZkTh 1931, 605/21 (Sunday and the Christian week). L. L. MCREAVY, EphThLov 1935, 291/323 (Sunday observance until 700). J. DANIÉLOU, RechSR 1948, 382 ff. (typology of the week in the fourth century; and in Le Jour de Seigneur, Paris 1948, 107 ff. (patristic teaching regarding Sunday). J. A. JUNGMANN, Liturg. Jahrbuch, 1951, 48 ff. (anticipation of the Easter vigil in Christian antiquity).

the East and West. Most probably it originated at Jerusalem shortly after the edict of Milan. In the East, it commemorated the birth of Christ and the manifestation of His Messiaship and divinity to the Magi, at Cana, and His baptism in the Jordan; hence it was called Theophany. In the West, while the threefold manifestation was not positively excluded, the feast of the Epiphany stressed the Adoration of the Magi as signifying the call of Christ to the pagan world. The birth of Christ was soon commemorated by a special feast on December 25[1]. The first mention of this date is found in the calender of the Roman chronographer Dionysius Philocalus compiled in 354. But since Philocalus uses sources dating from 335 and 336, it is quite possible that the feast was celebrated at Rome before 336. It was introduced at Milan in 377 and at Antioch and Constantinople about the same time. Strangely enough, it did not become popular in the East or West until Emperor Justin II (565—578) prescribed that it be celebrated throughout the Roman Empire. Armenia alone refused to admit the new feast and even to the present day commemorates the birth of Christ together with His baptism on January 6. The choice of December 25 for the **feast of Christmas** was very probably determined by the fact that the pagan world celebrated the birth of the *sun god* (natalis solis invicti) at the winter solstice (Brumalia). Since the reign of Emperor Aurelian the cult of Sol invictus had spread to every part of the Empire. By assigning December 25 as the feast of the birth of Christ, "the Sun of Justice" (Mal. 4:2), "the true and everlasting Sun" (Zeno of Verona, Ambrose and others) it was hoped that a great Christian feast would eventually supplant a most popular pagan one. The introduction of the feast of "Holy Lights", the feasts of the Epiphany, in the East was perhaps also influenced by the symbolism of light (§ 25, 2).

Since the fifth century the Church of Gaul observed a fast three times a week (Monday, Wednesday and Friday), beginning on November 11 as a *preparation* for Christmas. And even before Gregory the Great, a period including the four Sundays before Christmas was set aside in the Church of Rome to prepare for the feast. In the East (Syria and Egypt) the preparation lasted three to four weeks. Since the end of the fourth century the day after

---

[1] H. USENER, Religionsgeschichtl. Untersuchungen I, [2]1911. E. VACANDARD, Études de critique etc. III, Paris 1912. G. RIETSCHEL, RE XXI, 47/54. G. ALLMANG, Pastor bonus 1912/3, 129 ff. 257 ff. A. MEYER, Das Weihnachtsfest, s. Entstehung u. Entwicklung, 1913. M. P. NILSSON, ArchRelW 1918, 50/150. E. CASPAR, ZKG 1927, 346/55 (origin of the feast). A. HOLLARD, RevHPhR 1931, 256/74. B. BOTTE, Les origines de la Noël et de l'Épiphanie, Louvain 1932. H. FRANK, JbLW 12, 1932, 145 ff.; 13, 1933, 1 ff. (Christmas and Epiphany in Ambrose). K. PRÜMM, StZ 135/1939, 207/25 (origin of Epiphany and Christmas). H. LECLERCQ, Nativité de Jésus, DictAC XII, 905/58. F. J. DÖLGER, AntChrist 1940, 1/56 (Christ the true and eternal Sun). O. CULLMANN, Weihn. in der alten Kirche, 1947. J. A. JUNGMANN, ZkTh 1937, 341/90 (Advent in Gallic and Roman liturgy). C. A. KNELLER, StML 1904 II, 538/56 (feasts related to Christmas); cfr. H. LIETZMANN, Petrus und Paulus in Rom, [2]1927, 126 ff. A. BAUMSTARK, RLAntChrist I, 112/25 (Advent). F. BÜNGER, Gesch. der Neujahrsfeier in der Kirche, 1911.

Christmas was kept in the East as the feast of *St. Stephen*, the first martyr, and in the fifth century the feast was introduced into the West. The lectionary of Bishop Victor of Capua (546) and the Synod of Tours in 567 speak of the feast of the *Circumcision* on the octave of Christmas — another example of the Church's efforts to keep recent converts from joining in the dissolute pagan feast observed on the Calends of January.

3. Two new feasts were now intercalated in the Easter season: *Palm Sunday* and the *Ascension of the Lord*. It is known that Palm Sunday was kept with special ceremonies at Jerusalem about the year 400; but the feast and the procession with palms was not adopted at Rome until the seventh century. Formerly the commemoration of the Ascension[1] together with the Descent of the Holy Ghost had been made on Pentecost Sunday. All the days of *Holy Week* (hebdomada magna) and *Easter week* were feast days in the sense that no work was permitted and divine services were held every day. But *Holy Thursday* and *Good Friday* (παρασκευή, parasceve), the latter a day of deep mourning, were marked by special ceremonies. The three minor *Rogation days* with processions (litanies) were known quite early, but their present place in the calendar just before the Ascension as well as the manner in which they are now observed dates back to Bishop *Mamertus* of Vienne who prescribed intercessory processions throughout his diocese about the year 470. They were introduced at Rome about 800. The procession with the major litany on April 25, now the *feast of St. Mark*, was known at Rome in the sixth or seventh century. It was introduced to replace the Robigalia of the pagans held annually on April 25. Some scholars are of the opinion that rogation processions before the Ascension replaced the Ambarvalia or pagan processions through the fields.

4. While the **martyrs** were formerly given special honor on the *anniversary of their death* at their tombs or places of martyrdom, some of them were honored annually throughout the Church. Thus the feasts of *St. Stephen* and of *Sts. Peter* and *Paul* were observed everywhere, and in the Greek Church a feast of *All Martyrs* was celebrated on the octave of Pentecost. As devotion to the **saints** spread, not only martyrs, but holy bishops, monks and confessors (§ 70, 3) were specially commemorated on the anniversary of their death. About the year 600 the day of the death of *St. Martin* of Tours (§ 72, 6) was observed throughout the Church of Gaul and in the city of Rome. *St. John* the Baptist was an exception, since besides the day of his death, the day of his birth was also kept because he had been sanctified before birth. In honoring the saints, the practice was not everywhere the same. About the year 475, Bishop Perpetuus of Tours prescribed vigils for the feasts of ten popular saints.

5. In keeping with the veneration paid to the Mother of Christ (§ 70, 3) many **feasts of the Blessed Virgin**[2] were introduced during this period.

---

[1] M. JUGIE, Échos d'Orient 1929, 257/71.

[2] Candlemas: A. BAUMSTARK, ThGl 1909, 89/105; D. DE BRUYNE, RevBén 1922, 14/26; E. MICHELSEN, Festgabe R. Haupt, 1922, 149/96; F. J. DÖLGER, AntChrist 1936, 76 f. Assumption: F. X. FUNK, ThQ 1891, 328; F. CABROL, RClFr 63, 1910, 385/97; B. CAPELLE, EphThLov 1926, 53/45; MUSÉON 1943, 1/33. M. JUGIE, L'année théologique 1943, 11/42.

## § 69. Feasts and Fasts.

The oldest of these is the feast of the *Purification* or *Candlemas day*, which, among the Greeks was accounted a feast of Christ and called Ὑπαπαντή or Ὑπαντή, The Meeting (of Christ with Simeon). There is evidence of its celebration at Jerusalem in the fourth century, in Syria in the fifth century and in Egypt and at Constantinople in the sixth century. It was considered the Quadragesima de Epiphania and originally was kept on February 14; but with the introduction of Christmas, was transferred to February 2. A procession with lighted candles had long been known at Rome, but only later (sixth or seventh century) was it combined with the feast of the Purification. About 430 the Church of Constantinople appointed the Sunday before Christmas as the feast of the *Divine Maternity of Mary* and the Conception of the Eternal Word. About the same time or a little later the feast was introduced at Jerusalem and in Asia Minor — and in the beginning of the sixth century at Antioch. It was also celebrated at Milan and in the Spanish Church. The Synod of Toledo in 680 (can. 1) transferred the feast to December 18. During the reign of Justinian (527—565) the Marian cycle of feasts was developed at Constantinople with the *Nativity of the Blessed Virgin* (September 8), the *Annunciation* (March 25) and the *Assumption* (August 15). The latter feast (Κοίμησις, dormitio, pausatio) originated at Jerusalem about 450. A law of Emperor Maurice (582—602) ordered it to be observed throughout the Empire. In the seventh century it was kept on January 18 in the Church of Gaul. The Western Church instituted many feasts in honor of Mary or gradually adopted those of the Greek Church. There is evidence that all four of the principal feasts (Purification Nativity, Annunciation and Assumption) were celebrated at Rome as early as the pontificate of Pope Sergius (687—701).

6. General agreement was eventually reached on the question of the date of **Easter**[1]. The General Synod of *Arles* in 314 (can. 1) ordered that the feast be kept on Sunday and on the same day everywhere and that the Bishop of Rome notify all the churches regarding the date. This decree, however, had little effect. But since the matter concerned the whole Church, the question was again examined at the Council of Nicaea in 325 with some degree of success. The Council ordered (Socrates, H.E. I, 9; Theodoret, H.E. I, 8) that the Eastern brethren, that is, the Christians of Syria, Cilicia, and Mesopotamia, who formerly "kept Passah with the Jews" (the Protopaschites § 25, 3; 50, 6) henceforth celebrate the feast with the Romans and other Christians (on the first

---

A. RAES, OrChrPer 1946, 262/74. Feast of the Maternity: M. JUGIE, La première fête Mariale, Paris 1923; cfr. J. BRINKTRINE, ThGl 1924, 384/6. Nativity of the B.V.M.: J. LEROY, RechSR 1938, 282/89. G. MORIN, RevBén 1945/6, 9/11 (in seventh century Gaul).
[1] J. SCHMID, Die Osterfestberechnung auf den brit. Inseln, 1904; Die Osterfestfrage auf dem Konzil v. Nicäa, 1905; Die Osterfestberechnung in der abendländ. Kirche vom Konzil v. Nicäa bis c. 800, 1907. E. SCHWARTZ, Christl. u. jüd. Ostertafeln, Abh. Göttingen NF. VIII, 1904/5, 104 ff. J. BACH, Die Osterfestberechnung in alter und neuer Zeit, 1907. C. W. JONES, Sp 1934, 408/21 (the Easter tables of Victorius and Dionysius Exiguus). P. GROSJEAN, AB 1946, 200/44 (beginnings of the Celtic Easter controversy. Cfr. § 25.

Sunday after the full moon of the spring equinox). Shortly after the Council most of the bishops conformed. The Synod of *Antioch* in 341 threatened with penalties those who refused and the subject is never again mentioned in any of the Eastern synods. Nicaea further ordered that the Church of Alexandria *compute the date* every year and that the Bishop of Rome inform the whole Church. This order, however, was not immediately observed. The Synod of Sardica in 343 (§ 48, 3) fixed a period of 50 years during which a suitable plan could be worked out. But it was not until the sixth century that perfect agreement was reached. In 525, on the recommendation of Dionysius Exiguus, Rome adandoned her method of reckoning and accepted that of Alexandria. (Rome's reckoning was based on an 84 year cycle, with the spring equinox falling on March 18, allowing for Easter to fall between March 25 and April 21, — Luna XVI—XXII, while Alexandria's was based on a 19 year cycle, with the spring equinox on March 21 and allowing the date of Easter to fall between March 22 and April 25 — Luna XV—XXI). The other Latin Churches soon followed the example of Rome.

In the seventh and eighth centuries the *Irish* and *Scotch* conformed to the Roman practice after having followed until then the British cycle of 84 years (with March 25 as the equinox and Luna XIV to XX as the limits for Easter, § 44, 1, 4). *Gaul* also adopted the Roman practice in the eighth century. From about the middle of the fifth century, the Church of Gaul had used a table of dates worked out by Bishop *Victorius* of Aquitaine which was approved by the Synod of Orleans in 541. It furnished the date of Easter for 532 years and was based on a cycle of nineteen years but agreed with Roman usage in taking March 18 as the equinox and Luna XVI as the earliest date on which Easter could fall. In the eighth century too, a part of *Spain* made the change; the other part had been in agreement with the Roman date since the sixth century. After the conquest of Wales by the Anglo-Saxons early in the ninth century, all of *Britain* followed the Roman practice.

7. The **Easter fast**[1] (§ 25, 4) which in the third century was observed quite generally for the six days of Holy Week, was extended in the first half of the fourth century to forty days — *Quadragesima* (Τεσσαρακοστή). This was evidently in imitation of the fast of Jesus in the desert. Athanasius became acquainted with it while in exile at Trier in 366 (§ 48, 2) and introduced it at Alexandria immediately upon his return. In the West, it lasted six weeks, in the East, seven, that is, six weeks before Palm Sunday, since in some churches (Antioch and Constantinople), Holy Week was not considered as included in the Quadrages.

---

[1] Cfr. literature § 25 (LINSENMAYER, SCHÜMMER etc.). Also: FUNK, AU I, 258/78. A. VILLIEN, Histoire des commandements de l'Église, Paris ³1936. E. VACANDARD, DictAC II, 2139/58. J. SALAVILLE, Échos d'Orient 1910, 65/72; 1911, 355/57; 1929, 257/71 (Lent in the Orient); cfr. H. KOCH, ZKG 1925, 481/6. A. BAUMSTARK, Oriens Christ. 1911, 53 ff. (Lent in Jerusalem). C. CALLEWAERT, RHE 1914/20, 23/43; RevBén 1920, 11 ff. 132 ff.; 1924, 200/28 (Lent in the West). ED. SCHWARTZ, ZNtW 1935, 131 f. (Origin of Lent). J. FROGER, MSR 1946, 207/34 (beginning of the Lenten fast transferred to Septuagesima in the fifth to the eigth century).

The number of actual fast days, however, was the same, since in the East, not only Sundays, but Saturdays as well, were non-fast days, Holy Saturday excepted (§ 69,1).

When the Easter fast was lengthened, the *Station fasts* on Wednesday and Friday (§ 25, 1) were no longer strictly observed. But Pope *Leo I* (440—461) prescribed a fast on Monday, Wednesday and Friday of Pentecost week for the Roman Church, and a similar fast of three days in the seventh and tenth months (September and December). The original purpose was to return thanks for the harvest and eventually these Quatember fasts became the regular days for the ordination of clerics. The present arrangement of the **Ember days** came later (§ 100, 2). The Ember days as observed in the Latin Church were never known in the Greek Church, although the latter has four quite similar annual fasts: two major and two minor fasts. The major fasts are kept before Easter and Christmas and the minor ones after Pentecost, one called the fast of the Apostles, to honor Sts. Peter and Paul, and the other before the feast of the Assumption. There is evidence that a jejunium Quinquagesimae in Pentecost week was observed in *Africa* in the fourth and fifth centuries. — Cfr. *L. Fischer*, Die kirchl. Quatember, ihre Entstehung, Entwicklung und Bedeutung, 1914. — *K. Holl*, Die Entstehung der 4 Fastenzeiten in der griech. Kirche, Abh. Berlin 1923, 5. — *C. Lumbot*, RevBén 1935, 114/24 (the fast in Africa).

## § 70.
### Devotion to the Saints. Relics, Images and Pilgrimages[1].

1. The love and veneration which Christians showed to the *martyrs* (§ 14, 4) did not cease with the persecutions. The teaching of the Church

---

[1] Cfr. the sources and literature in § 2, 8 and § 14, 4. A. EHRHARD, Überlieferung u. Bestand der hagiograph. u. homilet. Literatur der griech. Kirche bis z. Ende des 16. Jahrh., 1936 ff. J. P. KIRSCH, Die Lehre von der Gemeinschaft der Heiligen im christl. Altertum, 1900; Der stadtröm. christl. Festkalender im Altertum, 1924; RQ 1930, 107/31 (tombs and cult of the martyrs in Rome). A. DUFOURCQ, La christianisation des foules, Paris [3]1907; Études sur les Gesta Martyrum romains, 4 vol. Paris 1900/9. E. LUCIUS, Die Anfänge des Heiligenkultes in der christl. Kirche, 1904. H. DELEHAYE, Les légendes hagiographiques, Brux. [3]1927, Germ. transl. E. A. STÜCKELBERG, 1907; Les légendes grecques des saints militaires, Paris 1909; Les origines du culte des martyrs, Bruxelles [2]1933 (standard); Les recueils antiques des miracles des saints, AB 1925, 5 ff. 305 ff.; Sanctus, Essai sur le culte des saints dans l'antiquité, Brux. 1927; Loca sanctorum, AB 1930, 5/64; La méthode historique et l'hagiographie, Bull. de l'Acad. R. de Belgique, Lettres 1930, Nr. 5/7; Cinq leçons sur la méthode hagiographique, Brux. 1934. P. PEETERS, Le tréfonds oriental de l'hagtiographie Byzantine, Brux. 1950. H. LECLERCQ, Saint, DictAC XV, 373/462. H. GÜNTER, Legenden-Studien, 1906; Die christl. Legende des Abendlandes, 1910; Psychologie der Leg., 1949; Buddha in der abendländ. Leg. ? 1922 (also H. HAAS, Z. f. Missionskunde u. RW. 1923, 193 ff. 225 ff.). E. VACANDARD, Origines du culte des saints, in Études de critique et d'hist. relig. III, Paris 1912. FR. PFISTER, Der Reliquienkult im Altertum, 2 vols. 1909/12. M. V. WULF, Über Heilige u. Heiligenverehrung in den ersten christl. Jhh., 1910. P. DÖRFLER, Die Anfänge der Heiligenverehrung nach den röm. Inschriften u. Bildwerken, 1913. K. HOLL, Die schriftstell. Form des griech. Heiligenlebens, NJklA 29, 1912, 406/27. H.

regarding the Communion of the Saints developed into a living reality in the lives of the people who manifested their admiration for all the saints, but particularly martyrs, in many new and expressive devotions. The remains of the martyrs (λείψανα, reliquiae) were given special honor and curative or other miraculous powers were ascribed to them. Devout persons travelled long distances to visit the tombs of specially revered martyrs, erected churches or chapels (μαρτύρια, memoriae, basilicae) over their graves, and called upon their intercession in time of need. The translation of *relics*, especially of newly discovered ones, was celebrated with colorful religious ceremony and every altar contained martyr's relics (§ 71, 3). Devotion to some martyrs was well-nigh universal. The Greek Church established a feast to honor all martyrs (§ 69, 4) and in 609 or 610 Pope Boniface dedicated the Pantheon at Rome in honor of the Blessed Virgin and all martyrs, an event which led eventually to the introduction of the feast of All Saints. The *acts of martyrs*, though often legendary, gave rise to a very extensive literature (§ 14, 4). Since the fourth century it was customary in most of the principal churches to keep a list of the natalitia martyrum, sometimes called calendars. The calendar for Rome, compiled by Dionysius Philocalus in 354 (§ 78, 3), besides the Depositio Martyrum also contains a Depositio Episcoporum. Among many such lists, the best known are those of Carthage, Naples (the marble calendar) and Syria, the latter compiled about the year 400. New names were constantly added to these early records to form the present voluminous *Martyrologies*[1], or, as they are known in the East, Menologia and synaxaria. The most important work of this sort is the *Martyrologium Hieronymianum* which begins with Christmas and contains the names of almost 6000 martyrs

---

PRIESSNIG, Die biograph. Formen der griech. Heiligenleben, Diss. 1924. F. LANZONI, Genesi, svolgimento e tramonto delle legende storiche, Roma 1925 (Studi e Testi 43). KIRSCH, HOSP, KENNEDY, DONCKEL § 67, 3. K. KÜNSTLE, Ikonographie der christl. Kunst, 2 Bde 1926/8. J. BUREL, Anciennes pratiques de dévotion, Avignon 1927. E. FREISTEDT, Altchristl. Totengedächtnistage, 1928. E. SCHÄFER, § 64, 3 (P. Damasus). J. QUASTEN, ThGl 1933, 318/31 (reform of the cult of martyrs by Augustine). F. RÜTTEN, Die Victorverehrung im christl. Altertum, 1936. C. CECCHELLI, Atti Pontif. Acad. Rom. Arch. III, 1939, 125/34 (Synod of Carthage 401 against the abuse of relics). JOS. BRAUN, Die Reliquiare d. christl. Kultes u. ihre Entwickl., 1940. A. GRABAR, Martyrium. Recherches sur le culte des reliques et l'art chrétien antique, 3 vol. Paris 1946. B. KÖTTING, Peregrinatio religiosa, 1950.

[1] H. ACHELIS, Die Martyrologien, ihre Geschichte u. ihr Wert, Abh. Göttingen 1900. H. QUENTIN, Les martyrologes historiques du moyen âge, Paris ²1923 (standard). H. LECLERCQ, Martyrologe, DictAC X, 2523/2619; Ménologe, ib. XI, 419/30. J. BAUDOT, Le Martyrologe, Paris 1911; Le Martyrologe romain, Paris 1925 (popular). For the Greek-Oriental martyrologies see especially the great works of A. EHRHARD, Überlief. u. Bestand, mentioned above. H. LIETZMANN, Die 3 ältesten Martyrologien, 1903 (Kleine Texte 2). Editions of the Martyrol. Hieronym. by QUENTIN-DELEHAYE, § 2, 8; cfr. J. FERNHOUT, De Martyrologii Hieronymiani fonte (Martyrol. Syriacum), Groningen 1922; H. DELEHAYE, AB 1931, 22/50; K. MOHLBERG, Oriens Christ. 1932, 546/67. H. DELEHAYE, Étude sur le Légendier romain (novembre et décembre), Brux. 1936.

and other saints. It received its name from the fact that it was ascribed to St. Jerome; but it actually originated in Upper Italy about 450 and was revised in Southern Gaul about the year 600. The Byzantine calendar of saints was adopted at the Synod in Trullo in 692.

The favorite places of pilgrimage were the tombs of *Sts. Peter* and *Paul* (§ 44, 4) and of *St. Hippolytus* at Rome; of *St. Cyprian* at Carthage; of *St. Sergius* in the Syrian desert; of *St. Martin* at Tours (§ 72, 6); of *St. Felix* at Nola (Sts. Martin and Felix were not martyrs); of *St. Thecla* at Seleucia in Isauria and St. Menas in the desert of Mareotis, west of Alexandria. The sanctuary of this soldier-martyr was discovered during excavations from 1905 to 1907. — G. Bardy, AB 1949, 224/35 (pilgrimages to Rome in the fourth century). — C. M. Kaufmann, Die Menasstadt u. das Nationalheiligtum der altchristl. Ägypter I, 1910; Die hl. Stadt der Wüste, 1918. — H. Leclercq, DictAC XI, 324/97. — J. Drescher, Apa Mena, Cairo 1946.

2. The desire to venerate the saints is deeply rooted in human nature, and, when kept within proper bounds, is not only reasonable, but laudable. It is true that abuses are frequently met with, such as excesses in the celebration of feasts, superstious notions and practices, falsification and trafficking in relics; but it is also true that constant effort was made by ecclesiastical and civil authority, by synods and theologians, to check and punish every form of disorder. The vast majority of the people, even the uneducated, understood well the essential difference between *veneration* of the saints (δουλεία, τιμή) and *adoration* (λατρεία) of God. The Fathers and apologists of the period, such as Epiphanius, Cyril of Alexandria, Theodoret, Augustine, etc., clearly explain and convincingly justify veneration of the saints.

A group of modern scholars of *comparative religion* (Usener, Deubner, Lucius, Saintyves and others) assert that the veneration of the saints and their relics is merely a continuation of the ancient pagan *cult of heroes and the dead*; that many Christian saints are the immediate "successors" of pagan divinities and that veneration of the saints is simply another form of polytheism. Even though it be granted that there is a certain similarity between Christian devotion to the saints and the pagan cult of the dead and that during the days of mass conversions some pagan superstitions and customs did creep in here and there to corrupt Christian belief and practice; yet it can be proved that in origin and nature veneration of the saints bore a distinctly Christian character which makes it fundamentally different from everything pagan. The elevation of morals and the refinement of culture, the ennobling of literature and the other arts directly resulting from the veneration of the saints are in themselves cogent proofs that the Christian practice bore no direct relations to Paganism. Nor can it be proved in any single instance that pagan gods or heroes became the object of Christian veneration. Usener and others have endeavored to identify St. Pelagia and the goddess Aphrodite; Tychon and Priapus-Dionysius, Cosmas and Damian and Castor and Pollux; George and Mithras; Agatha and Penelope; Thecla and Athena, etc. etc. It must be admitted, although always with caution, that popular pagan devotions and practices were sometimes suppressed by substituting especially attractive devotions to Christian saints or by commemorating Christian mysteries on the days formerly dedicated to pagan rites. Recent and poorly instructed converts from paganism may have looked upon the patron saint of a locality as assuming the functions of the old tutelary deity. It is also possible that some poetic or romantic exploits of mythology were used at times in writing highly fictionalized lives of saints and were repeated in the legends of those saints through the centuries. — Besides the literature listed above (especially *Delehaye* and *Günter*) see also *St. v. Dunin-Borkowski*, ZkTh 1911, 213/52, and *J. Geffcken*, Der Ausgang des griechisch-römischen Heidentums, 1920, 224 ff.

3. New names were constantly being added to the calendar[1]. After the persecutions, when death by martyrdom became an extremely rare occurrence, even those who had not obtained the martyr's crown, but who had distinguished themselves by virtue and piety were honored as saints. *Hermits* and *monks*, who had been heroes of prayer and mortification, and holy *bishops* who had fought valiantly in defense of orthodoxy were given the general title of confessors (§ 14, 4). Moreover, the *angels*, especially the Archangel *Michael*, and many pious characters of the Old Testament (the prophets, the Machabees, etc.) were venerated and invoked. But the greatest veneration was

---

[1] J. TURMEL, RHLR 1898, 289 ff. 407 ff. (devotion to angels). K. LÜBECK, HJG 1905, 773/83 (Michael). F. A. V. LEHNER, Die Marienverehrung in den ersten Jhh., ²1886. J. LÉMANN, La Vierge Marie dans l'hist. de l'Orient chrétien, Paris 1904. E. LUCIUS, Die Anfänge des Heiligenkultes (see above), 420/522. H. LECLERCQ, Marie, Mère de Dieu, DictAC X, 1982/2043. A. L. DELATTRE, Le culte de la S. Vierge en Afrique d'après les monuments archéol., Paris 1907. PH. FRIEDRICH, Die Mariologie des heiligen Augustin, 1907. E. NEUBERT, Marie dans l'Église anténicéenne, Paris 1908. E. AMANN, Le Protoévangile de Jacques et ses remaniements latins, Paris 1911. J. NIESSEN, Die Mariologie des hl. Hieronymus, 1913. AD. EBERLE, Die Mariologie des hl. Cyrill v. Alex., 1921. H. KOCH, Adhuc Virgo, Mariens Jungfräulichkeit u. Ehe in der altkirchl. Überlieferung bis z. Ende des 4. Jh.s, 1929 (also A. EBERLE, ThRev 1930, 153/55; B. CAPELLE, RechThAM 1930, 388/95; G. JOUASSARD, RevSR 1932, 509/32; 1933, 25/37). H. KOCH, Virgo Eva, Virgo Maria, Neue Untersuchungen über die Lehre von der Jungfrauschaft u. der Ehe Mariens in der ältesten Kirche, 1937 (also K. ADAM, ThQ 1938, 171/89; J. LEBON, RHE 1938, 336/45). P. R. BOTZ, Die Jungfrauschaft Mariens im Neuen Test. u. in der nachapostol. Zeit, Diss. 1935. J. GARÇON, La Mariologie de S. Irénée, Lyon 1932. B. PBZYBYLSKI, De Mariologia S. Irenaei Lugdunensis, Rome 1937. O. MENZINGER, Mariologisches aus der vorephesinischen Liturgie, 1932. O. BARDENHEWER, Marienpredigten aus der Väterzeit, 1934. L. HAMMERSBERGER, Die Mariologie der ephremischen Schriften, 1938. V. A. MITCHELL, The Mariology of S. John Damascene, Kirkwood Mo. 1930. C. CHEVALIER, La Mariologie de S. Jean Damascène, Rome 1936; cfr. also V. GRUMEL, Échos d'Orient 1937, 318/46. W. HALLER, Jovinianus, TU 17, 2, 1897. F. VALLI, Un eretico del sec. IV (Jovinianus), Torino 1925 (from Didaskaleion 1925). A. RÉVILLE, Vigilance, Paris 1902. T. TRZCINSKI, Die dogmat. Schriften des hl. Hieronymus, 1912. E. BICKEL, Das asket. Ideal bei Ambrosius, Hieronymus u. Augustinus, 1916. PH. FRIEDRICH, Festgabe A. Knöpfler, 1917, 89 ff.; Kath. 1917 II, 145 ff. 232 ff. 319 ff. (Ambrose on the virginity of Mary). A. PAGNAMENTA, La Mariologia di San Ambrogio, Milano 1932. J. ORTIZ DE URBINA, OrChrPer 1940, 40/82 (development of Mariology in the Eastern Fathers). H. DE MANNOIR, Maria I, Paris 1949.

paid to Her who stood in closest relationship to the Savior, the Blessed Virgin **Mary**, as is seen in the many feasts established in Her honor (§ 69, 5). The Nestorians had denied Her dignity as Mother of God (§ 54, 1. 2); but the decisions of the Council of Ephesus in 431, held in a church dedicated to her, did much to increase devotion. Mary's perpetual virginity was attacked by the *Antidicomarianites*, a sect of Arabia; by Bishop *Bonosus* of Sardica (§ 50, 5); later in the fourth and fifth centuries by the layman *Helvidius*, the monk *Jovinian* at Rome and the priest *Vigilantius* of Aquitania, who also attacked asceticism and monasticism (§ 72, 6). But these attacks were frustrated by Ephraem, Epiphanius, Ambrose, Jerome, Augustine, Cyril of Alexandria, John Damascene and others, and served to make Mary loved the more. Devotion to Mary was fostered by those who, in ever increasing numbers, adopted an ascetical form of life and who saw in the sinless "second Eve" the ideal of Christian perfection.

Arabia not only produced a sect which attacked Mary, but also one which honored her to excess. About 370, the priestesses of this sect, called *Collyridians*, sacrificed cakes (κολλυρίς) to the Blessed Virgin in a highly pagan manner. Epiphanius describes their worship (Haer. 79) and denounces it trenchantly. They were probably the same as the *Philomarianites*, a sect mentioned by Leontius of Byzantium in the sixth century. But such isolated examples of reversion to pagan customs by no means prove that devotion to the Blessed Virgin was derived from the cult of "Magna Mater", Cybele, or any other of the mother-goddesses. — F. J. Dölger, AntChrist 1929, 107/42; K. Prümm ZkTh 1930, 572/80; Der christl. Glaube u. die altheidn. Welt I, 1935, 321 ff.

4. The strict prohibition of graven images in the Old Testament (Exod. 20:4) and the fact that paganism was a religion of idol worship explain why many early Christians were opposed to *religious pictures or images*[1]. Some of the Fathers and ecclesiastical writers of the first three centuries are apathetic toward such representations, while others positively condemn them and consider the Old Testament prohibition as still binding. It was either for these reasons or to correct an abuse that may have arisen that the Synod of *Elvira* about the year 306 decreed (can. 36): Placuit picturas in ecclesia esse non debere, ne, quod

---

[1] N. MÜLLER, Christusbilder, RE IV, 63/82; XXIII, 308. E. V. DOBSCHÜTZ, Christusbilder, TU 18, 1899. J. E. WEIS-LIEBERSDORF, Christusu. Apostelbilder, 1902. H. GRISAR, Die röm. Kapelle Sancta Sanctorum, 1908. G. STUHLFAUTH, Die „ältesten Porträts" Christi u. der Apostel, 1918. K. HOLL, Sb. Berlin 1916, 828/68 (writings of Epiphanius against the cult of images); cfr. also J. WILPERT, HJG 1917, 532/5, and P. MAAS, Byz. Z. 1929/30, 279/86. H. KOCH, Die altchristl. Bilderfrage nach den liter. Quellen, 1917; also W. NEUSS, ThRev 1918, 157/62. W. ELLIGER, Die Stellung der alten Christen zu den Bildern in den ersten 4.Jhh., 1930. E. DINKLER, Die ersten Petrusdarstellungen, 1939. H. LECLERCQ, Culte et querelle des images, DictAC VII, 181/302. K. HOLL, Philotesia für P. Kleinert, 1907, 51/66, and in Ges. Aufsätze zur KG II, 388/98 (Stylites and the cult of images). G. OSTROGORSKY, Studien zur Gesch. des byzant. Bilderstreites, 1929. H. MENGES, Die Bilderlehre des Joh. v. Damaskus, 1938. On can. 36 of Elvira: FUNK, AUI, 346/52. H. KOCH, op. cit. 31 ff. L. V. SYBEL, ZKG 1923, 243/47.

colitur at adoratur, in parietibus depingatur. Later on, Eusebius of Caesarea, Epiphanius of Cyprus and, about the year 600, Bishop Serenus of Marseilles, plainly expressed their disapproval of religious pictures. Nevertheless as the pictures in the catacombs at Rome and elsewhere go to prove, not all Christians were of the same opinion, nor may they be indiscriminantly classed as "foes of art." With the decline of paganism, the principal reason for opposition to religious pictures was removed; hence from the fourth century we see an increasing use of pictures and images in the service of religion. They were used to *decorate* the churches where they served to instruct and *edify* the faithful. It is true, we hear of adoration, that is, *veneration* of pictures. And because of the danger of abuse, men who otherwise defended the use of pictures, such as Gregory the Great (Ep. IX, 105; XI, 13) sounded serious warnings. Still the veneration of pictures could be justified in so far as it was never paid to the picture itself but to the person it represented. Hence the use of pictures and images continued to spread and from the fifth to the seventh century all the churches of the East were profusely decorated. In this regard, the West always showed more restraint. In the Greek-Oriental churches, pictures were not only considered as symbols and signs, but often also as possessing supernatural powers. No doubt such notions were supported by certain pictures of supposedly miraculous origin, such as the *picture of Christ,* said to have been sent by the Savior Himself to King Abgar of Edessa (§ 12, 9), the picture at Camuliana in Cappadocia, the renowned *picture of the Savior* in Sancta Sanctorum chapel of the Lateran (rediscovered in 1903). Other pictures of the Lord, His Blessed Mother and the Saints piously believed "not to have been made by hand" (εἰκόνες ἀχειροποίητοι) made their appearance after the fifth century. The great *devotion to St. Peter* which prevailed at Rome during the Constantinian period is attested by the numerous representations of the Saint on Christian sarcophagi.

5. Far more popular than the tombs of the martyrs as places of pilgrimage were the places in *Palestine* sanctified by the presence of the Savior. The Itinerarium Burdigalense is a description of a pilgrimage to the Holy Land in 333. Another account in the *Peregrinatio ad loca sancta* of the fourth century is very important for the history of liturgy. Gamurrini (see below), the discoverer and first publisher of the Peregrinatio ascribed it to a noble lady of Aquitania named *Silvia*; but it appears rather to have been written by a nun named *Aetheria* (Egeria, Eucheria?) of Southern Gaul or Spain. As may well be imagined, some attached undue spiritual effects to such pilgrimages, so that some of the Fathers, as for example, Gregory of Nyssa (Ep. 2 De iis qui adeunt Jerosolymam) and St. Jerome (Ep. 58 ad Paulinum) were obliged to correct the mistaken notions. — P. *Thomsen,* Die Palästinaliteratur, internat. Bibliographie I—V (1895/1934), 1908/38. — Itinera Hierosolymitana s. IV to VIII, ed. P. *Geyer,* 1898. — Itineraria Romana I (Antonini Augusti et Burdigal.), ed. O. *Cuntz,* 1929. — A. *Baumstark,* Abendländ. Palästinapilger des ersten Jahrtausends u. ihre Berichte, 1906. — G. *Klameth,* Die neutest. Lokaltraditionen Palästinas vor den Kreuzzügen I—II, 1, 1914/23. — A. E. *Mader,*

Altchristl. Basiliken und Lokaltraditionen in Südjudäa, 1918. — *W. Kubitschek,*
Itinerarien, RE Pauly-Wissowa IX, 2308/63; Denkschriften der Wiener
Akad. 61, 3, 1919. — *H. Leclercq,* Itinéraires, DictAC VII, 1841/1922;
Pèlerinages, ib. XIV, 65/176. — *Peregrinatio* (Silviae sive Aetheriae) *ad loca
sancta,* ed. J. F. Gamurrini, Rome 1887; P. Geyer (see above), 35/101;
W. Heraeus, ³1929; H. Pétré, Paris 1948 with French transl.; German by
H. Richter, 1919. — *E. Löfstedt,* Philolog. Kommentar zur Peregrinatio
Aetheriae, Upsala 1911, reprinted 1936. — *W. van Oorde,* Lexicon Aetherianum,
Diss. Amsterdam 1929. — *F. Cabrol,* Étude sur la Peregrinatio Silviae, Paris
1895. — M. Fétotin et H. Leclercq, DictAC V, 552/84. — *A. Bludau,* Die
Pilgerreise der Aetheria, 1927. — Date of composition of the Peregrinatio:
J. Ziegler, Biblica 1931, 70/84; A. Vaccari, ib. 1943, 388/97; A. Lambert,
Revue Mabillon 1936, 71/94; 1937, 1/42; 1938, 49/69 (the nun Egeria, the
author ca. 414/6); E. Dekkers, Sacris erudiri 1948, 181/205 (514/8).

6. St. Ambrose, in his De obitu Theodosii (c. 43 ff.) written about 395,
was the first to relate the story of the finding of the *True Cross* by *Helena,*
the mother of Constantine the Great, on the occasion of her visit to the Holy
Places (after 324). Rufinus (X, 7—8), Socrates (H. E. I, 17) and other historians
tell the story substantially as told by Ambrose. The Itinerarium Burdigalense
and Eusebius both speak about the adoration of the True Cross at Jerusalem,
but are silent about the circumstances of the finding. St. Cyril of Jerusalem
in his Catecheses (IV, 10; X, 19; XIII, 4) written in 348, speaks of the True
Cross and its adoration at Jerusalem and adds that particles of it have been
distributed throughout the world. The feast of the Exaltation of the Cross
(September 14) appears to have been celebrated at Jerusalem toward the
end of the fourth century whence it spread throughout the East and was
observed in some localities of the West. A few decades before the feast of the
Exaltation was introduced into the West, the feast of the Inventio Crucis had
been assigned to May 3. This latter feast commemorated the recovery of the
Cross from the Persians by the emperor Heraclius in 614. — Cfr. *J. Straubinger,*
Die Kreuzauffindungslegende, 1913. — *R. Couzard,* Sainte Hélène, Paris 1915.
— *J. Maurice,* Sainte Hélène, Paris 1930. — *H. Leclercq,* DictAC III, 3131/39;
VI, 2126/45.

## § 71.

## Christian Art. Church Furnishings and Ecclesiastical Vestments[1].

1. During the preceding period, Christian art had been restricted
to very unpretentious efforts in the catacombs (§ 23, 5). But after

---

[1] See the collections on ancient Christian monuments listed in § 2, 1
(DE ROSSI, WILPERT, KRAUTHEIMER, DictAC etc.) and the works on ancient
Christian art in § 23, 5 (KRAUS, NEUSS, STYGER, KIRSCH, ELLIGER, WIRTH,
WILPERT et al.). Reallexikon zur deutschen Kunstgeschichte, ed. O. SCHMITT,
1933 ff. F. X. KRAUS, Gesch. der christl. Kunst, fortges. von J. SAUER, 2 vols.
1895/1908. A. MICHEL, Histoire de l'art depuis les premiers temps chrétiens,
8 vol. and Index, Paris 1905/29. K. WÖRMANN, Gesch. der Kunst aller Zeiten
und Völker, 6 vols. ²1915/22. M. DVOŘAK, Kunstgesch. als Geistesgesch.,
1924. B. KLEINSCHMIDT, Gesch. der christl. Kunst, ²1926. L. BRÉHIER,

Constantine's edict of 313 it was given free rein with a large field opened since, during the Diocletian persecution (§ 16, 4), almost all Christian churches had been destroyed. Now the Christian emperors, especially Constantine, and after him, Theodosius I and II and Justinian, bishops, popes and municipalities vied with one another

L'art chrétien, Paris ²1928. F. VAN DER MEER, Christus' oudste gewaad, Utrecht 1949. G. DEHIO u. G. V. BEZOLD, Die kirchl. Baukunst des Abendlandes, 2 vols. 1892/1901. H. HOLTZINGER, Die altchristl. Architektur, ²1899. J. P. KIRSCH, Die christl. Kultusgebäude im Altertum, 1893. V. SCHULTZE, Archäologie der altchristl. Kunst, 1895; Grundriß der christl. Archäol., ²1934. F. WITTING, Die Anfänge christl. Architektur, 1902. C. M. KAUFMANN, Handb. der christl. Archäol., ³1922. L. V. SYBEL, Christl. Antike, 2 vols. 1906/9; Frühchristl. Kunst, 1920. H. LECLERCQ, Manuel d'archéologie chrét., 2 vol. Paris 1907; Basilique, DictAC II 525/602. A. HEISENBERG, Grabeskirche und Apostelkirche, zwei Basiliken Konstantins, 1908. O. MARUCCHI, Manuale di archeologia cristiana, Rome ⁴1933, English by Vecchierello, Paterson, 1935. O. WULFF, Altchristl. u. byzantin. Kunst, 2 vols. 1914/6; Bibliographisch-krit. Nachtrag, 1939. C. ENLART, Manuel d'archéologie française I—II, Paris ²1919/20. J. SAUER, Neues Licht auf dem Gebiet der christl. Archäol., 1925. C. CECCHELLI, Archeologia della prima età cristiana e del medio evo I, Rome 1928; Studi e documenti nella Roma sacra I, Rome 1938. R. SCHULTZE, Basilika, Untersuchungen zur antiken u. frühmittelalterl. Baukunst, 1928. K. LIESENBERG, Der Einfluß der Liturgie auf die frühchristl. Basilika, 1928. M. HAUTTMANN, Die Kunst des frühen Mittelalters, ²1937. R. KÖMSTEDT, Vormittelalterl. Malerei, 1929. G. DE JERPHANION, La voix des monuments, Paris 1930; nouv. sér., 1938; Bull. d'archéologie chrétienne, Orientalia Christ. 28, 2, Rome 1932. J. WILPERT, Erlebnisse u. Ergebnisse im Dienste der Christl. Archäol., 1930. J. P. KIRSCH, RQ 1935, 1/22 (architecture of the old Roman basilica). G. WULFF, Byz.-Neugriech. Jbb. 1936, 61/96 (development of the basilica). TH. KLAUSER, Vom Heroon zur Martyrerbasilika, 1942. F. W. DEICHMANN, Frühchristl. Kirchen in Rom, 1948. TH. K. KEMPF, Forschungen u. Fortschritte 1950, 244/7 (Trier). J. STRZYGOWSKI, Orient oder Rom, 1901; Kleinasien, ein Neuland der Kunstgesch. 1903; Die Baukunst der Armenier u. Europa, 2 vols. 1918; Ursprung der christl. Kunst, 1920; L'ancien art chrétien de Syrie, Paris 1936. On the theory of orientation: A. BAUMSTARK, HpBl 152, 1913, 737 ff. 843 ff.; J. WILPERT, ZkTh 1921, 337/69; 1922, 1 ff. 177 ff.; E. WEIGAND, ZntW 1923, 233/56; H. LECLERCQ, DictAC VII, 547/94; ib. XII, 2610/57. CH. DIEHL, Manuel de l'art byzantin, ²1925/26; L'art chrétien primitif et l'art byzantin, Paris 1928; La peinture byzantine, Paris 1933. O. M. DALTON, Byzantine Art and Archaeology, Oxford 1911; East Christian Art, London 1925. TH. G. JACKSON, Byzantine and Romanesque Architecture, 2 vol. Cambridge ²1921. L. BRÉHIER, L'art byzantin, Paris 1924. J. EBERSOLT, Monuments d'architecture byzantine, ib. 1934. W. R. ZALOZIECHKY, Byzana u. Abendland im Spiegel ihrer Kunstanschauungen, 1936. JOHANN GEORG HERZOG ZU SACHSEN, Monumentale Reste frühen Christentums in Syrien, 1920. H. W. BEYER, Der syr. Kirchenbau, 1925. H. C. BUTLER, Early Churches in Syria, Princeton 1929. K. WATZINGER, Denkmäler Palästinas, 2 parts 1933/5. H. BROCKHAUS, Die Kunst in den Athosklöstern, ²1924. J. W. CROWFOOT, Early Churches in Palestine, London 1941. F. J. DÖLGER, Sol salutis, ²1925 (orientation); Ichthys, see § 22, 1. K. KÜNSTLE, Ikonographie der christl. Kunst, 2 vols. 1926/8. O. DOERING, Christl. Symbole, 1933. T. K. KEMPF, Christus der Hirt, Rome 1942. J. QUASTEN, Misc. G. Mercati I, Rome 1946, 373/406 (the Good Shepherd in sepulchral art). J. KOLLWITZ ThGl 1947/8, 95/117 (Christ the king in early Christian art and liturgy). A. W. DEICHMANN, RLAntChr I, 1157 ff. (the baptisterium); 1749 ff. (the basilica).

in erecting magnificent buildings for divine worship. A brisk building program was carried out in the East at Constantinople, in Syria, Palestine, Asia Minor and Egypt, and the West did not fall far behind. About 315 the oldest basilica, the Lateran, was built at Rome, followed shortly by St. Peter's, St. Mary Major, St. Paul's, St. Laurence's, St. Clement's, St. Sabina's, St. Agnes' and others. Excavations completed at *Trier* in 1950 revealed the foundations of a church measuring 110 × 112 meters (about 360 × 366 feet) which had been built in the Constantinian period. It was a double church, a style unique at that time. *Ravenna*, the residence of the emperors of the West after 407, later the residence of Theodosius the Great and the imperial exarchs, had many fine buildings. Some of these of the fifth and sixth centuries have been preserved; for example,the basilica of St. Apollinare Nuovo and S. Apollinare in Classe, together with several baptisteries and mausoleums (see below). *Syria* successfully developed a new type of stone building with massive pillars and rounded vaults and arches. *Constantine the Great* provided his new capital on the Bosporus with several beautiful churches (Eusebius, Vita Const. III, 48). The combination of Western (Greek) and Oriental architecture produced a new style called *Byzantine*. The most famous example of Byzantine architecture is the *church of St. Sophia*[1], built by Justinian from 532 to 537 and dedicated to Christ, the "Wisdom of the Father." Its interior represented the supreme triumph of artistic form and religious atmosphere. Since 1453 it has been a Turkish mosque.

2. From the very beginning of the period, the **basilica** (βασιλική scil. στοά = royal hall) was considered the ideal and normal type of the house of God. Although it took its name and its architecture from older models (market and court buildings, rather than places of pagan worship) it shows in general an entirely new creation of the Christian mind, uniting grandeur, dignity and utility. The nave was an *oblong* rectangle. In some basilicas, a *transept* extended in front of the sanctuary to facilitate the procession of the people to and from the altar in making their oblations. The nave was often paralleled on either side by two or four ambulatories or aisles, lower and narrower than the central nave. At the juncture of the nave and the transept there was usually a triumphal arch which served to direct and concentrate attention on the altar. The end of the building in which the altar stood formed a semicircle — the apse (ἀψίς, concha, tribuna) — in which stood the throne (θρόνος, cathedra) of the bishop, flanked by seats for the clergy. At the opposite or

---

[1] W. R. ZALOZIECKY, Die Sophienkirche in Konstantinopel, Rome 1936. TH. WHITTEMORE, American Journal of Archaeology 1938 , 219 ff. (cleansing of the mosaics of St. Sophia). A. M. SCHNEIDER, Die Hagia Sophia zu Konstantinopel, 1939.

entrance end there was often a small vestibule (νάρθηξ, porticus) or a quadran-
gular court (atrium) with a fountain (cantharus) in the center. The *practice
of orienting* the basilica, that is, of building the church so that the apse and
the altar would be *in the East* end took cognizance of a symbolism older than
Christianity, but followed by Christians from the beginning. However, up
to the fifth century many churches, especially at Rome, were given just the
opposite position or at least deviated from the "sacred line." In the East,
especially in Syria, *towers* were often appended to the church buildings. From
the sixth century on, they make their appearance in the West (Rome, Ravenna)
but they stand apart from the church (campaniles).

Besides the basilica-form of architecture, a **circular form** was sometimes
used, especially for **baptisteries** (Lateran at Rome; S. Giovanni in fonte and
S. Vitale at Ravenna; S. Lorenzo at Milan) and for *tombs* (S. Constanza at
Rome; the mausoleums of Galla Placidia and Theodoric the Great at Ravenna).
But in the East, the circular form was also used for large churches. As a rule,
a circular building had a domed roof or *cupola*. A *combination* of the circular
building with the basilic type, oblong or square was used frequently in the
East and forms the chief characteristic of the *Byzantine style*. Besides the
church of St. Sophia at Constantinople, many other churches of Asia Minor,
Syria and Armenia were built in this style.

As a rule the *baptisteries* (§ 66, 3) were erected quite near the church and
connected with it by a covered passageway. A large basin or pool for immersion (κολυμβήθρα = piscina, fons) was in the center of the floor and provided with steps. When infant baptism became general the *baptismal font*
in its present form replaced the basin and baptism was administered in
church.

For the reasons stated above, the **plastic arts**[1] developed even more
slowly than painting. Yet as early as the third century some marble statues
of artistic worth were carved, e. g., the Good Shepherd, St. Hippolytus of
Rome (§ 39, 4) and the statue or St. Peter in the Vatican Grottoes. During
the fourth and fifth centuries great progress was made in relief carving as
seen on the *stone sarcophagi* of noble and wealthy Christians. In general the
symbolism and typology of the figures are the same as found in the paintings
of the catacombs. *Other works* in bronze and clay, carvings in wood and ivory
are well represented in Christian art of this period. The ivory cathedra
of Bishop Maximian of Ravenna, of about 550, is a masterpiece of relief
carving.

Christian **painting**[2] which had reached a fair degree of development in
the catacombs in the pre-Constantinian period, was now called upon to adorn

---

[1] J. WILPERT, see § 2, 1. F. GERKE, Die christl. Sarkophage der vor-
konstantin. Zeit, 1940; Das hl. Antlitz, 1940; Christus in der spätantiken
Plastik, ³1948. G. W. MORATH, Die Maximians-Kathedra in Ravenna, Diss.
1941. J. KOLLWITZ, Oström. Plastik der Theodosian. Zeit, 1941.
[2] J. WILPERT, see § 2, 1. E. UEHLI, Die Mosaiken v. Ravenna, ²1939.
F. W. VOLBACH, Mosaïques chrétiennes primitives du 4ᵉ au 7ᵉ s. (Rome,
Naple, Milan, Ravenna), Paris 1946. O. G. V. SIMONS, Sacred Fortress:
Byzantine Art and Statecraft in Ravenna, Chicago 1948. S. BETTINA,
Frühchristl. Malerei u. frühchristl.-röm. Tradition bis zum HochMA., 1942.

the great churches springing into existence above ground. The walls of the nave, the triumphal arch, the apse, the ceiling of the dome were ornamented with pictures, often in a series, painted in fresco or in indestructable *mosaic*. The favorite subjects were: Christ as teacher or Pantocrater, surrounded by angels, the Apostles and other saints, the Lamb of God with the symbols of the Evangelists. The finest examples of mosaics are those preserved from the fifth and sixth centuries at Rome (S. Pudenziana, SS. Cosma e Damiano, S. Maria Maggiore) and Ravenna (S. Giovanni in fonte, S. Apollinare Nuovo, S. Vitale).

3. The most important article of furniture in the church — the *altar* — stood just before or at the entrance to the apse. The space around it, reserved for the clergy and chanters was called the presbyterium and was closed off from the nave by a grating (κιγκλίδες, cancelli) or by a row of pillars. In the East, after the sixth century, the grating developed into the *iconostasis*, usually of wood, seldom of stone, with representations of Christ, the Blessed Virgin, St. John the Baptist, the Archangels and other popular saints. In the forepart of the nave stood the *ambo* (pulpitum, suggestus), a raised structure of wood or stone from which the Scriptural lessons were read and from which the sermon was sometimes preached (§ 67, 4). In the pre-Constantinian period, the altar was a simple, unadorned, movable table (mensa) which had no significance outside of the Eucharistic celebration. After the fourth century it was usually made of stone. The old custom of visiting the graves of the martyrs and celebrating the Holy Mysteries as near the grave as possible (§ 23, 5) led, in the fourth century, to the practise of building a basilica on the spot so that the altar would stand immediately over the martyr's grave (confessio). This, in turn, gave rise to the custom of putting relics of the martyrs on the altars of ordinary parish churches within the city. The altar was then given the form of a sarcophagus and the table-shaped altar gradually disappeared. The altar then became, like the church, a res sacra, and an image of Christ, and before long a special consecration of the altar was introduced. Before the sixth century, each church had but *one* altar, as is still the case in the East; but after that date the Latin churches installed side altars for the private offering of the Sacrifice. A canopy-like structure, resting on four pillars, was erected over the altar (baldachin, ciborium, umbraculum). Between the pillars were curtains or drapes (tetravela) which were drawn around the altar at certain parts of the Mass. In the eighth century, a dove-shaped vessel (περιστήριον, columba) in which the Eucharist was preserved was hung from the *ciborium*. — *Fr. Wieland*, Mensa u. Confessio, 2 vols. 1906/12. — *J. Braun*, Der christl. Altar in seiner geschichtl. Entwickl., 2 vols. 1924 (standard); Die Reliquiare des christlichen Kultes und ihre Entwicklung, 1940; Stz 110, 1925, 161/72. — *K. Holl*, ArchRelW 1906, 365/84 (Iconostasis). — *Th. Klauser*, RQ 43, 1935, 179/86 (Constantine altars in the Lateran). — *G. Wunderle*, Um die Seele der hl. Ikonen, 1937. — *P. Batiffol*, Rev-SPhTh 1939, 58/73 (consecration of churches). — *F. J. Dölger*, AntChrist 1930, 161/83. (sanctity of the Christian altar). — F. Raible, Der Tabernakel einst und jetzt, 1908. — W. Lockton, The Treatment of the Remains of the Eucharist, Cambridge 1920. — L. Köster, De custodia Ss. Eucharistiae, Diss. Rom 1940.

The most important liturgical vessels were the **chalice** (calix offertorius, sacrificatorius) and the **paten** (δίσκος). During the Middle Ages it was prescribed that the chalice be of metal; but before then it was made of wood, clay, glass or any other suitable material. Besides the chalice which the priest used for Mass, there were much larger lay-chalices for the Communion of the people (scyphus, calix ministerialis, calix ansatus). — *J. Braun S.J.*, Das christl. Altargerät in seiner geschichtl. Entwicklung, 1931. — *D. Duret*, Mobilier, vases, objects et vêtements liturgiques, Paris 1932. — *J. Baudot*, Calice, DictAC III, 1595/1651.

4. Special **liturgical vestments** were unknown in the early ages of the Church. When taking part in divine service the clergy in the fourth century, wore the clothing then customary as holiday attire, especially the narrow-sleeved tunic, the dalmatic and the paenula, or sleeveless mantle. During the fourth and fifth centuries when different fashions were adopted for ordinary wear, the Church retained the former fashions which then became the distinctive liturgical dress of the clergy. The tunic became the alb and the paenula the *chasuble* (casula, planeta). The fourth Synod of Toledo in 633 (can. 28) mentions both as official garments of the clergy. Besides, the same synod mentions the *orarium*, corresponding to our present *stole*, and says that it is used by both priests and deacons. The orarium (ὡράριον) was mentioned earlier by the Synod of Laodicea about 380. In the Vita Sylvestri († 335) and Zozimi († 418) in the Liber Pontificalis mention is made of a pallium linostimum, an ornamented cloth from which the *maniple* developed. The Synod of Toledo mentioned above, speaks of the orarium as being part of the bishop's insignia as well as the *ring* and *crozier*. The *pallium* known in the East about 400 where it was called ὡμοφόριον, was originally perhaps the same as the lorum, a sort of scarf, worn by civil officials and was conferred by secular authority. In the West its use was restricted to the pope, but since the sixth century was conferred by him on other bishops, especially *metropolitans*, as a symbol of close union with Rome. It seems that Caesar of Arles was the first archbishop to receive the pallium. Pope Symmachus conferred it on him in 513. Besides the tunic, the pope and his deacons also wore a second *garment* with sleeves, called a *dalmatic*. It was worn at Ravenna since the sixth century and from the ninth century was used generally by bishops and deacons, the latter using it as an outer vestment. The *color* of all the liturgical vestments used in the early ages was white. It was only in the early Middle Ages (eighth to ninth centuries) that the various colors began to be used. — *J. Braun*, Die priesterl. Gewänder des Abendlandes, 1897; Die pontifikalen Gewänder des Abendlandes, 1898; Die liturg. Gewandung im Occident u. Orient, 1907 (standard); Die liturg. Paramente in Gegenwart und Vergangenheit, ²1924. — *J. W. Legg*, Church Ornaments and their Civil Antecedents, Cambridge 1917. — *H. Norris*, Church Vestments, Their Origin and Development, 1949. — *J. Baudot*, Le pallium, Paris 1909; cfr. *P. M. Baumgarten*, Festgabe Finke, 1925, 338/47, and *J. Braun*, Die liturg. Gewandung (1907) 620/76. — *Eidenschink*, see § 60. — F. Focke, Festgabe Al. Fuchs, 1950. 337/87 (Scepter and crozier). — *Th. Klauser*, Der Ursprung d. bischöfl. Insignien u. Ehrenrechte, 1949. — *D. Duret*, Mobilier etc., see above.

# § 72.

## The Rise of Monasticism and Its Devolopment in the East and West[1].

1. Christianity had made its first conquests in the cities; and before it advanced into the open country, monasticism was flourish-

---

[1] **I. General Works:** ROUET DE JOURNEL et DUTILLEUL, GUIBERT et al., see § 26, 2. H. U. V. BALTHASAR, see § 2, 7. G. GRAF, Geschichte der christl. arabischen Literatur I, Rome 1944. H. KOCH, Quellen z. Gesch. der Askese u. des Mönchtums in der alten Kirche, 1933. J. A. MÖHLER, Gesch. des Mönchtums in der Zeit s. Entstehung, Ges. Schriften II, 1840, 165/225. M. HEIMBUCHER, Die Orden u. Kongregationen der kath. Kirche, 2 vols. ³1932/4. P. POURRAT, La spiritualité chrétienne, 4 vol. Paris 1919/29, I⁹ 1926. CH. DE MONTALEMBERT, Précis d'histoire monastique, nov. éd., Paris 1934. U. BERLIÈRE, L'ordre monastique des origines au XIIᵉ siècle, Paris ³1924. Beiträge zur Gesch. des alten Mönchtums u. des Benediktinerordens, ed. I. HERWEGEN, 1911 ff. H. LECLERCQ, DictAC XI, 1774/1947 (Monachisme); ib. II, 3047/3248 (Cénobitisme); ib. XII, 1557/1615 (Nonnes). D. GORCE, La lectio divina des origines du cénobitisme à S. Benoît et Cassiodore I, Paris 1925. DictSpir = Dictionnaire de spiritualité ascétique et mystique, publ. p. M. VILLER, Paris 1952 ff.; in vol. II, 405/16; J. OLPHE-GALLIARD, Cénobitisme. H. EMONDS, RLAntChrist I, 45/55 (abbot). M. VILLER and K. RAHNER, Aszese u. Mystik in der Väterzeit, 1939 (valuable, extensive literature). O. ZÖCKLER, Askese u. Mönchtum, 1897 (also A. EHRHARD, HJG 1897, 867/70). A. HARNACK, Das Mönchtum, seine Ideale u. s. Geschichte, ¹⁰1921. H. B. WORKMAN, The Evolution of the Monastic Ideal (to 1200), London 1913. J. C. HANNAH, Christian Monasticism, London 1924. J. WAGEMANN, Entwicklungsstufen des ältesten Mönchtums, 1929 (lecture). H. V. CAMPENHAUSEN, Asket. Heimatlosigkeit, 1930 (lecture). W. SESTON, RevHR 108, 1933, 197/213 (Origen and the beginnings of monasticism). K. HEUSSI, Der Ursprung des Mönchtums, 1936 (standard; also L. TH. LEFORT, RHE 1937, 341/48). R. E. MALONE, The Monk and the Martyr, Wash. 1950. Enchiridion de statibus perfectionis I, Rom 1949.

**II. Oriental monasticism:** G. GRÜTZEMACHER, Pachomius u. das älteste Klosterleben, 1896. E. PREUSCHEN, Palladius und Rufinus, 1897. E. MARIN, Les moines de Constantinople (330—898), Paris 1897. P. LADEUZE, Étude sur le cénobitisme pakhomien, Louvain 1898. K. HOLL, Enthusiasmus u. Bußgewalt beim griech. Mönchtum, 1898. J. M. BESSE, Les moines d'Orient (to 451), Paris 1900. ST. SCHIWIETZ, Das morgenländ. Mönchtum, 3 vols. 1904/38. F. NAU, RevOC 1905, 1907/9, 1912, 1913 (solitaires égyptiens). D. A. PETRAKAKOS, Οἱ μοναχικοὶ θεσμοὶ ἐν τῇ ὀρθοδόξῳ ἀνατολικῇ ἐκκλησίᾳ I, Leipzig 1907. P. VAN CAUWENBERGH, Étude sur les moines d'Égypte (451—600), Thèse Louvain 1914. R. REITZENSTEIN, Historia Monachorum u. Historia Lausiaca, 1916. W. H. MACKEAN, Christian Monasticism in Egypt (to 400), London 1920. W. BOUSSET, Apophthegmata, Studien z. Gesch. des ältesten Mönchtums, 1923; Das Mönchtum der sket. Wüste, ZKG 1923, 1/41. H. G. E. WHITE, The Monasteries of the Wâdi 'n Natrûn, 3 vol. New York 1926/33. J. BREMOND, Les pères du désert, 2 vol. Paris 1927. R. DRAGUET, same title, ib. 1949. A. L. SCHMITZ, RQ 1929, 189/243 (archaeological researches on Egyptian monks and hermits). P. RESCH, La doctrine ascétique des premiers maîtres égyptiens du IVᵉ s., Paris 1931. W. BUDGE, Stories of the Holy Fathers of the Desert of Egypt (250—400), transl. of the Syriac, Oxford 1934. J. BIDEZ, Sb. Berlin 1935, 18 (Sozomen on the monks of Egypt and Palestine). F. KOZMAN, Textes législatifs touchant le cénobitisme égyptien, Rome 1935 (Codificazione canonica orientale, Fonti II, 1). N. ABBOTT, The Monasteries of the Fayjûm, Chicago 1937 (from American Journal of Semitic Lang. a. Lit. 53). P. KRÜGER, Das syrisch-monophysit. Mönchtum im Tur'Ab(h)din, OrChrPer 1938, 5/46.

ing in the deserts. This form of Christian life which was to mean so much to the Church and to the world through all future generations, did not come into existence suddenly. It was rather the development and organization of a wide-spread Christian *asceticism* (ἀσκηταί, continentes, virgines) which had been known in the Church since the Savior had enunciated the "evangelical counsels" (Matt. 19:12, 21; 1 Cor. 7:7 ff. 25 ff.; 19,5; 26, 3). From the third century many individuals desirous of leading a more perfect Christian life withdrew from the company of men into solitary places for a time, and finding there the fulfillment of their desires, resolved to remain permanently. Such ascetics were called *monks* (μοναχοί, μονάζοντες) from the solitary manner of their life, or *anchorites* (ἀναχωρεῖν to denote their withdrawal from the world) or *hermits* (from the places where they dwelt ἔρημος, the desert). Their choice of a life secluded from the world and devoted to a close union with God was not made because of fear of the persecutions, as Sozomen says (H. E. I, 12, 11), nor because of disgust at the superficial culture of the times, nor because of the fact that they saw their brethren in the faith yielding to a growing lukewarmness; it was simply that they saw it as the only form of life in which they could adequately realize their ascetical ideals. The climate of *Egypt*[1]

---

[1] H. DELEHAYE, AB 1926, 64/9 (Paul of Thebes); cfr. F. CAVALLERA, RevAM 1926, 302/5. Leben des hl. Antonius u. des hl. Pachomius übers. v. MERTEL, BKV 31, 1917. Vie sahidique de S. Antoine, ed. G. GARITTE, CSCO 118/9. Löwen 1949 (with French transl.). L. V. HERTLING, Antonius d. Einsiedler, 1929. L. BOUYER, La vie de S. Antoine, St. Wandrille 1950. J. LIST, Das Antoniusleben des hl. Athanasius, Athen 1930. H. DÖRRIES, Nachr. Göttingen 1949, 337/410 (Vita Antonii as an historical source. Cfr. also J. STOFFELS, ThGl 1910, 721 ff. 809 ff.; K. HOLL, NJklA 29, 1912, 406/27; R. REITZENSTEIN, Sb. Heidelberg 1914, 8. F. KLEJNA, ZkTh 1938, 309/48 (letters of St. Anthony and his disciple Ammonas); also G. GERITTE, Muséon 1939, 11/31; 1942, 97/123. S. Pachomii vitae (copticae), ed. L. TH. LE-FORT, OSCO SS. Copti III, 7—8, Paris 1925/36; Les vies coptes de S. Pachôme et de ses premiers successeurs, Löwen 1943 (cfr. Lefort, Muséon 193;, 75/80; 1936, 219/30; P. PEETERS, AB 1934, 286/320; 1946, 258/77; (Muséon 1946, 17/34). S. Pachomii Vitae graecae, ed. F. Halkin, Brux. 1932 (also F. HALKIN, Brux. 1932 (also F. HALKIN, AB 1929, 376/88; 1930, 257/301). S. Pachomii regulae monasticae, ed. BR. ALBERS, 1923 (Floril. pastrit. 16). A. BOON, Pachomiana Latina (Règle et épîtres), Louvain 1932. W. HENGSTENBERG, Pachomiana, in Festgabe A. Ehrhard, 1922, 228/52. H. LECLERCQ, Pakhôme, DictAC XIII 499/510. H. BACHT, Geist u. Leben 1949, 367/82. L. TH. LE-FORT, Muséon 1939, 379/408 (the first monasteries of Pachomius). GRÜTZ-MACHER, LADEUZE etc., see above. C. BUTLER, The Lausiac History of Palladius, in Texts and Studies VI, 1/2, Cambridge 1898/1904; Palladius' Leben der hl. Väter, übers. v. ST. KROTTENTHALER in BKV 5, 1912 (literature § 75, 7). J. LEIPOLDT, Schenute von Atripe, TU 25, 1, 1903. R. GÉNIER, Vie de S. Euthyme le Grand, Paris 1909. Kyrillos of Skythopolis ed. ED. SCHWARTZ, TU 49, 2, 1939 (lives of St. Euthymius, Sabas etc.). W. STROTH-MANN, Die arab. Makariustradition, 1935.

and the earnest disposition of its people (Copts) favored the eremitical life and caused the country to become the nursery of monasticism. Two names inseparably connected with early monasticism are *Paul* of Thebes († 347?) and *St. Anthony the Great* (251—356). The latter, born of wealthy Christian parents in a village of Central Egypt, became the "Patriarch" of monasticism, as well as a man of prayer, a "terror of demons," a healer of the sick and a director of souls. The Vita Pauli, a sort of romantic story of monasticism, was written by St. Jerome (376); and a highly idealized, but essentially trustworthy life of Anthony was written by his great admirer St. Athanasius, (about 357), who could scarcely have foreseen the effects of his little volume. It not only made monastic life known to a large circle of readers, but it also inspired an extensive literature on monasticism and exerted a lasting influence on the institution itself.

2. Monasticism may be said to have assumed the character of an institution when a *common life* began to take the place of the purely eremitical life. About the year 306, after St. Anthony had spent two decades in total solitude, he permitted disciples to erect cells near his hermitage and thus form a *band of anchorites* as yet without rule or stability and held together only by the words and personal magnetism of their leader.

With the third step, the introduction of the *cenobitical* form of life (κοινὸς βίος), monasticism became a permanent institution. This phase is always closely associated with the name of *St. Pachomius*. He had served some time in the army and upon being released, received baptism and lived for three years as a disciple of the hermit Palemon. About 320 he went to Tabennae (Tabennisi) in the Thebaid (Upper Egypt) where he founded a monastery, that is, a large group of cells surrounded by a wall (μάνδρα, μοναστήριον, κοινόβιον). He also gave his associates a *rule* in which prayer and religious exercises, clothing, work and discipline were regulated in detail. The spiritual head of a foundation, to whom the subjects owed unconditional obedience, was called *Abbas*, i. e., Father, a term originally used by the Pneumatici and implying charismatic gifts. Thus instead of the unregulated and unstable eremitical life, an organization was formed which better satisfied the religious and social needs of individuals, and monasticism was started on the path it was henceforth to follow and on which it would do great and good things for the Church and for civilization.

Christian monasticism, therefore, originated in *Christianity* itself and in Christian ideals of asceticism. The various attempts to derive it from apparently related non-Christian institutions are unhistorical. Thus it has been asserted that Monasticism within the Church had its origin in the Jewish sects of the *Essenes* and the *Therapeutae* (Eusebius, E. Lucius, § 6, 1); in Neoplatonism (Th. Keim); in *Neopythagoreanism* and *Gnosticism* (R. Reitzenstein); in *Buddhism* (A. Hilgenfeld, R. Garbe) or with the *penitential system* (κατοχή) at the sanctuary of Serapis at Memphis and elsewhere (H. Weingarten, W. Bousset and others). In all of these cases there may be analogy or parallels, but certainly no relation of dependence. Appreciation of a life of seclusion, devoted to union with God, is a natural tendency of the human heart and in any higher religion (as, later, in Islam) can lead to a form of monasticism. As far as the so-called *hermits of Serapis* (κάτοχοι) are concerned, whom Pachomius is supposed to have imitated, it is a question whether they were actually ascetics and penitents who became "prisoners" of Serapis (R. Reitzenstein, U. Wilcken) or whether they were sick persons who sought to recover health by sleeping in the temple (E. Preuschen) or were debtors or fugitives of all sorts seeking asylum (K. Sethe, F. v. Woess). At most there could have been some external resemblance based on common Egyptian customs (S. Morenz, ThLZ 1949, 423/9. — Besides the literature listed above cfr. also *H. Strathmann*, Gesch. der frühchristl. Askese I, 1914. — *Ph. Gobillot*, RechSR 1920, 303 ff.; 1921, 29 ff. 168 ff. 328 ff.; 1922, 46 ff. — *U. Wilcken*, Urkunden der Ptolemäerzeit I, 1927, 52/77. — *G. Heuser*, Die Katoche im Serapieion zu Memphis, Diss. 1933. — *L. Wenger*, Arch. f. Kulturgesch. 1938, 113 ff. (On the Katoche).

3. Once it had been established, monasticism grew with remarkable rapidity, especially in the *East*. *Pachomius* was obliged to build several monasteries to accomodate the disciples who flocked to him and several other monasteries placed themselves under his guidance. When he died in 346 his community numbered nine houses with several thousand members. The center of the congregation was the monastery at Pebou (Phebôou) which Pachomius had chosen as his residence. Monasticism was still highly concentrated in the *Thebaid* of Upper Egypt in the fifth century. The renowned Abbot *Schenute* (Schenudi † 466) governed over a thousand monks in the "White Monastery" at Atripe. Besides monasteries of men, many *monasteries* were founded *for women*. Monasticism, naturally in the form of cenobitism, met with a ready response on the part of women, especially since, as early as the third century, there were many virgines sacrae, virgines Christi, most of whom perhaps had taken a private vow of chastity (§ 26, 3). Pachomius established two monasteries for women, one at Tabennae of which his sister Mary was mother superior or abbess.

From the Thebaid monasticism spread to *Lower Egypt, Syria*

and *Palestine*. The Alexandrian Amun (*Ammon*, † c. 356) trained many disciples in the Nitrian mountains and *Macarius* the Elder or the Great (§ 75, 4) did the same in the nearby desert of Scete. St. Hilarion of Gaza († 371) introduced monasticism into Palestine where there were soon many flourishing monasteries. In the fifth century *Euthymius* († 473) was renowned as the father of monks in the Holy Land. In the first half of the fourth century there were monks and hermits in the neighborhood of *Edessa* in northeast Syria, whose manner of life was most probably not modelled after Egyptian monasticism. The mountains of West Syria near Antioch and the Desert of Chalcis (the "Syrian Thebaid") had colonies of hermits to which St. John Chrysostom and St. Jerome belonged for a time. *Eustathius*, Archbishop of Sebaste in Lesser Armenia († c. 380) fostered the cenobitic life in Asia Minor. But it was his disciple, *St. Basil the Great*[1], Archbishop of Caesarea in Cappadocia (§ 75, 2), who deserves the greatest credit for developing monasticism in the East. Before becoming bishop he had lived with like-minded companions on the banks of the Iris in the Pontus. He stressed the contemplative ideal, especially the pedagogical value of the common life, the duty of active charity, the obligation of higher learning and the study of theology. It was his endeavor to effect a combination of monasticism with Hellenic culture. Two monastic rules, known as the Greater and the Lesser Rules, are, for the most part, his work. And although he never founded a religious order, the monks of the East to the present day, follow his rules and are known as Basilians.

In some parts of the East, especially in Palestine, where the eremitical life predominated over the cenobitical, there arose a form which was a combination of the two. Many monks under the direction of one abbot lived in small individual cells (τὰ κέλλια) which formed a village and hence was called a *laura*[2] (λαύρα = vicus).

---

[1] E. F. MORISON, S. Basil and his Rule, London 1913. W. K. L. CLARKE, S. Basil the Great. A Study in Monasticism, Cambridge 1913. F. LAUN, ZKG 1925, 1/61 (Rule of St. Basil). F. M. GUÉTET, Recherches sur la texte des règles basiliennes, Thèse Lyon 1946. H. DÖRRIES, Symeon v. Mesopotamien 1941, 451/65. M. G. MURPHY, S. Basil and Monasticism, Diss. Washington 1930. P. HUMBERTCLAUDE, La doctrine ascétique de S. Basile de Césarée, Paris 1932. D. AMAND, L'ascèse monastique de S. Basile, Maredsous 1949. G. BARDY, S. Basile, DictSpir I, 1273/83. L. V. HERTLING, ZkTh 1932, 148/74 (profession of clerics and the three vows). L. MEYER, RevAM 1933, 232/62 (perfection and monastic life in John Chrysost.). See literature § 75, 2.
[2] H. LECLERCQ, Laures palestiniennes, DictAC VIII, 1961/88.

The great or old laura of St. Sabbas († 532; § 58, 4) near Jerusalem was especially famous. Many Greek Fathers of the fourth and fifth centuries, especially Evagrius Ponticus, Palladius, Isidore of Pelusium and Nilus the Elder (§ 75, 6. 7) fostered monasticism by composing ascetical works. Widely circulated lives of monks and collections of "Sayings of the Fathers" (Apophthegmata patrum) were read by monks and laymen. Thus monasticism became increasingly important in the internal and external life of the Greek Church, eventually affecting its asceticism and ministry, its social relations and even its ecclesiastical policy (§ 54; 55; 58; 59).

4. At this time, most of the *monks* were *not priests*. They all wore the same kind of garb — a linen undergarment with a leather girdle and outer garment of sheepskin with a hood. They occupied themselves with work and prayer (§ 67, 7). In Egypt, besides cultivating the earth, they wove baskets, mats and other such articles as could be made from the rank growth of reeds. In the larger monasteries almost every art and trade was represented. The products of their toil were sold in nearby cities and the proceeds used to support the monastery and relieve the poor. As a rule there was in the community only a sufficient number of priests — often but one — to conduct the divine services. Pachomius excluded priests from his foundations so as to remove every occasion of ambition and engaged priests from neighboring towns and villages for the necessary priestly ministrations. — *Ph. Oppenheim*, Das Mönchskleid im christl. Altertum, 1931 (RQ Suppl. 28); Symbolik u. religiöse Wertung des Mönchskleides im christl. Altertum, 1932. — H. Dörries, Festschr. Joh. Ficker, 1931, 17/39 (monasticism and work). — A. T. Geoghegan, see § 26.

Not infrequently the *monasteries of women* were built next to those of men or at least in close vicinity, so as to assure the necessary spiritual direction, the necessary economic assistance and the necessary protection from the attacks of brigands, then a real threat to life in the desert. Such an arrangement, however, was not without moral danger. The Synod of Agde in 506 (can. 28) and Emperor Justinian (Cod. I, 3, 43 of the year 529; Nov. 123, 36 of the year 546) forbade such *double monasteries*; the second Synod of Nicaea in 787 (can. 20) forbade the founding of new ones and made special regulations for those in existence. Such establishments were also known throughout the West until the end of the Middle Ages. The scant favor shown by the Church toward the system caused a decline in the tenth century, but there was a revival in the twelfth century. — *St. Hilpisch*, Die Doppelklöster, Entstehung und Organisation, 1928.

At the time of St. Pachomius *children* were sometimes placed in monasteries, usually with the understanding that they would eventually become monks. The Synod in Trullo in 692 (can. 40) demanded ten years as the minimum age, but this law was never strictly observed. (Cfr. *R. Riepenhoff*, vide infra no. 6).

At the General Council of *Chalcedon* in 451 both the ecclesiastical and civil authorities endeavored to *legislate* against some abuses which had arisen in Greek Oriental *monasticism*. It was decreed that all monks whether in the city or in the country be subject to the authority of the bishop in whose diocese their monastery was located; and that no monastery be established without the permission of the bishop. The monks were commanded to devote themselves to prayer and fasting and were not to leave their monastery except in case of necessity and then with the bishop's permission. Slaves were not to be received except with the consent of their master (can. 4) and to return to the world to accept an office or to marry was forbidden under pain of excommunication (can. 7.16). The Synod in Trullo (692) and *Justinian* supplemented the legislation for monasteries of the Greek Church. — Cfr. *W. Nissen*, Die Regelung des Klosterlebens in Rhomäerreiche, 1897. — *B. Granič*, Byz. Z. 1929, 6/34; 1930, 669/76; 1931, 61/9 (monastic legislation in Byzan.). *Petrakakos* et al., see above, also § 58 (Lit.).

5. Due to lack of a unified system, especially in the *Orient*, monasticism sometimes appeared in forms entirely unlike those already mentioned or, more correctly, as *serious deviations* from the original forms. The *Sarabaites* or *Remoboth* (Jerome, Ep. 22, 34) lived in small groups of two or three without a superior or rule. They were also fairly numerous in the West (Regula S. Bened. 1: monachorum deterrimum genus sarabaitarum). The *Gyrovagi* wandered about from monastery to monastery, remaining as guests for three or four days in each place (genus monachorum gyrovagum ... per omnia deteriores sarabaitis, l. c.). The *Grazers* (Βοσκοί) in Syria and Mesopotamia had no fixed abodes but moved through the fields and ate nothing but herbs. The *Audians* and *Messalians* (§ 50, 6. 7) were heretical sects with a monastic-like organization. Some singular types appeared among the anchorites and cenobites. *Recluses* (ἔγκλειστοι inclusi, reclusi) walled themselves in a small cage for a definite period or permanently. This form of ascetical life, embraced by both men and women, was not uncommon in both East and West from Christian antiquity to the sixteenth century. (See bibl. below). The *Stylites* or *Pillar Saints* lived on the tops of high pillars, *St. Simeon* († 459) spent 30 years on a pillar more than 50 feet high near the city of Antioch and became renowned as a spiritual adviser, a peacemaker and an advocate of the oppressed. Daily he preached to those who gathered around the foot of his pillar and converted many pagans. His example was imitated by *St. Daniel* († 493), *Simeon* the Younger († 596) and many others. In the ninth century a number of female Stylites lived on pillars in the Garden of Gethsemane at Jerusalem. The deacon *Wulflaic*, a Lombard by birth, undertook to live as a Stylite near the city of Trier, but the inclemency of the weather forced him to abandon the idea (Greg. Tur. Hist. Franc. VIII, 15). Finally a group of cenobites at Constantinople were known as *Acoemetae* — sleepless ones. They were divided into several choirs and chanted the office uninterruptedly throughout the day and night (ἀκατάπαυστος δοξολογία laus perennis). They were founded by *St. Alexander* († c. 440) a former officer at Constantinople who had retired to the desert. After founding a monastery on the banks of the Euphrates, he brought his monks to Constantinople, where no more than one such monastery was ever permitted. The famous monastery called *Studium* after its founder the consul Studius (463), which played an important role in the Iconoclast quarrel, did not follow the practice of Alexander's monks, although it accepted Acoemetae among its members. — Literature on **solitaries** (recluses): *L. Gou-*

gaud, Ermites et reclus, Ligugé 1928; RevBén 1933, 281/99 (bibliography). —
O. Doerr, Das Institut der Inklusen in Süddeutschland, 1934. — L. Oliger,
Speculum inclusorum s. XIV, Rom 1938 (Lateranum NS. IV, 1). — **Stylites**:
H. Delehaye, Les Saints Stylites, Brux. 1923. — H. Lietzmann, Das Leben
des hl. Simeon Stylites, TU 32, 4, 1908; cfr. W. E. Crum, ZntW 1927, 119/28;
G. de Jerphanion, RechSR 1931, 340/60. — P. Peeters, AB 1943, 29/71. —
M. Chaîne, La vie et les miracles de s. Sym. stilite l'ancien, Cairo 1948. —
E. Dawes and N. H. Baynes, Three Byzantine Saints, Oxford 1948. — **Acoe-
metae**: J. Pargoire, DictAC I, 307/21. — S. Vailhé, DictHE I, 274/82. —
H. Delehaye, AB 1934, 64 f. (not Studion, but Studios).

6. As early as the third century there were some Christian
ascetics in the **West**[1] who lived a sort of anchoretic life (thus for
a time, Novatian at Rome, cfr. F. J. Dölger, AntChrist 1940, 61/64).
But monasticism properly so-called was introduced and recommended to the West by *St. Athanasius* of Alexandria on the occasion
of his banishment to Trier from 335 to 338 (§ 48, 2) and through
the Latin translation of his Vita S. Antonii made by Evagrius of
Antioch (§ 50, 1) about 370 and even earlier by others. St. Augustine
(Conf. VIII, 6) speaks of the deep impression made in the West by
this work. At a very early date there were hermits on isolated islands
in the Mediterranean and in secluded spots in *Italy* and *Gaul*. But
climatic conditions and the western temperament which inclined
toward the practical and useful caused western ascetics to prefer
cenobitism which here, much more than in the East, became the
great agency of culture (learning) and of social and charitable works.
Monastic foundations for men and women were soon made in cities
or in country places with the support and encouragement of the
great churchmen of the age: Ambrose, Jerome, Augustine, Paulinus
of Nola and others. The bitter attacks on monasticism by Helvidius,

---

[1] Cfr. the general literature above. Also: CH. DE MONTALEMBERT, Les
moines d'Occident, 7 vol. Paris 1860/77; English: The monks of the West
(to 12th cent.) 7 vols. Edinburgh 1861—79 and 6 vols. London 1896. E.
SPREITZENHOFER, Die Entwicklung des Mönchtums in Italien bis Benedikt,
1894. G. GARITTE, Un témoin important du texte de la vie de S. Antoine
par S. Athanase, Rome 1939. J. M. BESSE, Les moines de l'Afrique romaine,
2 vol. Paris 1903; Les moines de l'ancienne France, Paris 1906. PH. SCHMITZ,
RevBén 1926, 189/95 (the first convents of nuns at Rome). F. ANTONELLI,
Antonianum 1927, 401/36 (monasticism according to the Dialogi of Gregory the
Gr.). A. ROBERTI, Scuola Catt. 1940, 140 ff. 236 ff. (Ambrose and monasti-
cism). P. ANTIN, Mél. bénédictins, Fontenelle 1947, 69/142 (Jerome and
monasticism). S. MERLIN, S. Augustin et la vie monastique, Albi 1934.
M. MELLET, L'itinéraire et l'idéal monastique de S. Aug., Paris 1934. C. LAM-
BOT, RevBén 1941, 41/58 (Augustine did not rewrite ep. 211 for men). C.
DEREINE, Scriptorium 1948, 28/36 (Rule of St. Augustine). A. ZUMKELLER,
Das Mönchtum des hl. Aug., 1950. J. PÉREZ DE URBEL, Los monjes españoles
en la Edad Media, 2 vol. Madrid 1933/4. L. UEDING, Gesch. der Kloster-
gründungen der frühen Merowingerzeit, 1935.

Jovinius and Vigilantius (§ 70, 3) in no wise impeded its progress. *Jerome* and *Rufinus* both wrote extensively in defense of monastic life; besides which Jerome published the lives of several famous monks (Paul, Malchus, Hilarion) and Rufinus published the Historia monachorum in Aegypto sive de vitis patrum, a translation and adaptation of a Greek work. These writings served to interest noble Roman ladies in asceticism and both authors spent several decades of their lives, the one at Bethlehem, the other at Jerusalem, in the midst of colonies of monks and nuns from the West. **St. Martin** of Tours († 397) did much to promote monasticism in Gaul.

*Martin*, the son of a Roman officer, was born in 316 or 317 at Sabaria in Pannonia. After serving a short time in the army, he was baptized at the age of 18, was ordained exorcist by Bishop Hilary of Poitiers and lived as a hermit on the island of Gallinaria, near Genoa. He returned to France about 371 and became a monk, but shortly thereafter was elected *bishop of Tours*. As bishop he worked zealously for the conversion of pagans still numerous in the country places of Gaul; and in spite of the opposition of the clergy, fostered monastic life which his disciples then introduced into Spain and Britain. The cell in which he had lived near Poitiers about 360 developed into the monastery of *Ligugé* and his hermitage on the Loire (about 375) grew into the famous *Marmoutier* (Majus Monasterium). His tomb at Tours became one of the most popular places of pilgrimage of the Middle Ages and his mantle (cappa) entrusted to the keeping of the court chaplains was the most treasured relic of the Frankish Kingdom. St. Martin may well be called the *national saint* of Merovingian France; but churches erected in his honor were to be found all over the Christian world. — The Vita S. Martini written about 390/400 by *Sulpicius Severus* with three letters and Dialogi, ed. C. Halm, 1866; German by P. Bihlmeyer, BKV 20, 1914; W. Rüttenauer, 1941; French by P. Monceaux, S. Martin, Paris 1926. — *Gregory of Tours* (§ 78, 4) wrote four books De virtutibus S. Martini. — Monogr. on St. Martin: *A. Lecoy de la Marche*, Tours ²1890; *A. Regnier*, Paris ⁷1929; *E. Ch. Babut*, Paris 1912 (from RHLR 1910/2, hypercritical). Opposing Babut: H. Delehaye, AB 1920, 5/136; C. Jullian, Revue des Études anciennes 1922/3; Hist. de la Gaule t. VIII, Paris 1926, 255 ff.; agreeing with Babut: E. M. Bolch, RHLR 1921, 44/57. — L. de G. Martin, Paris 1948. — *E. K. Rand*, Bull. of J. Rylands Library Manchester 1927, 101/9. — F. L. Ganshof, AB 1949, 203/23. — *J. M. Besse*, Le tombeau de S. Martin de Tours, Paris 1922. — *P. de Montsabert*, Le monastère de Ligugé, Ligugé 1931. — *H. Delehaye*, AB 1937, 29/48 (miracles of St. M.) — *P. Grosjean*, ib. 300/48 (Scotch-Irish and British devotion to St. Martin). — Cfr. § 43, 7 (Lit.).

About the year 410, *St. Honoratus*, later Bishop of Arles founded a monastery on the island of *Lérins*[1] off the coast of Southern Gaul,

---

[1] H. MORIS, L'abbaye de Lérins, Paris 1909. A. C. COOPER-MARSDIN, History of the Islands of Lérins, Cambridge 1913. H. LECLERCQ, Lérins, DictAC VIII, 2596/2627.

which became a famous institution of higher learning and a training school for a long series of excellent bishops (§ 60, 2). Not long thereafter John Cassian († c. 435)[1], said to have been a Scythian born in the Dobrudja, the opponent of St. Augustine (§ 57, 2), founded two monasteries at Marseilles, one for men and one for women. He had received his religious training in a monastery at Bethlehem and had spent about ten years with the anchorites of Egypt. Thus he himself became a master of the spiritual life and the link between East and West. His ascetical studies and experiences are contained in two works: De institutis coenobiorum and Collationes patrum. He held that the chief task of the monk is to overcome the eight capital vices. Perfection consists in charity; but his teaching on charity and contemplation is not entirely free from subjectivism. In the first half of the sixth century *Caesar* of Arles († 542; § 78, 4) reorganized monasticism in Southern Gaul and composed two excellent rules: one for monks and one for nuns.[2] He founded a convent of nuns at Arles with his sister Caesaria as abbess. Sometime before 600 Archbishop Leander of Seville (§ 74, 4) also wrote a rule for nuns.

The *arrangement* and *organization of monasteries in the West* were essentially the same as in the East. Since no one rule enjoyed wide acceptance, monasteries differed greatly in certain practices. Cassian (De instit. coenob. II, 2) said that almost every monastery had its own regulations. He mitigated many of the severe mortifications of Eastern monasticism, while retaining the general plan of life. *Children* were frequently accepted to be trained for the monastic life, a practice then justified by the example of Samuel (1 Kings 1:24 ff.) and the very extensive powers conceded to a father of a family by Roman Law. The young pupils were called *Oblati* or *Donati* while those who entered in mature age were called *conversi*. St. Benedict followed the practice, but did not, as is often asserted, originate it. About the seventh century, the oblati

---

[1] J. Cassiani Opera in PL 49/50; ed. M. PETSCHENIG im CSEL, 2 vol. 1886—1888; Selection in German: Weisheit der Wüste v. A. KAMMER, 1948. A. HOCH, Lehre des Joh. Cassianus von Natur u. Gnade, 1895. O. ABEL, Studien zu Cassian, Diss. 1905. L. WRZOT, Divus Thomas 1918/24 (Cassian's psychology and teaching on sin). BR. ALBERS, StMBenO 1925, 32 ff.; 1928, 12 ff. 146 ff. (Cassian and Benedict). M. OLPHE-GALLIARD, RevAM 1935, 255 ff.; 1936, 28 ff. 181 ff.; 1937, 141 ff. (contemplative life according to Cassian); Art. Cassien, DictApir II, 214/76. Monogr. on Cassian by L. CRISTIANI, 2 vol. Paris 1946; O. CHADWICK, Cambridge 1950. S. MARSILI, Giov. Cassiano ed Evagrio Pontico, Rome 1936. A. KEMMER, Charisma maximum, Untersuchungen zu Cassians Vollkommenheitslehre, Löwen 1938. ED. SCHWARTZ, ZntW 1939, 1/11 (chronology). H. J. MARROU, OrChrPer 1947, 588/96 (place of birth).
[2] S. Caesarii Regula Sanctarum Virginum, ed. G. MORIN, 1933 (Floril. patrist. 34); id. in RevBén 1932, 5/20; C. LAMBOT, ib. 1929, 333/41. S. Leandro de Sev., De institutione virginum, ed. A. C. VEGA, Escorial, 1948.

were considered obliged to become monks. Pope Gregory the Great (Ep. I, 50) ordained for the monasteries of Campanis and adjacent islands that they admit no candidates under the age of 18, but the old practice continued. The Synod of Toledo in 633 (can. 49) declared: Monachum aut paterna devotio aut propria professio facit. And this decree became a legal axiom (Decret. Grat. c. 3, C. XX q. 1) the validity of which remained unquestioned throughout the Middle Ages. — *J. N. Seidl,* Die Gottverlobung von Kindern in Mönchs- und Nonnenklöstern, 1872. — *M. P. Deroux,* Les origines de l'oblature bénédictine, Ligugé 1927. — *J. Schröteler,* Das Elternrecht in der kath.-theol. Auseinandersetzung, 1936, 35/136. — *R. Riepenhoff,* Zur Frage des Ursprungs der Verbindlichkeit des Oblateninstituts (to 17th cent.), 1939. — *H. Leclercq,* Art. Oblat. DictAC XII, 1857/77.

7. The truly great figure of Western cenobitism is **St. Benedict** of Nursia[1], often called the "Patriarch" of Western monasticism.

---

[1] Vita S. Benedicti in S. Gregorii M. Dialogi, ed. U. MORICCA, Rome 1924. Vita et Regula S. Benedicti, edd. R. MITTERMÜLLER et E. SCHMIDT, 1880. Leben u. Regel des hl. Vaters Benediktus, German by C. KNIEL, [4]1929. Leben des hl. Benedikt, German in BKV 2. R. III, 1933; by F. FAESSLER, 1949. Critique and sources for the life of St. Benedict: H. SCHRÖRS, ZkTh 1921, 169/207; ST. HILPISCH, ib. 1925, 358/86; L. HANSER, StMBenO 1927, 300/7; W. V. D. STEINEN, HZ 143, 1931, 229/56. S. Benedicti Regula, ed. E. SCHMIDT, see above; C. BUTLER, [3]1935; B. LINDERBAUER, 1922 (with philological commentary) and 1928 (Floril. patrist. 17); ed. J. KUCKHOFF, 1931 (school edition with commentary); C. KÖSSLER, 1931 (Text, transl. and commentary); PH. SCHMITZ, Maredsous 1945 (with French transl.); A. LENTINI, Monte Cassino 1947 (with Italian. transl.). G. ARROYO, (with concordance), Silos 1947; H. KOENDERS, Concordantiae s. Regulac, Westmalle 1947. English transl. by F. A. Gasquet, London, 1908; German by E. SCHMIDT, [4]1914; P. BIHLMEYER in BKV 20, 1914, and sep. [4]1934; B. LINDERBAUER, 1928; E. PFIFFNER, 1947. C. SELMER, Middle-High-German Translationes of the Reg. s. B., Cambridge (Mass.) 1933. W. BETZ, BeitrGdSL 1941, 182/5 (Old High German). A. ALBAREDA, Bibliografia de la Regla Benedictina, Montserrat 1933. L. TRAUBE, Textgesch. der Regula S. Benedicti, Abh. München 21, 3, 1898; ib. 25, 2, 1910. H. PLENKERS, Untersuchungen z. Überlieferungsgesch. der ältesten lat. Mönchsregeln, 1906; StMBenO 1929, 183/95 (on the editions of BUTLER and LINDERBAUER). M. ROTHENHÄUSLER, ib. 1917, 1/17; 1918, 167/70 (sources of the Rule). G. MORIN, RevBén 1922, 119/34; 1931, 145/52. BR. ALBERS, see under Cassian. O. GRADENWITZ, Die Regula S. Benedicti nach den Grundsätzen der Pandektenkritik behandelt, 1929; ZKG 1931, 257/70; 1932, 228/37. D. DE BRUYNE, RevBén 1930, 316/42 (Benedict's first Rule); also G. MORIN, ib. 1931, 145/52. H. S. BRECHTER, StMBenO 1937, 157/226; RevBén 1938, 89/135 (Title, Text and Effect of the Rule). P. HOFMEITESR, StMBenO 1936, 185 ff. 342 ff. (influence of the Benedictine Rule on other monastic rules). J. CARD. SCHUSTER, Scuola catt. 1945, 3/16 (first appearance in France). PH. SCHMITZ, Bénédictine règle, Dict. de droit canon. II, 1935, 297/349. Literature on the relation of the Reg. Benedictini to ,,Reg. Magistri'' (PL 88, 943 ff.) see B. ALTANER, Patrologie, [2]1950, 434; also E. FRANCESCHINI, Aevum 1949, 52/72; F. VANDENBROUCKE, RechThM 1949, 186/226. P. BLANCHARD, RevBén 1950, 25/64. H. VANDERHOVEN, RHE 1950, 707/10. Monogr. on St. Benedict by I. HERWEGEN, [3]1926; S. DU FRESNEL, Maredsous 1926; J. CHAPMAN, London 1929; L. SALVATORELLI, Bari 1929, German by G. KÜHL-CLAASSEN, 1937; F. CABROL, Paris 1933, J. MCCANN, London 1937; CARD. SCHUSTER, Milan [2]1946; T. F. LINDSAY, London 1949. PH. SCHMITZ, S. Benoît, DictHE VIII, 225/41;

He was born about 480 at Nursia in southern Umbria, the son of a wealthy Roman nobleman. As a youth he devoted himself to the study of the liberal arts at Rome, but, as Gregory the Great says (Dial. II praef.): "scienter nescius et sapienter indoctus" he fled to escape the evil influence of dissolute fellow students. The next three years were spent in a cave of the Sabine mountains near *Subiaco* where he lived as a hermit. The monks of the nearby monastery of Vicovaro prevailed on him to become their abbot. Forced to leave by the intrigues of unruly monks, he went back to his cave until the number of his disciples became so great that he built twelve monasteries each with twelve monks under a superior, while he, as abbot of the complex, lived in a thirteenth monastery with a few chosen companions. About 529 he built a larger monastery on the site of an old temple of Jupiter on *Monte Cassino*, which became the cradle of the *Benedictine Order*[1]. Here Benedict died

---

id. and P. DE PUNIET im DictSpir I, 1371/409. G. GRÜTZMACHER, Die Bedeutung Benedikts und seiner Regel, 1892; ib. in Harnack-Ehrung, 1921, 212/18. BR. ALBERS, Der Geist des hl. Ben., [2/3]1921; StMBenO 1915, 535/42 (scienter nescius, sapienter indoctus). W. FINK, StMBenO 1924, 247/53; 1925, 183/91 (B. the hermit); ib. 1929, 105/12 (B. on Monte Cassino). C. J. VIDMAR, St. Benedikts Leben u. die kulturelle Tätigkeit seines Ordens, 1933. E. V. HIPPEL, Die Krieger Gottes. Die Regel Benedikts als Ausdruck frühmittelalt. Gemeinschaftsbildung, 1936. I. HERWEGEN, Väterspruch u. Mönchsregel, 1937; Sinn u. Geist der Ben.-Regel, 1944. O. CASEL, Benedikt als Pneumatiker, in „Heilige Überlieferung", Festgabe I. Herwegen, 1938, 196/23. H. GRÜNEWALD, Die pädag. Grundsätze der B.-Regel, 1939 (cfr. ThGl 1942, 149/55). R. SPILKER, see § 68. V. STEBLER, Die Regel des hl. B. als Norm beschaul. Lebens, Diss. Freiburg Schw. 1947. The year of his death: L. SALVATORELLI, Ricerche religiose 1928, 543/7 (546 or 547); H. FRANK u. H. EMONDS, StMBenO 1938, 77/103; 1939, 51/54 (547 or shortly thereafter). R. BAUERREISS, StMBenO 1947, 12/9 (day of his death). E. MUNDING, in Texte u. Arbeiten (Beuron) I, 15/18, 1930 (translation of the relics to Fleury). For the year of Jubilee 1947: Benedictus, der Vater des Abendlandes, ed. S. BRECHTER; Vir Dei Benedictus, ed. R. MOLITOR; Zeugnis des Geistes, by the Archabbey of Beuron; Studia benedictina, Rome; Mél. Bénédictines, S.-Wandrille; Horae Monasticae, Thielt 1948.

[1] J. MABILLON, Annales Ordinis S. Benedicti (to 1157), 6 fol. Paris 1703/39; Lucca [2]1739/45; J. MABILLON, Acta Sanctorum Ord. S. Benedicti, see § 2, 8. C. BUTLER, Benedictine Monachism. London [2]1924; German, 1929. ST. HILPISCH, Gesch. des Benediktin. Mönchtums, 1929; Das Benediktinertum im Wandel der Zeiten, 1950; Gesch. der Benediktinerinnen, 1951. PH. SCHMITZ, Hist. de l'ordre de S. Benoît, 6 vol. Maredsous 1942/9, German by L. RAEBER, 1947 ff. A. ZIMMERMANN, Kalendarium Benedictinum. Die Heiligen u. Seligen des Benediktinerordens u. seiner Zweige, 4 vols. 1933/9. PH. SCHMITZ, Bénédictin ordre, DictHE VII, 1060/234. M. MAEHLER, DictSpir I, 1410/38. L. H. COTTINEAU, Répertoire topo-bibliographique des abbayes et prieurés, Mâcon 1935 ff. Bull. d'histoire Bénédictine in RevBén. M. HEIMBUCHER, (s. § 72, 1) I[3], 154/314; II[3], 650/5. M. ROTHENHÄUSLER and I. HERWEGEN, Studien zur benediktin. Profess, 1912. U. BERLIÈRE, L'ordre monastique, Paris [3]1924; L'ascèse Bénédictine des origines à la fin du XIIe s., Maredsous 1927. PH. SCHMITZ, B. CAPELLE et autres, Mél. à l'occasion du

on March 21, most probably in the year 547. Pope Gregory the Great also relates the life of Benedict's sister *Scholastica,* who seems to have been the abbess of a convent of nuns. It was probably after 534 that Benedict wrote his rule for which he drew on extant monastic tradition (Pachomius, Basil, Cassian, Caesar) and on a source used for the Regula Magistri attributed to the school of Cassiodorus; but he drew most heavily on his own rich experience and sound judgement. It is possible that Pope Agapitus (535—536) encouraged Benedict in the undertaking. At any rate, the sancta regula is characterized by pedagogical wisdom, well-balanced asceticism, adaptability, and carefully formulated method. Its purpose was to guide the monk in the perfect following of Christ. A few decades after the death of the founder the monastery at Monte Cassino was destroyed (581 or perhaps 577) by the Lombards and the monks fled to Rome. It was restored in 717. Before the restoration the remains of St. Benedict were transferred to the Frankish monastery of Fleury on the Loire. In the meantime the Benedictine rule spread rapidly with the full approval of popes, especially of Pope *Gregory the Great,* who himself was a Benedictine and who dedicated the second book of his Dialogi (§ 64, 7) to St. Benedict. Kings were as enthusiastic as popes in recommending the rule and in encouraging the spread of the Order so that soon it supplanted the other rules such as that of Cassian and Columbanus (vide infra). It offered the young Germanic and Romanic nations a fixed norm of asceticism and common life and enabled them to accomplish great things for the cultural advancement of their people. Up to the twelfth century it was the only form of monasticism in the West and in the following centuries new religious orders were guided in their formation by the Benedictine rule. According to St. Benedict

---

XIVᵉ Centenaire de la fondation du Mont-Cassin, Louvain 1929. Casinensia, Misc. di studi Casinesi, 2 vol. Montecassino 1929. R. MOLITOR, Aus der Rechtsgesch. benediktin. Verbände I, 1928. T. P. MCLAUGHLIN, Le très ancien droit monastique de l'Occident de S. Benoît de Nursie à S. Benoît d'Aniane, Thèse Strasbourg 1935. A. LIEBLANG, StMBenO 1931, 413 ff.; 1932, 109 ff. (economic administration in the Ben. Rule). G. SCHNÜRER, Kirche u. Kultur im MA. I³, 1936, 110 ff. H. S. BRECHTER, StMBenO 1938, 109/50 (Monte Cassino destroyed in 577, not in 581 or 589). H. W. KLEWITZ, QFItalAB 28, 1938, 36/47 (monks of Monte Cassino in Rome). GRÜTZMACHER, Vidmar, v. Hippel, above. G. H. HÖRLE, Frühmittelalterl. Mönchs- u. Klerikerbildung in Italien, 1914. W. KALBERER, Die Anfänge der Schule des Benediktinerordens, Diss. 1920. A. AMELLI, Revista storica Benedettina 1920, 168/72 (Cassiodorus and B.). A. VAN DE VYVER, RevBén 1941, 59/88 (Vivarium and the Institutiones). P. COURCELLE, Les lettres grecques en Occident. De Macrobe à Cassiodor, Paris ²1948, 313/48; MélAH 1939, 259/307 (site of Vivarium). R. RIEPENHOFF, above.

the purpose of monastic life is to glorify God (ut in omnibus glori-
ficetur Deus, Reg. c. 57), the chief task of the schola dominici
servitii being to cultivate liturgical worship (opus Dei, officium
divinum § 67, 7). Besides this he stressed the obligation of manual
labor and spiritual reading (lectio divina) which demands some
education. Thus prayer and work (Ora et labora) are organically
united. The fundamental principles of monastic life and at the
same time the object of the vows taken at profession are perseverance in the monastery (stabilitas loci), the improvement of
conduct (conversatio [later] conversio morum) and obedience under
the fatherly direction of the abbot (Reg. c. 58). By the vow of
*stability* Benedict not only restrained irresolute characters from
returning to the world but especially corrected the grave abuse of
monks wandering about aimlessly outside the monastery (vide
supra no. 5). Except for the lectio divina, Benedict had no thought
of promoting study; for the Migration of Nations then at full tide
scarcely allowed serious application to books and the majority
of monks were simple laymen. But a change soon took place. The
noble Roman *Cassiodorus* after resigning his offices in the Ostrogoth
Kingdom retired to his estates in Calabria and founded the monastery of Vivarium about the year 540. He not only instructed his
monks in the *classics* and *theology*, but assigned to them the task
of collecting and copying old manuscripts. Many Benedictines
imitated this example so that as the Order of St. Benedict spread,
it became the great benefactor of mankind in the field of learning.
Just as the Benedictine monk taught the unskilled tribes of Europe
how to cultivate the soil and thus brought them material prosperity,
so he opened for them the literary treasures of the past and rescued
some of the most precious works of classical antiquity and the
patristic age from the ravages of the Migration of Nations. The
Benedictine became the great educator of the West and Benedictine
monasteries were the schools of higher learning, especially of theology in the early Middle Ages. Assigned to the work of the missions
by Gregory the Great, the Benedictiones rendered inestimable services to the Anglo-Saxons and other Germanic peoples.

8. Toward the end of the sixth and the beginning of the seventh
century, **St. Columbanus**[1], an Irish monk, revived monasticism as

---

[1] JONAS V. BOBBIO, Vita S. Columbani, ed. B. KRUSCH, 1905; Kolumbans
Regel, ed. O. SEEBASS, ZKG 1895, 366 ff.; 1897, 215 ff. — 1922, 132 ff.; cfr.
B. KRUSCH, NA 1925, 148/57. Monogr. on Columban by E. MARTIN, Paris
1905; J. LAUX, 1919; FR. BLANKE, 1940. J. LAPORTE, MSR 1949, 49/56.

well as Christian life in Gaul. In 590 he left the monastery of Bangor (§ 44, 2) with twelve companions and preached penance and asceticism with the ardor of an Old Testament prophet, first in Bretagne and then for twelve years in Burgundy where he founded the monasteries of Aunegray (Anagrates), *Luxeuil* (Luxovium) and Fontaines (Fontanae) and took up his residence as abbot at Luxeuil (§ 43, 8). A penitential book (poenitentiale) which exerted a powerful influence at the time and later, is in great part the work of Columbanus. After a disagreement with the Frankish episcopate over the date of Easter (§ 69, 6), he further came into conflict with the immoral King Theuderic and the king's ambitious grandmother Brunhilde and was expelled from Luxeuil. From 610 to 612 he devoted himself to work among the Alemanni around the shores of the lakes of Zurich and Constance, but when Austrasia came under Theuderic's rule in 612, Columbanus crossed the Alps into Upper Italy. In the valley of the Trebbia southwest of Piacenza he founded the monastery of *Bobbio* where he died in 615. Columbanus' *rule* demanded extraordinary practices of penance; corporal punishments were inflicted for even slight faults. Yet it was highly regarded in France and Upper Italy for some time and many youths of both countries embraced it. But from the end of the seventh century Columbanus' rule began to give way to the more adaptable rule of St. Benedict especially after several monasteries had endeavored unsuccessfully to combine the two rules.

## § 73.
### Influence of Christianity on Social and Moral Life[1].

1. During the days of the persecutions, the Church had little opportunity to influence public life. But once she was given full

M. MASSANI, Didaskaleion 1928, 81/112; 1929, 1/157. G. MORIN, RevBén 1926, 164/77 (Columban's commentary on the Psalms). L. GOUGAUD, Revue Mabillon 1935, 169/78 (devotion to Columban). A. MALNORY, Quid Luxovienses monachi ad regulam monasteriorum etc. contulerint, Paris 1894. H. LECLERCQ, DictAC IX, 2722/87 (Luxeuil). J. B. GAI, § 43, 7. J. P. FUHRMANN, J. RYAN etc., § 44, 2. L. UEDING (monastic foundations), see no. 6, above.
[1] W. LECKY, History of European morals from Augustus to Charlemagne, 2 vols., London and New York, 1810. Reprint, London 1911. G. GRUPP, Kulturgesch. der röm. Kaiserzeit, 2 vols. 1903/4. I²ᐟ³, 1921; Kulturgesch. des MA.s I³, 1921. G. KURTH, Les origines de la civilisation moderne, 2 vol. Paris ⁷1923. R. V. POEHLMANN, Gesch. der sozialen Frage u. des Sozialismus in der antiken Welt, 2 vols. ³1925. CH. BIGG, The Church's Task under the Roman Empire, Oxford 1905. E. TROELTSCH, Die Soziallehren der christl. Kirchen u. Gruppen, 1912 (Ges. Schriften I); Augustin, Die christl. Antike

liberty, a new and limitless field of activity was opened to her.
Her preaching and teaching, her sacraments and discipline had a
stimulating, purifying and stabilizing effect on the religiosity and
morals of the peoples of ancient culture and served to form and
educate the still half-civilized nations. The national virtues of
the Germans with their self-reliance and love of liberty and the
ancient Roman love of order were merged in the Christian philosophy of life to form a well-balanced unity. Supported by the State,
the Church worked unceasingly to remove abuses and introduce
reforms. Even the imperial authority was obliged to yield to the
moral demands of the Church. As a result of mass conversions,
often carried out under threat of civil penalties, with superficial
religious instruction, if any, there were very many merely *nominal
Christians*. As St. Jerome expresses it (Vita Malachi c. 1), the
Church had grown richer and more powerful but had grown weaker

u. das MA., 1915. O. SCHILLING, Naturrecht u. Staat nach der Lehre der
alten Kirche, 1914; Die christl. Soziallehren, 1926 (vs. Troeltsch). B. A. FUCHS,
Der Geist der bürgerlich-kapitalist. Gesellschaft, Grundlagen u. Voraus-
setzungen, 1914. A. DOPSCH, Wirtschaftl. u. soziale Grundlagen der europ.
Kulturentwicklung von Cäsar bis Karl d. Gr., 2 vols. ²1923/5. O. DITTRICH,
Gesch. der Ethik I—II, 1923/6. M. WEBER, Die sozialen Gründe des Unter-
gangs der antiken Kultur, in Ges. Aufsätze zur Sozial- und Wirtschaftsgesch.,
1924. G. SCHNÜRER, Kirche u. Kultur im MA., I³, 1936. E. SALIN, Civitas
Dei, 1926. J. STIGLMAYR, StZ 115, 1928, 81 ff. 170 ff. (city life according to
Joh. Chrys.). FR. HEILSBERG, MIÖG Erg.-Bd. 11, 1929, 31/63 (Christianity
and late antiquity). S. J. CASE, The Social Triumph of the Ancient Church,
London 1934. CHR. DAWSON, The Making of Europe, London 1948 (to c. 1000).
L. HUGHES, The Christian Church in the Epistles of S. Jerome, London 1923.
P. V. SOKOLOWSKI, Der hl. Augustin und die christliche Zivilisation, 1927. A.
SCHULTZE, Abh. Leipzig 38, 4, 1928 (Augustine and the Germanic law of inheri-
tance). M. M. GETTY, The Life of the North Africans as Revealed in the Sermons
S. Augustine, of Diss. Washington 1931. J. ZELLINGER, Aug. u. die Volksfröm-
migkeit, 1933. G. METZGER, § 12, 6. P. ANDRES, Der Missionsgedanke in den
Schriften des hl. Joh. Chrys., 1935. F. J. DÖLGER, AntChrist 1936, 44/75 (popular
piety in the life of St. Nonna, mother of Gregory of Naz.). BR. KRUSCH, Sb.
Berlin 1934 (superstition in Gregory of Tours). H. PIRENNE, RevBén 1935,
165/177 (education of the laity in Merovingian times). A. L. VEIT, Antik-
sakrales Brauchtum im meroving. Gallien, in „Volk u. Volkstum" I, 1936.
121/37. G. UHLHORN, Die christl. Liebestätigkeit, 3 vols. 1882/90. L. LALLE-
MAND, Hist. de la charité, 4 vol. Par. 1902/12. U. BENIGNI, Storia sociale
de la Chiesa I—V, Milano 1907/33. F. MARX, Zur Gesch. der Barmherzig-
keit im Abendland, 1917. W. LIESE, Gesch. der Caritas, 2 vols. 1922.
W. SCHÖNFELD, ZRGkan 1922, 1/54 (hospices in Italy and France). D. GORCE,
Les voyages, l'hospitalité et le port des lettres dans le monde chrétien des
IVe et Ve siècles, Paris 1925. KÖTTING, § 70, 1. FR. MEFFERT, Caritas
u. Krankenwesen bis zum Ausgang des MA.s, 1927. J. DECLAREUIL, Revue
hist. du droit français et étranger 1925, 26/53 (duties of the clergy in the
later Empire). S. MOCHI ONORY, Vescovi e città sec. IV—VII, Bologna 1933.
G. VISMARA, Episcopalis audientia, Milano 1937; also V. BUŠEK, ZKGkan
1939, 453/92. C. HOHENLOHE, Der Einfluß des Christentums auf das Corpus
iur. civ., 1936. M. ROBERTI, Cristianesimo e diritto Romano, Milan 1935.
Cfr. literature in § 5, 26, 41, 43, 58.

in virtue (potentia quidem et divitiis major, sed virtutibus minor). That the moral level among Christians had sunk disgracefully low at this time is a fact that can not be denied. Discipline was relaxed and Christian life became shallow. Many forms of superstition (magic, astrology, etc.) and pagan vice flourished openly or in secret. And due to the rapidity with which the development went forward; due to many hindrances especially during the troublous times of the *Migration of Nations*, the Church, in spite of her efforts, was not always able to eradicate them. Although Emperor Theodosius' acceptance of a public penance imposed by Ambrose (§ 76, 1) represented a triumph of the Church as a moral power, yet the full rigor of the Church's penitential discipline was applied only in exceptional cases (§ 68). *Salvianus*, a priest of Marseilles († c. 480), the Jeremias of his age, bewailed the corruption and vice among the inhabitants of cities (De gubernatione Dei) and endeavored to shame the Romans by extolling the moral lives of pagan and Arian Germans.

In spite of these shortcomings, the superiority of Christianity over decadent paganism in religious, moral and cultural relations was very evident. Personalities such as Athanasius and Chrysostom in the East, Ambrose and Augustine in the West, to mention but a few among many, by their loftiness of mind and nobility of soul exercised a tremendous power of attraction. In the West, it was the Catholic Church that saved civilization from the surging waves of the Migration of Nations and became the bond of unity for the peoples of the old Empire (§ 64, 3). The spirit of Christian charity and devoted self-sacrifice which had once so impressed the pagan world was by no means dead. Rather the needs of the times called forth new efforts in the service of *Christian charity*. History records innumerable examples of practical works of mercy. The Church was a social power in the declining culture of those days. The *bishops* were obliged to substitute for a corrupt and decrepit officialdom; to assume the duties of *public welfare* servants; to supply the needy and suffering with food, clothing and shelter; and in many instances, even to organize the defense of cities. The *administration of justice* came almost entirely into their hands, especially after Constantine the Great gave them the legal status of judges (§ 61, 3). The *relief of the poor*, the care of slaves, of prisoners (vide infra) and of travellers became their concern. A part of the Church's income was set aside to aid the poor (§ 60, 4). In the large cities such as Constantinople and Antioch the Church's work among the poor was to a great extent highly organized. There arose many institutions for the relief of every human need: *hospitals, poor houses, orphanages, foundling homes, shelters for travellers*, etc., which had been entirely unknown in pre-Christian times. The blessing conferred by these institutions is best seen from the unsuccessful attempt of Julian the Apostate to introduce them among the pagans (§ 41, 3). The most famous foundation was that of *St. Basil* at Caesarea in Cappadocia (369), called "Basilias." It became the model for similar foundations in Cappadocia and elsewhere, even in the West.

A beautiful example of Christian charity and asceticism was set by *St. Melania* the Younger and her husband Pinianus, both of the Roman nobility. About 404 they disposed of their vast fortune in favor of the poor, churches and monasteries and Melania († 439) became superior of the convent she founded at Jerusalem, while Pinianus († 431 or 432) lived as a monk on the Mount of Olives. — Vita S. Melaniae of Gerontius, ed. Card. *Rampolla* del Tindaro, Roma 1905; German by St. Krottenthaler, BKV 5, 1912. — Monogr. on Melania by G. Goyau, Paris 1908; E. da Persico, German by R. Banz, 1912. — H. Leclercq, DictAC XI, 209/30.

2. The assertion that the Fathers of the Church not only severely condemned *business* and *commerce*, but also rejected *private property* and favored communistic ideas is false or highly exaggerated. Some of them, such as *St. Ambrose* and *Gregory of Nyssa*, do, in fact, say that business is a degrading and unworthy way to make a living; and the Arian compiler of the Opus imperfectum in Matthaeum (§ 76, 10) says: Nullus christianus debet esse mercator. But on the one hand, they were influenced by the general disdain in which business pursuits were then held; and on the other hand, they were moral preachers warning against the commercial spirit and the dishonest gain usually connected with speculation. But they did not forbid lay persons to engage in honest business as Valentinian III forbade clerics (§ 60, 4). It was chiefly among the class of artisans, tradesmen and merchants that Christianity found its first and most loyal adherents. Many sayings attributed to the Fathers in which private property is condemned are ungenuine. Very frequently the Fathers do condemn the improper use of material goods and stress the law of Christian charity. Sometimes, too, without denying the right of private property, they recommend the *ideal of Christian communism* as practised in the first community at Jerusalem as a reaction to the greed and materialism so prevalent in the large cities. The frequently cited sentence of St. Jerome: Dives aut iniquus aut iniqui heres, is a pagan saying used by Jerome in satire. *St. Augustine* speaks with great clarity about the moral sanction of property, wealth and business and explains the idea and obligation of Christian civilization in regard to property. *Gregory the Great* and *Isidore* of Seville enlarged on Augustine's opinions and passed them on to the Middle Ages. — Cfr. *I. Seipel*, Die wirtschaftsethischen Lehren der Kirchenväter, 1907. — *O. Schilling*, Reichtum u. Eigentum in der altkirchl. Literatur, 1908; Die Staats- u. Soziallehre des hl. Augustinus, 1910; ThQ 1910, 214 ff. (on the Opus imperf.

in Mt); Naturrecht und Staat nach der Lehre der alten Kirche, 1914; Der christl. Eigentumsbegriff, ²1930, 43 ff.; ThQ 1933, 481/92 (Collectivism of the Fathers). — *F. X. Funk*, Handel und Gewerbe im christl. Altert., AU II, 60/77; Reichtum u. Handel im christl. Altert., ib. III, 150/9 (versus L. Brentano). — *J. A. Ryan*, Alleged Socialism of the Church Fathers, New York 1913. — *M. Huebner*, Untersuch. über das Naturrecht in der altchristl. Lit. bis Augustin., Diss. 1918 (also O. Schilling, HpBl 164, 1919 II, 640/7). — *Fr. Tillmann*, Eigentum und Besitz bei Basilius d. Gr., Festschrift J. Mausbach, 1931, 33/42. — *H. Larmann*, Christl. Wirtschaftsethik in der spätröm. Antike, 1935 (faulty). — St. Giet, Science religieuse 1944, 95/128 (Prohibition of interest in 4th cent.). — *G. Squitieri*, Il preteso communismo di S. Ambrogio, Sarno 1946.

3. The Church found **slavery** a deep-rooted and apparently indispensable institution in the social life of the world upon which she entered; but at first there was nothing she could do to alter the situation. She, therefore, recognized slavery and even retained slaves on some of the estates which had been inherited. Acting on the conviction that all men are equal in the sight of God (1 Cor. 12 : 13; Gal. 3 : 28) she endeavored from the beginning to change the relation between master and slave from a purely legal to a *moral* one and to mitigate the severity of Roman law by Christian charity. Among the members of the Church, class distinction simply did not exist. The slave was considered the brother of the master, enjoying the same means of grace; even ecclesiastical offices and dignities were open to the slave provided he obtained his freedom (§ 60, 5) — a necessary condition in the circumstances of the times. On the other hand, the master was subject to the same penalties as the slave in case he offended against the Christian code of morality. Under the influence of a Christianity which stressed the universal *law of labor* and ennobled even menial work, the number of slaves gradually decreased; for the *emancipation* of slaves was recommended as an act pleasing to God and many Christian slave owners needed no other motive. During the reign of the so-called "good" emperors in the second century, civil *legislation* had somewhat improved the lot of slaves. But what had begun from purely humanitarian reasons was now carried out enthusiastically from higher religious motives. *Constantine the Great* punished the willful killing of a slave the same as murder. He further decreed that the emancipation of a slave in Church or at any assembly of Christians have the same legal effect as a solemn manumission. Clerics could free their slaves by any testamentary act or even by an informal declaration. *Justinian* removed all legal restrictions to emancipation, granted the individual thus freed full rights of citizens and permitted a slave with the consent of the master to marry a free person. During the Migration of Nations, when laws and the old order of things were generally disregarded, many freed men were illegally forced back into slavery. But when the Christian spirit was once more able to assert itself, the slave again received the special protection of the Church. By the early Middle Ages, serfdom and bondage in varying degrees had taken the place of slavery. — *J. A. Möhler*, Ges. Schriften II, 1840, 54/140 (abolition of slavery). — H. Wallon, Hist. de l'esclavage dans l'antiquité, 3 vol. Paris ²1879. — *P. Allard*, Les esclaves chrétiens, Paris ⁵1913; Les origines du servage en France, Paris 1912; DictApol I, 1457/522. — *A. Stein-*

*mann,* Die Sklavenfrage in der alten Kirche, 1910; Sklavenlos und alte Kirche, ²/³1922. — *F. Schaub,* Studien z. Gesch. der Sklaverei im Frühmittelalter, 1913. — *P. Bernard,* Étude sur les esclaves et les serfs de l'Église en France du VIᵉ au XIIIᵉ s., Paris 1919. — *J. J. Koopmahs,* De servitute antiqua et religione christiana capita selecta I, Diss. Groningen 1920. — *J. Manquoy,* L'Église et l'esclavage antique, Paris 1927. — A. D'Amia, Schiavitù romana e servitù medievale, Milano 1931. — *E. J. Jonkers,* Mnemosyne 1934, 241/80 (Christianity and legislation regarding slavery). — *Westermann,* Art. Sklaverei, RE Pauly-Wissowa Suppl. VI, 1935, 894/1068. — *G. Damizia,* § 64, 7. — A. Gyürki Kis, Gedanken des hl. Augustin über die Sklaverei, Dissertation 1942.

Constantine the Great also mitigated the former cruel *system of punishments* by abolishing some of them altogether, especially branding on the forehead and condemnation to the death struggle in the circus. During the fourth century, *crucifixion* ceased to be resorted to as a form of execution. It is quite possible that it was also abolished by Constantine. The same emperor demanded that *prisoners* be given a more humane treatment. Later the pagan rhetorician Libanius pleaded the same cause. By a law of 409 bishops were commissioned to visit the prisons regularly in order to observe the treatment given prisoners and to investigate complaints of unjust incarceration. The Synod of Orleans in 549 (can. 20) decreed that the material needs of prisoners be supplied from the funds of the churches. The *right of asylum,* which developed during the fourth century and which was recognized by the emperors, had a very pronounced effect on the penal system and made precipitate and unjust punishments practically impossible. It is true that pagan temples had formerly enjoyed the right of asylum; but under Christianity the right became a prescriptive law and had its effect from the general reverence for the church and altar as res sacrae and from the intercession of the clergy. — *K. Krauss,* Im Kerker vor u. nach Christus, 1895. — *J. Gröll,* Die Elemente des kirchl. Freiungsrechtes, 1911. — *M. Siebold,* Das Asylrecht der röm. Kirche, bes. auf german. Boden, 1930. — *H. Niemax,* Antike Humanität im Kampf mit dem röm. Gefängniselend, Diss. 1933. — *E. Herman,* OrChrPer 1935, 204/38 (right of asylum in Byzantium). — *P. Timbal Duclaux de Martin,* Le droit d'asile, Paris 1939.

4. Much was done for the preservation of **human life.** *Suicide,* which had been theoretically justified by Stoic philosophy with the result that it had become quite common, was severely condemned by the Church. In the City of God (I, 22—27), *St. Augustine* convincingly proves it to be grievously sinful. The Synod of Braga in Spain in 563 (can. 16) excluded the suicide from commemoration in Mass and denied him Christian burial. From the very beginning, the Church opposed the pagan custom of *killing the child* in the womb or at birth as well as the practice of exposing infants (§ 26, 3). The Synod of Elvira about 306 (can. 63) punished abortion with perpetual excommunication and Ancyra in 314 (can. 21) punished it with public penance for ten years. These efforts of the Church received the support of the State. A father's absolute power over the child was restricted. *Constantine the Great* declared the killing of the child by the father to be infanticide and ordered it to be punished as such. He also endeavored to stop the *practice of exposing*

infants, first by conceding the rights of parents to the finder or the one who raised the child and later by decreeing severe penalties for those guilty. The vast majority of Christians abominated the inhuman *gladiatorial combats* (§ 26, 1); and Constantine (325) expressly forbade criminals to be used as victims. They were entirely abolished during the reign of Honorius (395—423). The story told by Theodoret (H.E. V, 27) about the monk *Telemachus* (or as the name is given in Martyrol. Hieron., *Almachius*) who came from the East to stop the gladiatorial spectacles at Rome (391? 404?) is probably historical except for some details (cfr. J. P. Kirsch, RQ 1912, 207/11; DictHE II, 630 ff.; H. Delehaye AB 1914/19, 421/9.

5. Pure concepts regarding **sex life** were not entirely unknown in the pagan world; but at the time that Christianity first appeared such concepts were an exception. In general, the greatest laxity prevailed. Only adultery was censured and that not always. The demoralizing effects of pagan mythology and literature, the nature of the public celebrations and theatrical performances are well known. Christianity, on the other hand, immediately made the demand for a higher morality. It *elevated woman* and recognized her as the autonomous equal of man and explained the *marriage bond* in the light of the supernatural. In the writings of some ascetics of Christian antiquity and the Middle Ages, views are sometimes expressed derogatory of woman and marriage; but these are the narrow views of individuals and not the official teaching of the Church. From the beginning the Church unconditionally demanded fidelity of the husband as well as of the wife; and in the penitential discipline sexual relations of unmarried persons were visited with the same penalties as adultery (§ 24 and 68). During the reigns of the first Christian emperors gross public vice was effectively checked. The Church went even further than the State in forbidding the marriage of relatives; but it was not an easy task, nor soon accomplished, to obtain general recognition and compliance with the *principle of the indissolubility* of marriage. In the East where the civil law granted divorce under certain circumstances, the Church often showed undue complaisance. In the West, great churchmen such as *Augustine* (De bono conjugali) and Pope *Innocent I* vigorously defended monogamy and the indissolubility of the marriage bond. However, lax views and practices prevailed for centuries among the Germanic peoples or rather among the princes and nobles of those nations. — *K. Böckenhoff*, Reformehe u. christl. Ehe, 1912. — *J. Peters*, Die Ehe nach der Lehre des hl. Augustinus, 1918. — *B. Alves Pereira*, La doctrine du mariage selon S. Augustin, Paris 1930. — *D. Lindner*, Der usus matrimonii, seine sittl. Bewertung in der kath. Moraltheologie alter und neuer Zeit, 1930. — *L. Anné*, EphThLov 1935, 513/50 (marriage in tradition and legislation of the Latin Church to 500). — *H. Pappe*, Methodische Strömungen in der eherechtsgeschichtl. Forschung, 1934. — *J. Dauvillier* et *C. de Clercq*, Le mariage en droit canonique oriental, Paris 1936. — *C. J. Jonkers*, Invloed van het Christendom op de romeinsche wetgeving betreffende het concubinaat en de echtscheiding, Wageningen 1938.

An incident which occurred at the *Synod of Mâcon* in 585 is often adduced as proof of the Church's contempt for women. According to Gregory of Tours (Hist. Franc. VIII, 20), a bishop at that synod asserted: mulierem hominem non posse vocitari. But after cumulative proof from the Scriptures had been advanced, he was satisfied. Most probably the discussion was no more than a purely linguistic or etymological question: whether the word homo was undergoing a change in usage in the Romance languages then in formative state and whether the word (homme, uomo) could also be used to designate a woman. — Cfr. G. Kurth, RQH 51, 1912, 556/60; Études franques I, Brux. 1919, 161/9. — Hefele-Leclercq III, 1, 211 ff. — H. Finke, Die Frau im MA., 1913, 82 f. — M. Pribilla, StZ 127, 1934, 418/21.

## CHAPTER V
## ECCLESIASTICAL LITERATURE AND LEARNING[1]

### § 74.
### The General Character of Ecclesiastical Literature.

1. With Christianity's victory over the pagan State early in the fourth century, there began the *Golden Age* of ecclesiastical literature and learning — the period of the great *Fathers of the Church*. The many theological controversies promoted a brisk literary activity. A group of men entered into the movement who were distinguished alike by rare mental gifts and by the best schooling which the age afforded. Since their main task was to protect the faith against shallow innovations, the ecclesiastical literature of this period is primarily *dogmatic-polemic*. Yet other branches of theology were be no means neglected. Steady and brilliant progress was made almost up to the time of the Council of Chalcedon (451). From then on a decline in creative production is noted, due chiefly to increasing variations in language. However, the difficulty was eventually overcome and notable works appeared from time to time.

---

[1] See the literature listed before § 36 and § 40 (for more extensive literature on the matter in this chapter cfr. BARDENHEWER I—V and ALTANER, Patrologie, ²1950). G. GRAF, § 72. A. EHRHARD, Überlieferung und Bestand der hagiograph. u. homilet. Literatur der griech. Kirche von den Anfängen bis z. Ende des 16. Jh., 1936 ff. H. KIHN, Die Bedeutung der antioch. Schule auf dem exeget. Gebiete, 1866. PH. HERGENRÖTHER, Die antioch. Schule u. ihre Bedeutung auf dem exeget. Gebiete, 1866. J. GUILLET, § 54. E. V. DOBSCHÜTZ, Vom vierfachen Schriftsinn. Harnack-Ehrung, 1921. 1/13. G. RAUSCHEN, Das griech.-röm. Schulwesen zur Zeit des ausgehenden Heidentums, 1901. J. STIGLMAYR, Kirchenväter u. Klassizismus, 1913. L. RIBOULET, L'église et l'éducation, Avignon 1946. P. COURCELLE, Les lettres grecques en Occident. De Macrobe à Cassiodor, Paris ²1948. G. BARDY, RevSR 1934, 525/49; 1935, 1/27; 1939, 5/58; Irénikon 1937, 313/38 (the Church and learning in the 4th cent.); La question des langues dans l'Église ancienne I, Paris 1948; L'Église et les derniers Romains, ib 1948. É. GILSON, and PH. BÖHNER, Gesch. der christl. Philosophie I, 1936. O. PERLER, Patrist. Philosophie, 1950. M. VILLER and K. RAHNER, Aszese u. Mystik in der Väterzeit, 1939.

2. The centers of intellectual life in the East were *Alexandria* and *Antioch*, and the names of these cities at the same time designate the most important *theological schools* and trends of the age. Eusebius of Caesarea, Athanasius, Basil, Gregory of Nazianzus, Gregory of Nyssa, Didymus and Cyril belonged to the Alexandrian School; while Diodorus, Theodore, John Chrysostom and Theodoret are prominent representatives of the School of Antioch. The two schools differed in their philosophy as well as in their theological views. The Alexandrians as a rule were Platonists while the Antiocheans leaned more on Aristotle. In *biblical exegesis* Alexandria preferred the *allegorical-mystical* interpretation which Origen had popularized; Antioch, on the other hand, aimed at a *grammatical-historical* explanation of Holy Writ. The priest and martyr Lucius (§ 32, 3; 39, 5) is usually considered the founder of the Exegetical School of Antioch. In the fourth century when Arianism occasioned a more thorough investigation of the Scriptures, the Antiochian School reached the height of its development and raised exegesis to the rank of a special science. The Alexandrians knew well enough how to use the literal sense in scientific discussion, but their proneness to speculative theology and allegory stood in the way of real progress in exegesis. The two schools also differed on *Christology*. The Antiochians took a calm, reasonable view of Christian doctrine and strove cautiously to *distinguish* between the divine and human in Christ. In fact, some of them went so far in this direction as to endanger the oneness of Person in the Savior (§ 54). The Alexandrians on the other hand stressed the *union* of the divine and human natures. Their dogmatic speculation was productive of much good, but as in the case of some of the Antiochians, some Alexandrians carried their views to extremes until they led to Monophysitism (§ 55).

3. However, learning was not confined to these two schools; it was distributed fairly evenly throughout the Church. Although in the beginning the Latin Church relied almost entirely on Greek theology, it was not long until the West was ably represented by such men as *Hilary, Ambrose,* and *Jerome.* Finally, in the person of *Augustine,* the West brought forth a theologian beyond compare. Noteworthy contributions to the ecclesiastical literature of the period were also made by *Syria* and *Armenia.*

## § 75.
## Greek Theology of the Fourth and Fifth Centuries[1].
## Syrians and Armenians.

1. In order of time, **Eusebius**[*2], "the father of Church History" is the first of the Greek Fathers of this period. He had been the pupil (possibly the slave) of the learned priest Pamphilus of Caesarea (§ 39, 6) and always called himself Eusebius Pamphili. He died in 339 as Bishop of Caesarea in Palestine after having lived through the transition from the period of persecutions to the period of peace. It has been said of him that he was the proto-type of the weak characters who became court-bishops (Altaner). Constantine the Great held Eusebius in high esteem, while Eusebius on his part seized every opportunity to sing the Emperor's praise. He wrote a eulogistic Vita Constantini which because of the authentic documents quoted is a most valuable source for Constantine's reign. However, Eusebius is best known for his *Chronicle* and his *Church History* (§ 4, 1), the latter alone of sufficient importance to make his name immortal. He may also be considered the originator of scientific *apologetics*. Besides refuting the works of the Neoplatonists Porphyrius and Hierocles (§ 17, 1), Eusebius wrote two works, or rather one great work in two parts: Praeparatio evangelica and Demonstratio evangelica. In the former he shows that the revelation made to the Jews gave them a religion eminently superior to paganism; and in the Demonstratio he proves that Christianity is superior to Judaism and is the perfection of revealed religion. Like

---

[1] O. BARDENHEWER, GeschAL III—IV. O. STÄHLIN and A. PUECH III, § 36. K. STAAB, Pauluskommentare aus der griech. Kirche, 1933 (Fragments of Catenae from Didymus to Photius). FR. DIEKAMP, Analecta Patristica (zur griech. Patristik vom 4.—10. Jh.), Rome 1938 (OrChrAn 117).

[2] PG 19—24. Editions of chronicles and Church Histories, § 4, 1. Praeparatio evang., ed. E. H. GIFFORD, 4 vol. Oxford 1903. Demonstratio evang., ed. I. A. HEIKEL, 1913. C. MARCELLUM and De ecclesiastica theologia, ed. E. KLOSTERMANN, 1906. Selections in German in BKV 9 (life of Constantine, Martyr of Palestine), 1913; 2 vol. series 1 (KG.), 1932. R. LAQUEUR, Eusebius als Historiker seiner Zeit, 1929. J. STEVENSON, Studies in Eusebius, Cambridge 1929. F. J. FOAKES-JACKSON, Eusebius Pamphili, Cambridge 1933. ED. SCHWARTZ, Eusebius, RE Pauly-Wissowa VI, 1370/439. H. DOERGENS, Eusebius v. C. als Darsteller der phöniz. Religion, 1915; als Darsteller der griech. Religion, 1922. TH. ZAHN, NkZ 1918, 58/82 (Eus. born a slave). M. WEIS, Die Stellung des Eus. v. Cäs. im arian. Streit, Diss. 1920. A. MÖHLE, ZntW 1934, 87/9 (E's commentary on Isaias), cfr. R. DEVREESSE, Rev. Bibl. 1933, 540/55. P. HENRY, Recherches sur la Préparation évang. d'Eusèbe etc., Paris 1935. H. GRÉGOIRE, Byzantion 1938, 561/83 (Vita Constantini). J. DANIELE and H. EGER, § 41, 1. H. G. OPITZ, D. S. BALANOS and H. BERKHOF on Eus. as a theologian, § 47.

his historical works, which are also apologetic in character, the Praeparatio and Demonstratio give evidence of immense diligence, wide reading and a fair amount of learning. Eusebius was less fortunate in the field of theology proper. In the early dogmatic controversies he endeavored to steer a middle course. Like Pamphilus, he was an enthusiastic admirer of Origen and in the doctrine of the Trinity, held that the Son was subordinate to the Father. Although he eventually accepted the Nicene Creed, he was friendly toward the Arians and hostile toward those supporting Nicaea (§ 47, 3. 4), especially Athanasius and Marcellus of Ancyra. Two of his works, Contra Marcellum and De ecclesiastica theologia were open attacks on Marcellus.

**Athanasius**[*1], a younger contemporary of Eusebius, was one of the most important figures of the ancient Church and, unlike the Bishop of Caesarea, was the chief defender of Nicaea. His entire adult life was taken up with the struggle against the Arian heresy. He entered the conflict publicly while still a deacon at the Council of Nicaea in 325 (§ 47, 3) and when elevated to the See of *Alexandria* in 328, the consciousness of his graver responsibility lent him an increased zeal to continue the struggle; and neither sufferings nor vexations — not even five banishments from his see — could divert him from the defense of the orthodox faith (§ 48 and 49, 1). Very appropriately Gregory of Nazianzus called him the "pillar of the Church." Athanasius' writings are a reflection of his life. Most

---

[1] PG 25—28. The new critical Berlin edition of Athanasius' works (1934 ff.) § 47; also H. G. OPITZ, Untersuchungen zur Überlieferung der Schriften des Athanasius, 1935; ZntW 1934, 18/31. GUIDO MÜLLER, Lexicon Athanasianum, 1944 ff. S. Athanasii opera dogmatica selecta, ed. J. C. THILO, 1853. Selections in German in BKV 13 and 31, 1913/7. ATHANASIUS, Die Menschwerdung Gottes, selected and transl. by L. WINTERSWYL, 1937. Monogr. on Athanasius by J. A. MÖHLER, [2]1844; G. BARDY, Paris [3]1925; ib. in DictHE IV, 1313/40. X. M. LEBACHELET, DictThC I, 2143/78. BR. BECK, Die griech. Lebensbeschreibungen des Athanasius, Diss. 1912. F. LAUCHERT, Die Lehre des hl. Athanasius, 1895; Leben des hl. A., 1911. ED. SCHWARTZ, Zur Gesch. des A., § 47 (important). F. L. CROSS, The Study of St. A., Oxford 1945. E. WEIGL, Untersuch. zur Christologie des hl. A., 1914. A. STEGMANN, Die pseudoathanas. IV. Rede gegen die Arianer ein Apollinarisgut, 1917 (with critical text); ThQ 1914, 423/50 u. 1916, 227/31 (date of the orations I—III). ED. SCHWARTZ, Sb. München, 1924, 6 (Sermo maior de fide, not genuine); also J. LEBON, Muséon 1925, 243/60; R. P. CASEY, JThSt 1934, 394 f. ED. SCHWARTZ, ZntW 1935, 129/37 and M. PIEPER, ib. 1938, 73/6 (Paschal letter). R. P. CASEY, Sb. Berlin 1935, 33 and L. TH. LEFORT, AB 1949, 142/52 (De virginitate). J. LEBON, RHE 1935, 713/61 (letter to Epictetus). K. PRÜMM, ZkTh 1939, 350/9 (Mysterion in A.). L. BOUYER, L'incarnation et l'Église-Corps du Christ dans la théol. de S. A., Paris 1943. M. RICHARD, MSR 1947, 5/54 (psychology of Christ in A.). A. GÜNTHÖR, § 75, 4. Cfr. also § 47 and 48 (HAURET, GAUDEL, SEILER, HAGEL etc.).

of them are devoted to a clear exposition of the doctrines of the *Trinity* and the *Logos*, written with dialectic skill and precision but with little regard to style. His chief dogmatic work consists of three separate speeches against the Arians (a fourth speech ascribed to him is not genuine). Two works written while he was still young, the Oratio contra gentes and the Oratio de incarnatione Verbi actually constitute but one apologetic work. Other writings of Athanasius have been mentioned elsewhere: those against the Arians in § 48; the Life of St. Anthony in § 72, 1. 6 and the Creed falsely ascribed to him in § 49, 3. Some ascetical works on virginity, etc., were discovered recently. Like his predecessors, Athanasius wrote an annual Easter letter (§ 25, 3; 39, 3); at least 13 of these from 329 to 348 have been preserved in Syrian translations.

2. Like Athanasius, the *three great Cappadocians*[1] belonged to the Neo-Alexandrian School; and like him, they assumed the task of combatting the Arians and the Pneumatomachi (§ 48, 6; 49, 2). For the rest, their lives were cast in circumstances far different from his. **Basil the Great**[2], Archbishop of Caesarea in Cappadocia († 379) is renowned as an *administrator*, as the *organizer* of Eastern monasticism and as the founder of the greatest charitable institution in the early Church (§ 73, 1). He is equally renowned as a writer of

---

[1] F. BÖHRINGER, KG. in Bg.n VII—VIII, [2]1876. K. HOLL, Amphilochius 1904, 122 ff. (on the history of dogma). J. MAIER, Die Eucharistielehre der drei großen Kappadozier, Diss. 1915.

[2] PG 29—32. S. Basil Lettres, ed. R. J. DEFERRARI and MC GUIRE, 4 vol. London 1926/34 (Greek and English). S. Basile, Aux jeunes gens, éd. et trad. p. F. BOULENGER, Paris 1935; Homélies sur la richesse, éd. et trad. p. Y. COURTONNE, Paris 1935; Traité du Saint-Esprit, éd. et trad. p. B. PRUCHE, Paris 1947. San Basilio, Commento al Profeta Isaia, ed. with Italian transl. by P. TREVISAN, 2 vol. Turin 1939. D. AMAND, RevBén 1940/6 (critique of the Greek editions). Selected letters and sermons in BKV 46 and 47, 1925. Monogr. on Basil by: P. ALLARD, Paris [4]1903; J. RIVIÈRE, Paris 1925; R. JANIN, Paris 1929; M. M. FOX, Diss. Washington 1939. G. BARDY, DictHE VI, 1111/26; DictSpir I, 1273/83. Deutscher Gesamtkatalog, Sonderheft Basilius, 1938. J. SCHÄFER, § 48, 6. F. NAGER, Die Trinitätslehre des hl. Basilius, 1912. J. WITTIG, Des hl. Basilius geistl. Übungen 374/5, 1922; also P. HUMBERT-CLAUDE, RevSR 1930, 47/68. K. GRONAU, Das Theodizeeproblem in altchristl. Auffassung, 1922. L. V. JACKS, S. Basil and Greek Literature, Diss. Washington 1922. R. MELCHER, see below under Evagrius (no. 6). J. BESSIÈRES, La tradition manuscrite de la correspondance de S. Basile, Oxford 1923 (from JThSt 21/23). W. K. L. CLARKE, The Ascetic Works of S. Basil, London 1925. ST. GIET, RevSR 1949, 333/42 (rigorism of St. Bas.). A. CL. WAY, The Language and Style of the Letters of S. B., Diss. Washington 1927; American Journal of Philology 1931, 57/65 (correspondence of B. and Apollinaris). O. RING, Drei Homilien aus der Frühzeit Basilius' d. Gr., 1930; ZKG 1932, 365/83. Y. COURTONNE, S. Basile et l'Hellénisme, Thèse Paris 1934. G. F. REILLY, Imperium and Sacerdotium according to St. Basil the Gr., Washinghton 1945. Cfr. lit. § 72, 3 (KRANICH, MORISON etc.).

exegetical, ascetical and homiletic works. The following are deserving of special mention: Contra Eunomium (§ 48, 4) and De Spiritu Sancto, both dogmatic; nine sermons on the Hexaëmeron and many others of a dogmatic and exegetical nature; a treatise addressed to young men in which the author outlines a program of Christian Humanism; three hundred and sixty-five letters which reveal the author's perfect style and fine qualities of mind; the two monastic rules (§ 72, 3) and numerous treatises on liturgy (§ 67, 2). As a young man Basil joined his friend and fellow student **Gregory of Nazianzus**[1] († c. 390) in solitude on the banks of the Iris. Together they compiled the Philocalia, a collection of selected readings from the works of Origen. Later Basil consecrated Gregory bishop of the little town of Sasima, which see Gregory apparently never occupied. However, he became bishop of the orthodox congregation at Constantinople for a short time (379—381) where his theological discourses earned for him the titles of "the Christian Demosthenes" and *"the Theologian"*. Five of these sermons (27—31) are brilliant proofs of the divinity of the Son and Holy Ghost. His letters, written in polished classical style, were evidently intended for publication. Three of them (101, 102 and 202) addressed to the priest Cledonius are of importance for theology as constituting a forceful refutation of Apollinarianism. Gregory was also a poet of note. Most of his poems were written in his last years after he had retired to Arianzus, the place of his birth. The third of this illustrious group is Basil's talented younger brother, **Gregory of Nyssa** († c. 395)[2].

---

[1] PG 35—38. Orationes theologicae ed. A. J. MASON, Cambridge 1899. Q. CATAUDELLA, S. Gregorio Naz., Orazioni scelte con trad., Torino 1935. Gregors Reden deutsch I, BKV 59, 1928. Monogr. on Gregory of Naz.: C. ULLMANN, ²1867; A. BENOÎT, 2 vol. Paris ²1884; E. FLEURY, Paris 1930; P. GALAY, Paris 1943. F. J. DÖLGER, AntChrist 1936, 44/75 (Gregory's mother Nonna). A. DONDERS, Gregor v. Naz. als Homilet, Diss. 1909. M. GUIGNET, S. Grégoire de Naz. orateur et épistolier, Paris 1911. H. PINAULT, Le Platonisme de S. Grég. de Naz., Paris 1925. M. PELLEGRINO, La poesia di S. Gregorio Nazianzeno, Milano 1932. P. GALLAY, Langue et style de S. Grégoire de Naz. dans sa correspondance, Paris 1933. L. STEPHAN, Die Soteriologie des hl. Gregor v. Naz., Diss. 1938.

[2] PG 44—46. Berliner krit. Ausgabe: Contra Eunomium, ed. V. JAEGER, 2 vol. 1921/2; Epistulae, ed. G. PASQUALI, 1925. Oratio catech., ed. J. H. STRAWLEY, Cambridge 1903; ed. L. MÉRIDIER, Paris 1908 (mit franz. Übers.). Auswahl deutsch in BKV 56, 1927. Gregor v. Nyssa, Der versiegelte Quell, Auslegung des Hohen Liedes, in Kürzung übertragen von U. V. BALTHASAR, 1939; La vie de Moyse, trad. p. J. Daniélou, Paris 1942; La création de l'homme, trad. p. J. LAPLACE, Paris 1944. TH. GOGGIN, The Times of Gregory of Nyssa..., Washington 1947. F. DIEKAMP, Die Gotteslehre Gr. v. Nyssa I, 1896. J. B. AUFHAUSER, Die Heilslehre Gr. v. Nyssa, 1910. JOH. LENZ, Jesus Chr. nach der Lehre des hl. Gr. v. Nyssa, 1925. H. F. CHER-

His writings consist of theological, scriptural and ascetical treatises, together with sermons and letters. The "Great Catechism" contains 40 chapters and is a veritable "Summa Theologica". A dialogue De anima et resurrectione is a touching conversation with his dying sister Macrina regarding the soul, immortality and resurrection. The soul's union with God was a constant subject of Gregory's meditation. He is sometimes given the title of "the Mystic" and has always been considered one of the fathers of Christian mysticism. He found in the philosophy of his day the material with which to refute error and was particularly fortunate in finding expressions to describe the work of the Logos in perfecting in the soul the work begun in baptism. However, as an ardent admirer of Origen, he followed the latter in some of his peculiar notions, especially in regard to the apocatastasis (§ 39, 2) and in the denial of the eternity of hell.

3. **John** surnamed **Chrysostom**[1] ("golden-mouthed," a name applied to him since the sixth century) was born and educated

NISS, The Platonism of Gregory of Nyssa, Berkeley (Calif.) 1930. J. BAYER, Gregors v. Nyssa Gottesbegriff. Diss. 1935. E. V. IVÁNKA, Scholastik 1936, 163/95 (epistemology and theology). G. ISAYE, RechSR 1937, 422/39 (Gr. of Nyssa not a Tritheist). U. V. BALTHASAR, ib. 1939, 513/49; Présence et pensée, Paris 1942. M. GOMES DE CASTRO, Die Trinitätslehre des hl. Gr. v. Nyssa, 1938. L. GONZÁLES, § 48. J. B. SCHOEMANN, Scholastik 1943, 31 ff. 175 ff. (Anthropology). J. DANIÉLOU, Platonisme et théologie mystique (in Gr. of Nyssa), Paris 1944. J. T. MUCHLE, The Doctrine of St. Gregory of Nyssa on Man as the Image of God, Toronto 1945. A. LIESKE, Scholastik 1939, 485 ff.; ZkTh 1948, 1 ff. 129 ff. 315 ff.

[1] PG 47—64. De sacerdotio, ed. C. SELTMANN, 1887; ed. J. A. NAIRN, Cambridge 1906. De inani gloria et de educandis liberis, ed. FR. SCHULTE, Diss. 1914, German transl. by S. HAIDACHER, 1907. Omelie sulla lettera di S. Paolo ai Colossesi, ed. G. PIAZZINO, Turin 1939; Le omelie su S. Giovanni Evangelista I, Text and Italian transl. by C. TIRONE, Turin 1944. Lettres à Olympias, éd. et trad. p. A. M. MALINGREY, Paris 1947. K. J. HEFELE, Chrys.-Postille, ³1857. Selected works in German transl. by CH. BAUR et al., 8 vols. BKV 23, 25/27, 39, 42, 45; 2 R. 15, 1915/36. Monogr. on John Chrysost. by A. NEANDER, 2 vols. ⁴1858; A. PUECH, Paris ⁵1905; A. MOULARD, Paris 1923 and 1949; PH. E. LEGRAND, Paris 1924; CHR. BAUR, 2 vols. 1929/30 (standard); S. Jean Chrys. et ses oeuvres dans l'histoire littéraire, Louvain 1907 (bibliography). G. BARDY, DictThC VIII, 660/90. H. LIETZMANN, RE Pauly-Wissowa IX, 1811/28. A. NÄGLE, Die Eucharistielehre des hl. Joh. Chrys., 1900. A. NÄGLE, Byz. Z. 1904, 73/113 (John Chrys. and his relation to Hellenism); ThQ 1935, 117/42 (Homilien zu I/II Tim.). Χρυσοστομικά, Studi e ricerche, 3 fasc. Roma 1908. J. H. JUZEK, Die Christologie des Joh. Chrys., Diss. 1912. M. V. BONSDORFF, Zur Predigttätigkeit des Joh. Chrys., Helsingfors 1922. J. SEIDLMAYR, Die Pädagogik des Joh. Chrys., 1926. L. MEYER, S. Jean Chrys., maître de perfection chrét., Paris 1934. P. ANDRES, Der Missionsgedanke in den Schriften des hl. Joh. Chrys., 1935. E. R. SMOTHERS, RechSR 1937, 513/48 (Homilies on the Acts of the Apostles). E. HOFFMANN-ALEITH, ZntW 1939, 181/8 (Chrys. understanding of St. Paul). On De sacerdotio: A. NÄGLE, HJG 1916, 1/48; opposite opinion: J. STIGLMAYR, ZkTh 1917, 413/49. Cfr. also § 51, 3.

at Antioch. His pious mother Anthusa directed his early training and his polished classical education was received from the famous rhetorician Libanius (§ 41, 5). At the School of Antioch where John was the most brilliant pupil and of which he became the greatest Doctor, he associated with Basil, Theodore, the future bishop of Mopsuestia, Diodorus of Tarsus and Carterius. For four years he led a cenobitic life in the mountains and spent two years as a hermit. Returning home in enfeebled health, he was ordained deacon in 381 and priest in 386. His fame as a preacher spread far beyond Antioch and in 397 he was chosen to succeed Nectarius as Bishop of *Constantinople*. After only six years of a brilliant apostolate in the capital, the intrigues of Theophilus of Alexandria and the Empress Eudoxia forced him into exile (§ 51, 3). His friend and admirer the monk, Palladius (see no. 7 below), wrote his biography which is still a valuable source for John's life at Constantinople. John has always been considered the greatest *preacher* of the Greek Church as well as one of its most eminent *exegetes*. He followed the method of the Antiochian School in expounding the Scriptures, but he carefully avoided the Christological errors into which some members of the school fell. Among his many works — and with the single exception of Origen he was the most prolific writer of the East — his sermons and homilies occupy the first place. The homilies were methodical instructions on entire or almost entire books of the Bible: Genesis, Psalms, Isaias, Matthew, John and the Epistles of St. Paul. Some of the sermons preached on special occasions are of interest, especially the discourses on statues (21 sermons preached at the time the statues of Theodosius and the imperial family were destroyed at Antioch) and two delivered on the occasion of the dimissal of the minister Eutropius. His letters, about 240 in all, were written in exile and are of an intimate nature. De sacerdotio in dialogue form is considered the finest of all his writings. Several treatises deal with monastic life, one is on virginity and one on the education of children (cfr. § 67, 2 for the liturgy attributed to St. Chrysostom; and § 76, 10 for the spurious Opus imperfectum in Matthaeum).

4. The other Greek Fathers of the fourth century are not the intellectual equals of the three mentioned above, although some of them made valuable contributions to the ecclesiastical literature of the period. Bishop **Cyril of Jerusalem**[1] († 386) left the famous

---

[1] PG 33.  Pocket edition by W. K. REISCHL and J. RUPP, 2 vols. 1848/60;

Catechesis (§ 66, 2) or twenty-four lectures for catechumens and neophytes on the Creed, Baptism, Confirmation and the Blessed Sacrament. His teaching on the Logos was strictly orthodox although he disliked the word ὁμοούσιος. He was deposed and banished from his see three times during the Arian controversy. **Didymus the Blind**[1] († 398), although a layman and blind since the age of four, was the last master of the School of Alexandria before its removal to Side, and one of the most learned theologians of his day. Only fragments of his immense exegetical work have been preserved. Of his equally voluminous theological work, only three treatises are extant: On the Holy Ghost (in a not very precise Latin translation by Jerome), On the Trinity and Against the Manicheans. It may be that two works, De dogmatibus and Contra Arianos, found in an appendix to St. Basil's three books Against Eunomius are the work of Didymus. In his doctrine of the Trinity, Didymus always adhered closely to Nicaea, but he was never able to free himself entirely from the influence of Origen's teaching on the pre-existence of souls and the apocatastasis. Hence, the fifth Council at Constantinople in 553 anathematized his Origenistic errors. **St. Epiphanius**[*2] was born near Eleutheropolis in Palestine about 315. He founded and for thirty years governed a monastery

---

die mystag. Katech. im Florileg. patrist. 7, 2, ²1935. Sämtl. Katechesen deutsch in BKV 41, 1922. Reden der Einweihung (mystagog. Katechesen), transl. by L. A. WINTERSWYL, 1939. J. MADER, Der hl. Cyrillus, B. v. Jerusalem, 1891. B. NIEDERBERGER, Die Logoslehre des hl. Cyrill v. Jerus., 1923; cfr. J. LEBON, RHE 1924, 181 ff. 357 ff. W. J. SWAANS, Muséon 1942, 1/43 (the five mystogogical catecheses a work of Bishop John of Jerusalem, † 417).

[1] PG 39. F. ZOEPFL, Didymi Alex. in epistolas canonicas brevis enarratio, 1914. Fragments in K. STAAB, Pauluskommentare (see above), 1/45. Monogr. by J. LEIPOLDT, TU 29, 3, 1905,, G. BARDY, Paris 1910; W. J. GAUCHE, Diss. Washington 1934. FUNK, AU II, 291/329; III, 311/23 (De dogmatibus); cfr. J. LEBON, Muséon 1937, 61/83. E. STOLZ, Didymus, Ambrosius, Hieronymus, ThQ 1905, 371/401. A. GÜNTHÖR, Die 7 ps.-athanasian. Dialoge, ein Werk des Did. d. Bl., Rome 1941 (but see H. RAHNER, ZkTh 1941, 111 f.). W. DIETSCHE, Did. v. Al. als Verfasser der Schrift über die Seraphimsvision, 1941 (opp. view B. ALTANER, ThRev 1943, 147/51). On the recently discovered texts in Toura see RHE 1946, 618; ThQ 1947, 332.

[2] PG 41—43. ED. W. DINDORF, 5 vol. 1859/62. Best critical edition of principal works by K. HOLL, 3 vols. 1915/33; ib., Die handschriftl. Überlieferung des Epiph., TU 36, 2, 1910; Ges. Aufsätze zur KG. II, 1928, 204/24 (letter of Epiph. on Passionweek). R. P. BLAKE and H. DE VIS, Epiphanius de gemmis, London 1934 (Georgic with English transl.); also I. RUCKER, ThRev 1935, 329/35. Epiphanius, Treatise on Weights and Measures, Syriac version, ed. J. E. DEAN, Chicago 1935. Epiphanius, Interpretatio evangeliorum, ed. A. ERIKSON, Lund 1939; ib., Sprachliche Bemerkungen zu Epiphanius' Interpretatio evangeliorum, Diss. Lund 1939. Selections from Epiph. German in BKV 38, 1919. Cfr. literature in § 51, 2. 3 and 70, 4.

near his birthplace and in 367 was elected bishop of Constantia (Salamis), the metropolitan see of Cyprus. He was pious and learned but impetuous and excessively zealous. This latter characteristic was evident in his opposition to the Hellenistic culture, to the veneration of images and especially to Origenism. (§ 51; 70, 4). He is best known for the work Πανάριον (Medicine chest, usually cited under the title Haereses) a refutation of all (80) heresies of antiquity. In spite of unsound critique, the work is of great value because of the wealth of quotations from works now lost. For heresies which prevailed before his time, he relies on the accounts of Irenaeus and Hippolytus. Besides a Biblical Archeology, Epiphanius left a work called Ancoratus (well-anchored) which is an explanation of the doctrine of the Trinity with two Creeds (§ 49, 2 on the first of these Creeds). A Georgian translation and a fragment of a Latin translation are extant of his allegorical work De gemmis, on the precious stones which adorned the breastplate of the Jewish high-priests.

Bishop **Severian of Gabala** near Laodicea in Syria († after 408) was a contemporary, at one time a friend, and later a bitter opponent, of John Chrysostom. He was known as an exegete and preacher. His homilies on the hexaëmeron, some of which were delivered at Constantinople, and fourteen against the Arians have been preserved in the original Greek, others in translations into various tongues of the East. The Greek sermons are often falsely attributed to Chrysostom. — *J. Zellinger*, Die Genesishomilien des B. Severian v. Gabala, 1916; Studien zu Severian v. G., 1926. — *K. Staab*, Pauluskommentare, 213/351. — *Ch. Martin*, Muséon 1935, 311/22 (unedited Homily on Mt 26, 36).

**Macarius** the Great, also called the Elder and the Egyptian († c. 390), spent 60 years as a hermit in the Desert of Scete (§ 72, 3). Since the sixteenth century he has been considered the author of fifty "spiritual homilies" for monks and several letters which have given him the reputation of being one of the most ancient of Christian *mystics*. However, recent studies (Flemming, Stiglmayr) show the homilies to be a collection from various sources and one scholar (Vilecourt) considers them the works of the fanatical Messalians (§ 50, 7). Hence, Macarius' authorship can no longer be maintained. It seems that the homilies, at least in part, are the work of the Messalian leader Symeon of Mesopotamia. — PG 34. — An edition by *E. Klostermann* in preparation. — German transl. in BKV 10, 1913. — *G. L. Marriott*, Macarii Anecdota, Cambridge Mass. 1918; JThSt 1921, 259/62; HarvThR 1926, 191/8. — *J. Stoffels*, Die myst. Theologie Makarius des Äg., 1908; ThQ 1910, 88 ff. 243 ff. — *C. Flemming*, De Macarii Aeg. scriptis quaestiones, Diss. 1911. — *J. Stiglmayr*, Sachliches und Sprachl. bei Mak. v. Ägypten, Progr. Feldkirch 1912; ZkTh 1925, 244/60. — *L. Villecourt*, Comptes rendus de l'Acad. d. Inscript., Paris 1920, 250/7; RevOC 22, 1920/21, 29/56; Muséon 1926, 203 ff.

243 ff. — *A. Wilmart*, RevAM 1920, 58 ff. 361 ff.; 1922, 411/9. — W. Stroth-mann, Die arab. Makariustradition, 1934. — *Hausherr, Dörries, Klostermann* et al., see § 50, 7.

**Macarius** (Bishop?) of *Magnesia* in Lydia wrote Apocriticus (about 400), an apology in the form of a dialogue with a pagan polemicist. It is probably a refutation of extracts from the anti-Christian writings of Porphyrius (rather than Hierocles, § 17, 1). — Macarii Magnetis quae supersunt, ed. *C. Blondel*, Paris 1876. — *L. Duchesne*, De Macario Magnete, Paris 1877. — *L. Schalk-hausser*, TU 31, 3, 1907. — *A. Harnack* et al., see § 17.

5. Two native Antiochians of noble extraction, added lustre to the Exegetical School of Antioch (§ 74, 2): **Diodorus**[1], director of a monastery at Antioch and later (378) bishop of *Tarsus*; and his disciple **Theodore**[2] († 428), Bishop of *Mopsuestia* in Cilicia and friend of John Chrysostom (vide supra no. 3). The Syrian Nestorians call Theodore the "Holy Commentator" of Scripture. Because of the charges that both of these men were the fathers of Nestorianism (§ 54, 1. 5) and especially because of the sentence passed on Theodore after his death by Justinian and the fifth General Council (§ 58, 5. 6), the justice of which is strongly questioned today, their many

---

[1] PG 33. Fragments in K. STAAB, Pauluskommentare, 83/112. L. MA-RIÈS, Études préliminaires à l'édition de Diodor de Tarse sur les psaumes, Paris 1933; also M. JUGIE, Échos d'Orient 1934, 190/3. A. HARNACK, TU 21, 4, 1901 (four pseudo-Justinian treatises composed by Diodorus); opp. view FUNK, AU III, 323/50; J. LEBON, RHE 1930, 536/50 (written by Theodoret?). R. ABRAMOWSKI, ZntW 1931, 234/62; 1949, 19/69 (Diodorus' life, teachings and theological works). E. SCHWEIZER, ib. 1942, 33/75 (D. as an exegete). M. RICHARD, Mél. F. Grat I, Paris 1946, 99/116 (Dogmatic fragments of Diodorus and Cyril of Al. vs. D. and Theodore).

[2] PG 66. Theodori Ep. Mops. in epist. Pauli commentarii, ed H. B. SWETE, 2 vol. Cambridge 1880/2. Fragments in K. STAAB, Pauluskommentar, 113/212. R. DEVREESSE, Le commentaire de Théodore de Mopsueste sur les Psaumes (1—80), Rome 1939 (Studi e Testi 93). J. M. VOSTÉ, Angelicum 1942, 179/98 (commentary on the Psalms). Theodori M. commentarius in Ev. Joh. Ap. (CSCO, SS. Syri), Löwen 1940. R. DEVREESSE, Essai sur Théodore de M., Rome 1948 (Studi e Testi 141), in the same 287/419, the commentary on John. Theodore's sermons to the catechumens (Syrian), ed. A. MINGANA in Wood-brooke Studies V—VI, Cambridge 1932/3; also R. DEVREESSE, RevSR 1933, 425/36; E. AMANN, ib. 1934, 161/90; R. ABRAMOWSKI, ZntW 1934, 66/84; M. JUGIE, Échos d'Orient 1935, 257/71. R. TONNEAU et R. DEVREESSE, Les homélies catéchétiques de Théodore de M., Rome 1949 (Studi e Testi 145). F. J. REINE, The Eucharistic Doctrine and Liturgy of the Mystagogical Cate-cheses of Theodore of M., Washington 1942 (cfr. § 67, 2 A. RÜCKER and H. LIETZMANN on Theodore's Liturgy). M. RICHARD, Muséon 1943, 55/75 (Frag-ments of "On the Incarnation"); Mél. F. GRAT, see above. H. KIHN, Theodor v. M. u. Junilius Africanus als Exegeten, 1880. L. PIROT, L'oeuvre exégétique de Théodore de M., Rome 1913. L. PATTERSON, Theodore of M. and Modern Thought, London 1926. J. M. VOSTÉ, Rev. Bibl. 1925, 54 ff.; 1929, 382 ff. 542 ff. (Theodore's Life and writings). W. DE VRIES, OrChrPer 1941, 91/148 ("Nestorianism" in Theodore's teaching on the sacraments). E. AMANN, DictThC 15, 235/79. H. G. OPITZ, RE Pauly-Wissowa 2. R. V, 1181/90. Cfr. also § 54 and 58, 5.

exegetical and dogmatic-polemic writings have almost all been lost except for a few fragments. Diodorus wrote extensively on the principles of exegesis and commented on almost the entire Bible, but all is now lost save a few fragments in Catenae and the Commentary on the Psalms. Theodore's work fared somewhat better. The following have been preserved: Commentary on the Minor Prophets, on the Gospel of St. John (in Syrian), on ten of Paul's Epistles (in Latin) and a more recently discovered Liber de sacramentis et de fide ad baptizandos (in Syrian). The latter work is a valuable catechesis for the instruction of catechumens (§ 66, 2) and is quite orthodox in character.

The **Apostolic Constitutions**[1] (Διαταγαὶ τῶν ἁγίων ἀποστόλων) resulted from the revision and adaptation of older writings. As the work now stands, it is a collection of regulations for ecclesiastical discipline, law and liturgy. The first six books are no more than a revision of the Didascalia (§ 39, 5); the seventh book is taken from the Didache (§ 37, 1) and the eighth book, as has recently been shown (E. Schwartz, R. H. Connolly), is based on Hippolytus' Apostolic Tradition and the Egyptian Church Ordinance (§ 39, 4). The eighth and most valuable of the books, gives a description of ordination, the so-called Clementine liturgy (§ 67, 2) and the 85 Apostolic Canons (§ 65, 4). The entire work purports to be the work of Bishop Clement of Rome (§ 37, 3) undertaken by order of the Apostles; but it is actually of much later origin. The author or compiler was perhaps the same person who interpolated the Epistles of Ignatius (§ 37, 4) and belonged to the group of Apollinarians (§ 53) in Syria about the year 400. Some (E. Schwartz, H. Lietzmann) think that the collection was made or revised at Constantinople about 380. The work was condemned by the Synod in Trullo (can. 2) in 692, which retained the 85 Apostolic Canons. But in spite of this, parts of the work found their way into collections in the East.

---

[1] Didascalia et Constitutiones Apostolorum, ed. F. X. FUNK, 2 vol. 1905. Extracts from the liturgy of the Apost. Konst. in Floril. patrist. 7, 4—5, ²1936 (J. QUASTEN). F. X. FUNK, Die Apost. Konstitutionen, 1891; Das Testament unseres Herrn u. die verwandten Schriften, 1901; AU II, 236 ff. 359 ff.; III, 64 ff. 350 ff.; ThQ 1907, 226/41. H. LECLERCQ, DictAC III, 2732/95. ED. SCHWARTZ, Über die pseudoapostol. Kirchenordnungen, 1910. TH. SCHERMANN, Die allgemeine Kirchenordnung, früh-christl. Liturgien u. kirchl. Überlieferung, 3 parts 1914/6. W. H. FRERE, Early Ordination Services, JThSt 1915, 323/69. C. H. TURNER, JThSt 1929/30, 128/42 (the eighth book of the Ap. Const.). Lit. on the Traditio apostolica of Hippolytus § 39, 4.

Recent studies have made evident the kinship of several documents closely allied with the eighth book of the Apostolic Constitutions. But their interdependence is not yet clearly understood. The most important are: 1. the *Apostolic Church Ordinance*, Canones ecclesiastici apostolorum, in the Greek form in which they have been preserved, are from the first half of the fourth century if not from the end of the fifth century. This work gives a sketch of the Way of Life as found in the Didache 1—4 and various ordinances are represented as being given by individual Apostles. 2. *Constitutiones per Hippolytum*, should perhaps be considered as a *parallel text* to the eighth book of the Apostolic Constitutions of which they are an excerpt with some few additions. 3. The *Testament of our Lord*, dating from about 475 and the Prophecies of Christ after His Resurrection regarding the end of the world, also contain a church ordinance and a description of the liturgy. The principal part is a revision of the Egyptian Church Ordinance (Ausgabe des Testamentum Domini nostri Jesu Christi von dem Patriarchen Ephraem II Rahmani von Antiochien, Mainz 1899; cfr. id. Les orientales et occidentales, Beyrouth, 1929 [a new fragment of the testament]: *J. Quasten* in Florileg. patrist. 7, 235/73; *F. X. Funk*, Das Test. uns. Herrn, vide supra). 4. *Canones Hippolyti* of about the year 500 preserved in Arabic and Ethiopic versions likewise contain a revision of the Egyptian Church Ordinance (with perhaps other elements). — Cfr. K. Müller, ZntW 1924, 226/31.

6. **Amphilochius**, Bishop of Iconium († after 394), was closely associated with the three great Cappadocians and was probably a cousin of Gregory of Nazianzus. The three "Canonical Letters" of St. Basil are addressed to him. He was a man of action rather than a writer. Eight of his sermons known to be genuine have been preserved. — PG 39. — Monogr. by *K. Holl*, 1904. — *G. Ficker*, Amphilochiana I, 1906. — F. Cavallera, RechSR 1912, 68/74. — R. Abramowski, ZntW 1930, 129/35 (Symbolum of Amphilochius).

**Apollinaris**, Bishop of Laodicea († c. 390), was also a contemporary of the Cappadocians and like them was talented and had an excellent education. He was a strong opponent of Arianism, but later fell into serious Christological errors. (§ 53). He was a voluminous writer and composed works in the field of apologetics (against Porphyrius and Julian the Apostate), exegesis and dogma. He also wrote a number of poems, partly songs and partly metrical renditions of Old Testament material. The school laws of Julian (§ 41, 3) made it impossible for Christians to study the old classics. Apollinaris wrote his poems in an effort to offer a Christian substitute. A paraphrase of the Psalms in hexameter (ed. A. Ludwich, 1912) ascribed to Apollinaris is of doubtful authenticity. But a "detailed Creed" (ἡ κατὰ μέρος πίστις) by him is found among the writings of Gregory Thaumaturgus (§ 39, 3), another Creed presented to Emperor Jovian is ascribed to Athanasius (§ 53; 54, 1) and a treatise and a letter are ascribed to Pope Julius. The fact that these writings of the heretic are ascribed to orthodox Fathers account for their preservation. — Cfr. lit. in § 53. — Fragmente aus dem Kommentar zum Römerbrief bei *K. Staab*, Pauluskommentare, 57/82. — *J. Golega*, Byz. Z. 1939, 1/22 (his paraphrase of the Psalms not genuine).

**Evagrius Ponticus** († 399), a disciple of the Cappadocians, was ordained deacon by Nestorius for the church of Constantinople. About 382 he became a hermit in Egypt where he spent his last years. Even during his lifetime he enjoyed a reputation as an ascetic and a writer, but together with Didymus was condemned as an Origenist at the fifth General Council in 553 (§ 58, 6). Hence very few of his numerous writings have been preserved. His "Mirror for Nuns" and "Mirror for Monks" and a treatise On Prayer formerly ascribed to Nilus have come down in the original Greek text. Several other works exist in Syrian, Armenian and Latin translations. Evagrius was an ardent advocate of monastic *asceticism* and *mysticism* based on Origen. He cultivated the form of writing known as *Maxims* or *Spiritual Sayings*, which influenced Greek piety and mysticism down to Maximus Confessor and was not without influence on the West (Cassian, etc.) through the Latin translations of Rufinus and Gennadius. Finally, the eighth letter of St. Basil's correspondence is actually from the pen of Evagrius. — PG 40; PG 79, 1165/200 (De oratione). — *A. Wilmart*, RevBén 1911, 143/54 (Sententiae ad virgines). — *W. Frankenberg*, Abh. Göttingen NF. 13, 3, 1912 (several works in Syrian). — *H. Gressmann*, TU 39, 4, 1913 (the two "Specula" in Greek). — *J. Muyldermans*, Muséon 1929/34, 1938, 1940/1, 1946 (Greek, Syrian and Armenian fragments); cfr. E. Peterson, ZkTh 1933, 271/73. — *I. Hausherr*, Orientalia Christ. 22, 2, 1931; 30, 3, 1933 (Syrian and Armenian fragments); OrChrPer 1939, 7 ff. 229 ff. RevAM 1934, 34 ff. 113 ff. (De oratione). — *O. Spies*, Oriens Christ. 1932, 203/28 (on the eight evil thoughts). — *O. Zöckler*, Evagrius Pont. 1893. — *W. Bousset*, Apophthegmata, 1923, 281/341. — *R. Melcher*, Der 8. Brief des Basilius ein Werk des Evagrius Pont., 1923. — *M. Viller*, see below under Maximus Confessor § 77, 2; *M. Viller* and *K. Rahner*, Aszese u. Mystik in der Väterzeit, 1939, 97/109. — K. Rahner, ZAszMyst 1933, 21/38 (spiritual teaching of E. P.). — S. Marsili, Giov. Cassiano ed Evagrio Pontico, Rome 1936. — *H. U. v. Balthasar*, ZkTh 1939, 86/106; 181/206 (the Hiera of Evagrius Pont.); ZAszMyst, 1939, 31/47 (Metaphysics and Mysticism of E. P.). — *R. Draguet*, RHE 1946 321/64; 1947, 5/49 (influence on Hist. Lausiaca).

7. During the fifth century, the first place in the intellectual life the Greek Church was held by two bishops: Cyril, representing the School of Alexandria, and Theodoret, the School of Antioch. **Cyril**[1], Bishop of *Alexandria* (412—444), nephew and successor of

---

[1] PG 68—77. ED. SCHWARTZ, Acta concil. oecum. I, 5 vol. 1922/30. A. RÜCKER, Die Lukashomilien des hl. Cyrill v. Alex., 1911. Auswahl aus Cyrills Schriften, deutsch v. O. BARDENHEWER, in BKV 2. R. 12, 1935. Monogr. on Cyril by J. KOPALLIK, 1881; CH. PAPADOPOULOS, Alexandria 1933 (Greek). J. MAHÉ, DictThC III, 2476/527. A. REHERMANN, Die Christologie des hl. Cyrill v. Alex., 1902. E. WEIGL, Die Heilslehre des hl. Cyrill v. A., 1905; Christologie vom Tode des hl. Athanasius (373) bis 429, 1925. A. STRUCKMANN, Die Eucharistielehre des hl. Cyrill v. A., 1910. A. EBERLE, Die Mariologie des hl. Cyrill v. A., 1912. J. N. HEBENSPERGER, Die Denkwelt des hl. Cyrill v. A., 1927. J. B. WOLF, Commentationes in S. Cyrilli Alex. de Spiritu Sancto doctrinam, Diss. Rome 1934. P. RENAUDIN, La théologie de S. Cyrille d'Alex. d'après S. Thomas d'Aquin, Tangerloo 1937. H. DU MANOIR, RechSR 1937, 385 ff. 549 ff.; Gregorianum 1938/9 (the Church the Body of christ); Dogme et spiritualité chez s. C. d'A., 1944. Kyrilliana (444—1944), Cairo 1947; cfr. RHE 1948, 205/7. M. RICHARD, Mél. F. Grat, see above no. 5. N. CHARLIER, RHE 1950, 25/81 (Thesaurus de Trinitate). Cfr. § 54.

the cruel Theophilus (§ 51, 3), was the staunch champion of orthodoxy and defended the title of Theotokos against the Nestorians.
From 429 he attacked them in a series of writings and worked
energetically for the condemnation of Nestorius at the Council of
Ephesus in 431, at which he presided. However, for the sake of
union, he was obliged to make some purely formal concessions to
the Antiochians in 433 (§ 54, 2. 3). He wrote an apology Contra
Julianum Imperatorem (§ 41, 3), two great controversial dogmatic
works against the Arians, thirty Paschal letters or homilies (29 extant), several important works on ecclesiastical policy and numerous
Scriptural commentaries. The commentaries, by reason of their
extravagant allegory and typology are not altogether satisfactory;
but as a profound and sagacious *theologian* Cyril surpasses all the
other Oriental Fathers. — **Theodoret**[1], Bishop of *Cyrus* near Antioch
(423 — c. 458), was a versatile scholar and acquired lasting renown
as a *Church historian*, an *apologist, polemicist* and *exegete*. However,
suspected of being a partisan of Nestorius (§ 54, 2), he was deposed
by the Robber Synod at Ephesus in 449 but was reinstated by
Chalcedon in 451. Finally, he was condemned in the famous Three
Chapters because of his writings against Cyril (§ 58, 5. 6). Although
in the beginning his Christology did go beyond the limits of orthodoxy, since about 445 he corrected his errors and rendered great
service to the Church. His historical works include an Ecclesiastical
History which continues Eusebius down to 428; an Historia religiosa
with biographies of thirty famous ascetics of the East, and a Compendium fabularum haereticarum in five books, which is a history of
heretics from Simon Magus to Eutyches. The conclusion is a synop-
tic explanation of Christian morality and dogma. His Graecarum
affectionum curatio is one of the best apologies of ancient times.
The Eranistes seu Polymorphus is an attack on Monophysitism in

---

[1] PG 80—84.  Graec. affectionum curatio, ed. J. RAEDER, 1905. Auswahl
(Hist. relig. and c. hist.) deutsch in BKV 50 and 51, 1926. A. MÖHLE, Theodoret
von Kyros, Kommentar zu Jesaja, 1932. H. G. OPITZ, RE Pauly-Wissowa 2.
R. V, 1791/801.  G. BARDY, DictThC 15, 299/325.  JOS. SCHULTE, Theodoret
als Apologet, 1904.  L. SALTET, RHE 1905, 289 ff. 513 ff. 741 ff. (sources of
the Eranistes).  K. GÜNTHER, Th. v. C. und die Kämpfe in der oriental.
Kirche 444—449, Progr. Aschaffenb. 1913.  ED. SCHWARTZ, Zur Schrift-
stellerei Theodorets, Sb. München 1922, 1.  J. LEBON, RHE 1930, 523/60
(two pseudo-Cyrillian tracts and the pseudo-Justin. ecthesis written by Theodoret); R. V. SELLERS, ThSt 1945, 145 ff.  M. RICHARD, RevSR 1934, 34/61
(De unitate Christi written before 448/9); RevSPhTh 1935, 83/106 (literary
activity of Th. before 431); 1936, 459/81 (development).  KL. JÜSSEN, ThGl
1935, 438/52 (Christology of Th. according to the Com. on Isaias). M. WAGNER,
Dumbarton Oaks Papers 4, 1948, 119/81 (letters). Cfr. also § 54, 55, 58.

which the author shows the teaching to be a collection of errors borrowed from the earlier heresies: a myth in many forms. Theodoret was one of the most gifted *exegetes* of the Greek Church. His commentaries on the Psalms, the Canticle of Canticles, the prophets (the commentary of Isaias was but recently discovered) and the Pauline Epistles are thorough, methodical and written in elegant style.

Synesius of Cyrene († c. 414) is one of the strangest characters of Christian antiquity. He was born of wealthy parents and became an enthusiastic disciple of the famous Neoplatonic philosopher *Hypatia*, who was murdered by a fanatical mob at Alexandria in 415 (§ 41, 6). Although not yet baptized, Synesius was elected bishop of Ptolemais and metropolitan of Cyrenaica. He accepted the election on condition that he would not be obliged to renounce his *Neoplatonic* views regarding the pre-existence of souls, the eternity of the world and the allegorical interpretation of the resurrection; also that he be allowed to live with his wife whom he had married a short time before. As bishop he was a zealous shepherd and defender of the Church's rights but was never able to overcome the effects of his pagan studies. His writings include treatises, sermons, hymns and letters, all of which show an elegant style but very little Christian thought. — PG 66. — Hymni et opuscula ed. *N. Terzaghi*, 2 vol. Rome 1939/44. — *A. Fitzgerald*. Letters of Synesius transl., London 1926; Essays and hymns of Synesius transl., 2 vol. London 1930. — *W. Lang*, Das Traumbuch des Synesius v. Kyrene, 1926. — *X. H. Simeon*, Untersuchungen zu den Briefen des Synesios v. K., 1933. — *J. Hermelin*, Zu den Briefen des Bischofs S., Dissertation Uppsala 1934. — Monogr. on Synesius by R. Volkmann, 1869; *G. Grützmacher*, 1914 (cfr. also J. Stiglmayr, ZkTh 1914, 509/63). — *H. Koch*, HJG 1902, 751/74 (against A. J. Kleffner). — C. Bizocchi, Gregorianum 1944, 130 ff. 1946, 261 ff. (consecration). — *H. v. Campenhausen*, RE Pauly-Wissowa 2. R. IV, 1362/5. — On *Hypatia*: K. *Praechter*, RE Pauly-Wissowa IX, 1, 242 ff. — *H. v. Schubert*, Preuß. Jbb. 124, 1906, 42/60.

Palladius was a monk in Egypt and Palestine (c. 388—399) and later Bishop of *Helenopolis* in Bithynia († before 431). He was a disciple of Evagrius Ponticus. About 420 he wrote a history of monks which became immensely popular because of its charming ingenuousness and the natural interest of fifth century Christians in any writing dealing with monastic life. Palladius dedicated the work to Lausus the chamberlain of Theodosius II from which fact it has since been known as the *Historia Lausiaca*. Palladius also wrote a dialogue de vita S. Joannis Chrysostomi in imitation of Plato's Phaedo, which is a valuable source for the life of the Saint. — PG 65. Best edition of the Historia Laus. (with analysis) by *C. Butler*, 2 vol. Cambridge 1898/1904; next best by *A. Lucot*, Paris 1912 (with French transl.); German in BKV 5, 1912. — Critical edition of the Dialogus by *R. Coleman-Norton*, Cambridge 1928. — *E. Preuschen*, Palladius u. Rufinus, 1897. — *R. Reitzenstein*, Hist. Monachorum u. Hist. Lausiaca, 1916. — *W. Bousset*, Nachr. Gött. 1917, 173/217; ZntW 1922, 81/98. — *C. Butler*, Palladiana, JThSt 1920/21, 21 ff.

138 ff. 222 ff. — *F. Halkin*, AB 1930, 257/301 (Hist. Laus. and the Greek life of Pachomius). — *Ed. Schwartz*, Palladiana, ZntW 1937, 161/204. — R. Draguet, RHE 1946, 321/64; 1947, 5/49 (Hist. Laus. written in the spirit of Evagrius). — *E. Amann*, DictThC XI, 1923/30. H. *Leclercq*, DictAC XIII, 912/30.

**Isidore**, Abbot (?) of a monastery near *Pelusium* on the Nile († c. 435) was also a great admirer of Chrysostom. He wrote a great many letters of which more than 2000 are extant. Many of the letters deal with exegesis and asceticism and all of them prove the author to have been a highly cultured man. — PG 78. — *E. Schwartz*, Acta conciliorum occum. I, vol. IV, 1922. — Monogr. by D. S. Balanos, Athen 1922. (Greek). — *L. Bayer*, Isidors v. P. klass. Bildung, 1915. — *G. Redl*, ZKG 1928, 325/32 (Isidore as a "Sophist"). — *L. Früchtel*, Philol. Wochenschrift 1938, 764/68 (guide to sources). — *And. Schmid*, Die Christologie Isidors v. P., 1948.

**Nilus** the *Elder* († c. 430) formerly erroneously called Nilus Sinaita, was a disciple of John Chrysostom and superior of a monastery at *Ancyra* in Galatia. His literary production is considerable, including beautiful treatises on monasticism, virtues and vices, a collection of sentences and many letters (more than a thousand). Critics have not yet pronounced definitely on the authenticity of many works ascribed to him. One such work is the Narrationes de caede monachorum in monte Sinai. According to this story Nilus held a high office at Constantinople, but renounced it as well as his fortune and with his son Theodulus retired to a monastery at Sinai which was later attacked by hordes of brigands. According to Heussi this is a pure romance by an unknown author. — PG 79. — *Fr. Degenhart*, Der hl. Nilus Sinaita, 1915; Neue Beiträge zur Nilusforschung, 1918. — Opp. view: *K. Heussi*, Untersuchungen zu Nilus d. Asketen, TU 42, 2, 1917; Das Nilusproblem, 1921; RE Pauly-Wissowa XVI, 2186/87. — *M. Viller* and *K. Rahner*, Azese u. Mystik in der Väterzeit, 1939, 166/74. — *M. Th. Disdier*, DictThC XI, 661/74. — *J. Muyldermans*, Muséon 1939, 1942, 1943.

**Diadochus**, Bishop of *Photica*, about the middle of the fifth century, was the author of De perfectione spirituali capita centum (Greek and Latin text published by J. E. Weis-Liebesdorf, 1911; French translation by E. des Places, Paris, 1943). It is a masterpiece of spirituality and mysticism. In the course of the work Diadochus takes occasion to combat the false spirituality of the Messalians (§ 50, 7). — *F. Dörr*, Diadochus v. Ph. u. die Messalianer, 1937. — *M. Rothenhäusler*, Irénikon 1937, 536/53; Hl. Überlieferung, Festschrift I. Herwegen, 1938, 86/95. — *M. Viller* and *K. Rahner*, op. cit. 216/28. — *E. des Places*, Revue des études anc., 1943, 61/80.

8. Close relationship with the Greeks since the fourth century gave rise to a national Christian literature[1] in *Syria, Armenia,*

---

[1] For the most important collections of oriental Christian literature § 2, 9 g. R. DUVAL, La littérature syriaque, Paris ³1907. K. BROCKELMANN, F. N. FINCK, J. LEIPOLDT, E. LITTMANN, Gesch. der christl. Literatur des Orients (syr., armen., kopt., arab.), 1907. A. BAUMSTARK, Die christl. Literaturen des Orients, 2 parts 1911 (Samml. Göschen); Gesch. der syr. Literatur, 1922 (standard). J. B. CHABOT, Littérature syriaque chrétienne,

*Georgia, Egypt* and *Ethiopia.* However, it attained an independent and characteristic form only in Syria and Armenia, while the Georgians, Copts, Arabs and Ethiopians were satisfied to make translations of biblical, liturgical and canonical works from the Greek.

The oldest *Syrian* Father of the Church is **Aphraates**, surnamed the "Wise Man of Persia" and known also as Mar Jacob. He was a monk and later became bishop in Eastern Syria, probably at Mar Matthai near Mossul. He left a collection of twenty-three treatises variously known as sermons, discourses and letters, but usually called Demonstrations. They were composed between 336 and 345. — Edition of *J. Parisot* (with Latin transl.), 2 vol. Paris 1894/1907 (Patrologia Syriaca I, 1—2); German by *G. Bert*, TU 3, 3/4, 1888. — *P. Schwen*, Afrahat, 1907. — L. Haefeli, Stilmittel bei A., 1932. — *J. Ortiz de Urbina*, Orientalia Christ. 31, 1933, 5/140 (divinity of Christ according to A.). — *G. Richter*, ZntW 1936, 101/14 (discussion with the Jews).

**St. Ephraem** († 373) is the classical author of Syria. He was born at Nisibis where he became a monk and a disciple of Bishop James (not Aphraates) who ordained him deacon. About 365 he went to *Edessa* where he taught in the "School of the Persians" which he probably founded and was also active as a missionary among the pagans. He wrote a number of works both in *prose* and in *verse*. His grateful countrymen bestowed on him the titles "Prophet of the Syrians" and "Harp of the Holy Ghost." Pope Benedict XV declared him a Doctor of the Church in 1920. Long before the Council of Ephesus (431) Ephraem testified to the tradition of the Church in honoring Mary. Of his many exegetical works, the commentaries on Genesis and Exodus have been preserved in a Syrian version, while his commentaries on the Gospels, the Epistles of St. Paul and the Acts of the Apostles (rediscovered in 1919, cfr. A. Merk, ZkTh 1924, 37 ff., 226 ff.) are in Armenian translation. Besides these, several controversial dogmatic works of Ephraem against the Manicheans, Marcionites and Bardesanites (§ 30 B 1, 3) are extant in the original Syrian. However, his poetry is by far the most important part of his work. He is the great Christian poet of Syria and of the early Church. Even his sermons are metrical compositions of rare beauty. Many of his works were translated into Greek at an early date. — S. Ephraem Opera, ed. Jos. Simon et *St. Ev. Assemani*, 6 vol. Rome 1732/46 (with Latin transl.); ed. *S. J. Mercati* I, 1, Rome 1915 (Greek text). — *C. W. Mitchell*, S. Ephraim's Prose Refutations of Mani, Marcion and Bardaisan, 2 vol. London 1912/21. — *P. Krüger*, Oriens Christ. 1933, 13 ff. 144 ff. (E's prayer for rain). — *W. Heffening*, ib. 1936, 54/79 (exhortation against laughter). — *Jos. Molitor*, Der Paulustext des hl. E. aus seinem armen. erhaltenen Paulinenkommentar, Diss. 1936 u. Rome

Paris 1934. O. BARDENHEWER, GeschAL IV, 318/421 (Syrian); V, 177/219 (Armenian). E. R. HAYES, L'école d'Édesse, Paris 1930. TH. HERMANN, ZntW 1926, 89/122 (School of Nisibis). J. KARST, Gesch. der armen. Literatur, 1930; Littérature géorgienne chrétienne, Paris 1934 (cfr. also G. PERADSE § 42, 3). J. M. HARDEN, Introduction to Ethiopic Christian Literature, London 1926. O'LEARY, Littérature copte, DictAC IX, 1599/1635. G. GRAF, Gesch. der christl. arab. Literatur, Rome 1944 ff.

1938. — Selections in German by *P. Zingerle* in BKV 1. A., 3 vols. 1870/6, by *S. Euringer* and *A. Rücker* in BKV 2. A. 37 and 61, 1919/28. — Monogr. on Ephraem by C. Ferry, Paris 1877; *C. Emereau*, Paris 1919; *G. Ricciotti*, Torino 1925. — L. Hammersberger, Die Mariologie der ephremischen Schriften, 1938. — *E. Beck*, Die Theol. des hl. E. in s. Hymnen über den Glauben, Rome 1949. — *P. Krüger*, MissWRelW 1941, 8/15 (Mission in E.). Other writers of the Syrian Church who produced both prose and poetry are: **Cyrillonas**, who probably lived at Edessa in the fourth century; **Balai** (Baläus), a chorbishop from the district of Aleppo in the first half of the fifth century, some of whose poetry has been attributed to St. Ephraem; **Isaac** of *Antioch*, called *the Great*, often confused with two others of the same name: Isaac of Amida and Isaac of Edessa. Isaac of Antioch was probably a Monophysite and in his sermons attacked St. Augustine's teaching on grace. **James of Sarugh**, Bishop of Batnan († 521) called "the flute of the Holy Spirit and the harp of the believing Church" left few writings which have been edited, but scholars are not in agreement regarding his orthodoxy. — Excerpts of the works of these four in German transl. by S. Landersdorfer, BKV 6, 1912. — *C. Moss*, Z. f. Semitistik 1929, 295 ff.; 1930, 61 ff. (a Syrian homily of Isaac); Muséon 1935, 87/112 (Homilies of James of Sarug on spectacles). — *S. Euringer*, Orientalia Christ. 33, Rome 1934 (the Ethiopian Anaphora of James). — Jacobi Sarugensis Epistulae, ed. *G. Olinder*, Louvain 1937 (CSCO, SS. Syri II, 45); The Letters of Jacob of S., Comments on an edition, Lund 1939. — P. Peeters, AB 1948, 134/98 (James not a Monophysite).

9. **St. Mesrob**, also called Mashtots († 441) had been chancellor to the king of Armenia before becoming a monk and a missionary. With the encouragement of the Catholicos Isaac (Sahak III) he invented a new alphabet which was so admirably adapted to the complexities of the Armenian language that it infused new life into the literature of the country. Mesrob also directed a school of translators who translated the Bible into Armenian. Mesrob himself translated the New Testament. **Eznik of Golp**, Bishop of Bagrevand († c. 478), made many translations into Armenian and wrote a work "Against the Sects" which is considered one of the masterpieces of Armenian literature. **Moses**, Bishop of **Chorene** († c. 487), a disciple of Mesrob, is credited with being the author of a *History of Greater Armenia*, from its legendary beginnings to the year 428. A. Carriere and others hold that the work was written in the eighth century; but there are sufficient grounds for believing that the charming and valuable work was actually produced by Moses. — Ausgewählte Schriften der armenischen Kirchenväter (Eznik, Leben Mesróps von Koriun u. a.), deutsch v. *S. Weber*, BKV 57 and 58, 1927. — *Moses v. Choren*, Gesch. Armeniens, deutsch v. *M. Lauer*, 1869. — *L. Mariès*, Le "De Deo" d'Eznik de Kolb, Thèse Paris 1924. — On *Moses of Choren*: F. C. Conybeare, Byz. Z. 1901, 489/504; F. Haase, Oriens Christ. N. S. 9, 1923, 77/90; H. Leclercq, DictAC XI, 1689/98. — *V. Inglesian*, Das armen. Schrifttum, 1929. — *H. Leclercq*, Littérature arménienne, DictAC IX, 1576/99. — See above (*F. N. Finck, J. Karst* etc.) and § 42, 2.

## § 76.

## Latin Ecclesiastical Literature of the Fourth and Fifth Centuries[1].

1. The first Latin writer of note in this period is **Hilary** of Poitiers*[2] († 367), a theologian of sound doctrine and vigorous reasoning. He was born of wealthy pagan parents and did not become a Christian until he had reached maturity. He was elected bishop of Poitiers about 350 at a time when the Arian troubles were at their height. Like the Bishop of Alexandria, Hilary devoted his life and his talents to a defense of the orthodox faith and earned the surname "the Athanasius of the West." When Hilary refused to submit to Emperor Constantius' religious policy (§ 48, 3), he was banished to Phrygia where he spent four years (356—360). During the period of his exile he deepened his theological knowledge by a study of the Greek Fathers and upon his return applied himself to deepening Christian life especially by the spread of monasticism. It was due to his efforts (§ 48, 5) that many synods were held to check Arianism in the West. Most of his writings are concerned with the Arian controversy; but he also wrote commentaries on the Gospel of St. Matthew and on the Psalms, a Liber mysteriorum, explaining the figures of the Old Testament with respect to

---

[1] O. BARDENHEWER, GeschAL III—IV. B. ALTANER, Patrologie, [2]1950. M. SCHANZ, Gesch. der röm. Lit. IV, 1 (IV c.), [2]1914; IV, 2 (V—VI c.), by M. SCHANZ, K. HOSIUS and G. KRÜGER, 1921. Cfr. EBERT, KAPPELMACHER-SCHUSTER, BICKEL, MONCEAUX, DE LABRIOLLE, GUDEMAN, MORICCA, AMATUCCI etc., § 40. TH. HAARHOFF, Schools of Gaul, Oxford 1920. E. K. RAND, Founders of the Middle Ages (Ambrosius to Gregory the Gr.), Cambridge Mass. 1928. F. A. WRIGHT and T. A. SINCLAIR, A History of the Later Latin Literature (c. 350—700), London 1935. L. SALVATORELLI, Storia della letteratura latina cristiana (2.—5. Jh.), Milano 1936. E. M. PICKMAN, The Mind of Latin Christendom (373—496), Oxford 1937. G. M. DREVES, Ein Jahrtausend latein. Hymnendichtung, 2 vols. 1910. C. WEYMAN, Beiträge zur Gesch. der christl.-latein. Poesie, 1926. F. J. E. RABY, History of Christian Latin Poetry . . . to the Close of the Middle Ages, Oxford 1927. O. J. KUHNMUENCH, Early Christian Latin Poets (IV—VI c.), Chicago 1929. M. PELLEGRINO, La poesia cristiana latina dalle origini a S. Ambrogio, Torino 1947. J. MARTIN, Jahresber. über die Fortschritte der klass. Altertums-Wiss. vol. 221, 1929, 65/140 (Christian Latin Poets 1900/27).

[2] PL 9—10. CSEL vol. 22 and 65 by A. ZINGERLE and A. L. FEDER, 1891/1916. Auswahl deutsch in BKV 2. R. 5—6, 1933/4. Hilaire de Poitiers, Traité des Mystères, éd. et trad. p. J. P. BRISSON, Paris 1947. Monogr. by J. H. REINKENS, 1864; A. LARGENT, Paris 1902. X. M. LE BACHELET, DictThC VI, 2388/462. A. BECK, Die Trinitätslehre des hl. Hilarius, 1903. P. SMULDERS, La doctrine trinitaire de S. Hilaire de P., Rome 1944. H. LINDEMANN, Des hl. Hil. Liber mysteriorum, 1905. A. L. FEDER, Studien zu Hil., Sb. Wien 162, 4; 166, 5; 169, 5, 1910/2; StML 81, 1911, 30/45; Wiener Studien 1920, 51 ff. 167 ff. M. F. BUTTEL, The Rhetoric of S. Hilary of P., Washington 1933. J. E. EMMENEGGER, The Functions of Faith and Reason in the Theology of S. Hil. of P., Washington 1948.

the New, *De Trinitate*, a masterpiece of dogmatic theology and many hymns.

**Ambrose**[*1] († 397) was influenced by Greek theology even more than Hilary. His father, also named Ambrose, was Praetorian Prefect for Gaul, and the Saint was born between 330 and 340 probably at Trier. He studied rhetoric and law and about 370 was made Prefect (legatus consularis) of Upper Italy with residence at Milan, the capital of the West. Upon the death of Auxentius, the Arian Bishop of Milan, Ambrose, although only a catechumen, was elected by clergy and people. He was immediately baptized and within eight days received all orders including episcopal consecration. Under the direction of the priest Simplicius, who later succeeded him, Ambrose devoted himself to the study of theology, especially the Greek Fathers. As bishop, he was the true shepherd and teacher of his flock, the guardian of the Church against

---

[1] PL 14—17. In CSEL (5 vols. thus far) by C. SCHENKL and M. PETSCHE-NIG, 1897/1919. De virginibus, ed. O. FALLER, 1933 (Floril. patrist. 31). De mysteriis et De sacramentis, ed. J. QUASTEN, 1936 (Floril. patrist. 7, 3); ed. B. BOTTE, Paris 1950 (with French transl.). De officiis ed. A. Cavasin, Turin 1938; De virginibus etc., ed. M. SALVATI, Turin 1938 (each with Italian transl.). De obitu Theodosii, ed. M. D. MANNIX, Washington 1925; De consol. Valentiniani ed. TH. A. KELLY, ib. 1941 (each with English transl.). De spiritu sancto, ed. G. CRONE, 1948. Der Tod — ein Gut, ed. J. HUHN, 1949; De Nabuthe ed. J. HUHN, 1950 (Text and transl.). Hymns (14 genuine), edd. BLUME and DREVES in Analecta hymnica 50, 1907. Auswahl deutsch in BKV 17, 21, 32, 1915/7. Monogr. by BAUNARD, Paris [3]1899, German by BITTL, 1873; TH. FÖRSTER, 1884; A. DUC DE BROGLIE, Paris [5]1901; P. DE LABRIOLLE, Paris 1908; U. MORICCA, Torino 1928. H. V. CAMPENHAUSEN, J. R. PALANQUE (both important), WYTZES etc. § 41, 4. F. H. DUDDEN, The Life and Times of S. Ambrose, 2 vol. Oxford 1935 (standard). J. CARD. SCHUSTER, Milan 1940; A. PAREDI, ib. 1941; P. GORLA, ib. 1944. A. NAGL, 1940; L. CASTANO, Turin 1940. S. Ambrogio nel SVI Centenario della nascita, Milan 1940; cfr. ThRev 1941, 106/8. Ambrosiana, ib. 1942. On the Vita S. Ambrosii by Paulinus: G. GRÜTZMACHER, Festgabe A. Hauck 1916, 77/84; J. R. PALANQUE, RevSR 1924, 26 ff. 401 ff. On the penance of Theodosius: H. KOCH, HJG 1907, 257/77; CHR. BAUR, ThQ 1908, 401/9. G. RAUSCHEN, Jbb. der christl. Kirche unter Theodosius d. Gr., 1897. M. IHM, Studia Ambrosiana, 1890. J. E. NIEDERHUBER, Die Lehre d. hl. Ambr. vom Reiche Gottes auf Erden, 1904; Die Eschatologie des hl. A., 1907. P. ASSLABER, Die persönl. Beziehungen der 3 großen Kirchenlehrer Ambr., Hieron. u. Augustinus, 1908. M. A. ADAMS, The Latinity of the Letters of S. Ambrose, Washington 1927. J. HUHN, Die Bedeutung des Wortes Sacramentum bei A. 1928; Ursprung u. Wesen des Bösen u. der Sünde nach A., 1933. E. BÜRGI, in Stella Matutina-Festschr. I, 1931, 43/68 (De officiis). L. TH. LEFORT, Muséon 1935, 55/73 (De virginibus dependent on Athanasius). De sacramentis: O. FALLER, ZkTh 1940, 1 ff. 81 ff.; H. FRANK, ThQ 1940, 67/82; H. CONOLLY, Downside Rev. 1942 and 1946. K. SCHWERDT, Studien zur Lehre des hl. A. von der Person Christi, Diss. 1937. BICKEL, FRIEDRICH, PAGNAMENTA, § 70, 3. J. RINNA, Die Kirche als Corpus Christi myst. beim hl. A., Rome 1940. A. G. ROSE, Idee u. Gestalt der Kirche beim hl. A., Diss. 1942. G. FIGUERVA, The Church and the Synagogue in St. Ambrose, Washington 1949. W. WIL-BRAND, Festg. J. Hessen, 1949, 156/61 (A. and Judaism).

paganism (§ 41, 4), Arianism (§ 48, 6) and all other heresies. He gave valuable assistence to the emperors, Gratian, Valentinian II and Theodosius the Great in highly troublous times. He championed the independence of the Church against the power of the State, but always in such a way that he did not create or increase friction between them. He was resolute in applying the laws of the Church regarding the penitential discipline, even in the case of a guilty emperor. In 390 Theodosius had commanded bloody reprisals for a revolt in Thessalonica. Ambrose ordered the Emperor to do public penance and his firmess only increased the great admiration which Theodosius already had for him. Theodosius is reported to have said that Ambrose was the only bishop he ever met worthy of the name. As a Roman, Ambrose was not given to speculation; his teaching is above all else the practical application of Christianity to daily life. Most of his writing grew out of his *preaching* and *catecheses* in which he was particularly zealous and successful. In exegesis (The Hexaëmeron, commentaries on St. Luke and various Books of the Old Testament) he made use of Philo, Origen and Basil; and while tending toward allegory and typology, was chiefly concerned with drawing moral lessons. In his dogmatic works (De Fide ad Gratianum, De Spiritu Sancto, De Mysteriis, De Paenitentia, De Sacramentis [of doubtful authenticity]) he combatted error and expanded the doctrine of the Church. De Officiis Ministrorum is a moral-ascetical version of Cicero's De Officiis. Ambrose was most eloquent when writing on virginity. One of his five works on the subject, De virginibus, is dedicated to his sister Marcellina, who received the veil from Pope Liberius about 353. To him, Mary, the Mother of God, is the ideal of all purity and his constant and beautiful references to her helped much in spreading devotion to Mary in the West. Although Ambrose was the real creator of the liturgical hymn in the West and wrote a number of them, only four of those attributed to him are of undoubted authenticity. (Cfr. also 67, 1. 2. 6 and 7).

During the Middle Ages a commentary on the Epistles of St. Paul (except the Epistle to the Hebrews) was attributed to St. Ambrose. In the sixteenth century Erasmus first recognized the falsity of this attribution which is now admitted by all critics. Since that time the work is generally called **Ambrosiaster** or Pseudo-Ambrose. It was written during the pontificate of Pope Damasus (366—384) but the identity of its author is still a mystery and likely to remain so. G. *Morin* (RHLR 1899, 97/121) ascribed the work to *Isaac*, a converted Jew, the author of Fides Isaatis ex Iudaeo (publ. by

A. Souter, JThSt 1930, 1/9) and an opponent of Damasus. It is also generally believed that the author of the Ambrosiaster is the same as the author of the Pseudo-Augustinian work Quaestiones Veteris et Novi Testamenti (ed. A. Souter, 1908). Later, Morin changed his opinion (Rev. Bén. 1914, 1/38) and proposed as the author *Evagrius* of Antioch (§ 50, 1; 72, 6) or (Rev. Bén. 1928. 251/55) the Roman prefect Aemilius *Dexter*, the friend of St. Jerome. Still another name suggested is that of *Martini*, a convert and priest who lived at Rome under Damasus but was well known at Milan and in Spain. — PL 17, 45/508. — *A. Souter*, A Study of Ambrosiaster, Texts and Studies 7, 4, 1905; The Earliest Latin Commentaries on the Epistles of S. Paul, Oxford 1927, 39/95. — *J. Wittig* et al., in Kirchengesch. Abh., ed. M. Sdralek, 4, 1906; 8, 1909; *W. Mundle*, Die Exegese der paul. Briefe im Kommentar des A., Diss. 1921. — *H. Koch*, ZKG 1926, 516/51; 1928, 1/10. — E. Buonaiuti, Ricerche religiose 1928, 1/17. — *G. Bardy*, Ambrosiaster, Dict. de la Bible, Suppl., Paris 1926, 225/41; Revue Bibl. 1932, 341/69. — *C. Martini*, Ambrosiaster, Rome 1944. — P. Schepens, RechSR 1950, 295/9.

2. **St. Jerome**[1] was born of a Christian family at Stridon on the border between Dalmatia and Pannonia about the year 347.

---

[1] PL 22—30. SCEL vol. 54/56 and 59 by J. HILBERG and S. REITER, 1910/8. SS. Hieronymi et Augustini Epistulae mutuae, ed. J. SCHMID, 1930 (Floril. patrist. 22); cfr. H. LANGE, in Stella Matutina-Festschr. I, 1931, 257/80; D. DE BRUYNE, ZntW 1932, 233/48. Commentarioli, Tractatus s. Homiliae in Ps., ed G. MORIN, 3 vol. Maredsous 1895/1903; cfr. G. MORIN, Études, textes etc. I, ib. 1913, 220/93. De viris illustr., ed. C. A. BERNOULLI, 1895; ed. E. C. RICHARDSON, TU 14, 1, 1896 (both with Gennadius). De septem ordinibus ecclesiae (spurious), ed. A. KALFF, Diss. 1938; also G. MORIN, RHE 1938, 229/44. Auswahl deutsch in BKV 15, 1914; 2 R. 16 and 18, 1936/7. Röm. Vulgata edition 1926 ff. Lettres, Text and French transl. by J. LABOURET I, Paris 1949. M. PRONBERGER, Beiträge z. Chronol. der Briefe des hl. H., Diss. 1914. J. N. HRITZU, The Style of the Letters of St. Jerome, Washington 1939. Monogr. by G. GRÜTZMACHER, 3 vols. 1901/8; O. BARDENHEWER, 1905 (lecture); F. CAVALLERA, 2 vol. Louv. 1922; A. VACCARI, Rome 1921; U. MORICCA, 2 vol. Milano 1923; H. LECLERCQ, Louvain 1927; and in DictAC VII, 2235/304; P. MONCEAUX, Paris 1932. J. FORGET, DictThC VIII, 894/983. H. LIETZMANN, RE Pauly-Wissowa VIII, 1565/81; F. CAVALLERA, DictBibl Suppl. VI, 889/97. M. J. KELLEY, Washington 1944; P. STEUR, Nymwegen 1945; G. CONTINI, Alba 1948; A. PENNA, Turin 1949. Jubilee publications: Misc. Geronimiana, Roma 1920; Benedikt. Monatsschr. 1920, 333/552. ST. V. SYCHOWSKI, H. als Literarhist., 1894. C. A. BERNOULLI, Der Schriftsstellerkatalog des H., 1895; cfr. A. FEDER, Studien z. Schriftstellerkatalog des hl. H., 1927. J. BROCHET, S. Jérôme et ses ennemis, Paris 1906. P. ASSLABER, see above under Ambrose. J. N. BRUNNER, H. u. die Mädchenerziehung, 1910. T. TRZCINSKI, Die dogmat. Schriften des hl. H., 1912. J. NIESSEN, § 70. 3 (Mariology). A. FICARRA, La posizione de S. Girolamo nella storia della cultura, 2 vol. Palermo 1916/30. L. HUGHES, The Christian Church in the Epistles of S. Jerome, London 1923. G. MORIN, Strena Buliciana, Zagreb 1924, 421/32; RevBén 1926, 217/20 (place of birth). A. ALLGEIER, Die altlatein. Psalterien, 1928; Die Psalmen der Vulgata. 1940. G. VIOLARDO, Il pensiero giuridico di S. Girolamo, Milano 1937, E. SCHWARZBAUER, Die Kirche als Corpus Christi myst. bei H., Rome 1939. G. BARDY, RevBén 1934, 145/64 (J. and his Hebrew teachers); MSR 1946, 5/36 (J. and the Gospel of the Hebr.). R. GÉNIER, Sainte Paule (347 to 404), Paris 1917.

He studied at Rome under the renowned grammarian Aelius Donatus and was baptized when he was about 20 years old. After a short stay at Trier, he went to Aquileia where he spent some time either as a monk or at least in close contact with monks. About 373 he went to the East and lived several years as a hermit in the Syrian desert east of Antioch (§ 72, 3), where he studied Greek and made a beginning in the study of Hebrew. After some opposition, he allowed himself to be ordained priest by Paulinus of Antioch on condition that he would not be attached to a particular church. He then went to Constantinople where for two years he studied exegesis under the guidance of Gregory of Nazianzus. The next three years he spent at Rome as secretary and counsellor to Pope Damasus whom, it was thought, he would succeed. While at Rome he interested several noble Roman ladies (Marcella, Paula, Eustochium and others) in religious life. When Damasus died, Jerome left the city which he had always disliked and went to Palestine. In 389 he took up his residence in a monastery built by Paula near the grotto of the Nativity at Bethlehem and never left it until his death on September 30, 419 or 420. In the midst of a group of monks, mostly of the West, he spent thirty-five years in prayer, in teaching the monks whose superior he was, in study and especially in the great work of revising and translating the Scriptures. But the Origenistic controversy, the dispute with Bishop John of Jerusalem, the quarrel with Rufinus, the friend of his youth, (§ 51, 2) the terrors of the Migration of Nations and the Pelagian heresy (§ 56, 3) all came to disturb his studious retirement. The commentaries constitute the best part of Jerome's exegetical work, in which he followed the School of Alexandria. Even after he repudiated Origen, he remained dependent on him for the rest of his life; but was always careful to avoid Origen's errors. He also made translations and revisions of the text of the Scriptures. The *Latin version*, known as the *Vulgata* (sc. editio) was adopted practically throughout the West by the end of the sixth century. This followed his attempt to revise the old Latin Itala so as to give the real meaning as contained in the Hebrew and Aramacan versions. Besides his great work in the field of Scripture, Jerome wrote a number of controversial works against the Luciferians (§ 50, 3), against Helvidius, Jovinian and Vigilantius who denied the virginity of the Mother of Christ (§ 70, 3), against Rufinus and against the Pelagians (§ 56, 3). He also wrote De viris illustribus, which may well be called the first History of

Christian Literature, and which in spite of defects and inexactitudes is still of value. It was continued by Gennadius and others. He continued the chronicle of Eusebius from 325 to 378, wrote the biographies of several early monks (Pauli, Malchi and Hilarionis § 72, 1. 6), translated many Greek works and wrote many letters which are still of interest and value. (For the Martyrologium Hieronymianum erroneously ascribed to Jerome, see § 70, 1). Without doubt Jerome was one of the most learned of the Fathers and certainly the most versatile. He possessed a knowledge of languages (vir trilinguis), a brilliant style ("the grandfather of the Humanists") and a capacity for work which give him an uncontested position among the orthodox Fathers of the Church. He was not an original thinker, but kept strictly to what he found in tradition. Even the sense of the Scriptures had to be the sense taught by the Church, for that was the sense intended by the Holy Ghost, the author of the Scriptures. His very evident defects of character: his irrascibility, his resentment to criticism, his bitterness toward enemies can never obscure his more eminent virtues.

3. **Augustine** of Hippo\*[1], (354—430) Saint, Doctor of the Church, philosopher and theologian, influenced his own and subsequent

---

[1] E. NEBREDA, Bibliographia Augustina, Rome 1928 (not complete). Aug.-Bibliographie im Deutschen Gesamtkatalog, Sonderh. 1935. E. KALINKA, Sb. Wien 203, 1, 1925 (oldest list of the writings of Augustine). H. DÖRRIES, Theol. Rundschau 1929, 217/45 and G. KRÜGER, ZKG 1930, 494/501 and BL. SOTO, Archivio agostin. 39, 1933; 42, 1934 (recent literature). **I. Editions of the works of Augustine:** Ed. Benedictina, 11 fol. Paris 1679/1700 (cfr. J. GHELLINCK, Nouvelle Revue théol. 1930, 764/74); also in PL 32—47. In SCEL thus far 18 vols. 1887/1923. Deutsche Augustinusausgabe by C. J. PERL et al., 1940 ff. Deutsche Gesamtausgabe der moraltheolog. Schriften, ed. A. KÜNZELMANN and A. ZUMKELLER, 1949 ff. Augustin-Auswahl deutsch in BKV (1. and 2. series), 12 vols. 1911/35; briefer selections by J. BERNHART, 1922; A. V. HARNACK, 1922; H. HEFELE, 1923; O. KARRER, 2 parts 1925; E. PRZYWARA, 1934; H. U. V. BALTHASAR, 1942. Separate editions: Confessiones, ed. P. KNOELL, 1898; F. RAMORINO, Rome 1909; C. H. BRUDER, [2]1929; P. DE LABRIOLLE, 2 vol. Paris 1925/6 (with French transl.); J. GIBB and W. MONTGOMERY, Cambridge [2]1927 (with commentary); A. C. VEGA, Escorial 1930; M. SKUTELLA, 1934 (best edition); J. CAPELLO, Turin 1948. German transl. of the Confessions: G. V. HERTLING, [23/24]1928; A. HOFFMANN, BKV 18, 1914; H. HEFELE, [2]1922; C. J. PERL, 1948; H. SCHIEL, 1950. De civitate Dei, ed. B. DOMBART-A. KALB, 2 vols [4]1928/9; E. HOFFMANN, CSEL 40, 2 vol. 1899/1900; J. E. C. WELLDON, 2 vol. London 1924; C. WEYMAN, 1925. German transl. by A. SCHRÖDER, BKV 1. 16, 28, 1911/6; JOS. FISCHER, 1948 (excerpts). De beata vita, ed. M. SCHMAUS, 1931 (Floril. patrist. 27). Enchiridion, ed. O. SCHEEL, [2]1930; A. SIZOO, Den Haag 1947; German: A.s Handbüchlein, v. P. SIMON, 1948. De doctrina christiana, ed. H. J. VOGELS, 1930 (Floril. patrist. 24). De catechizandis rudibus, ed. G. KRÜGER, [3]1934; J. P. CHRISTOPHER, Washington 1926 (with commentary). S. Augustini textus eucharistici selecti, ed. H. LANG, 1933 (Floril. patrist. 35). S. Augustini textus selecti de poenitentia, coll. B. POSCHMANN, 1934 (Floril. patrist. 38).

times as it has been the lot of few men to do. The facts of his eventful life up to 387 have been reviewed with amazing frankness in the

G. MORIN, S. Aurelii Augustini Tractatus s. Sermones inediti, 1917 (cfr.
RevBén 1924, 181/99); S. Augustini Sermones post Maurinos reperti, Rome
1930 (Misc. Agostiniana I). C. LAMBOT, RevBén 1934/5, 1937/9, 1947,
1949/50; AB 1949, 249/66 (doubtful sermons etc.). De videndo Deo (= Ep.
147) and Ep. 120 ad Consentium, rec. M. SCHMAUS, 1930, 1933 (Floril. patrist. 23
u. 33). S. Augustini doctrina de cognitione, textus coll. L. W. Keeler, Rome
1934 (Univ. Greg., Textus et documenta). SS. Hieronymi et Augustini Epistolae mutuae, ed. J. SCHMID, 1930 (Floril. patrist. 22). J. H. BAXTER, S. Augustine Select Letters with English Transl., New York 1930. Augustinus, Über
die Psalmen, ausgew. u. übertragen v. H. U. V. BALTHASAR, 1936; Soliloquia,
German by L. SCHOPP, 1938; Christl. Ethos (De moribus eccl. cath.), transl.
by P. KESELING, 1948. **II. Biographies and Monographs,** general: POSSI-
DIUS, Vita S. Augustini, ed. H. T. WEISKOTTEN, Princeton 1919; better
in S. Possidii opuscula, rec. A. C. VEGA, Escorial 1935; German by AD.
V. HARNACK, Abh. Berlin 1930, 1 and by K. ROMEIS, 1930. Ed. Bened.
t. XI = PL 47. Modern Biographies: C. BINDEMANN, 3 vols. 1844/69;
FR. BÖHRINGER (KG. in Biogr. XI), [2]1877/8; C. WOLFSGRUBER, 1898;
G. V. HERTLING, [2]1904; L. BERTRAND, Paris 1913, German 1927 (popular);
C. BOYER, ib. 1932; H. LESAAR, 1930 (popular); E. KREBS, 1930; U. MORICCA,
Torino 1930 (= Storia della letteratura lat. crist. III, 1932, 278/695); A.
PINCHERLE, Bari 1930; G. PAPINI, German by P. STEPHAN, 1930; H. POPE,
London 1937; R. POTTIER, Paris 1945; G. BARDY, Paris [6]1946; R. V. KIE-
NITZ, 1947; J. D. BURGER, Neuchâtel 1948; M. F. SCIACCA, Brescia 1940.
Briefer studies: R. SEEBERG, 1930; G. KRÜGER, 1930; K. ADAM (the spiritual
development of St. Augustine), 1931. E. PORTALIÉ, S. Augustin, DictThC I,
2268/2472 (excellent); Augustinisme, ib. 2501/61. P. DE LABRIOLLE, DictHE
V, 440/72. CH. BOYER, DictApir I, 1101/30. P. MONCEAUX, Hist. litt. (§ 40)
VII, Paris 1923. Collection of Essays written for the Jubilee year 1930:
M. GRABMANN, J. MAUSBACH et al., Augustinus, Festschr. d. Görresgesell-
schaft, 1930. R. JOLIVET, CH. BOYER etc., Études sur S. Aug., Paris 1930
(Archives de philosophie VII, 2). Nouvelle Revue théolog., Tournai 1930.
C. D'ARCY, M. BLONDEL etc., A Monument to S. Augustine, London 1930.
Studi Agostiniani (Misc. Agostiniana, II), Rome 1931 (important). **III. Se-
parate essays and studies:** M. FASSBINDER, Monika, 1940. H. KARPP, Mo-
nika, 1941. F. WÖRTER, Die Geistesentwicklung des hl. Aug. bis zu seiner
Taufe, 1892. H. BEKKER, Aug., Studien zu s. geistigen Entwickl., 1908.
W. THIMME, A.s geist. Entwickl. 386/91, 1908; Aug., Lebens- u. Charakterbild
auf Grund s. Briefe, 1910. P. ALFARIC, L'évolution intellectuelle de S. Aug. I,
Paris 1918 (on the Index). CH. BOYER, Christianisme et Néoplatonisme dans
la formation de S. Aug., ib. 1920. P. GUILLOUX, L'âme de S. Aug., ib. 1921.
K. HOLL, A.s innere Entwickl., Abh. Berlin 1922, 4. J. NOERREGAARD, A.s
Bekehrung, German by A. SPELMEYER, 1923. E. HAENCHEN, Die Frage
nach d. Gewißheit beim jungen A., 1932. A. PINCHERLE, La formazione
teologica di S. Agostino, Rome 1948. M. I. BARRY, S. Augustine the Orator,
Washington 1924. B. LEGEWIE, A., eine Psychographie, 1925: also H. LANGE,
Scholastik 1926, 400/11. P. HENRY, La vision d'Ostie, Paris 1938. H.
I. MARROU, S. Aug. et la fin de la culture antique, 2 vol. Paris 1938/49.
V. NOLTE, Augustinus' Freundschaftsideal in s. Briefen, 1939. M. P. GARVEY,
S. Augustine: Christian or Neoplatonist?, Milwaukee 1939. G. BARDY,
Année Théol. 1940, 3/94 (L'âme de S. Aug.). G. METZGER, Die afrikan.
Kirche (according to A's letters), 1934; Kirche u. Mission in den Briefen
A.s, 1936. F. VAN DER MEER, Augustinus de zielzorger, Utrecht [2]1949.
J. FINAERT, S. Aug., rhéteur, Paris 1939. A. KUNZELMANN, Die zeitl. Fest-
legung der Sermones des hl. A., 1928. H. LIETZMANN, Sb. Berlin 1930, 29
(letters of A.). C. J. BALMUS, Étude sur le style de S. Aug. dans les Confess.
et la Cité de Dieu, Paris 1930. M. COMEAU, S. Aug., l'exégète du 4e évangile,

autobiography known as the Confessions. The remainder of his life has been recounted by his disciple and friend Possidius, Bishop

---

Paris 1930. M. PONTET, L'exégèse de S. Aug. prédicateur, Paris 1946. M. M. GETTY, The Life of the North Africans as Revealed in the Sermons of S. Aug., Washington 1931. C. MOHRMANN, Die altchristl. Sondersprache in den Sermones des hl. A., Nymwegen 1933. S. ZARB, Angelicum 1933/40 (Chronology of A's. writings). E. SCHUCHTER, Wiener Studien 1934, 115/38 (A's. style of preaching). J. LECLERCQ, RevBén 1947, 117/31 (preaching and rhetoric in A's. times). K. H. SCHELKLE, Virgil in der Deutung A.s, 1939. J. FINAERT, L'évolution littéraire de S. Aug., Paris 1939. B. ALTANER, Festschr. F. J. Dölgcr, 1939, 19/40 (the Greek language); ZkTh 1941, 81/90 (A. and Philo); Z. f. Rel. u. Geistesg. 1948, 71/9 (Greek text of the Fathers); ThRev 1948, 73/8 (A's library). É. GILSON, Introduction à l'étude de S. Aug., Paris ²1943; German: Der hl. Aug., eine Einführung in s. Lehre, von PH. BÖH-NER and TH. SIGGE, 1931. F. CAYRÉ, L'initiation à la philos. de S. Aug., Paris 1947. A. DORNER, Das theol. System A.s, 1873. J. STORZ, Die Philos. des hl. Aug., 1882. O. ROTTMANNER, Geistesfrüchte, 1908, 7/108. P. BATIF-FOL, Le Catholicisme de S. Aug., 2 vol. Paris ⁵1929. CH. BOYER, L'idée de la vérité dans la philos. de S. Aug., Paris 1921; Essais sur la doctrine de S. Aug., Paris 1932. H. EIBL, A. u. die Patristik, 1923 (Hist. of Philosophy). G. COMBÈS, Aug. et la culture classique, Paris 1927. R. JOLIVET, S. Aug. et le Néoplatonisme chrétien, Paris 1932. J. GUITTON, Le temps et l'éternité chez Plotin et S. Aug., Paris 1933. W. THEILER, Porphyrios u. A., 1933. W. VERWIEBE, Welt u. Zeit bei A., 1933. E. PRZYWARA, Aug., die Gestalt als Gefüge, 1934. P. HENRY, see no. 5 below under Firmicius Maternus; JThSt 1937, 1/23 (A. and Plotinus). J. BARION, Plotin u. A., 1935. J. RITTER, Mundus intelligibilis . . . neuplaton. Ontologie bei A., 1937. R. CADIOU, RechSR 1937, 597 ff. (A's early theology). A. DAHL, A. u. Plotin, Lund 1945. J. HESSEN, Die Philos. des hl. A., 1947. TH. PHILIPS, Das Weltbild des hl. A., 1949. H. WEINAND, Die Gottesidee der Grundzug der Weltanschauung des hl. A., 1910. M. GRABMANN, Die Grundgedanken des hl. A. über Seele u. Gott, ²1929. M. SCHMAUS, Die psychol. Trinitätslehre des hl. A., 1927. F. CAYRÉ, La contemplation Augustinienne, Paris 1927. G. COMBÈS, La charité d'après S. Aug., Paris 1934. H. ARENDT, Der Liebesbegriff bei A., 1929. J. HESSEN, A.s Metaphysik der Erkenntnis, 1931. G. WUNDERLE, Archiv f. Religionspsychol. 1931, 1/35 (concept of God). R. JOLIVET, Dieu soleil des esprits: la doctrine Augustinienne de l'illumination, Paris 1934; Le problème du mal d'après S. Aug., Paris 1936. E. BENZ, see no. 5 below under Marius Victorinus. J. STOSZKO, L'apologétique de S. Aug., Thèse Strasb. 1932. E. DINKLER, Die Anthropologie A.s, 1934 (also J. TERNUS, Scholastik 1935, 94/8). H. BARTH, Die Freiheit der Entscheidung im Denken A.s, Basel 1935. E. HENDRIKX, A.s Verhältnis zur Mystik, 1936. C. TERZI, Il problema del male nella polemica antimanichea di S. Agostino, Udine 1936. M. S. MULDONEY, World-Order in the Works of Aug., Washington 1937. G. MANCINI, La psicologia di S. Ag. e i suoi elementi neoplatonici, Neapel 1938. H. WOODS, A. and Evolution, New York 1924. N. MERLIN, S. Aug. et les dogmes du péché originel et de la grâce, Paris 1931. J. HENNIN-GER, S. Aug. et doctrina de duplici iustitia, 1935. O. SCHEEL, Die Anschauung A.s über Christi Person u. Werk, 1901. J. RIVIÈRE, Le dogme de la Rédemp-tion chez S. Aug., Paris ³1933. É. GILSON, Philosophie et incarnation selon S. Aug., Montréal 1947. J. VETTER, Der hl. A. u. das Geheimnis des Leibes Christi, 1929. FR. HOFMANN, Der Kirchenbegriff des hl. Aug., 1933. K. ADAM, Die Eucharistielehre des hl. A., 1908; cfr. also § 68. G. LECORDIER, La doctrine de l'Eucharistie chez S. Aug., Diss. Strasb. 1930 (also K. Adam, ThQ 1931, 490/536). D. ZÄHRINGER, Das kirchl. Priestertum nach dem hl. A., 1931. W. ROETZER, Des hl. A. Schriften als liturgiegeschichtl. Quellen, 1930. J. ZELLINGER, A. u. die Volksfrömmigkeit, 1933. H. EGER, Die Eschatologie A.s, 1933. N. MERLIN, F. M. MELLET, A. ZUMKELLER, § 72, 6.

of Calama (Vita S. Augustini written about 432). Augustine was born at Thagaste in Numidia on November 13, 354. His father, Patricius, was a worldly-minded pagan, who was baptized on his deathbed; his mother, *Monica,* a convinced Christian, was destined to exert a powerful influence on her son. At Madaura and Carthage, Augustine received the higher education to equip him for a teaching career. Although he had been received into the catechumenate as a child and instructed in the rudiments of religion by his pious mother, he joined the sect of the Manicheans while a student and for nine years (374—383) adhered to the sect, but never advanced in it beyond the rank of an 'auditor.' The great appeal which Manicheism held for him was the promise it gave of leading him to higher truth without the necessity of submitting to revelation. When the promise was not fulfilled Augustine began to wonder whether there was a way to true wisdom. But his craving for truth and a certain love for Christ which he had imbibed with his mother's milk and never entirely lost were important factors in turning his mind in the right direction. A conversion of heart and mind began to take place at *Milan* in 384 where Augustine held a position as teacher of rhetoric. The admonitions and prayers of his mother who had followed him to Milan, the preaching and powerful example of Bishop *Ambrose,* the study of Neo-Platonic authors — Augustine never entirely abandoned Neoplatonism — the reading of St. Paul's Epistles and the soul-stirring experiences in the garden at Milan in the summer of 386 when he heard a voice saying: 'Tolle, lege' Rom. 13:13 f.), all led to a momentous decision. He immediately resigned his post as teacher to be able to give his full attention

B. BLUMENKRANZ, Die Judenpredigt A.s, 1946.  F. X. EGGERSDORFER, Der hl. A. als Pädagoge, 1907.  J. HOGGER, Die Kinderpsychologie A.s, 1937. J. MAUSBACH, Die Ethik des hl. A., 2 vols. ²1929.  O. SCHILLING, Die Staats- u. Soziallehre des hl. A., 1910; Naturrecht und Staat nach der Lehre der alten Kirche, 1914.  B. ROLAND-GOSSELIN, La morale de S. Aug., Paris 1925. O. REUL, Die sittl. Ideale des hl. A., 1928.  H. JONAS, A. u. das paulin. Freiheitsproblem, 1930.  B. SWITALSKI, Neuplatonism and the Ethics of S. Aug. I, New York 1946.  W. ZIEGENFUSS, A., Christl. Transzendenz in Gesellsch. u. Gesch., 1948.  E. TRÖLTSCH, A., die christl. Antike u. das MA., 1915.  J. HESSEN, A. u. seine Bedeutung für die Gegenwart, 1924.  R. REITZENSTEIN, A. als antiker u. mittelalt. Mensch, Bibliothek Warburg, Vorträge I, 1923, 28/65.  M. GRABMANN, Mittelalterl. Geistesleben II, 1936, 1/62 (A.s influence on the MA.).  G. BARDY, A l'école de S. Aug., Ecully 1947.  A. MASNOVO, S. Agostino e S. Tommaso, Milan 1950.  L. SMITS, RHE 1950, 670/87 (Calvin and A.).  Cfr. lit. in § 56 and 57. Über den dreieinigen Gott, ausgew. und übertr. von M. SCHMAUS, ²1951.  B. CAPELLE, RLAntChr I, 981 ff.  F. VAN DER MEER, (see above) German transl. Aug. der Seelsorger by N. GREITEMANN, 1951.  P. COURCELLE, Recherches sur les Confessions de S. Augustin, Paris 1950.

to the step he had determined to take. With his son Adeodatus
(† 390) and a few friends he retired to Cassiciacum near Milan
where he spent his time in prayer and discussion. By Easter of
387 he was ready for baptism which he received from Ambrose.
The little party then set out for Africa, but Monica, her prayers
now answered, took ill on the way and died at Ostia in the autumn
of 387. After returning to Africa, Augustine did not long enjoy the
solitude he had planned. Called to the priesthood in an unexpected
manner, he was ordained in 391 for the church of *Hippo Regius*, a
Numidian port near the present city of Bône. Augustine's learning,
piety and eloquence caused Valerius, the aged bishop of Hippo,
to choose him as his coadjutor in 395 and a year later when Valerius
died, Augustine succeeded him in the see. He was then 42 years old.
As bishop he continued to live with his clergy the monastic life
he had begun at Thagaste before ordination to the priesthood
(§ 60, 2). Besides being a model shepherd of souls, he studied,
meditated and wrote so that even during his lifetime no name was
better known or more highly respected than Augustine of Hippo.
In the early summer of 430, the Vandals under Genseric besieged
the city of Hippo which held out for three months before surrender-
ing. Just as the enemy prepared for the final attack, Augustine
died, August 28, 430.

As a scholar, Augustine combined the idealism, the acute intelligence and mystical warmth of the Greeks with the practical
mind and psychological penetration of the Latins. His manifold
gifts which enabled him to deal with abstract problems or practical
issues, his dialectical skill which made him a formidable controver-
sialist, his style and power of expression as a writer, the diligence
with which he worked to the end of his life, especially the habit
he formed of seeing everything in relation to God, whom he loved
with all the ardor of his impassioned soul, explain the universal
influence he has exerted on all succeeding generations. The Protestant von Harnack says: "Even today we live by Augustine, by
his thought and his spirit." (Augustins Konfessionen). Much of
Augustine's attention was directed to questions of Christian anthropology: the relation of man to God; the problems of sin and grace,
and the Church as the institution for man's salvation. On all
of these questions Augustine's views developed as he studied and
meditated. At times he even reversed his former opinions. Much
of his work, especially after he became bishop, was devoted to

controversy, or more correctly, to an effort to show the truth of the Christian religion against the errors of the *Manicheans, Donatists* (§ 52, 3), *Pelagians* (§ 56) and *Semipelagians* (§ 57). It was while combatting the rationalistic teachings of Pelagianism that Augustine treated in greater extent and depth than any one before him the traditional doctrine of grace and merited the title "Doctor Gratiae." All of the heresies prevalent in his day were given special attention and one work, De haeresibus, treats of all heresies from Simon Magus to Pelagius. Eight of Augustine's philosophical works are extant, some written before and some after his baptism. Two works written by Augustine have long been classed as masterpieces of world literature: the Confessions and the City of God. The *Confessions*[1], written about the year 400 is a sort of autobiography, yet not so much a history as it is a prayer of praise and thanksgiving to God for the guidance and blessings vouchsafed the author. Although Augustine is unduly severe in judging himself, the account he gives of his life down to the date of writing is trustworthy. The twenty-two books of the *City of God*[2], written from

[1] Editions of the text, see above. A. HARNACK, Augustins Konfessionen, [3]1903 (lecture); Aus der Friedens- u. Kriegsarbeit, 1916, 67/91. J. NOERREGAARD, C. F. BALMUS, M. P. GARVEY, see above. M. ZEPF, A.s Confessiones, 1926. H. GROS, La valeur documentaire des Confessions de S. Aug., Paris 1928. F. BILLICSICH, Studien zu den Bekenntnissen des hl. Aug., 1929. W. THIMME, A.s Selbstbildnis in den Konfessionen, 1929. G. WUNDERLE, Einführung in A.s Konfessionen, 1930. P. SCHÄFER, Das Schuldbewußtsein in den Confessiones des hl. A., 1930. W. J. S. SIMPSON, S. Augustine's Conversion, New York 1930. A. D. NOCK, Conversion the Old and New in Religion from Alexander the Great to Augustine, Oxford 1933. G. BARDY, La conversion au christianisme durant les premiers siècles, Paris 1949. R. GUARDINI, Die Bekehrung des Aur. Augustinus, [2]1950; Antike 1934, 169/94; Anfang (Conf. I, 1/5), [2]1950. I. FREYER, Erlebte u. systemat. Gestaltung in A.s Konfessionen, 1937. P. HENRY, La vision d'Ostie, Paris 1938. M. HEIM, Der Enthusiasmus in d. Konf. des hl. A., Diss. 1941; also ThRev 1942, 114/7. Cfr. the essays by H. BÖHMER, NkZ 1915, 419 ff. 487 ff.; M. WUNDT, ZntW 1922, 53 ff.; 1923, 161 ff.; H. DÖRRIES, ib. 1924, 64/102; E. WILLIGER, ib. 1929, 81/106; J. STIGLMAYR, Scholastik 1932, 387/403; J. GEFFCKEN, ArchRelW 1934, 1/13 (on Tolle, lege); also J. BÖHMER, Bibl. Z. 1935, 58/61; A. PINCHERLE, see above: P. L. LANDSBERG, La vie spirituelle, Suppl. 48, 1936, 31/56.

[2] Editions of the text, see above. C. LAMBERT, RevBén 1939, 109/21 (an unedited letter of A. on De civit. Dei). H. SCHOLZ, Glaube u. Unglaube in der Weltgesch., ein Kommentar zu Augustins De civ. Dei, 1911. E. BERNHEIM, Mittelalterl. Zeitanschauungen in ihrem Einfluß auf Politik u. Geschichtschreibung I, 1918, 10 ff. J. N. FIGGIS, The Political Aspects of S. Augustine's City of God, London 1921. U. SCHRÖDER, A.s Ansicht vom christl. Staat als Glied der Civ. Dei, Diss. 1922. E. SALIN, Civ. Dei, 1926. H. FUCHS, A. u. der antike Friedensgedanke, 1926. P. V. SOKOLOWSKI, Der hl. A. u. die christl. Zivilisation, 1927. G. COMBÈS, La doctrine politique de S. Aug., Paris 1927 (also O. SCHILLING, ThQ 1928, 398/410). V. STEGEMANN, Augustins Gottesstaat, 1928. R. FRICK, Gesch. des Reichgottesgedankens in der alten Kirche bis Origenes und Aug., 1928. K. HEUSSI, Vom Sinn der Ge-

412 to 426, is both a magnificent outline for a philosophy of history
and an apology of Christianity in historical form. Beginning with
the collapse of the Roman Empire, Augustine sees society divided
into two groups — the Civitas Dei and the Civitas terrena — with
the destiny of the world dependent upon the Christian religion.
For although the two cities will always be in strife, God is not indifferent to the struggle and in everything that happens is preparing
for the ultimate triumph of the Civitas Dei. This *opus grande* had
a tremendous influence on the policy of Church and State during
the Middle Ages. The Enchiridion ad Laurentium or De fide, spe,
et caritate is a summary of dogma, while De Trinitate on which
Augustine spent 15 years, is a profound contemplation of the
Trinity. De doctrina christiana is a combination of a doctrinal
synthesis, a treatise on hermaneutics and a treatise on preaching
for the clergy. In the field of pastoral theology Augustine wrote
two treatises dealing with lying, five on marriage and virginity, two
model catechisms and a treatise on how to instruct catechumens.
Finally he left about 400 sermons and over 200 letters, many of
which are short treatises on philosophy and points of theology.
His correspondence with Jerome is particularly interesting. Toward
the end of his life (427) he wrote two books called Retractationes
which enumerate his ninety-three works, give the purpose, the
circumstances under which they were written and add some
corrections and explanations.

4. **Prudentius** Aurelius Clemens*[1], († after 405), a Spanish layman and high official under Theodosius, is the greatest Latin poet

---

schichte, Aug. u. die Moderne, 1930 (lecture).   E. GÖLLER, Die Staats- u.
Kirchenlehre As. u. ihre Fortwirkung im Mittelalter, 1931 (lecture).   H.
X. ARQUILLIÈRE, L'Augustinisme politique. Essai sur la formation des théo-
ries politiques du moyen âge. Paris 1934.   H. N. BAYNES, The Political Ideas
of S. Augustine's De civ. Dei, London 1936 (18 S.).   C. V. V. HORN, Beiträge
zur Staatslehre S. Augustins nach De civ. Dei, 1934.   RUD. SCHNEIDER,
Welt u. Kirche bei A., 1949.   J. H. S. BURLEIGH, The City of God, London
1950. Cfr. also the essays of H. LINDAU, ZKG 1918, 406/32; H. HERMELINCK,
Festgabe A. v. Harnack, 1921, 302/24; G. BEYERHAUS, HZ 127, 1923, 189/209;
H. LEISEGANG, Archiv f. Kulturgesch. 1926, 227/58; K. MÜLLER, ZntW 1928,
201/11; E. LEWALTER, ZKG 1934, 1/51; B. JANSEN, Der kath. Gedanke 1935,
74/79; E. HOFFMANN, in Essays presented to E. CASSIRER, Oxford 1936,
173/90 (Platonism in A.'s philosophy of history); W. KAMLAH, Philologus
1938, 248/64 (Ecclesia u. Regnum Dei in A.); Christentum u. Selbstbehauptung, 1940.   K. H. SCHELKLE see above.

¹ PL 59/60; ed. A. DRESSEL, 1860; H. J. THOMSON I, Cambridge Mass.
1949 (with English transl.).   R. J. DEFERRARI and J. M. CAMPBELL, A Concordance of Prudentius, ib. 1932.   Best edition of the Carmina by J. BERG-
MAN, 1926 (CSEL 61).   Monogr. by A. RÖSLER, 1886; A. PUECH, Paris 1888;
J. BERGMAN, Dorpat 1922.   E. K. RAND, Prudentius and Christian Humanism,

of the fourth century. The work called Cathemerinon, or hymns for every day, contains several hymns still used in the Breviary. The Peristephanon is a collection of hymns in honor of the martyrs. The Psychomachia or spiritual combat; the Hamartigenia, or origin of sin, the Apotheosis and Contra Symmachum, a refutation of paganism, are all single poems of some length. Prudentius, who seems to have been somewhat careless in the practice of religion in his earlier years, became more fervent as he grew older and sought to make reparation by writing his truly religious poems to glorify the faith and lead men to God.

5. **Juvencus**\*\* († c. 380) was a Spanish priest of noble birth who, about the year 330, wrote the Gospel story in hexameter. (Ed. by *J. Huemer*, 1891; F. Laganá, Giovenco, Catania 1947).

**Julius Firmicus Maternus**\*\*, a rhetorician of Sicily, while still a pagan (c. 336), wrote an apologetical work called Matheseos libri VIII. Later, as a Christian (c. 348), he addressed a rather violent pamphlet to the emperors Constans and Constantius called De errore profanarum religionum in which he attacks paganism (§ 41, 2), especially the mystery cults. G. Morin also ascribes to Maternus the anonymous Consultationes Zacchaei et Apollonii, which is a systematic exposition and defense of the faith with an instruction on Christian life in the form of a dialogue between Zacchaeus, a Christian, and Apollonius, a pagan philosopher. However, this latter work is known to belong to the fifth century. — Matheseos libri VIII, edd. W. Kroll, F. Skutsch et K. Ziegler, 2 vols. 1897/1913. — De errore prof. relig., ed. K. Ziegler, 1908; German by A. Müller in BKV 14, 1913. — *G. Heuten*, J. Firmicus Maternus, De errore prof. relig., texte avec trad. et commentaire, Brux. 1938. — *F. Boll*, RE Pauly-Wissowa VI, 2365/79. — *P. Henry*, Plotin et l'Occident. Firmicus Maternus, Marius Victorinus, S. Augustin et Macrobe, Louvain 1934. — *T. Wickström*. In Firmicum Mat. studia critica, Diss. Uppsala 1935. — Consultationes Zacchaei etc. in PL 20, 1071/166; critical ed. by *G. Morin*, 1935 (Floril. patrist. 39); cfr. id. in HJG 1916, 229/66; RevBén 1934, 456/9. — Vs. Morin: *B. Axelson*, Bull. de la Soc. des lettres de Lund 1936/7 IV, 107/32; B. Altaner, ThRev 1938, 55 f. — *A. Reatz*, Das theol. System der Consult. Zacchaei et Apoll., 1920. — *F. Cavallera*, RevAM 1935, 132/46 (spiritual life according to the Consult.).

Cajus **Marius Victorinus** († after 362), an African, taught rhetoric and Neo-Platonic philosophy at Rome during the reign of Constantius. His conversion at a ripe age created something of a sensation and his example and

Cleveland 1920. C. WEYMAN, Beiträge (see lit. at the beginning of § 76) 61/87. Z. G. VILLADA, Hist. eclesiastica de España I, 2, 1929, 155/209. G. MEYER, Prudentiana, Philologus 1932, 249 ff. 332 ff.; 1938, 377/403. M. MANITIUS, HistVS 1933, 142/53. M. LAVARENNE, Étude sur la langue du poète Prudence, Thèse Paris 1933; Prudence, 3 vol., Paris 1943/8 (Text and transl.). J. STAM, Prud., Hamartigenia (Text and transl.), Diss. Leyden 1940. J. RODRIGUEZ-HERRERA, Poeta christianus, Prudentius' Auffassung vom Wesen u. von der Aufgabe des christl. Dichters, Diss. 1936.

translations of Neo-Platonic works were not without effect on Augustine (cfr. Conf. 8, 2). After his conversion Victorinus, without sufficient theological knowledge, wrote against Arianism and commented on the Pauline Epistles. His notions regarding free will influenced Augustine and his philosophical terminology recurs at times in the language of the medieval schools. — PL 8. — *P. Monceaux*, Hist. litt. de l'Afrique chrét. III, Paris 1905, 373/422. — B. Citterio, C. M. Vittorino, Brescia 1948. — *A. Souter*, The Earliest Latin Commentaries on the Epistles of S. Paul, Oxford 1927, 8/38. — *E. Benz*, Marius Vict. u. die Entwicklung der abendl. Willensmetaphysik, 1932 (also M. Schmaus, ThRev 1933, 345/58). — *P. Henry*, see under J. Firm. Maternus; also JThSt 1950, 42/55 (Adversus Arium).

**Lucifer\*\***, Bishop of Cagliari († 370) was a vigorous opponent of the Arians and of Emperor Constantius (§ 50, 3). **Optatus\*\***, Bishop of Mileve († after 384) denounced the Donatists (§ 52). Pope **Damasus** (366—384) is known as the author of several poems, metrical sepulchral inscriptions and letters (§ 64, 3).

**Zeno**, Bishop of Verona († c. 372) left ninety-three sermons or sketches of sermons (PL 11; ed. by J. B. C. Giuliari, Verona ²1900; German by A. Bigelmair, BKV 2, R. 10, 1934; monograph by the same, 1904; A. Grazioli, Scuola catt. 1940, 174 ff. 290 ff.; M. Stephanich, The Christology of Zeno of Verona, Washington 1948). — *Filastrius* (Philastrius),\*\* Bishop of Brescia († c. 390) wrote a liber de haeresibus (PL 12; ed. of F. Marx, 1898).

6. **Pacianus**, Bishop of Barcelona († c. 390) opposed the Novatians and is said to have originated the expression (Ep. I, 4): Christianus mihi nomen est, Catholicus vero cognomen. Several of his extant letters and treatises throw much light on the doctrine of penance. — PL 13. — De similitudine carnis peccati gegen die Manichäer, ed. *G. Morin*, Études, textes etc. I, Maredsous 1913, 81/150; cfr. RevBén 1913, 286/93 (Liber ad Iustinum Manichaeum); contrary opinion *J. Madoz*, Estudios exclesiásticos 1942, 27/54. — *E. Göller*, RQ 1928, 245/61 (doctrine of penance). — L. Wohleb, in Span. Forschungen der Görres-Ges. II, 1930, 25/35.

**Gregory**, Bishop of Elvira († after 392), was a leader of the Luciferians (§ 50, 3). Recent research strongly indicates that he was the author of the following: Five sermons on the Canticle of Canticles; twenty sermons formerly ascribed to Origen; Tractatus (sermons) de libris SS. Scripturarum (ed. P. Battifol, Paris 1900) erroneously ascribed to Novatian (§ 40, 4); Tractatus de arca Noe on the Church and a treatise De fide orthodoxa contra Arianos. — Opuscula omnia, ed. *A. C. Vega*, I. Escorial 1944. — *A. Wilmart*, BullLE 1906, 233/99; RevBén 1912, 47 ff. 274 ff.; cfr. *H. Koch*, ZKG 1922, 132/39; 1932, 238/72. — A. d'Alès, RechSR 1919, 314 ff. — *A. Vaccari*, Biblica 1922, 188/93. — *J. A. de Aldama* (see § 49), 89 ff.

7. Tyrannius (Turranius) **Rufinus\*** of Aquileia was educated at Rome and, as a pupil of Didymus the Blind at Alexandria, became an ardent admirer of Origen. From about 378 to 390 he lived as a hermit on Mt. Olivet near Jerusalem where he and Jerome continued the friendship begun in the West. But when the Origenist controversy began in 393, the former friends parted company (§ 51, 2). In 396 Rufinus returned to Italy (Rome) and died at Messina in 410. He did little original work (a commentary on the Apostle's

Creed, ed. C. A. Heurtley, 2 vols. Oxford 1916, and an explanation of Jacob's blessing); but translated many Greek authors into Latin, e. g. Origen (§ 39, 2), Pamphilus (§ 39, 6), Eusebius' Ecclesiastical History (which he brought down to 395), the Clementine Recognitions (§ 28, 4), the Historia monachorum in Aegypto (§ 72, 6). However, in his translations he took great liberties with the original texts. — PL 21. — Cfr. lit. in § 51, 2 (Villain) and 76, 2 (*Brochet* etc.). — *H. Hoppe*, Studi ded. alla memoria di P. Ubaldi, Milano 1937, 133/50 (Ruf. as translator). — *F. X. Murphy*, Rufinus of Aquileia, Washington 1945. — *M. Wagner*, Rufinus, the Translator, Washington 1945.

The Spanish priest **Orosius\*\*** († after 417), friend and admirer of Augustine and opponent of the Priscillianists and Pelagians (§ 56, 3) and **Sulpicius Severus\*\*** of Aquitaine († c. 420), have already been mentioned as historians (§ 4, 2). The latter was also author of the famous biography of Martin of Tours (§ 72, 6).

**Nicetas**, Bishop of Remesiana in Dacia († after 414) was a zealous and successful missionary in the Balkan countries and a friend of Paulinus of Nola. He composed a series of instructions for catechumens in six books, of which the fifth book, Explanatio Symboli, is extant. Two of his sermons on the celebration of vigils and the singing of the Psalms have also been preserved. He wrote a number of hymns and is probably the author of the *Te Deum* (§ 67, 7). — Monogr. and edition by *A. E. Burn*, Cambridge 1905. — *W. A. Patin*, Niceta v. R., Diss. 1909. — *C. H. Turner*, JThSt 22, 1921, 305/20; 24, 1923, 225/52. — On the Te Deum see lit. § 67, 7.

**Paulinus\*\***, Bishop of Nola († 431) was born at Bordeaux of an illustrious patrician family and was the pupil and friend of *Ausonius*, the poet. At an early age he was appointed Governor of Campania, but after his baptism in 390 he resigned his high office and distributed his great wealth to the poor; and he and his wife retired to Nola to live as ascetics near the tomb of St. Felix of Nola, toward whom they had a special devotion. In 409 he was elected bishop of Nola. He was in correspondence with all the great writers of the day, a fact which lends his extant letters interest and value for historical study. His poems, many of which are in honor of St. Felix, are full of deep piety and charm. — *Ed. W. Hartel*, 2 vol. 1894. — P. Fabre, Essai sur la chronologie de l'oeuvre de S. Paulin de N., Paris 1948; S. Paulin de N. et l'amitié chrét., Paris 1949. — R. C. Goldschmidt, Paulinus' Churches, Amsterdam 1940 (Text and transl.). Monogr. by A. Buse, 1856; F. Lagrange, Paris ²1882, German 1882; *A. Baudrillart*, Paris ²1905. — G. Rizza, Catania 1947. — *P. Reinelt*, Studien über die Briefe des hl. Paulinus v. N., Diss. 1904. — *H. Leclercq*, DictAC XII, 1439/57.

8. **Marius Mercator** († after 451) seems to have been an African by birth and was probably a layman. His Commonitoria relating to the Pelagian controversy were mentioned in § 56, 4. The translations he made of various documents for the benefit of the West are quite exact. **John Cassian\*\*** († c. 435) distinguished abbot, ascetical writer and Semipelagian was mentioned in § 57, 2 and 72, 6. The writings of **Vincent**, priest of the monastery of Lèrins († c. 450) and of **Arnobius the Younger**, a monk at Rome about 450, both Semipelagians, are also described in § 57, 3. The layman **Prosper** of Aquitaine († 463) defended the views of St. Augustine (§ 57, 3). Besides polemical treatises

against the Massilians, he also compiled a chronicle of world history which is a summary of Jerome's Chronicle (§ 4, 1) up to 378. From then on to 455 it is an original and valuable work. (PL 51, Chronicon; ed. *T. Mommsen* MG Auct. antiq. IX, 1892, 341 ff. See bibl. § 57). It seems probable that he also wrote the charming work De vocatione omnium gentium. But the valuable and edifying work, De vita contemplativa (PL 59, 415/520; English translation by M. J. Suelzer, Westminster, Md), sometimes ascribed to him was written by the priest Julian **Pomerius** († c. 498) of Mauretania (J. C. Plumpe, VC 1947, 227/39).

**Eucherius\***, first a monk at Lèrins, then Bishop of Lyons († c. 450), wrote Formulae spiritualis intelligentiae and Instructiones, both of which were widely read during the Middle Ages. They aimed at providing a solution to various difficult passages in Holy Scripture. He also wrote the Passio Agaunensium martyrum (§ 16, 4). PL 50; ed. K. Wotke, 1894.

**Commodianus\*\***, a layman and ascetic ("mendicus Christi" Instr. 2, 39) probably from Gaza, composed Instructiones, eighty ascetical poems in rhymed hexameter in which he appeals to pagans and Jews to embrace Christianity and to Christians to lead lives pleasing to God. He also wrote Carmen apologeticum, an exposition of the Christian religion. The latter work shows him to have been a Chiliast and a Sabellian (§ 32; 33). His nationality and the time at which he wrote are still points of debate among scholars. Many think that he was a countryman and contemporary of St. Cyprian (*Zeller, Martin* and others); but there are equally good reasons for believing (*Brewer* and others) that he wrote in the second half of the fifth century and that he was a native of Southern Gaul (Arles). — *Ed. B. Dombart*, 1887. — *A. F. Van Katwijk*, Lexicon Commodianeum, Amsterdam 1934. — Monogr. by J. Durel, Paris 1912. — H. Brewer, 1906. Die Frage um das Zeitalter K.s, 1910; ZkTh 1912, 641 ff. 849 ff. — *F. Zeller*, Die Zeit K.s, Diss. 1909 (from ThQ 1909/10). — *J. Martin*, TU 39, 4, 1913; Sb. Wien 181, 6, 1917. — *Ed. Rein*, Schriften d. Univ. Helsingfors 1923, 1/89. — *L. Gasparetti*, Didaskaleion 1926, 1/48. — H. Lietzmann, ZntW 1939, 313.

9. Pope **Leo I the Great** (440— 461) (§ 64, 4) was renowned as a *preacher*; possibly the best after Augustine. **Peter Chrysologus**, Archbishop of Ravenna († c. 450) was also a preacher of great fame; but he adhered too closely to the pattern set by contemporary rhetoricians (PL 52; German BKV 43, 1923 and H. Franke 1946; Monog. by *F. J. Peters*, 1918 and *G. Böhmer*, 1919; cfr. *J. H. Baxter*, JThSt 1921, 250/58; D. de Bruyne, JThSt 1928, 362/68; *H. Koch*, RE Pauly-Wissowa XIX, 1361/72). **Maximus**, Bishop of Turin († after 465) (PL 57; C. H. Turner and A. Spagnolo, JThSt 1915/16/19; U. Moricca, Didaskaleion 1929 1/40; B. Capelle, RevBén 1933, 108/18; O. Heggelbacher, Maximus von Turin und sein Bibeltext, Diss. 1945). **Quodvultdeus**, Bishop of Carthage († c. 453) was a disciple of Augustine (§ 43, 6) and **Faustus\*\*** Bishop of Reji († c. 490), mentioned in § 57, 3 was an opponent of Augustine and a Semipelagian.

**Salvianus\*\***, a priest of Marseilles († c. 480) portrayed the moral conditions at the time of the collapse of the Empire and its clash with the invading Germans (§ 73, 1). He was noted as a preacher who called attention to the invasions as a punishment of God, and, like Augustine, saw God's providence in the confusion. He wrote De gubernatione Dei libri VIII; Ad ecclesiam vel Adversus avaritiam and several letters still extant. — PL 53; ed. *C. Halm*, MG Auct. antiq. I, 1, 1877; ed. *F. Pauly*, 1883 (CSEL 8); German in BKV 2. R. 11, 1935. — Monogr. by W. Zschimmer, 1875; M. Pellegrino, Rome 1939. — *G. Sternberg*, ThStKr 1909, 29 ff. 163 ff. — *L. Rochus*, La latinité de Salvien, Acad. R. de Belgique, Classe d. Lettres 30, 2, Brux. 1934. — *A. Schäfer*, Römer u. Germanen bei Salvian, 1930. — *O. Janssen*, L'expressivité chez Salvien de M. I, Nymwegen 1937. — *J. Fischer* and *P. Courcelle*, see § 43.

**Gennadius,** († c. 500), also a priest of Marseilles, continued Jerome's De viris illustribus under the same title (for editions see § 76, 2) and wrote a Liber ecclesiasticorum dogmatum (ed. *C. H. Turner*, JThSt 1905, 78/99; 1906, 103/14) which in its present form is perhaps only the conclusion of a larger work, Adversus omnes haereses, which has been lost. — PL 58. — *B. Czapla*, G. als Literarhistoriker, 1898. — *H. Koch*, Vinzenz v. Lerin u. Gennadius, TU 31, 2 b, 1907. — *A. Feder*, Scholastik 1927, 481 ff.; 1928, 238 ff.; 1933, 217 ff. 380 ff.

Two *Africans* belonging to the second half of the fifth century also deserve notice: **Vigilius,** Bishop of Thapsus, an opponent of Arianism and Monophysitism (PL 62. Monogr. of *G. Ficker*, 1897) and **Victor\*\*,** Bishop of Vita († c. 485), who wrote a history of the Vandal persecutions (§ 43, 6).

10. It is not possible to determine with any degree of certainty the authorship or date of composition of the **Peregrinatio ad loca sancta\*\*** (§ 70, 5) and the **Opus imperfectum in Matthaeum.** The latter is an important and interesting commentary (PG 56, 611/946) which as late as the sixteenth century passed as a work of St. John Chrysostom, but which Erasmus proved to be the work of an Arian. Since then it has been ascribed to *Ulfilas* († 383) or another bishop of the Goths named *Maximinus* who in 427 or 428 disputed with St. Augustine. *J. Stiglmayr* (ZkTh 1910, 1 ff. 473 ff.), thinks that it is a free rendition of a Greek original by a priest of Constantinople named Timothy (410—420). *G. Morin* (RevBén 1925, 239/62) thinks that the author lived about the middle of the sixth century in Illyria or Upper Italy and that he was the one who translated Origen's Commentary on Matthew. — *Th. Paas*, Das Opus imp. in Mt., Diss. 1907. — Fr. Kauffmann, Zur Textgesch. des O. i., 1909. — *E. Riggenbach*, Theol. Literaturblatt 1926, 33/5.

## § 77.
## Greek Theology of the Sixth and Seventh Centuries[1].

1. About the middle of the fifth century, after the long drawn out religious controversies, Greek theology became less productive

---

[1] O. BARDENHEWER, GeschAL V, 1932 (Leontius of Byzantium to John of Damascus). K. KRUMBACHER, Gesch. der byzant. Lit. (527—1453), ²1897; and pp. 37/218; A. EHRHARD, Die griech. Theologie; pp. 653/705: K. KRUMBACHER, Die griech. Kirchenpoesie. K. STAAB, Die Pauluskatenen, Rome 1926; Commentaries on St. Paul, § 75. R. DEVREESSE, Chaînes exégétiques grecques, Dict. de la Bible, Suppl. I, Paris 1928, 1084/233. J. REUSS, Matth.-, Markus- u. Joh.-Katenen, 1941. A. EHRHARD, Überlieferung u. Bestand usw., § 74. FR. DIEKAMP, Analecta Patristica, § 75. H. BECK,

and less original. Interest in the scientific study of dogma yielded place to interest in liturgy and ascetics. Collections of excerpts from the writings of Biblical commentators, exspecially the Fathers were strung together like links in a *chain* (hence, catenae) to give a connected interpretation of a text of Scripture. In like manner the dogmatic or moral teachings of eminent Fathers and theologians on a given subject were collected in *Florilegia*. The largest and most important work of the latter type was the *Doctrina patrum de incarnatione Verbi*[1] compiled about the end of the seventh century, most probably by Anastasius Sinaita (vide infra) and aimed chiefly at combatting Monophysitism and Monotheletism.

There were however, several writers of note in this period. The first important group of writings bore the name of Dionysius the Areopagite[2], later called **Pseudo-Dionysius** or **Pseudo-Areopagite.** Shortly before the year 500 he composed, apparently in Syria or Pa-

Vorsehung u. Vorherbestimmung in der theol. Literatur der Byzantiner (OrChrAn 114), Rome 1938 (important for theological literature).

[1] Ed. princeps von F. DIEKAMP, 1907. Cfr. J. STIGLMAYR, Byz. Z. 1909, 14/40; W. M. PEITZ, HJG 1917, 452 f.

[2] PG 3—4. PH. CHEVALIER, Dionysiaca, Suppl. à Migne (Latin translations), 2 vol. Paris 1937/50). A. VAN DEN DAELE, Indices Ps.-Dionysiani, Löwen 1941. On the Latin translations of the Ps.-Dionysius in the MA. (two in each of the IX, XIII and XV c.): G. THÉRY, Études Dionysiennes I: Hilduin, 2 vol. Paris 1932/7; M. GRABMANN, Mittelalterliches Geistesleben I, 1929, 449/68; M. BUCHNER, Die Areopagitika des Abtes Hilduin v. St. Denis, 1939. Auswahl deutsch von J. STIGLMAYR in BKV 2, 1911 u. 2. R. 2, 1933. English transl. by C. E. ROLT, London 1920; W. WATTS, New York 1944. French transl. by M. DE GANDILLAC, Paris 1943. J. STIGLMAYR, Der Neuplatoniker Proklus als Vorlage des sog. Dionysius Areop., HLG 1895, 253 ff. 721 ff. H. KOCH, Pseudo-Dionysius Areop., in seinen Beziehungen zum Neuplatonismus u. Mysterienwesen, 1900. Further works of STIGLMAYR and KOCH to 1909 are cited in BARDENHEWER, GeschAL IV, 282/99. H. F. MÜLLER, Dionysios, Proklos, Plotinos, ²1926. J. DURANTEL, S. Thomas et le Pseudo-Denis, Paris 1919. H. BALL, Byzantin. Christentum, 1923, 63/247. J. STIGLMAYR, Scholastik 1927, 161/207 (asceticism and mysticism in Ps.-Dionysius); 1928, 1 ff. 161 ff.; 1932, 52 ff. (Ps.-Dionysius = Severus of Antioch); contrary opinion J. LEBON, RHE 1930, 880/915; 1932, 296/313; R. DEVREESSE, ArchHistMA 1930, 159/68; G. BARDY, La Vie spirituelle 1931, 43/8. K. RICHSTÄTTER, StZ 114, 1928, 241/59 (Ps.-Dionys. the "Father of christian mysticism"). G. THÉRY, The New Scholasticism 3, 1929, 353/442 (on the Greek text). W. JAEGER, Der neuentdeckte Kommentar z. Johannesevangelium u. Dionysius Areop., Sb. Berlin 1930, 26. E. STEPHANOU, Échos d'Orient 1932, 446/69 (bibliography 1918/32); 1934, 125 ff. C. PERA O. P., Denys le Mystique et la theomachia, RecSPhTh 1936, 5/75; contrary F. CAVALLERA, RevMA 1936, 90/5. I. HAUSHERR, OrChrPer 1936, 484/90 (Eastern doubts about Dionysius). V. LOSSKY, RevSPhTh 1939, 204/41 (the "negative" theology of Ps.-D.); Essai sur la théologie mystique de l'Église d'Orient, Paris 1944. E. V. JVÁNKA, Scholastik 1940, 386/99 (second half of IV cent.). O. SEMMELROTH, ib. 1949, 367 ff.; 1950, 209 ff. 389 ff. (concept of God and Redeemer). L. BAUR, Nik. Cusanus u. Ps.-D., Sb. Heidelberg 1940/1, 4. J. M. HORNUS, RevHPhR 1947, 37/63 (mysticism).

lestine, four treatises and eleven letters in extremely poor, very often obscure, style. The treatises were entitled: De divinis nominibus, De mystica theologia, De caelesti hierarchia, De ecclesiastica hierarchia. The evident purpose of the treatises was to place *Neo-Platonic* theosophy at the service of the Christian Church, her worship, her sacramental system and her asceticism. The leading thought throughout is that the intelligent being comes forth from God and returns to Him. The ascent of man to a higher world, his union with God is accomplished by means of a three-fold process: purification, illumination and union. The author makes it appear that he is Dionysius the Areopagite of Athens, whom St. Paul converted (Acts 17:34). During the Middle Ages it was believed that he was the first bishop of Paris. In the religious conferences at Constantinople in 533 (§ 58, 2), the Monophysite Patriarch Severus and the Severians cited these writings as apostolic; but the Catholics rejected them as apochryphal and no one now defends their authenticity. *J. Stiglmayr* and *H. Koch* have definitely proved that the author was a disciple of the pagan Neo-Platonist *Proclus* († 485). Many scholars, too, see in the expressions used a resemblance to the vague language of the Henoticon of 482 (§ 55, 4); but no one has yet succeeded in identifying the author. Stiglmayr at one time thought that the works were possibly written by the Patriarch Severus, mentioned above. But no other scholars concurred in this opinion. C. Pera, even less convincingly, endeavored to find the author among the disciples of the Cappadocians of the fourth century, more specifically in the school of Basil the Great; and E. Elorduy (Estudios Ecclesiasticos 1944, 501/57) ascribed the works to Ammonius Saccas. After being rejected as apochryphal by the orthodox, the Pseudo-Dionysian writings were eventually accepted even by Catholics in the East but especially in the West. In the ninth century, Abbot Hilduin of St. Denis and John Scotus Eriugena translated them into Latin, and later, others did the same. They exerted a tremendous influence on Scholasticism, Mysticism and liturgics of the Middle Ages. The belief that they originated with a disciple of St. Paul gave them almost canonical status. Lorenzo Valla, the Humanist († 1457) was the first to question their authenticity, which was defended by a few scholars as late as the twentieth century.

The Patriarch **Severus**[1] of Antioch († 538; § 55, 5) must be rated as one of the great theologians of the sixth century. As a loyal

---

[1] Liber contra impium Grammaticum, ed. J. LEBON, 3 vol. Paris 1929/38

disciple of Cyril of Alexandria, he endeavored with the help of the theology and philosophy of the fifth century to systematize Christological dogma; but he persistently upheld Monophysitism against Chalcedon. He left a great number of theological works almost exclusively in Syrian versions, very few of which have ever been edited. His Liber contra impium Grammaticum, an unknown adversary, was probably written about 520. It is a veritable mine of theological learning and literary skill and contains a wealth of citations from the Fathers not found elsewhere. Besides numerous letters and sermons, he wrote liturgical hymns, many of which are included in the Octoëkos, or hymnal used by the Greek Church today.

2. **Leontius** of Byzantium[1] († c. 543) was a theologican of subtle and penetrating intelligence, acquainted with Aristotelian logic and Neo-Platonic psychology. However, he must not be confused with another of the same name who defended the Theopaschite formula (§ 58, 2). Only a few of his writings are extant, the principal one being Libri tres adversus Nestorianos et Eutychianos, in which he cited the Fathers at great length to refute the two chief errors of his day. He explained Cyril's Christology so clearly as to destroy the argument on which the Monophysites defended their theory. They maintained that the human nature of Christ was ἀνυπόστατος, i. e., was without a person to support it, therefore, it could have no existence. Leontius showed that the human nature was rather ἐνυπόστατος, i. e., that it had subsistence in the Logos.

During the reign of Justinian (527—565) the greatest hymnologist, not only of the East, but in the opinion of many scholars, of the whole Church, made his appearance in the person of **St. Romanus**, the Melodist[2] ὁ μελῳδός († c. 560). He was a Syrian by birth

---

(CSCO, Syri IV, 5/6 and 51); cfr. H. G. OPITZ, ThLZ 1940, 130/6. Orationes ad Nephtalium, ed. J. LEBON, Louvain 1949 (CSCO, Syri IV, 7). Homiliae cathedrales 52/119 in Patrologia orientalis 4, 8, 12, 16, 20, 22, 23, 25, 26, Paris 1906/48 (Syrian and French transl.). J. LEBON, Le monophysitisme Sévérien, Louvain 1909. G. BARDY, Mémorial L. Petit, Bukarest 1948, 15/31 (patristic texts in Severus); DictThC 14, 1988/2000. See lit. in § 55, 5.

[1] PG 86. Monogr. on Leontius by F. LOOFS, TU 3, 1/2, 1887 (cfr. RE XI, 394/97; XXIV, 15); J. P. JUNGLAS, 1908. V. GRUMEL, DictThC IX, 400/26; Échos d'Orient 1937, 385/97 (Soteriology). R. DEVREESSE, RevSR 1930, 545/76. S. REES, HarvThR 1931, 111/9 (Christology); JThSt 1940, 263/80 (life and character). M. RICHARD, RevSPhTh 1938, 27/52 (Leontius and Pamphilus); MSR 1944, 35/88 (L. of Jerusalem and L. of Byzant). B. ALTANER, ThQ 1947, 147/65 (L. of Byz. and the Scythian monk Leontius).

[2] J. B. PITRA, Analecta sacra I, Paris 1876. K. KRUMBACHER, Sb. München 1898, 1899, 1901, 1903; Abh. München 1907. ROMANO IL MELODE,

but was incardinated among the clergy of Constantinople (as deacon or priest?). He is credited with more than a thousand hymns composed for the liturgy, of which about eighty-five are still extant. They are all characterized by depth of inspiration and a noble simplicity of style.

3. **Maximus**[1], surnamed **Confessor** († 662) for his vigorous resistance to court theology, was the outstanding Greek theologian of the seventh century. He was born at Constantinople about 580 of a prominent family and after serving as secretary to Emperor Heraclius, became a monk and abbot of the monastery of Chrysopolis (Scutari). Throughout his life he defended the faith against the Monothelite heresy. In 645 he held a public disputation at Carthage with Pyrrhus, the Monothelite Patriarch of Constantinople who had been exiled to Africa. He died on August 13, 662 from tortures inflicted in an attempt to force him to accept Monothelitism (§ 59, 2). Maximus was a versatile scholar, a sharp dialectician and a mystic. He may well be considered the founder of Byzantine mysticism based on sound dogmatic principles, and with equal right may be considered a forerunner of the great Scholastics of the Middle Ages. He composed many exegetical, dogmatic, controversial, ascetical and mystical works. The Quaestiones ad Thalassium resolves certain difficult passages of Holy Scripture; the Mystagogia is a mystical explanation of the Church and her liturgy;

---

INNI, ed. G. CAMMELLI, Firenze 1930 (Text and Italian transl.). E. MIONI, Romano il Melode, Saggio critico e dieci inni inediti, Torino 1937. PH. MEYER, RE XVII, 124/31; XXIV, 432 f. P. MAAS, Byz. Z. 1923, 1/13. C. CHEVALIER, RechSR 1938, 48/71 (Mariology of R.).

[1] PG 90—91. S. L. EPIFANOVIC, Matériaux pour servir à l'étude de la vie et des oeuvres de S. Maxime le Confesseur (Russian), Kiev 1917 (contains unedited Greek texts, cfr. RHE 1928, 803 f.). R. CANTARELLA, S. Massimo Conf., la mistagogia ed altri scritti (with transl.), Firenze 1931. Buch v. geistl. Leben, German by M. GARBAS, 1926. H. U. V. BALTHASAR, Die ,,Gnostischen Zenturien" (Sammlungen von je 100 Sentenzen) des Max. Conf., 1941; Kosmische Liturgie, 1941. B. HERMANN, Weisheit, die betet, 1941 (ausgew. Texte). Centuries sur la charité, French transl. by J. PEGON, Paris 1943. J. A. WAGENMANN-R. SEEBERG, RE XII, 457/70. H. STRAUBINGER, Die Christologie des Max. Konf., 1906. J. DRÄSEKE, ThStKr 1911, 20 ff. 204 ff. (Maximus C. and Scotus Erigena). W. SOPPA, Die Diversa Capita unter den Schriften des hl. Maximus K., Diss. 1918. J. STIGLMAYR and W. M. PEITZ, see § 59. V. GRUMEL, DictThC X, 448/59. R. DEVREESSE, AB 1928, 5/49 (Vita S. Maximi Conf.); RevSR 1937, 25/35 (Ep. 8 of Maximus C.). M. VILLER, RevAM 1930, 156 ff. 239 ff. (Evagrius Ponticus the source of Maximus C.). M. TH. DISDIER, Échos d'Orient 1930, 296/313 (foundations of piety). É. GILSON, Festschrift M. Grabmann, 1935, 188/95 (Maximus, Erigena, S. Bernard). J. LOOSEN, Logos u. Pneuma im begnadeten Menschen bei Max. C., 1941. G. PIERRES, Formula S. Johannis Damasceni . . ., Rome 1940 (John Dam. dependent on Max.; Florilegium Synodi Lateran. 649 by Max.).

the Liber asceticus is a dialogue on the duties of religious life. Besides these works he commented on the exegetical works of Gregory Nazianzus and also on the writings of Pseudo-Dionysius which he purified of their crass Neo-Platonism and brought into harmony with tradition. Maximus exerted a powerful influence on Greek theology and the Latin translation of his works had a lasting influence on the West.

4. Two Alexandrian Monophysites, the grammarian **John Philoponus**, about the middle of the sixth century, and the theologian, **Stephen Gobarus**, toward the end of the century (§ 55, 5), were called Tritheists because they held three natures in God. Both applied Aristotelian philosophy to theology and Stephen collected contradictory statements from the Fathers, much in the same way that Abelard did in the Middle Ages.

**Cosmas,** because of his travels to Arabia and East Africa, surnamed **Indicopleustes,** had been a merchant and became a hermit and a monk. He composed several works now lost, but his Christian Topography, written about 547, is extant in two manuscript copies and was considered an important contribution to geography in the Middle Ages. — Ed. *E. O. Winstedt,* Cambridge 1909. — *J. Wittmann,* Altsprachl. Untersuch. zu Kosmas Ind., Diss. 1914. — *H. Leclercq,* DictAC VIII, 820/49. — M. V. Anastos, Dumbarton Oaks Papers 3, Cambridge (Mass.), 1946, 73/80 (Topogr. written in Alexandria).

**John Climacus,** called the Scholastic (lawyer), was a monk, and later, abbot on Mt. Sinai († 649). He was one of the most popular ascetical writers of his day. His Scala Paradisi (Κλῖμαξ, ladder) was translated into various languages and was widely read by monks. Under the figure of Jacob's ladder, John would lead the monk through thirty stages or steps of a ladder to perfection. — PG 88. — *H. Ball,* (see above under Ps.-Dionysius) 1/60. — I. Hausherr, Orientalia Christ. 9, 2 (Rome 1927) 134/48. — *M. Viller* and *K. Rahner,* Aszese u. Mystik in der Väterzeit, 1939, 155/64. — G. Hofmann, OrChrPer 1941, 461/79 (Climacus in Photius).

**Sophronius** of Damascus († 638) was a learned monk in the monastery of Theodosius near Jerusalem and in 634 became Patriarch of the Holy City. He was the first to recognize the dangers of Monothelitism (§ 59, 2) and endeavored to bring Cyrus back to orthodoxy. He wrote sermons, lives of the saints and poems in anacreonitic meter. He is most probably identical with Sophronius the rhetorician (sophist) mentioned by Moschus. During the Middle Ages, Sophronius was considered the author of the very popular work Λειμών, Pratum spirituale, a collection of edifying stories about famous monks and ascetics similar to the Historia Lausiaca (§ 75, 7). However, the work was actually written by his friend and travelling companion **John Moschus** († 619) and dedicated to Sophronius who published it after John's death. — PG 87, 3. — Latin transl. of the Pratum spirituale by Ambrosius Traversari in PL 74, 119/240. — S. Vailhé, RevOC 1902, 360 ff.; 1903, 32 ff. 356 ff. — H. Usener, Der hl. Tychon, 1907, 80 ff. — *H. Straubinger,* Kath. 1907 I, 81 ff. 175 ff. 251 ff. (Trinitarian and Christological teaching of Sophronius). — *G. Zuretti,* Didaskaleion 1926, 19/68. — *Th. Nissen,* Byz. Z. 1937, 66/85; 1938, 351/76

(Pratum spirituale); 1939, 89/115; 349/81 (studies on Sophr.). — *G. Cosmas*, De oeconomia incarnationis sec. Sophronium Hierosolym., Rom 1940.

**Anastasius Sinaita** († after 700), abbot of the monastery at Mt. Sinai and opponent of Monophysitism wrote a number of works chiefly against that heresy. The principal work which can be safely ascribed to him is called ʽΟδηγός or Viae dux. He is also most probably the compiler of the Florilegium 'Doctrina patrum de incarnatione Verbi' mentioned in no. 1 above. — PG 89. — *J. B. Kumpfmüller*, De Anastasio Sin., 1865. — *F. Spačil*, La teologia di S. Anastasio Sin., Roma 1923 (from Bessarione IX).

# § 78.
## Latin Writers of the Sixth and Seventh Centuries[1].

1. There was also a decline in interest and productivity in the field of theology in the West during this period. The disturbances created by the *Migration of Nations* naturally interfered seriously with literary or scientific pursuits. But here more so than in the East there was enough intellectual activity that one may speak of a *rebirth* of patristic literature. It aimed chiefly at making a practical use of the great productions of the past. Very successful efforts were made at collecting and revising profane and theological materials of antiquity for the, as yet, uneducated but keenly eager German tribes and thus the foundation was laid for the flowering of culture in the Middle Ages.

When speaking of Semipelagianism (§ 57, 3), mention was made of two works of **Fulgentius**[2], Bishop of Ruspe († 533). He was a gifted theologian and prolific writer, a disciple of St. Augustine and spokesman for the African Church. Besides combatting Semipelagianism in Gaul, he attacked Arianism in a number of works. He was twice exiled by the Vandal ruler Thrasamund (§ 43, 6). His two opuscula De Trinitate and De fide seu de regula verae fidei are excellent summaries of dogma.

---

[1] Cfr. lit. § 40 and 76 (especially the works of EBERT, SCHANZ, KAPPELMACHER-SCHUSTER, MORICCA). P. COURCELLE, § 74. O. BARDENHEWER, GeschAL V, 1932 (Eugippius to Isidore of Seville). M. MANITIUS, Gesch. der lat. Literatur des MA.s I (527—950), 1911; cfr. C. WEYMAN, HJG 1911, 333/49, and M. MANITIUS, Handschriften antiker Autoren in mittelalterlichen Bibliothekskatalogen, 1935. L. W. LAISTNER, Thought and letters in Western Europe (500—900), London 1931. H. AUBIN, Vom Altertum zum MA., 1949.

[2] PL 65. Vita S. Fulgentii by Ferrandus, ed. G. G. LAPEYRE, Paris 1929 (with French transl.); cfr. G. KRÜGER, in Harnack-Ehrung, 1921, 219/31. Auswahl deutsch in BKV 2. R. 9, 1934. Monogr. by O. FRIEBEL, 1911; G. G. LAPEYRE, Paris 1929. F. DI SCIASCIO, Rome 1941. B. NISTERS, Die Christologie des hl. Fulg. v. R., 1930. M. SCHMAUS, in Charisteria Al. Rzach, 1930, 166/75 (Trinitarian teaching of Fulg.). A. D'ALÈS, RechSR 1932, 304/16 (Commonitorium de Spiritu S.). C. LAMBOT, RevBén 1936, 221/34 (Abecedarius against the Arian Vandals).

Fulgentius **Ferrandus**, a deacon of Carthage († c. 546) was a disciple of Fulgentius of Ruspe. He was renowned as a theologian, but all that remains of his work is a life of St. Fulgentius and a Breviatio canonum, listing under special headings all the decrees of the Greek and African councils. **Facundus**, Bishop of Hermiane, and **Liberatus**, deacon of Carthage, both opposed the policy of Justinian in the affair of the Three Chapters. (PL 67/68; on the work of Facundus De defensione trium capitulorum cfr. W. Pewesin § 58, 5; new edition of the Breviarium of Liberatus by E. Schwartz also in § 58, 5). The work of the Roman deacon, later Pope **Pelagius I** (556—561) on the Three Chapters was mentioned in § 58, 5. 7. **Primasius**, Bishop of Hadrumentum († before 567) left a commentary on the Apocalypse. **Junilius**, a native African who held a high position at the court of Constantinople, although a layman, left an introduction to the study of Scripture. The work entitled Instituta regularia divinae legis was much used during the Middle Ages. It was based on the lectures of Paul of Nisibis and the views of Theodore of Mopsuestia. Cfr. *H. Kihn*, Theodor von Mopsuestia und Junilius Afrikanus als Exegeten, 1880.

2. Pope **Gregory the Great** surpasses all the other Fathers of this epoch, not by depth of learning but by the varied fields in which he worked and the powerful influence he exerted. See § 64, 7 for a sketch of his life and works.

The following writers lived in *Italy*:

**Ennodius\*\***, deacon and teacher of rhetoric at Pavia, defended Pope Symmachus during the Laurentian Schism (§ 64, 1. 2. 6) and about 514 became bishop of Pavia. Before becoming bishop he wrote a number of rather bombastic poems, speeches and letters and afterwards composed an auto-biography, Eucharisticum de vita sua, in imitation of Augustine's Confessions. — PL 63; ed. *W. Hartel*, 1882; ed. *F. Vogel*, MG Auct. antiq. VII, 1885. — *St. Léglise*, S. Ennodius, oeuvres complètes I (Lettres), Paris 1906. — *A. Dubois*, La latinité d'Ennodius, Thèse Paris 1903.

Anicius Manlius Severinus **Boethius**[1] of the ancient and famous family of the Anicii, was born at Rome about 480. He made his

---

[1] Boethius' works in PL 63/64; CSEL 48, 1906 (Commentary on the Isagoge of Porphyrius); 67, 1934 (De consol. philos.). Opuscula theologica, edd. H. F. STEWART and E. K. RAND, London 1918 and 1926 (with English transl.). De consolatione philosophiae, ed. R. PEIPER, 1871; ed. A. a FORTI SCUTO (Fortescue), London 1925; ed. EB. GOTHEIN, 1932 (with German transl.); German by K. BÜCHNER, 1939. L. COOPER, A Concordance of Boethius (Tract. theol. et Consol. philos.), Cambridge Mass. 1928. H. M. BARETT, Boethius, Cambridge 1940. E. VERNET, DictSpir I, 1739/45. H. USENER, Anecdoton Holderi, 1877, 37 ff. A. HILDEBRAND, Boethius u. seine Stellung z. Christentum, 1885. N. SCHEID, STML 1890 II, 374/92 (Weltanschauung of B.). M. GRABMANN, Gesch. der scholast. Methode I, 1909, 148/77. G. A. MÜLLER, Die Trostschrift des B., Diss. 1912. F. KLINGNER, De Boethii consol. philos., 1921. K. BRUDER, Die philos. Elemente in den Opuscula sacra des Boethius, 1928. A. AUER, Johannes v. Dambach u. die Trostbücher vom 11.—16. Jh., 1928. G. CHAPPUIS, Jubilé de A. Loisy III, Paris 1928, 15/40 (Theology of Boethius). R. BOUNAUD, Sp 1929, 206/13

philosophical studies at Athens and in 510 became consul. As he grew in favor with Theodoric the Great, he advanced in position until he finally held the post of royal chancellor. However, when the Romans became reconciled with Byzantium in 524, Theodoric became suspicious of all Romans. Boethius was denounced as a partisan of Byzantium, was cast into prison at Pavia and after being cruelly tortured, was executed in 524. He was a man of exceptional learning and is often called the *"last of the Romans"* and the *"first scholastic."* Except in his strictly theological works a strong Christian conviction is not always in evidence, so that some have argued that Boethius was a Christian only in name. But the theological works bear ample testimony to his faith and his philosophical works contain nothing anti-Christian. He translated and commented on the philosophical works of Aristotle and the Neo-Platonist Porphyrius (§ 17, 1). He also wrote several small theological treatises (Opuscula sacra s. theologica: De sancta Trinitate, Liber c. Eutychen et Nestorium, De fide christiana). The authenticity of the latter work is questioned by some. Finally, when he was in prison he composed De consolatione philosophiae, a work which was highly esteemed by the Scholastics of the Middle Ages. By bringing Aristotle to the Schoolmen, Boethius had a profound influence on Scholasticism down to the twelfth century. In his theological treatises one hears an echo of the Theopaschite controversy of 519—520 (§ 58, 2). They also show the beginning of the use of Aristotelean dialectic in dogma and stimulated further speculation in the Middles Ages.

**Dionysius**, who in humility called himself the Less, has been known by that name to all succeeding generations usually in its Latin form, Dionysius **Exiguus**. He was a Scythian by birth, but came to Rome while still young and lived there as a monk until his death about 540 or possibly later. During his stay in Rome, he was always closely associated with the papacy and was a friend of Cassiodorus, and possibly for a time a teacher in the monastery

---

(education of B.). R. CARTON, Revue de philos. 1930, 573/659 (Christianity and Augustinism in B.). G. B. PICOTTI, Archivio stor. ital. 89, 1931, 205/28 (trial of B.). H. J. BROSCH, Der Seinsbegriff bei B., 1931. V. SCHURR, Die Trinitätslehre des B. im Lichte der ,,skythischen Kontroversen", 1935. E. T. SILK, Saec. IX auctoris in Boethii Consolationem Philos. commentarius, Rome 1935. H. R. PATCH, Sp 1935, 393/404 (B. and Neoplatonism); The Tradition of B., A Study of His Importance in Medieval Culture, Oxford 1936. P. COURCELLE, MélAH 1935, 185/223 (B. and the School of Alexandria); ArchHist MA 1939, 5/140 (Commentary on De consolatione in the IX—XIV cent.). M. GALDI, Saggi Boeziani, Pisa 1938. W. BARK, Amer, historical review 1944, 410/26 (Theoderic and B.). E. RAPISARDA, La crisi spirituale di Boezio, Florence 1947.

of Vivarium. He supported the Scythian monks in their defense of the Theopaschite formula (§ 58, 2). He did much to promote the exchange of Oriental and Latin theological literature and collected and translated the synodal canons and papal decrees (§ 65, 4) in a work which rapidly attained authority throughout the West. However, his chief claim to fame is the introduction of the Christian Era (§ 3, 7d) with the birth of Christ as the central point in history, He also obtained the adoption of the Alexandrian cycle (§ 69, 6) and thus contributed toward the settlement of the Paschal controversy. — PL 67. — *Ed. Schwartz,* Acta concil. oecum. t. IV vol. 2, 1914; t. I vol. 4 u. 5, 1922/6. — *Strewe, Wurm, Peitz, Förster* see § 65, 4. — *Er. Caspar,* Gesch. des Papsttums II, 1933, 307 ff. — J. Rambaud-Buhot, Dict. de droit canon. 3, 1134/52.

Flavius Magnus Aurelius **Cassiodorus**[1] Senator, († c. 580), was born of a noble family at Bruttium in Calabria and held high offices of State under Theodoric and his successors (§ 43, 3). He endeavored most earnestly to reconcile the conquered Romans with the victorious barbarians. About 540 he retired to a monastery he had founded on his estates at Vivarium in Calabria where he devoted himself to practices of piety and intellectual pursuits and instructed his monks to do likewise. His writings, most of which were produced in monastic seclusion, show him to have possessed a *practical* mind and an *encyclopedic* knowledge of the ecclesiastical sciences. His Institutiones divinarum et secularium lectionum contain a methodology of theological studies and an introduction to the seven liberal arts. The Historia (ecclesiastica) tripartita (mentioned in § 4, 2), a summary of the then extant histories, and the Expositio in Psalterium were treasured textbooks of the Middle Ages. The Variae or collection of letters and rescripts written by Cassiodorus in the course of his public duties were put together in twelve books before he retired to Vivarium. They are still a source of history of the Ostrogoth Kingdom in Italy and during the Middle Ages served as a model in all the chanceries of Europe. The very impor-

---

[1] PL 69—70. Cassiodori Variae, ed. TH. MOMMSEN, MG Auct. antiq. XII, 1894. Institutiones, ed. R. A. V. MYNORS, Oxford 1937. Monogr. by AD. FRANZ, 1872; G. MINASI, Napoli 1895. P. LEHMANN, Cassiodorstudien, Philologus 1912/7. H. LECLERCQ, DictAC II, 2357/65. A. G. PUNZI, L'Italia del sec. VI nelle Variae di Cass., Aquila 1927. A. VAN DE VYVER, Sp 1931, 244/92 (Cass. and his work). A. HOFMEISTER, HistVS 1931, 13/46 (tradition of the Variae). H. THIELE, StMBenO 1932, 378/419 (Vivarium and C.s influence on the MA.). H. GOMOLL, Zentralblatt f. Bibliothekswesen 1936, 185/99 (C's library). B. GLADYSZ, Collect. Theol. 1936, 51/69 (C. and the medieval schools). E. K. RAND, Sp 1938, 433/47 (Cass.-Hass.). ED. SCHWARTZ, Sb. München 1939, 2 (Cass. and Procop). P. COURCELLE, § 74, 313/48 (knowledge of Greek). W. JONES, Sp 1945 u. 1947 (influence in MA.). G. BARDY, § 74, 2; Année théol. 1945, 383/425 (C. and the end of the old world). H. LÖWE, Roman. Forschungen 1948, 420/46.

tant History of the Goths, De origine actibusque Getarum (§ 43, 2) did not survive except in some rather imperfect excerpts made by Jordanis in 599.

3. The **Liber Pontificalis** is a *history of the popes* in biographical form, the first part of which, including the ponticate of Felix III (IV) (526—530) was probably written during the pontificate of Boniface II (530—532). The compiler, a Roman cleric, used the so-called *Liberian Catalogue* for the first centuries. This was a list of popes from Peter to Liberius († 366) found in the *chronography* of Dionysius Philocalus. (This chronography was of varied content, a sort of State almanac with lists of the consuls, Easter tables, anniversaries of Roman bishops and martyrs, lists of popes, a description of Rome, a chronicle of the City and world history, etc., etc.). Unknown hands continued the Liber pontificalis at various times down to the pontificate of Hadrian II († 872) and further additions were made, apparently by contemporaries, until Stephen V († 891). From the pontificate of Anastasius II (496—498) the work is a valuable source, but for the preceding period it is very often untrustworthy. Due to an unfortunate error on the part of the otherwise learned archeologist Onofrio Panvini († 1568), the Liber Pontificalis down to quite recent times has been wrongly ascribed to the Roman librarian *Anastasius* in the ninth century. — Best edition by *L. Duchesne* (with the later vitae to Martin V † 1431), 2 vol. Paris 1886/92; edited in part by *Th. Mommsen*, in MG Gesta Pontif. Roman. I, 1898. — Cfr. *J. M. March*, Liber Pontificalis prout exstat in codice Dertusensi, Barcinone 1925 (a Ms. at Tortosa offers a better and more complete text of the vitae from John VIII † 1130). — *A. Brackmann*, RE XI, 439/46. — *H. Leclercq*, DictAC IX, 354/460. — *F. G. Rosenfeld*, Über die Komposition des Liber Pontif. bis auf P. Konstantin I, Diss. 1896. — *M. Buchner*, RQ 1926, 141/65 (the Liber Pontif. in France in the IX cent.). *E. Caspar*, Gesch. des Papsttums II, 1933, 314 ff. 774 f.

4. *Gaul* and *Spain* also produced a number of writers whose names have lived in honor through the centuries. **Caesar**[1], Archbishop of Arles (502—542), a pupil of the monastery of Lèrins, a foe of Semipelagianism in Southern Gaul and a promoter of monastic life, has been mentioned several times (§ 57, 4; 72, 6). The forty years during which he was bishop of "Gallic Rome" were disturbed

---

[1] PL 39; 67; ed. G. MORIN, 2 vol. Maretioli (Maredsous) 1937/42 (definitive critical edition); cfr. A. D'ALÈS, RechSR 1938, 315/84. On the text tradition of Caesar.: G. MORIN, RevBén 1896, 1899, 1906, 1910, 1931, 1934 (Sermones); 1933, 43/61 (commentary on the Apocal.); 1934, 178/89 (Symbolum). Auswahl aus Cäsarius, deutsch v. C. F. ARNOLD, 1896. Monogr. by C. F. ARNOLD 1894; A. MALNORY, Paris 1894 and 1934; M. CHAILLAN, Paris 1912. P. LEJAY, Le rôle théologique de Césaire d'Arles, Paris 1906. F. HAUTKAPPE, Über die altdeutschen Beichten und ihre Bezieh., zu Cäs. v. A., 1918. E. GÖLLER, AkKR 1929, 45/110 (idea of penance). H. MILLEMANN, ZMW 1933, 12/27 (Caes. of A. and the early medieval mission sermon). F. HOPPMANN, Die christl. Frömmigkeit bei C., Diss. 1942. G. BARDY, RevHEFrance 1943, 201/36 (sermon of C.); 1947, 241/56 (political attitude). K. BERG, Die Werke des hl. Cäs. v. A. als liturgiegeschichtl. Quelle, 1946. S. CAVALLIN, Studien zur Vita Caesarii Arelat., Lund 1934.

by political, social and religious disorders of major proportions.
The Migration of Nations, the spread of Arianism among the German peoples, the appearance of Semipelagianism even among the
monks, called for extraordinary abilities in a pastor. Caesar met
the exigencies most competently. He presided at a number of
synods at which he did much for the *reform of ecclesiastical discipline*;
he *preached* untiringly, urging his people to the practice of their
religious duties and *wrote* on moral, dogmatic and ascetical subjects
for the instruction of the laity and the religious of his diocese. His
sermons, both in content and in form, are comparable to the best
efforts in the literature of homiletics. Many of his sermons have
been erroneously ascribed to St. Augustine. A new critical edition
of his sermons by G. Morin lists 238 as authentic. For the two
monastic rules written by St. Caesar see § 72, 6.

**Avitus**, Archbishop of Vienne († c. 518) was a great statesman as well
as a great churchman. The conversion of the Burgundians to the Church
(§ 43, 5) and their attachment to the Holy See were due chiefly to his efforts.
He left an epic poem of 2552 hexameters in five cantos: 1. Creation and the
earthly paradise; 2. the Fall; 3. the judgement of God; 4. the Deluge; 5. the
crossing of the Red Sea. Some think that Milton may have derived his inspiration for Paradise Lost from Avitus. Another poem on Virginity was
composed for his sister Fuscina, a nun. Avitus, also wrote against the Eutychians and Arians and left 85 letters which are important for an understanding of the history of his time. — PL 59. — *Ed. Peiper*, MG Auct. antiq. VI
2, 1883; ed. *U. Chevalier*, Lyon 1890. — Monogr. by *A. Charaux*, Paris 1876;
*P. N. Frantz*, see § 43, 5. — *M. Burckhardt*, Die Briefsammlung des Bischofs
Avitus v. Vienne, 1938. — *F. Vernet*, DictThC I, 2639/44. — *G. Krüger*, Die
Bibeldichtung zu Ausgang des Altertums, 1919. — Cfr. also § 43, 5.

**Gregory**[1], Bishop **of Tours** († 594), was born to a Christian
family of senatorial rank at Clermont-Ferrand (Arverna) and
governed the See of St. Martin with great prudence and self-
sacrificing solicitude. He wrote a number of biographies of the early
Fathers and of saints who were popular in his day; but he is best
remembered for his *History of the Franks*. This work contains
ten books, the first of which is a kind of introduction with an outline
of world history to the year 397. Books 2—4 relate the history of

---

[1] PL 71. An edition of the works of Gregory by W. ARNDT, M. BONNET
and B. KRUSCH, in MGSS rer. Merow. I, 1884/85. Gregorii Tur. Historiarum
libri, ed. II cur. B. KRUSCH, Fasc. 1, 1937. Frankengesch. deutsch von
W. GIESEBRECHT and S. HELLMANN, 3 vols. 1911/3. Monogr. J. W. LOEBELL,
²1869. H. LECLERCQ, DictAC VI, 1711/53. M. BONNET, Le Latin de Grégoire
de T., Paris 1890. R. A. MEUNIER, Gr. de T. et l'historie morale du centre ouest
de la France, Paris 1946. O. CHADWICK, JThSt 1950, 38/49 (Gregory of
Tours and Gregory the Great). Cfr. lit. § 43, 7.

the Franks from Clovis to Sigibert († 575) and the last six books
cover the years from 575 to 591. In spite of awkwardness of style
and language and in spite of the author's too great credulity and
penchant for relating the miraculous, the work is of immense value
as a detailed description of the political, ecclesiastical and moral
conditions of the nascent French nation.

**Venantius Fortunatus** († c. 601) was born in Upper Italy near Treviso
and studied grammar, rhetoric and law at Ravenna. He made a pilgrimage
to the tomb of St. Martin at Tours and stopped for some time at *Poitiers*
where he became acquainted with Queen Radegunde (§ 43, 8) and her nuns
at the convent of the Holy Cross. He was ordained priest and became chap-
lain of the convent and later bishop of the city. He was a *poet* with depth
of feeling and very real talent although in many of his numerous Carmina
he makes too many concessions to the vulgar tastes of the period. However,
in Pange lingua gloriosi, Vexilla regis prodeunt and Quam terra pontus
aethera, he created gems of lasting beauty. It is a tribute to his ability as
a religious poet that the Ave maris stella has been thought by some to be
a product of his pen. Venantius Fortunatus also wrote a number of prose
works, chiefly lives of saints: Vita S. Hilarii, S. Germani, S. Radegundis and
others. — PL 88. Best edition is by *F. Leo* and *B. Krusch*, MG Auct. antiq. IV,
1881/5. — F. S. Kopp, Ein neues Elogium v. Ven. Fort., Diss. 1938. — Monogr.
by *Ch. Nisard*, Paris 1890; *R. Koebner*, 1915; *D. Tardi*, Paris 1927; *G. M.
Dreves*, Hymnolog. Studien zu Ven. Fort. u. Rhabanus Maurus, 1908 (also
K. Strecker, Anzeiger der ZfdA 1909, 43/60). — *U. Moricca*, Didaskaleion 1927,
55/115. — *S. Blomgren*, Studia Fortunatiana, 2 parts Upsala 1933/4. —
*A. G. Amatucci*, in Studi ded. alla memoria di P. Ubaldi, Milano 1937, 363/72.

**Martin of Braga** (the old Bracara Augusta) was born in Pannonia. After
arriving in the West, he founded the monastery of Dumio over which he
presided and later became bishop of the same place. He died 580 as archbishop
of Braga in Galicia. He is known as the Apostle of the Suevi (§ 43, 2) and as
the guiding spirit in many synods of his day. His literary works are of a
practical nature: several moral-ascetical treatises (Formula vitae honestae,
De ira, etc.) strongly influenced by Seneca; and an interesting pastoral instruction (De correctione rusticorum) aimed at combatting superstition in
country places; a collection of synodal decrees (Capitula Martini) and the
translation of ascetical maxims of Oriental monks into Latin. — PL 72/73; 84.
De correctione rusticorum, ed. *C. P. Caspari*, 1883; cfr. E. Bickel, Rhein.
Museum für Philol. 1905, 505/51. — *R. Seeberg*, RE XII, 385/88. — *G. Jecker*,
Die Heimat des hl. Pirmin, 1927, 90 ff. (Martin's sermons to peasants). —
*S. McKenna*, Paganism and Pagan Survivals in Spain., Washington 1938,
75/107. — *P. David*, see § 43, 2.

**Isidore**[1], Archbishop of *Seville*, (c. 600—636) succeeded his older
brother *St. Leander* in that see (§ 72, 1). Isidore is considered the

---

[1] PL 81—84. Best edition of the historical works of Isidore is by TH.
MOMMSEN, in MG Auct. antiq. XI, 1894. Origines, ed. W. M. LINDSAY, 2 vol.
Oxford 1911. E. ANSPACH, Taionis et Isidori nova fragmenta et opera,

most renowned Latin writer of the seventh century and is often called the *last Father of the West*. Although he did little more than collect and compile, his services in making the vast learning of the past available to the new nations is something that can never be properly estimated. It is with good reason that he is called *"the great schoolmaster of the Middle Ages."* The Etymologies in twenty books sometimes called the Origines, to mention only one of his important works, is the first Christian encyclopedia. The Libri tres sententiarum is a manual of dogma and morals based on excerpts from the Fathers. De fide catholica contra Judaeos is not so much a controversial work as a dogmatic explanation of the effects of the Incarnation. De ecclesiasticis officiis describes divine worship and the various offices held by the clergy. De viris illustribus is a continuation of Jerome and Gennadius. Isidore's History of the Goths, Vandals and Suevi was mentioned in § 43, 2. It was compiled from earlier Christian authors. Although Isidore himself was a Roman he showed deep affection for the Visigoths, and more than any other individual was responsible for building up a consciousness of the cultural unity of the Germanic and Roman peoples (Vossler).

Madrid 1930 (contains the Vita Isidoii by Braulio). S. Isidori Hispan. Commonitiuncula ad sororem, rec. E. ANSPACH, Escorial 1935. S. Isidori De haeresibus liber, primum ed. A. C. VEGA, Escorial 1936; Quaestiones adv. Iudaeos et ceteros infideles, edd. A. C. VEGA et E. ANSPACH, ib. 1936. Monogr. by A. M. TORRADO, Sevilla 1936/8; J. PÉREZ DE URBEL, Barcelona 1940. G. BAREILLE, DictThC VIII 98/111. A. SCHMECKEL, Die positive Philosophie in ihrer geschichtl. Entwicklung II, 1914, cfr. RE Pauly-Wissowa IX, 2069/80. CH. H. BEESON, Isidor-Studien, 1913. P. LEHMANN, Philologus 1913, 504/17 (Isidore's dependence en Cassiodorus); ib. 1917, 357/83 (Cassiodorus-Isidore-Beda-Alcuin). P. SÉJOURNÉ, see § 65, 4. J. SOFER, Lateinisches u. Roman. aus den Etymologiae des I. v. Sev., 1930. J. R. GEISELMANN, Die Abendmahlslehre an der Wende der christl. Spätantike zum Frühmittelalter, Isidor von Sev. und das Sakrament der Eucharistie, 1933. Z. GARCIA VILLADA, Hist. ecclesiastica de España II, 2, Madrid 1933, 197/223. Misc. Isidoriana, Rom. Univ. Greg. 1936 (contains the following: pp. 1/32: B. ALTANER, Bericht über die Isidorforschung seit 1910; pp. 323/56: E. ANSPACH, Fortleben Isidors v. 7.—9. Jh.). H. KOEPPLER, JThSt 1936, 16/34 (De viris ill.). W. PORZIG, Hermes 1937, 129/70 (Recensions of the Etymologiae). A. C. LAWSON, RevBén 1938, 26/36 (sources of De eccles. off.). J. HAVET, EphThLov 1939, 32/93 (Sacraments and the H. Ghost in Isidore). J. MULLINS, The Spiritual Life According to S. Isidore of S., Washington 1940. K. VOSSLER, Hochland 39, 1947, 420/8.

# GENERAL INDEX

The numbers refer to the sections (§) and to the numbered paragraphs into which the sections are subdivided. An asterisk following a number indicates a principal reference. Thus: agape, 23,3* means that a principal reference to the agape will be found in the third numbered paragraph of § 23. The running headings on the right hand pages are preceded by the section number.

For general subjects consult the Table of Contents.